# Family, Self, and Human Development Across Cultures

## Theory and Applications

### Second Edition

# Family, Self, and Human Development Across Cultures

## Theory and Applications

### Second Edition

Çiğdem Kağitçibaşi
*Koç University*
*Turkish Academy of Sciences*

**LEA**

LAWRENCE ERLBAUM ASSOCIATES, PUBLISHERS
2007    Mahwah, New Jersey                    London

Lawrence Erlbaum Associates, Inc., Publishers
10 Industrial Avenue
Mahwah, New Jersey 07430
www.erlbaum.com

> Cover design by Tomai Maridou

**Library of Congress Cataloging-in-Publication Data**

Family, Self, and Human Development Across Cultures: Theory and
Applications

ISBN 978-0-8058-5775-7—ISBN 0-8058-5775-3 (cloth)
ISBN 978-0-8058-5776-4—ISBN 0-8058-5776-1 (pbk)
ISBN 978-1-4106-1656-2—ISBN 1-4106-1656-8 (e book)

Copyright information for this volume can be obtained by con-
tacting the Library of Congress.

Printed in the United States of America
10  9  8  7  6  5  4  3  2  1

To Oğuz

. . . and for the well-being of children everywhere.

# Contents

## CHAPTER 3
## SOCIALIZATION FOR COMPETENCE                          59

## CHAPTER 4
## CULTURE, SELF, AND INDIVIDUALISM–COLLECTIVISM          91

*91*
*−32*

# CHAPTER 5
# VALUE OF CHILDREN AND THE FAMILY    125

# CHAPTER 6
# PARENTING AND THE DEVELOPMENT OF THE
# AUTONOMOUS–RELATED SELF    165

# Preface to the Second Edition

I wrote the Preface to the First Edition more than 10 years ago. It was a personal account, and I named it so. I am keeping it in this Second Edition also, because it is still a valid prelude to my work and to my general outlook on life. Therefore, this Preface to the Second Edition is relatively brief.

Also included in this revised second edition is the Foreword to the first edition by Brewster Smith. It is maintained here because it is also valid currently and presents a thorough understanding of what this volume is about. It reflects the great wisdom and deep insights of a renowned senior psychologist who is my mentor.

During the last decade since the publication of the First Edition, cultural and cross-cultural research and theorizing on the self, family, and human development have expanded so much that the field is greatly transformed. The present volume is accordingly quite different from the former one. This is reflected in its title, though it is changed only slightly. Specifically *Self* is included in the title because there is now a great deal more emphasis on it than was the case in the first edition. Second, the subtitle is different. The subtitle of the first edition was "A View From the Other Side." This was because some 10 years ago, the book brought in a new and critical perspective from "the other side," that is, from outside of the dominant Western psychological perspective. With the greater acceptance of cultural and cross-cultural viewpoints and their greater integration into mainstream psychology today, this is no longer an "other side," though the critical perspective is still there. Instead, the new subtitle presents the two main emphases of this volume, theory and applications, in a synergistic relationship.

All of the chapters are updated and some are greatly modified. There is expanded coverage with two additional chapters, "Parenting and the Development of the Autonomous–Related Self" and "Immigration and Acculturation." The former presents my recent theoretical work on the self, which is also reflected in some of the other chapters. The latter covers a currently growing body of research and thinking that is of relevance to the thrust of the volume. The organization of the book as well as the contents of the chapters are described in the "Introduction" (chap. 1).

A main difference between the present volume and the previous one is that this one has a broader coverage of my theoretical perspectives on the self and family. These perspectives have developed mostly since the publication of the First Edition. They form the basis of this book, and several different topics revolve around them. Second, this volume presents a stronger view of a universal convergence toward a proposed "healthy model" in human development, family, and self. This viewpoint is seen throughout the volume, but especially in chapters 3, 5, 6, and 11. The emphasis on policy and applications is also relevant here. Thus this book has a thesis, and my views on various issues are made explicit. This is in line with my belief that social science cannot be "value-free" though values are often implicit. I further believe that it is better to make them explicit.

In presenting a topic, I tend to refer to earlier studies and theoretical viewpoints somewhat more than usually done in current writings in psychology. This is because I think it is important to understand and share with the reader the background of the thinking on a topic. I also believe that we have much to benefit from learning about earlier work, and this is how knowledge gets accumulated. Otherwise, there is the danger of repetition with a new label or "rediscovering the wheel." Thus, in this Second Edition, whereas on the one hand I have done considerable updating, I have also continued to refer to relevant earlier theoretical perspectives and studies. In dealing with a topic, I first give the historical antecedents and earlier formative research before I go on to more recent work. In this way, I hope to convey to the reader the fact that many issues are of long standing and that familiarity with the development of a topic over time should help understand its current status better.

All the chapters in the book are interrelated. At times there may also be some overlap between them, which is to be expected given the interwoven themes. This also helps each chapter to stand alone; thus in reading a chapter one can get an inclusive coverage of the topic.

There are a number of new features in this edition designed to make the book more reader- and student-friendly. At the end of each chapter, there is a "Summary and Main Points" section in bullet form. It aims to help the reader to have a better grasp of the significant points covered in the chapter. This is followed by a set of "Discussion Questions" to stimulate further thinking on the topics covered.

The important terms introduced throughout the volume are highlighted in bold. However, to prevent too much repetition of boldface presentation, a term is made bold only the first time it appears under a first- or second-level heading in the text. A further useful feature is the

"Glossary" at the end of the volume, which includes descriptions and definitions of these terms for quick reference. A very extensive bibliography is provided for the benefit of the reader and researcher.

## ACKNOWLEDGMENTS

I had written the First Edition during a sabbatical year from my former university, Bogaziçi, at the Netherlands Institute for Advanced Study (NIAS). I wrote most of this revised Second Edition on a second sabbatical leave at NIAS. I am truly indebted to NIAS for making this possible. Thanks are due for the kind services of Anneke Vrins-Aarts and Anne Simpson.

Koç University provided me with a precious 5-month sabbatical leave, which I appreciate greatly. At Koç University, my students Sinem Olcay, Elif Durgel, Selin Gulgoz, Bengi Keskin, Hande Sungur, Esra Gures, Uraz Oktay, Duygu Cakirsoy, Suzi Levi, and Ayca Atik helped with various aspects of the work toward this publication. In my "Culture and Behavior" and "Policy and Practice in Psychology" courses over the last years, I have developed my thinking and elaborated my views about the topics covered in this volume. I am indebted to my students who contributed to this process. The same is also true of my Turkish and international colleagues who taught me many things. I want to single out here my special gratitude to M. Brewster Smith, my mentor and friend.

I appreciated greatly to be asked by my publisher, Lawrence Erlbaum Associates, to prepare a revised second edition of my book. Lori Handelmann and Sondra Guideman were very supportive throughout the long process of publication. I thank them for that.

The first photograph at the beginning of the volume is that of my granddaughter Ece. The photos presented in chapters 8 and 9 are from the archives of Mother Child Education Foundation (MOCEF), except for the first one. They are pictures of children living in deprived environments in Turkey. Several depict instances of early enrichment provided to them, preparing them for a fair start at school and in life. Thanks are due to MOCEF for these wonderful pictures. I also want to express my appreciation and admiration for the superb contributions of MOCEF to human well-being in Turkey and abroad.

This is a culmination of my work over a long period of time, especially of the last two decades. Throughout my life career, many people, but especially my late mother, my husband Oğuz, and my whole family have been sources of strength and support to me. I feel much love for and gratitude to them.

—Çigdem Kağitçibaşi
Istanbul, 2006

# Foreword

M. Brewster Smith
*University of California, Santa Cruz*

This is an extraordinary book by an author who needs no introduction in the world of international psychology. Çiğdem Kağitçibaşi (*g* is silent in Turkish, lengthening the preceding vowel; *c* has the value of *ch, s* of *sh),* who is professor of psychology at Bogaziçi University in Istanbul and president of the Turkish Psychological Association, is also former president of the International Association of Cross-Cultural Psychology and two-term member of the executive committee of the International Union of Scientific Psychology. In 1993, she received the American Psychological Association's award for Distinguished Contributions to the International Advancement of Psychology. This volume represents the culmination of a distinguished career, which I have been privileged to follow with admiration ever since her graduate study at the University of California, Berkeley, some three decades ago. In that sense, as her preface attests, it is a very personal book.

But it is also an exemplary, up-to-the-moment exposition of a view of human and social development "from the other side"—from the perspective of what Kağitçibaşi aptly calls the Majority World (no longer sensibly labeled Third World) of countries that do not participate fully in the benefits and problems of the industrial and postindustrial West. Furthermore, it is an authoritative presentation of the cross-cultural perspective, as an essential corrective to the unthinking culture-boundedness of much Euro-American psychology. It is a searching analysis of perspectives on human development that escape the pitfalls of extreme relativism to which advocates of culturally contextual approach are vulnerable, in terms of criteria of cognitive competence and of developing selfhood in which autonomy and relatedness are in balance. It is an original contribution to the theory of family change, opposing the expectation of modernization theory that families in the developing world will converge on the Western individualistic model. It is a wise and constructive analysis of the role of psychology in inducing social change, focused on problems of the Majority World but just as relevant to the Euro-American context. And it is a critical review of research and theory on early childhood care and education (ECCE) in the United States and in the Majority World; ECCE is the particular mode of intervention, in the family context, with which she has been involved. In each of these widely dispersed topical areas, the breadth and depth of her command of the specialized literature is amazing. Readers who are already well acquainted with some of them (who else will be familiar with them all?) will respect her guidance to the very extensive bibliography in their own areas of competence and welcome it in the areas new to them.

All of the foregoing comes to concrete focus in her account of the Turkish Early Enrichment Project. This Lewin-style action-research, which Kağitçibaşi conceived and directed in the shantytowns of Istanbul, is exemplary in a number of respects. It was planned with sensitivity to the Turkish cultural context, but with nonrelativistic standards of cognitive and social competence in child development in mind. The intervention focused on the family, specifically the mother, as the primary context of socialization in the preschool years. The research design permitted appropriately controlled comparisons, with multiple outcome measures. Strikingly positive short-term results were obtained, expecially on cognitive and school-related measures, for the effects of training the mothers and of educational day-care centers. In the almost unprecedented 10-year follow-up, major effects of mother training persisted (including empowering benefits to the mothers themselves), whereas the advantages of day-care center experience dissipated with time. The findings make sense in terms of Kağitçibaşi's interpretation that intervention with the mothers reoriented the functioning of the family systems of participants in ways that were self-sustaining. She then draws the book together, making explicit how her project, which has had substantial impact on Turkish programming for early childhood enrichment, suggests useful ways in which psychology in the Majority World can become engaged with national and pan-human objectives of global human development.

I would like to highlight several respects in which Kağitçibaşi provides intellectual leadership that is much needed by psychology in the Euro-American and Majority Worlds alike. These are contributions of the book that I enthusiastically applaud.

For one, I am delighted with the way that she has enlarged on the recent critique of the individualism of Euro-American culture. Many voices in psychology and the social sciences, including feminists but not restricted to them, would give higher priority to values of relatedness, as complementing the individualistic values of agency or autonomy. From her Majority World perspective and her command of the large recent literature documenting the prevalence of "collectivist" values outside Euro-American cultural precincts, she challenges modernization theory when it predicts the supplanting of relatedness values in the less developed world by Western individualism. True, economic development with its accompanying urbanization is a strong corrosive for many aspects of traditional cultures. But the example of Japan and other East Asian "success stories" indicates that relatedness values can survive economic development. Addressing her colleagues in the Majority World, she calls for new goals of personal autonomy in a context that preserves the values of relatedness distincitve of non-Western cultures. Her mother-training early childhood development (ECD) project demonstrates that it is possible to apply psychology toward realizing this objective, which she sees as humanly desirable for the have-nots as it is for the haves.

Recently, a polarity has become salient contrasting the cross-cultural psychology of Triandis, Berry, Bond, and others with the cultural psychology of Cole, Rogoff, Shweder, and their associates. The former is charged by its critics with continuing the outmoded positivist tradition, employing imposed "etic" dimensions of comparison drawn inappropriately from individualistic Western culture; the latter is committed to contextual, "emic" treatment of experience and behavior in each culture's own terms, but is vulnerable to sometimes nihilistic relativism. Kağitçibaşi comes from the cross-cultural tradition, of which she is an acknowledged leader, but she insists, articulately and persuasively, that cultural and cross-cultural approaches are complementary, not competing; she believes psychology can give proper attention to cultural context without giving up its strategies of comparison or its aims to discover principles that transcend history and culture.

Her integrative approach comes to a focus in her insistence on the relevance of standards of human development that apply across nations and cultures and across the barrier between haves and have-nots in Euro-American societies. This attempt to combine cultural contextualism with universalistic standards is a complex, difficult intellectual maneuver, not an easy political compromise. I think it is the right choice. It has become politically incorrect to regard school-related cognitive competences as more "developed" than the less abstractive competencies of children in premodern rural societies or streetwise culture; the presently indispensable value of formal schooling is even disparaged. Kağitçibaşi reminds us that in the Majority World, universal schooling and literacy is a

*talk about*
*→ the gap*

consensual objective engraved in the Universal Declaration of Human Rights and the Convention on Rights of the Child but only very partially attained, expecially for girls and women. "Middle-class" cognitive competencies are very much needed to cope with the complexities of the contemporary world, whether on the part of disadvantaged minorities in the United States or the hordes of rural immigrants to the exploding cities of the Majority World. As she observes, it is only a step from the extreme relativism of some postmodern admirers of traditional culture to implicit advocacy of a double standard: first-class preschools and elementary schools for *our* children to prepare them for *our* world, but, for instance, rote learning in Koranic schools (or *no* schools, for girls) as preserving the valued culture of Those Others. The ethical/political issues are difficult, but Kağitçibaşi's position is courageous and clear.

Those who disagree in principle with her stance that calls for contextualism without complete relativism will not only have to contend with her argument; they will also have to come to terms with the implications of her intervention research on early childhood enrichment and mother empowerment. I have recently been involved in the armchair defense of scientific empiricism in psychology from postmodernist assault, trying to sustain the human effort to approach truth and goodness in formulations that transcend the particular historicocultural contexts from which they are derived. I am impressed that Kağitçibaşi's demonstration of the effectiveness of her mother-training intervention in a Majority World setting is a much stronger answer to the extreme cultural relativists than any other philosophical metatheoretical argument. The concrete example is persuasuve: Relevant culturally contextual scientific research *can* be done and it is useful and influential on public policy. Articulate elites in the developing countries will want to support interventions such as she exemplified; so will the participants themselves as they encounter such programs. This is the way to go!

*specifics*

This volume will immediately become obligatory reading and a valuable resource to the band of cultural and cross-cultural psychologists, still too few, who are committed to reshaping mainstream Euro-American psychology so as to make it more truly universal, less unwittingly culture-bound. It should have equal immediate interests to psychologists in the Majority World and Euro-American psychologists who want to collaborate with them in challenging enterprise of applying psychology to the problems of societal development. But the appropriate audience for this book as textbook and resource is much broader. Kağitçibaşi's view of family and human development "from the other side" is very relevant to the concerns of mainstream psychologists on "this" side of the great divide between have and have-not societies.

We Euro-Americans have parallel problems in relating to internal have-not minorities. In our current well-motivated wave of political correctness, we may be bemused by similar qualms of relativism concerning the relevance of middle-class cognitive standards to children and adults who have been systematically excluded from middle-class opportunities and benefits. The wave of support for early intervention projects peaked with President Johnson's Great Society programs, and these projects mostly neglected the family context of early child development. Perhaps Kağitçibaşi's hope-inspiring example from Instanbul may stimulate blasé American psychologists to take heart, and once more seriously address the problem of bringing excluded minorties into full citizenship. Certainly, she has given professors and students of developmental psychology and of family relations much to ponder.

# Preface to the First Edition

## A PERSONAL ACCOUNT

### Interpersonal Relations

A few years ago I was invited to participate in a symposium, at an international congress of cross-cultural psychology, to present a personal account of "How I became a cross-cultural psychologist," mainly in terms of how I came to be involved in cross-cultural research. That task helped me look back and delve into the background of my present academic involvement. It was an interesting process of reconstruction. While I tried to locate some point in my academic career where I could say my interest in cross-cultural or cultural psychology began, I kept going back more and more. So, an attempted academic reconstruction turned into an autobiographical reconstruction. Obviously, everyone's work must reflect something of her experience, though this is rarely made explicit. I would like to start this book by making this personal experience explicit. This is because I believe this exercise might help put what I have to say into some perspective—an international perspective at that.

I was a graduate student in the social psychology program at the University of California, Berkeley during the exciting 1960s. I was well-versed in the social-psychological literature of the 1950s and 1960s. But what intrigued me more than the highly popular cognitive dissonance theory and the lure of the experimental laboratory was the social, political, and the psychological implications of the then no-longer-in-vogue authoritarian personality theory (Adorno, Frenkel-Brunswick, Levinson, & Sanford, 1950). This was despite the influential methodological critique of Christie and Jahoda (1954). So, against my supervisor and mentor M. Brewster Smith's good advice, I undertook to do a cross-cultural comparative study for my PhD dissertation research, to test the cross-cultural generality of the authoritarian personality theory, instead of a clean laboratory experiment. Though calling myself a social psychologist, I was in fact already a cross-cultural psychologist at heart and in deed when nobody in my environment was using the notion of "cross-cultural psychology."

Yet, this was only a "natural" development, given the fact that I was a foreign student in America and was using, almost automatically, a cultural filter in my reading. Thus, my study emerged out of the realization, when I read the *Authoritarian Personality* (Adorno et al., 1950), that some of the characteristics of the so-called authoritarian *personality* were in fact *social norms* in Turkey. The following beginning paragraph of the resultant publication describes the general view underlying the study:

> Some findings of social psychology may refer to general panhuman relationships, others to relationships that hold only within specific sociocultural settings. Only systematic cross-cultural comparison can separate these or identify the limits within which particular generalizations hold. An example of findings that seem likely to be culturally specific are those in support of a general syndrome of "authoritarianism." In cultures in which social norms bear differentially on the components of this syndrome, one should expect different patterns of relationship to obtain. Such contrasts were anticipated between the United States and Turkey. This study examines the assumed inherent dynamic organization of personality attributes and attitudinal variables underlying "authoritarianism" in the light of a cross-cultural comparison. (Kağitçibaşi, 1970, p. 444)

I maintain the preceding view in a general sense some 25 years later. I believe it forms a *raison d'être* of cross-cultural psychology, which sheds important light on human behavior.

This early realization of cross-cultural variability in some "basic" personality characteristics, assumed to be universal, had something to do, I believe, with my own early experiences in culture contact, in addition to being a foreign student at Berkeley. When they occurred, they were simple events, though some quite powerful; only much later have I been able to put them into perspective, attributing to them a culturally situated meaning. I want to relate some of these experiences, going further back in time.

As a teenager I was a boarding student at an American school for girls in Istanbul, Turkey. There used to be much physical contact among girls (kissing on both cheeks, embracing, walking arm in arm in the corridors, in the garden, courtyard, etc.) as a natural part of interpersonal affection and warm peer relations.[1] We used to note and get a kick out of the shocked glances of the new American teachers (mostly young women) before they got acculturated to "the ways of the natives." Some mischievous girls among us used to overdo the show of affection in the presence of the "novice teachers" to shock them more.

During my last years at the American school in Istanbul I studied British and American literature and also took a course in 20th-century philosophy, which focused on phenomenology and existentialism. Apart from scholarly work by Kierkegaard, Jaspers, Husserl, Heidegger, and Sartre, I also read some plays by Sartre. These were my earliest scholarly contacts with the pervasive individualistic perspective in Western philosophy and literary tradition. The ending words of Sartre's play *No Exit,* "Hell is other people," got stamped in my memory at that time. This powerful statement was intriguing to me in its utmost strangeness. Today I see it as a reflection of extreme individualism.

My first impression of "suburban America" (Newton Center, Massachusetts), where I stayed with an American family, was beautiful homes, spacious gardens with lovely trees and flowers, clean streets, and no people. I often wondered where the people were. Not once did I meet any neighbors or see my host family visiting them.

I had a close friend at Wellesley, whom I visited and stayed with at her family's home during some short vacations. One day when she was very sad, I asked what was wrong. She said, "It is a personal matter." I was shattered. This was a clear indication of rejection for me; obviously she did not consider me very close if she could not confide in me. In my understanding, there couldn't be anything that I would withhold from my best friend; I would at least let her know the general nature of the problem even if the details might be unspoken. What for her was a simple assertion of her privacy, was for me a declaration of rejection. Even after more than 30 years the memory is still vivid.

These everyday events and experiences have all had to do with what I consider today a basic aspect of interpersonal relations that shows cross-cultural variation, that is, interpersonal connectedness (relatedness) or separateness. Looked at from another perspective, they have to

*[handwritten: └→ today, how are ppl interconnected?]*

---

[1]There is still much more physical contact among same-sex friends and kin in "contact" cultures such as Turkey than in "noncontact" Western cultures. However, the absolute amount of physical contact is probably less today than before, especially among the educated middle-class groups in those societies due to "cultural diffusion," especially through the media, of the Western models. After I graduated from the American school in Istanbul and was accepted at Wellesley College (in Massachusetts, USA), an important part of my self-induced preparation/orientation to life in America was to restrain myself from showing physical affection.

do with the self, again in terms of its level of individuation (separateness, boundedness) or connectedness with others. Obviously, there were many other culture contact experiences involving misunderstanding or readjustment throughout my student years in the United States and since then in many extensive international contacts. However, I find it important that most episodes that have left a trace in my memory, like these few I have mentioned, have to do with the connectedness–separateness dimension of interpersonal relations.

Some episodes may be eye opening even if one is no longer a "naive student." Thus, a few years ago during a social occasion, I was talking with a well-known Western cross-cultural psychologist friend and colleague and his wife. When I asked after their son, who was about 21 years old at the time, my friend said that their son was now staying with them in their home, but they were not charging him rent. I couldn't believe what I heard and wondered if he was joking; he was not.[2]

Yet another simple episode during my adult career years happened in the United States while I was on a sabbatical leave at Harvard University and Radcliffe College (Bunting Institute) some 10 years ago. I got acquainted with a renowned anthropologist, several years my senior. One day, getting into the back seat of a car, I attempted to let her go in first and to help her in. She was offended and said that she was not that old to need help to get into a car. My behavior was a reflection of my respect and appreciation for her age and accomplishments. She took it as an insult to her independence and autonomy. The interesting point here is that I, the cross-cultural psychologist, let my "old country values" take precedence over my knowledge of American values, and she, the highly experienced anthropologist, did not recognize that.

Experiences like these remind one of the cross-cultural diversity in the interpersonal-relations sphere that goes deep into cultural meaning systems and conventions. This diversity exists side by side a remarkable commonality, deriving from our common biologically based human nature and our immense intercultural-international communication systems, including similar educational experiences, working as strong converging and unifying forces. If even among educated people, culturally sensitive and internationally minded social scientists at that, there could be such differences in understanding, there would naturally be vastly greater differences among common people each immersed in their own culture.

[2]Another North American colleague interpreted this episode to mean that I was surprised my friend *was not* charging rent to his son! In case other Western readers also misinterpret what I have written, let me explain: I was surprised that it would even occur to my friend to charge rent to his own son.

The aforementioned experiential examples demonstrate how living in another cultural context or acculturation through early exposure to another culture sensitizes one to *culture,* as such. It is very much like "the fish in water"; you "see" culture when you get out of it. What is probably even more important, however, is that once you become conscious of it, you can't ignore it. This is probably the summary of my first involvement with cultural and cross-cultural psychology. It has important implications for the psychology that I do and that I think should be done.

Of particular significance to me is to understand the underlying dimensions of interpersonal relations, their variation across cultures, and their antecedents. The interpersonal connectedness–separateness dimension, as reflected in the preceding personal episodes, signals to me a clue to an understanding of the self and its development in context. This context is the family and, moving out from it, the sociocultural environment. The observed variations in self-construals and self–other relations appear to be deeply rooted in the cross-cultural diversities in contexts (Kağitçibaşi, 1990; Markus & Kitayama, 1991). How and why these variations come about is for me the key question to understanding an important aspect of human reality.

## Social Relevance

Another thread of influence running through both my personal life and professional career is a deep concern for and a commitment to social well-being. The roots of this commitment go back to my early socialization in family and school, which for me coincided. Both my parents were teachers who had a strong sense of mission to contribute to the education and development of a modern secular society out of the ashes of an old one based on tradition and religion.[3] They started their own private school with very limited funds, and I found myself in school at the age of 2 and have been in school all my life. I was brought up with the ideal of "doing something worthwhile for society," nourished especially by my mother.

In retrospect, such ideals were taken seriously by many young people in my generation, especially among the children of the educated teachers and civil servants who carried considerable responsibility for "building a modern nation." Indeed, early studies conducted in the post–World

---

[3]The republican secularist reforms were in full swing. They had been started by Atatürk and the founders of the Turkish Republic after the war for independence was won in the early 1920s, following the collapse of the Ottoman Empire after the First World War. The ties with the six centuries of Ottoman past were severed and by the 1940s the reforms were consolidated.

War II period in developing countries point to much higher "patriotism" and a great value put on "doing something good for one's family and country" among youth in these countries, compared with American youth. For example, Gillespie and Allport (1955) talked about the strong national loyalties of youth in newly emergent nations, in the process of nation building.

The historical context of nation building probably did make the loyalty felt to the nation more salient in young people's values. However, as evidenced by a great deal of subsequent research and current work, this is not the whole story. For example, in my comparative study of Turkish and American adolescents in 1966, I found the same high level of national loyalty among the Turkish sample, for whom nation building was not relevant. In contrast, American adolescents valued personal achievement and happiness (Kağitçibaşi, 1970). Furthermore, in a later study with Turkish adolescents (Kağitçibaşi, 1973), I found patriotism (loyalty to the country) to fit into a "modern" outlook and to be associated with belief in internal control of reinforcement, optimism, and achievement motivation. It was negatively associated with a more traditional outlook, characterized by religiosity, authoritarianism, and belief in external control of reinforcement.

Even when achievement motivation is studied, which is often assumed to focus on the self, the same loyalty to society can be seen. Thus Phalet and Claeys (1993) found Turkish adolescents (both in Turkey and in Belgium) to combine individual and group loyalties (Kağitçibaşi, 1987b) into a "social achievement motivation," contrasted with the individualistic achievement motivation of the Belgian youth. Similar findings of socially oriented achievement motivation have been reported for the Japanese (De Vos, 1968), the Indians (Agarwal & Misra, 1986), and the Chinese (Bond, 1986, p. 36; K.-S.Yang, 1986, pp. 113–114).

The preceding examples point to the continuing pervasiveness of the loyalty and commitment to entities transcending the self in the so-called collectivistic cultures. In the individualistic culture, however, it has been claimed that "the primary loyalty is to the self—its values, autonomy, pleasure, virtue and actualization" (Kagan, 1984). I do not mean to infer here value judgments about what is good and what is bad, but rather point to differences in emphasis in focusing on the self or on the larger collectivity in which the self is embedded. As is apparent in the following chapters, this is one of the central themes in the book.

There has been some recent questioning of the vulnerability of "lives organized around self-actualization and the pursuit of gratification" and a recognition of the fact that "human lives seem most meaningful and satisfying when they are devoted to projects and guided by values that transcend the self" (M. B. Smith, 1994, p. 7). Other critics have also expressed their concerns with too much individualism, especially in the United

States (e.g., Bellah, Madsen, Sullivan, Swindler, & Tipton, 1985; Cushman, 1990; Lasch, 1984; Sampson, 1987; C. Taylor, 1989). There have been pleas for a greater commitment to society (Etzioni, 1993; Sarason, 1981, 1988; Wallach & Wallach, 1983, 1990).

To some extent these recent developments have had an effect in making my own commitments more salient for me, which I have expressed here. The difference between the individualistic and the collectivistic concerns appears to be continuing. It is understandable, therefore, that much of Western academic psychology is still somewhat oblivious of societal problems,[4] but in contrast there is a loud cry from the collectivistic Majority World[5] for a more socially relevant psychology that assumes responsibility for societal development (e.g., Kağitçibaşi, 1991, 1994b; Nsamenang, 1992; D. Sinha, 1983; D. Sinha & Kao, 1988). Some Western cross-cultural psychologists have also joined in, as seen, for example, in an early call by Jahoda (1975).

The stress on the social relevance and applied significance of psychology is a key to my general orientation to it. This orientation is deepseated in both my personal and academic background and cultural context. Thus, I see psychological inquiry as an important tool not only in understanding behavior but also in changing it, at a macro level, to improve the human condition. This may be seen as an overly ambitious or presumptuous view of the field, if not also a naive one. Even though I am well aware of some truth in such an objection, as well as of the multiple causation of human phenomena, including to a large extent nonpsychological causes, I am, nevertheless, of the opinion that psychology does have the potential to contribute in its own right to the improvement of the human condition.

My work covering the last 15 years has involved research along two different but related paths. One of these has been theoretical in orientation whereas the other has been more problem oriented with an applied emphasis. These seemingly disparate research interests have been quite integrated in my own thinking, and I hope to reflect this integration in this book.

Thus, although on the one hand, I study self–family–culture interfaces and their modifications across time and space, on the other hand, I study planned change through an applied intervention project. This project, which is "action research" in the Lewinian tradition, is presented in this

---

[4]There are some signs that this may be changing. See chapters 7 and 8.

[5]I am using the *Majority World,* instead of the *Developing World* or the *Third World.* The developing countries are not getting any closer to the developed countries (if anything, the gap is widening), and with the collapse of the "Second World," the "Third" does not make much sense. Majority World, referring in fact to the majority of the world's population, emerges as a preferable term.

book both in its own right and also as a case study demonstrating the applied significance and policy relevance of psychology.

## ACKNOWLEDGMENTS

I wrote this book during a sabbatical leave in the 1993–1994 academic year at the Netherlands Institute for Advanced Study (NIAS). I appreciate this leave granted to me by Bogaziçi University. The perfect atmosphere and the superb support provided by NIAS contributed greatly to my work, for which I am truly grateful. Pilar van Breda-Burgueno of NIAS ably typed the whole manuscript through a few revisions.

Ype Poortinga read the first version of the manuscript and gave me much valuable feedback, which I appreciate very much. I also benefited greatly from the comments of John Berry, Pierre Dasen, Patricia Greenfield, and anonymous reviewers, as well as the support of Walt Lonner. I am thankful to Marc Bornstein for taking the initiative to contact Lawrence Erlbaum Associates for me, acting as a liaison. I appreciate the efficient assistance of Judith Amsel of Lawrence Erlbaum with the editing and the production of the book.

My students Asli Carkoglu and Nurcan Karamolla prepared the indexes and helped with the references. Throughout my work on the manuscript, my husband Oğuz Kağitçibaşi, as usual, provided me with invaluable moral support and encouragement. Without his support, I could not have finished this demanding task. I am indebted to all. I am also indebted to my colleagues and students who throughout the last 10 years have influenced my thinking on human development, the family, and cross-cultural psychology.

—Çigdem Kağitçibaşi
Istanbul, Turkey

# 1

# Introduction

## ABOUT THIS VOLUME

What does this volume have to offer the reader? What is it about? It is about human development in family and cultural context. It is about the development of competence and the development of the self, two important spheres of human development. It is about patterns of similarities and differences in these spheres. It is also about systematic changes in family, self, and human competence in conjunction with social change and in particular with socioeconomic development. I first stress the variability that is notable in self and competence. However, I then look into commonality or lines of convergence that are apparent or that can be predicted, given the global changes in lifestyles that include common features, such as urbanization. Thus, this book attempts to provide an understanding into a number of complex and interrelated topics that are of importance to us all in our ever-changing global society. Additionally, it aims to shed light on these multifaceted human phenomena from a cultural and cross-cultural psychological perspective.

This book is about human development, self, and human relations within a cultural context. The development of human relations and the self is situated within the family and society. In my thinking, the links between the person, family and society are crucial for an understanding of global human psychology. On the other hand, this volume is also about the **integration** of theory and practice. Specifically, I make an attempt to find out whether a culturally sensitive conceptualization of individual–family–culture links has any relevance for applications and policies designed to promote human well-being.

So, there are two different types of linkages here that need some clarification from the beginning. The first one has to do with some of the intersections between the different levels of analysis—the individual (self), the group (family), and the larger context in which both exist (culture and society). The second one relates theory and application. It is a defining and possibly unique characteristic of this volume to pursue simultaneously both of these types of linkages that derive from different research traditions. Thus in this book, I attempt to integrate important topics not usually dealt with together, particularly theory and application.

To start with, I should also point out that this is a rather personal book. In several places throughout the volume, I make my views explicit; at times these are political outlooks. Thus, values come into the picture on some important issues, particularly regarding applied or policy-relevant matters. This "involved" stance is a distinguishing mark of the volume and is made clear in both the Preface and the Foreword to the First Edition. Indeed, the Preface and the Foreword constitute an essential part of the book in introducing it from my perspective and in providing an understanding into its main features; that is why they are retained in this second edition also.

## Linking Self, Family, and Society

How do we link individual and society? This is an age-old goal of social philosophers and social scientists. From early on, recognition of the diversity of individual characteristics and interests brought forth the question, "How is social order possible?" (Allport, 1959). Many social theories have been devised to answer this question, but most important, the concept of culture has been construed to understand and make sense of the uniformity constructed out of diversity existing in human groups.

The links between individual and society have often been traced through middle-level contexts such as the family and child **socialization.** In this volume, I look into some aspects of family and family socialization within varying sociocultural contexts with a view to discovering their functional or causal links with human development. Thus, a **contextual-developmental-functional approach** is undertaken here that is also cultural and cross-cultural. It may be helpful at this point to briefly touch on these basic approaches that characterize my thinking in the field. They also constitute the defining features of this volume.

*A Contextual Approach.* The approach here is contextual in that the study of the person and human development automatically implicates the family as the context, and thus features the family explicitly in the conceptualization. Similarly, when the family is under focus, it is automatically situated in its sociocultural environment. This approach is very much in line with the original ecological orientation of Urie Bronfenbrenner (1979), with traces of the classical field theory of Kurt Lewin (1951), on the one hand, and with the later contextualist models, on the other

*in the context of the family*

(e.g., Featherman & Lerner, 1985; Hurrelmann, 1988; Lerner, 1998). Much thinking in cross-cultural psychology is also contextualistic, almost by definition, and the approach here is akin to the current theorizing in this field, particularly in dealing with human development (e.g. Berry, Poortinga, Seagall, & Dasen, 2002; Eckensberger, 1990; Gardiner & Kosmitzki, 2005; Greenfield & Cocking, 1994; Super & Harkness, 1994, 2002; Valsiner, 1989, 1994, 2000).

*more discussion*

*A Developmental Approach.* The approach here is also developmental. This is because it is not enough to note or even to establish with some certainty differences across contexts. *How* these differences emerge is just as important for psychological inquiry. Increasingly the significance of a developmental approach is being recognized, and a developmental orientation is seen as inherently complementing a cross-cultural one (Bornstein & Bradley, 2003; Eckensberger, 1990; Jahoda, 1986; Keller & Greenfield, 2000; Rogoff & Morelli, 1989; P. B. Smith, Bond, & Kağitçibaşi, 2006; Valsiner, 1989). This is not to say that all cross-cultural work takes cognizance of developmental processes, but that the recognition of the need to do so is increasing. It is interesting to note in this context that in her invited address at the centennial convention of the American Psychological Association, Anne Anastasi (1992) pointed to the progress of cross-cultural psychology and life-span developmental psychology as the two most important developments of the last decades in psychology.

*A Functional Approach.* The present approach is functional because social and psychological adaptive mechanisms are invoked to explain *why* a particular type of development occurs, rather than another one. I should note, however, that the functional approach I use is not deterministic and allows for flexibility and feedback mechanisms. Adaptive mechanisms are used as clues to understand why self–family–culture linkages get established in particular ways, showing variability as well as similarity across cultures. In particular, the following basic questions figure importantly throughout the volume: *Why* does a certain type of human development occur in a particular family context, and *why* does that type of family occur in a particular type of socioeconomic–sociocultural context? Such questions address the adaptability of psychological processes and behaviors to (changing) environmental demands. The contextual, developmental ,and functional approaches are elaborated where needed throughout the volume.

*A Cultural and Cross-Cultural Approach.* Finally, in forming the links among the self, family, and the larger sociocultural environment, I work from a cultural and cross-cultural perspective. A cultural approach is presupposed by contextualism, and a cross-cultural approach is required for the unambiguous interpretation of the observed cultural differences (Berry et al., 2002; Van de Vijver & Poortinga, 1990). To understand the functional relations among the society, the family, and the development of the self, the underlying dynamics need to be discovered. A cross-cultural comparative orientation provides the grounds for such an endeavor, as it supplies more variation than can be obtained in a single culture study (Berry et al., 2002; Rogoff, Gauvain, & Ellis, 1984; Segall, Dasen, Berry, & Poortinga, 1999). These basic approaches are elaborated further throughout the volume.

## Linking Theory and Application

The second basic task I undertake in this volume is integrating theory and application. By application, I do not mean the individual-focused psychological practice that readily comes to mind, but rather the use of psychology in large-scale efforts to improve human well-being and to contribute to societal development. Psychologists' contribution to development efforts focuses on its human aspects; therefore, any applied work would benefit from a knowledge of the cultural context in which human phenomena occur. Intervention attempts in the **Majority World** (see footnote 5 in the Preface to the First Edition) need to be especially sensitive to the human relations in the **culture of relatedness** (Kağitçibaşi, 1985a) prevalent in these societies. Thus, interventions may be expected to work better if they take into consideration and build upon the existing human connectedness, as reflected in closely knit family, kinship, and community ties, rather than counteracting them, for example, in building individualistic independence and competition.

    The emphasis on applied research occupies a central place in my orientation to psychology (Kağitçibaşi, 1995, 2002b; see also the Preface to the First Edition). Theory that is not put to the test of application has limited utility, and applications not informed by theory tend to be haphazard and expensive "shots in the dark" that cannot be afforded, especially in the Majority World countries with limited resources. In other words, I believe that psychology need not choose between theory and scientific rigor on the one hand and relevance on the other; both are needed, and it is incumbent on the psychologist, especially on one who lives in the Majority World, to be involved in efforts to contribute to human well-being. Culturally sensitive and both "socially and scientifically responsible" (Drenth, 1991) psychological research can go a long way toward contributing to social development efforts (see the Preface to the First Edition).

In this book I present, in some detail, an applied research project that I have carried out with my colleagues in Istanbul, Turkey. I believe this study deserves attention for demonstrating both the **integration** of theory and practice on the one hand, and the potential of psychology for contributing to human development on the other. This is the Turkish Early Enrichment Project and its long-term follow-up studies that together spanned over a 22-year period. I attempt to bridge the gap between theory and application by using this applied research and program implementations deriving from it as a case in point. I also delve into applied issues in dealing with **acculturation** and immigration.

Finally, I give considerable attention to policy issues and policy relevance. This is a natural next step of a keen interest in the social applications of psychology. For psychological knowledge to contribute to large-scale applications, it should be policy relevant. In this book, the policy implications of the development of competence, early enrichment, and education, in particular, are examined.

## A CULTURAL AND CROSS-CULTURAL PERSPECTIVE

The topics examined in this volume cover a wide scope and include extensive research and theory spanning the fields of cultural and cross-cultural psychology. I would like to give here a rather brief and general overview of the issues involved and examine the relevant concepts. My approach here is basically psychological, though I resort to anthropological and sociological conceptualizations, also, where appropriate.

### The Culture Concept

Anthropologists have been studying culture from early on. It is often quoted that some 164 definitions of culture have been made (Kroeber & Kluckhohn, 1952). Obviously, there are different views about how best to conceptualize culture and what aspects to emphasize. Only recently, in 2005, there was a heated discussion in an online communication network of cross-cultural psychologists about how best to conceptualize culture. So the debate continues. There appears to be agreement, however, regarding its comprehensive nature. Thus, the following characterizations, and others, have been proposed: "traditional ideas and especially their attached values," "the mass of learned behavior passing through generations," "shared learned behavior and meanings that are socially transferred in life-activity settings," "shared symbols and meanings," "different experiences of groups that lead to predictable and significant differences in behavior," "a 'gestalt' of ideas, practices, norms, and meanings that organize behavior as a system," "a superordinate organizer with a pervasive influence on its constituent elements," "a system, a set of interrelated and inextricably linked elements," and "mental programming or software of the mind."

Many psychologists tend to adopt Herskovits's all-inclusive definition of culture as "the man-made part of the environment," including both "physical culture" and "subjective culture" (subjective responses to what is human-made) (Triandis, 1980, p. 2). Various cultural conceptions have been elaborately discussed recently (e.g., Berry et al., 2002; Gardiner & Kosmitzki, 2005; Matsumoto, 2001b; Matsumoto & Juang, 2004; Segall et al., 1999).

*Utilizing Culture in Psychological Research.*    The important point is situating the psychological phenomenon to be studied in its cultural context. This appears as "obvious" because we know that every human behavior is in response to some aspect of culture. Nevertheless, what appears to be obvious turns out to be less so when indeed an attempt is made to integrate culture into psychological analysis (Van de Vijver & Hutschemaekers, 1990).

First of all, the diffuse, all-inclusive nature of culture presents a problem in research. As a superordinate entity, it cannot serve as an explanation or an independent variable (Segall, 1983). Such explanations can turn into empty tautologies, such as "Chinese are this way because of their culture." Thus, attempts have been made by psychologists to define culture in less molar and more molecular ways or to operationalize it (Poortinga, Van de Vijver, Joe, & Van de Koppel, 1987). In this more molecular conceptualization, culture is treated as a "set of conditions" (Segall, 1984), as quite different from culture as a system of meanings (Rohner, 1984). It has also been conceptualized as "shared constraints that limit the behavior repertoire available to members of a certain socio-cultural group" (Poortinga, 1992, p. 10).

Current experimental approaches, particularly in cross-cultural social psychology, "create" culture in the laboratory. This is done by priming certain cultural features, such as independence or interdependence, through experimental manipulations, and then the effects on behavior are examined (e.g. Gardner, Gabriel, & Lee, 1999; Kitayama, Markus, & Kurokawa, 2000; Kitayama, Markus, & Matsumoto, 1995; Kitayama, Markus, Matsumoto, & Norasakkunkit, 1997; A. Y. Lee, Aaker, & Gardner, 2000). Thus, culture can be conceptualized and operationalized as transitory, as well as enduring.

*Methodological Issues.*    Second, and as related to the aforementioned issue of definition, a perennial methodological problem and a longstanding issue is *how* to study behavior in culture. The two basic approaches here,

Box 1.1   Two Approaches to the Study of Behavior in Culture

| "From Within" | "From Without" |
|---|---|
| Emic | Etic |
| Relativist (indigenous) | Universalist |
| "unique" case | "typical" case |
| Cultural psychology | Cross-Cultural psychology |
| | Parallels in: |
| **Idiographic** | nomothetic (psychology) |
| Hermeneutic | positivistic (anthropology) |
| Qualitative | quantitative (sociology) |

*insider - outsider debate*

having traditional counterparts in psychology and sociology also, are those that prescribe studying the phenomenon either *from within* or *from without*. In general, the approach from within studies the particular phenomenon from within the system, whereas the approach from without studies the phenomenon from a position outside of the system. The approach from within treats the phenomenon as unique and studies it in its own right. The approach from without, however, sees the phenomenon as comparable to others. The two approaches have been the basis of "cultural" and "cross-cultural" psychology, respectively; these are discussed later. The two views have been expressed in different labels in different disciplines and orientations, but the basic similarities among them prompt me to group them together. The views from within and from without have their parallels in the *idiographic* and **nomothetic** approaches, respectively, in psychology. These go back to Cronbach's characterization of "the two disciplines of scientific psychology," and before him to G. Allport (1937), who traced them further back to the German philosopher Windelband. These perspectives also find parallels in the qualitative and quantitative research traditions in sociology and the hermeneutic versus positivistic approaches in anthropology. In cross-cultural psychology, the emic–etic debate and the indigenous (or relativist) versus universalist orientations (Berry et al., 2002), respectively, appear analogous. Finally, the debate between cultural and cross-cultural psychology reflects the same basic distinction (Box 1.1).

What is common in the idiographic, hermeneutic, emic, indigenous, relativist, cultural approaches is an emphasis on the uniqueness of concepts in each cultural context, because they derive their meanings from these contexts. There is also a stress on the variability and the uniqueness of the individual case (person, culture, etc.) that requires its study from within and in its own right, defying comparison. In contrast, the nomothetic, positivist, etic, universalist, cross-cultural approaches study the

*oh, I see*

*(?)*

*all different names for same idea?*

"typical," not the unique, which can be compared using a common standard or measure. The emphasis is on the underlying similarities that render comparison possible. There appears to be a basic conflict between the emic and the etic, if accepted as exclusive orientations, because being stuck in one would negate the other (Kağitçibaşi, 1992a, 2000b).

The 1990s witnessed much debate about whether cultural or cross-cultural psychology provides the better conceptual scheme for studying human phenomena (Markus & Kitayama, 1992; Shweder, 1990, 1991; Shweder & Sullivan, 1993; Van de Vijver & Hutschemaekers, 1990). The discussion revolved around some more basic methodological and conceptual issues such as whether a comparative (decontextualizing) or a holistic, contextualizing (situated) methodology is to be used in the study of human psychological phenomena and whether **universalism** or **relativism** of psychological functioning is to be assumed. It was paralleled by a discussion on universalist orientation versus **indigenous psychology** (Adair & Diaz-Loving, 1999; G. E. Enriquez, 1990; Kim & Berry, 1993; Nsamenang, 1993; D. Sinha, 1992, 1997). The debate still continues (Berry et al., 2002; Kim, Yang, & Hwang, 2006).

## Reconciling Assumed Opposites

Both the universalist and the relativist approaches have their challenges. The main problem the universalist approach faces is an inference of **false uniformity** across cultures on the basis of unicultural research. In other words, when a finding obtained in one sociocultural context is assumed to have universal validity, this may be false. A great deal of mainstream psychology is faced with this challenge. Indeed, cross-cultural psychology has emerged in reaction to this outlook. The relativist or **contextual approach** has its own share of challenges. Foremost among these is the reverse assumption of **false uniqueness** or specificity. This is the opposite of assuming uniformities where there are none; it claims that there are no uniformities where there may, in fact, be some. Taken to its extreme, this view considers all findings culturally relative and rejects all comparison, because every act is assumed to have a unique meaning deriving from its specific context.

For some time, psychology has ventured to integrate culture into its analyses, and it has striven to account for cultural diversity while claiming generality (Dasen & Jahoda, 1986, p. 413). In doing so, it is bound to "move out" from the individual into his or her interaction with the environment. Yet, this is where this basic conflict comes in. In the words of Lightfoot and Valsiner (1992), it is between "the need to conceptualize 'context dependency' of psychological phenomena and the 'context-eliminating' theoretical traditions of psychology" (p. 394). It can be resolved if there is a genuine understanding that eliminating the context or abstracting behavior from its environment is not the only route toward reaching generality. Indeed, it may be a route that does not lead to real generality but to pseudogenerality. This type of generality is assumed but not empirically demonstrated. The assumption is that the causal relation that is found in the behavior abstracted from the environment in the pure controlled laboratory condition holds across cultures or environments because it is independent of the latter. Yet, even the most ardent experimentalist knows that complete abstraction from the environment is impossible in research with human beings who bring their "culture" into the laboratory, in the form of expectations, habits, values, and so on.

The other, and surer, route toward generality, though laborious, is integrating context into psychological study and examining its impact. When this type of context-dependent study is conducted in other contexts, also, then the similarities in obtained causal relations can weave the path toward generalities. In other words, when studies that take context into consideration are repeated in different cultural contexts, and similar results are obtained, this provides grounds for possible universal patterns.

Thus, I do not subscribe to the "either–or" stance of the debate and believe that the two approaches can be, and should be, complementary (Kağitçibaşi, 1992a, 2000b). To my understanding, cultural psychology is psychology within the cultural context, and as such all human psychology should indeed be cultural psychology, because human phenomena always take place within culture. However, as we are far from this ideal, psychological inquiry that takes cognizance of the cultural context can be labeled cultural psychology. If in such inquiry a comparative approach is used and thus at least two cultures are implicated, even if implicitly, we are in the realm of cross-cultural psychology.

It is important to note that a comparative approach does not preclude a contextualistic orientation. Indeed, a contextualistic orientation and a comparative orientation are basic to my thinking (Kağitçibaşi, 2000a). In this, I am in agreement with Price-Williams (1980), who observed, "Contexts are not necessarily unique; they can be compared" (p. 82). That is why in this book I see myself involved in both cultural and cross-cultural psychology. However, for the sake of simplicity and to avoid using both terms together, I use *cultural psychology* unless specifically referring to cross-cultural comparison.

## The Growth of a Cross-Cultural Perspective

Human development always occurs within culture, but it has traditionally not been studied as such by academic psychology, despite some notable recent changes. The issue does not concern only **developmental psychology** but is true of all psychology whose unit of analysis is typically the individual. This outlook is in line with the goal of discovering universal regularities in psychological processes and behavior, which psychology inherited from physics. Accordingly, a physical science model is typically adopted adhering to a positivistic philosophy of science. This implies a methodological orientation isolating the behavior from its natural context to control for "unwanted" variation. Thus, social and cultural factors have often been absent in psychological analyses.

When the context is taken into consideration, it is often the proximal context, not so much the distal one, that appears too remote to the psychologist. This is noticeable from a cursory glance at developmental psychology textbooks. Most tend not to stress cultural differences, or they treat them as extraneous variables, and they view the individualistic trajectory as the normal way of developing. It is these textbooks that influence how development is viewed in American psychology and abroad, where it is exported. In other words, culture is still not seen as central to what is studied, but rather as the "distal" background. This is generally true even though some changes have been taking place more recently, and some texts do give a more central role to culture (e.g., M. Cole & Cole, 2001).

This state of affairs was noted by critics both within and outside psychology starting in the 1980s. For example, focusing on human development, the anthropologist T. Schwartz (1981) stated, "Developmental psychology has largely missed the opportunity to consider the child in the cultural milieu, which is the *sine qua non* of the developmental completion of human nature" (p. 4). Similarly, Jahoda and Dasen (1986) called for a "cross-cultural developmental psychology ... [which] is not just comparative [but] essentially is an outlook that takes culture seriously" and deplored the fact that "theories and findings in developmental psychology originating in the First World tend to be disseminated to the Third World as gospel truth" (p. 413).

In his classic work on the ecology of human development, Bronfenbrenner (1979) earlier complained about the "Marked asymmetry: a hypertrophy of theory and research focusing on the properties of the person and only the most rudimentary conception and characterization of the environment in which the person is found" (p. 16) and claimed that "developmental psychology ... is the science of the strange behavior of children in strange situations with strange adults for the briefest possible periods of time" (p. 19).

These views have been echoed in much writing up to the present by those who believe that a non-**contextual approach** to behavior in general and to human development, in particular, is inadequate (e.g., Bornstein & Bradley, 2003; Bronfenbrenner, 1986; Dasen, 2003; Eckensberger, 2003: Friedlmeier, Chakkarath & Schwarz, 2005; Kağitçibaşi, 2000a; Lerner, 1998; Rogoff, 1990, 2003; Saraswathi, 2003; Shweder et al., 1998). The extensive criticism, substantiated by insightful research, has aimed to be a corrective to the "narrow" focus of psychology. It has been an outcry, loud and clear, serving as the basis for the advancement of a wide range of disciplines and critical views spanning cross-cultural and cultural psychology on the one hand, and social constructionism and **indigenous psychology,** on the other (Kim et al., 2006).

Today the situation is surely undergoing change. Over the last two decades, significant advances have been made in broadening the perspective of psychological inquiry to encompass the context. The developments in cultural and cross-cultural psychology are substantial, and they do challenge the established scientific traditions of psychological research. The number of journals devoted to cross-cultural psychological research or having an international cross-cultural outlook has increased greatly. Reviews of cultural and cross-cultural research are increasingly published in the *Annual Review of Psychology* (Bond & Smith, 1996; Brislin, 1983; Cooper & Denner, 1998; Greenfield, Keller, Fuligni & Maynard, 2003; Kağitçibaşi & Berry, 1989; Shweder & Sullivan, 1993) and in several handbooks, encyclopedias, and other annual publications in psychology (Berman, 1990; Murphy-Berman & Berman, 2003, Pawlik & Rosenzweig, 2000; Spielberger, 2004). A second three-volume edition of the *Handbook of Cross-Cultural Psychology* appeared in 1997 (Berry et al., 1997), and biannual volumes of selected papers from the conferences of the International Association for Cross-Cultural Psychology are continuing.

Numerous books in cross-cultural psychology or cross-cultural *social psychology* have been published, including a number of textbooks that have made second or third editions (e.g. Berry et al., 2002; Lonner & Malpass, 1994; Matsumoto, 2001b; Matsumoto & Juang, 2004; Moghaddam & Taylor, 1993; Segall et al.,1999; P. B. Smith et al., 2006; Triandis, 1994). All this activity indeed points to a growing cross-cultural psychology. Side by side this comparative work, scholarship in cultural psychology also took place, at times in contention to it (e.g., M. Cole, 1996; Nucci, Saxe, & Turiel, 2000; Shweder, 1991; Stigler, Shweder, & Herdt, 1990).

Of greater relevance to the present volume, in recent years cultural and cross-cultural studies of human development have enjoyed significant growth, as is evident from a growing number of books on the topic (e.g. Bornstein & Cote, 2006; Friedlmeier et al., 2005; Gardiner & Kosmitzki, 2005; Greenfield & Cocking, 1994; Keller, Poortinga, & Schölmerich, 2002; Rogoff, 2003; Saraswathi, 2003).

## Trends in the Study of Culture and Human Development

In the early days of the cross-cultural study of human development, there was an affinity to an anthropological approach emphasizing the specific cultural context. Starting with the pioneering work of the Whitings and their associates on childrearing in six cultures (Minturn & Lambert, 1964; B. B.Whiting, 1963; B. B.Whiting & Whiting, 1975), a considerable amount of work was conducted by psychologists and anthropologists at times working together. Several publications in the 1980s and 1990s on cross-cultural child development provided overviews of this work (e.g., Munroe, Munroe, & Whiting, 1981; Stigler et al., 1990; Valsiner, 1989; Wagner, 1983; Wagner & Stevenson, 1982).

*A Move to Modern Nations.* Subsequently, some new trends have emerged in cross-cultural studies in general and in culture and human development in particular. The bulk of cross-cultural research today is less closely linked with anthropology. It is conducted more by psychologists and to a large extent in the Western world or in contemporary nation-states or "modernized" societies in the rest of the world and much less in preindustrial human groups, for example, in Africa or in Oceania, where cross-cultural research first started (see Berry et al., 2002; Segall et al., 1999). There are, of course, current exceptions (e.g., Greenfield, 1999, 2000; Keller, 2003; Nsamenang, 1992; Tape, 1994, cited in Dasen, 2003; Zeitlin, 1996), but their limited number relative to the ongoing bulk of cross-cultural research indeed makes them exceptions. Cultural variation in the study of human behavior and in particular of human development has become much more a part of mainstream psychological research.

Why this shift? A number of factors have contributed to this process. Globalization in general, coupled with greater international communication, immigration, and culture contact have made almost all Western societies multicultural. Thus, whereas some time ago psychologists interested in cultural diversity traveled to distant societies, now they find it in their own midst. Although there was always diversity in the world, what has challenged mainstream developmental psychology more than the international diversity is the increasing variety in Western societies themselves. Cultural diversity could no longer be ignored in

implications of cultural psych

the study of human development. Thus, there is a tremendous growth in research with different ethnic and cultural groups in the immigration countries of North America, Northern Europe, and Australia-New Zealand (see chapter 10). It is notable to see the topic of culture entering into mainstream psychology journals.

The earlier cross-cultural research conducted in preindustrial, even in isolated preliterate societies could easily be ignored by mainstream psychologists as irrelevant, with the possible exception of the cognitive area. This is because those societies were often remote and very different from contemporary societies. Also, as Azuma (1986) noted some time ago, "a limitation of such studies is that cultural variables covary with the degree of industrialization of the society" (p. 3). This confounding of socioeconomic structural factors (such as education, standard of living, **gross national product [GNP]**, etc.), that is, level of societal development, with cultural beliefs and values blurs interpretation. More recently, with the increased volume of comparative research emerging from contemporary nation-states, it has been possible to keep socioeconomic-level characteristics rather similar in cross-cultural comparison and to focus on other cultural differences. It is more difficult to ignore this type of research, for it often involves socioeconomically similar samples, such as urban educated groups, university students, and so on, with nevertheless different cultural orientations. For example, with the great economic growth in the "Pacific Rim" and the high mathematics-science achievement levels of Japanese and Chinese children, both in their own countries and in the United States, there is much interest in the West in discovering especially the Japanese culture (Japanese management, Japanese childrearing, Japanese education, etc.). Such interest leads to a greater appreciation of cross-cultural research.

*Majority World Researchers Join In.*     Another factor contributing to the changing trends in the study of culture and human development has been the greater involvement of psychologists from the **Majority World** (see footnote 5 in "Preface to the First Edition" in this volume) in research and publications. This is significant, when we consider the fact that traditionally psychology was a Western, and to a large extent, American preoccupation. The rest of the world typically followed suit, demonstrating a remarkable degree of "traditional acquiescence" (Kağitçibaşi, 1995, 1996b). Again starting in the 1980s, however, the progress of cross-cultural psychology and particularly of cross-cultural developmental psychology has benefited from scholarship in the rest of the world, especially in Asia. In addition to a growing number of contributions to journals and books containing cross-cultural psychological work from non-Western psychologists, some volumes have come out dealing specifically with psychology and human development in the Majority World (e.g., Curran, 1984; Kağitçibaşi, 1996b; Nsamenang, 1992; Pandey, 1988; Saraswathi, 2003; Saraswathi & Dutta, 1987; Saraswathi & Kaur, 1993; Suvannathat, Bhanthumnavin, Bhuapirom, & Keats, 1985). Currently research is conducted mostly with students and other "modern" urban populations in the rest of the world.

*Large-Scale Multinational Comparative Research.* The growing interest in large-scale multinational comparative work has also been an influential factor. Data sets obtained from a large number of countries have typically used university student samples or others such as teachers or business executives from the "modern" sectors of global society (e.g., M. H. Bond et al., 2004; Chinese Culture Connection, 1987; Georgas, Berry, Van de Vijver, Kağitçibaşi, & Poortinga, 2006; Hofstede, 1980; S. H. Schwartz, 1992, 2004; P. B. Smith, Dugan, & Trompenaars, 1996). Conducted mostly within cross-cultural social psychology, this work is of growing importance for the theoretical advances in cross-cultural psychology in general, particularly in the study of values (see P. B. Smith et al., 2006).

*An Applied Emphasis.* An applied emphasis has also increased the relevance of cross-cultural research on human development. Some significant social problems that require solutions are amenable to cross-cultural study. Among these, ethnic issues and global development efforts currently have high priority. Thus, with the need to improve ethnic relations and to contribute to the human aspects of global development, there is an increasing allocation of resources for applied intervention research both in the Majority World and also involving ethnic minorities in the Western world. This attracts the attention of mainstream psychologists to ethnic and cross-cultural research, as well. Nevertheless, cross-cultural developmental research, which has contributed significantly to theoretical advancement, cannot boast the same degree of success in serving the well-being of the world' s children (Dasen & Jahoda, 1986; Kağitçibaşi, 1991, 1992b, 1995, 2002a), for that has not been its intention. Much work needs to be done that is both informed by culturally relevant theory and is problem oriented in order to promote children's well-being globally. This is a basic theme in this volume.

*Indigenous Psychology.* Another trend emerging mainly from non-Western contexts is the so-called indigenous psychology (Adair, 1992; M. H. Bond, 1986; G. E. Enriquez, 1990; Heelas & Locke, 1981; Kağitçibaşi & Berry, 1989; Kim & Berry, 1993; Kim et al., 2006; D. Sinha, 1986, 1992). It purports that each culture should be studied within itself, as it forms the all-important context of psychological phenomena. In this approach "from within," the historical-cultural characteristics, symbols, and artifacts are used as materials to construct a meaningful portrait of a people. "Natural" rather than "imposed" categories are utilized, reminiscent of the typically *emic* approach of anthropology and cultural psychology, discussed earlier. Indigenous psychology has found ripe ground, especially in Latin America following the pioneering work of Diaz-Guerrero (1975) on the "psychology of the Mexican" (e.g., A. M. Padilla, 1995).

"Indigenization" or "indigenous psychology" has been proposed as an antithesis of the universalist orientation (Kim & Berry, 1993; Kim et al., 2006), typical of much of cross-cultural psychology. However as I discussed earlier, I believe these are complementary approaches (Kağitçibaşi, 1992a, 2000b), each providing feedback for the other. If indigenization is seen as an approach, rather than a goal in and of itself, then it is likely to be followed by a comparative approach. And when commonalities emerge out of such comparison among different indigenous realities, we begin to approach universality (Berry, 1989). This point is discussed further later.

*Similarity–Difference*

This brings me to a consideration of the meaning attributed to similarities and differences obtained in cross-cultural comparisons. It does not make much sense to insist on an either–or position (either **universalism** or **relativism**) because this is an empirical issue. It is the researcher's task "to know when it makes sense to emphasize likeness, [and when] difference" (to quote a phrase from Shweder, 1984, p. 60, which he later tended to abandon by rejecting likenesses; Shweder, 1990, 1991; Shweder & Sullivan, 1993). As I mentioned earlier, with the greater comprehensive coverage of variation in cross-cultural study, common and variable characteristics and biological and environmental factors can be distinguished more effectively than when a smaller range of variation is entailed.

However, it should also be noted that similarity across cultures does not *necessarily* imply genetic determination. It can be due to some universal (or commonly shared) psychological or social structural factors. For example, all societies have developed rules and social control mechanisms for maintaining intragroup harmony, care of the young, and **socialization** of children. Thus, there are similarities across cultures, as well as differences. These similarities may be due to analogous functional links among behaviors in different cultures, rather than to biological commonalities.

Yet, when similarities are found between cultures, an ethological (biological) explanation is commonly invoked (Papoušek & Papoušek, 1991; Sigman & Wachs, 1991); only when differences are found do they tend to be attributed to culture. One reason for this is the assumption of the uniqueness of each culture. This is a view that was derived from descriptive anthropology and was readily accepted by cross-cultural psychologists. It has led to the expectation that cross-cultural comparison should uncover *differences* in behavior. Thus cross-cultural research reports are replete with statements such as "the Indian self … , the Japanese mother … "; or "the Greek philotimo," the "Latin American simpatia," the "Japanese amae," or the "Mexican historic-sociocultural premises." Yet, study after study finds *similar* characteristics among behavior patterns in countries such as India, Korea, Mexico, Greece, Japan, and so on, that remain implicit. For example, Triandis (1989) noted sentiments in other collectivistic cultural groups similar to the "Greek philotimo," and a Turkish researcher (Ayçiçegi, 1993) found the "Mexican historic-sociocultural premises" (Diaz-Guerrero, 1991) regarding sex roles to be also typical in Turkey!

There is a need to go beyond the descriptive psychological portrayal of different peoples toward discovering underlying reasons for behavior that may be shared to some extent among them. Thus the current two-way thinking (difference implying cultural, similarity biological causation) needs to be expanded to at least a three-way thinking. When a difference is found in cross-cultural comparison, a contextual (environmental/cultural) interpretation would be implied, except for few known race differences. When a similarity is found, however, there is an ambiguity as either shared biology or shared structure (psychological, ecological, social, or cultural) may be the cause. Or there may be the further possibility of a combination or interaction of the two. The challenge is unraveling these influences. Recent work incorporating evolutionary perspectives into the study of culture and biology provides us with a more sophisticated understanding into the study of human development in culture (see Keller et al., 2002).

If we are interested in possible generalization, the comparison of two or more emic portrayals is needed. This is where an etic or cross-cultural comparative approach comes into the picture. It is important to note here that the ultimate aim of this approach should be more the discovery of shared characteristics than of differences, that is, if psychological theory aspires to universality. But interestingly enough, a focus on differences is prevalent here, also. There are, of course, exceptions as exemplified in the well-known studies utilizing data from a great number of countries in order to discover patterns of beliefs or values (e.g., M. H. Bond et al., 2004; Hofstede, 1980, 2001; Schwartz, 1992, 1994; Schwartz & Bardi, 2001; Schwartz & Bilsky,1990; P. B. Smith et al., 1996). However, in these studies, typically structures are imposed from outside rather than discovered in cultural (emic) study. What appears to be lacking are studies conducted within the cultural context that reveal functional/adaptive links among phenomena that may, in turn, repeat themselves in different contexts, thus pointing to some fundamental causal relations.

## Benefits of the Cross-Cultural Perspective

In concluding the introduction to the volume, I would like to dwell on the benefits of a **cross-cultural perspective.** The greatly increasing volume of cross-cultural research is a clear indication of the growing appreciation of the value of a cross-cultural perspective. The advantages involved have been repeatedly voiced by those conducting such research. Nevertheless, it may be valuable at least to remind ourselves of these benefits particularly as we start an extensive study of human development in a cultural context. The following are some of the oft-quoted benefits from a mainly developmental perspective.

A cross-cultural **developmental approach** uncovers a greater range of variation than any single culture study can. With a more comprehensive coverage of diversity, a wider perspective emerges according to which what is typical and what is atypical may need to be redefined.

With increased coverage of variation, it also becomes more possible to distinguish between biological and environmental influences. That is, the greater the commonality found in a developmental sequence or psychological process over highly varied cultural contexts, the greater the likelihood of its biological roots, though shared social structures may also be a cause. With a finding of increased diversity in a psychological phenomenon across cultures, environmental causation is implicated.

In view of the increased degree of variability in cross-cultural study, theories based on research with more limited samples may need to be revised if they are to hold up to their claims of universality. The theory-testing potential of cross-cultural research is thus very important. Any psychological theory claiming universality, as they all do, must be demonstrated to hold cross-culturally. Obviously, a theory can never be proven in absolute terms, as there is always the likelihood of one disconfirming case. Nevertheless, if a theory finds supportive evidence in highly diverse cultural contexts, its claim to "external validity" and universality would be a lot stronger than if it is tested in only a single cultural context. The more a theory receives cross-cultural confirmation, the more closely it approximates universal generality. Indeed, most cross-cultural research in human development has had such a theory-testing goal. This research has served theory very well; for example, Piagetian and Vygotskian theories have enjoyed cross-cultural extensions.

Such testing also helps refine theory. For example, as cross-cultural research showed that the "formal operations" stage of Piaget was very rare among illiterate adults, he changed his orientation and accepted

*[handwritten margin notes: — how many until applicable for all humans?]*

*[handwritten bottom note: meaning of diversity in a culturally psychological framework]*

that formal operations may not be a universal stage but may occur only in specific familiar domains. This reformulation was subsequently supported by research conducted in the United States (Kuhn & Brannock, 1977, reported in Rogoff, Gauvain, & Ellis, 1984; see also Fiati, 1992).

Another advantage of cross-cultural comparative research is the possibility of disentangling some variables highly associated in one culture by going to another society where this is less so. This allows for refined analysis by unconfounding variables. For example, it is difficult to study separately the effects of age (maturation) and the experience of schooling in Western contexts because these two variables are highly confounded (all children are at school). By conducting studies in cultures where this is not the case, the effects of maturation, as separate from schooling, can be studied (Kağitçibaşi, 2004; Rogoff et al., 1984; Rogoff, Mistry, Goncu, & Mosier, 1991).

As in the previous example, cross-cultural research has the potential to study naturally occurring cause–effect relationships that cannot be manipulated experimentally, by utilizing natural quasi-experimental studies. To follow up the preceding example, it is not possible to deprive some children of schooling in order to study the effects of age on cognitive development independently of schooling. However, if such is naturally the case, cause–effect relations can be pursued accordingly.

Cross-cultural study can also provide comprehensive descriptions of psychological phenomena. With an increased range of variation covered, for example, in age-specific human development, we can get a fuller spectrum of development, which is a prerequisite for explanation (Bornstein, 1984). Especially in the hands of anthropologists, who have contributed greatly to the study of cross-cultural human development, rich description can be a valuable source of knowledge and understanding.

Such comparative description and cross-cultural work generally provide insight into human adaptation (Keller, 2003; Rogoff et al., 1984, 1991). Such work brings into focus variation in ecological/environmental factors and how they are experienced by the people being studied. Functional relations among the ecological, economic, sociopolitical contextual variables and the psychological behavioral characteristics of people reflect biological/cultural adaptations (Berry, 1976; Berry et al., 2002; Keller et al., 2002).

Cross-cultural psychological study also works as a corrective for the researcher's ethnocentrism. This is mainly because it sensitizes the researcher to the cultural basis of his or her own beliefs. Cross-cultural psychologists are likely to realize that psychology, as it has been constructed historically, is indeed an **indigenous** psychology of the Western world. It needs to be tried out for validity in the non-Western world if its claim to universality is to be substantiated by evidence. A lot of psychological theories are cultural constructions, reflecting a particular orientation to and interpretation of "reality."

There are important implications of this view both in the explanation of human phenomena and in applications across cultures. For example, how sex roles or human competence are conceptualized within the prevalent "folk theories" of a people may be quite different from those of the psychologist armed with Western theory. It takes considerable sensitivity to work out differences in interpretation and to avoid blunders in applied work that may entail interventions to change behaviors. Here a psychologist with a cross-cultural orientation and experience would have a definite advantage over the one with a unicultural background.

Thus, probably a most important benefit that cross-cultural orientation is providing to general psychology is a "sensitization to culture." In a way, one could say that, it has taken the demonstration of cultural differences in comparative research to get the psychologists to take culture seriously. Both cross-cultural and ethnic psychological research has played an important role here. The **integration** of culture into psychological analysis promises to widen the scope of our understanding; it can be a breakthrough for psychology. There are significant signs that this has already started to happen.

## ORGANIZATION OF THE BOOK

In this introductory chapter, I have focused on cultural and *cross-cultural perspectives* in psychology, which I adopt in this volume to provide a general conceptual framework. Given the benefits of a cross-cultural approach especially in widening the scope of our understanding, I make frequent use of it in discussions throughout the book. Nevertheless, my main focus is on human development in a cultural context, as mediated by the family, with both a theoretical and applied emphasis. Its coverage here is quite varied and spans wide ground. The different chapters deal with different yet related topics.

The book is composed of two parts. The first part focuses on human development, family, and culture. The chapters in this first part mainly cover theory and research linking phenomena at the individual, group (family), and societal levels of analyses. Human development in a cultural context and the more specific process of the development of competence; the relations between culture and self, focusing on individualism–collectivism (I–C); family change through social change; and parenting and the development of the **autonomous–related self** are examined. Throughout the discussions a cross-cultural, contextual, functional, and developmental perspective is used.

In the first part there are five chapters, which deal with the central issues I have discussed in the Introduction. Within the framework of the complementary cultural and cross-cultural approaches put forward in the Introduction, chapter 2 studies "Development in Context." Numerous examples from across cultures and diverse theoretical perspectives point to the necessity of construing human development in context. Though the cultural context is stressed, an ecological perspective to context is used with different layers of embedded environmental influences, ranging from the family to societal values. Context is seen to impart meaning to human experience, as, for example, in the construal of "childhood" itself.

Chapter 3 examines "**Socialization** for Competence" and builds upon the previous chapter. Theoretical and cultural conceptions of **cognitive competence** are reviewed. There is a discussion of cultural variability in the meaning of *competence* and particularly cognitive competence. The difficult issues of **relativism** versus comparative standards and the danger of double standards in the study of competence across cultures are dealt with. A basic theme discussed in chapter 2 and later on in the book (chap. 7), is the culture gap between "traditional" childrearing values and the new environmental demands emerging with social change and urban lifestyles, which may result in a disadvantage for the child.

Chapter 4 provides a discussion of the concept of self across cultures and looks into the complex interplay of culture and self, focusing in particular on I–C. Several theoretical and disciplinary perspectives are examined, including a review of the earlier critique of individualism in the Western, particularly in the American, context, as well as the recent debates on I–C. A distinction is made between the *related self* and the *separate self,* which is another basic theme throughout the book. It is also conceptualized as a dimension of independence–interdependence in interpersonal relations. Correlates of I–C, including moral thinking, self-enhancement, cognitions and emotions, control, and achievement, are discussed.

Value of children and the family constitute the topic of chapter 5. Family is studied as the microcontext of development. Three prototypical family models are introduced, and a theory of family change is proposed through social change. The commonly accepted modernization view of convergence toward the Western model is questioned, and a shift toward a "model of psychological-emotional interdependence" is proposed, particularly in conjunction with urbanization socioeconomic development. This is a family/human model, as the development of the self within the family is also studied. There is a proposed shift toward the development of the **autonomous–related self** through changing lifestyles in the **culture of relatedness** (collectivism).

In the last chapter of Part I, parenting and the development of the autonomous–related self are examined. A developmental perspective is used to shed light on the self in the context of family and society deriving mainly from the **family change theory** proposed in chapter 5. Current debates in the field are addressed and a theoretical perspective is put forward. It is shown that pursuing either the macrosystem of socioeconomic change resulting in family change or the microsystem of the self with two basic human needs, the development of the autonomous–related self emerges as a viable process. Thus chapters 4, 5, and 6 fit together and build upon one another in dealing with self–family–culture dynamics.

Part II moves from theory to application. It focuses on induced change and the role of psychology especially with regard to two topical areas of current relevance: early enrichment and immigration. The second part of the book examines the applied significance of psychology in promoting healthy human development and analyzes the psychology (social science)–social policy interface. It addresses the implications of the theoretical perspectives proposed in the first part for social issues and applications. In particular, the materials covered in chapters 2 and 3 are relevant for chapters 7, 8, and 9, whereas the contents of chapters 4, 5, and 6 are relevant for chapter 10. The second part comprises five chapters.

Chapter 7, "Induced Change: The Role of Psychology," critically appraises the role of psychology in the light of the foregoing discussions; it forms a link between the two parts of the book. It asks the question how psychology can help promote "human development" and assigns a socially, as well as a scientifically, responsible role to psychology. There is a more extensive discussion here of the "political" issues of values, standards, and relativism in the study of human development across cultures. Some controversial topics are confronted, such as schooling, religious education, early development and school readiness, and the nature–nurture underpinnings.

The next chapter, "Intervention: Early Enrichment," narrows down the question to the early environment of the growing person and environmental enrichment. It provides an overview of the early childhood development (ECD) research and applications, in both the Western and the **Majority World.** This is seen as an area where psychological expertise, especially in the field of developmental psychology, can inform research and applications. Some issues in ECD are reviewed, such as the relative efficacy and cost-effectiveness of child-centered versus parent-centered approaches to providing support and building competence.

In chapter 9, the Turkish Early Enrichment Project is presented as a case in point. This is a longitudinal study of early enrichment, coupled with two follow-up studies, covering a period of 22 years. In this project, both the home and preschool environment and mother training are studied in terms of their differential effects on the development of children. Effects of the project intervention on the overall development and school achievement of children as well as on the mothers and the home environment are discussed. The holistic, interactional, contextual orientation of the project is seen as its main strength, leading to gains sustained over time.

Chapter 10 examines immigration and **acculturation.** It focuses on the self and the family in the immigration context. It builds upon the theoretical perspectives covered in chapters 4, 5, and 6. Acculturation is studied both in its own right and also as a field of policy-relevant applications; thus the chapter is included in the second part of the volume. Theoretical perspectives on acculturation and a selected number of issues are covered, including acculturation strategies, family, parenting and the self, and cultural transmission of values. Contextual as well as individual factors are examined.

The last chapter, "Search for Integration and Policy Relevance," builds upon the theoretical and the applied perspectives covered in the volume and examines the general issue of psychology and social policy. In particular, the policy implications of the Turkish Early Enrichment Project are reviewed. Policy relevance of psychology (and of social science) is discussed with a focus on global human development and well-being. **Integration** is searched for from the foregoing topics and discussions, especially with regard to the development of the self and of human competence in family and culture. In this integration an "involved" stance is assumed, in line with the socially relevant role of psychology.

All the chapters of the book are interrelated, yet each stands on its own, as well. As such, they may be seen as independent, and particularly the first and the second parts differ in theoretical and applied emphasis, respectively. Nevertheless, in my thinking the different parts of the book hang together, and I try to weave them together. Specifically, the theoretical perspectives set out in Part I serve as the theoretical underpinnings of the interventions and policy-relevant applications presented in Part II. Similarly, the call for the greater involvement of psychology in socially relevant research serves as the moral justification for the interventions. Theory, research, and policy need to be interrelated, and this is what this book is about.

## SUMMARY AND MAIN POINTS

This book is about human development, self, family, and human relations within a cultural context.

- It deals with two types of linkages: the links between the different levels of analysis—the individual, the group, and the larger context; and the links between theory and application.
- To study the links between individual and society, a contextual-developmental-functional, and cultural and cross-cultural approach is undertaken.
- Theory and application are both needed and interrelated.
- The universalist and the relativist/contextual approaches are basic to the study of behavior in culture. Each has its own challenges. The former carries the risk of false uniformity assuming the generality of unicultural research findings. The latter has the risk of false uniqueness, assuming there are no uniformities where there may be some. Two approaches can be complementary; there is no need to take an either–or stand.
- A comparative approach does not preclude a contextualistic orientation and they are both basic to this book.
- When the context is taken into consideration in psychology, it is often the proximal context. However, notable advances have been made to encompass the larger context, reflected in the growth of cultural and cross-cultural studies of human development.
- Some new trends in cross-cultural psychology emerged with globalization and the greater involvement of psychologists from the Majority World. There is a growing interest in large scale multinational comparative research as well as in the study of multicultural societies of immigration. Indigenous psychology has emerged mainly from non-Western contexts.
- Greater coverage of variation in cross-cultural study is helpful to distinguish common and variable characteristics and biological and environmental factors. Usually difference implies cultural, similarity biological causation. However, similarity may be due to either shared biology or shared social structure and norms.
- There are numerous benefits of cross-cultural perspective. With increased coverage of variation, it is easier to distinguish between biological and environmental influences. The theory-testing potential of cross-cultural research is important; any psychological theory claiming universality must be demonstrated to

hold cross-culturally. Cross-cultural research helps disentangle variables highly associated in one culture by going to another society where this is less so. Cross-cultural study also works as a corrective for the researcher's ethnocentrism, thus, contributing to a "sensitization to culture."

## DISCUSSION QUESTIONS

1. Why is it important to examine the link between individual and society?
2. How do theory and application feed into one another?
3. How do idiographic and nomothetic approaches differ?
4. What are the challenges of the universalist and the relativist/contextual approaches? How can these approaches be used as complementary to each other?
5. How did cross-cultural psychology emerge as a separate discipline from anthropology?
6. What are the benefits of a cross-cultural perspective?

# PART I

## HUMAN DEVELOPMENT, FAMILY, AND CULTURE

# 2

# Development in Context

Some time ago a Japanese psychologist, Azuma (1986), described the meaning of a common response by a Japanese mother to her stubborn child who refuses to eat a particular vegetable. She would often say, "All right, then, you don't have to eat it." How would you interpret this response? Most people would interpret it to mean that the mother did not feel very strongly that the child should eat the vegetable (could eat something else). Indeed, Azuma reports that this was his American research collaborators' interpretation, also. Yet, Azuma indicates that it was those mothers, in particular, who felt most strongly about the child eating the vegetable, and that is why they used the strong threat, "You don't have to obey me," which means "We have been close together. But now that you want to have your own way, I will untie the bond between us. I will not care what you do. You are not a part of me any longer" (Azuma, 1986, p. 4).

Clearly, the same words carry different meanings for the Japanese mothers and the American researchers. Do the words have correspondingly different meanings for the children in the two cultures? Azuma continued by saying that the Japanese mothers reported this strategy to be most effective in getting their children to cooperate. This is because in the family culture where *amae* (dependence of the child on the mother and the mother's complete indulgence in the child) is the key in early **socialization,** this statement would carry a meaning of rejection for the child. For American children, however, it would carry only the welcome meaning that they are free not to eat the vegetable. This simple example shows the importance of socially defined and contextually situated meaning.

## CONTEXT AS MEANING

Psychological phenomena always occur in context, not in a vacuum; therefore, context always figures in the psychological "reality." This is, of course, stating the obvious. Nevertheless, when it comes to studying human psychological functioning, a **contextual-interactionist perspective** is not commonly used. I have already pointed to this issue in the introductory chapter and have noted some criticism of traditional non-**contextual approaches** as well as recent significant attempts at contextual analysis. In this chapter, I want to elaborate these trends further, focusing on human development.

Human development is **socialization,** together with maturation. It encompasses the lifelong process of becoming social, becoming a member of a society. Thus, it involves constant interaction with the sociocultural environment. Any study of human development, therefore, must have contextual and temporal dimensions. Indeed, significant trends in these directions are becoming established with the rise of cultural and cross-cultural psychology on the one hand, and life-span developmental approaches on the other.

In cultural and cross-cultural study, culture is often invoked as the context of psychological functioning, though context can be conceptualized at other levels, also (physical, interpersonal, familial, etc.). One reason underlying the conceptualization of context as culture is the paramount role of culture as an "organizer" of meaning. I want to start the discussion of context, therefore, at the cultural level—context as meaning.

A contextual approach to the person–environment relations that focuses on culture considers culture as a source of meaning. Indeed, cultural context provides precious meaning to observed behaviors and their causal links, which can further expound the dynamics underlying the behaviors. Thus, the "same" behavior may assume different meanings in different contexts. The example provided by Azuma demonstrated how this may happen.

## Parental Warmth and Control as a Case in Point

Research examining the relations between **parental control** and parental acceptance as perceived by children is another case in point. In an early comparative study that I conducted (Kağitçibaşi, 1970), I asked Turkish and American adolescents how much parental control and affection they experienced while growing up. Although there was no difference in perceived parental affection, Turkish adolescents perceived more parental control than did American adolescents. In other words, the Turkish adolescents did not interpret strong parental control as lack of affection. This study provided early evidence for the independence of parental affection and control dimensions of childrearing. It also pointed to the social-normative and cultural basis of parental control, though not of parental affection.

Subsequent studies carried out in the 1980s in North America and Germany found parental control to be associated with perceived parental hostility and rejection (Rohner & Rohner, 1978; Trommsdorff,

1985). However, the same behavior of parental control was found to be associated with perceived **parental warmth** and acceptance in Japan (Kornadt, 1987; Trommsdorff, 1985) and in Korea (Rohner & Pettengill, 1985). In other words, American and German children and adolescents who thought their parents used strict discipline interpreted this as their parents not liking them, but Japanese and Korean children didn't. A current study comparing German and Turkish late adolescents found again that there was no difference between the two groups in perceived parental acceptance despite rather different parent–child relations (Hantal, Kağitçibaşi, & Ataca, 2006).

Why apparently the same behavior is attributed opposite meanings by children and adolescents in different cultural contexts is an intriguing problem. It can be addressed only with reference to the contextually situated meaning systems, that is, culture, that define what is and is not "normal." Specifically, in cultural contexts such as in the United States, nonrestrictive discipline is the norm in child **socialization** stressing autonomy. In this kind of context, strong parental discipline is the exception and is, therefore, more likely to be perceived as "not normal," and thus reflecting hostility or rejection on the parents'part.

From a **social comparison process** perspective, (Festinger, 1954; Gerard & Rabbie, 1961), which has been known for a long time in social psychology, one would expect that the behavior or experience that is different from others' would be interpreted as "not normal." This kind of comparison can be made only by children old enough to perceive the differences between their own situation and that of other children. Such deviant childrearing behavior can even function as pathology, precisely because the children and adolescents exposed to it would interpret it as "not normal" in comparing themselves to other children they know. Taking this reasoning one step further, deviant restrictive parental control can actually reflect parental hostility in such a cultural context.

In a different culture, where childrearing is characterized by strong parental control, as in Japan and Korea, however, the "same" strong parental control has an entirely different meaning. It is "normal" and therefore "good." When the child who is exposed to it compares herself with other children, she finds she is not different from them; that is, she is not rejected by her parents. Indeed Trommsdorff (1985) noted, "Japanese adolescents even feel *rejected* by their parents when they experience only little parental control and a broader range of autonomy" (p. 238, emphasis in original).

More recent work, especially with Chinese parent–child relations, concurs with earlier research. What is often interpreted as Chinese "authoritarian" parenting by psychologists is shown by Chao to be a socially valued parenting orientation designed to "train" the child toward moral

*[handwritten margin note: religion tie in in Asia, what about in N. America]*

maturity in the context of Confucian morality (Chao, 2000; Chao & Tseng, 2002). Similarly, research with other ethnic minorities in North America and Northern Europe points to more parental control, which appears to be accepted as normal by all concerned (Dekovic, Pels, & Model, 2006; Kwak, 2003; Oosterwegel & Vollebergh, 2002; Rudy & Grusec, 2001). Thus the same behavior can be attributed different meanings by parents and psychologists, with different cultural meaning systems and holding informal or professional knowledge.

Beyond the *meaning* attributed to parental control and as related to it, what actually is done, or the type of control may be important. Thus, Lau and his colleagues (Lau & Cheung, 1987; Lau, Lew, Hau, Cheung, & Berndt, 1990) differentiated between "dominating" and "order-keeping" parental control in their work with Chinese adolescents and adults. They found a negative relationship between dominating (restrictive) control and parental warmth but a positive relationship between order-keeping (and caring) control and warmth. This is in line with Moos's earlier distinction between dysfunctional and functional controls (Moos & Moos, 1981) and parallels Baumrind's (1980, 1989) and Maccoby and Martin's (1983) conceptualizations of **authoritarian** and **authoritative parenting,** respectively. In authoritarian parenting, there is an obedience orientation and no autonomy is provided to the child. In authoritative parenting, on the other hand, the child's autonomy is valued, and there is *induction,* that is, control with reasoning.

*[handwritten margin mark: ☆]*

In general, higher levels of control are common wherever childrearing does not stress the development of individualistic independence in the child. Over decades this has been demonstrated by research pointing to conformity-oriented childrearing in more closely knit familial and cultural contexts (Barry, Child, & Bacon, 1959; Berry, 1976; M. H. Bond, 1986; Dekovic et al., 2006; Kağitçibaşi, 1984, 1996a; Rothbaum & Trommsdorff, 2007). This is examined further later on.

*[handwritten margin note: what kind of negative outcomes]*

Recent studies point to the relevance of additional contextual factors. Comparing the long-term effects of strict parental control, even including physical punishment, it is found that this type of control leads to negative outcomes among Euro-American children and adolescents, but not among African American ones (Deater-Deckart & Dodge, 1997; Lansford, Deater-Deckart, Dodge, Bates, & Pettit, 2003). This is an important finding that challenges commonly held assumptions in psychology and shows that what is assumed to be human nature may be culture.

These studies point to the importance of how control is perceived, and whether or not it is seen as being "normal" and legitimate. It is an attribution that is, in turn, influenced by social conventions and norms. Thus, parental control in socialization is closely related to values and goals of

*[handwritten margin notes: "time is an important factor" / "factor 31 as well!"]*

socialization that show variation across cultures and through time. Parental affection, on the other hand, may be a candidate for a psychological universal, possibly based on biological/evolutionary processes involving protection and care of the offspring for the continuation of the species (Batson, 1990). As I have mentioned earlier, a key factor here is the desired level of dependence–independence in child socialization. This is one of the main themes in this book.

*[handwritten margin notes: "speaks to dynamic nature of culture"]*

These examples of culturally defined meaning point to the importance of integrating context (culture) into psychological analysis. Parental control and affection, key to the study of human development, acquire psychological meaning conveyed by "culture" and they, in turn, constitute "culture" at the proximal level.

*[handwritten margin note: "Everything in title is only for now"]*

## THEORETICAL PERSPECTIVES ON CONTEXT

*Historical Trends.* An interest in the context of development has a long history in philosophy, sociology, education, and psychology that goes back to the philosophers of the Enlightenment, like John Locke and J.-J. Rousseau, reemerges in the writings of John Dewey, and shows up in the early developmental and comparative psychology (Baldwin, 1895, 1909; Novikoff, 1945; Von Bertalanffy, 1933). A parallel emphasis emerged in the early Symbolic Interactionist School in sociology (Cooley, 1902; G. H. Mead, 1934; Thomas & Znaniecki, 1927).

The view positing the importance of the cultural context as providing meaning is ingrained in several theoretical perspectives in psychology and the social sciences. It is in line with the social-constructionist position, deriving from Berger and Luckmann (1967), that stressed "the processes by which people come to describe, explain, or otherwise account for the world in which they live" (Gergen, 1985, p. 3). In the 1980s, interpretive anthropologists who emphasized cultural symbols and meanings provided important insights into the cultural construction of "reality" (Kirkpatrick & White, 1985; Marsella, DeVos, & Hsu, 1985; Shweder & LeVine, 1984). Subsequent formulations of cultural psychology also emphasized the "implicit meanings that shape psychological processes" (Shweder & Sullivan, 1993, p. 507; see also Shweder, 1990, 1991; Stigler et al., 1990).

Thus, cultural context, as a source of meaning, was highlighted by social constructionists, interpretive anthropologists, and cultural psychologists alike. The basic idea shared by these scholars is that people attribute meaning to their environments; thus they create culture. Cultural symbols, such as religious ones, in turn provide meaning to people. In Shweder's (1990) words, "Culture and mind make each other up" (p. 27).

BOX 2.1.    Some Contextual Models and Research Traditions of Relevance to
Human Development

– Systemic models of person-environment interaction
– Ecological and Bioecological model of Bronfenbrenner (1979, 1999)
– Berry's eco-cultural theory in cross-cultural psychology (Berry, 1976, 1980;
  Berry et al., 2002; Segall et al., 1999)
– Early comparative anthropologycal research (Barry et al., 1959; LeVine,
  1974; B.B.Whiting, 1963; Whiting & Child, 1953; Whiting & Whiting, 1975)
– Vygotsky's socio-historical school of thought (1978)
– Life-span development theory (Baltes, Reese, & Lipsitt, 1980; Elder, 1985,
  1998; Lerner, 1989)
– Developmental contextualism (Featherman & Lerner, 1985; Lerner, 1989)
– "Everyday cognition and informal education" approaches of cultural psy-
  chologists and anthropologists (Cole, 1996; Greenfield & Lave, 1982; Nunes,
  Schliemann, & Carraher, 1993; Rogoff, 1990, 2003; Scribner & Cole, 1981;
  Serpell, 1976), informed by Vygotsky
– Problem and policy-oriented family research, informed by ecological the-
  ory (Bronfenbrenner & Weiss, 1983; Dym, 1988; Sameroff & Fiese, 1992;
  Weiss & Jacobs, 1988)
– Ethnic minority research from an ecological perspective (Coll, 1990;
  Harrison, Wilson, Pine, Chan, & Buriel, 1990; McLoyd, 1990; Ogbu, 1990;
  Szapocznik & Kurtines, 1993)
– Super & Harkness' developmental niche (1986, 1999)
– Valsiner's co-constructionism (1989, 1994)
– Kağitçibaşl's family change model (1985b, 1990, 1996a, b)
– Time and socio-historical change as context (Bronfenbrenner & Evans,
  2000; Crockett & Silbereisen, 2000; Elder, 1998; Kağitçibaşi's & Ataca, 2005;
  Keller & Lamm, 2005)

Over decades, other currents of theory and research also helped
bring context to the fore, both at the cultural level and at other levels.
They constituted independent academic traditions, spanning different
disciplines. Nevertheless, there have been some points of contact
among them; they have all shared a contextualistic thinking and emphasized an ecological orientation (see Box 2.1).

*Developmental Models.*    Given this philosophical and theoretical
background then, is developmental psychology heavily contextualistic? The answer, ironically, is not an unqualified "yes." This is because,

together with these various contextual perspectives, there have also been strong threads of "context-eliminating" theoretical traditions in psychology (Lightfoot & Valsiner, 1992), as mentioned in the Introduction. The prominence of the mechanistic and organismic models in developmental psychology is remarkable. These perspectives, together with the insistence on studying the individual as the unit of analysis have worked as deterrents to contextualistic conceptualizations (for reviews, see Dasen, 2003; Hurrelmann, 1988; Kağitçibaşi, 1990).

The mechanistic model espoused by behaviorism had a limited conceptualization of the environment as proximal stimuli. Though this model has been abandoned to a large extent in favor of cognitive models, its rather narrow focus on the individual has been maintained, with a shift from individual behavior to individual cognition. Even in social learning theory, it is the cognitive structuring of the social environment by the individual that is emphasized (Bandura, 1977, 1986).

The organismic model, in its turn, emphasized maturation, almost to the exclusion of context. Though in Piagetian theory, for example, interaction with the immediate environment through assimilation and accommodation is recognized, environment as the cultural context is assigned a secondary role. Nevertheless, in the face of cross-cultural evidence questioning the generality of the higher stages of cognitive development (formal operations), some of the theory's claims have had to be modified (Segall et al., 1999).

More recent developments in biological orientations to human development constitute new challenges to contextual approaches. The advances in biotechnology and computer technology as utilized in brain research, neuroscience, molecular biology, and genetics, including the completion of the human genome, are very important. They have contributed greatly to the unraveling of the biological underpinnings of human development and human behavior. The challenge is to continue to recognize the importance of culture in the face of this "biological shift." Recent evolutionary views stressing adaptive development as the interface between biology and culture are promising in dealing with the challenge (Keller et al., 2002).

*how one might frame psych. in a collectivist terms?*

## Theoretical Advancement and Problem-Oriented Research

Notwithstanding these strong individualistic traditions in psychology, contextual conceptualization in human development has acquired momentum, especially in the last two to three decades. Two theoretical developments have been especially important in this general paradigm shift. One of these is ecological theory; the other is life-span development theory.

The antecedents of ecological theory can be found in Lewin's (1958) topological psychology, Brunswik's (1955) "environment–organism–environment arc," and Barker's (1968) ecological psychology. However, it is subsequent theorizing and research that have paved the way for the rise of contextual conceptualization. In particular, Bronfenbrenner's (1979, 1986) conceptualization of environmental systems led to a general recognition of the multilevel bases of human development and functioning. This perspective is elaborated in the next section.

Life-span developmental approaches (Baltes, 1987; Baltes, Reese, & Lipsitt, 1980; Lerner, 1989; Lerner, Hultsch, & Dixon, 1983) also emphasized multilevel integrative organization of psychological functioning and the connections among levels. Change and plasticity in human development is also recognized as the environmental influences interact among themselves and change over time (Elder, 1985, 1995, 1998). Thus, there is a dynamic interaction both between the developing person and the environment, as well as among the different levels of influencing factors at the biological, psychological, physical, and sociocultural levels.

With this kind of a holistic approach to human development through time, several types of interactions among different variables become relevant. These may be at the intrapersonal, interpersonal, familial, social, cultural, and historical levels. Thus a great deal of complexity is involved in contextual theory, and integrating frameworks have been proposed to account for biological, psychological, and sociocultural changes in developmental processes (Featherman & Lerner, 1985; Lerner, 1989).

Apart from the aforementioned theoretical views stressing context, problem-oriented research has also contributed to the increasing relevance of context in human development in the last two decades. This has taken place quite independently of theory building, though Bronfenbrenner's ecological theory has been utilized as a general framework. Basically, research aimed at understanding children's sociocultural environments and designing programs to improve children's welfare have singularly focused on context variables. Family interactions, both internal and external, constitute the key contextual influence in this research (Brooks-Gunn & Duncan, 1997; G. W. Evans, 2004; Huston, 1991; McLoyd, 1990; R. S. Mistry, Vandewater, Huston, & McLoyd, 2002; Schorr, 1991; Slaughter,1988; Szapocznik & Kurtines, 1993). The contextualistic approach has been effectively used in this research mostly in studying child development in adverse environmental conditions, such as poverty. More recent problem-oriented research in the United States has focused on the long-term effects of poverty. This topic is examined further toward the end of the chapter.

focus on children
↳ what about reshaping
adult development, etc..?

The main point of this research is that there are mediating contextual variables (at the levels of the caregiver, family and community) between the macrolevel adverse conditions (such as poverty) and the growing child. Some of these are positive factors that can shield the child from adverse environments. The very existence of mediating variables allows room for action in favor of the growing child. For example, even if poverty cannot be arrested, the mediating family problems such as distress, abuse, and so on, can be reduced by intervention programs providing support to parents. Thus context, at different levels, assumes a key importance for applied research.

## Contextual Theories in Cross-Cultural Developmental Psychology

Much of this book involves the contextual study of cross-cultural human development. It is therefore important to provide a general overview of some of the main theoretical perspectives that share an ecological-contextual perspective, including my own. Whether they have emerged from cross-cultural developmental research or not, they have shed light on this research. I have already mentioned some of these perspectives in the previous discussion. Nevertheless, I take them up again because they have served as guidelines specifically for cross-cultural developmental research. This is a short overview; more detailed reviews have been provided by Dasen (2003), Gardiner and Kosmitzki (2005), and Mistry and Saraswathi (2003).

### Cultural Mediation

*Vygotsky.*    The sociohistorical theory of development propounded by Vygotsky (1978, 1986) is possibly the most thoroughly contextual theory of human development. Though Vygotsky's work became known in the West only after his death, he has had an enduring influence on cultural psychology and cognitive anthropology. He placed great emphasis on the social origins of human mental functioning in the sense that what is acquired by the growing child is that which exists in the sociocultural context, and thus is culturally mediated. This process works mainly through the use of language and expansion in the child's **zone of proximal development (ZPD).** ZPD refers to the child's potential for advancement beyond his or her present performance level if guided by an adult. Such guiding in a master–apprentice mode is called **scaffolding.** Thus, cognition is rooted in language and cultural experience. This contextual theorizing came as a challenge to the organismic and maturational models and the individual focus in Piagetian theory of cognitive development.

how did he discover this?

Vygotsky's focus on the cultural context also includes a historical perspective, referring to sociocultural changes over time that have direct impact on modifications in thought. In particular, his student Luria (1976) in his work with illiterate Uzbek peasants and those with some literacy living in collective farms pointed to the influence of these sociohistorical experiences in syllogistic reasoning. Vygotsky's influence is seen in cultural approaches studying "everyday cognition" (see chap. 3), which stress athat the scaffolding by adults of children's learning and **socialization** is society, in an apprenticeship mode (e.g., Nunes, Schliemann, & Carraher, 1993; Rogoff, 1990, 2003; Rogoff & Lave, 1984).

### Ecological Theories

*Bronfenbrenner.*   The ecological systems theory of Bronfenbrenner (1979, 1998,1999) has served as the basis of ecological-**contextual approach**es both in developmental psychology in general and also in the study of culture and human development. Culture comes into this model particularly at the macrosystem level, embedding the exo-, meso-, and microsystems that all embed the child, all nested within one another, like Russian dolls. The model is dynamic in the sense that there are mutual interactions between the active child and the immediate environment (microsystem), as well as mutual interactions and influences among the different environmental systems. Thus, changes in one system inevitably create changes in other systems. This is a basic characteristic of a systems model.

Though the direct interaction and experience of the child is with the immediately surrounding system, effects of the more embedding systems and culture as a whole are incorporated into the model. For example, a policy change regarding the provision of free child-care services for young children of working mothers is a macrosystem process. It would have effects on the exo-, meso-, and microsystems, for example, in increasing numbers of child-care centers (exosystem), encouraging more women with young children to seek employment, less extended family or neighbor caretaking of the child, less family caretaking of the child (all impacting the meso- and microsystems), and more peer and nonkin experience for the child in day-care centers.

Subsequently, Bronfenbrenner (Bronfenbrenner & Evans, 2000) incorporated "time" as an important component of the ecological system. Thus, as a second dimension to the spatial ecological systems, a "cronosystem" has been added. This reflects the influence of the "life course perspective" in sociology, in particular (Crockett & Silbereisen, 2000; Elder, 1995, 1998). This perspective addresses how macrosystem contextual factors such as an economic crisis or a change in political regime can impact different cohorts of adolescents and youth in different ways over time, depending on variability in timing and family characteristics and strategies.

*Berry.*    The ecocultural framework of Berry (Berry, 1976, 1980) emerged out of early work on cognitive style, and it has served as the main framework for two major textbooks in cross-cultural psychology (Berry et al., 2002; Segall et al., 1999). The main feature of the framework is distinguishing population and individual levels of analyses and to account for both cultural and biological adaptation/transmission of psychological characteristics and behaviors. The ecocultural context includes both the ecological and the sociopolitical context in which individual functioning is embedded through adaptation. The framework has been used to explain systemic differences between hunter-gatherer and sedentary agricultural societies in significant patterns of human behavior, such as psychological differentiation (cognitive style) and compliance orientation in childrearing. The latter deals directly with cross-cultural human development. More recently, the ecocultural framework has been extended to deal with differences among contemporary societies and families (Georgas et al., 2006).

Drawing on both Bronfenbrenner's ecological systems theory and Berry's ecocultural framework, Georgas (1988, 1993) developed an ecological and social cross-cultural model. Utilizing the concentric circles of Bronfenbrenner's theory, this model stresses the connections among the different embedding levels particularly in dealing with the family in context (Georgas et al., 2006).

### The Developmental Niche

Deriving the concept of "niche" from biological ecology where it refers to the habitat of a particular species, Super and Harkness (1986, 1994, 1997; Harkness & Super, 1996) devised a framework for the study of child development in context. Three components of the **developmental niche** surround the child. These are (a) the settings or the physical and social environment in which the child lives in daily life, (b) the cultural customs and childrearing practices of the caretakers, and (c) the psychology of the caretakers. This is an inclusive ecological framework focusing on the individual child, at the center of the developmental niche. Thus, the settings include the whole range of important environmental factors such as the physical setting, climate, nutrition, household and family size, language(s), and so on, in the child's environment. Customs and childrearing include childrearing practices, daily routines including play and work patterns, caretaking behavior, and formal and

*[handwritten margin note: Importance of informal education to culture!]*

informal education. Psychology of the caretaker includes basically parental beliefs (parental "ethnotheories"), values and orientations.

There is an understanding that the different components of the niche interact and act in a dynamic system. Again a systems approach is used, which entails some balance and coordination. However, this is easily disturbed when a change occurs in one of the components, usually introduced from outside. This framework has served as a heuristic device to study child development in context, especially from a comparative perspective. It has been valuable in providing the researcher with a systematic structure of what to look for and compare in different settings.

### Family Change Theory

*[handwritten margin note: self is general concept – universal?]*

I developed a theory of family change on the basis of a cross-cultural research on the value of children for parents (Kağitçibaşi, 1982a, 1985a, 1985b, 1990, 1996a). The theory has evolved over time and has led to the development of a model of self, as well. This theory serves as the main framework for quite a lot of the material presented in this volume, so I do not elaborate on it here. It is discussed in chapters 5 and 6. Briefly, note that this theory is similar to the other contextual models described previously in providing links among different levels of phenomena. In particular, it examines the connections between the different aspects of the background socioeconomic variables and lifestyles; family structure and family system; family interaction and childrearing; and the development of the self. It also deals with sociohistorical change and examines how different family models emerge in different environmental contexts.

## The Value of a Contextual Functional Perspective

This short overview of some contextual theories in cross-cultural developmental psychology points to a great deal of common ground. It also shows that we indeed have the theoretical tools to deal with human development in culture. Nevertheless, we also face some challenges. First of all, *where* culture is in the study of human development remains an issue. Particularly given the limitations of graphic representation of the models, misconceptions can occur. For example, in ecological models, culture is depicted to exist in the macrosytem or the distal environment. However, as Super and Harkness (1999) note, this locating of culture in the macroenvironment, for example, in Bronfenbrenner's model, misses its direct contact with the child. Even though surely culture has indirect impact on the developing human being through the institutions of the meso- and the microsystems such as family and school, it is also there in the innermost immediate context. Thus, the conceptualization of culture "out there" is misleading —a fact that psychologists need to remind themselves of.

Second, to be useful in explaining phenomena, our theoretical models need to go beyond the description of context and hypothesize causal relationships between contextual variables and child development outcomes. This can be a challenge where a myriad of influences complicate the picture. A developmental perspective benefits from a functional analysis, that is, an examination of the underlying reasons for behaviors and relations. In particular a theoretical perspective that entails a contextual, developmental and **functional approach** can go a long way in addressing the basic questions "What?," "How?," and "Why?"[1]

I illustrate this by taking up the example of self or **self-construal**, a concept widely used in current cross-cultural psychology. This concept is examined thoroughly in this book (chaps. 4 and 6); here I am using it as an example. As is discussed later, much recent research and theorizing has focused on the variability of the self across cultures. In particular, the distinction between an independent and an interdependent self has been stressed (e.g., Markus & Kitayama, 1991). These two types of self-construals have been shown to be more common in individualistic and collectivistic cultures, respectively. Of importance to cross-cultural theorizing, considerable research has been done treating the self-construal as the independent variable and examining its effects on various domains such as emotions, cognitions, communication styles, memory, resource allocation preferences, and the like.

The bulk of this social-psychological research deals with the question "What?" In other words, it examines what type of self-construal is associated with what type of behavior. This is important information but does not go beyond describing an association. If we want to know *how* this association comes about, we would need to delve into a more basic causal level of analysis. We would want to know *how* one or another type of self develops. This is a developmental approach that goes beyond establishing an association. The context of development becomes important here, such as family background, childrearing, and so forth. Such analysis would shed light on the contextual mechanisms involved in the emergence of a certain type of self.

---

[1] This section builds on the material of P. B. Smith, Bond, and Ka itçiba i (2006, pp. 80–81).

*How can you show more than a caused relationship when designing an experiment?*

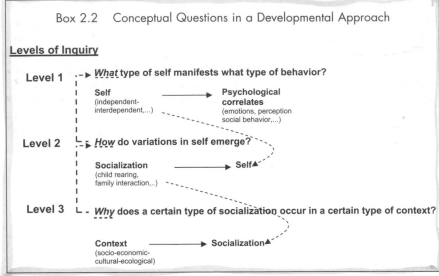

Box 2.2    Conceptual Questions in a Developmental Approach

**Levels of Inquiry**

Level 1    ┊-▶ **What type of self manifests what type of behavior?**

┊    **Self**                            ▶ **Psychological**
┊    (independent-                         **correlates**
┊    interdependent,...)                   (emotions, perception
┊                                          social behavior,...)

Level 2    └-▶ **How do variations in self emerge?**

┊    **Socialization**                   ▶ **Self**▲
┊    (child rearing,
┊    family interaction,..)

Level 3    └-- **Why does a certain type of socialization occur in a certain type of context?**

**Context**                          ▶ **Socialization**▲
(socio-economic-
cultural-ecological)

*Note.* From *Understanding social psychology across cultures (p. 81), by* Smith, Bond, & Kagitçibasi, 2006, London: Sage.

Even a third question can be asked regarding *why* certain types of background factors occur in some contexts but not in others. For example, why certain types of childrearing occur in certain types of family and society but not in others takes us into an inquiry regarding the functions of such childrearing. In other words, we would be examining the reasons underlying different childrearing orientations and their relative adaptiveness in different sociocultural contexts.

From this it should be clear that a developmental approach that is also contextual and functional can be a powerful tool in linking the individual (self), family, and society/culture. Such an approach can address and provide an understanding into the observed diversity in human patterns in different sociocultural contexts. Box 2.2 gives a schematic representation of this line of reasoning. This approach is used extensively in this book, and the particular example of self-development is elaborated further in chapter 6.

## FEATURES OF CONTEXT

The discussion up to now has focused on the theoretical developments that have helped bring context into the foreground of the study of human development, despite strong noncontextual academic traditions in psychology. Let us now consider context further, in relation to psychological functioning. In this discussion, I focus on what constitutes context.

The context of human development comprises numerous levels of influences, all interrelated with and embedded in one another. Because it may be impossible to integrate them all simultaneously into a single study, different "components" figure in different approaches. Which one of these different levels of ecological-environmental systems is to be studied at any one time and what variables in it are to be singled out for analysis are empirical questions. The answer often depends on the researcher's interests and the accessibility of the variable or the ecological system to scientific inquiry. In this section, I want to pick and discuss briefly two different contextual features, at different systemic levels, that I consider important and that have been studied extensively. These are societal values and parental beliefs and values.

## Societal Values Regarding Children

What is the place of the child in society? Do societal values regarding children show variability or is there a universal commonality, deriving from the nature of human evolution and procreation. The answer is both. Childhood, like any other concept, is socially defined and as such it is a cultural product that shows cross-cultural variation. Obviously, there are also universally shared aspects of the definition of childhood mainly based on our common biology (in terms of young age, small stature, dependence on adults, need for care; etc.).

Childhood has been studied through history and across cultures, and _still a_ remarkable variation and shifts in its conceptualization have been noted. _changing_ The historical treatise by Aries (1962) on the discovery and transforma- _role_ tion of childhood is well known. It showed that childhood in middle-class society in Western Europe, as a special conceptual entity unto itself, emerged only in late modern history. Although this view was later challenged by medieval historians (see Hanawalt, 2002), it has remained influential. Later studies of changes in the cultural definitions of childhood across time also point to diversities (LeVine & White, 1986; Woodhead, 1991). The main theme in all these works is that social-cultural conceptualizations of childhood, as reflected in social values, are not stable but change over time and space.

This has important implications about the place of the child in society, children's education, what is expected of them, how they are treated—in short, their complete lives. Examples of diversity in cultural conceptions of childhood and corresponding social values abound in the literature. I briefly discuss "child work" as an example.

*Child Work.* Early on, anthropologists (Munroe et al., 1984; B. B. Whiting & Whiting, 1975) studied children's work in different cultural contexts. In general, their findings showed that in agrarian societies children from a very early age onward are expected to do some household chores. The complexity and amount of work increase with the child's age. Thus, in middle childhood a large portion of a child's waking hours are taken up by some sort of work. This is in sharp contrast, for example, to the lifestyles of children in Western, urban, middle-class contexts, which are characterized by a preponderance of play. For example, B. B. Whiting and Whiting (1975) reported that 41% of the Nyansongo (Kenya) children's time was devoted to work, compared with only 2% of American children in Orchard Town, New England (United States.)

Subsequently, Nsamenang (1992) gave examples of children's work from West Africa, which start with small errands around the house from the time the children just begin to walk. Child work constitutes an important contribution to the household economy. It is also "an indigenous mechanism for social **integration** and the core process by which children learn roles and skills" (p. 156, emphasis added). Other research from Africa (Dasen, 1988a; Harkness & Super, 1992; Super & Harkness, 2002) presented a similar picture. Indeed, it is a familiar picture in many rural societies and even in urban contexts, where economic hardship prevails, and where children's material contribution in the form of household chores or economically productive work can make a difference to family well-being.

A nine-country comparative study on the value of children for parents, (Fawcett, 1983; L. W. Hoffman, 1987; Kağitçibaşi,1982 a, 1982b, 1998a) provided further evidence of the salience of children's work in agrarian economies. Children's material contribution (including help with household chores) was considered important by parents in less developed countries and among rural respondents, contrasted with very little salience of this value in developed countries and urban settings. This study and its recent replication are presented in chapter 5. The point to be made here is that in socioconomic contexts where the child's material contribution to the family is substantial, a utilitarian value is attributed to the child, and his or her work is seen as important.

With changing lifestyles, especially with urbanization and increased parental education, child work loses importance. This change is seen both in less actual child work and in less importance attributed to it by parents. Thus, values attributed to children and their place in the family and in society show variation. A most important dimension of variation is along rural–urban and socioeconomic-status (SES) differences, in short, level of development in societal terms.

*(handwritten margin note: care of the elderly)*

*(handwritten left margin: does that process have a role on a society?)*

The cultural conception of childhood obviously differs between contexts where childhood is *in fact* very different. Thus, in sociocultural domains where children, like other family members, carry heavy responsibilities, childhood may not be seen as a special, distinctive entity unto itself. In contrast, where children are in school and are an economic cost, rather than an asset, child work (even in household chores) is negligible (Rogoff, 2003). It is in this context that childhood is given a special, distinctive status and may even turn into a subject of "sentimental idealization" (Kessen, 1991; LeVine & White, 1991, p. 21).

When these two socioeconomic cultural contexts are compared, the main difference appears to be a shift from an emphasis on the material *value* of the child *for* the family to an emphasis on the *needs* of the child (Woodhead, 1991) (i.e., from a parent-family-centered to a child-centered outlook). It is also a shift from the utilitarian (economic) to the psychological value of the child, as I elaborate later on. These shifts in societal values take place both through time, as seen in Western modern history (Aries, 1962; Hanawalt, 2002; LeVine & White, 1991), and across space, through socioeconomic/rural–urban variations.

Thus the example of child work shows a general correspondence between a society's conception of childhood and children's actual lifestyles. Indeed, societies set up environments that are conducive to particular types of child behavior, reflecting parental-societal expectations from children, and by and large most children are socialized into those prescribed roles. Whether this fit between societal values and children's "developmental trajectories" is optimal for all involved (the children, families or the changing society) is a key question asked in this volume.

*(handwritten note: good)*

## Global Social Change

Child work also brings to the fore the problem of gaps or cultural lags between societal values that reflect traditions that may no longer be adaptive to changing socioeconomic conditions and the demands of new lifestyles. Child work has been debated extensively. It exists everywhere, but it is more common in Africa and other Majority World regions where there is widespread poverty. It often takes the form of domestic labor, agricultural labor, apprenticeship in manufacturing, and working as street vendors. Though some observers (Nsamenang, 1992) point to its value for the family and for the informal education and socialization of the child in society, studies also show that it interferes with the formal education of low-income children and adolescents. For example, Oloko (1994) points to "street work representing maladaptation to a modernizing economic, social and political environment" (p. 220).

The issue is when child work is a part of the common process of socialization for adult roles, as described by Nsamenang (1992), and when it turns into child abuse. In the previous pages, I gave some examples of variations in child work. When we look at global statistics, we see that child work is more extensive in poorer regions of the world. For the year 2000, the International Labor Organization (ILO, 2002) estimated that globally 211 million children (one fifth of all children) age 5 to 14 were working in economic activity; 73 million of these are under age 10 (ILO, 2002). Sub-Saharan Africa has the largest proportions, nearly one third of all children age 14 and under (48 million). Particularly with the declaration of "The Rights of the Child," there is a debate about the definition of child work and the borderline between child work and child abuse. This is a complex issue, which is also laden with value judgments. Boyden (1990) attempted an analysis by differentiating *child work* from *child labor*.

Thus, what was probably functional at one point in time may not continue to be functional at a later point in time, due to changed circumstances; it may even become dysfunctional. This issue has important policy implications, and it is a central theme of this book. All societies undergo social change; for many Majority World societies, the changes in lifestyles reach drastic proportions especially with large-scale migration from rural villages into urban areas (see Box 2.3). The graphic in Box 2.3 shows that only as recently as 1990, the number of young populations living in rural areas was twice that of the number living in urban areas of the Majority World. Soon after 2010 the two populations are expected to equal each other in numbers, and by 2025 the urban populations are expected to exceed the rural ones considerably. This global *urban shift* is of crucial significance in understanding contextual change. Nevertheless, it is not well recognized. It has tremendous implications for changing lifestyles from agrarian to urban ones with concomitant changes in the needs and behaviors of people. When studying psychological phenomena, therefore, this change and the possible gaps it creates need to be taken into consideration, rather than assuming stable environmental conditions. Societal change is of great relevance for all the issues covered in this book.

Other examples of culture lag in the face of societal changes abound around the world. For example, Boyden (1990) noted that the dowry system in India has led to the widespread abortion of female fetuses, with modern technology providing the information about the sex of the fetus (p. 202). With the continuing custom of providing a substantial dowry for the daughter at marriage, daughters are seen to be very costly in South Asia (Winkvist & Akhtar, 2000). This appears to be a major reason for the abortion of female fetuses, which is a growing social ill of alarming proportions in South Asia.

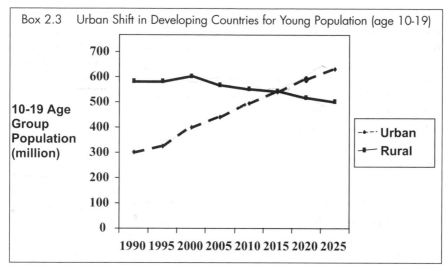

Box 2.3   Urban Shift in Developing Countries for Young Population (age 10-19)

*Note.* From World Energy Council (p. 5), 1999.

A politically and institutionally induced societal change of major significance is the one-child policy in China. In a society with traditional Confucian ideology of ancestor worship and the important role of the son in this tradition, a one-child policy has brought about tremendous social and familial challenges (e.g., Li, 1995; B. G. Rosenberg & Jing, 1996). Abortion of female fetuses is also seen in China, despite government measures against it. The implications for the future populations are awesome.

Another example of a politically induced social change of a very different type is that which followed the unification of Germany after the fall of the Berlin Wall. Crockett and Silbereisen (2000) studied the effects of this major societal change on the identities of adolescents who were directly affected by it. Each one of these issues and many others around the globe reflect the importance of looking into the macrosystem variables and particularly changes in these in studying human development in context.

## Parental Goals, Beliefs, and Values

Parental goals, beliefs, and values constitute an important component of the context of development. Parental values regarding children reflect societal values, but the former cannot be subsumed under the latter. First of all, there may be differences between the two value systems at different ecological levels, depending especially on the social-class status of the parents. Second, parental values have a more direct impact on the child, through parental behavior, than societal values. Nevertheless, it is

↳ can that be argued
against ?

also true that parental beliefs are cultural constructions. For example, Goodnow (1988, p. 297) found greater between-group differences than within-group differences in parental beliefs across social-class, ethnic, and cultural comparisons. Cross-cultural differences in parental values mirror more general cross-cultural differences in societal values.

Although it may appear obvious that parents hold beliefs about children and childhood and that these have an impact on the child, systematic study of these topics has been conducted only in the past few decades. Starting in the 1980s, U.S. research examining parental orientations (beliefs, values, and behavior) with mainly Latino, African American, and Anglo-American parents in the United States, pointed to complex belief systems about how children develop (Laosa & Sigel, 1982; Sigel, 1985; Sigel, Mc Gillicuddy-DeLisi, & Goodnow, 1992). Both ethnic and social-class differences emerged in this research.

Anthropological research studying parental beliefs about child development has stressed the importance of lay theories or beliefs parents have regarding various aspects of the development of children. These have been labeled "indigenous theories" (Chamoux, 1986), **"naive theories"** (Sabatier, 1986), or "ethnotheories" (e.g. Greenfield, Maynard, & Childs, 2003; Keller, 2003; Keller & Lamm, 2005). As described earlier, one of the three components of the **developmental niche** is "psychology of the caretaker" (Harkness & Super, 1993; Super & Harkness, 1986, 1994). Key aspects of the psychology of the caretaker are such parental belief systems.

Early on, LeVine (1974, 1988, 1989) pointed to adaptation to environmental requirements as a basis for parental goals and behaviors. For example, in agrarian societies, with high infant mortality and hazardous environments, parental goals of protection and survival of children lead to protective conformity-oriented child **socialization.** This is because in hazardous environments, obedience, rather than independence of children, is adaptive for ensuring their safety.

In all the aforementioned research, there is a common emphasis on the importance of parental belief systems both for parental behavior and for developmental outcomes. There is a growing confidence about the correspondence of parental beliefs and behavior (Bornstein & Bradley, 2003; D'Andrade & Strauss, 1992; Harwood, Leyendecker, Carlson, Asencio, & Miller, 2002; Sigel, 1992), which provides further impetus for studying beliefs. There is also a growing recognition of the need to situate parental beliefs, values, and behavior into their socioeconomic, social-structural contexts. This is especially important in understanding why certain belief systems show systematic variation across different parental groups. The answer often lies in underlying functional dynamics.

environments as well as culture play a huge role

Much research into parenting has investigated the relations between parental beliefs, characteristics of parenting, and the development of the child's cognitive and **social competence**. Parental orientations thus constitute an important feature of the developmental context. I discuss the specific issues involved in parenting in the coming chapters, especially in chapter 6. Another aspect of parental beliefs concerns the definition of parenting itself, as well as its conceptualization over time. For example, whether a mother defines her role only in terms of loving and caring for the child or also in terms of preparing the child for school and future school achievement appears to have a crucial significance both for her everyday behavior and for child outcomes (Coll, 1990).

Systematic social-class, ethnic, and cross-cultural differences have been found in research on just such self-role definitions. For example, educated middle-class Anglo-American mothers are found to consider it important to provide early stimulation to children, even during pregnancy, whereas lower-class Black mothers think it is the school's job to "teach children." Similarly, whereas Mexican-American mothers do not see themselves as "teachers," Chinese and certainly Japanese mothers work as teachers coaching and giving specific instructions to their children regarding schoolwork (Chao, 1994, 2000; Chao & Tseng, 2002; Coll, 1990; Jose, Huntsinger, Huntsinger, & Liaw, 2000; LeVine & White, 1986; Sameroff & Fiese, 1992). Similarly, an increasing number of educated middle-class Turkish mothers give endless drills to their children preparing them for competitive examinations to enter better schools, but low-SES Turkish mothers do not involve themselves because they believe they "don't know enough to help their children." In effect, the middle-class pattern is more conducive to school achievement.

This is not to say that coaching children is good. Indeed, it can involve too much pressure for both the child and the mother, when taken to an extreme. This is only an example of a class-related parental role definition and behavior. Similarly, Haight, Parke, and Black (1997) in the United States and Göncü (1993) in Turkey showed that middle-class parents' self-role definitions include "teaching their children" on the one hand, and engaging with their children as "peers" on the other. Social-class standing thus appears to cut across national differences, an issue that is taken up again in the next section.

Finally, the general view of the parental role and self definitions of it have implications for parent–child relations extending in time through the life cycle. For example, cross-cultural comparisons of traditional Japanese and American maternal role perceptions showed differences in definitions of responsibilities and in time perspectives (Shand, 1985). The American mothers' definition of maternal responsibility is of a relatively short term, until children reach adolescence, and involves physical care (with the husband's help) and love with no duties toward the patrilineage. The Japanese mother's self-definition of the maternal responsibility, on the other hand, is lifelong and is embedded in the husband's patrilineal or corporate structure where she is responsible for bringing up a respectful, cooperative child who is also highly achievement oriented. Studies conducted in other cultures (in "cultures of relatedness"; Kağitçibaşi, 1985a) have similarities to the Japanese pattern. For example, C. F. Yang (1988), in describing the close networks among the elderly and their offspring, as shown in surveys in China, noted that "they are indicative of the traditional parental protection of children until [parents'] death" (p. 109).

In general, lifelong conceptualizations of parental responsibilities go hand in hand with socialization values of interdependence, rather than independence. The latter, in contrast, implies an expectation of the self-sufficiency of the offspring, especially in adolescence, made possible by a stress on autonomy in childrearing. Though certain changes in these parental self-definitions may come about with education and lifestyle changes, the general patterns appear to be quite persistent (Georgas et al., 2006).

## SOCIAL CLASS AS CONTEXT

Running through the preceding discussion is social class, which is a major macrosystem variable that penetrates into all the ecological systems, including the immediate proximal environment of the child. Social class creates its own culture, and it is always there. Thus, it should figure importantly in all research on human development. However, until rather recently the "culture-eliminating" organismic and mechanistic theoretical perspectives (see chap. 1) of mainstream psychology tended to ignore social class.

Going beyond the insensitivity to context, there has been an ideological reason for avoiding the use of social class in psychological analysis. It is not politically correct to talk about social class in a democratic society that aspires for equality. This has been the case for much of the Western world. Thus, even when social class is addressed in research, socioeconomic status is the term most commonly used (Bornstein & Bradley, 2003). This sensitivity is certainly understandable, especially given the connotations of social class as fixed and unchanging, though not as rigid as caste. It may also remind the Western reader of the Marxist class-struggle concept. The point here is not to insist that we use the term social class rather than socioeconomic status; either can be used. The point is to stress its great significance in engulfing human development. That is why I use it to title this section.

It is also important to recognize that social class is indeed to a large extent stable and enduring over time, notwithstanding our wish to see it as flexible and changing. It tends to repeat itself through generations (Brooks-Gunn, Schley, & Hardy, 2000). This is demonstrated by a great deal of recent research on human development in poverty, some of which I describe in the next section.

Early studies on the effects of social class on human development seemed to go hand in hand with an interest in ethnic and cross-cultural differences in the 1980s. In a study of ethnic differences in parental beliefs and attitudes in Australia, Cashmore and Goodnow (1986) noted the importance of social-class standing. When this variable was controlled, the "ethnic" differences they had originally found disappeared. Similar results were obtained by Lambert (1987) in a cross-national study, by Podmore and St. George (1986) comparing New Zealand Maori and European mothers, and by Laosa (1978, 1980) comparing Anglo- and Hispanic-American mothers in the United States. These findings are also corroborated by subsequent research mentioned in the last section (Göncü,1993; Haight et al.,1997). They are important in pointing both to the significance of social class and also to a common methodological problem of confounding ethnicity/nationality and social-class standing. Because ethnic minorities often have lower socioeconomic status than the majority population, the obtained differences are difficult to interpret. These findings call for more care in situating the subjects of a study in socioeconomic terms and have relevance for immigration contexts (see chap. 10).

Early research also looked into parenting orientations as a function of social-class standing. A classic in this field is the rather controversial analysis by Kohn (1969) of British parental values and goals for children. He used the concept of **anticipatory socialization** into social class–based work roles, in other words, that parents socialize their children in such a way as to prepare them for their eventual adult roles in society. He showed that individual autonomy was encouraged in middle-class child socialization, because in middle-class jobs individual decision making is required; whereas working-class parents valued obedience and conformity in children, as these characteristics are more functional in working-class jobs.

A great deal of parenting research since then has corroborated these findings. Indeed social-class and ethnic differences are commonly found in compliance-oriented as opposed to autonomy-granting parenting; we cover them in this book. However, usually only the group differences are presented. Functional explanations of the sort Kohn used are not frequently proposed. One reason for this may be that the researcher is hesitant to go beyond data, to speculate. However, this type of functional reasoning, if supported by evidence, is valuable in understanding the underlying reasons for *how* the observed differences emerge (see Box 2.2). As mentioned in the previous section, LeVine's (1974, 1988) insightful analysis of conformity-oriented parenting in hazardous environments also uses a similar functional explanation. The **Value of Children Study** to which I referred earlier also used a similar **functional approach** in explaining parental values of children across different contexts characterized by different levels of socioeconomic development.

## Effects of Growing Up in Poverty

Globally, poverty is too well known, too real. What I can present here is only a very scanty sampling of developmental research results looking into its effects on the family, parenting, and most important, the child. Most of this psychological research comes from the United States, the richest country in the world. Though this may sound ironic, it is hardly surprising. First of all, there are more researchers and more research funding in the United States than anywhere else in the world. This is reflected in a high level of interdisciplinary and psychological research using large data sets that can provide conclusive evidence on such a social phenomenon. Second, despite its high **GNP,** there is large-scale poverty in the United States, particularly among women and children. The lack of effective public policies upholding social welfare to combat poverty in the United States distinguishes it from other affluent post-technological societies, for example, in Europe (Dohrn, 1993; Kamerman, 1991; McLoyd, 1997) (see chap. 11).

Countless studies have demonstrated correlations between children's poverty and various measures of child development, health, and psychological well-being in the United States (e.g. Brooks-Gunn & Duncan, 1997; Duncan & Brooks-Gunn, 1997, 2000; Keating & Hertzman, 1999; S. Mayer, 1997; Yeung, Linver, & Brooks-Gunn, 2002). Findings converge on the deleterious effects of poverty. In general, persistent poverty has a greater negative impact than transitory or intermittent poverty (Bolger, Patterson, Thompson, & Kupersmidt, 1995; McLoyd, 1998), as can be expected.

A less evident factor is the age of the child. Children at younger ages are more at risk (Duncan & Magnuson, 2003; L. W. Hoffman, 2003). They are more vulnerable to deficiencies in early nutrition and to environmental hazards that accompany poverty, such as lead poisoning and the like. They are also most directly affected by harsh parenting, which often results from parental distress accompanying poverty. Thus, household income is found to be a more important factor in early childhood. Classic studies on the impact of economic depression on different cohorts of children by Elder (1985, 1995) showed these age patterns in effects over time.

Another nonevident finding is the greater negative impact of family economic hardship on boys than on girls (Bolger et al., 1995; Huston et al., 2001). The explanations tend to refer to the relatively greater negative effects of poverty on boys with regard to behavior problems and the related difficulties with discipline that confront parents, particularly single mothers.

Apparently, there can be fast improvement when measures are taken to increase family income. For example, Huston et al. (2001) assessed the impact of the New Hope antipoverty program in the United States. With wage supplements sufficient to raise family income above the poverty threshold and subsidies for child care and health insurance to parents who worked full-time, strong positive effects were found for boys. These ranged from academic achievement, positive classroom behavior, prosocial behavior, and decreased problem behaviors, as reported by teachers, to the boys' advanced educational expectations and high occupational aspirations. Given these very significant gains, it was notable that no corresponding program effects were obtained for girls, who were apparently not doing as badly as the boys to start with.

Other evaluation studies show the positive effects of welfare programs on all the children. For example Gennetian and Miller (2002) studied the impact of welfare reform initiatives by assessing the specific effects of the Minnesota Family Investment Program on children. They found increased parental employment rates and decreased poverty with concomitant improvements in children reflected in less problem behaviors as well as better performance and more engagement in school.

Such results are useful in informing and evaluating policies to combat poverty. The policy-relevant studies are especially valuable when they use a rigorous experimental design, as this study did, that enables causal inferences to be drawn from the data. They also go a long way to show that even serious contextual problems such as poverty are not unsolvable. This is an important issue in this book.

Finally, going beyond the family, neighborhood characteristics and their effects have been studied extensively. This is in line with an ecological-contextual orientation, as the neighborhood embeds the family and the child. For example, a study by Kohen, Brooks-Gunn, Leventhal, and Hertzman (2002) showed the effects of neighborhood characteristics on preschoolers' verbal and behavioral competencies even after controlling for family socioeconomic status. Particularly the proportion of affluent residents, unemployment rates, and the degree of cohesion in neighborhoods emerged as key factors. Another study (Ceballo & McLoyd, 2002) pointed to the moderating role of the neighborhood between social support and parenting behaviors.

## MODELS RELATING DEVELOPMENT TO CONTEXT

The aforementioned studies on the effects of growing up in poverty show the importance of socioeconomic and ecological systems, which can make an impact on the growing child. In this chapter, I have been discussing the context of development, with some examples of that context. There are many other features of the context of development, of course, which are referred to throughout the book whenever relevant. In this section, I would like to conclude the discussion of the developmental context with a consideration of how to relate children's developmental outcomes to context.

Because the context of development is a multilayered multifaceted complex system of interacting influences, its conceptualization has emphasized its complexity (Bornstein & Bradley, 2003; Bronfenbrenner, 1979, 1986; Lerner, 1989; Super & Harkness, 1997, 1999). How this complex whole is to be related conceptually and in operational terms to developmental outcomes is a tough question, and some models have been developed to deal with it.

During the last few decades several models emerged out of research dealing with risk factors. Some of these have informed recent studies. Sameroff proposed a model of risk factors that stresses their *number* rather than their *nature* (Sameroff & Fiese, 1992; Sameroff, Seifer, Barocas, Zax, & Greenspan, 1987). Using the data of the Rochester Longitudinal Study in the United States, the researchers delineated 10 risk factors including mother's (low-level) education, mother's anxiety, (marginalized) minority status, unskilled occupation of household head, maternal mental illness, low level of mother–infant interaction, and so forth. A number of these factors are more common in lower-SES groups, thus social class is found to be associated with developmental risk. However the presence of multiple risk factors negatively affected the child's competence in all social classes, the higher the number of risk factors, the more deleterious the effect. In terms of preschool intelligence, for example, "children with no environmental risks scored more than 30 points higher than children with 8 or 9 risk factors" (Sameroff & Fiese, 1992, p. 349).

Thus, the number of risk factors work not in an additive but in a multiplicative fashion. For example, when two or more stresses occurred together, the chance of a damaging outcome went up at least fourfold, and when four risks were present, the chances of later damage increased tenfold (Sameroff & Fiese, 1992). More recently, similar views have been put forward, for example, in the family stress model of Conger (K. J. Conger, Rueter & Conger, 2000; R. D. Conger, Conger, & Elder, 1997). G. W. Evans (2004) has also stressed the particularly pathogenic effects of accumulated multiple environmental risks, a key harmful factor in childhood poverty.

This is similar to other risk models that are in common use in intervention programs in the **Majority World**. For example, in screening for children at risk and detecting potential risk cases, the *number* of existing risk factors can provide clues to health workers and others involved in intervention programs. In these programs, the conceptualization of developmental risk is commonly concentrated on health and nutrition status. However, there are attempts to expand its coverage to include also psychological factors (Kağitçibaşi, 1991; Landers & Kağitçibaşi, 1990; UNICEF, 2005).

*Family and Parenting as Mediating Factors.*   Models relating development to context typically attempt to delineate mediating factors between the macrolevel influences and the developing person (Linver, Brooks-Gunn, & Kohen, 2002; Masten & Coatsworth, 1998; Yeung et al., 2002). They also try to explain how these variables mediate, that is, to identify the processes involved. They are helpful in singling out which variables are important and what effects they may be expected to have. So they work as guidelines in applied research in pointing to ways in which interventions may be expected to have optimal effects. I briefly refer to some models relating developmental context to developmental outcomes as examples. They apply mainly to contextual variables associated with the development of low levels of cognitive and socioemotional competence in children.

The family emerges as the major mediating factor that links macro contextual factors and child development outcomes. The main point of these models is that life circumstances, such as low income, have an indirect impact on the developing child through the family. The importance of this, particularly for applications, is that because the family mediates and passes on these detrimental influences to the child, it can also shield the child from them. We deal further with this protective function of the family in Part II, where we examine applied issues of intervention.

The key factors used in the aforementioned studies are parental distress due to income loss or chronic poverty and the resultant problematic parenting. Several characteristics of such parenting are noted in research, such as less child centered and nurturant, more parent centered, rejecting and with inconsistent, sometimes harsh discipline (R. S. Mistry et al., 2002). Thus, Jackson, Brooks-Gunn, Huang, and Glassman (2000) showed that maternal education was positively associated with income, which together with instrumental support available to the mother, were negatively associated with financial strain.

Financial strain, in turn, was implicated in high levels of depressive symptoms, which were directly and negatively implicated in parenting quality. The quality of parenting was associated with children's behavior problems and preschool ability. Thus what we have here is a multilayered model explaining a chain of negative effects. The demographic factors of mother's educational attainment and earnings can be seen as the real causes here. However, it is the effect of the resultant parenting that impacts the child directly. Thus the key importance of the child's proximal environment is stressed by these models. Box 2.4. presents a general mediational model, based on the R. S. Mistry et al. (2002) study and other relevant research.

Patterson and Dishion (1988) used a multilevel family process model to explain the development of the antisocial problem child from mainly a clinical perspective based on research in the United States. At the family level, the relevant process is that depressed parents are more irritable in their discipline confrontations with their children. Irritable discipline is, in turn, causally related to antisocial traits in the child. This process, with parental discipline as the mediator, is found to repeat itself across generations (Belsky & Pensky, 1988; Patterson & Dishion, 1988; Simons, Whitbeck, Conger, & Chyi, 1991). Furthermore, a lower income and socially disadvantaged position aggravate this process through the mediation of increased stress, which in turn serves as an amplifier for the parental antisocial trait. Social disadvantage (low education, low income, low employment levels or unemployment) is additionally associated with lack of opportunity for developing effective social skills and parenting skills, which also serve as a negative mediator. Thus different contextual levels, through time, are used to explain, in interaction, a developmental outcome.

A similar complex multilevel process model was used by McLoyd (1990; McLoyd & Wilson, 1990) to explain how poverty and family income loss affect Black children in the United States. In a review of the research, poverty and economic loss are found to diminish the capacity for supportive, consistent, and involved parenting, with psychological distress as the major mediator variable. Negative life events, including disruption of marital bonds and economic hardship, affect children's socioemotional functioning through their negative impact on the parents' behavior toward the child. Parents' social networks are found to reduce emotional strain, decrease the tendency toward punitive parenting, and in this way foster positive socioemotional development in children.

The positive role of mothers' social-support networks and informational support in promoting more effective parenting is noted in much research carried out with families especially in disadvantaged

[Handwritten marginal note: Is it not telling that the 1st marker of social disadvantage is low education of social disadvantage mixed w/ financial]

*[handwritten annotation: same results w/ perceived economic pressure → for example, upper brackets to make more money]*

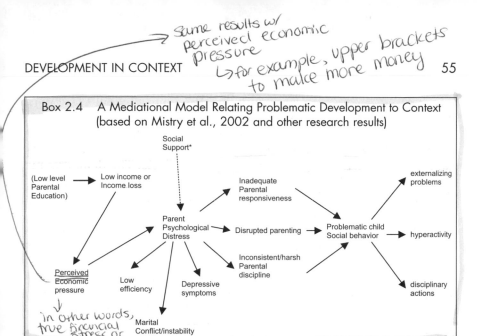

Box 2.4    A Mediational Model Relating Problematic Development to Context (based on Mistry et al., 2002 and other research results)

*[handwritten annotations on figure: "in other words, true financial stress or perceived financial strain"]*

*Note*: Emotional and Instrumental support from spouse/kin/neighborhood/intervention programs by public agencies etc. Counteracts negative chain of influences

socioeconomic conditions, often including father absence (e.g., Coll, 1990; Harrison, Wilson, Pine, Chan, & Buriel, 1990; Slaughter, 1988; Stevens, 1988; R. . Taylor & Roberts, 1995). This points to the value of family support programs. More recently, neighborhood characteristics are found to moderate the relation between social support and parenting behaviors. Specifically, the positive relation of both emotional and instrumental social support with better parenting is found to be higher in better neighborhoods (Ceballo & McLoyd, 2002).

In these examples of models relating contextual factors to developmental outcomes, there is first of all a recognition of different levels of contextual variables that affect the growing child. Second, they formulate hypotheses and make specific predictions regarding the processes that mediate the effects of macrosystem-level contextual variables and developmental outcome. This has direct implications for applied work and interventions.

Because socioeconomic conditions at the macrosystem level (social-class status, poverty, etc.) affect the child *through* the mediation of parental behavior, intervention is possible. It may be difficult to change the socioeconomic circumstances of a family, though every effort should be made toward this end. Nevertheless, even if change at this level is limited, parental distress may be ameliorated, and more effective parenting may be fostered through support programs for parents. Such intervention, if successful, would have a direct positive impact on children. Such support programs may build upon the existing resources of the family, promote social networks, provide information and emotional support, build up parental skills, and so on. This is a key theme in this book. Chapter 9 presents such an intervention project focused on the parent (mother). Parental behavior, mediating between the macrosystem variables and the child, is targeted in that intervention for the promotion of the child's overall development.

In this chapter, I have examined development in context, with examples of contextual factors. The family as the main microsystem (Bronfenbrenner, 1979) of developmental context has figured importantly in this discussion. It is considered to be the key aspect of context throughout this book, also. In chapter 5, it is studied more systematically, as it changes through social change and development. In the following two chapters, I examine more thoroughly two important spheres of development in context, that of competence and of the self.

## SUMMARY AND MAIN POINTS

- Culture is the context of psychological functioning; it provides meaning to observed behavior. Studies show that the same behavior (i.e., parental control) may carry different meanings for children and adolescents in different cultural contexts. Thus context (culture) should be integrated into psychological analysis.
- A basic idea shared by social constructionists, interpretive anthropologists, and cultural psychologists is that people attribute meaning to their environments; thus they create culture.
- Ecological theoretical approaches, life-span development perspective, and problem-oriented research have shared contextualistic thinking and have helped strengthen the contextual orientation in the study of human development.
- There have also been "context-eliminating" theoretical traditions. The mechanistic and organismic models have worked as deterrents to contextualistic conceptualization. Recent biological orientations to human development constitute new challenges to contextual approaches.
- Vygotsky's sociohistorical theory, Bronfenbrenner's ecological systems theory, Berry's ecocultural framework, Super and Harkness's developmental niche, and Kağitçibaşi's family change theory share an ecological-contextual perspective. A developmental approach that is also contextual and functional can be a powerful tool in linking the individual (self), family, and society/culture.

- The context of human development comprises numerous levels of influences, all interrelated and embedded in one another. Societal values regarding children and parental beliefs and values are contextual features at different systemic levels.
- Socialcultural conceptualizations of childhood change over time and space and have important implications for children's lives.
- Values attributed to children show variation depending on the level of socioeconomic development. The example of child work points to a general correspondence between a society's conception of childhood and children's actual lifestyles.
- Child work brings to the fore the problem of gaps or cultural lags between societal values that reflect traditions that may no longer be adaptive to changing socioeconomic conditions and the demands of new lifestyles.
- Parental orientations form an important feature of the context of development. Research into parenting has investigated the relations between parental beliefs, characteristics of parenting, and the development of the child's cognitive and social competence.
- Countless studies demonstrate the harmful effects of poverty on children. There can be improvement when measures are taken to increase family income.

Some models are devised to relate developmental outcomes to the context of development; they typically focus on the mediating factors between the macrolevel influences and the developing person. The family emerges as the major mediating factor. These models work as guidelines in applied research in pointing to ways in which interventions can have optimal effects.

## DISCUSSION QUESTIONS

1. Why is it important to take cultural context into account when examining psychological phenomena even though the unit of analysis of psychology is the individual, not society?
2. How have ecological theory and life-span development theory helped establish contextual conceptualization of human development?
3. How do societal values influence children's lives? How does the conceptualization of childhood differ in different contexts? What are the implications for the value of children for parents? What is the role of social change in this process?

— 4. Give examples of how parental belief systems influence both parental behavior and children's developmental outcomes.

— 5. Discuss the role of poverty on child development, health, and psychological well-being.

— 6. How can context be addressed in family intervention programs? Explain why and how intervention is possible.

# 3

# Socialization for Competence

In an early anthropological study of an isolated Turkish village, Helling (1966) noted the prevalence of a parental teaching style based on demonstration, imitation, and motor learning rather than verbal explanation and reasoning. As a husband–wife team, they observed informal teaching–learning activities and reported, for example, the case of a father "teaching" his son how to cut wood by just doing it himself, to be imitated, with no explanation. The Hellings returned to the same village 20 years later and did not observe any appreciable change in this nonverbal orientation to "teaching by doing" (G. A. Helling, 1986, personal communication). Recently a colleague did some observations in the same general area and found that some things had changed. In particular, all the children attended school. Nevertheless the typical parental "teaching" style had not changed much. I commonly tell my students at a Turkish university about Hellings's original observation and ask them whether it sounds familiar. They come up with more examples, usually not from their own lives but from what they have observed among "peasants" or "former peasants," now urban shanty town dwellers.

What is the meaning of these observations for **socialization**? In this chapter, I search for answers to this question. In doing this, I look at the global diversity in children's developmental trajectories. I also search for commonalities or possible convergences alongside enduring patterns. Finally, I present theoretical perspectives that make sense of the diversity and commonality. In presenting the topics, I first refer to earlier observations and research providing important conceptual background, as they show how this work contributed to our thinking; then I discuss more recent studies.

## SOCIALIZATION

**Socialization** is for competence. It is the human infant becoming social. Or to put it differently, it is the process through which the human infant becomes a member of the society. Toward that end, childrearing is goal oriented, though the goal is often not explicit and may not be consciously formulated. Because the long-range goal of socialization is, by definition, to become a competent member of a society, socialization is designed to accomplish whatever it takes to ensure this long-range goal. This view probably carries a too rational and goal-directed stance in view of the seemingly haphazard everyday childrearing behavior of many parents. It is not my intention to characterize all parenting behavior in a planned and rational framework, but rather to put it into a general perspective over time. Competence in this perspective refers to what is culturally valued and therefore shows variation across cultures.

The concept of socialization, once central, fell into some disrepute as implying a unidirectional process of "molding" a passive child. It should be noted from the outset that socialization, as construed here, does not imply a unidirectional causation with a passive child, but is an active interaction between the caregiver(s) and the child. Thus the child is actively engaged in her own socialization. A similar view was put forward earlier by M. B. Smith (1968) and later by many developmental psychologists. In this interactional perspective, the concept of socialization has reassumed importance in the cultural and cross-cultural study of human development.

In the psychological study of human development, cognitive and **social competence** are commonly differentiated and are conceived as positive developmental outcomes. This chapter focuses mainly on the development of **cognitive competence.** However, as the meaning of competence shows variation across cultures and developmental contexts, what I undertake to examine in this chapter expands beyond the conceptualization of cognitive competence in academic psychology. Furthermore, I examine socialization for competence, not only from the point of view of the child developing cognitive skills but in terms of the total interactive process of teaching and learning in cultural context and the meaning attributed to it by all those involved. Finally, I want to focus on socialization for competence in highly different socioeconomic-ecological contexts and examine its implications in the more general framework of social change throughout the world.

Indeed, the sociocultural perspectives on cognitive development, in particular those informed by the early sociohistorical school of Vygotsky (1978, 1986), Luria (1976), and their students (see chap. 2) do not differentiate cognitive from sociocultural aspects of human development. They address human development with a rather eclectic approach, grounding it in culture and history where culture mediates learning and cognitive development, particularly through language, tool use, and everyday teaching (**scaffolding**) by adults. The current neo-Vygotskian views continue with this tradition and the holistic understanding of the development of competence (M. Cole, 2005; Correa-Chávez & Rogoff, 2005; Karpov, 2005; J. G. Miller & Chen, 2005). Although this perspective is not used specifically in this chapter, the similarities are there.

It may be informative to review first some examples of socialization for competence outside of the Western middle-class family or school contexts, drawn from observations and research reports. They should provide us with some clues into the diverse processes involved in and the meanings attached to socialization for competence in different sociocultural–socioeconomic contexts.

## Everyday "Teaching and Learning"

As with the aforementioned Helling example, descriptions of nonverbal "teaching and learning" abound in anthropological reports from many cultures, especially among rural populations. For example, other early work pointed to similar patterns in Africa (Gay & Cole, 1967; LeVine & LeVine, 1966) and among the Maya in Mexico (Greenfield & Childs, 1977); it was also noted among the Australian aborigines (Teasdale & Teasdale, 1992). These patterns are clearly widespread, and they work. Children learn to cut wood or weave cloth and in time develop manual skills to produce exquisite handicrafts, mainly through imitation and commonly without verbal instruction or positive reinforcement (LeVine, 1989; Morelli, Rogoff, & Angellilo, 2003; Rogoff, 2003). In Western urban contexts, similar nonverbal and less praising parental teaching styles have been also noted among, for example, Hispanic minorities in the United States (Laosa, 1980) and Turkish minorities in the Netherlands (Leseman, 1993).

More recent work continues to report less parental verbalization in low-income and immigrant groups with lower levels of education, for example, in Europe and North America (e.g., Duncan & Magnuson, 2003; Leseman, 1993; Van Tuijl & Leseman, 2004). In particular, maternal speech is found to be a key factor that shows variation with socioeconomic levels and impacts child development outcomes in studies conducted in widely different countries, such as the United States (Hoff, 2003), Turkey (Aksu-Koç, 2005), and Argentina (Peralta de Mendoza & Irice, 1995). The implications of this issue with regard to creating a developmental disadvantage are addressed later on in the chapter.

Social skills are also often learned through observation of adult activity or from older children. For example, Nsamenang and Lamb (1994) describe child-to-child interactions where younger children are cared for by their older siblings and peers while parents are involved in economic activities in the field or in the marketplace. Thus, they note, "Informal education offers opportunities to learn performance skills, particularly during play, as well as social skills such as learning to (a) collaborate or disagree, (b) lead and follow others, (c) cooperate in collective responsibility, and (d) disagree about diverse tasks and issues"; in this process, "Child caregiving is but one form of children's roles"(pp. 142–143). Children also learn effectively by observing each other's behavior, particularly older role models (Azmitia, 1988; Nsamenang & Lamb, 1994). They learn by guided participation in activities (Greenfield, 1996; Greenfield, Keller et al., 2003; Keller, 2003; Rogoff, 1990). In all this informal teaching and learning, the learner has the role of the "apprentice."

Whether there is extensive verbalization with the child may also have something to do with some general cultural conceptions of childhood. Specifically, whether caregivers see themselves in an active, child development–oriented, consciously goal-directed "childrearing" role or not appears to be important. This type of self-role definition is common among the educated middle class (especially Western and particularly American) parents (Coll, 1990; Goodnow, 1988; see chap. 2). In contrast, Kakar (1978), for example, noted that Indian caregivers emphasize pleasure between adult and child and experience little pressure to mold the child in a given direction. Similarly, many less-educated, traditional Turkish mothers talk about the child *growing up* (*büyür*), rather than *being brought up* (*yetistirilir*). If they mention childrearing, it is more in the sense of enabling the physical growth of the child (*büyütmek*) (the root verb *büyü*-mek means literally "to get bigger").

Learning by observation and imitation obviously occurs in all contexts and throughout the life span. It forms the basis of "social learning theory" where role learning from models is considered very important (Bandura, 1962; Zimmerman & Rosenthal, 1974). In most **Majority World** societies, children's everyday social world includes others of all ages, rather than being age-segregated, as in Western peer culture. This means that from early on children are in the presence of adults all the time and observe their behaviors. For example, Morelli et al. (2003) showed that in the Democratic Republic of Congo and in a Guatemalan Mayan town 2- to 3-year-old children had plenty of opportunity to observe adults working. Even at this young age their play emulated adult work. In contrast, U.S. children had much less access to adults working; instead they saw adults as playmates and conversation partners. Thus in children's daily lives what is learned and how learning takes place show cultural variation.

There are limitations to observational learning, however. For example, it is found to be ineffective for transfer to new tasks (Greenfield & Lave, 1982; Segall et al., 1999). Also observational learning is commonly only one type of learning among others, and at least some of these others involve verbal reasoning. If verbalization with the child, especially verbal communication involving adult reasoning and de-contextualized language is lacking or infrequent, there may be serious developmental implications. I elaborate this point later on.

*A Second Example.*    A second example of socialization for competence and adult roles comes from Anandalakshmy and Bajaj's (1981) study of childhood in the weavers' community in Varanasi, India. Describing girlhood, for example, the authors note that:

> Most of the girls by the time they are six years old are adept at sweeping, cleaning and washing dishes and looking after siblings. ... As soon as a girl reaches the age of nine, she is subject to clearly defined restrictions on dress and movement, and is strictly forbidden from loitering in the streets unaccompanied. ... Living in a fairly enclosed and restricted environment with nothing else to do, the girls imbibe the craft skills of filling spools for weaving by observing their mothers at work. ... The day's routine runs an uninterrupted course of spooling, interspersed with domestic chores, [and] the care of younger siblings. ... For girls, formal education was not deemed essential at all since all that they had to do was to manage the household. In fact, the adults said that there was the danger of the girls becoming clever and non-conforming as a result of education, and that was why they were not even sent to the *madrasa* to learn the basics in reading and writing. According to their interpretation of the strictures in the Koran, education was proscribed for girls. (pp. 34–35, 37–38)

In this rich description, there is evidence of a great deal of socialization for competence into socially prescribed roles. Indeed, there is no question that most children learn the roles and skills necessary to live as competent adults in this apparently self-sufficient community. Some questions come to mind, of course, such as the implications of this type of socialization for the cognitive competence of the girl child (boys are described to enjoy greater freedom of action and some schooling). Another question is what happens when changes in economic conditions endanger the self-sufficiency of the community and push young people out to look for other types of employment.

What happens with social and economic change is well demonstrated by a series of studies carried out by Greenfield in a Mayan community in Mexico over a period of some 20 years. In the 1970s, she studied the everyday teaching and learning of weaving, transmitted from mother to daughter in this community (Greenfield & Childs, 1977). The common parental teaching strategy was highly directive and detail-oriented guidance, based on imitation, which didn't allow freedom of action for the learner. However, her observations in the same weaving community 20 years later revealed some important changes (Greenfield, Maynard et al., 2003b). Now the mothers allowed more independent activity to their daughters. The weaving patterns also reflected this change in the type of teaching. The earlier constrained and repetitive patterns gave way to more creative ones with novel designs.

Why this change? In the course of two decades, this Mayan community shifted from subsistence economy to a cash economy. Weaving for tourist consumption became the rule. Thus, there was room for change and innovation; this was even required by the changing lifestyles in order to be competitive in the market. A similar change took place in indigenous mathematical notation systems and practices when monetary trade was introduced into a previously isolated area of New Guinea (Saxe & Esmonde, 2005). Clearly, socioeconomic change brings about changes in lifestyles that often implicate concomitant behavioral modifications. Social change is thus a very significant aspect of the context and the culture, as I discussed in the last chapter. This is a key concept in this book.

A very significant type of social change is rural to urban mobility. This is of immense proportions in the Majority World (see Box 2.2 in the last chapter), also feeding on to international migration. Such mobility is mainly because traditional rural agrarian economic activities no longer prove viable for the livelihood of growing populations. This is the main global, social structural change that is going on in the world that needs to be taken into consideration when studying human conditions.

## THEORETICAL CONCEPTIONS OF COGNITIVE COMPETENCE

The examples I have given of everyday teaching and learning, mainly through observation and imitation, are similar to a great deal of early cross-cultural description looking into the development of **cognitive competence** in preindustrial societies. The beginnings of cross-cultural psychology were largely based on comparative studies of cognition from preindustrial and at times preliterate societies in Africa and Australia. Anthropologists also studied cognition in these societies. The development of cognitive anthropology, also called ethnoscience, drew attention to indigenous knowledge systems. The corresponding interest in psychology was focused on cognitive systems (Berry, Irvine, & Hunt, 1988). Several reviews of the early research are available (Berry, 1985; Berry & Dasen, 1974; Rogoff, 1990; Rogoff, Gauvain et al., 1984). More recent reviews also draw attention to the importance of this formative research (Berry et al., 2002; Matsumoto & Juang, 2004; Rogoff, 2003; Segall et al., 1999).

*this is one of the most basic procedures*

## The Cross-Cultural Background

The roots of some of the present-day debates in the cross-cultural study of competence go back to the 19th- and early-20th-century views of cultural evolution on the one hand and the contrasting views of Lévy-Bruhl (1910, 1922) and Boas (1911) on the other. Early claims of qualitative differences between logical (Western) and "prelogical" (primitive) thinking versus psychic unity of humankind, espoused by Lévy-Bruhl and Boas, respectively, still have their followers. However, this debate has subsided in importance today, to be replaced by another one that partly overlaps with it. This is whether competence (intelligence) is a central process that shows consistency, generalization, and transfer over different conditions or whether it is context-specific learning and represents an adaptation to specific environmental requirements. It is possible to trace the influence of Spearman's "g" in psychology and of Boas's **psychic unity view** in anthropology in the central process model that has been more dominant in cross-cultural psychology. Lévy-Bruhl's legacy, on the other hand, is acknowledged in the cultural psychology framework (Shweder, 1990), stressing the contextual specificity of each cognition (learning) and therefore claiming it to be qualitatively different from and not comparable to others in different contexts.

The **central processor model** is the traditional view of academic psychology, as seen in learning theory, differential psychology, and cognitive psychology. It considers **cognitive competence** (intelligence) as a basic psychological process, internal to the individual, that is treated as independent of sociocultural processes (J. G. Miller & Chen, 2005). It is understood to act uon different events (stimuli) in the same way, thus enabling transfer of learning from one situation to another. In cross-cultural psychology, this view underlies, for example, Piagetian approaches to cognitive development. Thus Piaget's cognitive developmental stages (and the operations they involve) are expected to manifest themselves similarly in different situations (tasks). Although Piagetian theory has been revised in the light of cross-cultural research that pointed to the significance of contexts (Hatano & Inagaki, 2001), it nevertheless represents the academic view of individual cognitive development, based on organismic maturation. Thus comparisons across cultural contexts are possible.

The central processor model came under attack from an anthropological perspective, that is, the **specific learning model** or "everyday cognition," which considers context as crucial and studies the functional relations between learning experience and cognitive skills (Carraher, Schliemann, & Carraher, 1988; Dasen, 1984; Göncü, 1993; Nunes et al., 1993; Rogoff, 1990; Rogoff & Lave, 1984; Scribner & Cole, 1981; Shweder,

1990). This perspective is informed by the Vygotskian (1978) sociohistorical approach discussed earlier (see chap. 2), which stresses that behavior is adapted to fit the context, and the context is structured to support the behavior, deriving basically from the adaptation of humans to their environments through cultural history. In this tradition, there is a "monistic" view of culture and cognition, as making each other up (Cole, 2005; J. G. Miller & Chen, 2003; Rogoff, 2003; Shweder, 1990). Social interaction and cultural practices promote cognitive development (Greenfield, Maynard et al., 2003).

Research in this tradition focused on everyday cognition through "guided participation" within the **zone of proximal development,** where the child's actual level of development is extended upward toward the limits of his or her potential by the help of adult guidance or that of someone more capable. Thus such tasks as weaving, tailoring, practical categorization, and oral mathematical calculations that children learn in their everyday task-oriented interactions are studied as valuable specific learning experiences. This is also known as the "apprenticeship" model of learning (Chavajay & Rogoff, 2002; Greenfield, Keller et al., 2003; Rogoff, 1990), that is, informal teaching and learning through a "master–apprentice" interaction. Its primitive antecedents are seen in nonhuman primates, as well (Greenfield, 2000). This type of learning involves keen attention, observation, and imitation over time. Contrasting methods, such as curiosity, questioning, and skepticism, are not promoted; those are more characteristic of individualistic /independent modes of learning (Greenfield, Keller et al., 2003).

From this perspective, all learning is considered to be context-dependent and "goal-directed action," which is adaptive to practical problem solving. School learning is not considered as superior to or even different from any other type of learning, as it also involves adaptation to school-type tasks, even though its greater generalizability is granted (Segall et al., 1999). There is also a strong "social" aspect to the "competence" construed in the everyday-cognition paradigm. The achievement or competence is not necessarily owned by the individual but is somehow shared with others. A moral aspect of sharing and responsibility toward others is also an aspect of competence where there are closely knit human ties binding people. It has been named social intelligence. I discuss it separately later on.

This important body of thinking and research brought in a corrective to traditional work in mainstream developmental psychology, which was oblivious of culture. It also helped create recognition of the "indigenous" cognitive competence of people (children and adults alike) who were too readily labeled as lacking in competence because they did not perform well on standard psychometric tests, Piaget tasks, or school-related activities. Finally, it has contributed to a better understanding of the interactive nature of the learning process—a functional, goal-directed activity, which unfolds itself in a systematic way through "teaching" and "learning" by "guided participation," the unit of analysis being the total interactive activity rather than the individual.

## Issues in Everyday Cognition

Despite the great value of this approach, however, it is not without its problems. The main problem of the **specific learning model** is the observed lack of transfer to tasks in different situations unless there are similarities in specifics (Berry et al., 2002). As learning is in itself adapting to a specific environment, it is not readily transferable to a dissimilar situation, especially across different cognitive domains (Segall et al., 1999, p. 186). Nevertheless, there is some evidence that especially everyday formal reasoning and mathematical skills do transfer (Carraher et al., 1988; Nunes et al., 1993). It is to be noted that these skills are at higher cognitive levels. Rogoff (1990) also notes that learning for young children involves highly structured specific situations, although this changes with age, with older children having learned much more about the process of learning. Guided participation aims to impart this process of learning, which can be expected to generalize to new and different tasks and situations.

It appears that learning specific procedural skills (*how* to do something) does not easily transfer to new tasks, but when conceptualization is involved, transfer is seen (Hatano, 1982). Quite a bit of traditional everyday learning is procedural and is thus rather limited. Nevertheless, in the Ivory Coast, Tanon (1994) found the transfer of planning skills from an everyday learning task, that is, weaving, to another unrelated task in a context where innovation in weaving was valued. Similarly, in a series of studies in Brazil (Nunes, et al., 1993), the transfer of proportional reasoning was observed among minimally schooled adult fishermen and foremen in constructions from their everyday work experience to novel situations. Although the debate on generalization continues, the general conclusion appears to be that transfer from everyday learning to new situations can occur when conceptualization is involved and especially for persons who have also benefited from formal schooling (Schliemann, Carraher, & Ceci, 1997).

Thus, learning and cognition can and do happen in different ways in different sociocultural contexts. This should come as no surprise to those who are sensitive to the great variability in global human behavior and the importance of culture. Different types of learnings may be at odds with one another. For example, research found that Brazilian street vendor children were successful in oral (street) arithmetic but failed in written (school) arithmetic (Carraher et al., 1988; Nunes et al., 1993). In a recent overview, Nunes (2005) noted that despite their lower mastery of school arithmetic, these children chose to use it rather than oral arithmetic, risking failure. She attributed this to a more positive evaluation of school arithmetic. That is, schools not only teach specific information, but also serve as socializing agents regarding what is valued in society (see also Hatano & Inagaki, 1998).

This is an important point, as it shows that we cannot treat learning specifically and as abstracted from context. Societal values need to be taken into consideration as important contextual variables. A problem may arise, indeed, when in an attempt to show that there can be other valuable learning outside of school, these other types of learning are presented as viable alternatives to school learning. This is especially an issue when social and economic changes (rural–urban mobility, shifts in economic activities and job markets), accompanied by new societal values, require school like cognitive skills or competencies rather than those promoted by traditional lifestyles. For example, with the introduction of mass production, traditional tailoring skills may lose their economic importance, to be replaced by new skills utilizing modern technology.

Furthermore, there can be misfits between different types of "learning" activities. This has implications for child work or child labor. As I mentioned in the previous chapter, in Nigeria it was found that despite the popular belief that street trading facilitates greater arithmetical skills, nonworking students outperformed working ones most in arithmetic (Oloko, 1994). Similarly, in literacy tests both in English and in the mother tongue, working children did more poorly than nonworking students. On the basis of these findings, street work was considered to represent a maladaptation to a changing and modernizing socioeconomic environment, as it either interferes with the school performance of children or keeps them out of school. Also school-related cognitive skills and orientations are often required for urban jobs, which out-of-school learning may fail to impart.

Finally, there are political implications of conclusions such as, "Increasingly, school is seen as simply another context for learning, with specific cognitive outcomes" (Segall et al., 1999, p. 203, referring to "everyday cognition" research) or "The apparent superiority of school-based performances is to some extent an artifact of cross-cultural experimental design" (Greenfield & Lave, 1982, p. 185, referring to the research of Cole, Sharp, & Lave, 1976). It should be noted that although these views may be true in the context of the research conducted, they are also, in effect, referring to situations in countries where significant

[margin handwritten note: notion of school & formal education → how it is valued or not across cultures] efforts are being made to institute universal schooling for children, including attempts to persuade parents to send their children, especially their daughters, to school.

I should also mention that schooling is receiving critical consideration, as well. Its negative aspects have been noted, especially in contexts where "colonial" elements in schooling continue, rendering it "foreign" to the society (for a critical treatment of the topic, see Serpell, 1993). This issue is discussed again in Part II, particularly in chapter 7. There can be conflicts, also, between school and home culture. For example, schools often expect competitive achievement from individuals, whereas in collectivistic "cultures of relatedness" cooperation is valued (Greenfield, Keller et al., 2003). Innovative solutions to such problems are needed, such as more cooperative group projects. An early successful example can be found in the "jigsaw classroom" technique (Aronson, Stephan, Sikes, Blaney, & Snapp, 1978) where students are rewarded for cooperation in group work, not for competition.

## CULTURAL CONCEPTIONS OF COGNITIVE COMPETENCE

In the previous chapter, I discussed parental goals, beliefs, and values as an important aspect of the developmental context. Here I will build upon that discussion and also on the theoretical conceptions of **cognitive competence** that I have just reviewed, to examine cultural conceptions of competence. Looking into some examples may again provide insights.

In Turkish, the word *uslu* is used particularly as a characteristic of children, meaning a combination of good-mannered, obedient, quiet, not naughty, not boisterous. It is a highly valued characteristic, especially in girls, as evidenced in research (Macro, 1993).

The etymology of the word reveals that it is made of the root "us" and the suffix "lu," referring to belonging, meaning "with 'us'" or "having 'us.'" The "us" root, in turn, means "reason." Thus apparently the word *uslu*, meaning "rational" originally, shifted in meaning to its everyday use in childrearing. Probably restrained, quiet, obedient, good-mannered behavior was associated with being reasonable and rational to start out with, and therefore the term for the latter characteristics (*uslu*) was used to refer to the former characteristics, also. With time however, the more concrete behavioral meaning appears to have gained prominence and the original meaning (rational) got lost.

*Uslu* is a term used for children. For adolescents (and maybe young adults), the combined term *akilli-uslu* is used. Literally and on its own, *akilli* means "intelligent." However, the combined term has similar

*[handwritten margin note: interesting differences in language]*

behavioral connotations for adolescents as *uslu* has for children. Nevertheless, the connotation of *akıllı-uslu* also involves an explicit meaning of being "reasonable" and "reliable" in addition to proper demeanor (not being impulsive) in this older age period.

## A Social Definition of Competence

This very close association in connotative meanings referring to intelligence, reason, reasonableness, and being reliable and good-mannered (not impulsive or boisterous) for adolescents and the complete shift in the meaning of *uslu* from being rational to proper demeanor for children are intriguing. These connotations are concerned with a *social* or interpersonal behavioral dimension of **cognitive competence.** Because these terms are period specific (for childhood and adolescence, particularly), they concern childrearing or **socialization** orientations and values.

In the nine-country **Value of Children Study** (VOC study) to which I referred earlier and that I examine in depth in chapter 5, childrearing values were studied that shed light on the aforementioned. Among the characteristics of children that are most desired and second most desired, "obeying their parents" was chosen by 60% of the Turkish parents whereas "being independent and self-reliant" was chosen by only 18% (Kağıtçıbaşi, 1982a, 1982b). The responses from Thailand were very similar. The findings from Indonesia and the Philippines showed an even higher stress put on obedience, whereas in the fast-industrializing countries of Korea and Singapore, the valuing of independence and self-reliance surpassed even that in the United States (Kağıtçıbaşi, 1982a, 1982b, 1990).

*[handwritten margin note: characteristics most commonly valued]*

Similar findings were obtained in the Turkish Early Enrichment Project Kağıtçıbaşi, Sunar, & Bekman, 2001). This research is presented in the second part of the book (chap. 9); I just want to refer to one early finding at this point. We interviewed mothers with low income and low education levels in Istanbul. In describing a "good child," mothers stressed being polite (37% of the mothers spontaneously mentioned it) and obedient (35%) more than any other characteristic. Being "autonomous and self-sufficient," however, was a negligible response (3.6%). In line with the emphasis put on respect and obedience was the stress on harmonious relations. Among children's behaviors that please mothers most, good relational behavior, such as "being good to mother," was mentioned most frequently. Good social-relational behavior (including being obedient, showing affection, and getting along well with others) accounted for almost 80% of mothers' spontaneously mentioned desired behavior in children. Thus, in general a positive social orientation, proper demeanor, and in particular an obedient disposition, are highly valued.

*this, of course, varies*

More recent research with ethnic minorities who emigrated from traditional collectivistic "cultures of relatedness" (Kağıtçıbaşı, 2006a) to North America and Europe also finds similar results. Harwood with Puerto Rican ethnic minorities in the United States (Harwood & Feng, 2006) found an emphasis put on "proper demeanor" by mothers. Research with Turkish and Moroccon minorities in Northern Europe shows a similar valuing of good social relations, obedience, and good manners in children (Deković et al., 2006; Leyendecker, Schoelmerich & Citlak, 2006).

Obedience expectations from children show systematic cross-cultural variation. In more traditional family contexts, especially in rural agrarian and low socioeconomic conditions, a high value is put on obedience in childrearing, and this value is reflected in a cultural conceptualization of cognitive competence that includes a social component. In the last chapter, I also pointed to the functional or adaptive value of conformity orientations inculcated in children for survival (LeVine, 1974, 1988) or for occupational requirements (Kohn, 1969). With changes in lifestyles, however, this social component decreases in importance or is separated out from the cognitive component (as reflected in the VOC study findings from Singapore and Korea).

Commonly, I ask my students in my cross-cultural psychology course to inquire informally of some of the people they know what an intelligent child is like. I also ask them to talk about this with people who have different levels of education and occupation. Typically they report characterizations including social skills, such as *uslu,* obedient, and so on, from respondents with low education-occupation status, but not from highly educated ones.

The so-called "social" definition of intelligence, as seen in my examples from Turkey, was noted early on in research from Africa and was even called "African **social intelligence**" (Mundy-Castle, 1974). A classic study by Serpell (1977) in a Zambian village demonstrated the contrast between the "folk" conceptions of intelligence and what is measured by intelligence tests. He asked five adults to rate the village children of about 10 years of age in terms of which ones they would choose to carry out an important task. He also asked them to rank the children in terms of intelligence, using the local term for it. The children thus rated were given a number of intelligence tests, including three developed for use with nonschooled children in Zambia. The scores the children received from the intelligence tests did not correlate with the adults' ratings. This is because even though free of specific school bias, the tests measured pure cognitive skills and not social skill and social responsibility, which the adults used as criteria.

Similar findings emerged from other research in Africa, starting with the pioneering work of Irvine (1970), who first stressed the importance

*I think Am. adults would do that as well*

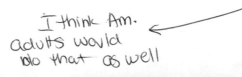

of studying the everyday meaning of "intelligence" for people. For example, Dasen (1984) showed that the Baoule of Africa stress social skills and manual dexterity in their childrearing because they define intelligence primarily in terms of these skills. Subsequent research also found it to be common in Africa, for example, in Cameroon (Nsamenang & Lamb, 1994; Tchombe, 2003, and Yovsi, 2001, both cited in Keller, 2003).

As obvious from the preceding examples from non-African countries, however, this is not unique to Africa but is commonly seen in "traditional" closely knit societies, where "socio-affective" aspects of cognitive competence are stressed. Similarly, Berry and Bennett (1992) noted that among the Cree of northern Canada, the cognitive and social/moral aspects of competence are not differentiated. As I mentioned earlier, in this type of a "shared" conceptualization of intelligence or competence, a moral sense of attentiveness to the needs of others and responsibility for their well-being are implied. This is in contrast to the purely cognitive conceptualization of intelligence in Western technological societies. Obviously, as intelligence tests are products of the Western technological society, they reflect the latter notions of intelligence.

More recent research continues to point to the same distinction between the individual cognitive competence and the more socially oriented competence that extends to others. For example, a study in rural Kenya confirmed the existence of two latent structures in an indigenous conceptualization of intelligence, namely, socioemotional competence and cognitive competence (Grigorenko et al., 2001). Only one of these, cognitive competence, correlated with scores on Western cognitive ability tests and school achievement.

Thus, over three decades similar findings emerge from research conducted in traditional non-Western societies. In particular, the continuity in the emphasis put on social sensitivity in the understanding of a competent person is notable. In general, this research has emphasized the importance of indigenous values and the adaptive nature of what is valued (Grigorenko et al., 2001; Harkness & Super, 1992; Super & Harkness, 1986, 1994, 1999). **Socialization,** in turn, aims to develop the valued characteristics in children, in this case social skills and social responsibility, rather than, for example, abstract reasoning, which is associated with intelligence by psychologists.

For example, Harkness and Super (1992) contrast the developmental results of differing parental conceptions of cognitive competence (ethnotheories) and their expression in the organization of daily life settings and customs of childrearing in Kokwet (Kenya) and in Cambridge, Massachusetts (USA). They describe that it is customary in Kokwet for 5-year-old children to take care of infants, for 3-year-old boys to drive cows from the garden, and for 8-year-old girls to cook dinner for the family, tasks in which children from Cambridge would fail badly. However, these children from Kokwet do poorly in simple cognitive tests (involving retelling a story), at which children from Cambridge have no difficulty. These descriptions are similar to those of children from the Cameroon in West Africa; another similarity is that children spend more time with one another than with adults and learn to talk from one another (Nsamenang, 1992, p. 143). Therefore the type of verbal competence they have tends to be rather limited compared with children exposed to a great deal of adult speech.

Comparable descriptions abound from many preindustrial societies. For example, Rogoff (2003) tells of Mayan Guatemalan 6-year-old girls as skilled caregivers for infants, and Efe infants in the Democratic Republic of Congo using machetes on their own. She contrasts this with Western habits. The latter even find expression in legal conventions; for example, it is an offence in the UK and in some other European countries to leave a child under age 14 alone at home without adult supervision.

## Changes in Lifestyles

Clearly, children's competence in culturally valued domains gets promoted whereas development in other domains lags behind, if it is recognized at all. Thus, learning is functional; it is adaptive to environmental demands. The main problem emerges, however, when stable functional relations or adaptive mechanisms get challenged by modifications in lifestyles, accompanying social structural and economic changes.

This problem becomes relevant in studies looking into ethnic and social-class differences in Western urban contexts, also. Most ethnic minorities in the industrialized countries of Europe, North America, and Australia are rather recent immigrants from less developed countries and especially from their rural areas (African Americans in the United States and native peoples being the main exception). Many of the childrearing patterns of these ethnic minority populations reflect the kinds of parental conceptions of **cognitive competence** that I have been discussing here. Specifically, a socially—rather than a cognitively—oriented conception of competence is valued, stressing conformity-obedience goals, and early learning in the family is based mainly on observation and imitation.

Indeed, research with ethnic-minority families points to this type of parental conception of competence and finds a misfit between this cultural conception and that of the school culture in the host society. For example, Nunes (1993) noted that immigrant Mexican parents in the

United Stastes believe, erroneously, that if their children are quiet and obedient and listen to the teacher, then they will succeed in school. Okagaki and Sternberg (1993) similarly found that for immigrant parents from Cambodia, Mexico, the Philippines, and Vietnam, noncognitive characteristics (i.e. motivation, social skills, and practical school skills) were as important as or more important than cognitive characteristics (problem-solving skills, verbal ability, creative ability) to their conceptions of an "intelligent first-grade child." However, this was not the case for Anglo-American parents. Furthermore, parents' beliefs about the importance of conformity correlated negatively with children's school performance, and American-born parents favored developing autonomy over conformity. Similarly, in recent research different ethnic-minority mothers in the Netherlands are found to have high levels of educational aspirations for their children, but they often don't know how success is to be achieved and how to support their children in this process (Dekovic et al., 2006).

Such research points to the importance of parental conceptions of cognitive competence and fits in with earlier work on parental beliefs and behavior (Laosa, 1982; Laosa & Sigel, 1982; Sigel, 1992; Sigel et al., 1992), referred to in the last chapter. Obviously, parental conceptions of cognitive competence are not the only factors affecting school-related developmental outcomes. Numerous influences, including the typical teaching and learning patterns in the early home environment, play a role. In this context, the role of social class is receiving more research attention and is figuring more importantly in studies of risk factors in the development of children's cognitive and **social competence** (Aksu-Koç, 2005; G. W. Evans, 2004; Hoff, 2003; McLoyd, 1990; Sameroff & Fiese, 1992). In the last chapter, I dealt with this issue in general; next, I examine it specifically with respect to its effects on the cognitive competence of children.

## DISADVANTAGE FOR COGNITIVE COMPETENCE

The last chapter discussed social class, poverty, and environmental disadvantage as an important context variable. Several characteristics of that context were examined and related to different aspects of child development. Here, I am focusing more specifically on environmental disadvantage as it impacts the child's cognitive development. The aforementioned research shows that some caregivers' conceptions of competence and their corresponding behaviors can conflict with mainstream (school) conceptions. If school performance is used as a developmental outcome variable, such home orientations may be considered a "disadvantage." A simple impressionistic example may provide an illustration.

*A Difference in Early Interaction.* Some time ago, at a European airport while waiting for luggage, I noticed a young Turkish family, father, mother, and two little boys. They were obviously living in Western Europe as an ethnic-minority family of lower socioeconomic status. The luggage didn't get processed for a long while, and I had a chance to do some naturalistic observation. The bigger boy was about 4 to 4½ years of age, and the smaller one was about 3. The bigger boy was trying hard to get his father's attention and to engage him in a conversation, as he was repeatedly telling the father some things and asking eagerly, "Isn't it so, Daddy?" The father was not responding, not even looking at the child. The mother did not intervene or respond in any way either; she, like her husband, looking aimlessly into space, as if the children were not there. The smaller boy, in turn, was actively searching for the attention of his older brother. After insistent repetitions, the bigger boy gave up on catching the father's attention and turned to his younger brother, and the two of them carried on chatting.

This behavior contrasts with Western (especially American) middle-class parental behavior. The greater verbal responsiveness of U.S.  middle-class parents compared with working-class parents has been documented in a great deal of research (Applegate, Burleson, & Delia, 1992; Haight et al., 1997; Hoff, 2003; Laosa, 1982, 1984; McLoyd, 1990, 1998; Tamis-LeMonda, Bornstein, & Baumwell, 1996). Again, I have personally experienced it on several occasions. I have felt surprised and even frustrated at not being able to carry on an uninterrupted conversation with an American colleague or friend, if a child was around. If the child says something, even while the other person is talking, the parent typically attends to the child, therefore tuning out the other person.

These two vignettes can be considered rather extreme; the difference, however, is unmistakably there. In a recent nationwide study in Turkey where interviews were conducted with more than 6,000 mothers (Macro, 1993),[1] a child behavior that 73% of the mothers reported as "not tolerated" was "the child interrupting adult conversation." Because a nationally representative sample was used, this finding reflects cultural standards, as discussed in the last chapter. In non-child-centered cultural contexts, where childhood is not considered as special, verbal responsiveness to children may be less intense. When one considers that the traditional motto "children are to be seen and not heard" was also widespread in the West until rather recently and is still present among lower-SES groups, changes over time as well as across cultures become apparent.

---

[1]Macro is a private research center; I supervised this large-scale survey that they carried out.

In the Early Enrichment Project (Kağitçibaşi et al., 2001) mentioned before, we interviewed mothers of young children, living in low-income areas of Istanbul. To find out the degree of mothers' involvement/interaction with their 3- to 5-year-old children, we asked them how often they gave their full attention to the child outside of mealtimes. Those who said "never" or "almost never" reached 22%. Together with those who said "seldom," low involvement was found among more than 40% of the mothers. In terms of what they commonly do when they are with their children at home, 90% of the mothers stated that they do household chores (or handwork such as knitting or embroidering), with little direct interaction with their children.

*Why Is There a Difference?*   Why is it that low-SES mothers tend *not* to verbalize with their young children as much as middle-class mothers? Could it be that, given the low education levels of the lower-SES mothers, their own verbal skills may not be as complex, as proposed by Applegate et al.'s model (1992)? Mother's education level is indeed an important factor. For example, research shows that parental education is more important than income for psychosocial stimulation at home and cognitive and school-related outcomes for the child (Duncan & Magnuson, 2003; Gottfried, Fleming, & Gottfried, 1998).

Though parental education appears to be a factor, it is not clear *how* this affects verbal interaction with the child. A high level of formal education is really not necessary to talk with a young child. What appears to be a critical factor is that the low-SES mothers with low levels of education are not in the habit of sitting down and talking extensively with young children as they do with other adults. This is not in the everyday behavior "repertoire" of these mothers, and when asked why not, they may even say that it is silly to do so because the young child won't understand "adult talk" (Kağitçibaşi et al., 2001). What we see here is an important social-class distinction in parental "ethnotheories" (see chap. 2), in the construal of everyday "teaching" and "learning," and more generally in parenting.

In the Early Enrichment Project (Kağitçibaşi et al., 2001), when we asked mothers if they *teach* anything to their young children, they often said, "No," adding that they themselves had not been to school for long and didn't know "things," and that the children would *learn* when they go to school. When further probed if they *taught* their children how to button a shirt or to put on shoes, they said, "Of course"; but this to them was not *real teaching*. Thus, what is often seen as a lack of a "child-focused and child-development-oriented approach" to childrearing in lower-SES groups appears to concern how teaching and learning are defined and understood. It also has to do with the definition of the

*interesting debate: Are parents teachers or not?*

parental role as nourishing and caring, but not as "teaching" the child in a conscious child-development-oriented manner, which is typical of the educated middle-class mothers.

Another example helps demonstrate this parental orientation further. I observed it a few years ago when I had the opportunity to give a lecture to a large group of Turkish women with low education levels living in the Netherlands as ethnic minorities. In the discussion that followed the lecture, they complained about the prejudice their children faced in schools, including low levels of teacher expectations from them. Though agreeing with their complaints, I told them about Leseman's (1993) study, mentioned earlier, where he found lower levels of language proficiency among Turkish ethnic-minority children in the Netherlands compared with the Dutch children at ages 3 and 3½, that is, *before* school and asked the audience to think together why there was this difference. Through discussion, the women indeed said that they talked less with their children than Dutch mothers did, and they eventually came to understand that this was a reason for the obtained difference.

Thus, the much reported social-class differences that I have already referred to and further present in this chapter may not be inevitable. They need not be "destiny" if well understood by all who are concerned and if concerted efforts are made to change them. It may indeed be possible to promote greater awareness among the caregivers of the value of certain types of interaction with children. This is one of the focal points of the second part of the book, "Implications for Social Issues and Applications," and in particular, the mother training intervention that is presented in chapter 8.

When does lack of responsiveness, especially in terms of verbal interaction, become a disadvantage for the child? Again research provides us with some answers. I have already referred to the misfit between school expectations and childrearing goals among marginal groups. A background of observational learning without verbal reasoning can be a disadvantage in school (Nunes, 1993). Indeed, early verbal interaction with adults appears to be a crucial antecedent of early language development (Hoff, 2003). Language skills are, in turn, indicative of better school performance.

*Studies on Language Development Over the Last Three Decades.* Studies on language development of young children point to the role of environmental factors. I first review here briefly the early studies that demonstrated this role; I next look into more recent work that corroborates earlier findings. In a pioneering study, Slobin (1972) noted that, compared to Western children in the United States, France, and Russia, non-Western children reach the two-word sequence of linguistic development at a substantially slower pace. He attributed this difference to the lower density of language addressed to young children in non-Western cultures. Similarly, subsequent anthropological and psycholinguistic research in preindustrial societies pointed to lack of child-focused conversations and low levels of verbal responsiveness to children (Harkness & Super, 1993; Ochs & Schieffelin, 1984; Schieffelin & Eisenberg, 1984).

Starting in the 1980s, research repeatedly showed the importance of parent–child (especially mother–child) verbal interaction. In a series of studies with Mexican-American mothers and their children, Laosa (1982, 1984) pointed to low maternal education, low social-class standing, and minority-language status as determinants of children's poor cognitive performance. Mothers' teaching strategies and verbal communication with the child were mediating factors. Specifically, less-educated Hispanic mothers typically had less verbal interaction with their young children; they also used less praise and less inquiring but more modeling directives and negative physical control than Anglo mothers. Laosa (1984) found differences between Hispanic and Anglo children's performance (on the McCarthy scales of children's abilities) as early as 2½ years of age, showing the importance of early language development.

Savasir and Sahin (1988) and Savasir, Sezgin, and Erol (1992) found persistent social-class differences in vocabulary and verbal competence of children in Turkey. Similarly, Slaughter (1988) noted the lack of decontextualized communication and play with young children in African American families in the United States. She pointed to this as a factor explaining why Black infants who surpass White infants in early sensorimotor intelligence fall behind in later language-based cognitive performance. Wachs and Gruen (1982) pointed out that verbal stimulation becomes especially important after the 1st year, and the amount of parent–child interaction after 24 months of age makes a crucial impact on developmental outcomes. The 2nd year appears critical for early syntactic and semantic development, and starting from age 2, the amount and complexity of parental verbal communication with the child is consequential for the child's cognitive development.

Ten years after Laosa's pioneering work with Hispanic parents and children in the United States, Leseman studied the same phenomenon among Turkish migrants in the Netherlands (1993), as mentioned before. Other studies on larger cohorts of Dutch and different groups of immigrant children in the 3- to 6-year age range also came up with similar results (reported by Leseman, 1993). Research from Argentina (Peralta de Mendoza & Irice, 1995) concurred in showing similar SES differences in the type of parental speech used with young children.

In the United States, Korenman, Miller, and Sjaastad (1995) found the amount (lack) of emotional support and cognitive stimulation in the

*I believe this! → mainly bk of exposure*

home to account for one third to one half of the disadvantages in verbal, reading, and math skills among persistently poor children. Lee and Croninger (1994) found home support variables such as literacy resources in the home, discussion about school matters, and mother's educational expectations to reduce the effect of poverty on reading achievement by more than half. Eccles and Harold (1993) and Epstein (1990) showed that variation in parental involvement contributes to disparities in achievement within and across income groups.

Applegate et al. (1992) proposed a model of communication development focusing on the complexity dimension. It claimed that the complexity of parental social cognition leads to the complexity of parental communication, which in turn leads to the complexity of the child's social cognition and finally to the complexity of the child's communication. The key in this process model is what they called "reflection-enhancing parenting," found to relate positively to mother's social class and social-cognitive development. This is also in line with Bernstein's (1974) earlier distinction between "elaborated code" and "restricted code," typical of middle-class and working-class home communication, respectively.

There are implications of Applegate's model for parental discipline, also. Whereas power-assertive/**authoritarian parenting** aims to control the child's behavior using negative reinforcement, inductive/**authoritative parenting** aims to influence the child's behavior through reasoning, especially by forming causal relations and drawing the child's attention to the consequences of his or her acts (Baumrind 1980, 1989; M. L. Hoffman, 1977). Thus, **reflection enhancing communication** with the child involves both inductive/authoritative reasoning with the child and also the complex (elaborated) language that this orientation necessitates. They found reflection-enhancing communication to be associated with social class.

Other research found consistent relations between authoritative parenting and adolescents' academic success and psychosocial competence (Dornbusch, Ritter, Leiderman, Roberts, & Fraleigh, 1987; Lamborn, Mounts, Steinberg, & Dornbursch, 1991; Steinberg, Elman, & Mounts, 1989), particularly with American middl- class samples. Thus, effects extend beyond childhood into adolescence. The distinction between dominating and restrictive **parental control** and an order-setting, adaptive parental control (Lau & Cheung, 1987; Lau et al., 1990) showed further that the latter has a positive impact on developmental outcomes. This is because order-setting control (authoritative, as opposed to authoritarian-restrictive control) involves extensive verbal interaction, in a rational, issue-oriented manner (Lau & Cheung, 1987. This is also in line with Goodnow's (1988) **parental modernity** construct. It is associated with "stimulating academic

(?)

*using a Western perspective though?*

*this could be differently interpreted everywhere you go*

behavior," "stimulating language," and "encouraging social maturity." Parents with such an outlook provide a stimulating environment for their young children and actively prepare them for school.

It is exactly this type of parenting that appears to be lacking in the lower social class and marginalized immigration contexts where especially maternal education is limited. For example, Gutierrez, Sameroff, and Karrer, (1988) found lower levels of complexity in parental reasoning about child development among lower-class and less acculturated Mexican-American mothers compared with more acculturated and middle-class mothers.

*Later Studies Focusing on Disadvantage.* In the last decade, more studies were conducted mainly in the United States and Europe examining the detrimental effects of poverty and ethnic minority status on child outcomes, often using large data sets. I referred to some of this research in the last chapter. There, I pointed to the overall harmful effect of lower social-class status and poverty on children, as revealed by American research. Here, I focus on cognitive competence and especially school performance.

Low income, by itself, is found to have deleterious effects on child outcomes. For example, McLoyd (1998) pointed to a number of studies that controlled for maternal education and IQ and other maternal behaviors and that reported the significant effects of poverty on children's cognitive and verbal skills. Thus poverty is a powerful risk factor for children's cognitive competence. There is general agreement, however, that this negative effect is mediated through proximate home variables.

Recent work on the development of oral language skills and literacy has continued to stress the importance of extensive adult–child verbal interactions, involving reasoning, asking and answering questions, storytelling, book reading, and discussions of ongoing events. Strong links are found between children's language and school performance and "family literacy" indicators, such as maternal verbal responsiveness, presence of books, and early book reading (Molfese, Molfese, & Modgline, 2000; Sénécal & Le Fevre, 2002; Whitehurst et al., 1994; Whitehurst & Fischel, 1999), and "middle-class ways of talking" at home (Martini, 1995, 1996). Clearly, early home experience with oral language skills and the "culture of literacy" (involving familiarity with printed media, world knowledge, vocabulary, etc.) predict advanced literacy achievement (Aksu-Koç, 2005; Hoff, 2003; Snow 1991, 1993). Children who lack such experience would be disadvantaged in school and as adults in literate society.

A recent volume on socioeconomic status, parenting, and child development (Bornstein & Bradley, 2003) includes studies by researchers studying many different aspects of SES particularly as it impacts the

*kids @ CLASP*

proximate environment of the child. For example, Duncan and Magnuson (2003) point to low levels of parental education as a key to cognitively nonstimulating home environments. This is highly consequential in explaining why children of less educated parents perform less well in school (Harris, Terrel, & Allen, 1999). In a dramatic demonstration of the contrasts in early environment, Hart and Risley (1995) observed the number of utterances (words) per hour that young children of professional parents, of working-class parents, and of parents on welfare to be very different—in the order of 2,000 to 2,500 words, 1,000 to 1,500 words, and 500 words, respectively. This is calculated to amount to "the early catastrophe of 30 million word gap by age 3" (Hart & Risley, 2003)! Hoff (2003) further demonstrated high-SES and middle-SES differences in the growth rates of 2-year-old children's vocabulary within a period of 10 weeks.

European research also points to less than adequate linguistic skills, such as vocabulary, among ethnic minorities in the Netherlands (Crijnen, Bengi-Arslan, & Verhulst, 2000), yet vocabulary is an important predictor of reading success. Van Tuijl and Leseman (2004), working with Turkish minority families in the Netherlands, pointed to the significance of mother–child interaction, and Aksu-Koç (2005) in a study looking into SES differences in home literacy environments in Turkey also stressed the importance of early environment for children's verbal competence. All this research reveals the key role of the caretaker and the proximate environment in mediating the detrimental effects of socioeconomic deprivation.

With a more holistic perspective, G. W. Evans (2004) has recently drawn attention to the accumulation of multiple environmental risks that in combination can constitute a pathogenic aspect of childhood poverty. This is in line with Sameroff's multirisk model (Sameroff et al., 1987; Sameroff & Fiese, 1992). Evans notes that psychological research has looked exclusively on the psychosocial factors in the family, particularly parenting. But a more encompassing ecological approach is called for that also takes into consideration the physical environment (toxins, water pollution, etc.), neighborhood variables (danger, crime, poorer municipal services, poor quality of child care, etc.), in addition to home variables. Less apparent variables may be added to these, such as prejudice and discrimination the ethnic-minority and low-income family and child may face in the larger society, as, for example, in terms of low expectations on the part of the teachers in school.

As the mediating factors are understood better, interventions to alleviate their negative effects may be undertaken. In the last chapter, I mentioned welfare programs in the United States that increased income and employment and had a strong positive impact on many aspects of children's behavior, including school performance and educational aspirations (Gennetian & Miller, 2002; Huston et al., 2001). More focused interventions involving teaching mothers to use more verbal stimulation, such as encouraging more comments during joint book reading with their children (Hockenberger, Goldstein, & Sirianni Haas, 1999) or through participating in an extensive mother-training program (Van Tuijl & Leseman, 2004) are shown to produce positive results. Intervention is an important topic in this book. I deal with it extensively in chapter 8.

The studies just discussed provide us with important information and thus a better understanding of the factors that constitute disadvantage for children's competence. We find different approaches, particularly with regard to how inclusive they are with regard to the ecological factors. Usually, reaching out into the distal environment involves more multidisciplinary perspectives including the physical, economic, and social variables in the environment, ranging all the way from chemical toxins to neighborhood crime rates. Psychological perspectives focus more on the proximal environment of the home, in particular parenting. However, the distal environmental variables have a great impact on and interface with the proximal ones. In such complexity, poverty plays a crucial role and is often the most consequential variable, either on its own or through its effects on other variables.

We should also note here that most of the research on this topic has been conducted in the United States, with low-income and minority populations, and marginally in Europe with ethnic minorities. Though the range of income and education differentials among different social classes is very large in the United States, it may nevertheless be seen as rather limited when compared with the global picture. Abject poverty, with concomitant high infant and child mortality and morbidity levels abound in the least developed countries. It is not possible here to deal with these overwhelming issues. Nevertheless, the research that I have touched on does provide some clues into the dynamics of disadvantage and the need to study it at different levels.

## Common Patterns and Mismatches

From the foregoing discussion, it may appear that I am lumping together different groups and that I am accepting Western, middle-class, White (school) culture as the *mainstream* culture. Some clarification may be in order on both points. My intention in the main discussion in this chapter is *not* to lump ethnic migrants, rural populations, immigrants, and socioeconomically disadvantaged populations together into any single social entity. Obviously, this would be a fallacious undertaking. What I have been trying to do is to point to certain aspects of the family culture shared to some extent by these groups that can be a potential source of disadvantage for the child. What these groups share within the macrosystem is a marginal and less powerful position vis-à-vis the more powerful mainstream. On this point there is probably agreement. It may be less apparent, however, that these groups also share some characteristics at the microsystem level of family and childrearing. It is to these characteristics that I have been referring.

As for what constitutes mainstream, I do not mean to identify it with Western middle-class (school) culture, only. Because the preponderance of research is carried out in the West, mainly in the United States, this is the appearance. However, urban–rural differences and social stratification based on SES levels are even more pronounced in less developed, non-Western contexts. The same problems of misfit, even in greater proportions, exist there. Indeed, that is why I started this chapter with some examples from Turkey and critically reviewed some of the policy implications of the "everyday cognition" research, based mainly in Africa.

What I have been discussing here with regard to verbal communication involving reasoning (causal explanation, inquiry, perspective taking, etc.) fits in with the **socialization** for **cognitive competence,** which I examined earlier. Specifically, "teaching and learning" limited to nonverbal observational learning and noninductive obedience-oriented child socialization appear not to be optimal for the promotion of high levels of cognitive/linguistic competence in the child. They may be seen to constitute a disadvantage for the child especially in contexts of social change, such as urban–rural mobility and international migration where the child has to adapt to new environmental demands, for example, in the school, for linguistic-cognitive competence, individual decision making, initiative, creative problem solving, and so forth.

Note, however, that the causes of problems of low school performance of some ethnic-minority and lower-SES children are inherent *not* in the families or individuals concerned, but in the general circumstances of majority–minority or social-class relationships in a society. For example, pervasive prejudice toward and low levels of expectations from minority and low-SES pupils on the part of teachers and school administrations work as "self-fulfilling prophecies." These issues are taken up in chapter 10 in particular.

It is not my intention here to explain all of the complex problems involved (elaborate analyses attempt at explanation; see, e.g., Guiraudon, Phalet, & Ter Wal, 2005; Ogbu, 1990). I am only pointing to some aspects that concern misfits between traditional cultural and parental conceptions of cognitive competence and mainstream conceptions of host society, urban culture, educational institutions, and the like. Whether we examine the situation of ethnic minorities in the industrialized countries, or of peasants and tribal people moving into urban areas or having to adjust to new economic activities, or of low-SES groups in a city, we find similar types of misfits.

The criteria for competence in the mainstream culture are to some extent different from those held by the minorities, immigrants, rural migrants, and lower-SES people. Given the existing power differentials, it is not realistic to expect mainstream culture (schools, businesses, professions, etc.) to change much, thus readjustments on the part of the less powerful are necessary. This is not to say that nothing changes in the mainstream culture; indeed no culture is static, and change is always with us. Furthermore, inequalities, exploitation, and so on, must be corrected, and psychologists, together with other social scientists must also work for change and improvement at the macro level, in addition to the individual or family level. For example, a motto in educational intervention work is "preparing children for school *and* schools for children" (Myers, 1992). As discussed before, there is an understanding here that there are many things in need of correction in the schools in both developing and industrialized countries. However, social institutional change is a slow process. Waiting for the institutions to change while doing nothing to help people (children and adults) to adjust to institutions is unrealistic and does not prevent frustrations and failures at the individual and group level.

Thus changes need to occur on both sides. However, some aspects of the school culture are not going to change because they are functional and inherently related to other modern social institutions and the prevalent urban literate culture. The schools' conception of cognitive competence in terms of verbal and mathematical ability and abstract reasoning, problem solving, and so on, are in line with what the industrial (and industrializing) society needs to develop these cognitive skills in young people. These are the skills that effectively fit the requirements of specialized functions to be carried out in modern society. It is especially in these realms that any mismatch between cultural/parental conceptions of cognitive competence and school requirements needs to be resolved by changes in the former.

Schooling is the prime route to upward mobility in most societies. With increased public education in the **Majority World,** children's school performance becomes a key factor in obtaining higher-status jobs and full participation in modernizing economies. In a changing environment, then, criteria for **social competence** also change. What may have been adaptive at one place and time may no longer be adaptive at another place and time. Given the increasing similarities in environments accompanying global urbanization, a universalistic perspective appears to better predict the common patterns of change than a relativistic perspective.

## ADAPTIVE CHANGES IN GLOBAL OUTLOOKS: TOWARD CONVERGENCE

The last point brings us to draw some conclusions based on the discussions in this chapter. Two of the themes that I have discussed, learning by observation-imitation (rather than verbal reasoning) and "social definitions of intelligence," can be briefly reconsidered. Though learning through observation-imitation can be effective, the importance of other types of learning, especially through verbal reasoning, explanation, reflection, and so on, need to be recognized by parents. This would bring with it other changes in orientation to the child, seen not only as a quiet observer and imitator of parental modeling but as an active participant in the learning process, who can verbalize about it. Such verbalization can involve causal relations, explanations, enquiries, and so forth. Effective and extensive use of language in child **socialization** would be a key mediating factor here.

As for social definitions of intelligence (or **cognitive competence**), what appears to be called for is not a decreased emphasis on social goals in child socialization but rather an increased emphasis on cognitive goals. In other words, *both* socially oriented competence *and* cognitive competence should be nurtured. The mismatch between parental values and school demands, for example, seems to derive from too little parental stress on cognitive skills and too much reliance solely on being good (obedient, quiet) for school success. There needs to be a recognition of the importance of cognitive and language skills, as well. Different realms of competence (social *and* cognitive), each important in its own right, would need to emerge for a better fit between the family culture and the school culture (Kağitçibaşi, 2002a).

To pursue this point further, **social intelligence** or a socially construed concept of competence is not seen only in traditional preindustrial societies, though they are most marked in such contexts. They are seen in "modern" societies with urban lifestyles and higher levels of education that have closely knit human ties, that is, a **culture of relatedness** (Kağitçibaşi, 1985a). Recent research conducted in collectivistic cultures of relatedness such as found in non-Western developed contexts or in immigration contexts points to it. For example, it is noted among Mainland Chinese and Chinese immigrants in the United States (J. Lin & Wang, 2002; Q. Wang & Conway, 2004), among Indians (Saraswathi & Ganapathy, 2002), and among Taiwanese (Yang & Sternberg, 1997). It is also reflected in the construal of socially oriented achievement (see the last chapter) among educated young people in the **Majority World** and immigrants in Europe (Phalet & Claeys, 1993; Yu & Yang, 1994). The point made in this chapter is *not* that this connectedness and its reflection in **social competence** need to be *replaced* by an individualistic cognitive competence. It is, rather, that social competence needs to be *complemented* by cognitive competence.

To borrow a terminology from economics and political science, what the disadvantaged groups lack is social capital (Coleman, 1990). If we understand the psychological underpinnings of the problems involved, it is possible to help ameliorate the problems even if the macrosituation does not change much. Mediating factors pointed to by models developed to describe the processes involved in disadvantage are helpful in this context. They tend to be shared to some extent in different disadvantage situations. Some examples are a high number of risk factors (G. W. Evans, 2004; Sameroff & Fiese, 1992) and the negative impact of poverty, stress, and social disadvantage on parenting skills and parental involvement (Duncan & Brooks-Gunn, 1997, 2000; Jackson et al., 2000; McLoyd, 1990; R. S. Mistry et al., 2002; Patterson & Dishion, 1988), which I have discussed earlier (see also the last chapter). Apart from these adverse conditions, parental conceptions of competence that are at odds with mainstream ideals and the corresponding parental orientations that are commonly found in rural/traditional society can also act as a disadvantage, especially in periods of social change.

*To Reiterate.*    In this chapter, we have discussed the insights that a sensitivity to the cultural context in general and the everyday cognition perspective in particular provide. We need to study socialization for competence in context. However, does recognition of the importance of context mean cultural **relativism**? If each context is treated as unique and the observed psychological processes are seen as inherent to it and therefore different from those in other contexts, we would end up with an unwieldy multiplicity of descriptions. This would not promote understanding of the possible systematic underpinnings of the differences and similarities in these processes.

As I also indicated in chapter 1, contexts are not necessarily unique; they can be more or less similar and thus can be compared, just as behavior in different contexts can be compared. This is not to say that we can ignore contexts. Thus my view is "**cultural contextualism** without relativism" (Kağıtçıbaşi, 2000b). This perspective is in line with the goal of discovering systematic patterns, even possibly universal regularities, in psychological processes through cross-cultural comparisons.

As must be clear by now, the aforementioned considerations are pointing in a certain direction, indeed a convergence. There is a global

Box 3.1.   Contextual Change and Change in Socialization for Competence

| | | |
|---|---|---|
| Context | Rural Subsistence ⟶ | Urban |
| | – less specialized work | – more specialized work |
| | – no/low schooling | – increased schooling |
| Teaching & | Demonstration and ⟶ | Verbal explanation |
| Learning | modeling | School-like learning |
| | Apprenticeship | |
| Competence | Social intelligence ⟶ | Social + Cognitive |
| | Practical/manual skills | Intelligence |
| | | School-like skills |

process of socioeconomic demographic structural change in contexts. This is the worldwide urbanization process (see Box 2.3 in the last chapter). It brings with it some similar patterns of lifestyles, including, among other things, increasing provision of public education, specialization in the workplace, and greater participation in a market economy, even in agriculture. This means that the environmental demands acting on people, and in particular, the growing person are becoming more alike. In other words, the similarity in contexts of human development across cultures is increasing.

The implications of this globalization process are far-reaching. They constitute the main topic of this volume as they impact the self, self–other relations, and the family, which I take up in the coming chapters. In this chapter, I have discussed the implications for the socialization of competence. Putting it all together, a summary is given in Box 3.1.

Note that in the urban context with increased schooling, social intelligence is not replaced by cognitive intelligence. Rather, cognitive intelligence is *added* to social intelligence. Social intelligence is adaptive in all contexts. Cognitive or school-like skills are functional for survival and success in school and in urban jobs. Social skills are also functional for adapting to the school environment (Okagaki & Sternberg, 1993). However, they need to be accompanied by cognitive skills that are adaptive to school and to more specialized modern economies.

What Box 3.1 shows is a convergence in lifestyles and the concomitant psychological perspectives and behaviors. This is not to claim that everyone will be the same through global urbanization. With socioeconomic changes bringing about increasing similarities in lifestyles, there are adaptations to rather similar environmental demands. However, these adaptations can be manifested in a myriad of different ways. So, although the underlying mechanisms become more similar, their manifestations in behavior can continue to be diverse. There can also be "culture lag" where some aspects of culture may change but others may remain the same, and even resist change. It is obviously not possible to deal with the complexities of societal changes here. What has been attempted here is to depict some common threads of influence on socialization for competence.

## SUMMARY AND MAIN POINTS

- The goal of socialization, is becoming a competent member of a society, so socialization is designed to accomplish whatever it takes to ensure this goal. Competence in this perspective refers to what is culturally valued and therefore shows variation across cultures.
- Socialization is an active interaction between the caregiver(s) and the child.
- Competence can be differentiated as cognitive and social competence; the former is the main focus of this chapter.
- Descriptions of nonverbal "teaching and learning" abound in anthropological reports, especially among rural populations. Whether there is extensive verbalization with the child may have something to do with cultural conceptions of childhood.
- The central processor model is the traditional view of academic psychology that considers cognitive competence (intelligence) as a basic psychological process that can act in different contexts in the same way, thus enabling transfer of learning from one situation to another.
- The specific learning model (which emerged as a contrasting view to "the central processor model) considers context as crucial and studies the adaptive relations between learning experience and cognitive skills. The main problem of the specific learning model is the lack of transfer to tasks in different situations unless there are similarities in specifics; however, transfer from everyday learning can occur when conceptualization is involved.
- In the traditional Majority World societies and among ethnic minorities and low-SES groups in Western societies, there is a socially rather than a cognitively oriented conception of competence. Conformity-obedience goals are stressed. Conceptions of competence held by caregivers and their corresponding behaviors can conflict with mainstream (school) conceptions.

- A number of studies show that level of verbal responsiveness to children shows variation depending on SES and mother's education. In non-child-centered cultural contexts, where childhood is not considered as special, verbal responsiveness to children may be less extensive.
- Since the 1970s, studies on language development point to the role of early home experience with language and the "culture of literacy" in predicting advanced literacy achievement. Verbal stimulation, especially after the 1st year, is found to have a crucial impact on children's developmental outcomes.
- Detrimental effects of poverty and ethnic minority status on child outcomes are found. Poverty is a risk factor by itself; however, it is mediated through proximate home variables. As mediating factors are understood better, interventions to alleviate adverse environmental effects would be more effective.
- Global changes in lifestyles accompanying increasing urbanization, education, and specialization require cognitive (school-like) competence to complement social competence. Both need to be nurtured in socialization.

## DISCUSSION QUESTIONS

1. What differences are observed in learning across different socioeconomic levels and cultures?
2. How do the central processor model and the specific learning model differ in their views on context and cognitive competence?
3. How do the different conceptions of competence across cultures and social classes shape children's cognitive development?
4. Discuss the relationship between maternal education and children's cognitive competence.
5. Discuss the role of early environmental factors on language development.

# 4

# Culture, Self, and Individualism–Collectivism

A Belgian psychologist, Karen Phalet, asked Belgian and Turkish adolescents in their late teens what would give them a feeling of pride in the future. Both groups referred to future achievement, such as being a successful doctor, lawyer, and the like. However, Turkish adolescents, but not Belgians, spontaneously and without being asked also said "and that would make my family proud, too" (Phalet & Claeys, 1993). In contrast is an item that measures individualism: "If the child won the Nobel Prize, the parents should not feel honored in any way" (Triandis, Bontempo, Villareal, Asai, & Lucca, 1988). What these examples reflect are different construals of the self, one that extends into the "other" and one that "separates" itself from the other, the topic of this chapter.

In the last chapter, it became clear that socialization for competence is understood differently in different cultural contexts. A social definition of intelligence prevails in contexts characterized by closely knit familial and communal bonds. Indeed, this covers most of the world outside of the individualistic West, though showing variations in degree. Thus, for most people even **cognitive competence** involves social competence; and social competence certainly looms large in a general conception of socialization for adult roles in a society. At the core of social competence, in turn, is the development of the self.

This chapter examines the interface between culture and self, a nebulous topic. Being quite selective in my orientation, I deal first with how the concept of self varies with culture, and reflects it. I then discuss some background psychological and anthropological approaches to the study of self and in particular the critical thinking in American social psychology that has brought the self to the foreground. These approaches combined with the more recent cultural and cross-cultural research within the individualism–collectivism paradigm point toward a basic dimension along which there is cultural variation in **self-construals**. This is the

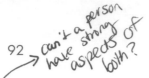

*can't a person have strong aspects of both?*

independence–interdependence dimension, reflected in the **separated** or **related self.** This dimension concerns basic human merging and **separation.** In this chapter, this dimension and its implications are discussed in some detail, as they constitute one of the main themes in this book. Further theoretical elaboration and a search for a possible convergence in the self across cultures are examined later on in chapter 6, where another dimension, that of **agency,** are introduced.

## CULTURALLY VARYING CONCEPT OF SELF

I am using self in this book as a construct that encapsulates the notion of the person and to some extent personality. It is a social product in the sense that it emerges out of social interaction and is socially situated at any point in time. This differentiates self from personality, the latter more often referring to rather enduring, stable characteristics, relatively unaffected by changing social situations. Self is also reflective, in the sense of the person's awareness of it as self-perception and self-awareness ("I," "me"). This is possibly the most important marker of the self and what has been more recently called **self-construal** (see P. B. Smith et al., 2006). An emphasis on the social origins of the reflective self-awareness is not new; it goes back to William James and G. H. Mead (1934), as well as to Fromm (1941), Murphy (1947), and Erikson (1959). Nevertheless, it is a currently important topic, especially in social and cross-cultural psychology (for an overview, see M. B. Smith, 2003).

In the 1980s, the cultural construal of the self became more evident. As a social product, self was seen as a culturally shared model of the person (Heelas & Lock, 1981; Lakoff & Johnson, 1980). It is this latter characteristic of self that has captivated recent cultural and cross-cultural work on the self and is the main focus of this chapter. I first refer to ideas emerging from studies conducted in the 1980s. Subsequently, I consider more recent developments that have gone beyond reporting variability toward forming theoretical conceptualizations of it. Indeed, this is where the field of psychology presently stands; in M. B. Smith's (2003) words, "We can now accept the challenge to understand what is invariant transculturally and what is culture specific in selfhood, and to understand the processes by which environing symbolic culture has its influence"(p. 175). This challenge is taken up in this chapter as well as in the coming two chapters.

### How Is Self Understood?
### Insights From the Last Few Decades

The concept of self is variously understood in different cultural contexts. This is the case even though self is a basic psychological concept and is commonly assumed to have a fundamental and universal nature. By now a vast body of research emerging from different disciplinary traditions provides definitive evidence of diversity. A well-known early expression of this diversity can be found in the following oft-quoted passage from Geertz (1975):

> The Western conception of the person as a bounded, unique, more or less integrated motivational and cognitive universe, a dynamic center of awareness, emotion, judgement, and action organized into a distinctive whole and set contrastively both against other such wholes and against a social and natural background is, however incorrigible it may seem to us, a rather peculiar idea within the context of the world's cultures. (p. 48)

In Bali, Geertz noted that it was not the individual persons, as actors, that were important but rather the roles they are assigned in society and that they enact in relation to others. Thus, "the masks they wear, the stage they occupy, the parts they play, and most important, the spectacle they mount remain and constitute not the facade but the substance of things, not least the self" (Geertz, 1975, p. 50). Geertz was referring to a relational conceptualization of self, where individuals are not known by their names (some nonsense syllable, they may, themselves, have forgotten) but in terms of whose sons they are—that is, their place in society.

Pursuing further the aforementioned parallel with the social definition of intelligence (see chap. 3), one would expect that where social definitions of intelligence prevail, some relational conceptualization of the self would be common, also. This is because the development of social competence, especially sensitivity to others and social responsibility, would be stressed in child training in cultural contexts where human relations are of supreme importance. I gave some examples of these in the last chapter (Dasen, 1988a; 1988b; Harkness & Super, 1992; Harwood et al., 2002; Kağitçibaşi, 1982a, 1984; Kağitçibaşi et al., 2001; Macro, 1993; Morelli et al., 2003).

Relational conceptualizations of the self were reported from other countries, also, though they were probably not as striking as in the Balinese case. For example, V. J. Enriquez (1988) described the concept of *Kapwa,* the core of Filipino interpersonal behavior, as "the unity of the 'self' and 'other'" (p. 139). It embraces both the categories of "outsider "(other) and "one of us"; thus it allows for the merging of the self and the other, in contrast to the common English usage pitting the two against one another. Similarly, much early work referred to the Japanese "group self," originating from the merging of the mother and the child in the *amae* relationship and continuing through life in a sense of connectedness and dependence (Caudill & Frost, 1973; De Vos, 1985; L. A. Doi,

1974; T. Doi, 1973; Hamaguchi, 1985; Lebra, 1976; Morsbach, 1980; Neki, 1976; Stevenson, Azuma, & Hakuta, 1986).

Nsamenang (1992) referred to **social selfhood** within the West African context, which starts with the naming of the infant until death in old age. Connectedness is also seen in the Chinese self, where the meaning of being human resides in interpersonal relationships (e.g., M. H. Bond, 1986; Hsu, 1985). Sun (1991) described "the Chinese 'two persons' matrix" in the sense that

> "a Chinese individual, far from being a distinct and separate *individuum,* is conceivable largely in the continuum of 'two persons.' ... The completion of One in the matrix of the Other is also reflected in the prime symbolism of Chinese culture—the complementarity of *yin* and *yan.* ... Confucianism is the philosophy *par excellence* of the 'Two'" (pp. 2–4, emphasis in the original)

Connectedness of the self is not only with others, but sometimes even with nature or the supernatural realm, as evidenced by much anthropological work especially in preindustrial, sometimes preliterate societies in Africa and Oceania. In these conceptualizations of the oneness of self with natural or supernatural forces, there is a continuity and extension of the self through time and space, and the individuals themselves are not necessarily in charge of their own life or actions, as noted by anthropologists and cultural psychologists (e.g., Marsella et al., 1985; Marsella & White, 1984; Nsamenang, 1992; Shweder & LeVine, 1984; Teasdale & Teasdale, 1992; White & Kirkpatrick, 1985).

From a psychoanalytic perspective, Roland (1988) distinguished the **familial self** of the Japanese and the Indians, "where the experiential sense of self is a 'we-self,'" as opposed to the Western individualized self (p. 8). Yet, "the West" is no homogeneous entity; for example, earlier Gaines (1984) contrasted the Northern European (Protestant) and the Mediterranean (Latin) concepts of the person as "referential" and "indexical," respectively. The latter self is perceived "not as an abstract entity independent of the social relations and contexts ... but as constituted or 'indexed' by the contextual features of social interaction in diverse situations" (p. 182). More recently, Harkness, Super, and Van Tijen (2000) also question the assumed uniformity of the "Western mind."

Cross-cultural studies conducted by anthropologists and psychologists provide us with many other accounts of this diversity. The main distinction drawn is between a self-contained, individuated, separate, **independent self** that is defined by clear boundaries from others and a relational, **interdependent self** with fluid boundaries. Furthermore, this distinction holds in both self-perception and social perception (perception of others).

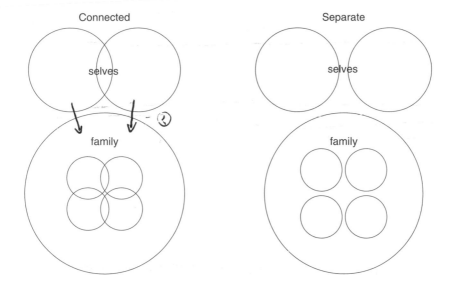

Figure 4.1.   Connected and Separate Selves/Family.

This distinction may reflect more a dimension of variability than a sharp duality. As mentioned before, the 1980s witnessed a rising awareness of this phenomenon, discussed mainly from an anthropological perspective.

At an absolute existential level, every person in every society is obviously aware of being a separate entity ("body" in Chinese terms, according to Sun, 1991). In other words, some line is drawn between what intrinsically is, or belongs to, the self and what is not. However, beyond this most basic existential level, extensive variability emerges. There is variability as to *where* that line is drawn and as to how sharply and clearly it is drawn. American (and Western) psychology, both reflecting and reinforcing the individualistic Western cultural ethos, has drawn the line narrowly and sharply, constituting a clear boundary between self and nonself. Other cultural conceptions differ from this construal of the self in varying degrees (Box 4.1).

Box 4.1 presents a schematic representation of connected or related selves and separate ones. The upper circles mirror self–other relations where the selves may be partially overlapping with permeable boundaries with regard to each other or separate from one another with well-defined boundaries. The degree of overlapping on the left-hand side may be more or less, ranging from almost total merging to barely touching. The right-hand-side separate selves can also range in the distance between them, from rather close to rather distant. Thus, *degrees* of self–other closeness is the key here, rather than a dichotomous construal. The lower figures depict the same variation within the family. This schematic representation can serve as a simple heuristic for the discussions in this and the following two chapters.

A growing body of cross-cultural research and thinking on the self appears to have converged on some such type of distinction, more recent views taken up later in this chapter. Partly as a reaction to American psychology's traditional emphasis on the **separate self,** the tendency in cross-cultural research and writing has been to construe the cultural differences in **self-construal**s as diametrically opposed realities rather than varying in different degrees on a continuous dimension. Because much work is also actually done in sociocultural contexts that are very different from those of the West, especially by anthropologists and ethno-psychologists, sharp polarities have predominated the cross-cultural discourse on the self. Even when this tendency is taken into account, however, diversity still appears to be more striking than commonality in conceptions of the self across cultures.

What is interesting in this context is that psychology of the self emerged as an area where American psychologists, especially those who were critical of the continuing mainstream conventions, started to make use of cross-cultural evidence (e.g., Pepitone, 1987; Sampson, 1988, 1989; M. B. Smith, 1991, 1993). Historical inquiry was also used (e.g., Baumeister, 1986; Cushman, 1990; Gergen, 1991; Sampson, 1989; C. Taylor 1989). For example, C. Taylor showed how an "inner" segregated self is "strange and without precedent in other cultures and times" (p. 114), reminiscent of Geertz's earlier (1974) claim. However, as M. B. Smith (1991) notes, "We can pursue our questions more rigorously, with better evidence, in cross-cultural comparison than is ever possible in historical retrospect" (p. 76; see also M. B. Smith, 2003). Indeed, the singular importance of cross-cultural analysis to the study of self is becoming more generally accepted.

## HISTORICAL TRENDS IN THE STUDY OF SELF

Here, I examine briefly some trends, especially of the last few decades, that have been influential in bringing self to the forefront of psychological inquiry. Two rather independent lines of thinking and research have contributed significantly to the current conceptualization of self and society relationships. One of these comprises American critical theory; the other emerges within cultural and cross-cultural psychological and anthropological thinking. The latter, in turn, covers different approaches.

## Soul-Searching in American Psychology

The 1970s marked the beginnings of increasing self-consciousness and soul-searching in American psychology, especially social psychology. With the rise of cognitive psychology, social psychology, despite its name, was also becoming a psychology of the cognizing "individual" and losing much of its social and interactionist character, stressed by its founders, such as Kurt Lewin and Muzafer Sherif. Both this trend and noncontextual, a-historical, laboratory-based methodology of social psychology came under attack, together with the questioning of the supremacy of the individual, as the unit of analysis. Recognition of the historical (contextual/ideological) nature of psychology and the dangers of excessive individualism for social well-being were important themes in this early auto-criticism (Gergen, 1973; Hogan, 1975; Lasch, 1978; Rotenberg, 1977; Sampson, 1977; M. B. Smith, 1978), which extended into psychology in general.

Also throughout the 1980s and 1990s, an increasing number of critics from among American psychologists and sociologists continued questioning mainstream psychology in general and the ideology of individualism that it upholds in particular. Bellah et al. (1985) wrote a seminal treatise on American society and its changes over time. Taking their clue from the French social philosopher Alexis de Tocqueville, who in the 1930s studied American character and society, they named their work *Habits of the Heart.* It is, basically, a critique of individualism "that has marched inexorably through our history ... that may be destroying those social integuments that Tocqueville saw as moderating its more destructive potentialities, that may be threatening the survival of freedom itself" (p. vii).

Critical thinking spread from the work of Sampson (1977, 1988, 1989), who differentiated between **self-contained individualism** (with firm boundaries of self–nonself and personal control) and ensembled individualism. The former is the prototype of the Western and especially American construal of the self. The latter, which he proposed as an alternative, is a definition of the self with permeable boundaries, and control located in the interpersonal *field,* and not necessarily within the person. Other critics deplored the empty self because of the loss of family, community, and tradition (Cushman, 1990), or the minimal self (Lasch, 1984), with a psychoanalytic orientation narcissistically turned unto itself but not able to prevent fragmentation (Kohut, 1977, 1984; Lasch, 1978), or the saturated self (Gergen, 1991), overwhelmed by the overload of information in the postmodern era.

M. B. Smith (1993; see also 2003) reviewed these critiques and talked about the vulnerability of the inflated self (p. 7) of which too much is expected as a source of life purpose and goals such as self-actualization, self-commitment, and so on. Given the fading of religious and moral values, the self is overburdened in having to replace these sources of life purpose, which Smith considered "basically unworkable as a frame for living our lives" (p. 8). This analysis is in line with those advanced by C. Taylor (1989) and Baumeister (1986, 1991). According to M. B. Smith (1993), the metaphors of both depletion and expansion of the self refer to the same problem. This is the problem of a self troubled with "inflated pretensions" of control and worth, lacking human nurturance and moral guidelines for action.

The negative social implications of this concept of self were further analyzed by critics, and psychology was blamed as being a part of the problem. For example, the Wallachs (1983, 1990) deplored psychology's sanctioning and promotion of selfishness, and made an effort to counteract it. In his APA Presidential Address, Donald Campbell had noted earlier, "Psychology and Psychiatry … not only describe man as selfishly motivated, but implicitly or explicitly teach that he ought to be so" (D. T. Campbell, 1975, p. 1104). Indeed, during the "me generation" in America (1980s) many "self-theories" developed, reinforcing and legitimizing the preoccupation with and exaltation of the individual self, unencumbered by any loyalties to others.

Batson (1990), who reviewed these theories, noted, "Each of these theories assumes motivation with an ultimate goal of maintaining or enhancing one's self image; social encounters [being] instrumental to this self-serving end" (p. 337). He also took issue with the assumed egoism of humans in psychology and endeavored to show, with a research program, the human capacity for empathy and caring. Etzioni (1993) proposed a manifesto, a new lifestyle, which he called communitarianism, reviving communal commitments and social responsibilities without puritanism or oppression. Communitarianism was an interdisciplinary endeavor, with philosophers (e.g., Taylor, 1989), sociologists (e.g., Etzioni, 1993), and psychologists (e.g., Sarason, 1981, 1988) attempting to combine the desirable attributes of individualism and collectivism. In political theory, it involves a critique of liberalism and its emphasis on individualism (Mulhall & Swift, 1982). Even those who considered individualism of value, warned of its excesses (Spence, 1985). Psychologists like M. B. Smith (1978, 1990, 1994, 2003) have devoted effort and continue to do so to promote a socially responsible psychology. Staub and Green (1992) gave an account of psychologists'work contributing toward the solution of global issues. More recently, B. Schwartz (2000) complained about the "tyranny of freedom," and the American Psychological Association and its presidents Zimbardo and Halpern have strongly reendorsed the social responsibility of psychology and "giving psychology

*difficult to be socially responsible & all the definitions of that*

away" to the public (Decade of Behavior, 2006). Socially responsible psychology is the topic of the second part of this volume.

It is interesting to note, however, that even the most outspoken American critics of individualism, when they proposed alternatives, coined new terms that qualified individualism rather than replacing it with another construct. For example, Rotenberg (1977) proposed reciprocal individualism (as opposed to alienating individualism); from a feminist perspective, Lykes (1985,) talked about "a notion of the self as 'social individuality'" (p. 373), more characteristic of the less powerful; and Chodorow (1989), in an attempt to reconcile psychoanalysis with feminist theory, developed the concept of relational individualism. Probably the best known and referred to among these is Sampson's ensembled individualism (1988). To the outsider these terms appear as a contradiction in terms because individualism connotes a particular worldview (ideology); thus another term like *self* would have fitted into these formulations better than individualism. Indeed, the debate *is* on individualism (Sampson, 1989) and given its importance in American culture and psychology, even its critics' alternative proposals don't seem to be able to exclude it. Nevertheless, and possibly in response to this wave of criticism, more attention has been directed to relatedness in more recent years. This is taken up later.

The discussion of the self in American psychology has thus focused on individualism and its place in both society and psychology. This has also been the core of social criticism and commentary. Both the disciplinary criticism and also social criticism shed light on the social implications of the prevalent psychological construal of the self. It is to be noted that the basic distinction between the related (interdependent) and the separate (independent) self found expression both in American thinking and in cross-cultural thinking. However, these two trends of thought pursued their separate paths for some time with little recognition of one another. American critics especially continued to refer only to American research, with some occasional reference to European work, in the true spirit of "self-contained American psychology." However, this situation changed in an important way starting in the1990s. This more recent work is examined later on.

## Cultural and Cross-Cultural Studies

Much anthropological and cultural/cross-cultural psychological work has focused on the concept of self and its development in diverse cultural contexts. This research and thinking has contributed significantly to the current views on the self in society and culture. I first review briefly the anthropological background and then cross-cultural psychological studies paving the way toward current work on individualism, collectivism, and the self.

   *Anthropological Background.*   The anthropological antecedents of "culture and self" can be found in the **Culture and Personality School.** "Culture and personality" was an outgrowth of Boas's early introduction of psychological themes into anthropology, which influenced his students, such as Kroeber, M. Mead, and Benedict. Starting in the late 1920s and 1930s and continuing for almost three decades, anthropologists looked into the interrelationships between culture and personality. Most of this work was designed to reveal the basic personality structure of a society, first construed as "configurational personality" (Benedict, 1934; M. Mead, 1928), then as "basic and modal personality" (Dubois, 1944; Kardiner & Linton, 1945), and continuing as "national character" (Gorer & Rickman, 1949; Inkeles & Levinson, 1954; C. Kluckhohn, 1957).

   All this work was characterized by an intensive and holistic study of single cultures. Starting in the 1950s, a cross-cultural comparative approach was introduced into the Culture and Personality School by Whiting, using the Human Relations Area Files (HRAF) (J. W. Whiting & Child, 1953). The HRAF had been founded by Murdock at Yale University and consisted of extensive ethnographic records on a great number of preindustrial societies, which allowed for comparison.

   The Culture and Personality School, which was later called Psychological Anthropology (Hsu, 1961), was informed mainly by psychoanalytic theory in psychology, which turned out to be a limitation, in terms both of the topics of study and of methodology. Another problem with this school of thought had to do with the assumptions of stability and societal homogeneity of basic personality, ignoring individual and subgroup differences and change over time. These are unwarranted assumptions even for an isolated tribe; they are clearly wrong for contemporary complex societies (for more detailed accounts of "culture and personality," see Berry & Bennett, 1992; Berry et al., 2002; Bock, 1988).

   Notwithstanding its problems, the Culture and Personality School contributed significantly to the study of self in a cultural context. It introduced the notion that some personality characteristics are shared by individuals in a society because they are adaptive to living in that society. This **functional approach** is also used in contemporary cultural and cross-cultural thinking, and provides insight into understanding the underlying reasons for cross-cultural similarities and differences.

   The cross-cultural comparative work of Whiting and his coworkers, especially, has produced important empirical findings regarding the development of self and paved the way to the current eco-cultural framework in cross-cultural psychology (Berry, 1976; Berry & Bennett,

1992; Berry et al., 2002). The general model used involved linear causal links among ecology, maintenance systems (settlement patterns, economy, etc.), childrearing, child personality, adult personality, and projective systems (cultural beliefs, religion, art, magic, etc.). Using this general framework, other studies looked into sex differences in child **socialization** (Barry, Bacon, & Child, 1957) and related child training to the economic functioning of the society (Barry et al., 1959), focusing on obedience, responsibility, nurturance, achievement, and self-reliance training. Some of the findings of this research program showed that girls were socialized more for responsibility and nurturance and boys for achievement and self-reliance. Also a general emphasis on compliance training was found in "high-food-accumulating" agricultural and animal-herding societies, whereas self-reliance training was seen among the "low-food-accumulating" hunters and gatherers (Barry et al., 1957, 1959).

Though this early work was challenged by later analysis (Hendrix, 1985), socialization for compliance in sedentary, agrarian, closely knit societies appears to be a common phenomenon as also evidenced in research on cognitive style (Berry, 1976, 1990; Witkin & Berry, 1975). The subsequent Six Cultures project (Minturn & Lambert, 1964; B. B. Whiting, 1963) also obtained similarities in childrearing among societies with subsistence agricultural lifestyles. Later work similarly noted dependency and conformity expectations from children in more traditional societies with extended or joint families characterized by closely knit bonds (Bisht & Sinha, 1981; Kağitçibaşi, 1984; see also chap. 5). These findings are akin to those about the importance given to social responsibility (and **social intelligence**) in child socialization in traditional societies with closely knit familial and communal bonds, noted earlier.

*Cross-Cultural Psychological Background.* As noted in chapter 1, there is a general shift in current cross-cultural study of the self from isolated subsistence societies to contemporary societies on the one hand, and to ethnic groups within these societies on the other. Even with this shift in emphasis, however, cross-cultural variability in conceptions of the self is the rule. In particular, two seminal comparative studies in the 1980s by American anthropologists focused on a relational conceptualization of the self contrasted with an **idiocentric** (self-contained) construal.

Shweder and Bourne (1984) studied person concepts in the United States and in India. Whereas American subjects used individual (**egocentric**) constructs (46% of Americans' descriptions were of this type, compared with only 20% of the Indians'), Indian subjects used more context-specific and relational (sociocentric) person descriptions, where "units" (persons) are believed to be necessarily altered by the relations they enter into" (p. 110). This distinction reflects the Western view of the self as comprising stable and abstract traits that have generality over time and situations, as opposed to a more situational understanding of the changeable self. Thus, whereas Americans tend to use more trait descriptions ("she is friendly"), Indians contextualize ("she brings cakes to my family on festive days") (p. 119).

J. G. Miller (1984), again comparing Americans and Indians, showed that relational concepts of self also figure in attributions made about others' behaviors. She asked her subjects to give reasons for others' deviant (asocial) and prosocial behaviors. Her results showed a preponderance of dispositional (person) attributions for Americans and situational (contextual) attributions for Indians, especially marked for deviant acts (of the American subjects, 36% made dispositional, 17% situational attributions; for Indian subjects, the figures were 15% and 32%, respectively). Clearly, there is a stronger situating of the person in the interpersonal context for Indians, for whom the self is affected by the situation (others' expectations, etc.) Americans, on the other hand, understand self and explain behavior in terms of context-independent, stable, enduring personality dispositions.

Relational or separate construals of the self also have implications for self-perceptions. Cousins (1989) used the Twenty Statements Test (TST; M. H. Kuhn & McPartland, 1954; which repeatedly asks "Who am I?") with American and Japanese students. He found that the American subjects used psychological trait or attribute descriptions of themselves whereas the Japanese subjects were more concrete (situational) and role specific. This is similar to the difference Shweder and Bourn found between Americans and Indians in describing *others*.

The reverse result was obtained, however, when a modified version of the test was applied specifying situations (in relation to others) in which to describe oneself. Because this was more "natural" for the Japanese, they could give enduring trait descriptions more easily, but the Americans felt the need to qualify their self-descriptions to make sure that their self-images could be independent of the situational constraints (Cousins, 1989). Other studies using the TST also found that Americans use more trait descriptions of self than the Japanese (M. H. Bond & Cheung, 1983) and the Chinese make more references to self as a member of a group (Triandis, McCusker, & Hui, 1990).

## INDIVIDUALISM–COLLECTIVISM (I–C)

This discussion brings us to individualism–collectivism (I–C), arguably the most significant construct that has stamped its mark on cross-cultural psychological research of the last 25 years (Kağitçibaşi & Berry, 1989). Kağitçibaşi (1994a) called the 1980s "the decade of individualism–collectivism." The 1990s could also be similarly labeled. In fact, there does not seem to be much of a reduction in research using this paradigm even though there is increasing criticism and debate. Whereas some see the construct as having served its term (Berry et al., 2002; M. H. Bond, 1994) or of dubious validity (Matsumoto, 1999; Takano & Osaka, 1999), others (Oyserman, Kemmelmeier, & Coon, 2002a, 2002b; Schimmack, Oishi, & Diener, 2005) find it valuable in showing systematic differences in self, values, and thinking and relating to others, despite its shortcomings. Still others (Allik & Realo, 2005; Yamagishi, Cook, & Watabe, 1998) claim that individualism, far from being a selfish orientation, is actually associated with social capital, which entails civic engagement and trust in people. Particularly the last view forms a contrast to the rather critical perspectives on the excesses of individualism in "soul-searching" in American psychology, as discussed previously.

Clearly, we are faced with a complex phenomenon involving multiple conceptualization and operationalization in research. I–C has stimulated a tremendous amount of research in cross-cultural psychology within the last two and a half decades, thus extensive reviews are available, including full volumes (Kağitçibaşi, 1997a; Kağitçibaşi & Berry, 1989; Kim, Triandis, Kağitçibaşi, Choi, & Yoon, 1994; Oyserman et al., 2002a, 2002b; Triandis, 1988, 1990, 1995). I give here only a short overview and touch on some points of relevance to the previous discussion.

The roots of individualism in the Western world have been traced in the history of ideas, in political and economic history, in religious history, and in psychosocial history. It has been traced as far back as ancient Greece and medieval Europe. Indeed individualism has been the hallmark of European social and intellectual history (see Kağitçibaşi, 1990, 1997a). In North America, also, it dates back to the preindustrial era. It is important to keep in mind this history of an individualistic ethos in the Western world that distinguishes it from most of the rest of the world's cultures. The implications of this history for family and family change are examined in the next chapter.

In midcentury sociology and anthropology, I–C dichotomy found expression in Parsons' (1951) writings as pattern variables of "self-orientation" or "collectivity-orientation" and in F. R. Kluckhohn and Strodtbeck's (1961) views on the "pursuit of private interests" and the "pursuit of common interests of the collectivity." The best-known antecedents of I–C in the social sciences are Tönnies's (1957) **Gesellschaft** and **Gemeinschaft**. Throughout these writings and particularly with its inception in cross-cultural psychology with Hofstede's (1980) *Culture's Consequences* two decades later, I–C has referred mainly to cultures

(Hofstede, 2001). It has been considered "the single most important dimension of cultural difference in social behavior" (Triandis, Leung, Villareal, & Clark, 1985, p. 395). It has also been used at the individual level of analysis, as characteristics of individuals, "idiocentrism–allocentrism" (respectively) (Triandis et al., 1985). However, this multi-level usage has at times caused some confusion.

The popularity of I–C for cross-cultural psychologists derives from its use as a culture-level explanation for observed differences in behavior. In particular, it has served as a theoretically meaningful construct to make sense of the observed human diversity in the world. Additionally, its apparent simplicity as a single dimension has contributed to its popularity. There is an inherent attraction to single key explanations. Actually, I–C is anything but simple or unidimensional.

Individualism and collectivism, as "isms," are basically ideological concepts and have come to acquire some social-normative content. For example, individualism is seen as akin to modernity and is associated with modern values such as sex-role equality, human rights, and freedoms, and so on, whereas collectivism is seen to embody traditional, conservative ideology (Kağıtçıbaşı, 1994a; K.-S. Yang, 1988). Such normative attributions do not follow from a psychological-level conceptualization. Thus, I–C carries considerable excess meaning.

## A Refinement: Normative and Relational I–C

In fact, we can differentiate two main orientations to the study of I–C, a values orientation and a self-orientation (Kağıtçıbaşı, 1997a). The values orientation emerged earlier and has remained more dominant, particularly in cross-cultural social psychology. It addresses mainly the **normative I–C,** as reflected in social norms, values, conventions, and rules. It deals mainly with whether individual interests should be subordinated to group interests (C) or should be upheld (I). In other words it refers to hierarchical or egalitarian human relations. The self-orientation, on the other hand, deals with **relational I–C,** focusing on self–other relations. Here the degree of separateness-connectedness with others emerges as important.

On the basis of this distinction, I have proposed two types of I–C, normative and relational. Normative collectivism puts the emphasis on the group or collectivity that serves as the person's in-group and whose needs have priority. Normative individualism, in contrast, upholds individual needs, rights, and prerogatives. These are often pitted against one another. This construal of I–C has permeated research and theorizing in cross-cultural social psychology from the 1980s on, emerging in the work of Hofstede (1980, 2001) and Triandis (1988, 1989, 1990, 1995) and further reinforced in the values research of S. H. Schwartz (1992, 1994; Schwartz & Bilsky, 1990; P. B. Smith & Schwartz, 1997), M. H. Bond (1988, 2002; Chinese Culture Connection, 1987) and others.

Normative I–C gets confounded with modernization/tradition. Because social norms and customs tend to change with socioeconomic development, normative collectivism gets weaker with changing lifestyles and is replaced by normative individualism, as predicted by **modernization theory.** For example, with increased affluence, old people become more self-sufficient financially and materially less dependent on their adult offspring. Together with this, hierarchical family roles would be expected to weaken, as found, for example, by Georgas et al. (2006) and Kağitçibaşi (1982a, 1982b, 1990; Kağitçibaşi & Ataca, 2005). This is because respect and loyalty to parents is no longer required for family livelihood. Decreased family hierarchy means decreased normative collectivism. However, the close emotional bonds between generations may continue, even though material interdependencies and hierarchy weaken. The emotional bonds reflect the other construal of collectivism, that is, **relational collectivism.** This process is discussed further in the next chapter.

Normative collectivism reflects tradition and conservative ideology (see Kağitçibaşi, 1997a). Thus, for example, conservatism regarding gender is closely associated with tradition rather than modernity, and this latter dimension overlaps with Hofstede's (normative) collectivism. Similarly, S. H. Schwartz had first labeled his "conformity, tradition, and security" values factor as "collectivism" but changed it to "conservation" afterward (1994). Together with tradition and conservatism go "power distance" and hierarchy. Thus, normative collectivism refers to collectivism combined with power distance (Hofstede, 1980, 2001) and hierarchy (S. H. Schwartz, 1992, 1994), as well as to vertical collectivism (Triandis, 1994; Singelis, Triandis, Bhawuk, & Gelfand, 1995).

A similar distinction to that of normative and relational I–C is proposed by Triandis (1994; Singelis et al., 1995); it is that between **horizontal** and **vertical I–C.** It refers mainly to equalitarian versus hierarchical relations respectively, and is also akin to Hofstede's power distance dimension. This distinction has been used in research and promises to bring a refinement into the broad I–C construct. The similarity between vertical I–C and normative I–C is quite apparent. In the same way, horizontal I–C is akin to relational I–C (see next paragraph). This point is elaborated further in chapter 6.

Relational I–C refers to **self-construals** and self–other relations. The main distinction is between a relatively self-contained, **separate self** defined by clear boundaries from others, and a relational self with permeable boundaries. This is the same distinction that I made earlier in this chapter when discussing the diverse understandings of the self across cultures, in particular the contrasting self-construals in the Western (middle-class) contexts and in most of the rest of the world (Kağitçibaşi, 1990; Markus & Kitayama, 1991). This distinction holds in both self-perception and in the perception of others (social perception) as exemplified by the early work of Shweder and Bourne (1984), J. G. Miller (1984), and Cousins (1989), described earlier, and by a great volume of research conducted since then. This research is reviewed later on.

From the very start, the normative I–C and a corresponding values orientation have dominated research in the field, mostly in the sense of whether the individual is or is not subservient to the group (family, collectivity). Subsequently, however, a number of researchers have recognized the more important psychological relevance of relational I–C (M. H. Bond, 1994; Kağitçibaşi, 1994a, 1997a; S. H. Schwartz, 1994). This has led to the "self" orientation in the study of I–C, which is the more prominent research paradigm today. The self-orientation and its implications for cognition, emotion, and motivation were first put forward by Markus and Kitayama (1991). Their seminal review helped establish I–C as a basic dimension underlying the cross-cultural variations in psychological processes studied by social psychologists.

The degree of correspondence between the normative and the relational I–C is an empirical question. Indeed, different types of measures assessing attitudes/values (normative) and social orientation (relational) may not relate to one another. For example, Chan (1994) found that Schwartz's collectivist (conservation) value index did not correlate with a measure of social content of the self (% Social on the M. H. Kuhn & McPartland, 1954, "Who am I?" Test).

Accordingly, a conceptual and methodological problem arises when the two different types of I–C, relational and normative, get confounded. This is particularly an issue in measurement in that many I–C scales include items that tap both normative and relational I–C. Yet it is possible that these two different I–C show variation within the same culture, even the same individual. Findings from the United States are a case in point. Since Hofstede's original comparative research, the United States has been labeled as the "arch individualist" culture. Most of the findings concurring with this view used a values orientation and normative I–C. Given the strong intellectual ethos upholding individual rights, equality, freedom, and the like in the United States, the scores obtained showed high individualism. However, the extensive meta-analysis by Oyserman et al. (2002b) of recent studies in fact found a high level of relatedness in the United States. Oyserman et al. also pointed to I–C as not falling on a single dimension. It appears that different types of I–C had been tapped in these studies, and the two basic ones appear to be relational and normative I–C.

Triandis (1989) suggested a probabilistic framework explaining when the private, collective, or public selves become more salient over three dimensions of cultural variation (individualism–collectivism, tightness–looseness, and cultural complexity). After Baumeister (1986) and Greenwald and Pratkanis (1984), Triandis defines **private self** as cognitions that involve traits or behaviors of the person ("I am introverted"); the **public self** as cognitions concerning generalized others' view of the self ("People think I am introverted"); and the **collective self** as cognitions concerning a view of the self that is found in a collective, such as the family ("My family thinks I am introverted") (Triandis, 1988, p. 507). Also E. S. Kashima and Hardie (2000) differentiated among the relational, individual, and collective self-aspects.

Most relevant for the present discussion is the prediction that the more individualistic the culture (i.e., the more self is construed as separate), the more frequent is the sampling of the private self (i.e., the private self is more salient in the person's experience), and conversely, the more collectivist the culture, the more the collective self is sampled. Societal tightness (which reflects closely knit familial-communal bonds) is also associated with the higher sampling of the collective self.[1]

There are other issues involved in the I–C paradigm particularly with regard to the dimensionality, generality, and the levels of measurement (see Kağitçibaşi, 1997a, for a review). For example, whether I–C forms a single dimension has been much debated. If I–C formed a single dimension, its two poles (individualism and collectivism) would be negatively related to each other and would be equally and inversely related to other variables. This is often not found to be the case (Kağitçibaşi, 1997a).

Hofstede (1980) originally derived individualism empirically as a unidimensional construct at the cultural level (lower scores denoting collectivism). Triandis and Suh (2002) also claim that at the cultural level individualism is the polar opposite of collectivism. However, research at the individual level of analysis points to the multidimensional (at least bidimensional) nature of I–C, with the two constructs being independent of one another (orthogonal) (Realo, Koido, Ceulemans, & Allik, 2002; Rhee, Uleman, & Lee, 1996). Thus, I–C can coexist in individuals or groups at the same time in different situations or with different target groups or toward different interactional goals (Gudykunst & Bond, 1997; Ho & Chiu, 1994; Oyserman et al., 2002a; 2002b; Singelis, 1994; Uleman, Rhee, Bardoliwalla, Semin, & Toyama, 2000). For example, a common finding is that individuals in collectivistic cultures behave differently with their in-groups than with out-groups. This is seen in behaviors ranging from conformity

---

[1]Triandis (1989) also relates cultural complexity to the sampling of the "private" self, which I find problematic (see Kağitçibaşi, 1994b, for a discussion on this point).

*this is something to explore more* (handwritten note in left margin)

*Conformity* (handwritten note in left margin)

(R. Bond & Smith, 1996) to equity-equality orientation in reward allocation (Leung & Bond, 1984) to trust (Yamagishi et al., 1998). Although this may be a general human tendency, research shows that it is more marked in collectivistic than in individualistic contexts.

The I–C paradigm has been challenged, particularly with reference to its questionable empirical base. For example, Takano and Osaka (1999) reviewed 15 studies comparing American and Japanese participants on I–C and found no evidence supporting "the common view." Matsumoto (1999), with a more extensive review of 18 studies, showed that I–C and the **independent–interdependent self**-construals lacked empirical support. These critical findings appear to be due at least in part to problems in conceptualization and operationalization of I–C and the independent–interdependent self that are dealt with later on.

Other methodological problems may also be involved in the conflicting findings. Oyserman et al. (2002b) pointed to measurement problems in I–C, in particular the lack of convergent validity (correlations) between Hofstede's (1980) individualism scores (at the cultural level) and more recent measures of individualism at the individual level. However, Schimmack et al. (2005) point out that this is due to response set variations across cultures. Whereas Hofstede corrected for response sets, more recent studies at the individual level of analysis have not. Because Oyserman et al. used these uncorrected scores in their meta-analysis, they could not get convergence. When Schimmack et al. corrected response sets statistically, they found convergent validity, also including correlations with national development levels and individualism, just as Hofstede had found. They conclude that I–C is a valid and important dimension of cross-cultural variation.

The debate continues. Notwithstanding the issues, the important body of research conducted within the I–C framework has provided insight into a better understanding of the separateness–relatedness dimension of the self and self–other relations. There is consideable overlap in the thinking involved in the two areas. Separateness–connectedness of the self may be construed as the psychological core dimension of individualism–collectivism.

## RELATED SELF–SEPARATE SELF

There is a great deal of convergence in the research and theorizing reviewed in this chapter. Whether in the form of speculative theory, social commentary/criticism, anthropological in-depth culture study, or cross-cultural psychological research, spanning different academic disciplines over considerable time and space, views about the self distinguish

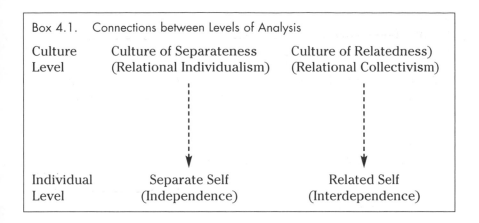

Box 4.1. Connections between Levels of Analysis

| Culture Level | Culture of Separateness (Relational Individualism) | Culture of Relatedness) (Relational Collectivism) |
|---|---|---|
| Individual Level | Separate Self (Independence) | Related Self (Interdependence) |

between (degrees of) relating to and separating from others. Whether the self is well bounded and separate or whether it is expansive and its boundaries are permeable is of crucial significance for the psychological and social functioning of the individual. Thus, the degree of relatedness–separateness of the self has emerged as a basic dimension.

I noted this dimension first at the cultural level, in terms of **culture of separateness–culture of relatedness** (Kağitçibaşi, 1985a), referring to general closeness–distance in human relations. Since then I have focused more on the separateness–relatedness of the self and its antecedents (indeed, going back to some of my own culture contact experiences, which I related in the Preface). I prefer this conceptual dimension to the more popular individualism–collectivism mainly because separateness–relatedness of the self is a basically psychological dimension whereas individualism–collectivism is not. Nevertheless, there are clear parallels between the cultural and the individual levels of analysis (see Box 4.1 in the next section).

The psychological domain within which I have noted a great convergence of research and thinking on the self can be called the **psychology of relatedness** (Kağitçibaşi, 1994a). It has to do with general self–other relations and their **integration** with how the self is conceptualized. This is in line with the **relational** type of individualism–collectivism that I have discussed before at the cultural level. From a disciplinary point of view, this domain bridges personality and social psychology. It is also a cross-cultural psychological domain because both the **self-construal** and also its integral interpersonal relations show cross-cultural variation, as evidenced by research. Indeed, if systematic cross-cultural variations can be established, and if they can be related to distinct antecedent conditions, we may be on our way to discovering a possibly universal dimension of human behavior.

There are clear parallels between the cultural, familial (group-interpersonal), and individual levels of analysis with regard to the psychology of relatedness. Thus, the culture of separateness refers to the contexts (cultural-familial) and interpersonal relational patterns characterized by relations between separate selves, with clearly defined boundaries (making them self-contained). The culture of relatedness, on the other hand, refers to contexts and relational patterns identified by relations between connected, expanding, and therefore partially overlapping selves with diffuse boundaries. There are, furthermore, different degrees of separateness–relatedness between these two polar opposites; thus what we have here is a dimension of variation.

## Independence–Interdependence

The **psychology of relatedness** can also be conceptualized as a dimension of interdependence–independence. Indeed, in an earlier analysis, looking into the development of the **related** and the **separate self**, I proposed independence–interdependence as a basic dimension (Kağitçibaşi, 1990, p. 154ff). Quite independently, Markus and Kitayama (1991) also proposed the independent and the interdependent construal of the self to refer to the same distinction. These are very similar concepts, which refer to the basic human relations–self interface. The concepts of interdependence–independence are obviously not "new"; they have figured for a long time in developmental research, personality theory, and the study of childrearing and **socialization.** I have referred to some of the latter in this chapter (Barry et al., 1959; Berry 1976, 1990; J. W. Whiting & Child, 1953; Witkin & Berry, 1975). However, an exclusive focus on this dimension in the study of self is rather recent.

The independence–interdependence dimension can be conceptualized at different levels. At the level of the self, it is equivalent to separateness–relatedness. It can also be studied at the familial or cultural levels, similar to the **culture of relatedness–culture of separateness** (Kağitçibaşi, 1985a). At this level, it can be useful in understanding, for example, childrearing and socialization orientations. It is at this level, especially that of the family, that an independence–interdependence dimension provides the links between the background (cultural, social-structural) variables and the self. It is thus an important concept in studying the development of the self.

*"Conflict Theories" of Personality.* The independence–interdependence dimension, just like the separate–related **self construal**, has to do with basic human merging and **separation.** In American psychology, it

finds its first expression in the "conflict theories" of personality (Angyal, 1951; Bakan, 1966, 1968; Rank, 1945), which proposed two basic and conflicting needs for merging with others and separation from others. Within the psychoanalytic point of view, reinterpreted by object relations theory, it derives from the "resolution" of the individuation-separation issue (e.g., Blos, 1979; Chodorow, 1989; Mahler, 1972; Mahler, Pine, & Bergman, 1975; Panel, 1973a, 1973b). It is considered a natural early developmental process of attaining object constancy and mental representations of objects (mainly of comforting others) in their absence, thus leading to autonomy from the environment.

This view is also shared by ego psychologists (Hartman, 1939/1958), who earlier posited this process as the development of the rational, autonomous ego. From a different perspective, that of family systems theory (Guerin, 1976; Minuchin, 1974), there is an emphasis on clear boundaries separating the selves (subsystems) within the family system. Thus, both for healthy development of the self and for healthy family functioning, **individuation-separation** and well-defined boundaries of the self are considered crucial in much of personality theory and clinical psychology.

As I discussed earlier, some early cognitive process of differentiation must take place for everyone, because every person is aware of being a separate entity from others. However, the individuation-separation hypothesis does not deal only with this basic existential level; it goes beyond it in defining healthy and pathological human development and family functioning. It works at a psychological level throughout the life span, proscribing "symbiotic" relationships (overlapping selves in Box 4.1) as pathological and prescribing separate selves as healthy. Other theoretical orientations in mainstream personality psychology, deriving from Freud, Erickson, and others share similar views.

Thus, Western psychology affirms one type of self—the separate self—as *the* healthy prototype. It is the prescriptive nature of psychology that empowers it; it can be used to contribute to human well-being; but if misguided, it can do more harm than good. This is what the critics of American psychology have complained about: that psychology is a part of the problem, rather than the solution, of selfishness and lack of social commitment.

*A Note of Caution.*   It is to be noted that throughout this chapter I have been examining relatedness–separateness as a basic dimension of self and interpersonal relations. I have called this psychology of relatedness (Kağitçibaşi, 1994a). As discussed before, this is the basis of a relational construal of I–C. It does *not* refer, however, to emotional ties. In other words, related selves do not necessarily like/love each other more than separate selves. It has to do with the *structure* of self–other relations, where one self ends and the other begins, or whether self-boundaries are clearly defined or not. This can be thought of as the "identity" of the selves being distinct or connected/overlapping, as depicted in Box 4.1.

Second, in the last decade my views on the dimension of relatedness– separateness and the corresponding **interdependent–independent self** have evolved to differ from some influential perpectives on the topic (Kağitçibaşi, 1996b, 2005a). In particular, I question the claim that you have to separate in order to develop autonomy, that is, the assumed close overlap, even identity of separateness and autonomy. This is commonly assumed by researchers in the field and appears to be a remnant of the psychoanalytic separation-individuation hypothesis (Mahler, 1972; Mahler et al., 1975), as mentioned earlier. I believe that including both separateness and autonomy (**agency**) in the construal and measurement of individualism/independence and conversely relatedness and lack of agency in collectivism/interdependence creates a conceptual and methodological problem. This problem is responsible, at least in part, for the conflicting results obtained from studies in the field. This issue is dealt with in greater detail in chapter 6, which approaches the self from a developmental perspective.

Next, we consider briefly research that has investigated some of the behavioral correlates of the I–C or independent–interdependent self. Indeed, this is one of the most researched topics in cross-cultural study of the self. Most of the work is conducted within a social psychological framework. It shows how far the I–C paradigm has reached and how it has been integrated into mainstream social psychology.

## CORRELATES OF I–C OR RELATED–SEPARATE SELF IN PSYCHOLOGICAL FUNCTIONING

Starting in the 1980s, research investigated the implications of the connectedness–separateness of the self. A great deal of research has been conducted to investigate how I–C and **self-construals** are reflected in different psychological outcomes. For example, early studies showed that a tendency to perceive interpersonal harmony rather than competition in social episodes (Forgas & Bond, 1985), less social loafing (Earley, 1989, 1993; Gabrenya, Wang, & Latane, 1985), and a more cooperative rather than competitive orientation (Eliram & Schwarzwald, 1987) are associated with a more relational construal of the self. Most of this research was conducted within an "I–C framework." Other tendencies in cognitive, emotional, and motivational realms were also found, as reviewed extensively by Markus and Kitayama (1991). The main determining factor in these studies was the degree of connectedness–separateness of the self.

Here, I examine some further spheres of psychological functioning where there is ongoing theoretical and empirical research. Given the enormous amount of empirical work within this paradigm, the presentation here is necessarily highly selective. It is designed to provide some examples of thinking and research in the field.

## Moral Thinking and Social Justice

I have already referred to how culture shapes self-perceptions and person perceptions, studied by Shweder and Bourne (1984) and by J. G. Miller (1984). How the self is construed also has implications for moral thinking. J. G. Miller, Bersoff, and Harwood (1990) compared Indian and American subjects' moral reasoning regarding hypothetical nonhelping situations. They found that Indians consider social responsibilities as moral issues, but Americans do not, except in cases of life-threatening emergencies and in parent–child interaction; they consider them as matters of personal choice or decision. Thus, for the Indian **related self,** the welfare of others (beneficence) is an integral aspect of moral code, invoking social responsibility. For the American **separate self,** however, moral code is limited to justice and individual freedom; it does not include beneficence, as also evidenced in Kohlberg's theory (1969; discussed later). Indeed, beneficence can be seen to conflict with the individual freedom of choice. There are clear implications of this finding for the issue of egoism–altruism, which is salient in the criticism and social commentary within American psychology, noted before.

Subsequently, J. G. Miller (1994) linked these differences in self-construals to cultural differences in duty-centered and individual-centered moral codes of the Hindu and American cultures, respectively. She further suggests different types of morality; for example, duty-based caring may constitute "community morality" whereas caring based on individual choice would constitute "voluntaristic morality." A third qualitatively different morality may involve an "empathy-based responsiveness to others," which is emphasized in Japan, for example (J. G. Miller, 2002; see J. G. Miller, 2001, for an overview).

These views are quite different from the main theoretical perspective on moral development in psychology, that of the Kohlbergian model. Based on Piaget's (1948) two-stage theory of moral development, from "heteronomous" to "autonomous" morality, Kohlberg (1969, 1984) formulated a three-level, six-stage sequence of moral development. This is a cognitively based model claiming universality, like Piaget's. It claims a progression from a hedonistic preconventional level (avoiding punishment) to a conventional level focused on social obligations, care for others, and the rule of law to a postconventional level upholding individual rights and principles of justice. The Kohlbergian model of moral judgment was very influential until it was challenged by the feminist critical perspective of Carol Gilligan (1982), Kohlberg's doctoral student. The challenge emerged from research with the obtained gender difference in moral levels of development. Higher stage responses occurred mostly within middle-class Western urban groups, especially among men. Women typically scored lower, at the "social" level, reflecting the "relational" morality of "care for others," rather than the highest level of "justice morality," which reflects an individualistic worldview. This criticism of individualistic male bias challenged the validity of the theory and made an impact on the thinking in this field.

What is notable from a cross-cultural psychological perspective is that together with gender differences, cross-cultural differences in moral development were also being found. For example, in early studies in the Lebanon, Mexico, China, and Turkey with urban groups and rural peasants (Kohlberg, 1969; Obermeyer, 1973) and afterward with the Kipsigis in Kenya (Harkness, Edwards, & Super, 1981), social conventional type of morality (second level) was commonly found, but this was not seen as challenging the theory. In other words, when American female participants were found to score lower than American men, the theory was challenged. However, when other groups in traditional non-Western societies were found to score lower than Western groups, this did not lead to a questioning of the universal validity of the theory (see J. G. Miller, 2001). It was assumed that those people were just less "developed"![2]

Today, it is generally agreed that there may be different bases of morality. In particular, the **culture of relatedness** appears to have a deep impact on moral understanding and moral responsibility. The moral basis of justice may involve a sense of responsibility for others, as found among the Chinese by Ma (1997). A related "socially oriented" morality may be based on role obligations in judgments of responsibility, found to be more salient in Japan (Hagiwara, 1992) and India (J. G. Miller, 2003) and other collectivistic cultures than in the United States.

It is to be noted, however, that a socially oriented morality based on a sense of duty does not mean lack of **agency.** As J. G. Miller shows (2003), for a person in a collectivistic context, meeting social expectations may be experienced as agentic and integral to self; such behavior

---

[2]Gilligan also did not take this seriously. After a lecture she gave at Harvard University in 1984, I pointed at findings of cross-cultural differences paralleling gender differences, but she dismissed the point.

may be motivationally satisfying rather than perceived as coerced. For example, she found that when American and Indian adults were asked to help a friend, where there was either strong expectation or little or no expectation of help, Americans expressed lesser satisfaction and lack of a sense of choice in the presence of strong social expectations (as when the other person directly asked for help). For Indians, there was no difference between the two conditions in either satisfaction or sense of choice (J. G. Miller, Schaberg, Bachman, & Conner, 2006). Similarly, Menon and Shweder (1998) in ethnographic research in India observed that acts of meeting social obligations involved a sense of personal agency and moral choice, not "blind conformity."

Social justice is related to morality; indeed, it is a manifestation of the morality of fairness in the distribution of resources. The first cross-cultural research examining social justice in collectivistic societies found equality rather than equity orientations in distributive justice (Y. Kashima, Siegel, Tanaka, & Isaka, 1988; Leung, 1987; Marin, 1985; Triandis et al., 1985). This is because social harmony is of great importance, and equal distribution among the in-group is seen to contribute to group solidarity; with out-groups, however, they use equity distribution, just like individualists (Leung, 1997; Leung & Bond, 1984). Thus, I–C appears to be situation and target specific, rather than having traitlike generality over situations and targets.

Maintaining relationships or justice concerns can also play a role in how disputes are resolved. Thus, it is found that Americans consider a justice goal (restoring fairness) as more important whereas Japanese find a relationship goal (maintaining a good relationship) more important in dispute resolution (Ohbuchi, Fukushima, & Tedeschi, 1999).

## Self-Enhancement

Another consequence of I–C or **independent–interdependent self-construal** is variability in self-enhancement or "self-serving bias" (Y. Kashima & Triandis, 1986). A great deal of research points to a greater tendency toward self-enhancement in individualists compared with collectivists. Americans in particular are noted for their tendency to self-enhancement, for example, in seeing themselves as better than most people on various attributes (Kitayama et al., 1997; Markus & Kitayama, 1991; Matsumoto, 2001a), and most research involves American–Japanese comparisons, the latter group forming a contrast. Cultural values and beliefs work as folk wisdom and are often reflected in practices that reinforce self-enhancement tendencies. Thus, American schools, parents, teachers, workplaces, and so on, reinforce self-confidence, self-esteem, and an optimistic belief in one's self-efficacy as a sure path toward success.

In other sociocultural contexts, however, a "self-improvement' orientation may be preferred. This would involve focusing on failure and trying hard to improve the next performance. Such a distinction in orientations is found in research comparing Japanese and Americans (Heine, Kitayama, Lehman, & Takata, 2001).

The social norm of modesty is relevant here. In sociocultural contexts where bragging is frowned on, as in many traditional collectivistic societies, modesty can function as impression management or public-display rule. However, if internalized, its effects can go deeper and function even when the person is alone (Heine, Lehman, Markus, & Kitayama, 1999). Indeed, research with Chinese and Japanese children/adolescents (M. H. Bond, Leung, & Wan, 1982; Yoshida, Kojo, & Kaku, 1982) showed the modesty norm to be internalized early, such that humble persons are liked and valued more. This may be reflected in how early memories are experienced and reported even in childhood. Q. Wang (2004) studied preschool to second-grade children's autobiographical memories and found that American children focused on their own roles, preferences, and feelings in a positive light, whereas Chinese children stressed social interactions and described themselves in terms of social roles and context-specific characteristics in a neutral and modest tone.

Kitayama et al. (1997) found a substantial difference between American and Japanese students' tendencies toward self-enhancement and self-criticism, respectively, in imagined positive and negative situations likely to increase or decrease self-esteem. Recognizing the modesty issue, they changed the instructions in a second study to refer not to "self" but to a "typical" student. The results were no different, which the researchers interpreted as reflecting real differences in self-enhancement rather than a modesty effect in self-presentation. This is in line with the earlier Heine et al. (2001) finding. It also has to do with the relative emphasis put on the value of hard work and self-discipline, rather than self-confidence, which are found to be strong in Confucian morality.

Other research, however, finds self-enhancement to be a universal human motive, but it is achieved through different socially acceptable ways. For example, Sedidikes, Gaertner, and Toguchi (2003) in two studies showed that Americans and subjects with **independent self-**construals self-enhanced on individualistic attributes whereas Japanese and interdependents self-enhanced on collectivistic attributes. Kurman (2001) obtained similar results with Chinese in Singapore and Jewish and Druze subjects in Israel, where she found that modesty interferes with self-enhancement on agentic individual traits. Muramoto and Yamaguchi (1997; cited in Yamaguchi, 2001) found that Japanese make self-effacing attributions about their own performance but group-enhancing attributions for their group's performance. In this way, they use indirect strategy of positive self-evaluation (or self-enhancement) by praising their group, while not boasting and thus maintaining harmonious relationships with the group members. This appears to reflect an in-group-enhancing bias rather than an individual self-serving bias. It is akin to the concept of "collective self-esteem" (Crocker & Luhtanen, 1990), as different from an individual self-esteem. On measures of individual self-esteem, Japanese typically score low.

The debate is continuing. A whole special issue of the *Journal of Cross-Cultural Psychology* (2003, no. 5) is devoted to it. It contains studies that generally show that when anonymity is assured or when there is a competitive environment, even modest individuals show self-enhancement. Furthermore, self-enhancement or positive self-regard is found to be associated with well-being. The weight of the evidence appears to tilt toward the pancultural existence of a need for basic self-regard, which, however, may not be expressed as explicit selfenhancement but in other forms, given cultural diversity in values, norms, and proper demeanor.

## Cognitions and Emotions

One could say that mainstream social psychologists started to pay serious attention to culture mostly when cultural differences in social cognition and emotions were found. Thus, Markus and Kitayama's influential review (1991) includes much U.S.–Japanese comparison on cognitions and emotions, and motivation. All this work has come to show that culture is not just "out there," an exotic thing that other people have, but is here, penetrating everyone. I have already dealt with some cultural differences in cognitive processes, mainly in attribution, moral thinking, person perception, and self-perception. The general finding is that collectivists tend to pay greater attention to relational-contextual factors in making attributions and judgments, as well as in describing themselves and others (Cousins, 1989; J. G. Miller, 1984; Shweder & Bourne, 1984).

More recent laboratory experimental research uses priming and other experimental manipulations to make culture and/or independence–interdependence salient. Experimentally produced cultural factors or the cultural backgrounds of the experimental participants are found to play a role in cognitive processes such as memory or judgments. For example, Q. Wang (Wang, 2004, 2006; Wang & Conway, 2004) studied episodic memory in adults and found that whereas Americans had more memories of individual experience, focusing on their own roles and emotions, Chinese had memories of social and historical events and emphasized social interaction and significant others more. These studies have important implications for memory–self interplay (see also Wagar & Cohen, 2003).

Gardner et al. (1999) found that participants primed with interdependence displayed shifts toward more collectivistic social values and judgments, mediated by corresponding shifts in their self-construals. Similarly, Cross, Morris, and Gore (2002) found that the subjects with interdependent self-construals, compared with independents, tended to have tighter cognitive schemas of relational terms, evaluated them more positively, and had a better memory for relational information. They also described themselves and a friend more similarly.

Another basic aspect of cognition that has been studied in relation to I–C/Independent–Interdependent self is flexibility and cognitive dissonance effects. There is evidence that East Asians are more tolerant of contradictions and tend to be more comfortable with the coexistence of opposite trends, which Westerners find contradictory, in line with their intellectual heritage of Cartesian dualism (D. Sinha & Tripathi, 1994). This has been explained in terms of the greater tendency of the collectivists to pay attention to the situational demands including the expectations of others in affecting one's behavior. Thus, inconsistencies in behavior may be due to a greater need of the collectivist East Asians to accommodate different environmental demands. This is in line with the findings of greater situational (external) attribution made by collectivists in making judgments about behavior (J. G. Miller, 1984). Given this tendency toward situational flexibility, it may also be reflected in self-perceptions. Indeed I. Choi and Choi (2002) found that Koreans displayed inconsistent beliefs about the self, unlike Americans.

Given that cognitive dissonance is based on a motivation to justify one's behavior and to be congruent particularly with a positive sense of self (Aronson, 1968; Stone & Cooper, 2001), it may be predicted that collectivists who have a flexible sense of self might experience it less. This is because there would be a greater acceptance that behavior can be inconsistent due to environmental factors (i.e., situationally determined). Indeed, Heine and Lehman (1997) found this to be the case for the Japanese, who appeared not to experience cognitive dissonance. However, individualists who make internal attributions for behaviors, that is, think that behavior is determined by personal dispositions rather than situational demands, would expect to behave in the same way across different situations.

More recently, Kitayama, Snibbe, Markus, and Suzuki (2004) reasoned that the cultural difference found may be due to the variation in the salient self-construal. Thus, Euro-Americans would tend to experience dissonance and justify their choices regardless of whether social others were made salient or not through priming; the Japanese did so only when self-relevant others were primed. These results showed that the tendency to experience cognitive dissonance and to justify one's choices may be universal but this would be manifested in terms of upholding culturally endorsed aspects of the self. For the independent Euro-Americans, such aspects are individual competence or efficiency; for the interdependent Japanese, they are positive appraisal by others. Questions regarding universality or culture specificity have also been asked in research on emotions.

In cross-cultural I–C research, emotions have been classified as encouraging independence or interdependence of the self (Kitayama et al., 1995). Some positive emotions such as pride and negative ones such as anger tend to make inner attributes salient and contrasted against the relevant social context; thus they are labeled *socially disengaged emotions*. Others, such as respect or guilt, encourage the interpersonal bond and are labeled *socially engaged emotions*. These were earlier called *ego-focused* and *other-focused* by Markus and Kitayama (1991), who found a greater prevalence of the former among independent selves and of the latter among the interdependent selves. A recent study (Kitayama et al., 2000) found that Japanese reported experiencing a higher frequency of socially engaged emotions than socially disengaged emotions, and Americans reported experiencing a higher frequency of positive than negative emotions. Furthermore, it was also found that "good feelings" were associated more with socially engaged positive emotions for the Japanese but with socially disengaged positive emotions for the Americans. Thus, feeling good or happy appears to be a more socially shared emotion for the Japanese self than for the American self.

The breadth of cross-cultural research on emotions is impressive. It ranges from the recognition of emotions to judgments of emotions and attributions based on emotions (Markus & Kitayama, 1994; Matsumoto, 2001a). As mentioned previously, a basic debate has been the universality versus the cultural construction of emotions. The weight of the evidence appears to tilt toward the universality of emotions (Berry, et al., 2002). Nevertheless, even with biological roots, emotions are manifested within contexts and therefore are influenced by them, for example, in terms of rules and norms about their expression. Thus, I–C research on emotions provides insight on how cultural variance in emotions emerges.

Emotion regulation has also been studied across cultures. A commonly accepted view here is that in individualistic cultures, emotion regulation is based on whether the control or expression of an emotion contributes to a person's well-being and serves to reach a personal goal, whereas in collectivistic cultures social norms and others' expectations play a role in emotion regulation (N. Eisenberg & Zhou, 2001). Therefore, expression of ego-focused emotions such as anger and frustration may be inhibited more in collectivistic cultures, as they are in sharp conflict with cooperative and harmonious social interactions. Studies comparing

U.S. children with Nepali and Japanese children (P. M. Cole & Tamang, 2001; Zahen-Waxler, Friedman, Cole, Mizuta, & Hiruma, 1996) indeed found that U.S. children display an underregulation of negative emotions. This issue is directly related to control, discussed in the next section.

## Control

The topic of control has been a subject of research and debate especially in Japanese–American comparisons. Weisz, Rothbaum, and Blackburn (1984) showed that whereas in the United States "primary control" (influencing existing realities) is emphasized and valued, in Japan "secondary control" (accommodating to existing realities) assumes greater importance. This distinction is reminiscent of the earlier conceptualization of belief in internal and external control of reinforcement, respectively (Rotter, 1966). From an individualistic point of view, belief in internal control has always been considered to be "better" (indicative of greater autonomy). Accordingly, from early on when the less powerful groups (women, lower-SES groups, people in traditional societies, ethnic minorities) were found to have less belief in internal control (more belief in external control), they were often considered to be deficient (traditional, weak, fatalistic, etc.) (e.g., Kağitçibaşi, 1973). Though depending on the situation, there could be some truth in this interpretation, it also tends to ignore the objective reality of less scope for control that is commonly available for the less powerful and thus tends to "blame the victim."

In the Japanese case, the lack of primary control was interpreted by the American researchers as relinquishing control, which may result in excessive conformity (Weisz, et al., 1984). However, Azuma (1984) pointed out that "secondary control" involves different categories of control: "In a culture like Japan, where tact concerning yielding is positively valued, highly differentiated perceptions are likely to emerge" (p. 970). In other cultures where similar values upholding interpersonal (group) harmony rather than individual self-assertion prevail, similar psychological processes involving adjustments, such as yielding when needed for ensuring social harmony, may also emerge as alternatives to direct control.

More recently, Yamaguchi (2001) reiterated these views and pointed to other types of control, that is, *indirect, proxy,* and *collective control,* which are alternative strategies to direct personal control. However, these strategies are not secondary control and certainly not relinquishing control because they are designed to change the environment and produce desired outcomes rather than change the self to fit into the environment. They involve such strategies as people "hiding or playing down their agency by pretending that they are not acting as an agent while they are actually doing so" (p. 227) or exerting control through someone else or through one's group, which serve as an agent of control. In particular, in order to enhance group harmony, individuals can use these indirect forms of control, which are all agentic but not self-assertive or self-enhancing. The latter strategies are not used because thay can be a threat to harmonious interpersonal relations.

There can also be alternative motivations. For example, an alternative to control may be "detachment,", studied by Naidu (1983) as a form of indigenous Indian form of "voluntarily giving up control," as distinguished from "involuntary" lack of control in Western theorizing. In his criticism of mainstream psychology's **self-contained individualism** construct, mentioned before, Sampson (1988) was also critical of the view of control as inhering in the individual and claimed that control is located in the interpersonal field in ensembled individualism. Earlier, I examined the work of J. G. Miller (Miller, 2003; Miller, Schaberg, Bachman & Conner, 2006) and Shweder (Menon & Shweder, 1998) in the discussion on socially oriented morality. That research showed that it was possible for persons in collectivistic cultures to be autonomous or agentic while meeting social obligations. This is quite relevant here. Thus, conceptions of agency and control can vary across cultures, which have direct implications for child **socialization** and the development of the self, taken up in chapters 5 and 6.

## Achievement

Whether autonomy and control are construed in a more individualistic or a more interpersonal (social) sense also has implications for the conceptualization of achievement motivation. Since the early work of McClelland, Atkinson, Clark, and Lowell (1953), achievement motivation in American psychology has been conceived in terms of *individual* striving, agency, and competition with others. This is congruent with an individualistic ethos but may be at odds with a culture of relatedness where interpersonal harmony and group loyalties are of prime importance. Indeed, efforts to instill competitive individualistic achievement motivation in a collectivistic setting such as India were not successful (McClelland & Winters, 1969; J. B. P. Sinha, 1985). So should we conclude that people in collectivistic societies lack achievement motivation? On the contrary, some of the greatest feats of economic achievement at societal levels have been seen in the collectivistic societies of the Pacific Rim in the last decades. The industry and high achievement of Japanese and Chinese students are also well known.

The nature and meaning of achievement motivation appears to be different in a collectivistic culture; it extends beyond the self and merges with others very much parallel to the related self expanding toward others through diffuse boundaries. This was found by Phalet with Turkish students, as presented in the example at the beginning of this chapter. Thus, a "socially-oriented achievement motivation" is proposed to be common in societies where interdependent human relations prevail (Agarwal & Misra, 1986; M. H. Bond, 1986; Phalet & Claeys, 1993; K.-S. Yang, 1986; Yu & Yang, 1994). Early research showed that when achievement is construed and measured in individualistic terms, people in cultures of relatedness emerge as lacking it (Bradburn, 1963; Rosen, 1962). This is mainly because a different, more socially oriented achievement motivation is not tapped by measures devised to assess an individualistically construed achievement motivation (Yu & Yang, 1994).

Thus, the achievement motive appears to be a complex construct, possibly involving different types of achievement needs, functioning singly or in combination. A **socially oriented achievement motive** would involve upholding group achievement, transcending the self, in such a way that achievement would not only exalt the self but *also* some other social entity encompassing the self. It is to be noted, however, that this is not debasing the self or sacrificing self-interest for the group, but rather merging the self with the group so that achievement elevates *both*. The individualistic self-oriented striving, in contrast, is again what the critics of American psychology and society deplore, calling for "values that transcend the self" (M. B. Smith, 1993 p.7).

The type of child socialization that engenders such a combination of self-and-other-oriented achievement motivation is probably itself rather complex, involving a combination of different goals. For example, C.-Y. C. Lin and Fu (1990), in a comparison of Chinese, immigrant Chinese, and Anglo-American parents, found the two Chinese groups to be higher than the Anglo group on *both* **parental control** *and* encouragement of independence (with an emphasis on achievement). These complex socialization orientations may be considered to be at odds with one another and involving conflicting elements, when viewed from an individualistic perspective. However, such an interpretation pits the individual against the group. Indeed "loyalty to the self" and "self-realization" need not conflict with "loyalty to the group" (Kağitçibaşi, 1987a) in the familial-cultural context that is conducive to the development of the relational self.

Such developmental questions bring us to the context in which the self develops. This is mainly the family, the topic of the next chapter. The present chapter focused on cultural variation in the self and its behavioral outcomes. A closer look at the macrosystem variables and their intersections with the family provides us with an understanding of how the culturally varying self comes about.

## SUMMARY AND MAIN POINTS

- The concept of the self includes the notion of the person and to some extent personality, but the most important marker of the self is that it is reflective, in the sense of self-perception and self-awareness.
- Starting in the 1980s, the social and the cultural construal of the self has become an important topic in social and cross-cultural psychology. Cross-cultural research has studied self and its development in different cultural contexts examining childrearing and socialization.
- American (and Western) individualistic culture draws a narrow and sharp line between the self and the other, constituting a clear boundary between self and nonself. Other cultural conceptions differ from this construal of the self in varying degrees.
- Separateness–connectedness of the self may be construed as the psychological core dimension of individualism–collectivism (I–C).
- Two types of I–C are defined: normative I–C as reflected in social norms, values, conventions, and rules; and relational I–C as focused on self–other relations. The culture of relatedness–separateness refers to relational I–C at the cultural level.
- The culture of relatedness refers to cultural and familial contexts and relational patterns identified by connected, expanding, and therefore partially overlapping selves with diffuse boundaries. The culture of separateness refers to the contexts and interpersonal patterns characterized by separate selves with clearly defined boundaries (self contained).
- The (inter)dependence–independence dimension, just like the related–separate self-construal, has to do with basic human merging and separation.
- A great deal of research has investigated how I–C and self-construals are reflected in different psychological outcomes.
- A culture of relatedness–separateness appears to have an impact on moral understanding and moral responsibility.
- A great deal of research points to more self-enhancement in individualists compared with collectivists, whereas other research finds self-enhancement to be a universal motive that is manifested through different socially acceptable ways.
- Collectivists tend to pay greater attention to relational-contextual factors in making attributions and judgments, as in describing themselves and others.
- Cross-cultural research on emotions covers recognitions and judgments of emotions, attributions based on emotions, and

emotion regulation. It has shed light on the issue of the universality versus the culture-boundedness of emotions.

- Conceptions of autonomy and control vary across cultures with direct implications for child socialization and the development of the self.
- Achievement motivation in American psychology has been conceived in terms of individual striving, agency, and competition with others; whereas a socially oriented achievement motivation is common in societies with interdependent human relations.

## DISCUSSION QUESTIONS

1. How does the meaning of self vary across cultures?
2. What important trends have influenced the current conceptualization of self?
3. Describe the culture of relatedness and the culture of separateness in terms of the different types of self that characterize them. What type of I–C is implied here? Do you find Kağitçibaşi's differentiation of normative and relational I–C helpful? Why or why not?
4. What are some psychological correlates or behavioral outcomes of individualism–collectivism and different self-construals?
5. Explain the implications of the culture of relatedness on moral understanding and moral responsibility.
6. What implications does the construal of autonomy and control have for the conceptualization of the achievement motive?

# 5

# Value of Children and the Family[1]

"God should give daughters to rich families only." This is the title of a paper by Winkvist and Akhtar (2000) on attitudes toward childbearing among low-income women in Punjab, Pakistan. What is the meaning of this expression? It reflects strong **son preference** in a society where women have a subordinate position and their work is not valued. It reflects a lifestyle where there is a dependence on the sons' contributions for the family livelihood, particularly in old age (Kağitçibaşi, 1982a, 1998a). How would such values impact parental orientations toward children and the family? And how does change in all this come about? These are the topics of this chapter.

In the Introduction to this volume, I said that one of the main things I attempt to do in this volume is to link the self, family, and society. Up to now, I have been trying to form some links mainly by examining human development in context and the culture–self interface. Societal conceptualizations of childhood, of competence, and of the self emerged as important; so did the corresponding parental construals of competence and of the self, mediating between societal conceptions and childrearing patterns. In this discussion, though the family was often invoked, this was not explicit. In this chapter, I want to focus on the family as the central component of the self–family–society interface. I propose a theory of family and family change, through socioeconomic development, entailing a causal/functional analysis of the development of the self. This theory should help throw light on some of the antecedents of the separate and the relational selves.

Though **parental ethnotheories,** values, and behaviors are of great significance in understanding how societal values link with developmental outcomes, including the self, they constitute only some aspects of the family. Other aspects of the family need to be studied also to complete the picture. Of particular importance is situating the family

---

[1] Some parts of this chapter are based on my earlier writings (Ka itçiba i, 1990, 2005a).

within the macro systemic ecological context by examining its links with social-structural-economic factors. Such an analysis should help provide some explanations for the contrasting childrearing orientations among the middle-class/urban/educated groups and the low-SES/rural/marginal immigrant groups that I have discussed earlier (see chap. 2).

My approach to the family is multidisciplinary, where I make use of sociological and demographic concepts and evidence in addition to psychological ones. This is because especially the family–society interface has not been studied much by psychologists. Sociological perspectives are valuable in situating family processes into their socioeconomic, cultural, and historical context. Dealing with the different levels of analysis spanning individual–family–society interface is a difficult task. The complexity of the family as an intergenerational system moving through time has been a deterrent to its study within academic psychology (McGoldrick & Carter, 1982). It has been difficult for psychologists, given their focus on the individual and their experimental methodology, to treat the family as a unit of analysis. That is why few psychologists have tried to link society, family, and individual systems empirically until the emergence of recent policy-oriented studies using large data sets and sophisticated multivariate models that I presented at the end of chapter 2 (e.g., Bolger et al., 1995; Brooks-Gunn & Duncan, 1997; Ceballo & McLoyd, 2002; Duncan & Brooks-Gunn, 1997, 2000; Gennetian & Miller, 2002; Huston et al., 2001; Kohen et al., 2002). The recent work by Georgas et al. (2006) is also a new development in the field.

It is important to understand the relationships and possible causal links underlying the self, family, and society. Such understanding would, for example, unravel the reason that certain socialization values and goals are seen in certain societies and not in others, and how and why change comes about. There is a dearth of psychological theory and research on the family, except in the more applied fields of family studies, social work, policy research, clinical psychology, and family therapy. In this latter field, family systems theory (e.g., Fisek, 1991; Minuchin, 1974) has informed thinking and applications, particularly in providing a holistic approach to the family. Given the lack of theory in academic psychology to throw light on family functioning and family change, the prototypical Western (middle-class, nuclear) family has been adopted implicitly as "the family."

## MODERNIZATION THEORY ON THE FAMILY

Family is an integral part of society and is inherently tied to its social structure, values, and norms. As these social and cultural characteristics vary through time and across societies, families vary too. Faced with family diversity researchers have, until rather recently, typically either ignored it, regarding it a topic appropriate for sociological or anthropological inquiry, or have dismissed it as transitory. The latter view adheres to the **modernization theory** prediction that there is a convergence of the diverse patterns in the world toward the Western prototypical pattern and thus, whatever is different from this pattern will be modified in time to resemble it. Thus, in the absence of challenging cross-cultural theory of the family, there is an assumption of a unidirectional change toward the Western model with social development, as originally proposed by modernization theorists (Dawson, 1967; Doob, 1967; Inkeles, 1969, 1977; Inkeles & Smith, 1974). Even though modernization theory lost its popularity in sociology, in the face of serious criticism (Bendix, 1967; Gusfield, 1967), it is still ingrained in a great deal of thinking regarding social change and the family. Its expectation of a unidirectional shift in the human/family characteristics toward the Western pattern is shared by many psychologists and social scientists (Georgas, 1989; see Kağitçibaşi, 1994a, 1998b, 2005b, for a further discussion of this issue). Thus, for example, developing countries are often characterized as "transitional societies," with the transition implied to be toward the Western pattern.

To reiterate the main characteristics of the "prototypical" Western family, it is a system of "independent" relationships. It is independent of kin and forms a separate nucleated unit onto itself, and also its subsystems (members) are separate from one another by well-defined boundaries. It may be argued that not all Western families fit this pattern completely. This is certainly true. Nevertheless, this is the "prototype" that has been promoted especially in psychology, reflecting the Western (particularly middle class American) individualistic ethos, as I discussed extensively in the last chapter. Despite much criticism emerging from among psychologists and other social scientists, the prototype remains strong and colors much of the thinking regarding family and family change (see Georgas et al., 2006). *this is true*

The modernization view of change is tenacious. It adheres to an evolutionary model of progressive improvement, eventually to reach the fixed goal–the Western prototype, in the tradition of social Darwinism (Mazrui, 1968). Underlying it is the implicit assumption that whatever is different from the Western prototype is deficient and is, therefore, bound to change with development. This view has been rather influential especially in debates regarding economic development. It is commonly assumed, for example, that in line with the Weberian thesis, collectivistic (inter)dependent orientations are not compatible with economic development (Weber, 1958, as discussed by Hoselitz, 1965; D. Sinha, 1988). Indeed, Hofstede (1980) found a close association between individualism at societal level and economic affluence.

*development = Westernization*

## Challenges to Modernization Assumptions

Though pervasive, this assumption has been challenged over the last few decades by the striking examples of economic growth in East Asia with its collectivistic cultures, Japan, Korea, Taiwan, Hong Kong, and Singapore, with Thailand and Malaysia following suit. The interdependent family patterns in these societies do not appear to deter development or to be "deficient" in any sense. Neither do they manifest any significant changes toward the Western individualistic-separate family patterns. For example, in the 1980s a number of studies provided evidence of continuity in human relations and family patterns (M. H. Bond, 1986; Iwawaki, 1986; Sinha & Kao, 1988; Sun, 1991; Suzuki, 1984; C. F. Yang, 1988). Furthermore, these family patterns are found to be conducive to economic success, as, for example, in Japan where they are successfully adopted into the workplace and in Chinese societies where family businesses flourish. More recent research has also pointed to continuities in family patterns and values (Georgas et al., 2006; Kim et al., 2006; Kim, Park, Kwon, & Koo, 2005; Stewart, Bond, Deeds, & Chung, 1999).

A second assumption underlying the **modernization theory** and its **convergence hypothesis** is that the Western family patterns have themselves evolved toward nucleation and individualistic **separation** as a necessary outcome of industrialization. Therefore it is claimed that industrialization in non-Western contexts will also engender the same changes in family patterns. This common assumption has also been challenged by a great deal of historical evidence that clearly documents that the nuclear family and individualism predated industrialization in Western Europe, particularly in England, by several centuries.

Historical and historical demographic records and court rolls are excellent sources for the study of the family in terms of interactions (cooperation–conflict), relations (similar surname forms), marriage patterns, residence patterns, and several family functions (Razi, 1993). This research has shown that the typical British family was nuclear rather than extended; that the bond between family and land was weak; wider ties of kinship were also weak so that villagers relied on institutional support rather than on the assistance of kin; rural society was highly mobile; children often left home in their teens and spent a few years as live-in servants in other families before starting their own families; women married late and some never married (see Razi, 1993, for a review).

These are all demographic-structural characteristics that are associated with nuclear, separate, individualistic human and familial relational patterns. There is also evidence of secular individualism, individual control of sexuality, and later age at marriage, which led to marital fertility decline starting in the 18th century. Though most marked in Britain, similar early individualistic themes predating industrialization in Western Europe and the United States are also found in historical research and travelers' records (Aries, 1980; Furstenberg, 1966; Lesthaeghe, 1980; Thorton & Fricke, 1987). Some recent accounts of childhood in medieval Western Europe concur (Hanawalt, 2002; Orme, 2001).

On the basis of such historical research, some historians claim that the nuclear family and individualistic patterns date all the way back to the medieval period (13th century) in Britain (Bennett, 1984; Hanawalt, 1986; Laslett, 1977; MacFarlane, 1978, 1987). But even those who do not trace the individualistic familial system so far back in history, agree that it was prevalent by the early modern period (beginning of the 16th century) (Lesthaeghe, 1983; Lesthaeghe & Surkyn, 1988; Razi, 1993; Thadani, 1978; Thorton, 1984). Given this historical evidence, it is clear that Western individualism was not an outcome of industrialization; it predated it by centuries. Therefore, the argument by analogy that individualism will spread in the non-Western world as an inevitable outcome of industrialization does not hold.

This does not mean that the non-Western family patterns, characterized by interdependence, do not change. Change is going on in all societies at all levels of human phenomena, but it may take different forms rather than necessarily following a single path toward the "Western model," as claimed by the convergence hypothesis. In order to ascertain what kind of change in family patterns is most likely, we must understand why and how change takes place.

## VALUE OF CHILDREN STUDY I (1970s)

Of particular importance in understanding family dynamics and change over time and through societal socioeconomic development is the nine-country Value of Children (VOC) Study. This study constituted the basis of my **family change theory,** described in this chapter. That is why it is covered in some detail in this chapter.

The VOC Study was carried out in 1970s with more than 20,000 married respondents, mostly women of reproductive ages from Korea, the Philippines, Singapore, Taiwan, Thailand, Turkey, Indonesia (Javanese and Sudanese), the United States, and Germany (only women in one province in Germany). Motivations for childbearing, values attributed to children, fertility preferences, and so on, were studied (Bulatao, 1979; Darroch, Meyer, & Singarimbum, 1981; Fawcett, 1983; L. W. Hoffman, 1987; Kağıtçıbaşi, 1982a, 1982b, 1998a). Recently, a partial replication in many of these countries has been conducted in a project initiated by Trommsdorff and Nauck (Kağitçibaşi & Ataca, 2005; Kağitçibaşi, Ataca, & Diri, 2005; Trommsdorff, Kim, & Nauck, 2005).

In this section, I present some of the main findings of the original study that paved the way toward the development of my family change theory. I then discuss the model extensively in the next section. The recent VOC Study, particularly the Turkish partial replication, follows next, as it serves to test the model.

The original study was conducted by an interdisciplinary team of researchers, psychologists, demographers, and economists, who also collectively prepared the instruments, which were extensive face-to-face interviews including both open ended and closed-ended questions (scales). These interviews were carried out by trained local interviewers in the local languages and took anything between 1 and 3 hours. As nationally representative samples were drawn, there was a great deal of diversity in the regional developmental levels in terms of urbanization, industrialization, and so on, as well as in the individual-level characteristics of the respondents such as education, employment, and income. Most samples consisted of married women and about one fourth of their husbands. In Turkey, the sample size was about 2,300.

## Values Attributed to Children

The several values attributed to children by parents were factor ana-lyzed and were found to fall into three main value types—utilitarian, psy-chological, and social—based on a conceptual scheme by L. W. Hoffman and Hoffman (1973). Utilitarian values are basically concerned with the economic/material benefits of children, both while they are young and when they become adults. Of special significance here is the old-age security that adult offspring provide to their elderly parents. Psychological values have to do with such satisfactions as the joy, pride, love, and companionship that children give their parents. The social values of children refer to general social acceptance that married adults gain when they have children, in the sense that especially in traditional soci-ety people are really considered to be adults when they have children, but not necessarily when they get married. Continuation of the family name or family line is also a social value of having children, focussed on the son.

Of these three main types of values, **economic/utilitarian, psycholog-ical values,** and specifically **son preference** emerged as important in their differential relationships with macrosystem variables and out-come variables. In particular, it was found that the utilitarian/economic voc[2] and in particular old-age security voc was more important in less developed countries and in the rural, less developed areas within the countries. This is because in the context of poverty and lack of social security systems, children's economic contribution to the family is very important. Children contribute to the family economy while they are young, and in old age elderly parents depend on their children for their livelihood. Furthermore, the greater salience of the economic/utilitarian VOC is associated with greater son preference because it is mainly the son who provides the parents with economic support in old age in patriarchal family systems (Kağitçibaşi, 1982a, 1982b; Kağitçibaşi & Ataca, 2005).

Thus, **old-age security** as a reason for childbearing was considered very important among women by 93% and 98% of the two subsamples in Indonesia, by 89% in the Philippines, by 79% each in Thailand and Taiwan, and by 77% in Turkey; sharply contrasted by only 8% each in Germany and the United States. The percentages in Korea (54%) and Singapore (51%), though still high, were significantly lower than the other non-Western countries, in accordance with their higher levels of economic development. Other specific results and men's responses manifested similar patterns (Kağitçibaşi, 1982b).

Within-country variations also reflected similar patterns in terms of regional socioeconomic development levels. For these, I use the Turkish VOC Study findings as an example. As the development level of the area of residence rose in Turkey, the salience of old-age security voc decreased (100% in the least developed areas, 73% in medium-developed, 61% in more developed, and 40% in most developed large metropolitan centers). Similarly it decreased systematically with increased women's professionalization, involving education (100% among unpaid agricultural family workers in rural areas with little or no education; 91% among small-shop owners and artisans, typically "traditional" groups; 50% among wage earners and only 19% to 37% among white-collar workers, depending on their education levels). Again, similar patterns were obtained for men (Kağitçibaşi, 1982b).

Another utilitarian value, children's "help with household chores" lost salience for parents with increased parent education (28% at no education level; 22% at primary-school level; 11% at high-school level; and 0% at university level). Similarly, children's "material help" (i.e., contributing to family economy at young age, by working in the field/family business/marginal economy, etc.) also lost salience with parent's education (56% at no education level; 54% at primary; 15% at high school; and 20% at university levels) (Kağitçibaşi, 1982b).

---

[2]VOC (in capitals) refers to the study; voc (in small letters) refers to values attributed to children by parents.

*In contrast, psychological voc is found to be more salient in the context of greater affluence and urban lifestyles. This is because here children are no longer economic assets; they are indeed quite costly. In relative terms, their psychological value thus emerges as important as a reason for having a child, because it does not make much economic sense to have children, yet most people want to have children anyway. Thus, values attributed to children and their place in family and society show variation. A most important dimension of variation is along rural–urban and SES differences, in short, level of development in societal and socioeconomic terms.

The economic/utilitarian voc is positively associated with fertility (child numbers) but psychological voc is not. Thus, in the Turkish VOC study, psychological voc and the number of existing children were found to be negatively associated ($r = -.26$), but economic voc and the number of children were positively associated ($r = .24$) (Kağitçibaşi, 1982b, p. 77). This is because the material contribution of each child (while young and as an adult) can add up to that of every other child and thus increases with child numbers, but the psychological satisfactions children give their parents do not add to each other in the same way with more children. For example, parents can get all the love they need from one or two children without the need to have more. Indeed, in the Turkish VOC Study, women who had two children wanted to have additional children if they stressed the economic voc, but did not want more children if they stressed the psychological voc (Kağitçibaşi, 1982b, pp. 72–73). Similarly, in a comparative analysis of data from eight VOC countries, Bulatao (1979) found that women not using contraception with five or more children stressed the economic voc more than women using contraception with two or fewer children, the differences being quite large (some exceeding 30 percentage points).

Thus, in contexts of low-affluence, rural/agrarian/low-SES standing with material interdependencies favoring high fertility, socialization values include a stress on the utilitarian/economic voc, old-age security voc, and son preference. Son preference is closely associated with economic/old-age security voc because commonly, and particularly in patriarchal societies, sons are more reliable sources of economic benefits and old-age security (Caldwell, 1977; Fawcett, 1983; Kağitçibaşi, 1982 a, 1982b, 1998a). Son preference is also closely associated with fertility, because high fertility assures that at least some sons survive (Darroch et al., 1981).

These findings point to the dynamics underlying high fertility. In this context, socialization values also uphold family/group loyalties, rather than individual loyalties and investment in elderly parents, as these values are adaptive for the livelihood of the family in a pattern of total (intergenerational) interdependence. Accordingly, a particular type of family interaction is implicated in childrearing, entailing an obedience/ dependence orientation, characterized by control, rather than autonomy.

Thus, in the Turkish VOC Study, among characteristics most and second-most desired in children, "to obey their parents" was the most prominent, chosen by 61% of men and 59% of women, contrasted by much lower importance of "to be independent and self-reliant" (chosen by 17% of men and 19% of women) (Kağitçibaşi, 1982b). Similarly, even more contrasting results were obtained in countries such as Indonesia, the Philippines, and Thailand. This is in line with some of the discussion earlier in this book, pointing to obedience and conformity orientations in childrearing in societies where these characteristics are highly valued and are adaptive, as well as among ethnic minority groups from these societies in the Western world (e.g., Greenfield, Keller et al., 2003; Keller, 2003; Kohn, 1969; LeVine, 1974, 1988; Nauck & Kohlman, 1999; Serpell, 1977).

## A THEORY OF FAMILY CHANGE

The **VOC Study** led me through the path to develop a **theory of family change** and the three different family models that it entails (Kağitçibaşi, 1985b, 1990). In particular, the notable variations in values related to children and expectations from them, both among the different national samples and also across different social strata within nations, provided much insight into family and family change. The main dimension underlying the variability appeared to be societal socioeconomic development. The findings of the VOC Study thus served as the basis of this theory, though other research in psychology, demography, and sociology also contributed to it.

### The General Theoretical Framework

What I propose here is a general family theory, entailing three different models of family interaction patterns in context and the systematic changes toward one of these models. This theoretical framework, in its three different manifestations, is used as a heuristic device to understand the functional/causal links between society/culture, family, and the (resultant) self. It is a contextual theory that situates the self within the family and the family within the cultural and socioeconomic environment. The family is treated in terms of both its social and psychological characteristics. The former is examined in terms of the family structure, and the latter in terms of the family system, including interaction and **socialization.**

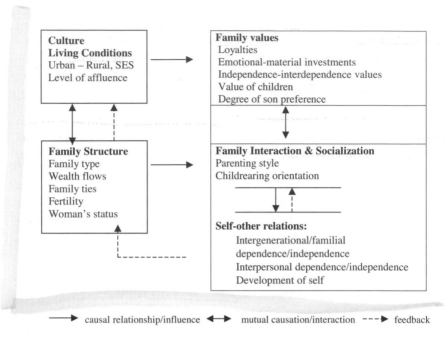

| | |
|---|---|
| **Culture**<br>**Living Conditions**<br>Urban – Rural, SES<br>Level of affluence | **Family values**<br>Loyalties<br>Emotional-material investments<br>Independence-interdependence values<br>Value of children<br>Degree of son preference |
| **Family Structure**<br>Family type<br>Wealth flows<br>Family ties<br>Fertility<br>Woman's status | **Family Interaction & Socialization**<br>Parenting style<br>Childrearing orientation<br><br>**Self-other relations:**<br>Intergenerational/familial<br>dependence/independence<br>Interpersonal dependence/independence<br>Development of self |

⟶ causal relationship/influence ⟷ mutual causation/interaction ---▶ feedback

Figure 5.1.    General model of family in context. From Kağitçibaşi (1996a).

*Note.* From Family and Human Development Across Cultures: A View from the Other Side, (p. 77), by C. Kagitcibasi, 1996a, Hillsdale, NJ: Lawrence Erlbaum

This is also a functional theory as causal relations and the dynamics underlying both the family interaction patterns and the socialization/development of the self are stressed.

The three different family models are proposed as prototypes of family patterns that are prevalent in different societal contexts. To understand the different family models, however, we need to look into their basic shared structure. This structure constitutes a general framework that situates the family, family interaction, and socialization in its sociocultural context, thus linking self and family to the context. I discuss this general framework first before I go on into the three different models.

In the general theoretical framework (Fig. 5.1), reflected also in the three specific models that follow, there is recognition of the primacy of the context in which the family is situated. The context is construed mainly in terms of the culture and the living conditions of the family and is seen as basically an influencing component. Culture is construed as mainly individualistic (culture of separateness) or as collectivist (**culture**

*too narrow terms?*

of **relatedness**), as I have discussed earlier. It refers to the existing culture base underlying the socioeconomic-structural factors and the family system. Urban–rural residence, socioeconomic development levels, and subsistence/affluence characteristics of the living conditions are taken up as significant indicators of context. However, they are not considered to be exhaustive.

In this contextual framework, there is a systemic approach to the family. The subsystems of the family are socialization values and interaction patterns in childrearing and in self–other relations. Family structure can be seen both as the context of family functioning (affecting it) and also as a part of the family system, in general. Social change and societal development impact the family with resultant changes in the family structure and the family system. Such changes may, in turn, feed back into the context, modifying some of the living conditions. This kind of a feedback loop would occur mainly through changes in family structure. Thus, a dynamic interaction takes place between the context and the family system through time.

*so far mainly talking about place of relation within each other*

Family structure comprises the structural-demographic variables that are established in sociological and demographic research to be important in affecting family functioning. These structural variables are also found to change systematically with socioeconomic development. For example, whether the family is extended or nuclear, with high or low fertility, and with high or low **woman's intrafamily status** appear to relate to socioeconomic contextual factors (living conditions).

The family system entails two interacting subsystems, socialization values and family interaction. Some of the main socialization values found to be important in research are included, again with no claim to comprehensiveness. They show variations along the independence–interdependence dimension and in terms of the emphasis put on the individual or the group and on the economic or psychological values of children for parents and the family.

Family interaction is differentiated in terms of parenting orientations and the resultant self–other relations and the development of the self. Parenting orientations are akin to those used by Baumrind (1971, 1980, 1989), authoritarian, authoritative, and permissive. The resultant familial/ interpersonal, independence/(inter)dependence and the **relational/ separate self** can be considered to be the final product of the overall system.

*doesn't realize the stress interconnect of family dynamics*

The general theory is not a linear one but is, rather, dynamic and interactive, involving mutual causal relations and feedback loops in addition to direct causal routes. Its contents, and therefore how it works, are more evident in its three different patterns of manifestation, which I next examine. Thus, the general theoretical framework is a heuristic device that attempts to analyze family functioning in sociocultural context, as it mediates between the macro sociocultural structural variables and the individual self.

The three specific family models that I propose are construed as prototypes of family systems and family functioning in different socioeconomic-cultural contexts. They are not to be seen as descriptions/ characterizations of existing families, but rather as approximations toward different theoretical configurations. The three models involve different combinations of characteristics, partially overlapping, though each is discernible as different from the other two. This difference is more one of degree than of kind. They can also be seen as human models, especially when the focus is on the type of self-development. They concern basic human relational patterns and their linkages to family and culture. Thus, where relevant, I refer to them as family/human models.

I first describe the ideal-typical **family model of interdependence**. This has been described to some extent already in the presentation of the VOC Study in the last section. It reflects the prototype of the "traditional family" and can serve as a baseline for the VOC Study findings. Then the contrasting model of independence is examined. These two prototypes are familiar, because they figure most commonly in the literature. I have discussed some aspects of these family patterns in the previous chapters, also.

The third model, psychological/emotional interdependence, is what I propose in my theory of family change to be a prototype of families undergoing modification through socioeconomic change in the **Majority World** with cultures of relatedness. However, I also discuss that it is not limited to these contexts. Indeed, on the basis of recent research, I believe that there may be a general convergence toward this model. I describe this model later on, after presenting the two contrasting models and after a discussion of how change from the prototype of traditional interdependence comes about. In presenting these three family/ human models, I try to explain why they exhibit their particular characteristics. Thus, I also deal with dynamics from a contextual/functional point of view.

## Model of Interdependence

An ideal-typical **family/human model of interdependence** (Fig. 5.2) is commonly found in rural/agrarian traditional societies with closely knit human/family relations, often characterized by patrilineal family structures. This is the ideal-typical **culture of relatedness** (collectivism) at both the societal and the familial levels and is a pervasive pattern in

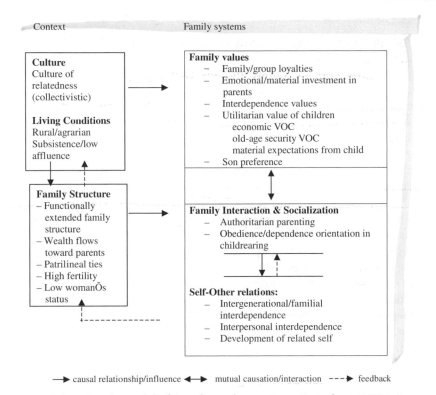

Figure 5.2. Family model of Interdependence. From Ka itçiba i (1996a).

*Note.* From Family and Human Development Across Cultures: A View from the Other Side, (p. 79), by C. Kagitcibasi, 1996a, Hillsdale, NJ: Lawrence Erlbaum

many parts of the **Majority World,** notwithstanding variation. I do not deal here with variations that may appear in family structures, kinship, and descent systems (e.g. polygamous marriages, matrilineal structures, etc).

This prototype typically entails either structurally extended or **functionally extended family** structures (Kağitçibaşi, 1985b, 1996a). Functionally extended means that even though the household may be nuclear, the family functions as if it were extended when carrying out such tasks as agricultural production, home production or consumption of goods, child care, and so on, jointly with kin. This is often made possible by the close proximity of immediate kin spanning different generations. Given the low affluence levels and agricultural lifestyles, such shared work is highly adaptive for survival. Thus, the family is interdependent with kin (other families).

The interdependence between generations is particularly notable, as adult offspring are the main sources of old-age security for their elderly parents, in the absence of wide-scale old-age pensions, social security systems, and so on. Thus, young adults provide financial assistance to their elderly parents; so in demographic terms, **wealth flows are toward** parents, especially through patrilineage. This has direct implications for **son preference** in a patrilineal (patriarchal) context where having sons is a great asset, because they are more reliable sources of old-age security. Such a family structure also entails high fertility, to ensure the survival of enough children, and particularly sons, in the face of high infant mortality. Having sons also increases the **woman's intrafamily status,** which is initially quite low, because she is, by definition, an outsider to the patrilineage at the beginning of the marriage. In the last section, we saw this pattern to be a main finding of the VOC Study.

The intergenerational dependencies shift direction during the family life cycle in the model of interdependence; first the child is dependent on the parent, this dependence to be reversed later on as the dependence of the elderly parent on the grown-up offspring. The child's dependence on the parent is ensured through an obedience-oriented **socialization** and **authoritarian parenting,** as substantiated by the VOC Study findings. Such parent–child interaction and socialization are adaptive for family survival through time. This is because a socialization orientation stressing family loyalties, control, and dependence/obedience of the child ensures the child's full **integration** in the family. When socialized this way, a child grows up to be a "loyal" adult offspring who would uphold family needs and would invest in his or her elderly parents, whereas an "independent" child might be more likely to look after his or her own individual interests. So, independence training is not adaptive in the family model of total interdependence.

The resultant familial and interpersonal relations in the family model of interdependence are characterized by interdependence along both emotional and material dimensions. The **relational self,** which I discussed in the last chapter, typically develops in this type of family system. Thus, the causal antecedents of socialization for a relational self are construed in this model to reside in the requirements of the family livelihood, based on intergenerational interdependence.

Socialization values and family interactions in this model further reinforce a functionally extended family structure. Thus, the general pattern is a self-perpetuating one unless the context, that is, living conditions, changes. It is possible, of course, for the family system (socialization values and family interactions) to change in response to other influences, also, such as intervention, culture contact as in the case of immigration, or cultural diffusion.

This brief description of a prototypical family structure is a capsule summary of a complex pattern, necessarily leaving out several important aspects. It involves mainly characteristics that are theoretically important for explaining family dynamics and interaction–the family system which shows predictable modifications through social change and socioeconomic development.

One such crucial characteristic, then, is the old-age security value of children for parents, which implicates **material dependencies,** together with **emotional dependencies** between generations. The distinction between material and emotional dependencies is important because these dependencies are differently affected by social change and development and modifications in lifestyles. Although material interdependencies across generations decrease with increased affluence, urbanization, education, and so on, emotional interdependencies do not change with socioeconomic development in the Majority World with cultures of relatedness. Again, the findings of the VOC Study provide direct evidence for this pattern, as discussed before.

## Model of Independence

I want to examine next the contrasting **family/human model of independence**–the ideal-typical model for the family in the Western, industrial, urban/suburban middle-class society with a culture of separateness (individualism) (Fig. 5.3). This model is also familiar, since it is the prototypical model of the Western individualistic, nuclear family, hailed or assailed by social critics, as the case may be.

This is the family model of independence of the family from other families and of its members from one another. It probably reflects more an ideal or abstraction than reality, given ample evidence regarding the existence of quite a bit of interdependence in the Western (American) family (see the section A Different Convergence). Nevertheless, the overall picture is obviously quite different from that of the model of interdependence. Indeed, there is almost no overlap between these two prototypical models in terms of shared characteristics. The dissimilarity reflects the dissimilarity of the contexts, in terms of high levels of affluence, urban/industrial technological society in the family model of independence contrasted with low levels of affluence, rural/agricultural/preindustrial lifestyles in the model of interdependence. It also reflects the difference between the underlying cultures of separateness (individualism) and relatedness (collectivism), respectively.

The family/human model of independence is distinguished by the separateness of the generations and both emotional and material investments channeled toward the child, rather than to the older generation.

⤷ hmm. Look toward the future, rather than the past

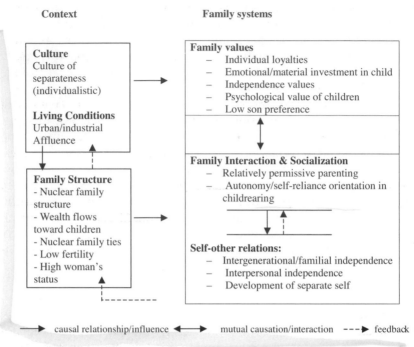

Figure 5.3.    Family model of Independence. From Ka itçiba i (1996a).

*Note.* From Family and Human Development Across Cultures: A View from the Other Side, (p. 83), by C. Kagitcibasi, 1996a, Hillsdale, NJ: Lawrence Erlbaum

The unit is the individuated nucleated family. The lack of commitment to the patrilineage and affluence providing **old-age security** goes along with woman's higher intrafamily status, low **son preference,** and low fertility. In this context, especially with mass education, having children entails economic costs, not assets. Accordingly, in the absence of children's **economic value,** their psychological value comes to the fore. **Psychological voc,** together with high costs of children, further implicates low fertility. This is particularly noticeable among educated professional couples for whom the "opportunity cost" of having children is considerable.

Socialization values and family interaction engender the development of the **independent, separate self,** with clearly defined boundaries. Interactions at both the individual and the family levels are among separate, nonoverlapping entities. There is less control in childrearing; it entails a relatively permissive parenting compared with the **authoritarian parenting** of the model of interdependence. Autonomy orientation is stressed in accordance with the prevalent individualistic ideology. This is because independence and self-reliance are valued in a sociocultural-economic context where intergenerational material dependencies are minimal. Elderly parents don't depend on their adult offspring for their livelihood; they have other sources of income and services in old age. Thus, children's loyalty to their elderly parents is not required for old-age security. This type of **socialization is conducive to both intergenerational (familial) and interpersonal independence**. Thus, we have in this model an analysis of the causal/functional antecedents of the independent separate self.

Many of the characterizations in this model, such as woman's status, permissive parenting, and independence of the family and the self, are to be understood in relative terms, especially in comparison to the **family model of interdependence.** They should not be taken at absolute levels and certainly they should not be considered typical of all Western middle-class families, but these characteristics are by and large reflective of the "mainstream" Western and more specifically American middle-class family. This is in keeping with the individualistic ethos, which constitutes the cultural context for the family and the self.

Furthermore, this model does not reflect the great diversity that exists in the Western and particularly the American scene with regard to ethnic and social-class variations. The same is true of the previous model of interdependence. They are provided as heuristic devices to understand some of the functional bases of family functioning in varying contexts and the differences among the families. For example, there is research evidence showing quite a bit of interdependence in the American family, particularly among the working class and among women (Cohler & Grunebaum, 1981; Keniston, 1985). However, given the pervasive normative individualism (see chap. 4), there is also a commitment to independence and self-sufficiency (Bellah et al., 1985; Kagan, 1984), at times resulting in ambivalence, as noted in chapter 2.

## WHAT KIND OF FAMILY CHANGE?

The previous section described two contrasting family models–total interdependence and independence. Given their disparate characteristics and the significant differences in their respective contexts, it is commonly assumed that there is a shift from one to the other. As discussed earlier, this is the **modernization theory** prediction of convergence toward the Western model. Apparently, because the family model of total interdependence is more common in rural/agrarian/low-affluence contexts, and the **family model of independence** is more common in urban/industrial/high-affluence contexts, a shift in both contexts and family patterns is assumed to take place from the former to the latter with socioeconomic development.

This assumption does not take culture into account. As I have explained in some detail, both the historical and current evidence point to some continuity in cultures while social and economic structures undergo modifications. Thus, individualistic familial and human relational patterns are seen in Western Europe long before, during, and following the industrial revolution. Similarly, collectivist patterns appear to be sustained in the Pacific Rim countries alongside significant economic growth and industrialization. Reviewing research from Mainland China, Taiwan, and Hong Kong, Kao and Hong (1988) concluded that there is a "general persistence of [the] cultural and **socialization** patterns, without being subject to much attenuation and erosion in spite of the impact of modern industrial life" (p. 262, emphasis added). More recent work from Korea finds "harmonious family" as the most important life goal (Kim, Park, Kim, Lee, & Yu, 2000, cited in Kim et al., 2005), and Kim et al. conclude, "Although social structures became modern, the core values of emotional relatedness and family harmony remain strong" (p. 351).

Given this continuity in basic culture, then, the question is what kind of change occurs in family patterns and why. Obviously, change is going on, and it would be rejecting reality to assert the persistence of all forms or aspects of family-human relations. As I have shown for example in discussing the VOC Study, systematic changes are seen in values attributed to children with socioeconomic development in both international and intranational comparisons. Specifically, with socioeconomic development, the old-age security and **economic/utilitarian value of children** (voc) decrease. There are also parallel decrements in expectations of specific financial support from children in old age (Kağitçibaşi, 1982a, 1982b).

At first sight, such systematic reduction in utilitarian/economic values of children and expectations of specific help from them appears to indicate that full nucleation and **separation** are occurring in the family with socioeconomic development[3] as claimed by modernization theory. However, a closer examination of the findings reveals that these changes are taking place only with respect to certain needs satisfied by children. Specifically, it is **material dependencies** that decrease with socioeconomic development, not **emotional dependencies.** This distinction led to a breakthrough in conceptually differentiating between material and emotional (psychological) dependencies in the family (Kağitçibaşi,

---

[3]This was my original interpretation of the VOC Study findings (Ka itçiba i, 1982b). However, later on I realized that this interpretation was too simplistic and refined it by distinguishing between material and emotional interdependencies.

1990), the former reflected in economic/utilitarian voc and the latter in **psychological voc.**

The VOC Study findings refer mainly to material dependencies, and not to emotional (psychological) dependencies. They provide clear evidence for decreasing economic voc with socioeconomic development. This is found to be the case for different indicators of economic/utilitarian voc (children providing **old age security;** specific financial support in old age; help with household chores; or material help while young) and using different indicators of socioeconomic development. (Kağitçibaşi, 1982a, 1982b).

However, the fact that material dependencies decrease with socioeconomic development does not imply family nucleation-separation. Psychological/emotional dependencies can continue even if material dependencies on children decrease with alternative old-age security benefits becoming available. Indeed, this was evidenced by the VOC Study findings that show that in contrast to economic voc, psychological voc either does not change (Fawcett, 1983) or even increases with development (Kağitçibaşi, 1982a, 1982b). For example, in Turkey the salience for parents of the "companionship" value of children increased with parent education (from 33% at high school to 43% at university level) and with the development level of the area of residence (20% in the least developed areas; 26% in medium-developed; 32% in more developed; and 51% in metropolitan areas).

Subsequent research provided further evidence for decreased material (inter)dependencies without a corresponding decrease in emotional (inter)dependencies. For example, a study conducted in Turkey (Erelçin, 1988) compared the willingness of modern (young and urban) and traditional (old and rural) groups to give material and emotional resources to close others. There was no difference between the two groups in willingness to give emotional resources (e.g., to visit a person in the hospital) but the modern group was less willing to give material resources (e.g., money).

Intergenerational and close family/kin relations in developed/urban areas of the **Majority World** with cultures of relatedness continue. This is despite the fact that material dependencies have diminished, as many urban elderly are self-supporting (through old-age pensions, etc.) and may even themselves be providing financial support to their young-adult children (Georgas, 1993; Georgas et al., 2006; C. F. Yang, 1988). Thus, on the basis of his research in Turkey, Duben (1982) concluded that "the significance of kin relations seems not to be fading with increased urbanization or industrialization" (p. 94). Current research draws a similar portrait. For example, Georgas et al. (2006) in a 30-country comparative study find material interdependencies (instrumental roles) and hierarchy in the family to decrease in importance with increased affluence, but emotional bonds to remain strong. Similarly, Koutrelakos (2004) found decreasing material interdependencies but continuing emotional interdependencies with **acculturation** of Greek Americans.

What are the implications of a decrease in material dependencies but not in emotional dependencies, reflected in economic voc losing importance and psychological voc gaining importance? It would be expected that some aspects of the family system would undergo changes whereas other aspects are sustained. Therefore some combinations of characteristics not present in either the family model of total interdependence or the family model of independence would emerge.

## Model of Psychological or Emotional Interdependence[4]

The complexities of contextual and familial changes through socioeconomic development in the **Majority World** with cultures of relatedness implicates a third family/human model–the model of psychological/emotional interdependence. This model differs from, but nevertheless overlaps in some characteristics with the two other prototypical models. To reiterate, the distinguishing mark of the prototype of total interdependence is familial and individual interdependence in both material and emotional dimensions. The prototype of independence is distinguished by independence in both familial and individual levels in both material and emotional dimensions. The third model, however, manifests interdependence in the emotional realm in both family and individual levels but entails independence in both levels in the material realm (Fig. 5.4).

The model of psychological/emotional interdependence is typical in the more developed/urban areas of the Majority World with cultures of relatedness (collectivistic culture base). So, what we see here is social-structural and economic change alongside cultural continuity, as discussed previously. Given the continuity of the relational culture, the family in this pattern extends into other families (kin) in complex ways. These family links can occur bilaterally (with either spouse's kin), with the decreased importance of patrilineage and the correspondingly increased women's status, lower fertility, and lower **son preference.** However, the kind of shared activities would be different in this case than joint (agricultural) production or consumption (as seen in the case of the **functionally extended family** in the family model of total interdependence).

---

[4] I use psychological and emotional interdependence interchangeably, referring to the nonmaterial realm of family relations and interdependencies.

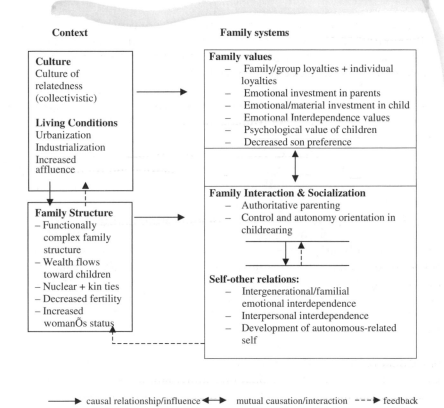

Figure 5.4.   Family Model of Psychological/Emotional Interdependence.

*Note.* From *Family and Human Development Across Cultures: A View From the Other Side* (p.88), by C. Kağitçibaşi, 1996, Mahwah, NJ: Lawrence Erlbaum Associates.

Given the sustained **psychological/emotional interdependencies** between generations, though not required for material survival, psychological/emotional investments of young adults go both toward their elderly parents and toward their children. Material investments (**wealth flows**), however, are directed mainly toward children who in this developed/urban context cost more. With the higher cost of children and their diminished economic voc, their psychological value becomes more salient. This is because economically it does not "make sense" to have children; thus the psychological satisfaction derived from children assumes greater importance as a reason for childbearing.

It is to be noted that *emotional* does not mean liking or loving; that is, there is no claim here that the family members in the family model of psychological/emotional interdependence like each other more than *need more clarification*

those in the other models. The differences between the models have more to do with the self–other relations, self-boundaries, or identities rather than with emotions, as such. That is why psychological is added to emotional, in contrast to material. There is connectedness of the selves as in the family model of (total) interdependence, but whereas in the interdependence model this connectedness is based on material interdependence, in this model, it is based on nonmaterial (psychological/emotional) interdependence.

Socialization values continue to emphasize family/group loyalties, given the sustained psychological/emotional interdependencies. However, individual loyalties are emerging, as well. This is especially important in implicating modifications in family interaction patterns, that is, childrearing entailing autonomy. Alongside **parental control** in **socialization,** reflecting the continued importance of closely knit family/human bonds, there is room in this family system for individual loyalties and autonomy as well. This is because with decreased material interdependencies, complete dependency of the child (and subsequent total loyalty of the grown-up offspring) is no longer required for **old-age security** of the parent and thus for family well-being.

It is important to understand why autonomy emerges in the family model of psychological/emotional interdependence. There are at least two reasons for this. First, given the decreased material dependence of the elderly parents on the adult offspring, the child's autonomy is no longer seen as a threat to family livelihood. It is now acceptable for the young person to look after his or her own (material) needs given that the elderly parents' needs are provided for by alternative means, such as old-age pensions and the like. Second, with changing lifestyles, autonomy of the growing child becomes functional. That is, autonomy becomes an asset for success in school and urban employment that require active decision-making, **agency,** and innovation rather than obedience.

Nevertheless, closeness of the child and the adult offspring are still highly valued, accordingly the relatedness of the self is characteristic of the family model of psychological/emotional interdependence. Thus, this model reveals the causal antecedents of the development of the **autonomous–related self** through societal and familial change. This type of self integrates within itself both autonomy and relatedness. The two basic human needs for agency and communion (relatedness) (Bakan, 1966, 1968) appear to find expression in the self engendered by the **family model of psychological/emotional interdependence.**

The individual interests (of the growing child) can be accommodated in this model alongside group (family) interests because the autonomy of the growing child is no longer seen as a threat to the family. The comparisons of childrearing values in different SES groups provide some evidence for this. For example, Imamoglu (1987) found urban upper-SES mothers in Turkey to value independence and self-reliance, whereas most middle- and lower-SES mothers emphasize obedience and loyalty to parents. Similarly, whereas upper-SES parents do not wish their children to feel much gratitude toward them, lower-SES parents do. In terms of old-age security and economic voc, "it is highly functional that children feel a high degree of gratitude toward their parents to keep up the family bond" (p. 143).

The modifications in values and orientations in the family/human model of psychological/emotional interdependence do not mean that family interests are unimportant or secondary at best, as in the **family model of independence.** A combination or coexistence of individual and group/family loyalties is the case here (Kağitçibaşi, 1987a, 1990). Accordingly, the familial/interpersonal relations continue to be interdependent ones, though in the psychological/emotional realm only, and the resultant self is again the **relational self,** though also entailing autonomy–the autonomous–related self. For example, Imamoglu (1987) found that all parents, even upper-SES ones who don't want their children to be grateful to them, want them to be more loving and close. Children are also desired to be more respectful as they grow older, pointing to the continuing psychological/emotional interdependence and relatedness.

The childrearing orientations and socialization values in this family model may at first sight appear as conflicting, even mutually exclusive. In particular, control and autonomy orientations in parenting may be seen as mutually exclusive. Also it may be considered unlikely for autonomy to emerge in a **family model of interdependence,** even if that interdependence is of a psychological nature. Such interpretations would be reflecting views pitting relatedness against autonomy. I deal with these issues at some length in the next chapter. Suffice it to say here that the family/human model of psychological/emotional interdependence presents a challenge to some long-standing perspectives in the psychology of personality, self, and self–other relations. Those perspectives are based on an individualistic world view.

## VALUE OF CHILDREN STUDY II (2000s)

Having presented my **family change theory,** I can now look into the recent **Value of Children Study.** A partial replication in many of the original VOC countries has been conducted in a project initiated by Trommsdorff and Nauck (Kağitçibaşi & Ataca, 2005; Kağitçibaşi et al., 2005; Trommsdorff et al., 2005; Trommsdorff & Nauck, 2005). The

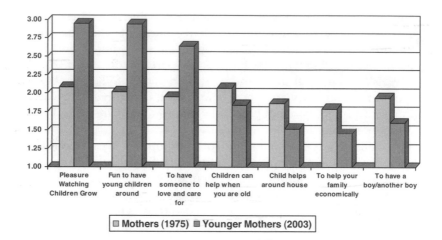

Figure 5.5.    Reasons for Wanting a Child: 1975 VOC Study Mothers vs. 2003 VOC Study Younger Mothers in Turkey.

Turkish partial replication in particular serves as a testing ground here for some aspects of the family change theory.

The second Turkish VOC Study was carried out in 2003, some three decades after the original VOC Study (Kağitçibaşi & Ataca, 2005; Kağitçibaşi et al., 2005). It was not designed as a full-replication study, therefore there are some methodological differences between the two studies. Whereas the original study utilized a nationally representative sample, the recent study used a purposive sample consisting of an urban middle/upper-SES, an urban lower-SES, and a rural sample. Nevertheless, the variations in the results obtained from the different regional and socioeconomic groups as well as the contrasts over time provide a great deal of information and insight into understanding the current situation and the dynamics of change over time.

In each stratum, there were younger mothers of preschoolers, older mothers of adolescents, and their mothers (grandmothers of the adolescents). The adolescent children of the older mothers were also interviewed. The total sample included 1,025 respondents. The younger mothers of the 2003 study were compared with the mother sample of the 1975 study, given the similarity in their mean ages, 31 and 28 respectively. It is mainly this comparison that I present here.

The most notable finding of the 2003 Turkish VOC Study was a decrease in the **economic/utilitarian value of children** (voc) and a sharp increase in the **psychological voc**'s over time. Figure 5.5 presents the comparisons of the reasons given by respondents for wanting to have a child in 1975 and 2003. Clearly psychological vocs such as fun, pleasure,

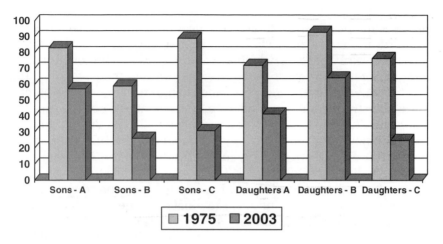

A: Financial assistance to siblings
B: Help with housework
C: Financial assistance to the mother

Figure 5.6.    Expectations of Financial/Material Help from Sons and
Daughters. 1975 VOC Study Mothers vs. 2003 VOC Study
Younger Mothers in Turkey.

and love as reasons for having a child are markedly more important in
the recent study. However, old-age security, other material benefits of
children, and the desire to have a son are less important as reasons for
having children.

In order to understand intergenerational **material dependencies,**
specific expectations of economic/material help from sons and daughters
were also examined in both studies (Figure 5.6).[5] The shifts in the
responses to these questions complement the aforementioned responses
on vocs in that overall there is less expectation of economic/material
help from children in 2003. Particularly, the reversal in the expectation of
financial assistance is remarkable.

A number of significant societal changes involving economic growth
and urbanization have occurred in Turkey during the last three decades.
The differences between the samples of the two studies optimize these
changes in that the 2003 sample was over two thirds urban, reflecting
lifestyle shifts from rural to urban, even for the low-income group.

___

[5]To agree with the 1975 format of dichotomous "yes–no," we combined the 1–2 ("not
at all" and "little") and 4–5 ("yes, some" and "a lot") scores on a 5-point scale.

Actually, though not a nationally representative sample, the VOC II sample is not out of proportion to the general population, which is now two thirds urban. Urban lifestyles entail old-age security resources, such as social security benefits, which are alternatives to adult offspring support. Also children are in school longer rather than working, thus increasing their "dependency age" and therefore their cost for parents. These objective conditions render children's material contribution less important. Education levels of the respondents in the VOC II Study are correspondingly higher. The average schooling of the 1975 mothers was 3 years; it was 9.5 years for the younger mothers of the 2003 sample.

These findings provide support to my family change theory and more specifically for the model of psychological/emotional interdependence in showing that it is material intergenerational dependencies that decrease with socioeconomic development, not psychological ones. The latter has increased as reflected in much stronger psychological vocs in 2003.

Beyond changes over time, the variations across the different strata in the VOC II Study provide further support to the model (see Kağitçibaşi & Ataca, 2005; Kağitçibaşi et al., 2005, for details). Specifically, the economic/utilitarian voc was most heavily endorsed by the rural respondents, followed by the urban low-income group, who are themselves mostly of rural origin. The urban middle/upper-SES groups considered it the least important. This is contrasted by psychological vocs being important for everyone, with low variances across groups. This finding is important in showing that the emotional bonds in the family are very important. Thus, what we see emerging in the urban middle/upper-SES groups is the psychologically/emotionally interdependent family model rather than the independent family model, as predicted by my family change theory. Expectations of help from (adult) children followed suit. The urban middle/high-SES mothers expected the least from their children followed by urban low-SES and rural groups.

Qualities desired in children were also inquired into. Whereas in 1975 "minding parents" (obedience) had the highest importance (together with "being a good person"), in 2003 this was one of the least important qualities desired in children, except for grandmothers. Independence/self-reliance was not at all stressed in 1975; in 2003, it emerged as a desired child quality especially for the urban high-SES group. This change reflects the emergence of autonomy in childrearing in the **family model of psychological/emotional interdependence,** again supporting the theory. Corresponding variations in parenting orientations are reflected in the comparisons across strata in 2003. The rural and the urban low-income groups were similar in endorsing "obeying parents," "popularity," and "success in school" more strongly and "independence/self-reliance" less strongly than middle/upper-income groups.

Generational differences were in keeping with those along social strata. Grandmothers considered economic/utilitarian voc more important than both mothers and adolescents whereas psychological voc was stressed by all generations. "Independence/self-reliance" was endorsed as a desired child quality more by mothers than by grandmothers, who stressed "obeying parents" more. Generational differences also point to systematic changes over time and further support the theory of family change.

Notwithstanding the variations, all the positive child qualities were strongly endorsed by the respondents, even those that can be seen as conflicting, such as "obeying parents" and "independence/self-reliance." This combination indicates the coexistence of "control" and "autonomy" orientations in childrearing, a finding that supports the family model of psychological/emotional interdependence.

With regard to gender preference in children, VOC Study II was distinctly different. On a forced-choice item in VOC Study I, there was overall 84% **son preference** contrasted with 16% daughter preference; among women it was 75% and 25% (Kağitçibaşi, 1982a, 1998a). In Study II, the forced-choice item was administered only to the urban sample. Among the younger urban mothers in 2003, the corresponding figures were reversed to 41.1% son and 58.9% daughter preference. The reversals are more marked for the urban middle/high- than for the urban low-SES samples. This striking difference reflects significant temporal and social-structural change, in keeping with the predictions of the family change theory.

Finally, actual, desired, and ideal numbers of children, reflecting fertility attitudes and behavior, fit in with the preceding findings and the predictions of my family change theory. The VOC Study II younger mothers have significantly fewer actual, desired, and ideal numbers of children than VOC Study I mothers. With regard to the different strata in 2003, the urban low-SES mothers had higher numbers than rural groups, and the urban high/middle-SES group had the lowest numbers. The higher numbers of the low-SES urban group may be due to better public health services in urban contexts, thus less infant mortality, together with the rural origins of these mothers conducive to high fertility.

In conclusion, we can say that VOC Studies I and II provide food for thought and support many aspects of my family change theory. Particularly, the changes evidenced in VOC Study II point to predictable modifications in every aspect covered by the theory, that is, living conditions (urban, rural, SES), family structure (fertility, **wealth flows**), socialization values (vocs, son preference, independence values), and parenting and family interaction (obedience vs. independence/self-reliance orientation). This constitutes strong support for the theory and more specifically for its model of psychological/emotional interdependence.

### Further Support for the Family Change Theory and Model of Psychological/Emotional Interdependence

A growing body of research provides support to the **model of psychological/emotional interdependence** and in general terms to the **family change theory.** Some of this comes directly from the recent **VOC studies** in the other countries. I refer to this research first before going on to other relevant work.

Kim et al. (2005) carried out the VOC Study in Korea. Similar to the findings of the Turkish VOC Study II, the findings from Korea point to changes from social and economic benefits to psychological and relational benefits. Compared with the 1970s VOC Study results from Korea, the psychological aspects of having a child appear to have become central in understanding why Koreans decide to have children and the number of children they have (pp. 351–352).

Sam, Peltzer, and Mayer (2005) conducted the VOC Study in South Africa. They report positive associations between **traditional/utilitarian voc** and fertility and negative associations between psychological (social/emotional) voc and fertility, in line with the original theoretical perspective of VOC (Kağitçibaşi, 1982a, 1982b) and the family change theory. This is found to be the case even though the three conceptually distinct vocs did not emerge in the South African study.

Sabatier and Lannegrand-Willems (2005) report some of the findings of the VOC Study in France. They point to a combination of autonomy values with solidarity in the family. Similarly, they find high levels of both individualism and also endorsement of family values in adolescents. They also note the shift in family values toward more emotional ties (p. 383). These findings are in keeping with the family model of psychological/emotional interdependence and the resultant **autonomous–related self** of this model. Similarly, the German VOC Study (D. Klaus, Nauck, & Klein, 2005; Schwarz, Trommsdorff, Albert, & Mayer, 2005) found lower instrumental vocs among more educated women and general shifts from more traditional vocs of grandmothers to more emotional vocs of the younger generations. Thus, the shift toward the psychological/emotional interdependence model may not occur only in the developed contexts of the **Majority World** with collectivistic cultures of relatedness. In the Western world, also, similar shifts may be seen. This topic is taken up again. Also the autonomous–related self is discussed at some length in the next chapter.

In Israel, the two samples of rural Moslems and urban Jews with lower and higher levels of education, respectively, were compared (Suckow, 2005). As expected, the material and social acceptance functions ("comfort" and "esteem") of children were stressed more by the Moslem

sample whereas there was no difference between the two groups in the **psychological voc** ("affection").

The Indian VOC Study had a city sample (Varanasi) and a rural sample from several villages (Mishra, Mayer, Trommsdorff, Albert, & Schwartz, 2005). The main difference between the samples was seen in the greater salience of the emotional voc in the city, whereas no difference was found among groups in the traditional voc (a combination of economic, old-age security, and social-normative vocs). Even in the case of India, which has not yet gone through a demographic transition (shift toward lowered fertility), the shift toward increased emotional voc with urbanization is important. It provides support to the theory of family change. Among the urban adolescents, only, traditional voc was low. This might signal further future change, however, as the authors note, it could also reflect a young life stage that does not involve the experience of having children.

The VOC Study in Indonesia (Albert, Trommsdorff, Mayer, & Schwarz, 2005) also found a general shift from more traditional reasons for having children to more emotional ones. The shift was apparent over both rural–urban and generational comparisons. Nevertheless, the continuing importance of the old-age security voc across groups is reminiscent of the 1970s findings from the original VOC Study in Indonesia, published in a monograph titled, "Two Are Not Enough" referring to the need to have more children to ensure old-age security for the parents (Darroch et al., 1981).

In China, the urban–rural and "floating" populations comparisons on the one hand and intergenerational comparisons on the other revealed variations in vocs that were similar to the other VOC countries (Zheng, Shi, & Tang, 2005). Both the rural and low-SES "floating" samples, as well as grandmothers endorsed material (substantive) vocs more than the urban, higher-SES and younger-generation samples. For the latter groups, "emotional" vocs were more important. The researchers also note that typically Confucian values such as "to have a boy," "to carry on the family name," and "older relatives feel that you should have more children" were losing importance. Clearly, together with socioeconomic changes, the Chinese "one-child policy" is an important exogenous factor augmenting the value change. Thus, VOC studies from different countries point to similar systematic connections between vocs and several background and outcome variables. These findings provide further support to the model of psychological/emotional interdependence.

Further support to the model and the general Theory of family change comes from a large-scale research study on the family carried out by Georgas et al. (2006). University students in 30 countries comprised the sample, and the comparative analyses were carried out with data from 27 of these countries on the relationships between ecological, sociopolitical, family, and psychological variables. Additionally collaborators from the 30 countries provided country portraits and qualitative analyses of the cultural features of their countries. The study emphasized the psychological variables of emotional closeness, self-construal, personality, family values, and general values and their relationships within ecological and sociopolitical features of societies, family roles, and family networks.

The level of socioeconomic development was found to be the most powerful source of variation of the family and psychological variables. It was composed of affluence, percentage of the population engaged in agriculture and education. The strongest relationship with the socioeconomic development level of countries in the project was with the family hierarchy; that is, less developed, primarily agricultural countries were found to have higher hierarchical family values as compared to more highly developed countries. Similar relationships in the same direction, but somewhat lower, were found with relationships with family and kin and S. H. Schwartz (1994; P. B. Smith & Schwartz, 1997) values Embeddedness, Hierarchy, and Harmony, as well as the Expressive/Emotional roles and some Instrumental/Expressive roles in the family.

The strong negative effect of socioeconomic development on family hierarchy points to increasing autonomy. Indeed, in most countries the university students rejected family hierarchy. Nevertheless, "emotional bonds" were the most robust universal. There was also a common distinction in all the countries between the emotional and the instrumental dimensions of family roles. Even in affluence, close family relations are found to exist, together with lessened/rejected family hierarchy. These findings from a great number of countries with considerable variance in socioeconomic development levels, religion, climate, and so on, provide support to my family change theory. The highly educated, mostly urban samples appear to have mainly the family model of psychological/emotional interdependence. This model appears to be a global converging point for different family patterns through socioeconomic development—a point further elaborated in the next section.

Coexistence of control and autonomy in the model of psychological/emotional interdependence is reflected in research by C.-Y. C. Lin and Fu (1990) in a comparison of Chinese, immigrant Chinese, and Anglo-American parents. The two Chinese groups were found to be higher on both **parental control** and encouragement of independence than the Anglo group. Similarly, Jose et al. (2000), again with Chinese, Chinese American, and Euro-American parents, found the Chinese groups to endorse both relatedness and autonomy. **Authoritative parenting**

(Baumrind, 1980, 1989), which combines order-setting control and autonomy (together with love), also entails some of these apparently conflicting orientations. Baumrind (1989) noted, "Authoritative parents represent a balance between **agency** and communion, as does the competent child type" (p. 370, emphasis added).

Other research has also found authoritative parenting to be more conducive than authoritarian and permissive parenting to both cognitive development and academic success and also to psychosocial competence (Dornbusch et al., 1987; Lamborn et al., 1991; Lau & Cheung, 1987; Lau et al., 1990; Steinberg et al., 1989). More recent research in the United States provides further evidence for the coexistence and distinctness of parental control and autonomy granting (e.g., Silk, Morris, Kanaya, & Steinberg, 2003). Such evidence provides support to the family model of psychological/emotional interdependence and shows that it is not confined only to the more developed contexts of cultures of relatedness. This topic is examined further in chapter 6.

This type of parenting is proposed to replace authoritarian (restrictive, obedience-oriented) parenting in the family model of psychological/emotional interdependence. This is because, as I have discussed before, with decreased material dependencies in this model, complete obedience (and loyalty) of the child is no longer needed for family survival, and there is room for autonomy in childrearing. However, at the same time, there is still firm control (rather than permissive childrearing as in the **family model of independence**) because full independence-separation is not the goal, either, in the context of continuing **emotional dependencies.** Thus, Stewart et al. (1999) found among upper-middle-class Hong Kong families a combination of autonomy, relatedness, and control.

In family psychology and clinical practice in the United States–an entirely different area of research and application–similar formulations are seen, combining independence and interdependence. For example, Vannoy (1991) found that stable marriages are more likely to be achieved only by those individuals who develop capacities for both autonomy and intimacy, and Selman (1989) focussed on fostering intimacy and autonomy in psychotherapy with children. Similarly M. L. Hoffman (1989) called for conceptions of adolescent development that simultaneously pose goals of relatedness and interdependence with autonomy and self-reliance. From a gender-role perspective, Barciauskas and Hull (1989) also recommended a new **integration** of individualism and relatedness, of independence and interdependence, both in the home and at the workplace. And Fu, Hinkle, and Hanna (1986) consider dependency a valued trait in adulthood, as it helps maintain close family ties.

Thus, emerging from a different (applied) academic tradition, the aforementioned views are similar to the criticisms of mainstream American psychology, which I have reviewed in the last chapter. They decry an excessive preoccupation with the self and call for greater social concern and interdependence, similar to Sampson's (1988) ensembled individualism or in Etzioni's (1993) communitarianism.

Research on **acculturation** provides further insights. The changes in family relationships with increased urbanization and socioeconomic development in many parts of the world are paralleled by similar changes in immigrant groups as they acculturate to Western lifestyles. For example, as mentioned before, Koutrelakos (2004) studying self-disclosure of Greek Americans found decreasing material interdependencies but continuing emotional interdependencies with acculturation. Similarly, research on "familism" among Hispanic Americans showed the same pattern of shifts from material to emotional bonds through generations and acculturation (Perez & Padilla, 2000; Sabogal, Marín, Otero-Sabogal, Marín, & Perez-Stable, 1987). These studies provide supportive evidence for some aspects of the family model of psychological/emotional interdependence and the general theory of family change. Further work on acculturation that reveals common patterns of change is considered in chapter 10.

Finally, a great deal of recent research on parenting in general and on parental control and warmth in particular has touched on family dynamics of relevance to the family models I discussed in this chapter. In particular, the coexistence of parental control and autonomy orientations in childrearing together with relatedness are found across cultures (Cha, 1994; Dekoviç et al, 2006; Jose et al., 2000; Kwak, 2003; Lansford et al., 2003; C.-Y. C. Lin & Fu, 1990; Phalet & Schonpflug, 2001; Smetana & Gaines, 1999; Stewart et al., 1999; Yau & Smetana, 1996). These studies have been conducted in various nations with cultures of relatedness and with ethnic minority groups in Western European and North American contexts. The common theme running through them is the type of family functioning that involves parental control together with an autonomy orientation and relatedness–the family model of psychological/emotional interdependence. The reflections of this family model in parenting and the self are examined further in the next chapter.

## A DIFFERENT CONVERGENCE?

The research and thinking covered in this chapter, and particularly the evidence cited in the previous section, follow rather parallel paths within American psychology and social science and within cross-cultural

psychology. In the cross-cultural scene, the research points to continuities in human/familial relational patterns despite socioeconomic
changes. These changes tend to decrease material interdependencies,
which are no longer necessary with changing lifestyles, especially with
urbanization. However, they do not affect psychological/emotional
interdependencies, because these latter continue to be adaptive and functional psychosocial mechanisms in the context of economic development.
The shift in family/human patterns, therefore, is toward psychological/
emotional interdependence entailing the **autonomous–related self.** In the
American scene, also, there is a recognition of the desirability of the psy-
chological/emotional interdependence and a search for it, in reaction to
the dominant independence model.

The common underlying assumption here is that the **family model of
independence** is prevalent in the American society, and it is endorsed
and reinforced by psychology. It is indeed the case that the independence model has traditionally been advocated by normative individualism (see chap. 4), that is, by the pervasive individualistic ideology in
the West and especially in the United States. Nevertheless, whether it is
really prevalent has been questioned. As I have mentioned earlier, the
family model of independence may reflect more the middle-class ideology
than the reality. ⟶ ✱important point

Bellah et al. (1985, p. 144) in their classic study of the American family
noted an ambivalence between professed ideology and actual behavior.
Though individualism, self-sufficiency, and independence are highly valued, much interdependence between generations and kin in many
American families has been observed for a long time (e.g., Cohler and
Geyer,1982; Fu et al., 1986), thus Keniston (1985) referred to "the myth of
family independence." This has been observed more among women,
who are socialized more than men into interdependence and relatedness in Western society (Chodorow, 1978; Gilligan, 1982), especially
among the low-income families who lack alternative sources of support.
Family support and three generational "extended" families (especially
of women) are particularly notable among lower-income Blacks in
the United States (Slaughter, 1988; Washington, 1988). Subsequent
research has also pointed to the value of social support networks (e.g.,
R. D. Taylor &Roberts; see chap. 2, this volume).

Social class and ethnicity make a difference because the dominant
normative values of individualism and self-reliance are internalized and
upheld more in the mainstream middle class than in lower-income
groups and ethnic minorities who tend to be rather marginal with regard
to those values (L. W. Hoffman & Youngblade, 1998; Solomon, 1993).
Thus, Blair, Blair, and Madamba (1999) found that the presence of kin in
African American households was related to better school performance

of children; the opposite was the case for middle-class Anglo-American homes. Nevertheless, given the cultural ideal of independence and self-sufficiency, which reflect normative individualism, interdependence tends to be psychologically problematic. Being dependent on someone can lead to feelings of inadequacy, loss of self-esteem, resentment, and so on. The ambivalence involved has been found to cause discomfort for each generation (Cohler & Geyer, 1982).

This is indeed different from the situation that is common in the **culture of relatedness,** especially in the family model of total interdependence. There, intergenerational interdependence is not only required for family survival, given **material dependencies,** but it is also a cherished value, a requisite of family honor. Thus, in the original **Value of Children Study** a common response of the traditional rural Turkish respondents to questions asking if they expected their children to take care of them in old age was, "Of course, if my son is worthy of his family name, he would take care of us," with no sentiment of ambivalence or resentment. On the contrary, they were offended that we would even question the loyalty of their children (Kağitçibaşi, 1982a, 1982b). The same questions in the United States and Germany annoyed parents, and a common response was, "I don't want anything from my children; if they can take care of themselves, I'll be glad" (L. W. Hoffman, 1987). Thus in the **culture of separateness,** dependence on anyone, particularly on one's children, may be seen as a sign of weakness or failure, even if it may be a reality of life among some groups.

I have reviewed research from several societies with cultures of relatedness undergoing economic development, which provides evidence for a shift toward the model of psychological/emotional interdependence. This is often manifested in terms of coexistence of seemingly opposing characteristics of human and familial relations and in the continuation of the **relational self,** which also entails autonomy. Thus, in the model of psychological/emotional interdependence combinations of control and autonomy orientations are posited in childrearing. This is also what is found in research conducted in the United States to be characteristic of **authoritative parenting.** Similarly, human/family interdependencies are reported in American research, and the relational self is called for by the critics of American psychology.

What does all this mean? Just as there is a shift in the **Majority World** with economic development from a family model of total interdependence to a model of psychological/emotional interdependence, is there also a shift in the postindustrial society from a family model of independence to one of psychological/emotional interdependence? As the model of psychological/emotional interdependence reflects a dialectic synthesis of the two basic human needs for merging and **separation** (relatedness and autonomy), such a shift may indeed be the case.

Note, also, that from a functional perspective, psychological/ emotional interdependence is not at odds with economic development and urban lifestyles. There is nothing incompatible between modern urban lifestyles and psychological/emotional interdependence. There is no need, therefore, for psychological/emotional interdependence to diminish in conjunction with socioeconomic development. It is different in this sense from material interdependence, which is not adaptive to the urban context because it is not conducive to the development of autonomy.

Thus, a new type of global convergence may be emerging, characterized by a shift toward the model of psychological/emotional interdependence from the model of interdependence in the Majority World together with a shift in the **Minority World** from the model of independence to the model of psychological/emotional interdependence, rather than the other way around. The latter shift from independence to psychological/ emotional interdependence is quite possible though counterintuitive. Some evidence that I have reviewed in fact supports this view.

European research in 1980s pointed to relational needs. Thus, Saal (1987) reported alternative communal living arrangements in the Netherlands that appear to reflect a need to re-create the community. Ekstrand and Ekstrand (1987) found that Swedish parents stress the value of group relations more than Indian parents, because the former miss them more. In Israel, Weil (1987) showed how proximal households function as alternatives to joint families among the "Bene Israel" who migrated to Israel from India.

Shifts from the family model of independence to even more individualistic nonfamily living arrangements (Liljestrom & Ozdalga, 2002a, 2002b) may also result in a swing back into more interdependent patterns approaching the model of psychological/emotional interdependence. Recent studies of postmodern values in the posttechnological society (Inglehart, 2003) find the increasing importance of human relational values, rather than individualistic competitive values. For example, N. Young (1992) describes postmodern discourse that sees the reconstruction of the self "through compassionate, abiding and deeply rooted relationship with others" (p. 144). Apparently, particularly in Europe the austere Protestant work ethic of the modern era is giving way to some "softer" values in the postmodern era. Greater concern with the environment, decreasing importance of work and fewer working hours, more leisure, and in general "a search for community" are some of the defining characteristics of this era in the Western posttechnological society. If we consider the specific elements of the two models, that of independence and of psychological/emotional interdependence, the latter indeed appears to better fit these new characteristics of the postmodern era.

This prediction of a shift from the model of independence to one of psychological/emotional interdependence in the Western world is rather tentative, given the still pervasive individualistic ethos in the Western world. Nevertheless, the signs of change are telling indeed. Because both autonomy and relatedness are basic human needs, models that integrate them would indeed be expected to prevail, a point laborated further in the next chapter. Whether or not there is a shift in the Western world from independence to psychological/emotional interdependence, there is no question that some synthesis similar to that found in the model of psychological/emotional interdependence is being seriously searched for in the Majority World. C. F. Yang (1988) has identified it as "something creative that takes in the new element of individualism while keeping the old family tradition intact" (p. 117).

Such a synthesis or coexistence of autonomy and relatedness (of **agency** and merging) have been recognized by others also (Mascolo & Li, 2004; J. B. P. Sinha, 1985; Wiggins & Trapnell, 1996; K.-S. Yang, 1986). At times it has been considered as utopic. For example, from a sociohistorical perspective, Westen (1985) traced societal development through four main phases: (a) primary communitarian collectivism of primitive society, (b) secondary communitarian collectivism (similar to Durkheim's mechanical solidarity seen in peasant societies with classical historic religions), (c) individuated collectivism (similar to Durkheim's organic solidarity; characterized by self-interest and modernity), and finally (d) synthetic collectivism in which both collectivity and the individual, both sociality and self-interest, and both self-interest and group feeling are legitimate (pp. 280–281). The last phase is seen by Westen as a logical possibility, though probably more a utopia than a reality. I believe recent research and thinking are showing that such a synthesis may indeed be a reality. It is what the **human/family model of psychological/emotional interdependence** involves.

A caveat is needed here. The theory of family change I have proposed in this chapter is based on a functional analysis and refers to what is to be expected on the basis of ongoing socioeconomic changes, as also evidenced in research. It is possible, however, that other factors not dealt with in the model can interfere with this "natural" process. One such exogenous factor could be the resistance of culture to change or "cultural lag."

It is possible, for example, that in the urban developed contexts in the Majority World with collectivistic cultures, authoritarian, obedience-oriented childrearing persists even though it is not required for family livelihood, because socioeconomic changes have decreased material dependency on the offspring. In this context, the obedience-oriented childrearing would not be functional for the family or adaptive for the growing person whose future lifestyle will require autonomy and individual decision making. This is an example of a mismatch that I have discussed between the requirements of new lifestyles and traditional childrearing.

Another factor that can counter the "natural" process of change based on functional dynamics could be "cultural diffusion." Global media are dominated by Western, mainly American, establishments, which project a particular worldview. Diffusion of the Western individualistic model may be so pervasive as to promote the emergence of the human/family model of independence, even though it is not necessitated by or even functional for the lifestyles in most sociocultural contexts in the world.

The theory of family change I have proposed here cannot deal with such exogenous influences, but it is important to keep in mind that they may play a role. Nevertheless, the functional relations underlying the internal dynamics of the self–family–society interface appear strong enough to cause the proposed changes in most cases. The supporting evidence further confirms them.

## SUMMARY AND MAIN POINTS

- Family is the central component of the self–family–society dynamics; it needs to be examined within the social-structural-economic context.
- Modernization theory proposes a unidirectional change, involving convergence of the human/family characteristics toward the Western individualistic pattern. This is because it holds that Western individualistic-separate family is a necessary outcome of industrialization and therefore that as the rest of the world industrializes, individualism will follow. This view is challenged by historical and current evidence.
- The nine-country Value of Children (VOC) Study (1970s) found three main types of values attributed to children: utilitarian/economic, psychological, and social. Utilitarian/economic voc, old-age security voc, and son preference were prevalent in the rural/agrarian/low-SES contexts. In contrast, psychological voc was more salient in the context of greater affluence and urban lifestyles.
- Kağitçibaşi's theory of family change is a contextual model; it situates the self within the family and the family within the cultural and socioeconomic environment. It is a functional model as causal links among lifestyles, dynamics underlying family interaction patterns, and development of the self are stressed.
- Three family/human models–model of interdependence, model of independence, and model of psychological/emotional

interdependence–are proposed as prototypes of family systems and functioning in different socioeconomic-cultural contexts.

- The family/human model of interdependence is commonly found in rural/agrarian traditional societies with closely knit human/family relations, characterized by culture of relatedness (collectivism). Material dependencies between generations promote economic and old-age security voc, as well as son preference, high fertility, low intrafamily status of women, obedience orientation in childrearing, and authoritarian parenting.

- As a result, relational self (as discussed in chap. 4) typically develops in the family/human model of interdependence.

- The family/human model of independence is commonly found in affluent, urban/industrial technological societies, characterized by culture of separateness (individualism). It is characterized by intergenerational and interpersonal independence, low son preference, emphasis on psychological voc, low fertility, higher intrafamily status of women, independence and self-reliance orientation in childrearing, and relatively permissive parenting.

- As a result, independent/separate self with clearly defined boundaries (as discussed in chap. 4) develops in the family/human model of independence.

- The model of psychological/emotional interdependence is a synthesis of two prototypical models. It is characterized by emotional interdependencies between generations, diminished economic voc, salient psychological voc, increased women's status, lower fertility, lower son preference, socialization values emphasizing family/group loyalties as well as individual loyalties, and childrearing entailing autonomy together with parental control. The resulting self is the autonomous–related self.

- As a result of economic growth and urbanization occurring in Turkey during the last decades, the 2003 Turkish VOC Study revealed significantly different findings compared to the original VOC Study, supporting Kağitçibaşi's family change theory.

- The findings of VOC studies conducted in different countries, and a growing body of research investigating family and psychological variables in relation to socioeconomic development and acculturation provide evidence for a general shift toward the model of psychological/emotional interdependence.

- Thus, a new type of global convergence may be observed, characterized by a shift from the model of interdependence toward the model of psychological/emotional interdependence in the Majority World, as well as a shift from the model of independence to the model of psychological/emotional interdependence in the Minority World.

- Although it is possible that exogenous factors like cultures' resistance to change and cultural diffusion can counter this "natural" process of change, the internal dynamics of the self–family–society interface appear strong enough to cause the proposed changes.

## DISCUSSION QUESTIONS

1. Explain how (material) independence and interdependence between generations shape "son preference," referring to the of Value of Children (VOC) Study.
2. How do socialization values and family interactions shape parenting styles in the family models of interdependence, independence, and psychological/emotional interdependence?
3. How do the three different types of self develop in the three prototypical family models?
4. How is modernization theory's prediction of convergence toward the Western model challenged by economic and historical evidence?
5. What is the reasoning behind Kağitçibaşi's alternative prediction of a convergence toward the family model of psychological/emotional interdependence from both the model of interdependence and the model of independence?
6. What factors may prevent this "natural" process of change?

# 6

# Parenting and the Development of the Autonomous–Related Self

In parent education classes in the United States, young mothers are often taught to "let go" of their toddlers. Compare this with Azuma's characterization of the mother–child interaction in Japan (reported in Kornadt, 1987, p. 133), where the mother's message to the child who is being difficult is "I am one with you; we can be and will be of the same mind." What is the contrast? American mothers are taught to let their toddlers separate from them. This early separation must go against at least some (natural?) tendencies of mothers to "merge" with their young children, because they are asked to make a calculated effort to control these tendencies and "let their children go." This is being done because psychological teaching, based on psychoanalytic theory, claims that unless early **separation-individuation** occurs, a pathological "symbiotic" relationship gets formed between the mother and the child. On the other hand, what the Japanese mother is telling the child reflects a symbiotic relationship of "oneness" of completely overlapping selves (see Fig. 4.1 in chap. 4). I sometimes ask my students to imagine themselves as a clinical psychologist fresh with a PhD degree from an American university carrying out an observation in a traditional Turkish village. What would they see? A lot of overlapping connected selves.

What is to be done? Do we declare Japanese society or Turkish society as pathological? Or do we declare the separation-individuation hypothesis to be wrong? What is wrong is probably a culture-blind application of the hypothesis. This is yet another example of the underlying human dimension of separation-relatedness. In this chapter, we examine the developmental processes underlying this dimension.

## NEED FOR A DEVELOPMENTAL CONCEPTUALIZATION

How the self is construed in a cultural context has direct implications for **socialization.** This is because childrearing and socialization are goal directed, the goal being culturally valued adult characteristics and optimal functioning. Several examples of this were examined in the previous chapters regarding parental values and cultural conceptions of competence. Indeed, it is often possible to see the links between cultural values and childrearing patterns. For example, in accordance with the American ethos of an **independent self,** autonomy orientation in childrearing is widely evidenced in research, especially among the middle-class Anglo-American mainstream. Western individualistic values as, for example, reflected in Western TV and films are also influencing the globalizing world. Additionally Western, mainly American developmental psychology is being exported to the world as the "gospel of truth" (Dasen & Jahoda, 1986). The issue is *what* is to change and *what* is to remain, and *how* this will be ascertained and *by whom.*

Early caregiver–child interaction, reflecting psychology of relatedness, can provide clues for understanding the development of the self. Systematic studies of this interaction across cultures are emerging in increasing numbers, but much more work needs to be done to unravel the antecedents of the related and separate selves. These behavioral antecedents mediate between the cultural and parental goals and conceptions of human development on the one hand, and the actual development of the self on the other. A small-scale psycholinguistic study of communicative socialization processes by S. H. Choi (1992) provides some insight into these antecedents. In observations of Korean and Canadian middle-class mothers' interactions with their young children, she noted a fundamental difference. The Korean mother–child interactions are found to have a "communicative pattern relationally-attuned to one another in a fused state" where the mothers freely enter the children's reality and speak for them, "merging themselves with the children." The Canadian mothers, on the other hand, are "distinguished by their effort to detach themselves from the children … withdrawing themselves from the children's reality, so that the children's reality can remain autonomous" (pp. 119–120).

This is reminiscent of Azuma's previous description of the Japanese mother's message to the child and quite similar to Caudill and Schooler's (1973) earlier findings. They noted that American mothers, holding culturally derived views of infants as potentially autonomous, encouraged them to express their own needs and desires. In contrast, Japanese mothers viewed their infants as "extensions of themselves" and stressed physical contact. Similarly, Coll (1990) argued that attachment and separation processes foster interpersonal dependency (rather than autonomy) in minority groups whose ideal for mature relationships is relative enmeshment.

Apparently, childrearing where the mother "merges herself with the child" paves the way for the development of a relational self, whereas childrearing that allows an "autonomous reality" to the child, mother "withdrawing" from it, engenders the development of a separate self (see chap. 4). In sociocultural-economic contexts where closely knit familial communal relations are important and where social responsibility training is stressed in socialization, the former type of early caregiver–child interaction may be expected to prevail (Greenfield, Keller et al., 2003; Keller, 2003).

## Key Questions

*this is important information to identify*

The preceding discussion points to some possible causal relations between cultural contexts where closely knit human bonds are important and the type of childrearing that engenders the emergence of the relational self. This is contrasted with the development of the separate self in cultural contexts characterized by individualism. Childrearing and socialization in general mediate between the cultural and social-structural-economic conditions on the one hand and the resultant self on the other.

However, the causal links may not be apparent. Descriptive approaches amount to showing that in individualistic cultures individualistic (separate) selves prevail, and in collectivistic cultures collectivistic (related) selves prevail. They do not address the question of *how* this distinction comes about. A developmental perspective is needed to answer such a question. Studies of childrearing, such as that of S. H. Choi (1992) on the communicative socialization processes, provide insight into the parenting and parent–child interaction that underlie the development of a particular type of self. However, childrearing by itself does not address the question *why?* A functional analysis and conceptualization is needed to understand why in some sociocultural contexts there is a particular type of childrearing whereas in others a different one prevails.

Thus, different types of conceptualizations are possible. For example, as we have seen, one could show that there are different types of selves, independent–interdependent or separate–related (varying in degrees) and that they differ from one another in several spheres of psychological functioning, ranging from self-perceptions to emotions (e.g., Markus & Kitayama, 1991). A second type of conceptualization could throw light on the kinds of socialization engendering the different selves. A third type of conceptualization could reveal why a certain kind of socialization occurs in a particular context and when a change in this process may be expected. I analyzed these questions in chapter 2 in discussing the value of a contextual-functional perspective (see Box 2.2).

Most current cross-cultural conceptualizations of the self do not deal with this third type of analysis. The causes or antecedents of the independent and the interdependent selves have not been adequately examined. Usually only individualism and collectivism are invoked, and the consequences or behavioral correlates of the different types of selves are examined. However, not much analysis is done on the antecedent conditions, underlying functional relationships, and especially how changes in these occur.

Such analysis requires an examination of the functional underpinnings of the society–family–socialization interfaces. For example, there is a need to understand how family interaction patterns and socialization values are influenced by the socioeconomic-cultural context and how the former, in turn, affect childrearing. Any changes in the context would have implications for changes in the chain of these causal relationships. This kind of conceptualization cannot remain only at the psychological level but has to situate the self and the family within the larger context. The family plays a key mediating role in the functional/causal relations between the self and society.

The theory of family change that we examined in the last chapter aimed to provide such a framework for understanding the societal and familial antecedents of the separate and related selves. It also proposed systematic changes in the family through socioeconomic development, impacting the development of the self.

## PARENTING

Parental orientations constitute an important feature of the developmental context and specifically of the family. Parenting is influenced by the macro-system factors and in turn impacts the developing child, mediating between societal values, beliefs, conventions, and norms and child development outcomes. Research shows that parenting does have a demonstrable effect on diverse developmental outcomes across cultures. A great deal of recent research has been conducted to reveal what types of parenting and **socialization** underlie the development of the self.

From the perspective of the **developmental niche** (see chap. 2), Harkness et al. (2000) refer to individualism and collectivism (sociocentrism) as a cultural *meta model,* "a cluster of ideas that characterize cultures at a broad level and that should logically have wide-ranging functions for the organization of human development and social relationships" (pp. 23–24). They see parental ethnotheories as mediating between these cultural metamodels and behavior. Ethnotheories refer to cultural beliefs that parents hold regarding the nature of children, their development, parenting, and the family. Thus, parenting is a key to addressing the *how* and the *why* questions I presented previously.

Earlier anthropological work reviewed in the previous chapters, especially in chapters 2 and 4, provided insights into the role of child care and socialization in leading to the development of the self and in cultural transmission of values and beliefs. Informed by these early insights, more recent cross-cultural and cultural psychological research has gone further in understanding the links between parenting and the development of the self in a more systematic way.

## Infancy and Attachment

*Parenting the Infant.* Quite a number of studies on parenting of infants focus on mother–infant interaction. There is much that is universal in this interaction, given the biologically based needs for care, nutrition, and protection. So, a great deal of infant caretaking involves biological/evolutionary aspects reflected in *intuitive parenting* (Papoušek & Papoušek, 2002), including carrying, nursing, responding to distress signals, stimulating, smiling, and talking with a high-pitched "baby talk" (Keller, 1997; Keller, Schölmerich, & Eibl-Eibesfeldt, 1988). There are four basic systems in this stage: the system of primary care (especially nursing), the body contact system (especially carrying), the body motor stimulation system, and the face-to-face interaction system (Keller, Lohaus, Völker, Cappenberg, & Chasiotis, 1999).

Notwithstanding this basic commonality, even in this early developmental stage, cultural diversity is seen. For example, Bornstein and his collaborators found significant cross-cultural differences in modes of parent–child interaction even in infancy. These variations in parental orientations are found to have consequences for children's cognitive development (Bornstein, 1989; Bornstein, Tal, & Tamis-LeMonda, 1991; Bornstein et al., 1992) and even for their physical/motor development (Bornstein, 1984, p. 245). Similarly, Roopnarine and Talukder (1990) noted cultural specificity of certain parent–infant activities in research in India. Working with Québécois, Vietnamese, and Haitian cultural groups in Montreal, Canada, Pomerlau, Malcuit, and Sabatier (1991) identified differences among beliefs about babies in these groups, controlling for SES differences. They noted variations in the social and physical environments that distinguish immigrants and natives. Thus, cultural differences appear to exist in childrearing environments from very early on even where typically substantial commonality is seen.

In an extensive research program, Keller et al. (1999) have shown that body contact and body stimulation are more prevalent in the collectivistic agrarian African cultures, whereas a face-to-face system is more prevalent in middle-class urban Western contexts. They further propose that close body contact is conducive to the development of close ties and relatedness with others, whereas face-to-face interactions with language use are conducive to the development of a sense of **independent self** and **agency.**

Research conducted with samples of mother–infant pairs from more similar sociocultural contexts provides further insights. Keller et al. (2003) compared Greek and German middle-class mothers who were both found to display face-to-face interactions with their infants. They also had more object play and less body contact and body stimulation. All these early parenting strategies are believed to lead to the development of independent agency in the child. Together with these similarities, however, there was an important difference between the two groups in that Greek mothers showed more warmth by smiling during face-to-face interaction than German mothers. Thus, whereas both groups showed parenting behaviors that might be expected to lead toward agency in the child, Greek mothers also built in relatedness through warmth, thus showing parenting that is conducive to the development of an **autonomous–related self** in the child.

There can be change over time, also. Thus Keller and Lamm (2005) compared similar groups of middle-class German mothers over a 25-year period. They found a significant increase in agency promoting parenting and a decrease in body contact and warmth, downplaying relatedness.

Keller's research is rich in conceptualization and careful in empirical detection of interactional systems in the proximal environment of the infant. It differentiates the two different paths toward independence and interdependence (Keller, 2003). However, as in the case of Greek mothers, combinations are also recognized. Nevertheless, there is also criticism of this framework. Neff (2003) questions Keller's tendency to tie "equality" versus "apprentice" models of parent–infant interaction to larger societal goals of independence or interdependence. In other words, there is a questioning of whether too much is being read into some early mother–infant interaction patterns in bringing about two different pathways of development with societal implications.

*Attachment.*    From a different perspective, that of *attachment theory,* mother–infant interaction has also been studied extensively. Based on an ethological tradition, early attachment theorists focused on the infant's and young child's proximity to the caregiver and parent's sensitivity to the child, which ensure a *secure base* for the infant to explore the environment (Ainsworth, 1963, 1976; Bowlby, 1969/1982, 1973). Although Ainsworth's research was conducted in Uganda, all the subsequent work on this theory was carried out by Western researchers who were rather "blind" to culture (LeVine & Norman, 2001).

Exploration is viewed in attachment theory as an early form of autonomy, which is made possible by the secure attachment the infant has formed with the caregiver. Hundreds of studies using the attachment paradigm have been carried out in many societies. To a large extent, these studies found support for it in that in general more *securely attached* than *insecure* patterns were observed everywhere, as well as secure attachment leading to autonomy (Van Ijzendoorn & Sagi, 1999). Importance of responsive and sensitive caregiving (Posada et al., 2002) and systematic and predictable variation across the "strange situation" settings were also found (Grossmann, Grossmann, & Keppler, 2005). There are also extensions into the adolescent period and adulthood.

Nevertheless, the attachment paradigm has also been criticized for being ethnocentric in that it is influenced by Western values and assumptions and that it has not attended to culture (e.g., LeVine & Norman, 2001; Rothbaum & Morelli, 2005; Rothbaum, Pott, Azuma, Miyake, & Weisz, 2000). Van Ijzendoorn and Sagi (1999) pointed to some important cross-cultural issues, particularly the universality assumption, the tripartite classification system, and the behavioral manifestation of maternal sensitivity. For example, what constitutes maternal sensitivity is a problem in that research with Japanese and Latino mother–infant dyads have found less *responsive sensitivity* but more *anticipatory sensitivity* toward the infant and more control and less autonomy fostering than in Western contexts (Harwood, Miller, & Lucca Irizarry, 1995; Harwood et al., 2002; Rothbaum, Weisz, Pott, Miyake, & Morelli, 2000). For example, LeVine (2004) found that Gusii mothers of Kenya are more responsive to distress signals from infants than are U.S. middle-class mothers, and the same difference was found between Cameroonian and German mothers by Völker, Yovsi, and Keller (1998) who also found, on the other hand, that German mothers are more responsive to positive signals from the infants.

There are also problems in the measurement of attachment in that the strange situation setting may have different meanings in different cultures. For example, in contexts where children are rarely left alone, as in traditional Japanese families or where there are multiple caregivers as in the Israeli kibbutz, high rates of anxious ambivalent attachment were found (Miyake, 1993; Miyake, Chen, & Campos, 1985; Sagi et al., 1985). Other research investigated the effect of socioeconomic standing on attachment in the United States. As in most other research reviewed in chapter 2, poverty emerged as a risk factor, particularly for less secure mother–child attachment relationships. The association between maternal sensitivity and attachment security was found to be moderated by SES, the strength of the association being less in lower-SES samples (De Wolff & Van Ijzendoorn, 1997). Nevertheless, proximal factors such as maternal depression and available resources made for a great deal of variability within the same SES context (Diener, Nievar, & Wright, 2003).

Though there is ongoing debate, there seems to be general agreement on the evolution-based universality of attachment between infants and their caregivers. However, beyond this, the meanings attributed to the specific behavioral manifestations of this relationship may show contextual variation in terms of both its antecedents and its consequents. Crittenden (2000) suggests to replace value-laden terms such as *secure* and *insecure* with *adaptive* and *maladaptive* and to define them with reference to the particular context. Thus, adaptive attachment would be a relationship that provides an optimal level of safety for the child within a specific context, which may differ from other contexts.

One reason for the focus on infancy and early attachment is that this may predict later self- and competence development. Though there is some evidence of early secure attachment leading to later social competence and adult secure attachment (Waters, Merrick, Treboux, Crowell, & Albersheim, 2000), there are also conflicting findings. For example, life circumstances such as divorce, serious illness in the family, child abuse, or a deteriorating financial situation, can have detrimental effects on attachment security (Hamilton, 2000; Weinfeld. Sroufe, & Egeland, 2000). Thus, a recent longitudinal study (Lewis, Feiring, & Rosenthal, 2000) found no relationship between infant insecure attachment and adolescent maladjustment.

An environmental focus tends to differ from an attachment perspective. In chapter 2, we reviewed contextual theories used in developmental psychology. Particularly contextual models, such as Bronfenbrenner's more recent formulation of bioecological theory, involving a process-person-context-time model (PPCT) (Bronfenbrenner & Morris, 1998), pay more attention to changing dynamics over time. This new formulation also puts the biopsychosocial person at the center stage whereaws Bronfenbrenner's original ecological model (1979) had somewhat underestimated the significance of the person (child). Thus the active person–environment dynamics progress and change over time. This perspective is endorsed by the developmental systems perspective on parenting (Lerner, Rothbaum, Boulos, & Castellino, 2002). It is not in tune with the emphasis on the early determination and stability assumptions of attachment theory. For example, research supporting a developmental systems perspective finds parental antecedents of attachment (i.e., sensitivity) and long-term consequences of sensitivity (i.e., social competence) to be different in Japan and the United States (Rothbaum, Pott et al., 2000; Rothbaum, Weisz et al. , 2000).

One possible resolution to the conflict might be an integrative synthesis (Kağitçibaşi, 1990) combining the concept of adaptive or optimal attachment as a person–environment interaction variable in the early microsystem that would feed into later development but that could also be affected by the ever-changing context.

## Parenting the Child

As we move from parenting of infants to parenting of children, the diversities become more marked. This is in line with the diversities in cultural values, beliefs, and lifestyles that require different adaptive mechanisms for well-being. In earlier chapters, particularly chapters 2 and 5, we examined instances of this diversity in such spheres as child work and **value of children** for parents. We dealt with parenting orientations as important elements of the *context* of development, playing a key role in mediating between societal values/beliefs and child outcomes, as well as transmitting these values and beliefs to the next generation. In this chapter, we look at parenting in more specific terms as directly impacting child outcomes.

The role of parenting in childhood is examined in numerous cultural and cross-cultural studies. In general, the findings and their interpretation mirror research with parenting of infants. Greenfield (Greenfield, Keller, et al., 2003; Greenfield & Suzuki, 1998) extend Keller's aforementioned work on early infant–parent interaction leading to different pathways of development. When applied to parenting in general, this is the view that the distinction between cultural pathways toward independence and interdependence is universal. They review three different perspectives, "the cultural values approach," "the ecocultural approach," and "the sociohistorical approach" and find evidence in each supporting the different developmental pathways. For example, research comparing U.S. mother–child interactions with the Puerto Rican (Harwood & Feng, 2006; Harwood et al., 2002; A. M. Miller & Harwood, 2002) and with the Japanese (Dennis, Cole, Zahn-Waxler, & Mizuta, 2002) point to greater mother–child physical distance and emphasis on autonomy and choice in the U.S. mothers, but more physical closeness and emphasis on relatedness on the part of Puerto Rican and Japanese mothers.

The very concept of independence and autonomy may be affected by culture also. For example, Osterweil and Nagano (1991) and Fujinaga (1991) found that Japanese mothers, like American and Israeli mothers, value independence in their children, but "independence" for the Japanese mother means that children are capable of interacting with other children or engaging in relationships of "mutual sympathy, trust, and consideration." Thus in a way, independence connotes interdependence in the development of the Japanese self. Befu (1986) also defines

Japanese "personhood" in terms of "interpersonalism" ("definition of self in terms of the relationship one has with others," p. 22), self-discipline, and "role perfectionism" (see chap. 4 for other relational construals of the self).

*yes!*

*Objections to Dichotomous Conceptualization.* Nevertheless, as Weisner (2002) notes, the studies on parenting of infants and children also point to the coexistence of autonomy and relatedness, in line with the **autonomous–related self** construal of Kağitçibaşi (1996b, 2005a) that we discussed in the last chapter and elaborate further in this chapter. For example, Q. Wang and Tamis-LeMonda (2003) comparing childrearing values of American and Taiwanese mothers found that "independence and interdependence are not in opposition or mutually exclusive. ... Rather, mothers in the two societies embraced both individualist and collectivist values" (p. 640). Such complex patterns belie the assumed homogeneity of I–C as a cross-cultural dimension of comparison. As I noted earlier, Harkness et al. (2000) also question the dichotomizing particularly with respect to the supposed unity of the "Western mind." They find, for example, that Dutch parents are quite tolerant of children's dependency demands, such as attention seeking, whereas U.S. parents are not. Other research also points to variation within Western groups (Sabatier & Lannegrand-Willems, 2005; Suizzo, 2002).

Recently, the two pathways of development—the independent and the interdependent that is put forward by Keller, Greenfield, Rothbaum, and others (Greenfield, 1999, 2000; Greenfield, Keller et al., 2003; Keller, 2003; Keller et al., 2003; Rothbaum, Pott et al., 2000; Rothbaum, Weisz et al., 2000) has been questioned. This questioning also addresses the **independent–interdependent self** distinction of Markus and Kitayama (1991) that concerns individualism–collectivism. For example, Raeff (1997) stresses that "the self is constituted by autonomous **agency** and relationships with others" (p. 205, emphasis added), referring to several traditions in the social sciences that have also made this point. She notes, however, that independence and interdependence may be manifested in different ways across cultures. She further claims that "autonomy and connectedness may be conceptualized as multifaceted dimensions of the self" (Raeff, 2004, p. 66). Killen (1997) is similarly critical of the dichotomous cultural templates, independent and interdependent, and Neff (2003) objects to Keller's generalization from mother–infant interaction to societal goals of independence–interdependence.

Notwithstanding objections to dichotomies, variations are noted by all. The middle-class Euro-American patterns tend to reflect "Western" normative individualism and dominate psychological teaching and practice. The emphasis on the development of the child's autonomy as well as on self-esteem, self-expression, self-reliance, and self-assertion is well documented (Dennis et al., 2002; Friedlmeier, 2005; Kağitçibaşi, 2005a; Rothbaum & Morelli, 2005; Rothbaum & Trommsdorff, 2007). The same emphases are not typically found in non-Western contexts or among the working-class and ethnic-minority populations in Western societies.

*Authoritarian and Authoritative Parenting.*    An element of parenting that is considered important for developmental outcomes and that has been shown to vary with social class and culture is parental control and the associated parenting styles—authoritarian, authoritative, and permissive (Baumrind, 1971, 1980, 1989; Maccoby & Martin, 1983). In chapter 2, we considered **parental warmth** and **control** as an important aspect of the context of development. A main point there was that in general, higher levels of parental control are seen in sociocultural contexts where independence of the child is not a goal of parenting.

The meaning of parental control, both for the child and for the parent, however, is to some extent borne by culture. Thus, for some time we have known that in sociocultural contexts where parental control is common and accepted, children perceive it as normal, and not as reflecting parental hostility or rejection (Kağitçibaşi, 1970; Rohner & Pettengil, 1985; Trommsdorff, 1985; see chap. 2, this volume). Nevertheless, mainstream child development literature has to a large extent ignored the role of culture. It tends to see strong parental discipline as reflecting an authoritarian form of parenting that is also assumed to lack warmth and is seen as detrimental to healthy development. More recent research with African American families (Deater-Deckart & Dodge, 1997; Lansford et al., 2003) and with ethnic minorities in the United States and Europe (Chao, 1994; Decoviç, Pels, & Model, 2006; Harwood, Handwerker, Schoelmerich, & Leyendecker, 2001) serves as a corrective here. These studies show that family control, even physical discipline, and connectedness and warmth can go together.

The normative context may even influence the "nature" of control and its meaning for the parent, which influences the child even at a very early age. Carlson and Harwood (2003) found that the "highest rates of physical control" were associated with secure attachment in 1-year-old Puerto Rican infants, but with insecure attachment in Anglo-American infants. In other words, where physical control is accepted as normal, this behavior of the mother may not involve hostility or rejection. However, where physical control is unacceptable, such behavior may reflect a negative sentiment, at times even pathology. The effects on the child would be different accordingly.

In many sociocultural contexts, what "appears" from the outside to be authoritarian control may in fact be more attuned to an **authoritative**

**parenting** that combines parental control with warmth. Thus Gonzales, Cauce, and Mason (1996) report that often the ethnic-minority parenting is labeled authoritarian because it appears too controlling. Similarly, comparing Egyptian Canadian and Anglo-Canadian parents, Rudy and Grusec (2001) found that collectivism predicted **authoritarian parenting** in both groups, but lack of warmth predicted it among Anglos, but not among Egyptians. Thus they concluded that "higher levels of authoritarianism are not necessarily accompanied by overall lower levels of warmth" (p. 202). Indeed, as I showed in an early study (Kağitçibaşi, 1970) parental control is independent of parental warmth; therefore the two can coexist (see chap. 2, this volume). We saw many examples of such coexistence in research covered in the last chapter providing support for the **family model of psychological/emotional interdependence.** Respect for age (and parents) as a childrearing value is also often seen to indicate a domineering hierarchy, but it may rather reflect a different understanding of decency and ethics, upholding family integrity and loyalty as well as sensitivity to others' needs (Kağitçibaşi, 2006a, 2006b).

## The Adolescent–Parent Relation

Adolescence is a period that presents even greater challenge for conceptual endeavors reconciling a context-independent developmental perspective and a contextual perspective. The question posed in this period is whether adolescence involves a universal phase in human development or whether universality diminishes in the face of increasing cultural diversity in lifestyles of adolescents. Since the classic study of Margaret Mead (1928) in the Samoa putting forth a different portrait of adolescence as a period of bliss rather than turmoil, this question has remained with us. The commonly accepted view is that this is the period when the adolescent becomes independent of the parent and where the reference group and attachment shifts from parents to peers. However, there is a growing body of research showing this not to be the case everywhere (e.g., Kapadia & Miller, 2005; Kwak, 2003; Larson, Verma, & Dworkin, 2003; Schlegel, 2003). The picture is more complicated than a separation and distancing process, with much cultural variability.

Even without the cultural concern, however, an ongoing theoretical debate in parent–adolescent relations addresses autonomy and relatedness dynamics. Two opposing views here have to do with how autonomy and relatedness interface. One view, called *emotional distancing model,* derives from a psychoanalytic perspective and and is based on the work of Douvan and Adelson (1966) and Blos (1979). It considers this stage a second **separation-individuation** (after infancy) (A. Freud,

1958; J. A. Hoffman, 1984; Kroger, 1998) where the adolescent moves away from the parent. This view is upheld by object-relations theorists (Kegan, 1994; Mahler, 1972) and is reflected in Erikson's (1959) theory of identity formation. It is prominent in much applied psychology, particularly in clinical and counseling areas. It is also in tune with the general Western individualistic worldview. Thus, this view may in fact be a product of normative individualism of the West and in turn feeds into it (see chap. 4). From such a perspective, distancing and detachment from the parent constitutes the "healthy pathway" toward the development of autonomy. Thus, Steinberg and Silverberg (1986) put forward the influential concept of emotional autonomy from parents as a key to adolescent individuation. Others (J. A. Hoffman, 1984; Kroger, 1998) have concurred. Recently, Steinberg and Silverberg's Emotional Autonomy Scale has been shown to have poor construct validity, questioning the emotional-distance model on methodological and conceptual grounds (Schmitz & Baer, 2001). Nevertheless, the model continues to be popular.

A contrasting view has also been proposed, espoused especially by attachment theory and self-determination theory (SDT). This view holds that autonomy develops out of secure attachment and close relationships with parents (e.g., Allen et al., 2003; Bretherton, 1987; Chirkov, Ryan, Kim, & Kaplan, 2003; Grossmann et al., 2005; Grotevant & Cooper, 1986; Ryan & Deci, 2000; Ryan & Lynch, 1989). This perspective is a challenge to assumptions regarding the necessity of adolescent separation for autonomy. It has also enjoyed cross-cultural research support. For example, many recent studies in diverse cultures point to adolescent autonomy and well-being as being associated more with close ties and attachment to parents than with detachment from them (see Box 6.1). This is found to be the case even in the United States where adolescent separation from parents is considered normal, even desirable.

*Conceptual Problems.*    Nevertheless, the individualistic view is tenacious. At times, even researchers who are critical of the emphasis put on detachment or separation still consider the main developmental task of adolescence to be separation-individuation (Kroger, 1998; Noom, 1999). As a possible solution, a distinction was drawn by Daniels (1990) between therapeutic and nontherapeutic separation-individuation, the former involving connectedness, also. Some semantic and conceptual issues arise here. If there is connectedness, then why is the process called separation? For example, Daniels recognizes that "becoming an autonomous individual and maintaining an interdependent relationship with one's parents are not mutually exclusive" (p. 107). Nevertheless, the process is still called separation-individuation.

---

Box 6.1    Relatedness is compatible with Autonomy

Several studies have found that relatedness is associated with auton-omy in both 'collectivistic' and 'individualistic' cultures:

- **Ryan & Lynch (1989) and Ryan Decin & Golnick (1995)** in the United States found positive rather than negative links between relatedness to parents and autonomy in adolescents.
- **Hodgins, Koettner & Duncan   (1996)** found a positive relation between autonomy and relatedness with parents and others among U.S. college students.
- **Kim, Butzel, & Ryan (1998)** showed a more positive relation between autonomy and relatedness than with separateness in both Korean and American samples.
- **Beyers & Goossens (1999); Chen & Dornbush (1998); Garber & Little (2001)** showed separateness from parents to be associated with developmental problems.
- **Chou (2000)** in Hong Kong found individuation to be associated with depression in adolescents.
- **Aydin & Öztütüncü (2001)** found depression to be associated with separateness in Turkish adolescents, but not with high parental control.
- **Meeus, Oosterwegel, & Vollebergh (2002)** found with Dutch, Turkish & Moroccon adolescents that secure attachment fosters agency.
- **Kwak** (2003) in review of research noted the common preference of adolescents for both autonomy and family relatedness.

---

Separation-individuation has accorded with an individualistic world-view; therefore it has been generally accepted without much question-ing. Even when it is recognized that the term does not describe the total adolescent growth process, it is still retained, but connectedness is added to it. This results in separateness and connectedness being together, which is a conceptual anomaly because these two constitute opposite poles of the same dimension, **interpersonal distance.** A related problem emerges in the construct of individuation, also. Here, too, there is an understanding that the individual achieves a sense of being sepa-rate from significant others but is also connected with them (Bartle & Anderson, 1991). Again this is problematic, because separation and con-nectedness fall on the same dimension, as, for example, empirically demonstrated by Frank, Avery, and Laman (1988).

Why then is this called individuation, only? Also, how is the state of being less individuated defined? Is it defined in terms of less separateness or less connectedness? We have here a conceptual confusion. It is reflected in individuality being construed at times to include connectedness (Grotevant & Cooper, 1986) but at times not. A recognition of the two underlying dimensions of interpersonal distance (separateness–relatedness) and **agency** (autonomy–heteronomy) would bring in clarification.

## AUTONOMY AND RELATEDNESS AS BASIC NEEDS

How autonomy and relatedness are construed is of key importance in understanding the development of the self as well as the conflicting findings and perspectives in the field. In chapter 4, we examined the related and separate self as well as independence–interdependence. The psychology of relatedness formed the general framework in that discussion. Here I am introducing "autonomy" into the picture. I now focus on the autonomy and relatedness interface in an attempt to put forward a systematic perspective on the self and self–other relations. The following discussion paves the ground toward a theory of self that I have developed deriving from the theory of family change (Kağıtçıbaşi, 1990, 1996a, 2005a) that I discussed in the last chapter. So, this discussion forms a natural link with chapter 5.

Autonomy and relatedness have long been considered basic human needs. This is seen in many areas of psychology ranging from psychoanalytic thinking and conflict theories of personality to evolutionary psychology (Assor, Kaplan, & Roth, 2002; Baumeister & Leary, 1995; Chirkov et al., 2003; Erikson, 1968; Franz & White, 1985; Guisinger & Blatt, 1994; Ryan & Deci, 2000). As mentioned in chapter 4, we see an early emphasis on these basic needs construed as conflicting by the "conflict theories of personality," originally espoused by Rank (1929, 1945), and then by Angyal (1951) and Bakan (1966, 1968). These theories posited the needs for independence from others and for interdependence with others, variously called "autonomy," "**agency**." or "separation-individualization," versus "surrender," "communion," "union," "fusion," or "dependency," respectively. A dialectic synthesis of these merging and separating tendencies is considered to engender a healthy personality, whereas too much stress put on one of these needs, at the cost of the other, is seen as a problem. However, Angyal and especially Bakan (1966, 1968) stressed particularly the dangers of denying only *one* of these needs—communion, possibly in reaction to dominant American individualism.

Other early theoretical views carried similar themes, for example, Deutsch's (1962) promotive interdependence (cooperation) versus contrient interdependence (competition); Benedict's (1970) high- or low-synergy societies; and expressiveness versus instrumentality in gender theories (Chodorow, 1974, 1978; Gilligan, 1982). In chapter 4, I pointed to criticisms of the individualistic stance of American psychology. From 1970s on, the critics proposed formulations combining the two basic needs for relatedness and autonomy, reminiscent of the model of psychological/emotional interdependence. For example, "ensembled individualism" (Sampson, 1988), "reciprocal individualism" (Rotenberg, 1977), "social individuality" (Lykes, 1985), and "relational individualism" (Chodorow, 1989) were suggested. Subsequently, utilizing an evolutionary perspective, Guisinger and Blatt (1994) proposed two basic developmental lines, through natural selection: "interpersonal relatedness" along with "self-definition," which interact in a dialectical fashion. This is very much in line with the thesis being proposed here.

In each one of these views, a "relational" conceptualization of the self is proposed, similar to the resultant "relational self" in the **family model of psychological/emotional interdependence.** Furthermore, in some of these formulations and also in the model of psychological/emotional interdependence, autonomy is attributed to the relational self. Excesses of individualism (and independence from others) are deplored by these critics as well as by others within American psychology and social science to whom I have already referred (Batson, 1990; Baumeister, 1986, 1991; Bellah et al., 1985; D. T. Campbell, 1975; Cushman, 1990; Etzioni, 1993; Hogan, 1975; Lasch, 1978, 1984; Sampson, 1977, 1988, 1989; M. B. Smith, 1993; C. Taylor, 1989; Wallach & Wallach, 1983, 1990) (see chap. 4).

As related to autonomy, agency has also been of key importance, especially in the social-cognitive theory of Bandura (1989). Indeed, it has received the greater attention in social psychology, at times at the expense of relatednesss. This has been the case in almost all Western psychology, including also European scholarship (e.g., Crockett & Silbereisen, 2000; Eckensberger, 1995; Neubauer & Hurrelmann, 1995). Thus, in response to this, for example, Baumeister and Leary (1995) saw the need to assert the fundamental nature of the "need to belong" or the relatedness motive. Similarly, Quintana and Kerr (1993) stressed the need to maintain attachment with parents in late adolescence.

I define autonomy as willful agency. This is also the dictionary definition of autonomy, which is "self-governed or ruled," rather than being ruled by someone else. In other words, it is to be an agent and to willingly carry out this agency, without a sense of coercion. The definition of self-determination theory (SDT) is very close, when it claims that

*[handwritten: self-determination theory]*

"true agency requires autonomy" (Ryan, Deci, & Grolnick, 1995, p. 624). Thus autonomy and agency overlap to such a great extent that they may be used interchangeably. In fact, this has often been the case.

Beyond their basic nature and therefore universality, the compatibility of autonomy and relatedness has also been asserted (e.g., Blatt & Blass, 1996; Cross & Madson, 1997; Guisinger & Blatt, 1994; Hodgins, Koeatner, & Duncan, 1996; Kağitçibaşi, 1996b, 2005a; Markus & Kitayama, 2003; J. G. Miller, 2003; Raeff, 1997; Wiggins & Trapnell, 1996). In their recent meta-analysis, Oyserman et al. (2002b) provide evidence for the independence and compatibility of autonomy and relatedness, showing that Americans are high in both individualism/personal agency and also in some aspects of relatedness. SDT as well as attachment theory have also been influential in this respect. I have noted these points in discussing adolescent–parent relations earlier. If autonomy and relatedness are basic needs, they should indeed coexist. So, why should it be necessary to assert this compatibility? This is because though considered basic needs, autonomy and relatedness have also been seen as conflicting, ever since the conflict theories of personality (Angyal, 1951; Bakan, 1966), as discussed previously. Therefore, given their presumed conflicting nature, the claims of coexistence have not been heard sufficiently well.

Thus, on the basis of several theoretical perspectives, we know that autonomy and relatedness can coexist; they are not antithetical to one another. These theoretical perspectives range from attachment theory to the psychological/emotional family model presented in chapter 5. However, the construal of autonomy and relatedness as opposing orientations has interfered with the recognition of their compatibility. Thus, the assumption of the necessity of separation for autonomy development is the key issue here. As mentioned before, this assumption derives mainly from psychoanalytic theory and reflects an individualistic worldview that stresses the separate individuality of the person.

## Two Underlying Dimensions

From such an individualistic perspective, autonomy is often seen to combine two distinct meanings. One of these concerns an agentic disposition to be able to act willfully, as mentioned earlier. The other has to do with being separate from others/being unique. When combined, the portrait of autonomy that emerges greatly resembles the **independent self** or individualism that we examined in chapter 4. Indeed some definitions, particularly emerging in cross-cultural scholarship on the study of self, show that these concepts are used to form a single prototype. Autonomy and separateness are thus seen to be intertwined.

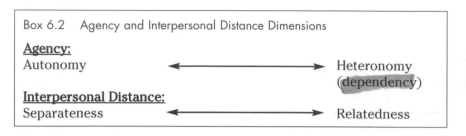

Box 6.2    Agency and Interpersonal Distance Dimensions

**Agency:**
Autonomy ←——————————→ Heteronomy
(dependency)

**Interpersonal Distance:**
Separateness ←——————————→ Relatedness

However, a closer look reveals that underneath the two meanings of being an agent and being separate from others lie two distinct dimensions. These may be called **agency** and **interpersonal distance** dimensions (Kağitçibaşi, 1996b, 2005a) (Box 6.2). Agency extends from autonomy on the one pole to heteronomy on the other. I use these terms in a way similar to Piaget's (1948) classic use of autonomous and heteronomous morality. Autonomous morality means subject to one's own rule or being self-governing; heteronomous morality means subject to another person's rule or being governed from outside.

Interpersonal distance dimension has to do with self–other relations, specifically with the degree of connectedness with others. It extends from relatedness to separateness poles (see Box 6.2). These dimensions are both logically and psychologically distinct; they are probably orthogonal (independent). They could be correlated, too, or fit together, loading on the same factor, in sociocultural contexts such as middle-class North American or Western European, where being both autonomous and separate is valued (Beyers, Goosens, Vansant, & Moors, 2003). However, they would not be associated in sociocultural contexts where being connected is valued and does not imply lacking autonomy (Kağitçibaşi, 2005a).

At this point we can draw some parallels between autonomy–heteronomy, relatedness–separateness, and normative and relational individualism–collectivism that I discussed in chapter 4. To summarize briefly, normative I–C concerns a *values orientation,* upholding either individual (I) or group interests (C). As such, normative individualism appears parallel to autonomy, whereas normative collectivism is akin to heteronomy. Another parallel can be seen with the vertical–horizontal I–C dimensions (Singelis et al., 1995; see chap. 4, this volume). Normative I–C is similar to vertical I–C; therefore, vertical individualism would be analogous to autonomy and vertical collectivism to heteronomy.

On the other hand, relational I–C has to do with a *self-orientation,* focusing on self–other relations. As such, relational individualism appears similar to separateness, whereas relational collectivism is akin to relatedness. Here, too, the further parallel with vertical–horizontal I–C is apparent. Relational I–C is similar to horizontal I–C; therefore, horizontal individualism would be comparable to separateness and

Box 6.3   Parallels among concepts

Normative I–C // Agency (Autonomy-Heteronomy)
Relational I–C // Interpersonal Distance (Separateness-Relatedness)

**More Specifically:**

| Vertical/<br>Horizontal I–C | | Normative/<br>Relational I–C | | Agency/Interpersonal<br>Distance Dimension |
|---|---|---|---|---|
| Vertical<br>individualism | // | Normative<br>individualism | // | Autonomy |
| Vertical<br>collectivism | // | Normative<br>collectivism | // | Heteronomy |
| Horizontal<br>individualism | // | Relational<br>individualism | // | Separateness |
| Horizontal<br>collectivism | // | Relational<br>collectivism | // | Relatedness |
| // : parallel to | | | | |

horizontal collectivism to relatedness (see Box 6.3). These parallels may help put the agency and interpersonal-distance dimensions and their opposing poles into perspective. This is in the sense that normative and relational I–C and horizontal–vertical I–C are conceptualized by different researchers but referring to somewhat similar phenomena. Seeing the similarities that exist among these concepts may help provide a better understanding of the common underlying structures and patterns through the apparent complexity in the field.

Coming back to the two dimensions of agency and interpersonal distance, we can say that if they are orthogonal, then it is possible for each pole of each to coexist with each pole of the other one, bringing out four possible alternative combinations. In other words, a person's standing on one of these dimensions does not affect or imply his or her standing on the other one. Accordingly, the interrelationship of agency and interpersonal distance dimensions is an empirical matter, not a logical or necessary one. This has significant implications for self-construal because it means that a person can be high in both autonomy (one pole of the agency dimension) and relatedness (one pole of the interpersonal-distance dimension)—thus the viability of the **autonomous–related self** (v, 1996b, 2005a).

## THE AUTONOMOUS–RELATED SELF AND A MODEL OF SELF-DEVELOPMENT

In the last chapter, we examined the autonomous–related self as emerging in the **family model of psychological/emotional interdependence** mainly because it is adaptive in changing lifestyles that imply this family model. This family model reflects a global pattern of urbanization and socioeconomic development in the **Majority World.** It is important to reiterate that in this family context psychological VOC is prevalent, reflecting closeness and warmth between parent and the child. There is also recognition of the need for autonomy in childrearing. There is, however, also strong **parental control,** which is basically "order setting" rather than domineering. This combination is adaptive in socioeconomic contexts with urban lifestyles, involving education and specialized work but where the culture is one of relatedness (relational collectivism). This is because urban lifestyles require individual decision making and initiative, that is, autonomy. However, the **culture of relatedness** with closely knit self–other relations also prevails. There is therefore parental control in childrearing rather than a permissive "letting go" that aims for the separate independence of the child. Thus, parental control that also allows for autonomy, rather than being oriented toward obedience, may function as a centripetal rather than a centrifugal force. The resultant self of the person developing in this type of family is the **autonomous-related self.**

In this chapter, we have come upon the autonomous–related self through a different conceptual path, that of the two basic needs for autonomy and relatedness and the two underlying dimensions of **agency** and **interpersonal distance.** Whether we pursue the path of the changing macrosystems of socioeconomic change, which imply changes in family patterns discussed in the last chapter, or that of the microsystem of the self, the development of the autonomous–related self emerges as a viable process (Box 6.4).

The left and the right sides of Box 6.4 summarize the two theoretical models I have developed and presented in this chapter and the previous one. They derive from different research backgrounds and perspectives. On the left-hand side, theory of family change derived from the **Value of Children Study** of the 1970s and was reconfirmed by both its original findings and those of its recent partial replication. It is further supported by a great deal of other work across cultures. The right-hand side presents the model of the self based on a logical and psychological conceptualization of two basic human needs and their underlying psychological dimensions. What is notable is that both theoretical routes point toward the viable autonomous–related self.

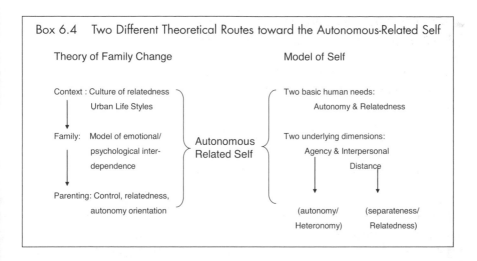

Box 6.4    Two Different Theoretical Routes toward the Autonomous-Related Self

We are now in a position to integrate these two theoretical perspectives. The basic dimensions of agency and interpersonal distance form the structure of such **integration**. When we consider the family models, parenting style and childrearing orientation, and the resultant self, and we juxtapose the two underlying dimensions of agency and interpersonal distance, we come up with a fourfold model (Kağitçibaşi, 1996b, 2005a). This is a general theoretical conceptualization that integrates the different family models that we saw in the last chapter, as well as the different parenting orientations and the resulting selves, which all go together (Box 6.5).

The orthogonal presentation of the two dimensions in this framework is made for the purposes of the theoretical argument. As I indicated before, their distinctness is the main point here. Though distinct, the two dimensions may be related in some sociocultural contexts (Beyers et al., 2003), but not in others; this is an empirical matter. They are suggested to be orthogonal across many domains of behavior (Wiggins & Trapnell, 1996). For example, Huiberts, Oosterwegel, Valk, Vollebergh, and Meeus (2006) find autonomy and connectedness to be independent of one another in both Moroccon and Dutch adolescents. We see in Box 6.5 that four different types of prototypical self-development are possible, varying in terms of their levels of autonomy and relatedness and systematically associated with their family and childrearing backgrounds. Again, for the purposes of the theoretical presentation, they appear as categorically different. However, it is more correct to think of them as varying from each other in terms of degree, rather than being categorical types. They differ from one another in degree along the two dimensions of agency and interpersonal distance.

Box 6.5    Agency, Interpersonal Distance and the Types of Selves in Context

**AGENCY**

**Autonomy**

| | |
|---|---|
| Family model of independence | Family model of psychological/ emotional interdependence |
| Self-reliance orientation | Order setting control and autonomy orientation |
| Autonomous-Separate self | Autonomous-related self |

**INTERPERSONAL DISTANCE**

**Separation**                                              **Relatedness**

| | |
|---|---|
| Hierarchical neglecting family | Family model of interdependence |
| Neglecting, indifferent orientation | Obedience orientation |
| Heteronomous- separate self | Heteronomous-related self |

**Heteronomy**

Note. From Autonomy and Relatedness in Cultural Context. Implications for Self and Family *(p.412), by* C. Ka itçiba i, 2005a.

The fourth pattern in Box 6.5, that of the **heteronomous–separate self,** may reflect a pathological case. It may emerge in the context of parental indifference or neglect (Baumrind, 1980; Maccoby & Martin, 1983). It has been reported in families characterized by hierarchy, rejection, and obedience orientation (Fisek, 1991). This type of a family context is not conducive to the development of either relatedness or autonomy.

In this chapter, it has become clear once again that the development of the autonomous–related self need not be constrained to the urban, developed contexts of the Majority World. Indeed, if autonomy and relatedness are basic needs, any family context that satisfies and reinforces these two needs would be expected to result in this type of self-development. There are many trends in this direction. Thus, we saw in the last chapter the example of the postmodern society searching for communal relatedness or soft human values (Inglehart, 2003; N. Young, 1992) possibly reflecting a shift from the **family model of independence** to the family model of psychological/emotional interdependence. Similarly, we discussed in chapter 4 social criticism in American psychology calling for a greater recognition of the need for relatedness and for community. More recent perspectives such as the SDT, attachment theory, and cross-cultural research on the development of the self, which I have discussed in this chapter, also strongly imply and endorse the autonomous–related self.

Of the four patterns of self-development, the autonomous–related self promises to be psychologically optimal, as it involves the satisfaction of both basic human needs for autonomy and relatedness. Research that I have reviewed earlier supports this claim (Blatt & Blass, 1996; Chirkov et al., 2003; Chou, 2000; Grotevant & Cooper, 1986; Ryan & Deci, 2000; Weisner, 2002). The other two, the **autonomous–separate self** and the **heteronomous related self** both leave something to be desired; one or the other of the two needs remains unfulfilled. From an analysis of the self reaching out to the macrosystem of societal values, one could claim that both the individualistic and the collectivistic worldviews have erred somewhat in emphasizing one of the needs at the cost of the other one. A balanced coexistence would promise to serve human well-being better. Indeed, balanced perspectives have been put forward that are rather similar to the views I have presented here (Imamoglu, 1998, 2003; Raeff, 2004, Ryan & Deci, 2000; Ryan & Lynch, 1989).

## THEORETICAL DEBATE AND CLARIFICATION

To reiterate, I have put forward a theoretical perspective on the two dimensions underlying self and self–other relations, namely **agency** and **interpersonal distance,** which derive from the two basic needs for autonomy and relatedness. These two dimensions range from autonomy to heteronomy and separateness to relatedness (Box 6.2). Autonomy, in turn is defined as willful agency, without any implication regarding separateness from others. I also pointed out that this is not how autonomy is understood by a number of researchers. Specifically, the common tendency is to define autonomy as agency *plus* separateness. I indicated that this tendency derives from two main theoretical backgrounds pitting autonomy against relatedness. One is the individualistic psychoanalytic perspective, reflected for example in object relations theory and adolescent research. The other one is early conceptualizations of conflict theories of personality. We can see that cross-cultural research and theory have also been influenced by these views, especially in conceptualizations of individualism–collectivism/independence–interdependence. The theoretical model that I have posited here questions these views.

## Two Types of Relatedness?

Recently, Rothbaum and Trommsdorff (2006) reviewed these issues and provided a conceptual framework to reconcile the contentious viewpoints. They note the conflicting orientations, supported by what they call Western (basically American) and cross-cultural research. The former, claimed by attachment theory and SDT, is that autonomy and relatedness are compatible, and even that for autonomy to emerge, relatedness is required. The latter (Markus & Kitayama, 1991; Triandis, 1995), looking at cultural differences, "*depict autonomy and relatedness as in opposition* to one another" (Rothbaum & Trommsdorff, 2006, emphasis in the original). Furthermore, conflicting research results provide evidence for these conflicting views.

Following Yamagishi's (2002) distinction between *trust* and *assurance*, Rothbaum and Trommsdorff (2007) proceed to reconcile this controversy by noting that there are different *types* of relatedness, based on trust or assurance. They claim that generalized trust is prevalent in Western and assurance in non-Western (collectivistic) societies, that individualistic and collectivistic societies are *qualitatively* different. They then theorize that assurance is inversely associated with autonomy whereas trust is compatible with it. Therefore, they reason that Western research finds an association between relatedness and autonomy because Western theories define relatedness in terms of general trust. By contrast, they note that in cross-cultural research a negative relation is found between relatedness and autonomy because cultural psychologists tend to equate relatedness with assurance.

Though thought provoking, there are some problems in this thesis. First of all, not all Western theory and research posits and finds a positive association between relatedness and autonomy. On the contrary, as I have discussed previously, and also earlier in chapter 4, from the start, conflict theories of personality (Angyal, 1951, Bakan, 1966, 1968; Rank, 1945), as well as psychoanalytic and object relations theoretical perspectives stressing **separation-individuation** have pitted autonomy against relatedness (A. Freud, 1958; Blos, 1979; J. A. Hoffman, 1984; Kroger, 1998; Mahler, 1972; Mahler et al., 1975; Panel, 1973a, 1973b; Steinberg & Silverberg, 1986). I also noted that this view reflects the normative individualism of the West. This has been a powerful perspective, particularly informing adolescent research and influencing *individualization* theory (Crockett & Silbereisen, 2000; Neubauer & Hurrelmann, 1995) as well as feminist scholarship (Chodorow, 1989; Gilligan, 1982; see Kegan, 1994). It has been and still is the prominent theoretical perspective behind clinical/counseling practice.

Rothbaum and Trommsdorff (2006), rightly, point to the attachment and SDT theory and research that have come to show a close association, even mutual reinforcement, of autonomy and relatedness. As I have discussed earlier, however, this can be seen as a reaction to the widespread emphasis put on separation and independence in American psychological thinking and teaching. Especially SDT emerged in reaction to Steinberg and Silverberg's (1986) concept of *emotional autonomy* defined as *detachment* of the adolescent from the parent as necessary for healthy development (Ryan & Lynch, 1989). To reiterate the conflicting perspectives, they are presented in Box 6.6 (see also Box 6.1).

A second issue concerns the conceptualization of *trust* and *assurance.* It may be claimed that perceived assurance is presupposed by trust. For example, to be able to trust someone to care for you, you would need to have at least a minimal level of assumption that she or he will. If you don't have this implicit sense of assurance of the other's readiness to support you, then you wouldn't trust that person. So to my mind, trust and (presumed) assurance make each other up in interpersonal relations.

The more important factor here may be the in-group–out-group distinction. Indeed, the main point that Yamagishi makes is that strong in-groups (intense group ties) prevent trust developing beyond the ingroup (Yamagishi et al., 1998). Because people with strong in-groups trust their in-groups totally, they turn to them when they need help and do not reach out to others. The in-group–out-group distinction appears to be more marked in more traditional societies that are also collectivistic. In-groups and out-groups are treated very differently. In-groups are both trusted and are also perceived to provide the assurance of support. Neither of these hold for out-groups. In individualistic contexts, on the other hand, the in-group–out-group distinction tends to be less evident, which may lead to the observed greater tendency for expanded trust and taking risks and trusting out-groups, to withdraw from them, however, at the first indication of evidence to the contrary.

Does this mean, however, that individualists and collectivists have qualitatively different relations? It may not be quite right to interpret Yamagishi's theory to mean that there is trust in individualistic contexts (and not in collectivistic ones) and assurance in collectivistic contexts (but not in individualistic ones). Rather, both would appear to exist in conjunction in all contexts, but *with whom?* and *to what extent?* is the issue. This is an empirical issue that needs to be clarified through further research.

There is a further problem of psychological interpretations of findings deriving from culture-level studies examining trust (Inglehart, 2003). These studies find a positive relation between individualism and trust. This is often explainable by the greater affluence of individualistic nations that enter into these national surveys (e.g., Allik & Realo, 2004; Gheorghiu & Vignoles, 2005). Indeed, the economic development dimension is often confounded in studies looking into the concomitants of

---

Box 6.6    Perspectives on Autonomy-Relatedness Dynamics

| Autonomy **versus** Relatedness | Autonomy **and** Relatedness |
|---|---|
| Psychoanalytic Theory | Attachment Theory |
| Conflict theories of personality | Self Determination Theory |
| Feminist Theory | Family Change Theory and Autonomous-Related Self Model |
| Cross Cultural Theory/research | |
| Values orientation to I-C; independent-interdependent self | |

---

individualism (Georgas et al., 2006). Trust may very well be one such case, as it may be argued that affluent people can better afford to trust others because they have less to lose; the same amount of possible risk is less significant for them than for the less affluent.

Finally, it is possible to propose different types of relatedness based on other factors than trust-assurance. For example, Raeff (1997) suggests that Hispanic, African American, and Euro-American samples may all value interdependence but of different types. Though this may well be the case, these typologies of relatedness appear rather problematic. First of all, it is not parsimonious to come up with different types. Second, it may prevent revealing possible common systematic underpinnings of theoretical importance.

*Two Types of Agency?*    A different typology is put forward by Markus and Kitayama (2003). Their seminal paper (Markus & Kitayama, 1991) greatly contributed to the popularization of the constructs of **independent–interdependent self** in cross-cultural psychology and to the development of a cultural awareness in mainstream social psychology. At the same time, however, objections were raised (e.g., v, 2005a; Killen, 1997; Mascolo & Li, 2004; Matsumoto, 1999; J. G. Miller, 2003; Raeff, 2004) on mainly two accounts. One is that East Asian "interdependent selves" are presented as selfless and without autonomy; the other is the more general dissatisfaction with the dichotomous thinking involved. To be fair, Markus and Kitayama (1991) pointed out that interdependence does not mean lack of **agency** (p. 228); nevertheless, they did stress the contrasts for the sake of their theoretical argument and claimed that for the **independent self** "autonomy [is] secondary to, and constrained by, the primary task of interdependence" (p. 227), thus in effect pitting autonomy against relatedness.

Recently they distinguished two types of agency, *disjoint* and *conjoint* (Markus & Kitayama, 2003). Disjoint agency is the "dominant American middle class model of agency ... as personal and bounded within the individual" (p. 7). Conjoint agency, on the other hand, is group based, akin to Bandura's (1989) collective efficacy and is shared with others. It is also reminiscent of Sampson's (1988) "ensembled individualism." This distinction implies that there are two ways of being an agent. Independent selves have disjoint agency whereas interdependent selves have conjoint agency. Markus and Kitayama think that autonomy, as, for example, stresses by self-determination theory (Deci & Ryan, 1995; Ryan & Deci, 2000), is disjoint agency.

This is also a thought-provoking view that promises to clarify certain issues in the field. However, it is again a dichotomous conceptualization, and it is not parsimonious. Just as Rothbaum and Trommsdorff (2006) proposed two types of relatedness, based on trust and assurance, here we see two types of agency. Instead of assuming different types of agency and relatedness, it would be more parsimonious to recognize agency and interpersonal distance as two dimensions of self–other dynamics and allow for variation on each. Thus, higher standing on both agency (autonomy) and interpersonal distance (separateness) would imply disjoint agency; whereas higher standing on agency but lower standing on interpersonal distance (relatedness) would imply conjoint agency. In other words, when autonomy is together with relatedness we have conjoint agency; when not, it is disjoint agency. Given the fact that both agency and interpersonal distance in my theory are *dimensions,* one can stand at different levels on each. This possibility for *variation* avoids dichotomizing or categorization.

Finally, as I explained before, in my theoretical perspective, autonomy is not necessarily a lone individual affair because it does *not* imply separateness from others. It is, therefore, agency, as willed and felt by the person (not coerced). In this sense, it has validity in both separate and related contexts as, for example, when the person makes an independent decision *or* when he willingly consults others and makes a decision on the basis of this consultation. Similarly, there is autonomy when the person is helpful because she chooses to do so *or* because she has internalized societal norms that uphold helpfulness. More recently, this view is finding greater acceptance with changing outlooks that question the assumed association between agency and unique separateness (Markus & Kitayama, 2003; J. G. Miller, 2003).

## Accounting for the Conflicting Perspectives

How can we account for the aforementioned conflicting perspectives and findings then? I believe that some of the problems noted may be due at least in part to confounding conceptualizations and measurement used in the field (see Kağitçibaşi, 2005a, for a review).[1] In particular, how can we explain why autonomy and relatedness are considered and found to be conflicting in cross-cultural research?

The implicit individualistic assumptions of mainstream (American) psychology have cast their shadow on cross-cultural research as well, particularly in how I–C /**independent–interdependent self** are construed. I have discussed this issue to some extent in both chapter 4 and in this chapter, but pursue it further here, particularly looking into how the concepts are operationalized in research. In cross-cultural research, we see the prevalence of the construal of individualism/independent self as including *both* separateness *and* autonomy. This is clearly influenced by an individualistic stance based on the conflict theories and psychoanalytic views of **separation-individuation** that assume separation to be a requisite of autonomy. Accordingly, as Rothbaum and Trommsdorff also note, in many (cross) cultural theories, individualistic separation is understood as autonomy (Hofstede, 1980, 1991; Rothbaum, Pott et al., 2000; S. H. Smith & Schwartz, 1997; Triandis, 1995). For example, S. H. Schwartz (2004) recast I–C as autonomy–embeddedness, pitting autonomy–embeddedness (connectedness) against one another.

This is particularly the case for normative I–C perspectives. As I discussed before, **normative I–C** is parallel to **horizontal–vertical I–C** (V–H I–C) (see Box 6.3), addressing whether the individual is or should be subordinate to the group or not. However, both the conceptualization and the measurement of H–V I–C have also included relational I–C regarding the self being related or not. Combining normative with relational I–C is commonly done, and it is confounding; for example, Singelis et al. (1995) state:

> Vertical or horizontal collectivism includes, perceiving the self as a *part of a collective*, either accepting inequality or stressing equality, respectively; vertical or horizontal individualism includes the conception of an *autonomous* individual and acceptance of inequality or emphasis on equality, respectively. (p. 240, emphasis added)

There is no room for relatedness in individualism or for autonomy in collectivism here. Similarly, Hofstede (1991) describes collectivism in

---

[1] This section and the following ones are based on Ka itçiba i (2005a).

terms of ingroups "which throughout peeople's lifetime continue to protect them in exchange for *unquestioning* loyalty" (pp. 260–261, emphasis added), expressing an assumption of lack of autonomy. This description appears to reflect "traditional" peasant society, typical of the **family model of interdependence** (see last chapter) rather than relational collectivism (**culture of relatedness**) that can exist in developed, urban socioeconomic contexts, as we have seen before.

Even in construals of **relational I–C**, however, an independent–interdependent self still combines **agency** and **interpersonal-distance** dimensions. Thus, although Markus and Kitayama do not claim that autonomy and interdependence are mutually exclusive, they nevertheless construe them in oppositional terms, thus their definitions, "[independent self] involves a conception of the self as an *autonomous,* independent person" (1991, p. 228) and, "The cultural press in the [interdependent model] is not to become *separate and autonomous* from others but to fit-in with others" (1994, p. 97, emphasis added).

The measures developed to study independence and interdependence empirically have followed Markus and Kitayama's conceptualization. Therefore, we find items in the same scale measuring both interpersonal relatedness and agency dimensions, with interdependent-self scales including both relatedness and lack of agency (heteronomy) and independent-self scales including both separateness and agency (autonomy) (Kitayama, Markus, Kurokawa, Tummala, & Kato, 1991; Singelis, 1994). Regarding the latter, for example, Gudykunst, Matsumoto, Ting-Toomey, and Nishida (1996) state, "All items on the independent self construal scale clearly reflect individuals being autonomous, unique people" (p. 527). The same thing has been the case with I–C scales (Hui & Yee, 1994; Matsumoto, Weissman, Preston, & Brown Kupperbusch, 1997; Triandis et al., 1988; Yamaguchi, 1994).

This situation has been responsible, at least partially, for some of the conflicting findings in the field (see Kağitçibaşi, 2005a). For example, Uskul, Hynie, and LaLonde (2004), in a comparison of Turkish and Canadian university students, found a difference between them on interdependence (Turks scoring higher) but not in independence on Singelis's (1994) scale. They attribute this partially to the fact that the scale measures autonomy and assertiveness, rather than interdependent self-construal.

The two dimensions of agency and interpersonal distance may be correlated and may fit together in some cultural contexts where being both autonomous and separate are valued, but they may not in other cultural contexts where being related does not mean lacking autonomy. In other words, the relationship between these two dimensions and their poles is empirical, not logical, or we can say that they are in a probabilistic, not a necessary relationship to one another.

## MEASURING THE AUTONOMOUS–RELATED SELF

What is needed, therefore, are different measures that assess **interpersonal distance** (relatedness–separateness) and **agency** (autonomy–heteronomy). Box 6.7 gives some measures that have been developed for this purpose: relatedness (related self), autonomy (autonomous self) and **autonomous–related self** measures.

It is possible to use the Relatedness and Autonomy scales, only, and to look at a person's standing on these, such that if she or he gets an above-median score on both scales, this would point to an autonomous–related self. A person scoring below median on both scales would be considered to have a **heteronomous–separate self**. Higher than median on Relatedness and lower than median on Autonomy would connote a **heteronomous–related self**, and the reverse would point to an **autonomous– separate self**. It is important to note here that the two dimensions of interpersonal distance and agency are not confounded in the same measure. Each scale is therefore conceived to be unidimensional with a single factor. Factor analyses confirmed this. These scales were used with Turkish university students (Kağitçibaşi, Baydar, & Cemalcilar, 2006).

We have also devised parallel scales of autonomous, related, and autonomous–related self in family context. This was done in order to deal with self-construal from a developmental perspective. Particularly in view of the formative significance of family dynamics and relationships during adolescence, these scales contain items that refer to the time the respondent was "growing up" (Box 6.8).

This scale was used with university students and business executives in Turkey with varied socioeconomic standing (Tuncer, 2006). The different construals of self-in-family were found to predict attitudes toward paternalistic leadership style (Aycan, 2006) in both samples. The related self was positively associated with positive attitudes toward the paternalistic leadership style; the autonomous self was negatively associated, and the autonomous-related self was in between. The Traditional Family Ideology Scale (Georgas,1993) mediated these relationships. These scales are currently being used in other cross-cultural research also (Güngör, v, & Phalet, 2006; see also O. Otyakmaz & Kağitçibaşi, 2006).

## EMPIRICAL EVIDENCE TOWARD A CONVERGENCE

In this chapter, I have put forward an integrated perspective on the self and its development, which also built upon the material I have covered in the last two chapters. In this last section on the self, I provide more

Box 6.7   Autonomy – Relatedness Scales (Ka itçiba i)

**Autonomous Self Scale**

1. People who are close to me have little influence on my decisions.
2. I do not like a person to interfere with my life even if he/she is very close to me.
3. I feel independent of the people who are close to me.
4. I lead my life according to the opinions of people to whom I feel close. (R)
5. The opinions of those who are close to me influence me on personal issues. (R)
6. While making decisions, I consult with those who are close to me. (R)
7. On personal issues, I accept the decisions of people to whom I feel very close. (R)
8. I usually try to conform to the wishes of those to whom I feel very close. (R)
9. I can easily change my decisions according to the wishes of those who are close to me. (R)

**Alpha = 0.74**

**Related Self Scale**

1. I need the support of persons to whom I feel very close.
2. I prefer to keep a certain distance in my close relationships. (R)
3. Generally, I keep personal issues to myself. (R)
4. The people who are close to me strongly influence my personality.
5. I think often of those to whom I feel very close.
6. I do not worry about what people think of me even if they are close to me. (R)
7. Those who are close to me are my top priority.
8. My relationships to those who are close to me make me feel peaceful and secure.
9. I do not share personal matters with anyone, even if very close to me. (R)

**Alpha = 0.78**

**Autonomous-Relational Self Scale**

1. It is important to have both close relationships and also to be autonomous.

Box 6.7    (Continued)

2. Even if the suggestions of those who are close are considered, the last decision should be one's own.

3. A person who has very close relationships cannot make his/her own decisions. (R)

4. A person should be able to oppose the ideas of those who are close.

5. Giving importance to the opinions of those who are close to me means ignoring my own opinions. (R)

6. Being very close to someone prevents being independent. (R)

7. A person can feel both independent and connected to those who are close to him/her.

8. In order to be autonomous, one should not form close relationships. (R)

9. A person may be attached to those who are close, and at the same time, expect respect for any differences of opinion.

**Alpha = 0.84**

---

Box 6.8    Autonomous-Related Self- in-Family Scales (Ka itçiba i)

**Autonomous Self-in-Family Scale**

1. I feel independent of my family.
2. I usually try to agree with the wishes of my family. (R)
3. I do not have to think the way my family does.
4. People should receive approval from their families for their future plans. (R)
5. avoid making decisions with which my family would not agree. (R)
6. On personal issues, I accept the decisions of my family. (R)
7. I would not be close to someone whom my family does not agree. (R)
8. Independent of my family, I can not make my decisions easily. (R)
9. I can easily change my decisions according to the wishes of my family. (R)

**Alpha = .84**

**9 Items, Lowest factor loading: Item 1: .53**

---

Box 6.8    (*Continued*)

**Related Self-in-Family Scale**

1. I prefer to keep a certain distance in my relationship with my family. (R)
2. During hard times, I would like to know that my family will be with me.
3. The time that I spend with my family is not important for me. (R)
4. Feeling very close to the family is a good thing.
5. My family is my top priority.
6. I feel myself closely attached to my family.
7. My relationship with my family makes me feel peaceful and secure.
8. I am very close with my family.
9. I don't enjoy spending much time with my family. (R)

**Alpha = .84**

**8 items, Lowest factor loading: Item I: 49**

**Autonomous-Related Self-in-Family Scale**

1. One should not hesitate to express his/her own ideas, even if he/she values his/her family.
2. A person may be very close to his/her family and at the same time can make his/her decisions.
3. A person can feel both independent and emotionally connected to his/her family.
4. A person may be attached to his/her family, and at the same time, expect respect for any differences of opinion.

**Alpha = .77**

**4 Items, Lowest factor loading: Item 1: .59**

---

empirical evidence to substantiate the theoretical perspectives I have put forward. Some of this evidence was mentioned before, but it may be helpful to present it again in a more coherent way.

A great deal of recent research points to the distinctness of the **agency** and **interpersonal-distance** dimensions and the compatibility of autonomy and relatedness. In a recent structural modeling of autonomy (Beyers et al., 2003), separation and agency emerged as two independent dimensions. Other work also finds relatedness and autonomy to be independent of one another (Huiberts et al., 2006; Wiggins & Trapnell, 1996). In particular, SDT, attachment theory, and adolescent research informed by them have emphasized the compatibility of autonomy and relatedness, as I discussed earlier in the section titled The Adolescent–Parent Relation (e.g., Allen et al., 2003; Bretherton, 1987; Chirkov et al., 2003; Grossmann et al., 2005; Grotevant & Cooper, 1986; Ryan & Deci, 2000).

Thus, more positive relations are found between closeness to parents and autonomy than between separation from parents and autonomy even in the United States, where separation from parents is culturally endorsed (Ryan et al., 1995; Ryan & Lynch, 1989). Relatedness is found to be associated with well-being, for example, among Dutch, Turkish, and Moroccon adolescents in the Netherlands (Meeus, Oosterwegel, & Vollebergh, 2002). In contrast, Chou (2000) found two components of "emotional autonomy" (Steinberg & Silverberg, 1986), separation and de-idealization of parents, to be associated with depression in Chinese adolescents, and Aydin and Öztütüncü (2001) found depression and negative schema to be associated with separateness but not with **parental control** in Turkish adolescents. Separateness from parents was found to relate to developmental problems in various other groups (Beyers & Goosens, 1999; Chen & Dornbush, 1998; Garber & Little, 2001). Finally, Kwak (2003), reviewing a great deal of research from immigrant groups in the United States, noted a common preference of adolescents for both autonomy and relatedness. All of this work indicates the viability, indeed the optimal nature, of the **autonomous–related self** across cultures, including those of the United States.

From another perspective, research examining the family provides supportive evidence. Parenting that integrates control, warmth, and autonomy is seen in the psychologically/emotionally interdependent family context, and it engenders the autonomous–related self. As discussed in chapter 5, the coexistence of parental control and autonomy orientations in childrearing together with relatedness are found across cultures (Cha, 1994; Deković et al., 2006; Jose et al., 2000; Kwak, 2003; Lansford et al., 2003; C.-Y. C. Lin & Fu, 1990; Phalet & Schonpflug, 2001; Smetana & Gaines, 1999; Stewart et al., 1999; Yau & Smetana, 1996). These studies have been conducted in various nations with collectivistic cultures of relatedness and with ethnic-minority groups in Western European and North American contexts. The common theme running through them is the **family model of psychological/emotional interdependence.**

Furthermore, as we saw in the last chapter, research emerging from the United States and Northern Europe also points to the viability of parental control and warmth, together with endorsement of autonomy. For example, Silk et al. (2003) in their study with American adolescents showed that parental control and parental autonomy granting are distinct parenting constructs, not opposite ends of a continuum. Thus, we may indeed be observing a convergence here. This convergence is toward the family model of psychological/emotional interdependence rather than the **family model of independence,** in contrast to the modernization perspective. It is also toward the autonomous–related self, rather than the **autonomous–separate self**. The recent 27-country comparative study of Georgas et al. (2006) studying educated urban young people provides further evidence for such convergence.

In another recent study (Kağitçibaşi, Baydar et al., 2007), university students from the United States, Hong Kong, Sweden, and Turkey all endorsed the compatibility of autonomy and relatedness, agreeing with the statement, "A person can be both autonomous and closely attached to someone," thus recognizing the autonomous–related self construal. In Turkey, adults also agreed with the statement, the level of agreement being higher among the younger and more modern urban groups. This may be seen as evidence for the emergence of the autonomous–related self-construal emerging with socioeconomic development in the family model of psychological/emotional interdependence. It is in line with the aforementioned VOC Study results over three decades in Turkey (v & Ataca, 2005; v et al., 2005) and other VOC studies (see chap. 5). Specifically, there are intergenerational, rural–urban, and temporal differences/changes in values attributed to children and expectations from children. These all show decreasing **material interdependencies** but continuing or increasing **psychological/emotional interdependencies** in the family with socioeconomic development, increased education, urban standing, and young age. The family model of psychological/emotional interdependence is the emerging model, which engenders the autonomous–related self.

## From Diversity to Convergence

From the very beginning, I have pointed to diversity across cultures. For any culturally valid psychology, it is important to recognize and try to understand this diversity. This is what I have done, especially in the last three chapters with regard to the self. In the process of making sense of the diversity, however, we have also seen the underlying dimensions of self and of human relations. At both the level of the family and that of the self, these underlying dimensions provide the structures that make for similarities and differences across cultures.

Of key importance here is the concept of adaptation. The functionality of a pattern of behavior for optimal adaptation to the environment is what makes that behavior be maintained over time. Thus, a **heteronomous-related self** is maintained as long as it is functional for adapting to environmental demands. In a relatively stable agrarian subsistence economy, for example, this would be the case. Also, the family model of (total) interdependence would be sustained over time in the same type of sociocultural economic context.

When environmental conditions change, however, change is also implicated in family and the self. This change may not be in a one-to-one
fashion; there can be delays or mismatches. Nevertheless, the general
pattern of change would be expected to correspond roughly to the contextual changes. This is why there is a general tendency toward convergence in the world. This is because globally lifestyles are becoming more
similar in many ways. Thus, more similar environmental demands
emerge, and to adapt to them, some convergence in family/human patterns appears to be emerging. A great deal of research from many countries that I have reviewed here and in the last two chapters shows that it
is toward the **family model of psychological/emotional interdependence**
and the **autonomous–related self.** At the basis of such a convergence lie
a number of significant factors.

One is the two basic human needs for autonomy and relatedness,
which when recognized and satisfied, imply the autonomous–related self.
The compatibility and coexistence of these apparently conflicting needs is
the main reason for the convergence toward this type of self. Otherwise,
at least one of these needs remains unfulfilled. The other significant factor
is the global social change. In particular, the shifting of populations from
rural to urban lifestyles renders certain family and human patterns
more adaptive. In particular, decreasing **material interdependencies**
among generations imply less family hierarchy and obedience orientation
in childrearing, allowing autonomy to emerge. Autonomy also emerges in
response to environmental demands for more individual efficacy and decision making with increased levels of education and specialization in the
workplace.

Though deriving from different perspectives, the basic needs on the
one hand and globally converging environmental demands on the other,
indicate the same point of convergence, the family model of psycholog-
ical/emotional interdependence and the autonomous–related self. This
appears to be a healthy human model.

There are two important points to be noted here. One is that this is a
*theoretical* prediction; it is a statement of what should happen. Obviously,
a myriad of factors are involved in real-life situations that complicate
them immensely. It is impossible to foresee them all. The other is that this
theoretical prediction is not exclusive of others; neither does it claim to
be all-inclusive. In other words, all kinds of other theoretical perspectives
can obviously be formulated and predictions can be made accordingly.
What I propose is *one* healthy human model; there can be others.

Regarding the first point, there is indeed a caveat, here. As I indicated at
the end of chapter 5, this "natural" tendency toward convergence may be
counteracted by exogenous factors that work toward another kind of convergence. Specifically, the American-dominated mass media can work as a

force toward the **family model of independence** and the **autonomous–separate self**. This could happen through cultural diffusion or a general process of imitation of the American or Western model by the rest of the world, as it is assumed to be the most "modern" or "developed." This would create a less than optimal condition for human well-being, because one of the two basic human needs, that for relatedness, would not find adequate expression. As we have seen, there is ample evidence emerging from the United States or the West in general that stresses the importance of this need. Nevertheless, often what is reflected in the mass media is normative individualism or individualistic ideology, which does not necessarily reflect 'reality."

Given this risk, psychologists and developmental scientists and other social scientists would do well to make an effort to disseminate their knowledge and to "give psychology away." In the second part of the book, I am going to elaborate on such applications of the theoretical perspectives presented in the first part.

## SUMMARY AND MAIN POINTS

- The links between cultural values and childrearing patterns can provide clues for understanding the development of self. Parenting is the key here.
- Notwithstanding common features in parenting, interpreted as intuitive parenting, cultural differences exist in modes of parent–child interaction even in infancy (e.g., body contact vs. face-to-face interaction), which may influence the development of the self.
- Similarly, from the perspective of attachment theory, evolution-based attachment between infants and their caregivers is universal, but its specific behavioral manifestations may differ from one context to another.
- Cultural and cross-cultural research on parenting of children mirrored research on parenting of infants, tracing two pathways of development—toward autonomy and relatedness.
- Recently, this dichotomous conceptualization has been questioned, and findings on parenting of infants and children have evidenced the coexistence of autonomy and relatedness, in line with Kağitçibaşi's autonomous–related self construal.
- Parenting styles (authoritarian, authoritative, and permissive) is an important aspect of parenting, which should be investigated by taking into account sociocultural contexts.
- Two contrasting perspectives inform research on adolescence. One view deriving from psychoanalytic theory emphasizes the necessity

of adolescent separation for autonomy, whereas the contrasting view is upheld by attachment and self-determination theories and claims that autonomy develops out of secure attachment and close relationships with parents.

- Although assumed to be conflicting, autonomy and relatedness are basic needs.
- From an individualistic perspective, autonomy has meant both being an agent and being separate from others. However, agency and interpersonal distance are two distinct dimensions underlying self and self–other relations. Agency dimension extends from autonomy on the one pole to heteronomy on the other, and the interpersonal-distance dimension extends from relatedness to separateness. Autonomy concerns only the agency dimension.
- Confounding conceptualization and measurement may be the reasons for construing autonomy and relatedness as conflicting. Different measures assessing autonomy and relatedness are needed.
- Among the four patterns of self-development, the autonomous–related self is psychologically optimal as it fulfills both of the basic human needs for autonomy and relatedness. The autonomous-separate self and the heteronomous-related self are both lacking in the satisfaction of one or the other of the two needs. The fourth pattern, the **heteronomous–separate self,** may reflect a pathology case because it fulfills neither of the two basic needs.
- Two types of relatedness based on trust and assurance (Rothbaum & Trommsdorff) and two types of agency as disjoint and conjoint (Markus & Kitayama) have been construed. However, it is more parsimonious to use agency and interpersonal-distance dimensions to account for these variations.
- Recent cross-cultural research points to the compatibility of autonomy and relatedness with a convergence toward the family model of psychological/emotional interdependence and toward the autonomous–related self.

## DISCUSSION QUESTIONS

1. How do different childrearing patterns characterized by connectedness or separation shape self development? Give examples referring to cultural differences.
2. Why have autonomy and relatedness been construed as conflicting?

3. What does cross-cultural research on parent–infant and parent–child relations reveal with respect to autonomy and relatedness?
4. Explain how psychoanalytic perspective on the one hand, and attachment and self-determination theories on the other deal with autonomy and relatedness in adolescence.
5. What are the two dimensions underlying self and self–other relations? Given these dimensions, what are the four patterns of self-development proposed by Kağitçibaşi? Among them, which one is psychologically optimal? Why?
6. What are the factors that may be expected to lead to a convergence toward the family model of psychological/emotional interdependence and the autonomous–related self.

# II

# IMPLICATIONS FOR SOCIAL ISSUES AND APPLICATIONS

# 7

# Induced Change: The Role
# of Psychology

## ABOUT PART II

"If the times don't fit you, you fit the times" is a saying attributed to the prophet Mohammed, which if understood properly, could be a golden rule of change and progress. It refers to the value of adaptation to changing contexts that has been a main theme of this book. To develop an insight into the processes of adaptation particularly in the context of social change, individual–society links need to be revealed. This was attempted in the first part of the book. In the second part, the emphasis is on applications regarding how adaptation and change can occur and how they can be promoted and facilitated. However, focusing on applications does not mean that theory is relegated to a secondary role. Indeed, there is much wisdom in K. Lewin's (1951) classic words that "there is nothing as practical as a good theory" (p. 169). The emphasis on theory is not opposed to but is parallel to an applied emphasis because applications have to be based on sound theory and research. If not informed by theory, applied work runs the risk of turning into blind empiricism or "shots in the dark" that cannot be afforded, especially not in the **Majority World.**Part I of this book has dealt with the theoretical linkages between the self, family, and society, focusing mainly on human development within a cultural context. The discussions have been mainly theoretical though I have often looked into the implications of the viewpoints for applications and policies. The present chapter elaborates this approach further and serves as a link between the first and the second parts of the book. In Part II, the interface between theory and application is stressed, and the emphasis is on applications. In this chapter I consider the role of psychology vis-à-vis applications/interventions/policies designed to improve human well-being. This discussion provides the basic perspectives and leads to the examination of some social problems and intervention studies in the following chapters.

Another main theme in this book from the very beginning is social relevance, which has to do with an involved stance. Here I pursue this theme further and also discuss at length the political implications of an involved stance. In the following two chapters, two different applied topics are presented. They constitute important cases in point for the present discussions. Chapter 8 deals with intervention involving the early enrichment of children's lives for their overall healthy psycho-social development and well-being. It integrates some of the points made in chapters 2 and 3 with the views presented in this chapter. Chapter 9 presents a specific longitudinal intervention research and its follow up covering a 22-year period. This research that I conducted with my colleagues demonstrates that early intervention can have sustained positive effects over a considerable period of time. Chapter 10 deals with immigration and **acculturation** as a topic of much current interest. My treatment of it will be in the light of the conceptualizations put forward in chapters 4, 5, and 6. The final chapter attempts an overall integration of theory and policy-relevant application. It attempts to synthesize and put a closure on the research, theory, and applied emphasis of the volume.

## PSYCHOLOGY AND DEVELOPMENT

For most psychologists, development means child development or human development through the life span, at most. In either case, the unit of analysis is the individual, though there is a growing recognition of the context of development. I have examined these issues in some detail in the previous chapters. Here I want to focus on a different conceptualization of development in current usage by social scientists, planners, and policymakers throughout the world. This is the construal of human development at the societal level.

For some time, development, in this sense, was equated with economic growth and operationalized in terms of purely economic indicators, such as the per capita GNP. Today there is a questioning of economic growth as the main indicator of societal development and a growing recognition of the dynamic link between human development and societal development. For example, the World Bank is focusing more and more on the role of education in improving the efficiency and motivation of the labor force, and on the well-being of women with implications for better child care and lower fertility. This long-overdue recognition that social development cannot be subsumed under economic development has paved the way for a new concept of human development (at the macro level) to emerge from the United Nations Development Program (UNDP).

Since 1990, UNDP has been publishing *The Human Development Report* on an annual basis to present the global situation and to rank the countries by selected human development indicators. One hundred and seventy-seven countries are included in the ranking. Several indicators are used for this purpose such as life expectancy at birth, access to health services, access to safe water and sanitation, adult literacy, combined primary and secondary school enrollment rates, daily newspaper circulation, televisions, and GNP per capita. These indicators are used to form three main components of the Human Development Index (HDI)—health, education, and income. HDI, which is used as the overall indicator, can further be adjusted for gender disparity.

Is this all beyond the scope of psychology? At first glance it appears so. However, a closer scrutiny of some of the indicators involved and their wide-ranging implications discloses the relevance of psychology, alongside the other social science disciplines, to the issues under question. This is as it should be, because the focus is on *human* development, even if macro (aggregate) criteria are being used in its conceptualization and operationalization. It has also been referred to as social development. Yet, psychologists themselves appear to have hardly recognized the relevance of their discipline for global human development.

A number of reasons come to mind to explain this situation; I review them briefly, to relate them to some of the issues in the global applications of psychology that I discuss in this chapter.

- The definition of psychology as a pure science and the condescending attitude toward applied research have caused a "distancing" from real problems. This has also led to the perceived and at times real conflict between scientific rigor and social relevance. The original adoption by psychology of the physical science model, aspiring to discover universal laws of behavior, has meant the abstraction of behavior from its total environment and its reproduction in pure form in the laboratory. Though this scientific orientation has served psychology well for decades, particularly in certain areas of specialization, it has at the same time entailed a neglect of the existing diversity in the world and the "real-life problems" not easily amenable to the scrutiny of the experimental laboratory.
- These basic characteristics of psychology, as it developed first in Europe and then permeated North America and flourished there, were soon after transferred in ready-made form to the rest of the

world. They were accepted by the Western-trained psychologists in the Majority World with acquiescence and without questioning. Though there are significant exceptions today emerging in many parts of the Majority World, the overall picture remains more or less the same.

- The traditionally applied area within psychology—clinical psychology—has not been relevant for development efforts, given its individual focus and exclusive involvement with psychopathology.

- Psychology has remained rather "estranged" from the important societal issues in the Majority World also because it is an imported discipline. As such, it has typically adopted Western psychology's theories and problems, being content in "transferring" knowledge, rather than "producing" knowledge. Often the transferred knowledge has been of limited use, being the product of another cultural milieu.

- Majority World psychologists, trained in the West, continue to work on similar issues when they return to their countries. This is because of their Western socialization into the field and because Western psychological circles remain their main reference groups and American journals their main publication targets.

- Even when dealing with issues of social importance, psychologists, given their basically individual level of analysis, tend to locate the "problem" in the individual and do not deal adequately with contextual factors. For example, Nunes (1993) complained about school psychologists' explanation of school failure in Brazil in terms of lower capacity of the working-class children (who score lower on adapted intelligence tests), ignoring the social context in which they grow up and the misfit between the home and the school cultures. There are similar complaints in Europe regarding ethnic-minority students. Such a tendency toward "blaming the victim" does not help to change the unfavorable environmental conditions either at home or at school.

- Indeed, the individualistic stance of Western psychology can be used (or misused) to justify existing social inequalities by "blaming the victim," or in terms of the "just world hypothesis," which claims that people get what they deserve. This is a problem related to seeing individuals as solely responsible for what happens to them and can be relevant for a wide range of explanations spanning from psychological health/pathology to attributions of economic success/failure (Leahy, 1990). This view presupposes initial (equal) opportunity and choice; where this assumption does not hold, it is not warranted.

- Given the previous characteristics of psychological research, psychologists have typically shied away from confronting problems of development, such as population, education, health, migration, and so on. The large-scale proportion of such problems, not amenable to an individual level of analysis, has been a deterrent for psychologists. Yet, these are all human problems with distinct cognitive, motivational, and behavioral aspects that in fact require psychological inquiry to be better understood,
- Finally, the lack of involvement of psychologists with human problems also derives from an unawareness of the relevance of their knowledge for such problems, on the one hand, and a hesitation to act on the basis of insufficient knowledge, on the other (Suedfeld & Tetlock, 1992). Yet, psychology is relevant to human problems, and there is indeed accumulated psychological knowledge, even if insufficient in some respects, that can be used to solve them.

These interrelated factors all play a role in the low levels of involvement of psychologists in development efforts in the Majority World. This situation has meant that psychologists have not in fact contributed what they could and should to the solution of important human development problems. Correspondingly, it has also had some significant implications for psychology, itself, as a discipline. Because societal development is often the first item on the agenda in developing countries, scientific disciplines that are seen to contribute to societal development have a high status and enjoy priority in allocation of resources for research, recruitment in large-scale projects, and so on. J. B. P. Sinha (1993) noted, "Psychology has yet to develop as a policy science. ... It has neither a macro database, nor a national perspective, nor a planning model to claim any attention" (p. 146). It lags behind, as it is seen to be irrelevant to societal development issues.

Just as serious are some of the implications of psychology's noninvolvement for social policies drawn up in the Majority World. In effect, it means that social policies are *not* informed by psychological knowledge and expertise. There is commonly a lack of scientific expertise in Majority World government agencies and ministries. If the existing expertise in a few universities is not tapped either (because it is not considered relevant), poorly formulated policies emerge, entailing a great waste of economic and human resources. There are many examples of such poor policymaking in population, health, and education areas in the Majority World.

The result of all this is often slow social development, which tends to lag behind economic development (Moghaddam, 1990; UNESCO,

1982). One factor is the relatively low contribution of human sciences, especially of psychology, to *social* development efforts, compared with the contribution of physical and material sciences and engineering to economic and technological development. Psychology has tended to be "modulative" (in reacting to societal change) rather than "generative" (in instigating societal change) (Moghaddam, 1990); this timidity has been costly. To remedy the situation, it is incumbent upon the psychologists in the Majority World to take the initiative without waiting to be asked, to make their knowledge available and to partake in policy-relevant projects.

## Theory and Application

The gist of the preceding discussion is not a call to **Majority World** psychologists to do only applied research. There has been this kind of a call for a problem-oriented, non-theory-driven approach for developing countries (Connolly, 1985; Moghaddam & Taylor, 1986). But this is a patronizing stance, reflecting the conventional habit of looking "West" for theory and "East" for data (Kağitçibaşi, 1995). More important, theoretical work is crucial in informing policy-relevant research. To be of value, the theory should be culturally valid. This is an issue of crucial significance, given the fact that most psychology in the Majority World is imported.

Formulating a theory that has cultural validity requires the production of knowledge. Both cross-cultural theory testing and indigenous theory construction would contribute to this process. Indeed, this is well recognized by a number of socially concerned psychologists from developing countries in a call for a more integrative approach involving endogenous psychological knowledge and culture-sensitive theory development (e.g., Kağitçibaşi, 1995; Nsamenang, 1992; D. Sinha,1989; D. Sinha & Kao, 1988; J. B. P. Sinha, 1993; Z. M. Wang, 1993). The concept of **endogenous development**, first proposed by UNESCO (Huynh, 1979), is now receiving wide acceptance. It centers on humans and takes into consideration the characteristics and inherent strengths of the societies involved.

However, when theories or models are used implicitly in development plans, they tend to be those transferred from the West. Thus in development "recipes," there are often tacit assumptions about the underlying human factors—a human model for development. This, in turn, is often based on the Western experience and is informed by Western psychology. Though the model is assumed to hold universally, it may in fact be quite at odds with the local reality. An example of such a misfit was the failure of attempts at promoting economic growth through an individualistic competitive achievement motivation model in collectivistic cultures such as India (J. B. P. Sinha, 1985) where "social achievement motivation" is pervasive (Agarwal & Misra, 1986). What is required is a different human model, one that combines achievement with extension needs. The need for extension refers to relating to others; thus when combined with the need for achievement, the need for *social* achievement emerges, "which is shown to facilitate collective efforts for development" (J. B. P. Sinha, 1993, p. 145).

This example fits in with the discussion of achievement in chapter 4 and the family/self models in chapters 5 and 6. Specifically, an individualistic achievement motivation model is in line with the family/self model of independence, whereas social achievement motivation fits in better with a model of psychological/emotional interdependence. As discussed in chapter 5, there are unidirectional change expectations of the tenacious modernization theory, toward the Western model. Most tacit assumptions about human factors in social development models subscribe to the family/self model of independence. Yet, as I have shown, the main shift in the world with socioeconomic development is *not* toward the model of independence but toward the model of psychological/emotional interdependence. What is needed is culturally valid theory to be developed and used in development models rather than tacit assumptions, based on imported knowledge.

Up to this point, I have been discussing the problems of lack of involvement of psychologists in development efforts and the need for the integration of culturally valid theory into applied work in the Majority World. There is a related issue, which is not as readily apparent but which nevertheless has something to do with the modulative, rather than the generative stance of psychology, noted by Moghaddam (1990). This is the role definition of the psychologist-scientist as the "student" of human behavior, trying to understand and explain phenomena, with the ultimate ambition of predicting them, which is to be contrasted with another possible role definition that in addition to the aforementioned goals, would also entail being an "agent of change" (Suedfeld & Tetlock, 1992). Obviously, this is again the distinction between "pure" and "applied" research orientations. However, it is also worthy of discussion in its own right, for it becomes relevant also in the types of interpretations made of any research results and concerns values, standard setting, and relativism.

In this chapter, I have been focusing on the situation in the Majority World, in particular. Similar complaints may also be made about the rather inactive role of Western psychology in social policymaking and societal issues, combined by an overactive emphasis on the individual. It should be noted, however, that there are some psychologists who are keenly aware of social issues and who have been involved in pioneering service oriented research in such areas as public health, family planning, education, rehabilitation in war and conflict, and so on. For example, an issue of *The American Psychologist* (February 1994) contains reviews and evaluations of psychological contributions to early educational intervention in the United States. More recently the *Decade of Behavior* (2000–2010) initiative of the American Psychological Association makes the point that psychology contributes significantly to human well-being. Still the numbers are limited, especially in the Majority World, where such involvement is most needed.

## VALUES, STANDARDS, AND RELATIVISM

This discussion begins with examples of two contrasting approaches. Nutrition researchers who study the nutritional status of children in a village in a developing country may encounter malnutrition. They would note the situation, establish the severity of the problem, analyze the type of nutrition deficiency, and so on. Together with such analysis, they would also recommend that some measures be taken to ameliorate the malnutrition, such as the provision of nutritional supplementation and the like. The level of malnutrition is established using growth monitoring techniques, based on age-specific norms, though there may be problems in devising norms that are appropriate for the specific population in question. The nutritionists pass a judgment, based on a standard, even if approximate, and often try to induce change to correct an unhealthy state. Indeed, quite a number of recent nutrition studies compare different intervention methods to the nutritional status of children in terms of their relative long-term effectiveness (e.g., Behrman, Cheng, & Todd, 2004; Behrman & Hoddinott, 2005). They do not construe this situation in relativistic terms, for example, viewing the children's malnutrition in comparison to their possible normal status in some other sphere of development, such as manual dexterity in pottery making.

An early example of research with such an approach, where an involved orientation of the researcher is seen, is a large-scale nutrition project carried out in a number of villages in northern Thailand (Kotchabhakdi, Winichagoon, Smitasiri, Dhanamitta, & Valya-Sevi, 1987). The presence of wide-scale malnutrition was established in this study. In addition to providing nutritional supplementation to children, the researchers also undertook to sensitize mothers to the importance of early psychosocial stimulation and more effective feeding techniques to decrease malnutrition. More recent work across a number of **Majority World** countries follows suit (e.g., Armecin et al., 2005; Behrman et al., 2004).

The other example is one that I related in chapter 3 and reflects the contrasting approach of the cultural psychologist/anthropologist who studies child development. Specifically, Harkness and Super (1992) note the inability of children in Kokwet (Kenya) to retell to an adult a story or to do other simple cognitive tasks. This low level of performance of Kokwet children is viewed with a relativistic stance, however, as compared to their developed skills in child care or household chores. Explanations of this situation are made (rightly) in terms of parental ethnotheories and their expression in the organization of daily life settings and customs of childrearing, and no action is taken to induce any change to "correct" the low level of performance in cognitive tasks.

Yet another example of an uninvolved approach is the study of childhood in a weavers' community in India by Anandalaksmy and Bajaj (1981), which I also presented in chapter 3. The authors note the restrictive and cognitively unstimulating environment of especially the girl child, who is also deprived of schooling. However, again no action is taken to induce change.[1]

The contrast between the two approaches is obvious. In the first case, a *judgment* is made about normal (acceptable) and subnormal (unacceptable) growth on the basis of a *standard,* and *change is induced to bridge the gap.* This is not done in the second approach. Where does this difference emerge from? Are the issues involved so different in kind that a comparison is nonsensical? This is unlikely. Some of the points discussed in this chapter are relevant here, especially the role of the psychologist (and also of the anthropologist) as a distant scientist who observes (understands, explains) phenomena but who does not instigate change. Apart from this definition, however, there is the additional factor that to instigate change, one needs a standard with which to compare the case under study, much like the nutritionist's standard of "normal" growth, based on growth norms. Are psychologists (or anthropologists) able or willing to develop such standards? This is a basic issue I have touched on in this book in different contexts, especially with regard to **relativism-universalism** in the study of socialization for competence (see chap. 3), and in the cultural versus crosscultural approaches in the Introduction.

## Is Relativism the Only Alternative to Ethnocentrism?

It also became clear in chapter 3 that researchers are generally unwilling to pass judgments or to use standards in the study of human development

---

[1]It should be noted, however, that later on Anandalaksmy (1994) actually got involved in an action research to improve the situation of the girl child in the family.

in cultural context; this is especially true of anthropologists. A number of factors appear to play a role here. One is the fear of being ethnocentric (or Euro-American-centric). Because most of the child development researchers doing cross-cultural/cultural psychology/anthropology are in fact Euro-Americans, this is understandable (the smaller number of non-Western researchers are also so imbued with the Western psychological/anthropological outlooks that they are mostly not very different).

This is actually a respectable sensitivity, especially in view of the remnants of the colonial past and the social evolutionary views of the "primitives" as "childlike," "prelogical," and "less developed," in general. Thus, passing judgments about the (inferior) capacities of non-Western preindustrial groups on the basis of their poor performance in Western tests (or even in any tasks that are not culturally meaningful to them) is not warranted. It is reminiscent of a biased outlook that cross-cultural and cultural researches rightly want to avoid. However, is the only alternative to this unacceptable position a rampant relativism where anything is as good as anything else?

As I discussed in chapter 3, this appears to be the view of some cultural psychologists and cognitive anthropologists. It is particularly strong in hermeneutic anthropology and in postmodernism, in general, which are so committed to subjectivity and therefore relativism that even the existence of any "facts" or "knowledge" is denied. Gellner (1992) seriously criticized postmodernism as an "ephemeral cultural fashion ... of interest [only] as a living and contemporary specimen of relativism which as such is of some importance and will remain with us for a long time" (p. 24). M. B. Smith (2003) refers to the "perils of postmodernism" (p.151), spreading from the humanities to the social sciences, taking on an antiscientific direction and hitting psychology, as well.

Relativism is of course not confined to postmodernism. It is quite noticeable in the **specific learning model** and **everyday cognition** tradition informed by the Vygotskian sociohistorical school of thought. In this approach, all learning is "goal-directed action," which is functional for adapting to the context and for practical problem solving required by the particular context in which it takes place. Thus, a great deal of everyday learning "through guided participation" within the child's **zone of proximal development** is studied *in* context, and the context-specific requirements on the development of specific cognitive skills are emphasized (see chap. 3).

This body of research has provided us with rich description and insight into the adaptive nature of cognition. However, if this view of context-specific learning is seen to define *all* learning (Shweder, 1990), then we are left with no shared attributes, no common standards, and no possibility of comparison–total relativism.

School has been considered by some cross-cultural researchers as just another context for learning and not superior to any other specific learning (Greenfield & Lave, 1982, p. 185). This is a relativistic approach that does not see any problem with a child who cannot perform simple cognitive tasks but, for example, is skilled in carrying out household chores or with girls developing skills for household chores and filling spools for weaving but remaining illiterate. It is interesting to note that this type of relativistic interpretation (nonjudgment) tends to be made for children (or adults) in preindustrial, less developed contexts of the **Majority World** but not for those in industrial environments. For the latter, comparative standards are used, involving cognitive skills and school performance, and arrears in these are not interpreted in relative terms, compared with their skills in noncognitive, non-school-like tasks.

*The Issue of Double Standards.* It could be claimed that this is as it should be, because noncognitive tasks are more adaptive and valued in preindustrial traditional settings whereas school-like tasks are more adaptive for living in urban industrial society. Though this may be true, it is also the crux of the matter. Indeed, by *not* using comparative standards and *not* passing judgments about the state of the children in the preindustrial traditional society, ironically, a value judgment *is* being made by default. Expressed rather bluntly, this value judgment states that in the industrial society with mass schooling, universal cognitive standards of achievement apply, but in preindustrial societies they don't. What we have here is relativism leading to *double standards*.

A number of problems are involved here. A basic one is social change. As mentioned earlier, preindustrial even preliterate societies, like all societies, undergo change. Shifts from rural to urban lifestyles are occurring globally (see Box 2.3 in chap. 2). Change often involves the opening up of traditional economies to cash economies, greater integration with national and international markets, rural to urban migration, introduction of public schools, and so on. Many of the traditional skills lose their adaptive values in the process of change. Relativistic values stressing the importance of these traditional skills presume static societies, which do not exist, especially today, given the tremendous ongoing socioeconomic structural changes and globalization. Furthermore, emphasizing these skills alone would help perpetuate the status quo.

This can be a dilemma especially in contexts where people *want* to change their lifestyles, for example, rural peasants aspiring to migrate to cities. In such situations, researchers should be especially careful about their conclusions and interpretations. It can be just as patronizing to claim that the traditional ways are valuable and should not change (when people would like to change them), as it is to insist that people should change when they don't want to change. This type of dilemma can be resolved if the researcher does not make interpretations of the situation on purely theoretical grounds but tries to find out people's genuine preferences.

A related dilemma concerns the hesitation to impose "middle-class values" on non-middle-class populations. It is interesting to note here that the so-called middle-class values or behaviors are those that research shows to be beneficial for children's development in general (S. A. Miller, 1988, p. 271) and for their **cognitive competence** and school performance in particular (Aksu-Koç, 2005; Duncan & Magnuson, 2003; Goodnow, 1988; Gottfried et al., 1998). I have reviewed a great deal of research showing this in chapters 2 and 3, especially in dealing with the concept of disadvantage (see also Martini & Mistry, 1993, and Sénécal & LeFevre, 2002). The question to be asked is why such positive parental values and behavior should be in the monopoly of the middle classes. If they are beneficial for children, then it is desirable to promote them in all parents as much as possible. _Not_ to do this is again to affirm the existing inequalities, which work against the children of the marginalized groups. It is important to make sure that tolerance of diversity and relativism do not impede efforts to improve the environments of socioeconomically disadvantaged children.

_A Dilemma._  The issue in hand can be seen as a dilemma. Many enlightened and well-meaning social scientists avoid focusing on the lower performance of socioeconomically disadvantaged children because they don't want to label these children "inferior." This is an admirable concern. However, taking note of the inadequate performance of children need not entail labeling them as inferior. In fact, to do so would be making the **"fundamental attribution error"** (or **"correspondence bias"**) (Rotter, 1990). This type of "dispositional" attribution is _not_ the correct interpretation in the context of disadvantage. Rather, a situational attribution would be in order. In other words, one would need to point at the environmental factors that are accountable for the less than adequate performance, as they hinder the phenotypical realization of the genotypical potential. This would not be "blaming the victim" but rather recognizing that there are environments that victimize children, and that something should be done about this.

The natural outcome of the concerned hesitation is, to take refuge in a relativist interpretation, showing that these children are indeed capable, because they are good in other things, such as household chores, child care, manual skills, and so on. There is also the further tendency to see these practical skills as being just as valuable as cognitive skills. This final interpretation can in turn help legitimize and perpetuate the status quo, which in fact deprives children of valuable school-like skills. This is something of a trap that the researcher can fall into, with serious consequences for the children in question.

Related to this is the commonly observed misfit between indigenous skills and the requirements of formal schooling. An example is the traditionally valued social skill of quiet obedience, which does not guarantee and may even detract from school success. The same is true for the contrasting case of cognitive skills, such as preliteracy skills, including verbal reasoning, vocabulary, and so on, which are conducive to school performance but are not typically valued or stressed in traditional childrearing. For example, research in Nigeria (Haglund, 1982), in Turkey (Aksu-Koç, 2005), and in the United States (Hart & Risley, 2003; Hoff, 2003; Martini, 1995,1996; Sénécal & Le Fevre, 2002; Tamis-LeMonda et al., 1996) points to the mismatch between the concrete language and classification skills at socioeconomically disadvantaged homes and the abstract and representational language and classification skills required in school (see chaps. 2 and 3).

It does not help to claim that school learning is just another specific learning, not superior to any other. First of all, school learning is more conducive to generalization and transfer to new learning situations (Scribner & Cole, 1981; Segall et al., 1999), though some higher level everyday cognitive skills are also transferable (T. N. Carraher et al., 1988; Nunes et al., 1993; see also chap. 3, this volume). And just as important, schooling (school attainment and performance) is more instrumental than traditional skills for advancement in urbanizing societies. Ironically, then, whereas cultural psychologists and anthropologists shun using Western-type school-related standards in their research with traditional peoples, in those same societies, those standards are often used as yardsticks for advancement in social status, economic well-being, and so on.

The point I am trying to make here is that research may be conducted for academic purposes only; however, because it is conducted in the real world, it cannot stay at a distance from social values and policies. Indeed, social science cannot be "value-free." As Bellah et al. (1985) rightly noted some time ago, "To attempt to study the possibilities and limitations of society with utter neutrality, as though it existed in another planet, is to push the ethos of narrowly professional social science to the breaking point" (p. 302). Absolute neutrality is not possible, for even when the researchers do not intervene or prescribe change, they are in fact taking a stand with political implications. As in the earlier example, stressing the importance of traditional ways may have the effect of perpetuating the status quo and not change, which is a value-laden view and even a political stand.

*The Role of Social Science Research.*    It might be argued that social science research does not really have the power I am attributing to it. Such power may not be readily observable, but it is there, at least potentially. In fact, given the high prestige of science, any conclusions or interpretations made by a researcher carry quite a bit of weight, especially when published and available through the mass media. They are certainly liable to be used by politicians and policymakers to legitimize their positions. Thus, social science research carries social responsibility, whether or not it chooses to do so.

Actually, a socially responsible role is also demanded of social science. This is certainly the case in the Majority World where effective development models, including human models, are being searched for, and human potential development is high on national agendas. Most cross-cultural research in child development, for example, has been knowledge-driven, mainly with the goal of testing "universal" theories of child development or developing new theories. Though highly beneficial for academic advancement, this substantial amount of research has contributed little to the well-being of children or to societal development in the Majority World (Dasen, 1988b; Kağitçibaşi, 1995; Wagner, 1986).

There is some resentment in the Majority World of research conducted by foreigners (especially anthropologists) that only gathers information and thus benefits from the local resources but gives back nothing in return. What are needed are insights into how improvement in human conditions and human potential can be achieved. This is because societal (national) development is the most important goal in these societies, and human resources are often their most important resources for development. Yet, this is what many cultural psychologists and anthropologists are *not* equipped or willing to provide, given their relativistic views avoiding judgments based on (comparative) standards and their role definitions as uninvolved scientists.

## Politics of Education

Societal aspirations need to be taken seriously. Universal literacy and schooling are pervasive aspirations in the **Majority World.** The World Conference on "Education for All" met in Jomtien (Thailand) in 1990, and a second meeting was held in New Delhi in 1993, focusing on "quality education for all." The year 1990 was declared the International Literacy Year. In early 1994, "The Education for All Summit" witnessed the governments of some of the most populous nations of the world (China, India, Indonesia, Bangladesh, Pakistan, Brazil, Mexico, and Egypt) commit themselves to provide schooling for all their children. In 1996, representatives of 73 countries met in Amman, Jordan, for a mid-decade evaluation, and in 2000 the "World Education Forum" was held in Dakar. At the beginning of the second millennium, it has been painfully admitted that the overall goal of universal basic education has not been reached, and the 1990–2000 has been called the "lost" decade (UNESCO, 2005; UNICEF, 2000). The United Nations Literacy Decade began in 2003 with renewed concerted effort. All this is in response to gross inequalities in educational opportunities and provisions in the world that are too painfully recognized in many parts of the Majority World. For example, whereas in North America primary school completion reaches 99%, it is only 60% and 63% in South Asia and Sub-Saharan Africa, respectively. Secondary school enrollment ratios of the age group are at 94% for boys and 92% for girls in the United States. The corresponding figures for South Asia are 51% and 39% and for Sub-Saharan Africa, they are merely 29% and 23%, respectively (UNESCO, 2005).

Education is also a basic human right. Article 26 of the Universal Declaration of Human Rights states: "Everyone has the right to education. Education shall be free, at least in the elementary and fundamental stages. Elementary education shall be compulsory." Accordingly, all efforts to expand literacy and schooling must be supported and governments should be urged to invest more in education to significantly increase educational opportunity for some 150 million children, more than two thirds of them girls, who have no access to basic education (Bennett, 1993, p. 12). Apart from the vast proportions of the problem, there are other reasons for concern. For example, the 1980s witnessed declining investments in health and education with economic difficulties in the world, especially in Africa and Latin America, called by some "a lost decade for development" (Jolly, 1988). In this context, the negative effects of the IMF and World Bank policies of structural adjustment and privatization of education should also be mentioned. The situation in Africa has not improved much since then. Finally, most foreign aid from the affluent industrial societies is *not* to education; only Sweden allocates more than 5% of its aid to education.

Together with the urgency and the serious nature of educational issues in the world go controversies and political debates on education. For example, governments may invest inadequate resources to formal education, which is a long-term investment, allocating resources, instead, to other areas with faster returns. Thus, they may fail to meet their commitments and be eager to relegate the responsibility to nonformal communal organizations, religious groups, and so on. Every effort should be made, by psychologists among others, to force governments to face their responsibilities. Alternatively, genuine efforts by governments to make education available to all may be frustrated or counteracted by conservative or reactionary forces who oppose modernization and especially the education of girls and women.

*Religious Education as a Case in Point.*   An example of the latter is the rising political power of religious fundamentalism in the world, especially in Moslem societies (Gellner, 1992). In early 1980s, Wagner (1983) already noted that "Koranic schooling [is] in more direct competition with the modern secular school systems of many Moslem societies" (p. 80). Indeed, there have been efforts to *replace* regular schooling by Koranic schooling, often financed internationally by theocratic governments such as those in Iran, Libya, and Saudi Arabia with the intention of undermining secularism in Moslem societies. Such reactionary movements are impediments to societal development, as, for example, measured by the human development indicators of the United Nations Development Program (UNDP). It is also to be noted that widescale religious education is being advocated only in Moslem societies in the world, which points to some political issues involved.

Many governments and particularly the secular, educated sectors in Moslem societies are struggling hard and against great odds to overcome the rise of fundamentalism. Much is at stake, with fundamentalist terror also emerging in the picture.[2] Yet, research by Western cross-cultural psychologists and anthropologists came up with statements supporting and legitimizing Koranic schooling (Wagner, 1983, 1988).

As supplementary education (*not* replacing formal schooling), Koranic schooling might contribute to literacy in Arab countries (Wagner, 1988). However, it cannot serve this function in other Moslem societies with other languages. Even in the case of Arabic-speaking countries, however, the goal should be "education for all" in modern schools. In fact, some of the highest proportions of illiteracy in the world are found in Arab countries, 40% (UNESCO, 2002; Verhoeven, Rood, & Laan, 1991), especially among women. In poorer and more populous Arab countries, the figures are even higher. In Yemen, for example, 54% of the country's 9 million people are illiterate, and the figure increases to about 90% among women and 76% among men in rural areas (UNESCO, 2002). Clearly, Koranic schooling has not helped to achieve literacy.

Actually, any positive effects of Koranic schooling (at the preschool level) obtained in research were very limited and specific: only on a serial memory task using digits. Even this specific effect diminished "when

---

[2]Most of this chapter is taken from the previous (1996) edition of this volume. Considering what we have experienced in the world since then with 9/11 and other terrorist attacks, what I have written in this section has assumed even greater urgency.

Koranic names were used instead of digits or when these items were used incrementally rather than in longer randomized spans" (Wagner & Spratt, 1987, p. 1217). Among adults also Koranic schooling did not improve overall memory but only specific incremental recall (Scribner & Cole, 1981). In Moslem societies with languages other than Arabic, it is doubtful that it would even have this specific effect because it amounts to memorizing text in an incomprehensible language. In contrast, pervasive and consistent positive effects of formal schooling are found on diverse cognitive and memory tasks (Ceci, 1991, 1999; Ceci & Williams, 1997; Oloko, 1994; Scribner & Cole, 1981; Segall, et al., 1999; Serpell, 1993)

Given the flimsy evidence of any positive cognitive effects, it appears unwarranted to draw conclusions about traditional education as "appropriate education" that has a definite contribution to make, "given the needs of Third-World countries" (Wagner, 1988, p. 106). Again we are faced with relativistic double standards. Religious education has declined in the world, especially in the industrialized West, and no one is proposing a return to it; but it is seen as "appropriate" for the Third World (Moslem societies). Religious education cannot serve the functions of public schooling in promoting societal development; therefore, it should not be considered as an alternative, but only as a supplementary form of education to universal schooling.

I have discussed education in some detail within the Majority World perspective both because it is very important in its own right and also because it presents a particularly striking example of the political implications of research. Schools are possibly the most important institutions for societal development, despite their weaknesses. They don't just provide cognitive skills or specific learning. For example, much evidence is obtained over the last decades indicating that formal education, especially for girls, has far-reaching long-term effects, such as later age at marriage, lower fertility, lower infant mortality, and better nutrition/health of future children (Caldwell, 1979, 1980; Cochrane, 1979; LeVine, 1983; UNESCO, 2002), in addition to the "obvious" benefits such as better literacy skills and higher levels of employment. Furthermore, these long-term benefits obtain with only primary school education, even with a few years of formal schooling, particularly in the least developed countries (Cochrane & Mehra, 1983). Min (1994) reviewed a great deal of research pointing to the empowering effects of public schooling for girls/women.

Thus, belittling expressions such as school learning not being superior to any other kind of everyday specific learning are not helpful to global efforts to provide "education for all." On the contrary, psychologists can contribute to efforts to expand schooling by disseminating scientific evidence showing the enhancement of human performance through schooling (e.g., Ceci, 1991, 1999; Ceci & Williams, 1997).

Similarly, religious education does not just impart specific memory skills. It inculcates a religious worldview that is often antithetical to a scientific worldview. This is particularly the case in Islamic education, because Islam encompasses not only "the faith" but also "the law," which regulates everyday life, including gender, economy, government, and so forth. In countries such as Turkey, Egypt, and Tunisia that have opted for secularism, religious education tends to promote reactionary conservatism. In an early research with adolescents in Turkey (Kağitçibaşi, 1973), I found "religiosity" to be associated with authoritarianism and belief in external control of reinforcement and to correlate negatively with optimism and achievement motivation.

There are also problems in countries of immigration such as those in Western Europe where there are large numbers of ethnic migrants from Moslem societies. Tolerant educational and social policies allow, even support religious educational institutions for the children of these minorities. However, this leads to the even greater separation of these children and adolescents from the mainstream society and gets in the way of their reaching the same levels of intellectual performance as the children of the dominant society. This issue is taken up in more detail in chapter 10.

Given the serious issues involved, it is incumbent on cross-cultural researchers to be aware of the politics of education in the world and the far-reaching implications of their own work. As mentioned earlier, schooling has its problems, also, and has been criticized for them. Indeed, in most of the Majority World schools are inadequate (Myers, 1992; Serpell, 1993). The inequality of access to schools; the poor quality of instruction, often involving rote learning and recitations; overcrowded classrooms; lack of educational materials; at times the irrelevance of the curriculum to local/national realities are among the many problems in the Majority World. This calls for greater efforts to invest in schools to work toward improving them.

Furthermore, problems of schools reflect the existing societal problems, rather than causing them, as sometimes assumed. For example, it is not schooling that causes rural-to-urban migration but basic social-structural and economic changes, such as the mechanization of agriculture replacing human labor, too high a population pressure on cultivable land, and so on—which push people out of rural areas in search of urban jobs. Again, commonly, it is not schooling that creates unemployment, but mainly economic and population problems in a society. However, schooling may be inadequate in solving issues such as unemployment that call for more investment and better planning to upgrade schools and to enable them to train youth in line with the employment requirements in the society.

Schooling has been found to induce individualistic orientations, which in collectivistic societies can result in the weakening of interdependent family ties (Greenfield, 1994; Oloko, 1994; Serpell, 1993). However, this may not be inevitable, because interdependence values can be integrated into school learning, as, for example, generally seen in East Asian cultures (Greenfield, 1994) or in the Pueblo Indian classrooms (Suina & Smolkin, 1994). Even in individualistic contexts such as the United States, experimental school programs such as the "jigsaw classrooms" (Aronson, Stephan, Sikes, Blaney, & Snapp, 1978) have been shown to help create cooperation rather than individualistic competition. In this type of intervention, group projects are used where success requires mutual cooperation among the group members. This is reminiscent of Sherif's (Sherif, Harvey, White, Hood, & Sherif, 1961) well-known Robber's Cave experiment on cooperation that showed that both competition and cooperation can be brought about by situational factors.

Schooling promises to be a powerful instigator of societal development when it is rendered socially relevant and culturally appropriate, for example, disposing of colonial components where applicable. I would further propose discontinuance of the term *Western schooling* in most Majority World societies where national educational policies and plans have been established and applied for some time. What used to be Western (or the property of the Western world) is now globally shared education. It is an inherent part of endogenous development (Huynh, 1979; Tripathi, 1988) that encompasses *both* the culturally relevant *and* the globally shared knowledge.

## WILL PSYCHOLOGY HELP?

Up to now, I have been discussing issues involved in linking theory and application, with a special focus on the role of the cross-cultural researcher. I have also stressed the problems of values and politics, inherent in research that informs policy and social action. There is, of course, no guarantee that research findings will be used to promote human well-being. Because science is public, it can be used or misused, and there is probably not much that the scientist can do about it.

Social scientists or psychologists who are involved in cultural/cross-cultural research have the additional problem of evaluating and interpreting their research findings within the cultural and political context of the societies in which they work. A call for an "involved" stance is not a sanction for a foreign visitor to intervene whenever they find something disturbing. A good way of preventing misunderstanding is to work in partnership in team research with local researchers. Indeed, as noted by Greenfield (1994), "an insider's perspective [may be] essential to the valid description of socialization and development" (p. 23). This is not to say that an insider's view is perfect; it has its own weaknesses. Nevertheless, it can serve as a corrective to the outsider's possible ethnocentrism and possible misinterpretation of events. It promises to be especially valuable in policy-relevant research and interventions.

A second way of avoiding imposing one's own views on the situation is involving "subjects" of the research as participants in evaluation/interpretation as well as asking their opinions and aspirations regarding the issues relevant to the research in question. These approaches are particularly helpful in tackling some difficult decisions in applied research. For example, in intervention research or applied research designed to provide some solutions to human problems, decisions about change are involved. Difficult questions such as "what is to change, what is to remain, how is this to be ascertained, and by whom?" can be better handled by using the informed opinions and insights of the insiders.

Caution is called for in intervention research. We should be able to differentiate between what constitutes good social science involvement in social policy and what constitutes psychological imperialism and unwelcome paternalism. This is not always easy to achieve, and some of the procedures recommended earlier may help by bringing in the insider's perspective.

**Endogenous development** does *not* mean perpetuation or strengthening of traditional ways. Indeed, this type of an indigenization may carry the danger of turning into a revivalistic movement (Dalal, 1990, p. 116), as in the case of religious fundamentalism. Though on the one hand, endogenous development involves aligning development with societal values, on the other hand it also entails development of effective systems that can cope with global changes. Both "openness" and "embeddedness" are thus required for social change to qualify as "development" (Tripathi, 1988).

Examples of such development are reflected in some psychological constructs that can be seen as "integrative syntheses." These constructs bring together and integrate some concepts that are not commonly construed together in mainstream psychology. However, in a different cultural context they may coexist. I have been discussing and proposing some of these. They are the nurturant-task leadership (J. B. P. Sinha, 1980); **social achievement motivation** (Agarwal & Misra, 1986; Phalet & Claeys, 1993; Yu & K.-S. Yang, 1994); the **autonomous-related self;** the **family model of psychological/emotional interdependence,** also entailing autonomy and interdependence (chaps. 5 and 6); and emphasis on language-cognitive development alongside **social intelligence** in childrearing, that is, **cognitive-social intelligence** (chap. 3).

These issues are relevant, for example, in intervention research designed to improve the early environment and to promote optimal human development. Chapter 3 examined "disadvantage," and chapter 2 discussed some models relating human development to context. A main point made was that because adverse socioeconomic conditions at the macro level affect the growing child through the mediation of parental behavior and the family, psychological intervention is possible. Such interventions at the family level, extending into other in-groups and the community, are even more likely to be effective in collectivistic cultures than individual-level interventions (Sinha & Kao, 1988, p. 25).

## School Readiness and Early Development Indicators

A serious human development problem many countries in the **Majority World** face is school failure and school dropout. It leads to high rates of repetition of 1st-year classes and low retention rates until the last year of the basic educational cycle due to school dropouts (UNESCO, 2005; UNICEF,2000) (e.g., Bangladesh retains only 20%; Bennett, 1993, p. 12). Especially in the context of underdevelopment, where universal schooling is not yet achieved, this problem entails great economic and human costs. Thus the World Bank (1988, p. 50) reported that the cost of each completer of primary school in Sub-Saharan Africa is on the average 50% higher due to repetition and dropout; in some countries in the region this is the case even today (UNESCO, 2005).

Obviously many factors are involved, such as low-quality schools with overcrowded classrooms, their uneven distribution, involving long commuting distances for some children, and so on. Among the factors involved also are inadequate school preparation by the child and inadequate family support of the child's "student role" and school performance. I discussed this issue in chapters 2 and 3. Here I want to examine how psychological research can address the issue, together with other issues of human development. As Myers (1992) noted, "Improving the readiness of children for school can improve the quality and efficiency of school systems ... [for] children are probably the most important 'input' into schooling as well as its most important 'output'" (p. 221).

Inadequate preparation for school can be seen as a developmental problem that is based on the assumption of some standard of adequacy that can be established and measured. School readiness is defined in terms of the child's (a) activity level (health and nutritional status, affecting both school attendance and concentration in class), (b) **social**

**competence** and psychological preparedness (affecting adaptation to and coping with school requirements), and (c) cognitive abilities, including preliterary and prenumeracy skills. Readiness is also reflected in the positive outlooks and expectations of the family as well as their support (Myers, 1992).

Though different terms may be used for some of these concepts, and/or some slightly different or more refined categories may be utilized, these concepts constitute in general a characterization of the child's school preparedness. Their combination can form an "index" or measure of where the child stands in terms of such a standard. We can thus talk about adequate or inadequate school readiness. Within developmental psychology, there is much accumulated knowledge regarding both the conceptualization and the assessment of the aforementioned aspects of human development. Much research has informed us about language/communication; problem solving, concept formation, and other cognitive processes; social competence/maturity; emotional development; life skills development, and so on in the years preceding school entry, which altogether contribute to school readiness.

*Assessment and Developmental Indicators.* All this knowledge is yet to be used optimally in intervention work in different sociocultural contexts. Culturally sensitive and appropriate measures of age-specific development in different spheres need to be devised in order to ascertain any retarded development, which needs to be acted on to promote school readiness. These measures should be based on culturally valid conceptualizations of human development that, in turn, would be informed by both international research in the field and also research within each sociocultural context.

The current dependence on Western conceptualizations and especially on Western measures is an impediment for advancement in this area. Related to this is the problem of the lack of measures that do not require much time and expertise for their application to large numbers of children. Given the scale of the problem in many developing countries, large numbers are involved. Screening and detection instruments are often needed to pick out children at risk of debilitated or delayed development in order to attend to their needs. Individual intelligence tests or other assessment techniques that are costly in terms of time and professional expertise for their application are not suitable for such use. This is the type of assessment in which psychologists have been traditionally involved. Therefore, a different kind of approach is called for to address the needs arising in real-life situations.

For example, a UNICEF workshop held in Brazil some time ago concluded that "a simple instrument to measure children's psychosocial development needs to be perfected and applied in the different countries of the region. Current methods are considered, by and large, to be inadequate" (Consultative Group, 1986, p. 2). The statement is instructive in reflecting the needs felt by fieldworkers. Psychological expertise, especially in psychometrics and cross-cultural developmental psychology, can contribute a great deal to efforts to devise reliable and culturally sensitive assessment instruments, for example, to ascertain school readiness. This is a new challenge for psychologists that has not yet been met (Kağitçibaşi, 1991; Landers & Kağitçibaşi, 1990).

Indeed, a current initiative by UNICEF (2005) attempts to devise child development indicators that can be used across cultures. These are designed for specific ages and are construed to provide general (minimal) standards against which a child's standing can be established. If it is found to be less than the standard, necessary action can be taken, such as providing support to the caregivers, referral to professional help, and the like. The challenge here is to come up with indicators of (minimal) overall child development that can be used as a standard in diverse sociocultural economic contexts.

Typically the health professionals, mainly nutritionists and pediatricians, have been involved in large-scale assessment of children for screening and detection purposes. There is a growing need now to devise psychological developmental assessment techniques to parallel the existing measures of physical growth. Similarly, there is a need to establish culturally valid norms of psychosocial development to parallel physical growth norms. Such norms are crucial for monitoring child development (very much like growth monitoring) and for ascertaining developmental delays.

So far psychologists have not had a significant presence in large-scale health projects and have not made a "niche" for themselves in multidisciplinary efforts in promoting health and education in the world. Nevertheless, significant attempts have been made in research, for example, in Latin America, India, and Turkey to establish culturally valid age-specific developmental norms (Dasen, Berry, & Sartorious, 1988; Landers & Kağitçibaşi, 1990; Myers, 1992; Pandey, 1988; Saraswathi & Kaur, 1993; Savasir et al., 1992; UNICEF, 2005). Box 7.1 gives some development indicators for a 5-year-old child.

In some large-scale projects involving several developing countries, establishment of psychosocial indicators of development is pursued within health or mental health contexts where mainly health professionals are involved. One of these was the World Health Organization project for the development and use of psychosocial indicators, started in 1983 and carried out in Argentina, China, India, Pakistan, Senegal, and Thailand. By 1990, more than 31,000 children had been measured for

Box 7.1    Suggested Development Indicators for a Five Year Old Child

### Child Indicators at Age 5 (Kağıtçibaşı)

Physical well-being
(immunizations; no parasites; well-nourished; satisfactory physical growth; satisfactory energy/activity level; gross and fine motor development; sensory development)

Language development
(vocabulary; comprehensible narrative language)

Cognitive development
(concept formation: sorting/categorization, if-then statements used; pre-numeracy-literacy skills; social intelligence*)

Emotional security
(sense of being loved; sense of belonging; low aggression)

Autonomy/competence
(Ability to do things on his/her own, ability to relate positively to adults and other children- -play, share; realistic self-assessment)

*Note. Social intelligence includes knowledge of (and adjustment to) social norms and rules; it also refers to sensitivity to others' needs*

both growth and psychosocial development (World Health Organization, 1986, 1990). This large-scale undertaking involved test development, reliability checks, tester training, repeated administration and refinement, including the integration of culture-specific items, and so on. It was a major international effort toward cross-cultural conceptualization and assessment of early (age 0–6) human development. However, the academic psychological community was hardly involved.

*Environmental Indicators.*    In addition to indicators of psychological development, environmental indicators are also greatly needed. These entail the assessment of the physical environment, environmental stimulation, caretaker attitudes and behavior, child–caretaker interaction, and so forth. Environmental indicators were also integrated into some large-scale health projects, again mainly carried out by health professionals (DeSilva, Nikapota, & Vidyasagara, 1988; Nikapota, 1990; Sockalingam, Zeitlin, & Satato, 1990; World Health Organization, 1986, 1990). A most important component of intervention work involves parent education, community programs, and so on, designed to act on the environment to make it more conducive to healthy human development. For interventions to be effective, environmental indicators are crucial to ascertain high-risk environments. General indicators such as socioeconomic status are not adequate; more refined indicators are needed because there is much variation, for example, in parental behaviors within the same socioeconomic context.

The UNICEF (2005) initiative to devise child development indicators, mentioned before, also includes setting up environmental indicators. The environmental indicators are based on the revised HOME Scale (Bradley & Caldwell, 1988), which has been validated in many Majority World countries. However, the HOME Scale requires time and expertise for application. The UNICEF effort is coming up with a simple instrument that does not have this drawback in large-scale applications. This is a step in the right direction.

Psychological expertise is also called for in the establishment of environmental indicators. The very concept of environmental risk is in need of better conceptualization and operationalization. This is a challenging task in a cross-cultural context. Culture-specific aspects need to be addressed; but it may be possible to establish some basic categories in areas such as caregiver interaction styles, expectations, and beliefs; cognitively stimulating environment and verbal stimulation; physical characteristics of the environment; autonomy granting and affection in childrearing, and so on. Box 7.2 gives an example of environmental indicators.

An adequate conceptualization of human development has to be complex, integrating both physical growth maturation and also total psychological development (including socioemotional, language, cognitive development) *within* context and through time, starting from the very beginning. With the serious problems of infant mortality in the Majority World, for some decades a heavy emphasis was put on nutrition and health needs of children, concentrating on early ages (0–3). With recent shifts from medical to social science models of health, there has been a greater recognition of the social-behavioral aspects of health and well-being. Thus, the World Health Organization constitution defines health broadly as "a state of complete physical, mental and social well-being, and not merely the absence of disease or informity." The broader conceptualization of health is both in terms of the synergistic relationship among nutrition, health and psychosocial development (Myers, 1992) and also in terms of the contextual-interactional aspects of human development. Thus, psychological development and the importance of the mediating factors in the environment are now recognized as important. Research conducted in different parts of the world has contributed to this long-overdue recognition.

Box 7.2    Suggested Environmental Indicators

**Environmental Indicators (Kağıtçıbaşı)**

Physical Environment
(clean, orderly, safe environment; some things owned by child)

Environmental (cognitive) stimulation
(availability of books/magazines; toys and or play materials; radio, television; child being read/told stories, level and extent of adult verbalization to child)

Positive orientation to child
(parental educational aspiration for child; realistic/positive parental assessment of child's capacity; parental acceptance - - pleased with child; attentiveness/responsiveness to child)

Mother/caretaker's cognitive/language capacity
(mother's speech comprehensible; mother's education)

Low-conflict environment
(no drug addiction/alcoholism/crime, low spousal conflict; no wife battering or child abuse; mother having social support network)

The interactive relationship among nutrition, health, and psychosocial development and the direct impact of environmental factors are relevant from the very beginning and affect children's school readiness. For example, research shows that malnourishment breeds malnourishment, unless counteracted by caregiver sensitivity and behavior. Because sick and malnourished children are less active and demanding, they end up getting less food, leading to more malnourishment in a vicious circle, whereas active, healthy babies demand and therefore get more food. The immediate environment is a part of this synergism because reluctant babies can be fed more if, for example, mothers stimulate them during breastfeeding, whereas a less stimulating environment is less conducive to nutrition-health and psychosocial development from early on (Brazelton, 1982; Myers, 1992; M. E. Young, 2002).

*Proximal Environment.*    Since the 1980s, there has been a growing focus on the proximal environment. For example, an early study by Carvioto (1981) was an "eye-opener" in showing the crucial role the proximal environment plays in shielding the growing child from the general adverse influences of deprived environments. This study was conducted in a remote mountain village in Mexico; it drew attention to "caregiver's radio-listening habit" as a factor that plays a role in affecting the child's nutritional status. In this village with considerable poverty and child malnutrition, it was found that some children were not malnourished and were growing at the normal rate. The only environmental factor that differentiated these children from the malnourished ones was their mothers' greater exposure to the radio. How can this unlikely result be explained?

A number of factors might have played a role. These mothers might have learned from the radio programs information about childrearing and children's developmental needs. Or the radio might have served as a general stimulant, keeping these mothers more alert and attentive. Or these mothers might have been those with a greater openness to experience or higher intellectual ability that predisposed them to both listening to the radio and responding to their children's needs. Or a combination of these factors might have been important. In any case, it was found that these mothers provided a higher quality of home stimulation and were more responsive to their children than were the mothers of malnourished children.

Similarly, a child stimulation project by the Ford Foundation in Central Java (reported by Landers & Kağitçibaşi, 1990) found that the quality of mother–child interaction (mothers' level of understanding of and responding to their children's developmental needs) was related to positive growth and development outcomes (better nourishment, higher physical and cognitive development of children), in spite of deprived environments. A large-scale nutrition intervention project in Thailand, mentioned earlier, provided mothers in villages also with awareness of the importance of early stimulation and interaction with infants, with beneficial results for nutrition, health, and development (Kotchabhakdi et al., 1987).

The concept of **positive deviance** was proposed by Zeitlin, Ghassemi, and Mansour (1990) to refer to children who survive, even thrive in adverse environments whereas others don't make it. Reviewing 16 studies, they concluded that positive caretaker–child interaction "enhances the child's tendency to exercise its developing organ systems and hence to utilize nutrients for growth and development" (p. 33). Psychological stress has adverse effects on the use of nutrients whereas psychological well-being stimulates the growth-promoting hormones. "Psychosocial factors, such as the positive affect between mother and child, are associated with adequate growth and development" (p. 34). All this evidence indicates the importance of the proximal environment (caregiver–child interaction) and its mediating role in safeguarding the growing child against negative macrolevel influences, such as poverty.

The synergistic relationship between nutrition, health, and psychosocial development is noted in research conducted with school- or preschool-age children also, with direct relevance for school readiness or school performance (E. Pollitt & Metallinos-Katsaras, 1990; Seshadri & Gopaldas, 1989). More recent work on nutrition, health, and psychosocial stimulation and development corroborates earlier findings, with long-term consequences well into adulthood (Armecin et al., 2005; Behrman et al., 2004; Behrman & Hoddinott, 2005).

These studies point to the need to assume a holistic as well as an interactional-**contextual approach** to human development in both conceptualization and operationalization. Such an approach promises both to offer a better understanding of the factors involved and to provide clues for more effective interventions to promote healthy human development, also involving better school readiness.

## Recent Research on the Impact of Early Environment

More recent work points to the importance of early environmental adversities and early psychosocial stimulation for the health and overall development of children. Of particular significance is the very early environment, both before and after birth. The biological factors involved are now much better understood with advances in neuroscience, brain research, and biotechnology.

At birth, the human infant's nervous system is only partially assembled. All its subsequent development, so-called "fine-tuning," comes through interactions with the environment. The impact of environmental influences ranges from stress to language, from immune system to memory and cognition. In particular, early stimuli affect the hypothalamic-pituitary-adrenal gland (HPA) axis, setting it into action, which in turn affects cognition, memory, behavior, the immune system, and other neural pathways (Mustard, 2002). There is a growing amount of neuroscience research on experience-based brain development conducted with animals and humans. I present here only a few examples to reiterate the importance of the environment, particularly early environment, as well as environment–genetics interaction. This time the focus is on the biological underpinnings of the environmental influences on the organism.

*Animal Studies.* One such pathway is that which leads to early anomalies in response to stress, involving high cortisol levels. Research with Rhesus monkeys and rats (Black, Jones, Nelson, & Greenough, 1998; Coe, 1999) showed that newborn monkeys and rats exposed to early poor (nonstimulating) mothering had high fearfulness, high level of stress reactiveness, and high cortisol levels, as well as stress-related immune deficiency. Thus, early experience has a powerful impact on the immune system and behavioral responses to stress, and especially if prolonged, changes the brain's sensitivity to stress hormones. In the monkey, poor mothering in the first 6 months of life was also associated with high impulse aggression and violent behavior, alcohol consumption (self-medication), and subsequently poor mothering behavior on the part of the grown-up female offspring.

There is also plasticity, however, in that if the vulnerable baby rats and monkeys, exposed to early poor mothering, are placed with "good" foster mothers that stimulate and nurture them, they improve and become normal. Even those with genetic vulnerability benefit from good mothering and develop normally, whereas those with poor mothering show unhealthy responses (Suomi, 2000). The implications of plasticity for intervention are immense.

*Human Studies.*    Similar results are found with humans that point to the alarming impact of severely deprived early environments. Phillips (2004) reports findings of higher cortisol levels in children abused during the first few years of life, in children severely neglected in Romanian orphanages studied 6.5 years after adoption, and in children from Russian and Eastern European orphanages studied 2 to 3 years after adoption. Other extensive reviews of research provide an understanding of the processes involved (Gunnar, 2000; Thompson & Nelson, 2001).The case of children "rescued" from extreme deprivation in orphanages or from other severe adversity point to the severity of harmful environmental impact in all aspects of early development. In general, the longer this type of damaging experience, the greater its negative impact and the less the likelihood of a resilient return to normality (Clarke & Clarke, 1999). For example, Rutter and his research team (1999) working with Romanian orphans adopted into English homes found that those adopted within the first 6 months of age developed normally. Those adopted later, especially after 12 months of age, however, showed about one standard deviation of cognitive deficit at age 4 years.

In less extreme circumstances, also, high cortisol levels in children are found in adverse environments. For example, Dawson et al. (2000) found this to be the case among 3-year-old children whose mothers had been clinically depressed during the child's 1st year of life. There is also evidence that shows that a secure attachment relationship with mother/caregiver works as a buffer against cortisol increases in the face of novel events.

Thus, accumulated evidence points to the crucial role of the early proximal environment, for both negative and positive influences on the growing human being. A better understanding of the biological underpinnings of how such processes work provides clues with regard to determining when there is a problem and what type of an intervention is required to deal with it.

## NATURE–NURTURE UNDERPINNINGS

Underlying the discussions in this chapter is the basic principle of malleability of human nature by environmental influences. This is assumed in any intervention research. From a contextual-interactional perspective, and in line with the evidence I have reviewed, the familial factors, such as caretaker–child interaction, that mediate between the macro-level social structural factors and the child appear to be the best targets for psychological interventions.

This view does not imply a rampant environmentalism, rejecting constitutional influences including genetic factors. For some time, studies on the effects of environment and genetics to psychological outcome have stressed "the multiple contributions of organismic and environmental variables to the processes that result in particular behaviors and particular developmental outcomes" (Horowitz, 1993, p. 350), and "non-additive synergistic effects in genetic–environment interaction" (Bronfenbrenner & Ceci, 1993, p. 314). There is a call for "multideterminant research" to develop a better understanding of the covariance and interaction among the genetic, biomedical, nutritional, environmental, and individual determinants ( Thompson & Nelson 2001; Wachs, 1993).

The long-standing debate on nature *versus* nature is a misnomer. As Anastasi (1958) urged half a century ago, instead of seeking to establish how much of the variance in outcome variables is attributable to heredity and how much to environment, the question "how?" should be addressed. In Hyman's words (1999):

> In the dance of life, genes and environment are absolutely inextricable partners. On the one hand, genes supply the rough blue-print for the brain. Then stimulation from the environment, whether it's light impinging on the retina or a mother's voice on the auditory nerve, turns genes on and off, fine-tuning those brain structures both before and after birth.

The recent advances in behavior genetics and a general shift toward organismic explanations in psychology, however, have led to the tendency to undermine the role of the environment, with far-reaching implications for social and political agendas. Specifically, if environment is inconsequential, then interventions are not needed or even justifiable. It is a short step from this to asserting that intergroup differences, say in intelligence or achievement, cannot be helped, because they reflect the "natural" unfolding of the different genetic pools (Herrnstein & Murray, 1994)—thus it is a "just world," with those having lower genetic potentials doing less well. Even though responsible behavior geneticists are careful to note the limitations of the claims that can be made from data regarding genetic control of behavior (Plomin, 1989), easily popularized statements can be misused, with significant potential harm to the marginal groups in society. Though the current debate is mainly occurring in American psychology, and to some extent in the American public discourse, it also has global implications. For example, recently some statements have been voiced in the European media regarding the "biological" inferiority of ethnic-minority children!

The well-accepted **genotype → environment** theory (Scarr, 1992) is of relevance here. This theoretical perspective claims that environment has an influence on developmental variability only at the extremes. In "normal families," therefore, environmental variability is considered to be unimportant. A problem here is the determination of what is "normal" and what is "extreme." Scarr defines normal as "families in the mainstream of Western European and North American societies" (p. 10). Obviously, the **Majority World,** constituting some 80% of the world's population, as well as those families outside of the "mainstream" in the **Minority World** remain outside. Yet this is proposed as a "general" developmental theory. A basic claim of the theory is that individuals "choose" their environments, and therefore it is their genetic endowment that creates the environments they constitute for themselves. Though in a footnote Scarr admits the theory is based on the assumption that people have varied environments from which to choose their experiences, she does not seem to think it detracts from the external validity of the theory that a great many people in the world are in fact not in a position to choose much at all.

This view reflects the individualistic stance of American psychology that explains outcomes in terms of individual characteristics (even innate ones) and holds the individual responsible for them. What we see here is a "dispositional attribution" or "**correspondence bias**" (Jones, 1990; Rotter, 1966), which does not take the situational factors into account. Yet those situational factors can be powerful influences that make a great difference to people's lives from the very beginning. This type of an outlook assumes initial equal opportunity and the existence of choice. When we consider the diverse environments children are born into, some with great opportunities and choices, others with very meager ones, the limitations of the theory become apparent. Indeed, we have seen in this chapter as well as in chapters 2 and 3 the devastating effects of poverty, especially at an early age.

Actually, studies have shown that even in normal, nonextreme families, specific environmental factors relate to specific aspects of development (Bornstein & Tamis-LeMonda, 1990; Gottfried et al., 1998; Wachs, 1987, 1993). A great deal of evidence that I presented in this chapter and in chapters 2 and 3 is relevant here. All this research shows that when specific mediating variables in the environment are adequately conceptualized and operationalized, they are found to relate to developmental outcomes.One of the problems of genetic deterministic explanations is a rather global treatment of the environment, with inadequate assessment. A better and more standardized measurement of *specific* environmental components is therefore badly needed and promises to throw light on some of the "masked" influences (Horowitz, 1993). This needs to be done cross-culturally. The environmental indicators approach that I described previously aims to do this (see Box 7.2).

Another problem with some of the interpretations of behavior genetics has to do with the concept of **heritability (H)**. High heritability is often understood to mean high genetic causality and therefore a negligible role of the environment. Yet, even with extremely high heritability, environment can still have a powerful influence. For example, some time ago Greulich (1957) reported a surge in the heights of second-generation Japanese children raised in the United States. Heritability of height is over 0.90, yet the American-reared sons were substantially taller than they would have been if they had been reared in Japan. Similarly, it is reported that the heights of young-adult men in Japan increased by about 3½ inches since the Second World War. If a trait as highly heritable as height can show such fluctuations in relatively short periods and across societies, other traits with lower levels of heritability, such as intelligence and personality, can change even more (Ceci & Williams, 1999; Neisser et al., 1996).

The fact of the matter is that a great number of children in the world grow up in environments that do not actualize their potential; that is why environmental intervention is important. More than a decade ago, Bronfenbrenner and Ceci (1993) put it succinctly:

> Humans have genetic potentials ... that are appreciably greater than those that are presently realized, and progress toward such realization can be achieved through the provision of environments in which proximal processes can be enhanced, but which are always within the limits of human genetic potential. (p. 315)

Environmental adversity can prevent the genotypical potential from being realized and manifested in the resultant phenotype. Not much can be done about unfavorable genetic influences; however, adverse environmental influences can be ameliorated to a considerable extent.

The earlier and sustained interventions can go a long way in counteracting detrimental environmental influences that pull down children's potentials. Even interventions that take place later are better than no intervention at all. This is because development and change are possible throughout the life span, given considerable human plasticity and the potential to learn (Thompson & Nelson, 2001). So a positive and constructive role psychology can play is to show how this can be done effectively. This is how psychology can help promote better human functioning and human well-being—global human development.

## SUMMARY AND MAIN POINTS

- This chapter examines the role of psychology vis-à-vis applications/interventions/policies designed to improve human-well being in the world.
- A new concept of "human development" at the macro level has emerged from the United Nations Development Program (UNDP). Indicators of health, education, and income comprise the Human Development Index (HDI). Since 1990, the HDI is used for ranking countries in the world and presenting the global situation in terms of human development.
- Although psychology is relevant to global human development issues, psychologists often do not recognize the relevance of their discipline for human development. "Distancing" from societal problems, limited applicability of the transferred psychological knowledge from the West, and the individualistic stance of Western psychology are some of the reasons for the lack of involvement of psychologists in the global development efforts.
- Theory is crucially important. However to be of value, theory should be culturally valid.
- Whether there is an attempt to induce change constitutes the difference between the "involved" and "uninvolved" approaches in research.
- One reason for the unwillingness of researchers to develop standards and to assume an involved stance is the fear of being ethnocentric. To avoid ethnocentrism, a relativist approach tends to be adopted. However, this may lead to the emergence of double standards.
- Education in the Majority World is an important cause for observing the political implications of research. Cross-cultural researchers should be aware of the politics of education to prevent negative consequences.

- A serious "human development" problem many countries in the Majority World face is school failure and school dropout, which cause economic and human losses. Children's inadequate school preparation and inadequate family support for the child's "student role" are among the many causes of this problem.
- "Readiness for school" is a construct that involves the child's activity level, social competence, psychological preparedness, and cognitive abilities.
- Culturally sensitive and appropriate measures of age-specific development in different spheres are needed. Psychological expertise, especially in psychometrics and cross-cultural developmental psychology, can help devise culturally sensitive assessment instruments to ascertain school readiness.
- Many studies conducted on animals and humans point to the crucial role of the early proximal environment for both negative and positive influences on the developing human being.
- A nature-deterministic approach is not right because development and change are possible throughout the life span, given considerable human plasticity and capacity for learning.

## DISCUSSION QUESTIONS

1   What are the reasons for psychologists' low levels of involvement in issues of global human development?
2.  Discuss the political implications of the relativistic approach of researchers in studies conducted in the Majority World.
3.  Explain, why traditional religious education cannot be accepted as "appropriate" in the Third World Moslem societies by referring to the dilemma between Koranic schooling and secular school systems?
4.  Explain in what ways psychology can contribute to human development especially considering the situation in the Majority World.
5.  What are the consequences of a genetic approach to explain psychological phenomena?

# 8

# Intervention: Early Enrichment

When we look at the world today, we see an "increasing problem of inequality. ... As noted by Nobel laurate Amartya Sen (1999), the core of human development is really a question of choice and freedom—which millions of children in the world today still do not have" (Iglesias & Shalala, 2002, p. 363). This is a global crisis; however, its massive scale should not intimidate efforts to ameliorate the conditions that create it. As we discussed in the last chapter, psychology has indeed a role to play here, especially regarding the individual and the proximate environment.

We examined development in context in chapter 2 and **socialization** for competence in chapter 3; then in the last chapter we dwelt on the role of psychology in inducing change. Where do we stand now? We are ready to delve into applications designed to ameliorate early disadvantage and promote human development. This is the topic of the present chapter. It represents "an involved stance" on the part of the researcher that was called for in the earlier chapters.

Applied research and interventions can pursue two main routes toward policy and applications. One route would be directed toward improving environments, that is, increasing environmental resources and decreasing environmental constraints, for example, providing better educational facilities, a more stimulating home environment, better parenting, and the like. The other route is building individual resources, for example, enhancing the cognitive skills and performance of children and youth. These two routes interact and complement one another, as improving the environment helps build individual resources from early on.

In this chapter, we deal with early intervention and see how the two routes are pursued in research and applications in a particular area where I have conducted an intervention project with my colleagues over the last 22 years. This is the area of early enrichment to promote better child development and competence. This chapter aims to provide the background theory and research as well as the state of the art in the field. Chapter 9 presents our intervention research as a case in point. What is covered here is related to the issues of human development discussed in chapters 1, 2, 3, and 7. To a great extent it derives from them, focusing on the development of competence, and bringing in intervention. In line with what has been discussed up to now, the main thrust of the chapter is that intervention in the form of providing the child with early environmental enrichment can contribute in a significant way to his or her overall development.

## EARLY CHILD DEVELOPMENT (ECD) PROGRAMS

**Early Child Development (ECD)** is a general term used to refer to early childhood development, education, and care. Formerly **Early Childhood Care and Education (ECCE)** was the term adopted (N. van Oudenhoven, 1989) to describe education-related services to the young child. The more general ECD is currently used to refer to all aspects of early human development and programs to support it (M. E. Young, 2002). It involves meeting basic needs in all spheres, that is, health, nutrition, and socioemotional and cognitive development. This is an important area of research and application and is receiving increasingly greater attention as an interdisciplinary field that integrates theory, application, and program development. First in the United States and growing in numbers and expanding to other countries, a great deal of research has been conducted in this field. A brief overview is provided here of some main research issues and the state of the art in ECD programs.

ECD programs constitute an important example of early environmental support and building resources for the child. It assumes great value for the low-SES context in counteracting the adverse effects of that context. ECD programs cover various types of interventions ranging from early nutrition supplementation and health interventions to preschool educational enrichment for school preparation. More and more intervention programs are designed to include nutrition, health, and psychosocial development components, pursuing a **whole child approach.** Some were referred to in the last chapter (Armecin et al., 2005; Behrman et al., 2004; Behrman & Hoddinott, 2005). Additionally, both child-centered and parent-centered approaches can be used. The time and duration of interventions also vary, ranging from very early interventions starting in infancy to school readiness programs just prior to primary school entry.

In this chapter, I focus more on educational interventions carried out mainly for children from 3 to 5 years of age though some of the programs also cover earlier ages. The main aim of these programs is to promote children's cognitive and socioemotional development to enable them to demonstrate good social adjustment and school performance and to attain overall well-being. They are considered to be "interventions" because commonly they concern children in adverse conditions who are at risk of not realizing their full potentials.

The large body of literature on intervention projects and programs has been reviewed, mostly covering work conducted in the United States (Blok, Fukkink, Gebhardt, & Leseman, 2005; Bridges, Fuller, Rumberger, & Tran, 2004; Meisels & Shonkoff, 1990; Reynolds, 2004; Sweet & Appelbaum, 2004; M. E. Young, 1997, 2002) and to a much lesser extent in the **Majority World** (Haddad, 2002; Myers, 1992; M. E. Young, 2002). I do not attempt a comprehensive review here but rather focus on some of the main developments in this field and the basic issues involved.

## State of the Art in ECD Research

Most of the reviews and evaluations of early intervention work have been conducted in the United States, although this does not mean that the most comprehensive ECD programs exist in the United States (Kamerman, 1991). There is a higher coverage in "preprimary education" in Europe than in the United States (80%, and 70%, respectively; UNESCO, 2005). Early childhood education can be provided in nonformal family and child-care contexts as well as in preschool centers, especially for younger children. Informal care is often not represented in the statistics. In many European countries there is universal, or close to universal, formal (center-based) ECD provision, particularly in France (écoles maternelles), Sweden, and some Eastern European countries.

However, systematic evaluations of these programs are not easily available. This may be because in these countries preschool education is considered as an inherent part of normal (public) education, and there seems little need to test its effectiveness. Nevertheless, there are some studies from Europe looking especially into long-term effects of early day care (e.g., Andersson, 1992) and early enrichment programs for ethnic minorities (Blok et al., 2005; Eldering & Leseman, 1993; Van Tuijl & Leseman, 2004).

Compared with the almost universal provision of center-based ECD Programs in Europe for 3- to 5-year-old children, there is greater diversity in the services for the 0- to 3-year-olds. Family day-care homes and care in a child's own home through parental leaves of absence from the workplace are widespread for this younger age group. The same is true in the United States.

ECD programs in the **Majority World** lag behind. In Latin America and the Caribbean, the figure reaches a high of 54%, followed by a large margin by developing countries in East Asia and Oceania: 29%. It is down to 15%

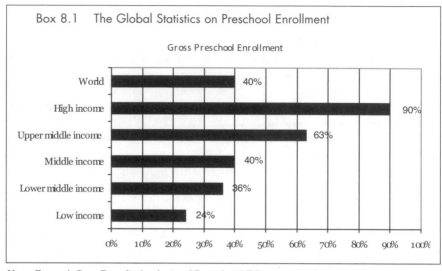

Box 8.1    The Global Statistics on Preschool Enrollment

Note. From *A Cost Benefit Analysis of Preschool Education in Turkey* by M. Kaytaz, 2005, Istanbul: AÇEV.

in Arab countries, 11% in South Asia, and a mere 9% in Sub-Saharan Africa (UNESCO, 2005). Again, these statistics do not cover informal care. Still, the very low coverage of ECD programs particularly in Africa and South Asia is notable, and should be taken seriously in view of the importance of early stimulation for school readiness. Box 8.1 gives the global statistics on preschool enrollment. The clear linear relationship between overall societal affluence and access to ECD services is notable. It shows that just as in the case of primary education and above, preschool education is also very closely connected with general macroeconomic characteristics of societies, and in particular, with affluence.

Starting in the 1980s, great strides were made in many developing countries, doubling and tripling available ECD services (e.g., in Brazil and Thailand), increasing even five- or sixfold in some (Burkina Faso, Oman, and the Dominican Republic) (Myers, 1992, p. 24). However, because in many countries the baselines were very small, even today the coverage is still grossly inadequate. Given this situation and the limited available funds, alternative nonformal ECD programs such as non-center-based services and innovative community-based programs often involving nonprofessional caretakers are being tried out in many countries in the world. In this context, the American programs and their evaluations serve as a model. These programs often take the form of interventions for early support in the context of socioeconomic adversity.

## The American Experience: Head Start and Other ECD Projects

The roots of the ECD programs in the United States are to be found in the "War on Poverty" initiative of the Johnson era in the 1960s. It aspired to open up opportunities for poor families, especially poor African American families, and to enable them and their children to benefit from these enhanced opportunities. **Head Start**, sponsored by the Office of Economic Opportunity, synthesized several aspects of this massive endeavor, including preschool education, meals, service brokerage for families, and parent participation, but not parent education. Detailed accounts of Head Start appeared in the several extensive reports and evaluations coming out of the program, as well as in other writings (Halpern, 1990; Kassebaum, 1994; Woodhead, 1988; Zigler & Berman, 1983; Zigler & Weiss, 1985).

*Early Evaluations.*   An early evaluation of Head Start, the Westinghouse Report (Cicirelli, Evans, & Schiller, 1969), concluded prematurely that Head Start had failed, followed by a review by Bronfenbrenner (1974) that also expressed disappointment. These early reviews focused mainly on the problem of the dissipation of immediate gains in IQ scores over time. A subsequent report based on the initial evaluations was prepared for the World Bank (Smilansky, 1979). It was so critical of early enrichment programs that it resulted in a policy decision by the World Bank not to allocate funds to early intervention. This is an example of the heavy social responsibility carried by the social scientist. The main problem with the report was that it referred mainly to the first wave of rather negative evaluations, based on the work of the 1960s. It did not use the later information providing evidence of positive long-term effects. Nevertheless, it had a significant effect directing the World Bank away from ECD.[1]

The unfavorable early evaluations of Head Start and other ECD programs in the United States had a number of conceptual and methodological problems. Among these were the vague criteria of success; exclusive dependence on IQ measures; thus a unidimensional conceptualization of child development in terms of **cognitive competence** (narrowly defined in psychometric terms); abstraction of the child from the environment and focusing only on individual child outcomes; and the short time span used for evaluation. I deal with these issues later on. Underlying these problems was an unrealistic and unnecessary goal attributed to Head Start—raising IQs. This was greatly reinforced by the popular media, as

---

[1]The situation has changed since then, and the World Bank is now actively involved in ECD (see Young, 1997, 2002).

well. IQ as a "magic" yet concrete target was singled out, to the exclusion of other beneficial outcomes.

*Second Wave of Evaluations.*    A second wave of evaluations subsequently brought forth a different and more positive picture. More than 1,600 documents on Head Start formed the basis for the Head Start Synthesis Project, which utilized a meta-analysis of 250 research reports. Seventy-two studies showed evidence of gains in cognitive competence, school readiness, and school achievement, which were sustained for 2 years after attending Head Start. There was also evidence of positive effects on children's socioemotional development and health status (McKey et al., 1985). However, IQ and achievement differences (from the control groups) tended to dissipate over time.

The great diversity of Head Start programs and the methodological flaws of some of the studies involved, notably, noncomparability of groups, detracts somewhat from the overall value of the meta-analysis (Woodhead, 1988). Nevertheless, the trends all pointed to positive effects, especially notable in large-scale studies. For example, a study with thousands of sixth through eighth graders who had attended Head Start in Philadelphia found that they had better school adjustment than peers without such experience (Copple, Cline, & Smith, 1987). Another study of three Head Start cohorts, totaling more than 1,900 children, found the oldest cohort to perform better academically than a control group at the end of high school (Hebbeler, 1985). Yet another study supplemented a regular Head Start program with an emergent literacy component resulting in beneficial outcomes (Whitehurst, Zevenbergen, Crone, Schultz, & Velting, 1999).

Other carefully planned early enrichment projects utilizing experimental designs produced evidence of sustained effects in 1990s. Such studies predated Head Start, paving the way for it, and they have been continuing up to the present. Some of them involved massive and costly intervention, often starting out in infancy. Long-term effects have been found. Some important examples include the *Early Training Project* (Gray, Ramey, & Klaus, 1983; R. A. Klaus & Gray, 1968), the *Abecedarian Project* (Wasik, Ramey, Bryant, & Sparling, 1990), *Ypsilanti Perry Preschool Project* (Berrueta-Clement, Schweinhart, Barnett, Epstein, & Weikart, 1984; Schweinhart, Barnes, Weikart, Barnett, & Epstein, 1994), *Success for All Program* ( Madden, Slavin, Karweit, Dolan, & Wasik, 1991), and the *Mother–Child Home Program* (Levenstein, O'Hara, & Madden, 1983; Scarr & McCartney, 1988).

The longitudinal results of these studies showed better school performance and social adjustment for the experimental group of children compared with control group, including lower rates of grade retention and referral to special classes; higher rates of high school completion and employment; and lower incidence of crime and teenage pregnancy. There are also indications of motivational gains and psychological well-being such as higher achievement motivation; higher occupational aspirations and expectations; and more positive self-concept. These are reflected in parental outlooks that also show higher aspirations and expectations for their children, as well as indicating more satisfaction with their children's school progress, even when grade retention and referrals to special classes are controlled. These results come from some single-study evaluations, especially of the Perry Preschool Project (Berrueta-Clement et al., 1984; Schweinhart et al., 1994, 2005). They also derive from pooled findings, in the form of meta-analyses conducted by the Consortium for Longitudinal Studies (Lazar, Darlington, Murray, & Snipper, 1982). Bronfenbrenner (1979) also conceded that his earlier conclusion, that there were no lasting intervention effects, had been premature.

The explanations proposed for the positive long-term effects focused on interactions between immediate cognitive gains from enrichment programs and environmental factors such as teachers' and parents' expectations and school requirements (Lazar et al., 1982; Woodhead, 1985). Specifically, it appears that children who go through preschool enrichment programs gain immediate cognitive skills as well as other skills such as attentiveness to teachers, ability to follow instructions, task perseverance and sustained focused attention, ability to work in groups, and they also relate well to others. All these school-relevant skills help them adjust to the demands of classroom procedures and the school system better than children from similar socially disadvantaged backgrounds. These positive attitudes and behaviors are in turn perceived by the teachers and further reinforced, producing feelings of competence and higher aspirations for success in children, as well as higher expectations on the part of teachers and parents, thus triggering a virtuous circle—a "positive" Pygmalion effect (Rosenthal & Jacobson, 1968) leading to sustained satisfactory school performance.

Longer-term effects are of great value, as sustainability is a true test of impact over time. Although these effects do not involve raising children's IQs, they are important in terms of long-term real-life consequences, such as better social adjustment, reflected in less delinquent or antisocial behavior, higher school attainment, higher earnings, and the like (Kassebaum, 1994; Reynolds, Chang, & Temple, 1998; Schweinhart et al., 1994; Yoshikawa, 1994; Zigler & Styfco, 1994; Zigler,Taussig, & Black, 1992).

*Third Wave of Evaluations.* What may be termed a third wave of evaluations has recently been coming out. A recent meta-analysis by Blok et al. (2005) used more exact measures on 19 studies published from 1985 onward and examined a total of 85 different outcomes in the cognitive and the socioemotional domain. The programs were grouped into three different delivery types, center based, home based, and a combination of the two. They found greater effects on cognitive child outcomes in the center-based and combination types of interventions compared with home-based programs. However, no differences among the delivery types were found in the socioemotional domain where generally weak effects were obtained. Coaching of parenting skills was further found to relate positively to cognitive child outcomes.

A rather different portrait is drawn by Sweet and Appelbaum (2004), who conducted another meta-analysis of home-based intervention studies conducted in the United States. Sixty home-visiting programs from the United States were covered in this study. Ten standardized effect sizes were computed for treatment versus control comparisons, and 6 of these positive-outcome effects were found to be significant. Longer-term tracing studies of well-known early intervention studies also point to sustained gains. For example, the *High-Scope* (Schweinhart et al., 2005), the *Abecederian* (F. A. Campbell, Ramey, Pungello, Sparling, & Miller-Johnson, 2002; Ramey & Ramey, 1998), the *Comprehnsive Child Development Program* (Goodson, Layer, StPierre, Bernstein, & Lopez, 2000), and the *Chicago Longitudinal Study* (Reynolds & Ou, 2004) long-term follow-ups reconfirm longer school attainment and other school-related benefits, such as less retention and referral to special classes, together with better overall adjustment extending into adulthood. For example, the Abecedarian Project experience resulted in an almost 50% decline in the likelihood of children repeating a grade in primary school (Ramey et al., 2000).

On the other hand, some European early intervention programs with ethnic-minority mothers and children have produced variable outcomes (Van Tuijl & Leseman, 2004; Van Tuijl, Leseman, & Rispens, 2001). Issues in implementation and selection of outcome variables appear to be factors responsible for some of the weak effects obtained. These issues are addressed later on.

Given the varied outcomes from intervention programs, some recent overviews of the field reflect on what went wrong with the earlier efforts, pointing in particular to the unrealistic expectations of lifelong gains from limited short-term investments (Brooks-Gunn, 2003; Zigler, 2003). Others examine the important factors that make an impact in "quality" interventions (Ramey & Ramey, 1998). Meta-analyses and comparisons attempt to ascertain commonalities and differences that are important to arrive at generalizable conclusions (Layzer, Goodson, Bernstein, & Price, 2001; Love, Schothet, & Meckstroth, 2002). Box 8.2 presents some features proposed to contribute to the success of ECD programs.

---

Box 8.2 Features of a Successful ECD Program

Child-centered approach

- Parental involvement and family support
- Community ownership
- Cultural and financial sustainability
- Training and capacity building
- Integration within a broader framework of development
- Private-public partnership

---

*Note.* From Communities can make a difference: Five cases across continents (p.298) by S. Kirpal, 2002, In M. E.Young (Ed.), *From Early Childhood Development to Human Development* (pp. 293-360). Washington, D.C.: The World Bank.

## Majority World Experience

As indicated before, ECD programs lag behind in the **Majority World,** with great diversity in the provision of services. Nevertheless, the recent increases are notable and the sheer numbers of children in programs are impressive. Thus, in Brazil and Indonesia several million children are served. At the beginning of the 1990s, China was providing preschool services to 16.3 million children (a number larger than many European countries' total populations, but nevertheless still constituting a relatively low percentage coverage) (Myers, 1992). The largest ECD program in the world is the *Integrated Child Development Service* (ICDS) of India, serving a remarkable 32 million children (M. E. Young, 2002, p. 6).

There is great variety in programs. Some involve integrated health, nutrition, and early education services, as, for example, in the massive ICDS in India. Others are smaller-range experimental programs; some entail mainly nursery school activities; many include home and community involvement. The quality of care and early education provided varies greatly.

Starting in the 1980s there has been an important trend toward coordinating different approaches and diverse orientations underlying services for young children, women, and families. An early example of this was the *Thai Nutrition Project* (Kotchabhakdi et al., 1987), discussed briefly in the last chapter. In this large-scale project, a community-based primary health care program was integrated with a growth-monitoring, supplementary food program, nutrition education, and a psychosocial education program (sensitizing mothers to the early development of sensation-perception in the infant, the value of early stimulation, and the importance of mother–child interaction). Other integrative attempts were also made in the 1980s to meet the intersecting needs of (working) women and children (Engle, 1986; J. L. Evans & Myers, 1985).

In general, early childhood programs have been conceptualized in formal preschool terms, following the traditional Western experience. However, preschools tend to be expensive because they entail building/grounds maintenance, expensive materials, and especially professional salaries. Consequently, in less developed countries they are limited in number and those that exist mainly cater to the children of the urban middle-class families who can pay for such services. Thus there is considerable need for innovative and cost-effective approaches in ECD in the Majority World to reach large numbers of poor children who need these services the most. This need is slowly being recognized and alternative ECD models are being experimented with, sometimes in large-scale service programs.

Myers (1992) differentiated five different approaches and program/policy options: center-based programs, parent support/education, community development, strengthening institutions, and creating awareness and demand for ECD programs. These approaches also continue to be valid today. Therefore, I present a short summary of the different types of ECD programs in the Majority World following this grouping.

Center-based programs provide services to children within an institutional context and constitute the traditional model of ECD. They vary greatly, however, in terms of their degree of formality, ranging from formal preschools to nonformal home day care, where a child caretaker (child minder) cares for a number of children, including her own. Whereas preschools focus on education, home care is mainly oriented toward custodial care. Between these two are different types of centers. Some of them are designed mainly to support children's health and nutrition needs whereas others try to integrate early education and school preparation with food supplementation and health care. Some centers function at the workplace, mainly to support working mothers, whereas some are "mobile crèches," serving the children of seasonal workers who move from one site to another, such as construction workers.

Moving beyond centers, parent/caregiver support and education is an important approach to ECD. Here the target is the caregiver and the goal is to support her, in order to promote, in turn, better child development. A holistic contextual orientation underlies this approach. Educating/supporting caregivers can be done through home visits, adult education in groups, the mass media, or child-to-child programs. The last alternative is a typically non-Western model where older children are trained/supported to care for younger children and prepare them for school.

Another approach to the provision of ECD services is to integrate them into community development programs. Community development programs aim to strengthen the material conditions of a community and its capacity for self-help. So, they build on existing resources, and the whole community, together with the children, benefit. But there is the danger that **early child development** may be treated simply as a residual in a larger program and not attended to adequately.

Strengthening institutions and creating awareness and demand for ECD in populations are other complementary approaches. In general, they have to do on the one hand with integrating child development into the formal training of medical professionals, nutritionists, and others whose work is relevant to children. On the other hand, improving child-care provisions by introducing educational materials and better care/training skills among caretakers all promote good ECD services. Finally, creating a higher level of awareness of the importance of ECD services among parents and in the general public is of crucial significance.

*Early Evaluations.* A general issue addressed in the evaluation of early intervention programs is whether they work in Majority World conditions and whether the "Western experience" can be generalized to non-Western contexts. Indeed, given the great contextual differences, this type of generalization is problematic. However, there is a growing body of evaluation research emerging from the Majority World that needs to be attended to.

Myers (1992) reviewed the early evidence regarding the effects of early educational interventions in developing countries on progress and performance in school. Six of the 13 studies examined showed a difference in school promotion rates, being dramatic in some cases. For example, in Brazil repetition of the first grade was only 9% for children who had had a nutrition and education intervention, compared with 33% for a control group. Another study from Brazil showed a high first-grade repetition rate of 36% for children with a kindergarten experience but a much higher rate (66%) for those without such experience. Studies from Colombia showed higher gains from intervention among the most impoverished groups of children, where 60% of the program children reached the fourth grade of primary school, compared with only 30% of the comparison group. Similarly, in India and Argentina, the most impoverished groups benefited the most. In Argentina, 36% of poor rural children repeated the first grade if they had a preschool experience, compared with 77% of those without such experience. In India, the children who participated in the ICDS had higher intellectual aptitude test scores, better school performance, better school attendance, and better overall adjustment (Chaturvedi, Srivastava, Singh, & Prasad, 1987). Finally, in 6 of the 10 studies where information was available on academic performance, children who had had early educational intervention performed better than comparison groups.

The early results of ECD interventions from the Majority World show that early enrichment can improve children's school performance. Though long-term effects are not available, the shorter-term results are encouraging. They are particularly notable for the most disadvantaged children, and they appear to be materializing despite unfavorable conditions in primary schools. Multifaceted programs integrating nutritional-health aspects together with early education are found to have a greater impact, particularly in the most impoverished areas. These findings have clear policy implications for promoting human development in the Majority World.

*More Recent Evaluations.*   More recent evaluations of ECD programs in Latin America continue to show the benefits of early interventions. A decrease in grade repetition is a very important gain from ECD interventions. Grade repetition in primary schooling is a serious global problem with high individual and social costs. For example, a UNESCO Institute of Statistics study in Latin America showed that one in four primary school students repeated the 2001 school year in Brazil, 14% in Guatemala, and 11% in Peru. Repetition is a factor in an estimated 18% of the students in the region not completing primary schooling. The cost of repetition is estimated at over $11.1 billion a year in the region. Brazil fares the worst, with $8.3 billion. This amount is equal to 1 year of schooling for almost 10 million secondary students or 2 million university students in Brazil (UNESCO, 2004, p. 15).

ECD evaluations from Brazil (Barros & Mendonca, 1999) showed that poor children who attended 1 year of preschool attained 0.4 years more schooling than children who didn't have the preschool experience. Additionally, for each year of preschool, in adulthood they achieved a 7% to 12 % increase in lifetime earnings. These gains were greater for children whose parents had the lowest levels of schooling. This is clear evidence for the compensatory function of intervention programs in providing the greatest gains to children from families with the least education.

In a comparative analysis of school outcomes in 13 Latin American countries (Willms, 2002), Cuba emerged with the highest scores on almost all measures of standards on family and school variables. It was attributed in no small degree to the fact that almost all children in Cuba have access to preschool day care (94%). Together with high parental education, high parental involvement, and high school standards such as good classroom climate, the fact that children enjoy ECD support make for overall success.

ECD intervention can be combined with other services to the parents, families, and communities ranging from income-generating activities to health services. Kirpal (2002) reviewed five diverse programs in widely different countries, *the Montessori Preschool Project* in Haiti; *the Mother–Child Day Care Center Services* in Uganda; *Servol* in Trinidad and Tobago; *the Madrasa Resource Centers* in Kenya, Uganda, and Zanzibar; and *the Step by Step Program* in Central and Eastern Europe, the former Soviet Union, Haiti, Mongolia, and South Africa.

The Montessori program trains scholarship students in Haiti to be Montessori preschool teachers and then helps them establish preschools. The Uganda program aims to improve the condition of young children by providing them with a safe and stimulating environment thus empowering poor mothers to work; varied services are provided such as counseling on child health, parenting skills, and literacy. SERVOL provides ECD services to young children as well as conducting parent outreach programs and training programs for adolescents and young adults. The Aga Khan Foundation supports Madrasa Resource Centers in Africa and improving preschool and primary education in South Asia. Community awareness and mobilization is aimed for. The Step by Step Program, started and supported by the Open Society Institute, especially helps address the problem of a decline in services for young children after the collapse of communism. In an effort to reform the educational system, interventions at all levels of education are carried out, including preschool education, teacher training, and so on.

Despite their diversity, these programs also have common aspects. They all provide direct center-based ECD services to young children, all involve teacher and/or caregiver training, and all rely on community support. Thus they build both individual and environmental resources. All of the programs are seen to be effective (Kirpal, 2002), however, their long-term evaluations have not been conducted.

Putting it all together, we can say that ECD provides significant benefits to children. Evaluation research in diverse settings has pointed to gains in the areas of education, health, social capital, and greater equality. Both immediate benefits and long-term gains render these interventions highly valuable and worth the investment. Van der Gaag (2002) summarizes this situation (Box 8.3).

## ISSUES IN ECD RESEARCH

The previous overview of ECD research both in the United States and in the **Majority World** shows that the main debate has revolved around

Box 8.3  ECD Benefits for Children, Adults, and Society: Summary

**Pathways linking ECD to HD**

| Benefits of ECD | Education | Health | Social Capital | Equality |
|---|---|---|---|---|
| For Children (immediate) | Higher intelligence, improved practical reasoning, eye and hand coordination, hearing and speech; reading readiness; social | Less morbidity, mortality, malnutrition, stunting, child abuse; better hygiene and health care | Higher self-concept; more socially adjusted; less aggressive; more cooperative; better behavior in groups; increased acceptance of instructions | Reduced disadvantages of poverty; improved nutritional status, cognitive and social development and health |
| improved school performance; less grade repetition and dropout; increased schooling | | | | |
| For adults (long-term) | Higher productivity; increased success (better jobs, higher incomes); improved childcare and family health; greater economic well-being | Improved height and weight; enhanced cognitive development; less infections and chronic diseases | Higher self-esteem; improved social competence, motivation, acceptance of norms and values; less delinquency and criminal behaviour | Equality of opportunity, education, health and income |

Box 8.3 *(Continued)*

**Pathways linking ECD to HD**

| Benefits of ECD | Education | Health | Social Capital | Equality |
|---|---|---|---|---|
| For Society | Greater social cohesion; less poverty and crime; lower fertility rates; increased adoption of new technologies; improved democratic processes; higher economic growth | Higher productivity; less absenteeism higher incomes | Improved utilization of social capital; enhanced social values | Reduced poverty and crime; better societal health; increased social justice; higher sustainable economic growth |

*Note.* From 'From child development to human development' *(p 73)* by J. van der Gaag, 2002, In M. E. Young (Ed.), *From Early Childhood Development to Human Development* (pp. 63-78). Washington, D.C.: The World Bank.

*Note.* ECD, Early child development; HD, human development.

the question of whether early intervention works. This is of course the key issue in intervention. Interventions are carried out to achieve a goal. Every intervention is designed to promote optimal development, however, whether it achieves it is an empirical question. If programs do not achieve their goal, they have to be changed, improved, or relinquished. Therefore, evaluation is of key importance to establish whether interventions make an impact or not.

The goal in ECD interventions is to improve the environment and to build individual resources, as mentioned before. Several issues are involved in evaluation research entailing important conceptual and methodological points. Some of these were mentioned briefly in discussing the problems with the early evaluations of **Head Start.** I want to elaborate on them and introduce others in this section.

*Child-Centered Versus Parent-Centered Approaches.* A long-standing issue that appears to have assumed renewed importance is the relative focus on the child or the parent. This is known as child- versus parent-centered or center-based versus home-based approaches in early intervention. For example, the recent meta-analysis of Blok et al. (2005), mentioned earlier, focused on this comparison while also adding a third category, their combination, as three different delivery modes of ECD support. They found center-based or a combination of center- and home-based approaches to be superior to home-based approaches. They also showed, however, that promoting parenting skills related positively to cognitive child outcomes.

Similarly, a review of home-visiting programs also reported meager outcomes (Home Visiting, 1999). Does this mean that home-based intervention does not work and therefore should be relinquished? As mentioned before, different and more positive results have been obtained in the meta-analysis conducted by Sweet and Appelbaum (2004). The general conclusion drawn was that "home visiting does seem to help families with young children" (p. 1448). Other recent evaluations concur (Layzer et al., 2001; Reynolds, Wang & Walberg, 2003). As we see in the next chapter, in the **Turkish Early Enrichment Project (TEEP)** we also found valuable long-term effects of a home-based intervention (Kağitçibaşi, Sunar, & Bekman, 2001; Kağitçibaşi et al., 2007). So, how do we explain the variable findings?

Home-visiting programs that try to build parenting skills without directly providing early enrichment to children are often categorized as parent-focused or home-based and are contrasted unfavorably with child-focused or center-based programs in terms of child cognitive outcomes (e.g., Blok et al., 2005; Farran, 1990; Ramey & Ramey, 1998). However, a child focus can be integrated with a parent-focused approach.

In fact, a combination of child education with parent support/education is found to be highly beneficial, especially in counteracting the detrimental effects of poverty (Behrman et al., 2004; Hadeed, 2005; Kağitçibaşi et al., 2001; Yoshikawa, 1994). An earlier review of community-based early intervention (Halpern, 1990) also pointed to the value of more **holistic/contextual approaches** and showed evidence of success in programs where specific outcome domains were stressed and intensive enrichment was provided. Recent research has shown that children's cognitive development doubled when intervention programs involved education for both mothers and children (Dearing, McCartney, & Taylor, 2001; Layzer et al., 2001).

Home visiting programs tend to be more prevalent for the younger ages, 0 to 3. Accordingly, they also often have a more holistic approach, providing early stimulation and play activities, education and support to parents, community involvement, and the like. For example, Scott-McDonald (2002) reviewed three home-visiting programs from Jamaica. These programs serve children and families, mostly single teenage mothers, who live in poverty. A number of elements of quality are singled out that have contributed to the success of the programs, among them are: linkage of child-care supports with family supports; recognition of women's multiple roles as mothers, homemakers, and income earners; and proactive measures to ensure sustainability and institutionalization.

Clearly, home-visiting programs are often multifaceted and contain complex service provision. However, their research and evaluation component is often not well developed. Thus Sweet and Appelbaum (2004), in their rather positive meta-analysis, also noted that the complexity of the programs and targeted outcomes as well as program designs that don't have an evaluation component create difficulties in arriving at clear-cut generalizations. On the other hand, it is possible to build up the research and evaluation component as well as the intensity and quality of the education or enrichment that is provided to the child while the parent is being supported.

*The Value of a Contextual Approach.*    Usually the child focus is rather marginal in home visiting, but this need not be the case. Furthermore, combined parent and child orientation need not be confined to home visiting only. What is important is that *both* the child *and* the child's immediate environment (parent) are targeted. If this is not done, then focusing on the child out of context would ignore that context. Yet, there is a great deal of evidence showing that support of the child's immediate social environment is of great importance. In chapters 2, 3, and 7, we saw many examples of this. Thus, in cognitive enrichment programs targeting the child that also help the mother build self-esteem and competence so that she can engage in cognitively oriented, affectively based communication with her child can help support the continued cognitive development of the child. When both the mother (caregiver) and the child benefit from the intervention, the impact is more likely to be sustained over time through a process of continued mutual reinforcement.

Particularly in sociocultural contexts where close-knit family, kinship, and community ties exist, as in most parts of the Majority World, it would make sense for an enrichment program to build on these ties as support mechanisms. Such an approach would be more likely to succeed than an individualistic orientation that treats the child separately from the environment and ignores the existing family and community ties. A contextual approach, which includes support of the child's immediate environment, provides other advantages as well. For example, it avoids the creation of two different and possibly incompatible environments—the preschool and the home/community—for the child. Another advantage is the possibility of the generalization of gains from enrichment efforts to other individuals in the family, particularly younger siblings, and possibly other relatives, neighbors, and other members of the community.

Despite these advantages of contextual models of early intervention, the debate is continuing about the relative effectiveness of child-focused versus caregiver-focused approaches. This is because child-focused approaches also have some advantages such as direct impact on the child, which can include the enhancement of the child's autonomy and reflectiveness, as seen, for example, in the high-quality Perry Preschool Program (Schweinhart et al., 1994, 2005). In Sweden, where child care is of high quality, it is found that the earlier a child enters day care (within the 1st year of life), the more beneficial are the long-term benefits (at 8 and/or 13 years of age) (Andersson, 1992). Thus, *quality* in care in child-focused center-based approaches appears to be of key importance. Finally, a problem with a home-based approach has been noted in that parents may not be competent teachers (Eldering & Vedder, 1993), decreasing the impact of parent-focused interventions.

As Seitz and Provence (1990) noted some time ago, without longitudinal research it is difficult to resolve this debate. On the basis of the existing evidence, at least for populations at poverty level, caregiver-focused approaches are found to be effective, because by changing the family environment, they can bring about a broader range of beneficial outcomes for children.

Actually, even so-called child-focused approaches inevitably involve parents, at least to the extent of informing them and getting their endorsement. In many cases, parent involvement is of a much higher level. Often programs entail home visits to involve parents or inform them in other ways. Thus, rather than asking whether child-focused or caregiver-focused programs are more effective, it may be better to look into how the needs of both parents and children can best be met. TEEP, covered in the next chapter, provides one answer to this more important question.

*Unidimensional Conceptualization Versus Whole Child Approach.* A continuing problem in ECD research is the unidimensional conceptualization of child development solely in cognitive terms. The easy availability of intelligence tests and other cognitive measures, and their wider acceptance in comparison with the less well-established measures of socioemotional development, have contributed to the disproportionate emphasis on cognitive development.

Apart from the methodological weakness of single-criterion measures, and their vulnerability to statistical artifacts such as ceiling effects and regression toward the mean in repeated testing, a unidimensional conceptualization is theoretically too simplistic. Cognitive development is but one aspect of total human development. There is an inherent interdependence among the different aspects of overall development. Thus a "whole child" approach is called for. Focusing exclusively on the IQ gains of a child diverts attention from other possible developmental benefits of preschool intervention programs. An impoverished environment that is not conducive to the full development of the child's cognitive potential is also detrimental to his or her socioemotional development. For example, a child's lack of self-confidence may underlie a low level of motivation to excel in intellectual tasks, which may in turn result in low IQ scores and poor school achievement. This low self-confidence is itself a reflection of how "significant others" in the environment view the child.

The dissipation of IQ gains after the completion of enrichment programs may, ironically, be due to the exclusive concern of these programs with IQ gains. The cognitive development spurred by the directive cognitive approach is often not supported by the induction of corresponding growth of the child's self-confidence, initiative, motivation, and autonomy, so that the cognitive gains turn out not to be self-sustained after the completion of the program. It is therefore necessary to support the child's *overall* development. If the child's immediate social environment, which could provide the child with continued support, is not fostered by the intervention, cognitive gains are likely to be short-lived.

This has been a major problem in early-intervention research. Although it is generally accepted that human development is multifaceted and should be studied as such, certain measurable outcome measures are given a disproportionate weight in evaluation studies. For example, home-based parent–child education programs for ethnic-minority populations in the Netherlands have been labeled as ineffective by researchers (Blok et al., 2005) because they apparently do not affect fifth-grade standardized test scores. This evaluation is made despite the fact that the children who participate in this intervention program are found to repeat fewer grades in primary school than control children. This judgment is made because test scores are considered to be more important outcome measures than class repetition. Yet, as discussed before, repetition of a school year is a serious problem with high individual and economic costs (UNESCO, 2004). Thus, this appears to be a questionable judgment. Nevertheless, it is influencing policy in that the Dutch government tries to exclude home-based programs that support ethnic-minority mothers and children from funding (personal communication, C. van Tuijl, February, 2006).

*Timing of Effects.*    A third evaluation issue in intervention research is timing. Because human development is a continuous process, we are faced with the question of deciding when to assess an effect. Typically, immediate effects of an intervention program are measured, yet this approach leaves questions of sustainability unanswered. This is especially problematic given the fact that immediate gains in IQ scores tend to dissipate over time. Ideally, long-term effects in different spheres of development should be assessed. When such evidence is available, it can provide a better understanding of whether lasting gains obtain and *how,* for example, through motivational and better adjustment mechanisms or through higher cognitive skills. Thus, with early enrichment, the child's positive orientation to school, initial good performance (cognitive skills) and parents' high aspirations may all combine to initiate a positive cycle of development.

A considerable amount of time has now passed since some important ECD interventions began, especially in the United States. Thus, longer-term effects are emerging in repeated evaluation studies. These studies now provide us with plenty of insight into effects well into adulthood. Such long-term effects constitute real "proof" of the effectiveness of early intervention. They are more meaningful than shorter-term IQ gains or other cognitive measures, as intervention is after all for building lifelong "competence" and well-being.

Assessing long-term effects can also reveal **sleeper effects** or effects consolidated over time, which may not be immediately apparent at program completion. For example, a particularly intensive caregiver-focused program, the *Yale Child Welfare Program,* obtained stronger long-term than short-term effects (Seitz & Provence, 1990; Seitz, Rosenbaum, & Apfel, 1985). *The High-Scope* (Schweinhart et al., 2005), the *Abecederian* (F. A. Campbell et al., 2002; Ramey et al., 2000) and the *Chicago Longitudinal Study* (Reynolds & Ou, 2004) long-term follow-ups reconfirm longer school attainment and other school-related benefits, such as less retention and referral to special classes, together with better overall adjustment extending into adulthood.

*Definition of the Outcome Variables.*    Another problem that is related to some of the previous points is the definition of the outcome variable (dependent variable) in intervention research. As indicated before, this is commonly construed in terms of the child's cognitive development, most narrowly operationalized in terms of IQ. Somewhat broader conceptualizations may entail other indicators of cognitive capacity, such as Piaget tasks. Expanding further, school-related performance (school success and attainment) is included in the dependent variable. Assessment of noncognitive psychological development as outcome variable is less common, though it is gaining importance, especially in longer-term evaluations. An example is the longitudinal results of the Perry Preschool Program, providing evidence for better social adjustment of the experimental group compared with the control group over time (Schweinhart et al., 1994, 2005).

Even with such expansion, however, it is clear that the dependent variable is commonly construed in terms of the child alone. This is despite the fact that interventions are often directed to the family and parents (caregivers) as well as the children. As I noted before, in many cases parents are involved in one form or another, and they are influenced by the intervention. However such impact is usually not construed as an outcome variable and is not assessed. This is a conceptual and methodological weakness, particularly in home- and community- based programs.

For example, a positive outcome of Head Start has been on families and the employment of parents. Thousands of low-income parents have obtained jobs through Head Start, and more than 35% of the staff were found to be parents of Head Start children or graduates (Collins, 1990). Head Start programs were also found to enhance communities' capacities to meet local needs (McKey et al., 1985). Thus, both a whole child approach and a more contextual approach, entailing different types of dependent variables, are needed. These would shed light on the dynamics of change produced in different spheres and levels of outcome variables.

This is especially relevant in Majority World contexts. Indeed, the programs there tend to be multifaceted targeting both the child and the family, especially the mother. Often community mobilization and capacity enhancement are also aimed for, for example, in terms of income generation activities. Furthermore, these different outcomes are often in a synergistic relationship, mutually reinforcing one another. Therefore, operationalization of all the outcome variables in these different spheres needs to be planned from the start.

*Program Implementation.* Another issue in intervention research concerns program implementation. Conclusions are often drawn regarding the effectiveness of a *type* of intervention (e.g., child-focused vs. caregiver-focused delivery) on the basis of the results obtained from a program. However the impact of the program may have more to do with the quality of implementation than with the approach or delivery mode used. The intensity of the intervention, the level of training and supervision of the fieldworkers, the availability of good materials, the rapport between the targets (families, caregivers) and the implementers of intervention, the participation level of the caregivers (including their attrition rates), and so forth, are all important in affecting the outcome.

At times, the same program content together with the same approach used in two different programs may produce different outcomes, mainly due to variations in implementation. For example, the Home Instruction Program for Preschool Youngsters (HIPPY) (Lombard, 1981) achieved good results in Israel and in Turkey (as a part of our Early Enrichment Project, presented in the next chapter). However, its effects in a program with Turkish, Moroccan, Surinamese, and Dutch immigrants in the Netherlands were negligible (Eldering & Vedder, 1993). Among the reasons for such different outcomes were implementation problems in the Netherlands (such as high attrition rates, language problems in program application, etc.)

Even though it is recognized that quality of implementation is as important as the type of intervention per se, it tends to be overlooked in drawing conclusions about programs. This is especially a problem inherent to meta-analyses. Given the great number of programs covered in meta-analytic studies, the researchers cannot examine in detail the actual implementation of any of the programs. Rather, only some broad program characteristics are utilized comparatively as categories, and the focus is on the outcomes.

## Cost-Effectiveness and Potential for Expansion

A final issue in intervention research is cost-effectiveness and, as related to this, the potential for expansion of a program to scale. The goal of intervention research and in general of ECD programs is to reach the families and children who are in greatest need of such services and who can benefit most from them. Thus large numbers are potentially involved and therefore the capacity of the program to expand or "to go to scale" assumes great importance. Cost effectiveness enables going to scale. This has been the case from the beginning of ECD interventions and has shaped policy decisions. For example, in his highly critical early report on preschool interventions, mentioned earlier, Smilansky (1979) recognized that some good programs could produce longer-term results but dismissed them as being too costly. The resultant policy shift away from funding of ECD programs reflected this judgment.

Cost-effectiveness analyses are valuable for the advocacy for early intervention and provision of ECD services to young children. As is the case for all policy decisions, evidence showing that an intervention works and is well worth its cost is crucial for ECD services. Policy relevant research is, therefore, progressively focusing on the cost-effectiveness of ECD programs.

Calculations of the cost-effectiveness of intervention programs are thus increasing in number, though still not very common. A notable one is the Perry Preschool Project. As part of the follow-up evaluation, the first cost–benefit study was carried out when program children reached age 19 (Berrueta-Clement et al., 1984). Benefits were construed in terms of cost savings and increased economic productivity (earnings) over the lifetime. Cost savings included child-care savings, reduced school costs due to less remedial education, savings in welfare expenditures, and savings due to the reduction in crime and delinquency. Increased earnings were both actual earnings of program children between the ages of 16 to 19 and also projected earnings after the age of 19. The overall benefit-to-cost ratio was found to be very high: 7 to 1, indicating a very high pay-off from the program. This is despite the very high actual cost of this intensive, high-quality program.

A later cost-effectiveness analysis of the Perry Preschool Program when the "children" reached the age of 27 corroborated the earlier ratio (Barnett, 1995; Schweinhart et al., 1994). Cost-effectiveness analysis has been conducted on the Abecederian Project, also, when children reached the age of 27. Both analyses included the quantifiable benefits and costs in health, employment status, criminality, and education. The benefit-to-cost ratio in the Abecederian Project is found to be 4 to 1 (Masse & Barnett, 2002). The high ratio was mainly due to the lower criminality among the adults who had participated in the preschool programs in early childhood.

As for the **Majority World,** Myers (1992) provided some examples of early cost calculations from India (the *ICDS*), Peru (*PRONOEI*), and Chile (*The Parents and Children Project [PPH]*) and a cost–benefit analysis from Brazil (*PROAPE*). More recently, more detailed cost–benefit analyses have been conducted, based on projections or scenarios, as longitudinal data are lacking. Van der Gaag and Tan (1998) calculated the benefit to cost ratio of the *PIDI* program in Bolivia. This is an ECD program providing nutrition, health, and education services to children living in urban slums. Based on different scenarios regarding decreases in under-5 mortality rates, increases in primary school enrollment, and decreases in repetition and dropout rates, they found benefit-to-cost ratios between 1.38 and 2.26 (between 1.38:1 and 2.26:1). A World Bank study in Egypt focusing on regional differences found ratios varying between 1.20 and 5.81, based on increases in enrollment and decreases in class repetition and dropout rates (World Bank, 2001). M. E. Young and Van der Gaag (2002) found ratios between 1.49 and 3.06 in Jordan, based on decreasing child mortality rates and increasing enrollment in primary and secondary education. Finally, Kaytaz (2005) calculated the benefit-to-cost ratio of the Turkish Early Enrichment Project, which is presented in the next chapter.

What do these benefit-to-cost ratios show? They show that investing in ECD programs is beneficial in economic terms as well as being worthwhile in terms of human development. Kaytaz (2005) demonstrates this by showing that benefits ensuing from ECD programs compare favorably with those arising from viable economic investments such as factories, forestation programs, livestock and other agricultural projects, and so on. This is very important for policy advocacy for ECD programs. A main point here is that more important than the absolute cost of a program is its cost-effectiveness or its benefit-to-cost ratio. An expensive program is a good investment if it produces highly beneficial outcomes, whereas an inexpensive program may be a poor investment (and more "costly") if it produces no effect.

Nevertheless, absolute costs cannot be ignored, either, especially in the Majority World where resources are very limited. In general, non-formal home- and community-based programs, employing paraprofessionals, volunteers, parents, and so on, tend to be less costly than formal, center-based preschool programs, employing professionals. Because early enrichment is usually understood as formal preschools, many governments in developing countries have typically considered early education a "luxury." This view does not hold up any longer, given the recent evidence all over the world on less expensive but effective alternatives to the formal traditional preschool.

Programs with multiple outcomes promoting cognitive and personality-social development of children, as well as their physical growth, better school adjustment and performance, better social and economic competence later on, and so on, and with multiple beneficiaries (children, their parents, siblings, whole families, communities) appear to be good investments. Particularly in the Majority World, such multipurpose approaches to early intervention and ECD have great potential to contribute to human development, defined in societal terms.

On the basis of this discussion, it appears that there is no one best early enrichment approach, but different approaches have their relative strengths. The characteristics of the situation and the goals set for intervention need to be taken into consideration. A conceptualization of child development as a multifaceted process is of crucial importance, as well as a contextual construal of this development.

## ECD in Turkey

As indicated earlier, the next chapter presents the **Turkish Early Enrichment Project (TEEP)** as an ECD intervention program and its applications. As background information for this, the state of ECD services in Turkey is briefly covered here. It also serves as an example of a situation from the **Majority World,** including efforts that lead toward the establishment of ECD programs.

In Turkey, preschool education is available for only about 16% of the preschool-age children. The shortage is even more critical for children from deprived socioeconomic backgrounds because many of the preschool facilities available are privately owned and charge for tuition. National resources have been allocated to primary education to raise literacy levels, leaving government-sponsored preschool services at a rudimentary level. Turkey has been undergoing rapid social change involving massive migration from rural to urban areas. This has created a demand for child care and a consequent recent increase in the number of child-care centers. However, the ECD provisions for the children of low-income working parents mainly provide custodial care, in contrast to the educational preschools catering to the middle classes. The former are mostly crèches at the workplace to provide working women with child care during working hours.

In the period 1978 to 1980, I directed a team of child development specialists and early childhood educators in the *Turkish Preschool Project* (Kağitçibaşi, 1981) conducted for the Ministry of Education. The team studied the state of ECD in Turkey, developed alternative working models for preschool services, and prepared resources for use in preschools, teacher training, and parent education. The materials included the texts *Child Development, Yearly Program in the Preschool, Preschool Activities, Cognitive Activities,* and *Your Child and You* (all in Turkish). These books, published by the Turkish Ministry of Education, provided valuable source material for preschool teachers and parents, but they did not reach a wide audience. The project also provided the Ministry with detailed recommendations regarding the promotion of preschool services and their synchronization with primary school education and teacher training. It paved the way for our subsequent longitudinal study,

TEEP, and consequently to policy-relevant outcomes emerging from this project.

The ECD provisions in Turkey are much too limited considering the country's level of development. This is mainly because of conservative values about the family, the continuing low levels of urban women's employment, despite recent increases, and in general, a lack of public opinion with regard to the importance of the early stimulation/learning for later school performance. It may be said that psychologists, child development specialists, and educators have not yet succeeded in sensitizing the public to the needs of the growing child, especially of children growing up in adverse conditions.

More recently, there have been attempts to advocate greater public provision of ECD utilizing alternative models. This is important, because it goes beyond the traditional center-based preschool model, which is costly and bound to remain rather limited in coverage. It entails home- and community-based nonformal enrichment through mother–child training. This may be seen as an outgrowth of our Early Enrichment Project (TEEP), presented in the next chapter.

## SUMMARY AND MAIN POINTS

- ECD programs constitute an important example of early environmental support and building resources for the child; they cover various types of interventions.
- Early evaluations of Head Start concluded prematurely that Head Start had failed. These evaluations contained conceptual and methodological problems. A second wave of evaluations showed evidence of gains in cognitive competence, school readiness, and school achievement.
- The longitudinal results of several early enrichment projects using experimental designs showed better school performance and social adjustment for the children in the experimental groups as well as lower incidence of socially maladaptive behaviors such as crime and teenage pregnancy.
- A third wave of evaluations has pointed to sustained benefits over a long time period. The main delivery types of ECD programs include center-based, home-based, and combination of center- and home-based approaches.Their relative effectiveness is a debated issue.

- ECD programs in the Majority World lag behind. There is much need for innovative and cost-effective approaches to reach large numbers of children.This need is being recognized slowly, and alternative ECD models are being experimented with.
- Myers (1992) differentiated five different approaches and program/policy options: center-based programs, parent support/education, community development, strengthening institutions, and creating awareness and demand for ECD programs.
- In the Majority World better academic performance and lower grade repetition are observed among children who had early educational intervention compared to the control groups.
- Some conceptual and methodological issues in ECD programs concern delivery modes (how the service is delivered), conceptualization of child development, timing of effects, definiton of the outcome variables, program implementation, and cost-effectiveness evaluation.
- A long-standing issue in evaluation research is the relative focus on the child or the parent. Targeting both the child and the child's immediate environment (parent) is crucial. Also a "whole child" approach is needed.
- Long-term effects in different spheres of development are more meaningful than shorter-term IQ gains.
- At times quality of implementation may be more influential than the approach or delivery mode used.
- A program's cost-effectiveness or its benefit-to-cost ratio is more important than its absolute cost.

## DISCUSSION QUESTIONS

1. Why has there been a tendency to assess the effectiveness of ECD programs with IQ tests?
2. What is wrong with this tendency?
3. What kinds of measures should be used to assess the effectiveness of ECD programs like the Head Start?
4. How do the outcomes of the ECD programs vary according to the deprivation levels of the subjects? What may be the implications of this?
5. The relative effectiveness of the different delivery modes are debated. What are the advantages and the disadvantages of the specific ECD delivery modes?
6. What does cost-effectiveness imply? How would you interpret it?

# 9

# The Turkish Early Enrichment Project (TEEP)

The previous chapter presented an overview of the field of **early childhood development (ECD)** interventions where psychology can contribute to applications designed to promote human development. The present chapter presents the **Turkish Early Enrichment Project (TEEP)** as a case in point. This project also serves as a case study of intervention and an "involved" orientation which has a central place in this book. The perspectives on the development of competence set out in chapters 2 and 3 serve as the theoretical underpinnings of the intervention presented here.

TEEP[1] is in the tradition of the ECD intervention studies and spans a period of 22 years (1982-2004). The original study was a 4-year intervention project, utilizing a field experiment. The two follow-up studies were carried out 6 years after the end of the original study (7 years after the intervention) and again 12 years later. I conducted these studies with my colleagues Sevda Bekman and Diane Sunar (Bekman, 1998a , 1998b; Ka itçiba i, 1997a, 1997b; Ka itçiba i et al., 2001). This chapter presents both the original study and the two follow-up studies.

## THE ORIGINAL 4-YEAR STUDY

The original study was a 4-year longitudinal project involving early childhood enrichment and mother training in low-income areas of Istanbul. The effects of both center-based day care and home-based early childhood education were studied, separately and in combination. The center-based child care was not introduced by the Project; rather, existing day-care centers were selected in terms of their basic orientations (custodial or educational day care). Groups of children in each type of center and a third group of children undergoing care in their own homes were studied. Because children were not randomly assigned to these three contexts, this aspect of the study involved a quasi-experimental, rather than an experimental design. In each of these groups, 3- and 5-year-old children were included.

The intervention undertaken by the Project was mother training introduced in the 2nd and 3rd years of the Project for a randomly selected number of the mothers in each group. The research design used,

[1]Funded by the International Development Research Centre (IDRC) of Canada. Project director: Cigdem Ka itçiba i; research associates: Diane Sunar and Sevda Bekman. See Ka itçiba i, Sunar, and Bekman (2001). The first follow-up study was funded by the MEAwards Program of the Population Council (Grant MEA 272). The second follow-up study was funded by MOCEF. The follow-up studies were conducted by the same research team, with the addition of Z. Cemalcilar in the second one.

**TABLE 9.1**
*Design of the Original (4-year) Study*

| | Number of subjects in each group | | | | | | |
| | Educational Day Care | | Custodial Day Care | | Home Care | | Total |
|---|---|---|---|---|---|---|---|
| Age of child | 3 | 5 | 3 | 5 | 3 | 5 | |
| Mother training | 11 | 16 | 23 | 17 | 16 | 7 | 90 |
| No mother training | 18 | 19 | 30 | 35 | 34 | 29 | 165 |
| Total | 29 | 35 | 53 | 52 | 50 | 36 | 255 |

*Note. $F = 3.55$; $p = .03$; d.f. 2, 244*

therefore, was a three (context: custodial, educational, home care) by two (age: 3 or 5) by two (mother training or no mother training) factorial design (Table 9.1). In the 1st year of the project, baselines were established through assessments of children, mothers, mother–child interaction, and demographic/socioeconomic variables. In the 2nd and 3rd years, the project intervention was applied, and in the 4th year reassessments were carried out.

The study was conducted in five low-income districts of Istanbul where factories employing large numbers of women ran day-care centers for their young children. Initially 3- and 5-year-old children were selected randomly in the day-care centers and in some where the numbers were small, all the 3- and 5-year-olds were included in the project. Their mothers constituted the mother sample. Families of the home-reared children were neighbors of the families where the mothers worked at the factories. Most of the mothers of home-reared children did not work outside the home. The mean age for mothers (in the 1st year) was 29 (32.8 for fathers). The mean years of school attendance for mothers was 5.4 (5.8 for fathers). All the families had low income and similar living conditions, which consisted largely of squatter housing.

Most of the population in these five regions are blue-collar workers or are involved in cottage industry or the marginal economy. The sample of parents consisted mainly of former villagers who had moved into the city. Only 27% of the mothers and 26% of the fathers had been born in the city. Nevertheless, most of the sample had been living in the city for a substantial period, having migrated in their teens. Previous research in Turkey had shown that where a person lives and where her family originates (large city, small town, or village) is an important factor in the degree of her modernization (Kağitçibaşi, 1982a, 1982b). The sample can thus be characterized as "semiurban." The majority (two thirds) of the sample of mothers were unskilled or semiskilled factory workers; one third were nonworking women (some of whom were involved in home production or cottage industry).

## Procedure and Measures

Mother training constituted the project intervention. After the establishment of the baselines through assessments in the 1st year, a randomly selected portion of the mothers of children in educational, custodial, and home care were provided with mother training in the 2nd and 3rd years of the project. This was the main independent variable, the other being the preschool context (custodial, educational, home care).

In the 4th (and last) year of the original study, reassessments were carried out to examine both pre- and post-, and experimental (mother trained) versus control (nontrained) group differences. Most of the 1st-year assessments were repeated, except for those that became inappropriate for use with the now older children (7 and 9 years old). Additionally, other measures were used, including extensive school-related assessments. In line with our whole child and contextual orientation, a variety of assessments were carried out to obtain detailed and comprehensive information on the children, mothers, and families, including the testing of children, observation of children's behavior and mother–child interaction, and extensive interviews with mothers.

Assessments of the children and their families were conducted in four main areas: cognitive development, socioemotional development, family context, and day-care context. Cognitive measures included: (a) IQ scores (with a Turkish adaptation of the Stanford-Binet Intelligence Test); (b) Piaget tasks of classification and seriation; (c) complexity of behavior (assessed through time-sampled observations at the day-care centers in the 1st year), cognitive style, and analytical thinking (the "analytical triad," consisting of "Block Design" from the Wechsler Preschool and Primary Scale of Intelligence [WPPSI] and "Object Assembly" and "Picture Arrangement" from the Wechsler Intelligence Scale for Children–Revised [WISC–R], as well as Children's Embedded Figures Test [CEFT]); (d) academic achievement (standardized tests of achievement in mathematics and Turkish and a general ability test in the 4th year); and (e) school grades: 1 year of primary school grades for the younger group (the original 3-year-olds) and 3 years of grades for the older group (5-year-olds).

The measures of socioemotional development included: (a) autonomy–dependence (assessed through time-sampled observations at the day-care centers and through mothers' reports); (b) aggression (again through observations and interviews with mothers); (c) level of social participation (observation and mother interviews, using a subscale on aggression from Rohner's [1980] Parental Acceptance–Rejection instrument [PARI]); (d) indicators of emotional problems (Goodenough Draw-a-Person test with the Koppitz [1968] scoring system); and (e) self-concept/self-esteem (some items from Rohner's [1980] PARI, asked in mother interviews).

Measures of family variables included: (a) background demographic and socio-economic information; (b) home environment (an **environmental stimulation index** including father's and mother's education, mother's language skills, frequency of reading/telling stories to child, number of toys present, and whether there are any books in the home); (c) information about the mother, including her childrearing attitudes and behaviors, lifestyle, self-concept, satisfaction with her life/environment, (assessed through the interviews), and teaching style (measured by the Hess & Shipman [1965] Toy and Block Sorting Task observations). In the 4th year, the mothers' intrafamily status was also assessed, in terms of decision making, role sharing, and communication between the spouses.

Measures of day-care and teacher variables included ratings of the main orientation of the day-care centers, that is, providing preschool education or only custodial care to children. The ratings were based on direct observation of centers and teachers and on interviews with directors.

Every effort was made to make the measures acceptable to the mothers and the children. Much time was spent in developing "rapport" for testing and interviewing and in rendering these as "normal" activities. In general, there was a good level of acceptance of these assessments on the part of the subjects, and no significant problems were encountered.

The reader may find an inconsistency between a main theme in this book—the importance of cultural context and culture sensitive orientations in research and the use of many Western measures in this research. Three explanations are in order here. First of all, as I have stressed repeatedly, common standards of cognitive development, in particular, need to be used for school preparation. However, they have to be made ecologically valid (Bronfenbrenner, 1979), which we tried hard to achieve. Thus, there is an attempt here to integrate universal standards with cultural appropriateness. Second, for some of the variables, we decided to use already-existing measures (with established reliability and validity), if we judged them to be appropriate for use with our subjects, rather than invent new ones from scratch. For each such measure, however, we conducted further reliability tests in a pilot study. Third, particularly for the noncognitive variables, such as family variables, parental orientations, and so on, we developed our own measures. This is because the cultural context was of more direct relevance here.

*Mother Training*

The project intervention comprised "mother training" given to a randomly selected group of mothers for 60 weeks over a 2-year period (30 weeks each year). Mother training was composed of two programs: the **Cognitive Training Program** and the **Mother Support Program**.

*The Cognitive Training Program.*   To foster the cognitive development of children, the Home Instruction Program for Preschool Youngsters (HIPPY) was used. This program was originally developed by the Research Institute for Innovation in Education at the Hebrew University of Jerusalem (Lombard, 1981). We translated and adapted it for use in Turkey. It focuses on three main areas of cognitive development (language, sensory and perceptual discrimination skills, and problem solving) for 4- to 5-year-old children. It can be considered a school preparation program, including preliteracy and prenumeracy skills.

The materials were supplied to the mothers on a weekly basis, 1 week at home and 1 week in a group setting. Explanations and role playing were used to teach the mothers how to use the materials with their children. The mothers then worked with their own children on a daily basis (about 20 minutes a day) to complete the week's task, including in total 60 weekly work forms of 25 to 30 pages each and 18 storybooks.

Mainly paraprofessionals worked in the program, trained and supervised by the research team. Two levels of paraprofessionals were employed. "Group leaders," one for each of the five localities, were rather well educated (at least high school education), middle-class women and were specially trained and supervised by the research team. "Mothers' aides" were no different from the mothers in education and SES status. They were selected to provide the program to the mothers at home every other week and also to help them in the group setting. They were trained and closely supervised by the group leaders on a weekly basis. Mothers' aides first applied the program to their own children before teaching it to the mothers at home.

*The Mother Support Program.*   At the biweekly group meetings, guided group discussions were conducted, in addition to working on the Cognitive Training Program. Group discussions were designed to sensitize mothers to the needs of the growing child and to enhance their communication skills to promote better verbal interaction with the child. The goal was to enhance the child's overall development, but supporting the mother was also of great importance. Group leaders led the group discussions, and the mothers were active participants; they asked questions, expressed opinions, and shared ideas and experiences. Following group discussions, group decisions were frequently taken regarding some course of action to be taken in the home. In the following meeting, the results of the decision would be discussed, reassessed, and possibly a new decision made.

Thus, techniques of group dynamics in the Lewinian tradition (1958) were utilized to enable the mothers to provide their children with support for overall development. In the 1st year, the emphasis of the group discussions was on children's health, nutrition, and creative play activities. In the 2nd year, the stress was on discipline and mother–child interaction and communication. Expressing and "listening to" feelings while interacting both with the child and with others were also emphasized. Throughout the program, the mothers were encouraged to develop a positive self-concept. Empowerment of the mothers in coping with problems and attending to their children's needs as well as their own needs was aimed for. Specifically, health and family-planning needs were addressed.

A special effort was made to render the program culturally sensitive. For example, the close-knit family ties and the relatedness values were reinforced, but a new element, "autonomy," was also introduced into childrearing. The goal was to work toward the ideal of the **Autonomous–Related Self.** The fact that the program was original, rather than imported from abroad, was an asset in rendering it culturally sensitive. One hour was usually spent by the group on the Cognitive Training Program, and 1 to 1½ hours was spent on the Mother Support Program. All the mothers were expected to attend all the group meetings; absenteeism was quite low.

Throughout the 2 years of the mother-training program there was close supervision of the group and home activities to ensure adequate implementation of the program. In addition to the Project team, selected university students also participated in group observations. Every effort was made to ensure regular monitoring, supervision, and good record keeping of the progress of the program.

## The 4th-Year Results

As mentioned earlier, extensive assessments were used in the **Turkish Early Enrichment Project,** in line with our **whole child** and contextual orientations. They are summarized here in terms of both child outcomes and mother outcomes. The findings pertaining to the project intervention (mother training) are stressed, though the effects of context (educational, custodial, home care) are also briefly covered. All the results refer to statistically significant findings, unless otherwise specified.

*Cognitive Development (Child Outcomes).* In the 4th year, a significant difference was obtained on the Stanford-Binet Intelligence Test between the children whose mothers underwent training and the control group of

**TABLE 9.2**

**4th-Year Comparative Standing of Children on Various Cognitive Measures by Context and Mother Training**

| Measure | | ED | CUST | HOME | Total | *F Values* | |
|---|---|---|---|---|---|---|---|
| | | | | | | *Environ.* (2, 244) | *Training* (1, 244) |
| I.Q. | MT | 94.19 n = 27 | 90.80 n = 41 | 92.89 n = 22 | 91.21 | 3.60* | 18.37** |
| | NMT | 89 n = 34 | 82.72 n = 60 | 86.12 n = 60 | 85.43 | | |
| | Total | 91.30 | 86.00 | 87.66 | | | |
| | | | | | | *Environ.* (2, 245) | *Training* (1, 245) |
| Analytical Trian | MT | 14.85 | 11.76 | 8.35 | 11.82 | 16.09** | 7.81* |
| | NMT | 11.63 | 9.84 | 8.09 | 9.58 | | |
| | Total | 13.03 | 10.60 | 8.16 | | | |

*(Continued)*

**TABLE 9.2** (Continued)

| Measure | | ED | CUST | HOME | Total | F Values | | |
|---|---|---|---|---|---|---|---|---|
| | | | | | | Environ (2,254) | | Training (1,246) |
| | MT | 16.06 | 15.22 | 13.54 | 14.86 | | | |
| **Block Design** | NMT | 14.39 | 13.57 | 10.45 | 12.63 | 16.09** | | 16.68** |
| | Total | 15.14 | 14.32 | 11.16 | | | | |
| | | | | | | Environ. (2,245) | | Training (1,245) |
| | MT | 8.41 | 5.98 | 7.22 | 7.02 | | | |
| **CEFT** | NMT | 7.37 | 5.40 | 6.66 | 6.32 | 5.68** | | 1,598 |
| | Total | 7.82 | 5.63 | 6.84 | | | | |
| | | $N = 61$ | $N = 101$ | $N = 83$ | Total $N = 246$ | | | |
| | | | | | Total Mother trained: 90 | | | |
| | | | | | Toal not mother trained: 156 | | | |

$*p < .05, **p < .01$

279

children whose mothers did not have training in the s2nd and 3rd years of the project (see Table 9.2).

This is notable, given the fact that no direct training was provided to the children; rather, mothers trained their own children. Mother training made a substantial difference especially for children at home (Table 9.2). The effect was less for children in educational day care (possibly showing a ceiling effect), because they received cognitive training in day care. This is in line with other research, mentioned in the last chapter, showing greater effects of ECD programs on the more deprived children.

The analytical triad results are parallel to IQ scores. The educational preschool children whose mothers were trained had the highest scores, and significant effects were found for both mother training and context (educational/custodial day care or home care). Similar positive effects of both mother training and context were found on the Block Design and the CEFT tests. Finally, the children of the trained mothers performed better than the control group on Piagetian classification tasks ($\chi^2 = 7.54$; $p = .02$). These differences on cognitive performance show that the "experimental" group of children who were trained by their mothers benefited from this enrichment.

In the 4th year, further assessments were undertaken with special age-graded achievement tests in general ability, mathematics, and Turkish. School performance was also assessed through the first grade for the younger group and through the third grade for the older group. On all the achievement tests, the children whose mothers had been trained performed better than the control group. Particularly the younger children who were in the first grade during the posttesting in the 4th year surpassed others in mathematics ($F = 10.59$; $df = 1$, 91; $p = .002$), and the mother-trained group (both ages) surpassed the control group on the general-ability test ($F = 3.9$; $df = 1$, 212; $p = .05$).

The positive effects of mother training began to appear in the children's school grades even after only 1 year of training, with higher grades achieved by this group in all subjects though not reaching significance levels. After the 2nd year of mother training, the effects increased overall, and significantly better grades were achieved in Turkish and nearly significant in social studies ($F = 11.19$; $df = 1$, 80; $p = .001$; and $F = 3.29$; $df = 1$, 79; $p = .074$, respectively). Furthermore, even 1 year *after* the end of mother training the positive effects on children's school achievement continued to increase with the mother-trained group having a higher academic average ($F = 4.5$; $df = 1$ 80; $p = .037$) involving better grades in all subjects. Their deportment/adjustment grades were also higher ($F = 4.22$; $df = 1$; 79; $p = .043$), pointing to better school adjustment.

As for the preschool context, again the superiority of the educational day care over the others (custodial and home care) can be seen. Children from educational day care outperformed the others on the achievement tests as well as in school achievement and school deportment/adjustment grades (Kağitçibaşi et al., 2001).

Overall, the results pertaining to cognitive development and school-related achievement show the positive effects of mother training and educational day care. The children who were trained by their mothers surpassed the control group on all measures of cognitive development and school-related achievement, significantly so on most. Similarly, the educational day-care context was found to be superior to custodial and home care on almost all of the cognitive measures. Children from the educational day-care setting whose mothers were trained consistently performed the best on virtually every measure. However, an interaction effect was not found. This shows that the effects of mother training and educational day care were additive and/or that there may have been a "ceiling" effect for the educational day-care children, given their initially higher level of cognitive performance.

*Socioemotional Development (Child Outcomes).* The socioemotional developmental outcomes are not as notable as the aforementioned cognitive outcomes. Nevertheless, the differences between the mother-trained and control groups of children on socioemotional measures were all in the expected direction, showing some benefit from the mother-training program. The effects of child-care context are less clear-cut, though children cared for at home were found to be more dependent than children in day care ($F = 4.29$; $df = 2, 196$; $p = .015$) and to exhibit more emotional problems ($F = 4.82$, $df = 2, 198$; $p = .01$).

On the Rohner (1980) subscale of aggression, used in mother interviews, the mother-trained group of children were rated as less aggressive than the control group ($t = 2.59$; $p = .01$). Similarly, on the Rohner (1980) subscale of autonomy/dependence, the mother-trained group of children was rated as less dependent, though the difference did not reach significance level ($t = 1.75$; $p = .08$). On the Rohner subscale of self-concept, the mother trained group was rated as having somewhat higher self-concept than the control group, approaching significance ($F = 3.19$; $df = 1, 191$; $p = .07$). Finally, on a measure of school adjustment, the mother-trained group received slightly higher scores ($F = 3.06$; $p = .087$).

*Mother's Orientation to the Child.* Fourth-year results showed a number of important differences between the trained and nontrained mothers in their orientation to the child. The trained mothers were more attentive to the child (34.7% vs. 18.6 % of the control group showing "frequent" or "very frequent" attention to the child at other than meal-times). They also reported more interaction while at home with the child (26.6% vs. 9.6% of the control), whereas 57.1% of the nontrained mothers (compared with 38.9% of the trained mothers) reported that the child played alone ($\chi^2 = 14.6$; $df = 4$; $p = .005$).

The trained mothers reported reading or telling stories to the child more than the nontrained mothers (87.7% vs. 62.6%; $\chi^2 = 40.8$; $df = 3$; $p = .0001$). They also helped the child with his or her homework more ($t = 3.54$; $p = .001$), and cognitive activities figured more prominently in what they taught to their children compared with the nontrained mothers (32.2% vs. 25.6%), even though there was no difference between the two groups in teaching practical skills to their children.

Attitudes toward, and expectations of the child, also differed between the experimental (trained) and control (nontrained) group of mothers. Trained mothers had higher expectations for their children, especially regarding success in school ($F = 2.84$; $p = .09$), years of schooling aspired for ($t = 2.03$; $p = .04$), and realistically expected of children ($t = 2.11$; $p = .04$) compared with the control group. Similarly, expectations of things the child should be able to do on his or her own without asking for help differed between the two groups ($\chi^2 = 14.85$; $df = 5$; $p = .01$), school success being the most frequent response for the trained mothers (48.8% vs. 18.6% for the control group). Clearly, such high expectations have something to do with the higher actual school-related achievement of the experimental group of children discussed before.

In systematic observations of mother–child interaction on structured problem solving (Hess & Shipman task), conducted by raters blind to the study hypotheses, trained mothers were found to have more positive and supportive interaction styles, involving encouragement, praise, positive feedback, reasoning, and cognitive/rational appeals in teaching the task to their children, compared with non-trained mothers ($t = 1.67$; $p = .09$). Trained mothers also had more positive current general evaluations of their children compared to the past (2/3 years earlier) than the nontrained mothers ($t = 2.16$; $p = .03$).

Finally, mothers exposed to the enrichment program were found to verbalize with their children more than nontrained mothers. This was apparent in both expressing satisfaction (73.5% vs. 58.1%; $\chi^2 = 6.01$; $df = 1$; $p = .02$) and dissatisfaction with the child, especially the latter (40.7% vs. 21.9%; $\chi^2 = 9.79$; $df = 1$; $p = .002$), compared with a greater use of physical punishment among the nontrained mothers (36.8% vs. 17.6% among the trained mothers; $\chi^2 = 10.11$; $df = 1$; $p = .002$). Also more of the trained mothers (61%) than nontrained mothers (39%) took into consideration the child's intentions in responding to his or her behavior, and they used "induction" (reasoning and making the child understand the consequences of his or her behavior) in child discipline more than the nontrained mothers (26.4 and 16.1%, respectively; $\chi^2 = 3.77$; $df = 1$; $p = .05$).

These differences between the experimental and control mothers, emerging from the mother interviews, appear to be indicative of different orientations to parenting in the two groups. In view of theory and research discussed in this book, the kind of parenting demonstrated by the experimental group can be characterized to promote better overall development and school performance, involving less physical punishment and more reasoning/verbalization with the child; being more responsive to the child; supportive interaction with the child through reasoning, praise, and encouragement; high expectations of the child; reading or telling stories to the child; helping the child with homework; and being more pleased with the child. It is quite similar to what Goodnow (1988) called **parental modernity** (see chaps. 2 and 3). It is notable that both self-report results and those based on observations of mothers' interaction with the child on structured tasks pointed in the same direction, providing confirming evidence for the positive effects of mother training on parenting.

Apart from experimental–control group comparisons, before–after comparisons also provide insights. The 1st-year baselines showed strong relational needs of the mothers together with much value put on social-harmonious-compliant child orientations. For example, when asked about children's behavior that pleased them, "being good to mother" was mentioned most frequently. Together with showing affection, being obedient, and getting along well with others, relational behavior comprised almost 80% of desired behavior in children. Thus, clearly the social/relational aspects or **social intelligence** was emphasized by the mothers. In contrast, "autonomy" was among child behaviors that annoyed mothers. Seen as self-assertion and being "headstrong" and disobedient, it accounted for more than half of the unacceptable behaviors. Complaints about dependence (of the child on the mother) was strikingly low (1.2%). In describing a "good child," also, mothers stressed being polite (37%) and obedient (35%) more than any other characteristics; being autonomous and self-sufficient again were negligible requirements (3.6%).

In the 4th year, it was found that trained mothers valued autonomous behavior in their children more than the control group ($F = 12.5$; $p = .02$). Additionally, in responding to an open-ended question about which child behaviors mothers find pleasing, more than twice as many trained mothers than nontrained mothers mentioned autonomous child behavior as pleasing them (21% vs. 9.7%; $\chi^2 = 6.04$; $df = 1$; $p = .01$). Even within the trained group, the percentage spontaneously mentioning autonomous behavior as pleasing was still not high. However, in comparison with the 1st-year baselines, there was a noticeable difference.

The great majority of mothers in both groups continued to stress affectionate and positive relational behavior in children as pleasing and otherwise demonstrated close-knit ties as reflected in their behaviors and values. Thus, some of the trained mothers appeared to acquire a new positive orientation toward the child's autonomy while remaining as close to their children as the nontrained mothers, demonstrating a trend toward the acceptance of the **autonomous–related self.** Thus, these before–after comparisons provide some clues to possible changes among the trained mothers that are indicative of an integration or synthesis of some new values stressing autonomy with continuing relatedness values. It is in line with the family model of **psychological/emotional interdependence** and the autonomous–related self proposed in chapters 5 and 6. This finding shows that such a synthesis of autonomy and relatedness orientations can be brought about through an intervention program.

*Direct Effects on the Mother.* The mother-training program was also found to have direct effects on the mother, even though this was not the professed goal of the program. In the 4th year, the trained mothers enjoyed a higher intrafamily status vis-à-vis their husbands, compared with the control group (Kağitçibaşi et al., 2001). I had developed an index of **intrafamily women's status** in earlier research (Kağitçibaşi, 1982a, 1982b). High intrafamily status of the woman indicates an egalitarian relationship between the spouses. A high score on this index shows shared decision making between the spouses (rather than exclusive husband decision making), communication, and role sharing between them, rather than man's and woman's roles being clearly different, with separate activities and functions. Compared with the national averages I obtained earlier on the **Value of Children Study** (chap. 5), the trained mothers in this project fared quite well on this index. Compared with the control group, the trained women also expressed greater satisfaction with their current life situation, compared with 3 years earlier ($t = 1.98$; $p = .05$), and they had more positive expectations for the future ($t = 2.61$; $p = .01$). As a reason for the more favorable evaluation of their present condition, compared with 3 years earlier, the trained mothers said that they were now "better educated" and better able to cope with problems, as a result of the Mother Support Program.

## Discussion and Rationale for Follow-Up

The 4th-year results of the Turkish Early Enrichment Project provided evidence of the beneficial effects of both mother training and educational day care on the children's overall development. All the findings were in the expected direction and in none of the measures used did the non-mother-trained (control) group of children fare better than the experimental group, nor did the children in custodial and home care outperform educational day-care children. The gains in school performance from mother training could be seen within the 1st year of the intervention and continued to increase even a year after the completion of the program.

As discussed in the last chapter, a common problem in intervention research is the dissipation of gains over time (especially in IQ scores). Among the factors underlying the dissipation of gains is the double approach of focusing on cognitive development alone and focusing on the individual child alone. Because cognitive gains are not supported by other gains in the "overall development" of the child and because the child's environment has not been changed and does not provide continued support to the child, the positive effects of the program may not be sustained over time. With a **whole child** and especially a contextual-interactional approach, we tried to overcome these weaknesses.

We reasoned that the changes brought about in mother's orientation to the child and parenting behavior would constitute important environmental changes for the child. Furthermore, to the extent that these changes persist over time, they would continue to support the changes brought about in the child. Thus the gains from the program would be self-sustaining. This reasoning is based on the assumption that mother training affects not only the child but also the mother. The findings related to mothers' orientations toward their children as well as the direct effects on mothers provided evidence for changes in mothers.

There was every indication from the 4th-year assessments (posttesting) of the Turkish Early Enrichment Project that a positive cycle had started when the children began primary school. It is evidenced from better school adjustment and liking of school, higher scores on achievement tests, and higher school achievement of the experimental group of children whose mothers had been trained, and of those who had been in educational day care. It is also evidenced from the trained mothers' expression of greater satisfaction with their children, their higher expectations of their children's school success, and both higher aspirations and expectations of more years of schooling for their children.

In addition to the aforementioned school-related behaviors and orientations, the trained mothers' interaction styles with and general orientation to their children were also found to be conducive to the overall success and well-being of the child (particularly valuing autonomy more than before, being more attentive to and interacting with the child, helping with the child's homework, more verbalization and reasoning with the child, and more reading/telling stories to the child). The fact that the mother-trained children's school performance *continued improving* even 1 year after the end of mother training provided evidence of self-perpetuating positive change.

Even though these findings were encouraging, the real test of sustained impact requires a longer-term follow-up study. Our expectation was that the effects of mother training would hold up better than those of educational day care. This expectation derived from our contextual orientation, as has been discussed. It was based on the assumption that the changes in the mothers would be sustained over time, which the follow-up study undertook to test.

One reason for this assumption was that the mother-training program was a community-based intervention that capitalized on women's networks in group discussion sessions. These networks would be expected to continue after the completion of the program and to provide support to the women. Another reason for expecting sustained effects was the adaptive nature of the changes in women and in their interactive styles with their children and spouses. Because the mother-training program provided the mothers with better communication skills, these newly acquired skills should be inherently reinforcing in solving problems effectively and might, therefore, be expected to "stamp in" and be self-sustaining. For example, in the 4th year the trained mothers reported that when they learned to express their own feelings instead of blaming the other person or when they learned behavior modification techniques in changing some undesirable behavior of their children instead of resorting to physical punishment, they were more effective, more in control of the situation, and less frustrated.

## THE FIRST FOLLOW-UP STUDY

A follow-up study was initiated 6 years after the completion of the original study (7 years after the end of the project intervention—mother training). The aim was to assess the overall condition of the children (experimental and control), now adolescents, and of their mothers and families and to relate these to the original intervention.

The design of the follow-up study was essentially the same as that of the original study (see Tables 9.1 and 9.3), except that the age category was dropped. It is a 3 × 2 factorial design with three categories of early context (educational day care, custodial day care, and home care) and two categories of mother training (training or no training).

A major task was tracing the original families, which is difficult after so many years. Out of the original 255 families we were able to reach 225 (with a very low attrition rate of 10%), 217 of whom agreed to participate in the follow-up study (Table 9.3). One hundred and eight of the young adolescents were about 13 years, and 109 were about 15 years old at the time of the interviews; 117 were boys and 100 were girls. One hundred and sixty-one of them were still in school; 56 had dropped out. Compulsory education was 5 years when these children were in the fifth grade (it is now 8 years).

Extensive individual interviews were carried out in the follow-up study with the adolescents, with their mothers, and also with their fathers. The adolescent interviews covered topics such as attitudes toward school/education, relations with parents (current and retrospective), expectations for education and occupation, self-concept, and social adjustment. The mother interviews included questions on the child's educational orientation and social adjustment, childrearing, family relations, mother's educational and occupational aspirations for her child, mother's self-concept, and role sharing/communication/decision making vis-à-vis the spouse (intrafamily woman's status). The fathers were given a shorter version of the mother interview.

The adolescents were administered individually the Vocabulary subtest of the WISC–R, standardized for Turkish (Savasir & Sahin, 1988)[2] and the EFT (Embedded Figures Test) standardized for Turkish subjects (Okman, 1982). Their full school records were also obtained.

---

[2]We decided against an academic achievement test or an individual intelligence test, given the dependence of such measures on schooling. Because compulsory education was only 5 years in Turkey, a good number of the adolescents (36% of the total sample) were out of school, some of them for a number of years. This would have been a confounding factor. Also previous research (Berrueta-Clement et al., 1984) showed that the IQ differences between trained and nontrained groups did not persist after the sixth grade. A vocabulary measure was, therefore, chosen. Vocabulary is also subject to the same problem of being affected by schooling, but less so at this age (13–15) in an urban center where adolescents are constantly exposed to the radio, television, magazines, and so forth. Also research on human abilities in this part of the world (reviewed by Ka itçiba i & Savasir, 1988) has pointed to the greater disadvantage of lower-SES subjects on performance tests in general and the higher variance explained by the verbal factor of the WISC–R, as evidenced by research from Greece, Israel, and Turkey. Finally, the Turkish standardization of WISC–R has been done with urban low-SES norms, which fits with our sample. It is also reported (Savasir & Sahin, 1988) that the vocabulary subtest, which has been devised on the basis of Turkish word counts and extensive research, had high validity, reliability, and discriminating power.

**TABLE 9.3**
*Design of the Follow-Up Study*

|  | Number of Subjects in Each Group | | | |
|---|---|---|---|---|
|  | Educational Day Care | Custodial Day Care | Home Care | Total |
| Mother Training | 24 | 37 | 22 | 83 |
| No Mother Training | 31 | 50 | 53 | 134 |
| **Total** | 55 | 87 | 75 | 217 |

## The First Follow-Up Results

Extensive results were obtained in the follow-up study. Both the findings relating to mother training and also to preschool context (educational/custodial day care and home care) are next summarized. Interview items were rated on a scale of 1 to 5, unless otherwise noted.

*Cognitive Development and School Performance.* In a context where compulsory schooling is only 5 years, as was the case for these children, probably the most important indicator of a positive orientation to education in low-income areas is "being in school." This is because, given the economic pressures, especially the children who don't do well in school and those who are not highly motivated get out at about the age of 11 to 12, upon the completion of the compulsory primary school attendance. On this crucial indicator of school attainment, a significant difference was obtained between the children whose mothers had been trained in the original study and those whose mothers had not been trained, with 86% of the former but only 67% of the latter still in school ($\chi^2 = 9.57$; $p = .002$).

This is a finding that, in itself, as an objective outcome measure, speaks for the policy implications of our contextual model of early enrichment (mother training). No significant difference was found in school attainment among the children who had had educational, custodial, or home-care experience.

Primary school academic performance is the second objective academic indicator on which significant differences were obtained between the experimental (mother-trained) and control groups. Based on report card grades over 5 years of primary school, the mother-trained children surpassed the control group on Turkish, mathematics, and overall academic average (Table 9.4). This finding shows that the gains obtained from the

**TABLE 9.4**
*Adolescent's Academic Performance*

| Primary School GPAs | Mother Trained[a] | | Not Trained[b] | | t | p |
|---|---|---|---|---|---|---|
| | Mean | SD | Mean | SD | | |
| Turkish | 8.85 | 1.36 | 8.18 | 1.41 | 3.08 | .001 |
| Mathematics | 8.15 | 1.75 | 7.32 | 1.75 | 3.01 | .001 |
| Overall academic | 8.56 | 1.45 | 7.89 | 1.53 | 2.82 | .002 |

[a]$N$ = 83. [b]$N$ = 134.

intervention were not short lived. Five years of better school performance must have contributed to the higher level of school attainment of the experimental group. It signifies a better school experience in the beginning, which paves the way for higher educational achievement and more years of schooling.

The difference between the academic performances of the two groups is not significant after primary school. This appears to be due to the greater self-selection factor in the control group, where the less successful students tend to drop out after primary school, and the better ones continue in school.

The preschool context does not relate to grades. However, the custodial-care group had a significantly greater number of grade retentions (failed 1 or more years of school) than the educational or home-care children ($F = 4.69$; $df = 2, 216$; $p = .01$).[3] As indicated in the last chapter, grade retention is a serious negative-outcome variable.

The mother-trained children surpassed the control group on the standardized WISC–R Vocabulary test, which is an indicator of verbal cognitive performance. This finding is important particularly in view of previous research showing a more limited vocabulary among children from lower-SES families in Turkey (Kağitçibaşi & Savasir, 1988; Savasir et al. 1992; Savasir & Sahin, 1988) and in the world (Aksu-Koç, 2005; Bernstein, 1974; Hoff, 2003; Laosa, 1984; Leseman, 1993; Van Tuijl & Leseman, 2004). The key importance of vocabulary and language proficiency for school performance was also discussed in chapters 2 and 3. In a two-way analysis of variance (ANOVA), the mother-trained group of children obtained a significantly higher mean score (45.62) than the control group (41.92) on this test (over a range of 0–68, the standard deviations being 10.23 and 13.39, respectively). The main effect for mother training was significant at the .03 level ($F = 4.63$; $df = 2, 216$).

---

[3]Retentions are not reflected in grades, because the grades of the year failed are deleted.

Early-care context also produced a significant main effect at the .01 level ($F = 4.78$; $df = 2$, 216), with the educational day-care group scoring highest (47.06), followed by the custodial group (43.22), and the home-care group showing the lowest performance (40.11). An interaction effect was also obtained, with mother- raining making a greater difference for the custodial day-care and home-care groups than for the educational day-care group. Again, a ceiling effect may have affected the educational group, whereas those starting from a lower level of performance (custodial and home groups) benefited more from the mother-training intervention.

*Adolescent's Academic Orientation.* The effects of intervention are also seen in adolescents' academic orientation, their self-esteem regarding academic performance, and their retrospective assessment of how well prepared they were for school at school entry.

Compared with the control group, those adolescents whose mothers had been trained were more pleased with their school success and thought that their teachers were pleased with them, too; they also felt that they could be the best in class if they studied hard (academic self-esteem). Negative or external-pressure reasons for going to school, such as having nothing better to do or parents' wishes, were endorsed more by the control group (Kağitçibaşi et al., 2001). Thus, a positive orientation to education and academic self-esteem appear to be concomitant with good academic performance.

The mother-trained children were also perceived by their parents in a more positive light regarding academic orientation than were the control children. Thus, the experimental group of children were perceived by their fathers as more motivated to succeed in school, compared with the controls (4.00 vs. 3.26; $t = 3.03$; $p = .003$), and by their mothers as actually having greater school success (3.54 vs. 3.32; $t = 1.8$; $p = .04$).

The preschool context made a difference also, mainly in terms of a negative effect from the custodial day-care experience. The custodial group perceived their parents ($F = 3.67$; $df = 2$, 214; $p = .027$) and their teachers ($F = 3,53$; $df = 2$, 214; $p = .031$) as being less pleased with their school performance than educational day-care and home-care children.

As for school preparation, many more of the experimental group felt that they were prepared when they started school, compared with the control group (97% vs. 77%; $\chi^2 = 15.1$; $p = .0001$). It is to be noted that all types of preparation were referred to in the question, including day care (two-thirds of both the experimental and control groups had attended day care). Among those adolescents who felt that they were prepared for school, the mother-trained ones, compared with the controls, believed that their preparation helped them more in school (4.42 vs. 4.15; $t = 2.07$; $p = .02$), and that it helped them for longer (5.2 years vs. 4.3 years; $t = 3.01$;

$p = .002$). Thus, the home intervention was perceived retrospectively as helpful by the adolescents.

The preschool context also had an effect on retrospective assessment of school preparedness. Home-cared children, compared with those in educational or custodial care, were much less likely to think that they had been prepared for school (32 % vs. 96% and 93%, respectively; $\chi^2 = 27.42$; $df = 2$; $p = .0000$).

*Socioemotional Development and Social Integration of the Adolescent.* The experimental group fared better than the control group in some indicators of socioemotional development and social integration. The adolescents whose mothers had been trained demonstrated greater autonomy, as reflected in making their own decisions ($t = 1.73$, $p = .05$). They also gave evidence of better social integration and social adjustment, in terms of their ideas being accepted by friends ($t = 2.06$, $p = .02$), mothers' approval of their friends ($\chi^2 = 9.02$, $p = .03$) and having had less trouble with the law ($\chi^2 = 3.69$, $p = .05$). Juvenile delinquency was rare among these young adolescents, most of whom had intact families; nevertheless, the few who had had trouble with the law (6%) were all from the control group.

As for the preschool context, again the negative effects of custodial care were apparent. Adolescents with a custodial day-care experience tended to have less self-confidence than others. For example, they rated themselves as less intelligent than their classmates ($F = 3.68$; $df = 2, 214$; $p = .027$), and had a near-significant tendency to have less confidence in their ability to cope with difficult situations ($F = 2.4$; $df = 2$, $214$; $p = .093$). With regard to juvenile delinquency, also, six of the eight adolescents who had been in trouble with the law were from the custodial-care group; the other two had been in home care; none were from an educational day-care background. Though the numbers are too small for statistical significance, the pattern is suggestive of a difference.

Compared with the 4th-year findings, where the socioemotional outcomes were not very clear-cut, the longer-range effects appear more marked.

*Adolescents' Perception of the Mother.* Adolescents' retrospective perception of their mothers demonstrated what our Mother Support Program accomplished. The adolescents whose mothers had been trained perceived their mothers to have been significantly more nurturant and more responsive than the control group. Specifically, the former group perceived their mothers to talk with them, to console them, to help them, to be interested in them, and to appreciate them more, and to spank them less than the latter (Kağitçibaşi et al., 2001). Obviously the trained

CHAPTER 9

mothers manifested a different, more supportive style of parenting. This was probably the key difference between the human environments of the two groups of children.

*Parents' Perception of Child and Family Relations.*   Responses of mothers and fathers to the questions in interviews provide further evidence that substantiates the findings obtained from the adolescents. They imply that the changes in the mothers meant changes in family emotional atmosphere and family relations, with corresponding changes in children, already described. Significant differences between the two groups emerged in many basic family variables, parent–child interaction and perception of children by the parents. Thus in the mother-trained group, better parent–child communication, better adjustment of the child in the family, less physical punishment, and in general closer and better family relations were reported by both mothers and fathers (Kağitçibaşi et al., 2001).

An index measuring **woman's intrafamily status** also differentiated the experimental and control groups. This is the same measure used in the 4th year of the original study. It consists of communication, shared decision making, and role sharing between the spouses. The higher intrafamily status enjoyed by the trained mothers following the intervention in the 4th year was found to continue 6 years later. This is an important finding attesting to an enduring favorable position of the woman in the family as a result of mother training.

*Parents' Academic Orientation/Perception.*   A final category of findings concerns parental orientations/expectations regarding the child's educational status (student role, educational attainment, and so on).

Both mothers' and fathers' educational expectations for their children were found to be higher in the mother-trained than in the control group. Additionally, fathers in the mother-trained group reported greater interest in what was going on in school. All of the trained mothers thought that the child had been prepared for school at the start, compared with only 65% of the control mothers, and that this preparation had been helpful, confirming further their children's independent assessments, presented earlier. Thus the mother-training program was seen in retrospect by both mothers and children as valuable school preparation.

Two measures served as an indication of the existence of support at home for the child's student role, which is indirectly related to parents' academic orientation. One of these is the existence of help with the child's homework at home. The other is the environmental stimulation index. The latter index was also used in the original 4-year study and includes father's and mother's education, mother's verbal skills, the frequency of buying newspapers and magazines, and the presence of books at home. On both of these indicators, the mother-trained group fared better than the control group, reflecting that a literate home environment is more likely to promote educational achievement.

## Discussion and Rationale for the Second Follow-Up Study

The first follow-up study pointed to significant gains sustained over a period of 7 years. These results led to important revisions in the program and its wide-scale applications that are described later on. However, alongside such applied work, we were drawing conclusions from our follow-up study and already looking at the future.

*Relative Effects of the Two Interventions.* When we started the original study, we were interested in studying both center-based (child-focused) and home-based (mother-focused) early enrichment. That is why we studied the effects of both context (educational, custodial day care, and home care) and mother training. Our original view was that having *both* an educationally oriented day-care experience *and* a supportive, stimulating home environment (through mother training) would provide optimal early enrichment.

Our 4th-year results had indeed showed that children who had *both* an educational day-care experience and mother training outperformed the others in almost all the measures of cognitive development (Table 9.2) and school achievement. Whereas the main finding was that the effects of the educational day care and of mother training were both positive, their combined effect was additive, not multiplicative. In other words, a significant interaction was not obtained between them. Indeed, as indicated before, often the more deprived custodial-care and home-care children benefited more from the mother training. Thus, mother training served a *compensatory* function for enhancing the capacity of the more deprived children. It did not contribute as much to the educational day-care children because of ceiling effects in their cognitive gains. That is, the educational day care apparently already helped the children to realize their potentials or to come close to doing so. Therefore, the two interventions (educational day care and mother training) emerged as possible alternatives rather than being complementary to one another.

The two types of interventions were ingrained in our original research design. The relative effectiveness of these two approaches is an ongoing debate in ECD research, as discussed in the previous chapter. It is rather difficult to reach conclusive results regarding the relative merits of the center-based and home-based approaches because these approaches may not be mutually exclusive. As pointed out before, often there is parent involvement in center-based (child-focused) approaches, and there can be a direct child-focused orientation in a home-based intervention. The latter was the case in our project.

Nevertheless, our research design allowed us to examine the relative effectiveness of the two types of interventions we had in our original study. Taking up the 4th-year results again, and examining cognitive-school achievement outcomes that are more clear-cut than the socioemotional outcomes, we find that both interventions were effective. In specific terms, the children with educational day-care experience showed a significantly superior performance on 23 measures and a positive though nonsignificant trend on 5. By contrast, the custodial group was superior on only three measures, whereas the home-care group never had the highest score. Likewise, the mother-trained group was superior to the nontrained group on 12 measures and showed a nonsignificant positive trend on 15, whereas the nontrained group was in no case superior to the mother-trained group.

Indeed, both mother training and educational day care were found to be effective in the 4th year, and if anything, the gains from the educational day care were even more notable, in terms of being reflected in a greater number of significant differences. In view of this, what is notable is that when we move from the 4th year to the longer-term effects, there emerges something of a reversal in the relative effectiveness of the two types of intervention. More of the gains from mother training are sustained compared with those from educational day care. This is found to be the case for school attainment, school achievement, and academic orientation, on the one hand, and for socioemotional development and social adjustment/integration on the other. Only in vocabulary (WISC–R) were there significant main effects for *both* mother training and the day-care context, with the educational day-care group scoring the highest. The custodial day-care group fared better in this measure than the home-care group. However here too, the mother-trained children in both custodial and home-care groups performed better than the non-mother-trained children as shown by the interaction effect.

This dissipation of gains over the long term from educational day care is in line with other research findings that I reviewed in the last chapter regarding the situation where parental involvement is lacking or is minimal (as in our study for the nontrained group). It is possible that despite their clear superiority to the custodial day-care centers, the educational centers in our study may not have been of a sufficiently high quality to exert much long-term influence. This might have been the case even though we picked the three highest-quality centers catering to the children of the working classes that we could find in Istanbul. In fact, some research does provide evidence of long-term effects from high-quality center-based programs (e.g., Schweinhart et al., 1994, 2005), which, however, also entailed some parent involvement, even if not substantial.

It is to be noted, however, that the educational day-care centers in our study were of a sufficiently good quality to have substantial short-term effects (in the 4th year). It is indeed the difference obtained between the short- and the long-term effects of educational day care that is problematic. Although we have to allow for the possibility that an even higher-quality educational day care might have produced a broader range of long-term effects, we are left with the question of whether this is a realistic option. Particularly in the **Majority World,** it is unlikely to achieve such high quality in large numbers of day-care centers catering to the children of the poor, as evidenced by our experience in Istanbul and as noted in the literature (Myers, 1992). Thus the policy implications call for greater attention to be paid to more **contextual** approaches involving the caregivers rather than complete dependence on center-based care.

In this context, the relative ineffectiveness of custodial care also in the longer time perspective is a reason for concern. In too many cases, day care for the children of the poor, especially in the Majority World, tends to be mainly custodial care. Far from being beneficial for children's overall development, such custodial care can even do harm, as evidenced by our long-term results. Adolescents with custodial day-care background had more grade retentions, perceived their parents and teachers to be less satisfied with their school performance, had lower academic self-concepts, and displayed more delinquency. This is probably due, at least in part, to the authoritarian-restrictive orientation commonly found in custodial day-care centers (Bekman, 1993; Myers, 1992). Therefore, just "more day care," as often demanded, is not a solution unless the quality of care is seriously considered.

## THE SECOND FOLLOW-UP STUDY

Twenty-two years after the beginning of the original study, and 10 years after the first follow-up study, we carried out the second follow-up study of TEEP (Kağitçibaşi, Sunar, Bekman, Baydar, & Cemalcilar, 2007). This was an ambitious endeavor and a real challenge, because finding people after so many years is very difficult, especially as we did not have any contacts with them in between. Nineteen years had passed since the completion of the mother-training intervention. Now the original children were 25- to 27-year-old young adults. The second follow-up was designed to examine the long-term effects of both types of early education, center based and home-based (mother training). We were also curious to see if the results of the first follow-up would continue to hold 12 years later.

*Method and Procedure.*    Of the 217 participants in the first follow-up study, 133 were located and interviewed. So we were able to reach 61%. This means a high attrition rate, which is typical of long-range studies. To compare the respondents we could reach with those whom we couldn't reach, we carried out *t* tests on the two groups' 1st-year (preintervention) IQ scores, SES levels, and whether or not they were still in school at the time of the first follow-up study. No significant differences were found, assuring the comparability of the two groups and the representativeness of the respondents for the whole sample. Nevertheless, a smaller sample size reduced the probability of reaching statistical significance in outcomes; if we had been able to reach more people, we would have obtained results with higher significance levels. Taking the small sample size into consideration, as well as the long period of time between the treatment and the measurement of effects, we present probability levels of up to 0.10 in the results. The overall distributions of the conditions in the second follow-up study were comparable to that of the first follow-up (see Table 9.3).

Sixty-six female and 67 male young adults participated in the second follow-up study. Mean age of the respondents was 25.4. Thirty-eight percent of the young women and 27 % of the young men were married, mean age at marriage being 21.9 for females and 23.6 for males. Of those married, 21 had one child and 4 had two children. Females had an average of 2 more years of schooling than males.

Initial contacts were made by telephone with the mothers who provided their adult children's contact information. The adult children were interviewed individually using a structured interview in their homes or workplaces; 25% were interviewed by phone. The interview topics covered demographic information, educational history, occupational status, attitudes toward education, childrearing and family life, and social participation. Mostly closed-ended Likert-type questions were used. A vocabulary test was also administered.

Occupational status was measured by an index integrating income level and prestige (Kağitçibaşi, 1973). The vocabulary test (Gulgoz, 2004) measured knowledge of Turkish vocabulary (Cronbach alpha: .77).

## Results of the Second Follow-Up

Given that the sample of the second follow-up study consisted of adults, the outcome variables were quite different from those of the original 4-year study and the first follow-up. This is commonly the case in longer-term follow-up studies in the field. Of most interest are educational attainment, occupational status, and social participation/integration in modern socioeconomic life at this important life stage of young adults from very modest socioeconomic backgrounds; that is, how well have they done?

As in the two previous studies, the independent variables are the three preschool environments (educational, custodial, and home care) and mother training or no mother training. Note again that the assignment to the mother-training/no-mother-training conditions was done randomly in the 2nd year of the original study. Whether children attended an educational day-care center or a custodial one or were at home was based on what was available to them, mainly provided by their parents' workplaces. The parents were not in a position to choose.

Our main goal was to see if and what kinds of effects of early intervention still obtained after so many years. To address this basic question, we endeavored to study the effects of the main independent variables of the original study, that is, early enrichment provided by the mother-training intervention introduced by the project, that provided by the educational day-care experience, and their combination.

Thus, three types of comparisons were carried out:

1. To find out whether *any* type of early ECD intervention had long-lasting effects, we combined conditions of mother training (including respondents from all three preschool care environments whose mothers had been trained) and educational preschool (including those who had mother training or no mother training who had had educational preschool experience). In other words, respondents who as children were exposed to *either* mother training *or* educational preschool *or* both were treated as the "Early Intervention" group. These respondents were compared with those who had *neither* mother training nor educational preschool experience, that is, the "No Intervention" group.

2. To examine the specific effects of the project intervention, mother training, comparisons were made between the mother-training and no-mother-training conditions.

3. Finally, to examine the specific effects of preschool environment, comparisons were made among the educational-, custodial-, and home-care conditions.

## Effects of Early Educational Intervention

Several outcome variables were examined for differences between those participants who had any type of early intervention and those who had not. These can be grouped under two broad categories, academic success and socioeconomic success.

*Academic Success.*    General academic success was assessed in terms of school attainment and university attendance. At the time when our respondents were growing up, compulsory schooling was 5 years.

For the whole sample, mean school attainment was found to be 10.8 years, indicating that most of the respondents had graduated from high school (11 years). Thirty-five percent were still attending university or were university graduates. Figure 9.1 shows the school attainment of  the Early Intervention and the No Intervention groups. A one-way ANOVA was carried out with school attainment as the dependent variable and 1st-year IQ and physical conditions at home (measured in the 1st year of the original study as an index of SES) as covariates, to control for possible confounding due to sample differences. The analysis showed that participants in the Early Intervention group attended school longer than those in the No Intervention group—$F(1, 127) = 3.22$, $p = .07$, ($M_1 = 11.34$ years and $M_2 = 10.13$ years, respectively) (see Fig. 9.1). More than 1 full year of difference is substantial. Furthermore, it was seen that 44.1% of the participants in the former group who had some type of Early Intervention attended university compared to 26.6% of the participants in the No Intervention group ($\chi^2 = 4.43$, $df = 1$, $p = .03$) (Fig. 9.3). Thus higher educational attainment may be seen as the most significant long-term benefit of early intervention.

*Socioeconomic Success.*    Several indicators of socioeconomic success were used: age at beginning gainful employment, occupational status, monthly household expenditure, and social participation. Age at beginning of paid employment was examined, because an early start in the labor force indicates less educational attainment, less qualified jobs, and lower lifetime earnings. The Early Intervention group was found to start employment later, consonant with their longer years of schooling—$F(1, 121) = 4.71$, $p = .03$, $M_1 = 17.53$ years and $M_2 = 16.19$ years, respectively (see Fig. 9.3). This is another important difference early intervention made.

Respondents' jobs were coded on a prestige scale from 1 to 7. It was found that those in the Early Intervention group had higher prestige jobs than those in the No Intervention group. This is in line with the findings that children whose mothers did not have any training and who were raised at custodial-care centers or at home had a lower school attainment and started working to earn a living at an earlier age compared to their peers whose mothers had training and/or who attended an educational child-care center. As expected, there was a significant correlation between occupational status and school attainment: $r = .28$, $p = .001$.

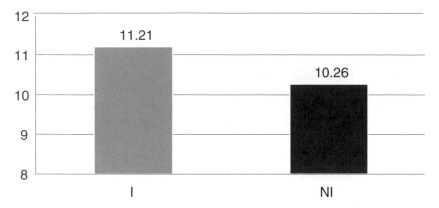

Figure 9.1.  School attainment (in years) of early intervention and no intervention groups in the second follow-up study.
Note: [ANCOVA F(1, 127) = 3.218, P = .07]

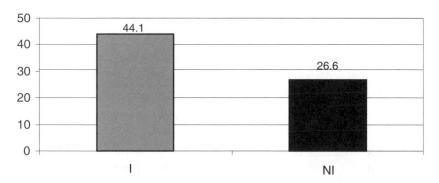

Figure 9.2.  University attendance of intervention and the no intervention groups (%).
Note: [x2 = 4.432. df = 1, p = .03]

Monthly household expenditure was used as a proxy for income, because it was found in previous research to be a more reliable indicator of income, and people tend to report it more comfortably than their income. The intervention groups were compared in terms of the percentage reporting higher and lower figures than the overall sample median. There was a trend in the expected direction, with the Early Intervention group reporting somewhat higher figures.

Finally, owning a computer was used as an indicator of participation in the modern information society. A higher percentage of Early Intervention

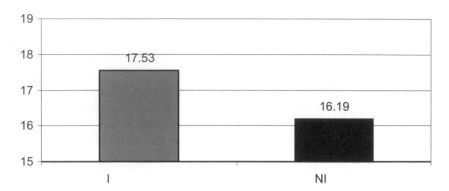

Figure 9.3.   Age of Beginning Gainful Employment
Note: [F(1, 121) = 4.708, p = .03]

group reported owning and using a computer (44%, compared with 24% of the No Intervention group), $\chi$ (1, N=131) = 5.98, p = .01.

### Effects of Mother Training

Specific effects of mother training compared with no mother training were seen in both cognitive/school outcomes and socioeconomic outcomes.

*Vocabulary Test Performance.*   A one-way ANOVA controlling for 1st-year IQ and 4th-year vocabulary achievement scores showed that participants whose mothers had been trained performed better in the vocabulary test than non-mother-trained participants—$F(1, 98) = 3.36$, $p = .09$, $M_1 = 14.11$ and $M_2 = 12.22$, respectively, on a scale of 0 to 24. This finding suggests that mother training produced a verbally more stimulating environment for the children while they were growing up. Furthermore, as can be expected, those who were more successful in the vocabulary test were more likely to have attended school for more years and had jobs of higher occupational status. Vocabulary scores correlated with years of schooling, $r = .35$, $p = .001$, and occupational status, $r = .18$, $p = .05$.

*School Attainment.*   Controlling for 1st-year IQ scores, a two-way ANOVA showed a significant interaction between preschool environment and mother training—$F(1, 125) = 3.51$, $p = .06$. Mother training had a greater effect on the school attainment of those who had attended custodial day care and those who had been in home care than on educational preschool participants. Custodial and home participants whose mothers had undergone training had almost 1.5 years more schooling than those whose mothers were not trained, whereas within the educational day-care group the difference between those whose mothers were trained and not trained was not significant. This showed that mother training provided compensatory benefits to those who did not have other early education, whereas it did not add much to those who already benefited from educational day care. This finding replicates that of the first follow-up.

*Socioeconomic Success.*    Participants whose mothers had mother training began gainful employment at a later age than non-mother-trained participants, $F(1, 121) = 2.66$, $p = .10$, $M_1 = 17.58$ years and $M_2 = 16.51$ years, respectively. Again a difference of a full year between the two groups appears substantial.

*Social-Economic Integration.*    Owning a credit card was used as an indicator of participation in the modern economy. A significantly higher percentage of those whose mothers had been trained had credit cards compared to those in the non-mother-trained group—$\chi (1, N=131) = 3.96$, $p = .047$.

### Effects of Preschool Environment

Specific preschool environment effects (educational day care, custodial day care, or home care) were seen mainly in socioeconomic outcomes. Reasons for leaving school also showed a difference between groups.

*Socioeconomic Success and Occupational Status.*    Participants who had had educational day care experience began gainful employment at a later age than those who had been in custodial day care and home care—$F(2, 120) = 2.51$, $p = .08$, $M_1 = 17.94$ years, $M_2 = 16.84$ years, and $M_3 = 16.12$. The educational day-care group also had higher occupational status— $F(2, 128) = 4.14$, $p = .02$. This was expected because the educational group had more years of schooling (though not significant—11.15 years) than the custodial day-care (10.78 years) and home-care (10.46 years) groups. There was also a trend for the educational day-care group to have higher monthly expenditures.

*Reasons for Leaving School.*    Many participants dropped out of school at some point before university graduation. They were asked about their reasons for discontinuing their education. The responses fell into two main categories. The first category consisted of reasons beyond the person's control, such as financial constraints or health problems. The second category consisted of reasons of personal preference, such as getting married or not liking school. It was found that participants who had attended any type of preschool day-care center were significantly more likely than those from the home group to give financial/health reasons for dropping out. The home group were significantly more likely to give reasons related to personal preference—$\chi$ (1, $N = 100$) = 4.20, $p = .04$—indicating that those who attended an educational or a custodial day-care center would have preferred to continue their education for more years if they had been able to do so.

## RESULTS AND DISCUSSION

The main finding of the second follow-up is that early childhood educational intervention has positive effects on the overall development of the child that carry over into adult life, affecting life chances through higher levels of educational attainment, delayed entry into the workforce, and higher status occupations. Both mother training and educational preschool day care were associated with more positive outcomes regarding academic success and cognitive skills, socioeconomic success, and indices of social and economic integration into the modern urban world.

Thus either type of ECD intervention, whether in the form of mother training or educational preschool, had beneficial effects. Children who had been exposed to either type of early educational intervention, compared to those who had not, subsequently exhibited higher school attainment, were more likely to attend university, began their working lives at a later age, had higher occupational status, tended to have higher monthly expenditures (a proxy for income), and were more likely to own a computer.

The policy implication of this finding is that "quality early education," whether home based or center based, is valuable. The delivery mode that is more appropriate and feasible in a particular context, taking into consideration constraints such as resources, costs, and the number of beneficiaries, is the one that should be used.

It is notable that long-term effects of this ECD intervention are sustained over a period of two decades. The results show that, on its own, mother training carried some effects over into early adult life, namely superior vocabulary and greater integration into middle-class economic life, as signaled by credit card use. In addition, mother training brought children with deprived custodial day-care and home-care experience up to the same level of school attainment as children from the educational preschool group.

Preschool day-care environment also had some independent effects, with children who had attended educational day-care centers having more favorable outcomes than those who had experienced custodial or home care in terms of later entry into the labor force, higher occupational status, and income. Simply attending preschool, whether educational or custodial, appeared to foster a greater desire for education, so that more young people from these groups gave "necessity" as a reason for leaving school, compared to those cared for only at home during the preschool period.

## Project Intervention (Mother Training)

TEEP can be characterized as having a multipurpose approach aimed to support both the mother and the child. Particularly, the Mother Support Program was an empowerment program that enabled mothers to develop better communication skills with their children and others, especially their husbands, to express their own needs and to understand others' needs better. The Mother Support component best reflects the contextual-interactional orientation of the project. The Cognitive Training Program (HIPPY) appeared to further enhance the mothers' sense of efficacy by providing them with the role of their children's teachers. The cognitive activities (such as reading books to their children, asking questions, following instructions, etc.) actually improved many mothers' rather poor literacy skills, as well. Thus mothers benefited from the program as much as children did.

Mother-child interaction constitutes a most important core element of TEEP. The use of group discussion was the main instrument of mother training, especially of the Mother Support Program component. Group dynamics greatly facilitated learning and attitude-behavior change, sustained over time. Group discussion was found to be an effective technique to bring about innovative change, with implications for use in wider applications.

The theoretical assumptions underlying our expectations are supported by the results of the follow-up studies. Indeed, a virtuous cycle was apparently set into action by mother training, which has proven to be self-sustaining. This is notable in view of the fact that the first follow-up data were collected 7 years after the end of the intervention and the second one 13 years later, and that there had been no contact with the families in the interim periods. The mothers (and children) were apparently empowered by the intervention, so that they could perpetuate the gains from the program on their own. Our **contextual-interactional approach** undoubtedly had a lot to do with this. It was not single individuals who had been the target of intervention, but rather individuals in interaction with one another in the family context. It was because the child's proximal environment had changed that the gains could be long-lasting. This is in keeping with a great deal of research from many countries pointing to the importance of the child's immediate environment above and beyond the general socioeconomic context for child development. In chapters 2, 3, and 7 we saw many examples of this.

It is also to be noted that the gains from early intervention were not only in the cognitive realm or school-related performance. They were also in family relations, as assessed in the first follow-up. The Mother Support Program (group discussions) focused on empowering mothers and improving their communication skills in interacting with their children. However, in group discussions the theme often expanded to cover communications with others, also, especially with the spouse, which was an area where many women had problems. The impact was seen 7 years later in better family relations and in general greater well-being of mothers and children, as seen, for example, in higher academic self-esteem, greater autonomy and better social adjustment of children, and higher intrafamily status of the mothers. Further impact was realized later on in better overall adjustment of the young adults.

It was the combination of our whole child approach and contextual-interactional approach that produced the obtained effects in such a wide range of developmental realms and touching on the whole family. There is a consistency of positive findings relating to the project intervention (mother training). This was the case covering a wide scope, from adolescents' and young adults' school attainment to social integration, from vocabulary competence to harmonious family relations.

School attainment, as discussed before, is of key importance for this group of people for whom access to continued education is the road to social mobility. In turn, primary school achievement is an important factor in determining whether a child from a poor family will go on to middle school or leave education to take up work. The superiority of the mother-trained group in both primary school performance and overall school attainment, therefore, constitutes objective outcomes with significant policy implications. The superior vocabulary competence of the mother-trained group is another important objective outcome, indicative of a higher level of **cognitive competence.**

On the basis of these long-term results, it may be proposed that a contextual-interactional approach to early enrichment has potential for promoting human development, particularly in the Majority World. Especially if a multipurpose approach is undertaken, it promises to have wide-ranging beneficial effects. TEEP has been presented here as an example of a theoretically informed applied research that has significant policy implications. Those implications have, in fact, materialized as public service. The mother-training program is now in actual use throughout Turkey in the adult education centers of the Ministry of Education. It is also being implemented in a number of other countries in Europe and the Middle East. I present next these applications deriving from TEEP.

## EXPANDING APPLICATIONS

Even before the completion of the original 4-year study of the Turkish Early Enrichment Project, interest in the mother-training program began to emerge on the basis of preliminary reports. A first initiative was taken by some of the mothers participating in the mother-training program who encouraged us to prepare a television program "to reach more mothers and childre"; they also volunteered to take part in this undertaking. An 11-session series was prepared of the **Mother Support Program** component in the form of small-group discussions (of the mothers in the program). It was shown on the then single-channel state television and was very well-received. Partial and full applications of the mother-training program were then carried out as a public service mainly in Istanbul. These applications were funded by various groups, such as parent-teacher associations, women's groups, and private business. They also entailed the training of more paraprofessionals and the revision and improvement of the program content.

After the initial phase of limited applications, the main developments started with the cooperation of the Turkish Ministry of Education and UNICEF. This was mainly in response to the evidence from the first follow-up study demonstrating beneficial long-term effects of the mother training-program. The Mother Support Program component was first adopted into the adult education programs of the Ministry to train child minders, and the training manual was published by UNICEF. Then when it became apparent that the whole mother-training program could find widespread application through the Ministry of Education Adult Education infrastructure, we undertook to devise a new **cognitive training program,** to replace HIPPY.

The whole program was changed into a 25-week program (from the previous 60-week one), concentrating on the year immediately preceding school entry. This was done for a number of reasons, most important, to reach the parent at a "touch point" (Brazelton, 1982) when the parent is most motivated to do something for the child to ensure better school performance, that is, the year just before school entry. Also there was a need to make the program less demanding in terms of mothers' time (1 year instead of 2 years) and to make it less costly. Regular individual home visits were discarded, and a complete-group orientation was adopted with weekly (rather than fortnightly) group meetings to conduct both the cognitive training program and the mother support program. As discussed before, our experience with mother training and our knowledge of the social psychology of groups pointed to the effectiveness of group dynamics, which is why this change was made. The resultant program is named **Mother-Child Education Program (MOCEP).**

These adjustments did not decrease the quality of the program because all training was now being carried out by the well-trained group leaders with higher formal education, rather than depending on the less educated mothers' aides who had previously conducted the training in fortnightly home visits. Nevertheless, this change did not increase the costs, because the Ministry of Education adult-education teachers were trained as group leaders. In most cases, this meant, in effect, the upgrading and optimized use of already existing personnel and facilities. Thus, the absolute costs are minimal. Close supervision and regular upgrading of the personnel and the materials were done to ensure quality. Evaluation studies, with the children and mothers (Aksu-Koç & Kuscul, 1994; Ayçiçegi, 1993; Ercan, 1993) provided evidence of significant benefits from the program.

In 1993, the **Mother-Child Education Foundation (MOCEF)** was established supported by a private Turkish bank. This foundation has been actively promoting MOCEF in collaboration with the Turkish Ministry of Education, with World Bank support. The aim has been to expand the program to reach mothers and children all over the country. The numbers of mothers and children reached by the program have indeed increased greatly since the establishment of MOCEF. By 2005, MOCEF and its extensions have "gone to scale," having reached 230,000 women and children in 73 provinces in Turkey, including some of the least developed areas. It is also being implemented in Europe (France, Belgium, and Germany) with Turkish immigrant families. It has been translated into Arabic and is in application in Bahrain, Jordan, Egypt, and Saudi Arabia.

An extensive evaluation study was carried out on MOCEP in four different provinces (Bekman, 1998a). Positive effects on children and mothers were found, parallel to the findings of the original **TEEP** study. This study showed that even with large groups, the quality of the program could be maintained and significant benefits could be produced.

The Turkish Early Enrichment Project and the applications deriving from it have influenced educational policy and have helped formulate new policy in Turkey. These recent policy-relevant developments entail mainly recognition and endorsement of nonformal family- and community-based models (mother and child training). There is also greater investment in expanding ECD services, as touched on briefly at the end of the last chapter.

## Cost-Effectiveness

As discussed earlier, cost-effectiveness is crucially important for policy and applications, particularly when programs are to "go to scale." Absolute costs are also important, however. Expensive programs, even if highly effective, have limited applicability for low-income groups. In general, home-based programs are less expensive than center-based ones, especially as in the case of TEEP where institutional investments and professional employment are not required, and paraprofessionals are used. Costs decrease further if a group-based, rather than an individual-based (home-visiting) approach is used.

A recent cost–benefit analysis conducted in Turkey (Kaytaz, 2005) calculated and compared the cost–benefit ratios of different models, home based and center based, under different scenarios. The calculated benefit–cost ratios ranged from 4.35 to 6.31 (to 1) for center-based education and from 5.91 to 8.14 (to 1) for home- and community-based MOCEP. In other words, whereas one unit of investment in center-based early childhood education services can be predicted to bring a return of up to 6.31 units over the person's lifetime, the return would be up to 8.14 units from home-based ECD services (see chap. 8). The implications of this simulation study parallel the findings from the current study: Both types of intervention can be expected to produce important social and economic returns in terms of the individual's increased productivity; one or the other might be expected to produce superior results in certain contexts, with somewhat higher expectations overall for mother and child education.

## CONCLUSION

Clearly **TEEP** and its extension **MOCEP** constitute an important case for the contribution of psychology to the promotion of human competence. It serves to demonstrate what can be done in ECD context to increase children's environmental resources and to enhance their developmental trajectories. The links with the discussions in chapters 2, 3, 7, and 8 are clear: Much can be accomplished by reaching children early in life to build both environmental and individual capacity that can be sustained over time. Improving the environment, while enhancing individual cognitive performance, helps in turn to support that performance further, in a synergistic interaction. In doing this, our accumulated knowledge and insights deriving from developmental science (Lerner, 1998) can provide us with possibly universal standards of healthy development.

## SUMMARY AND MAIN POINTS

- TEEP, conducted by Kağitçibaşi, Sunar, and Bekman spans a period of 22 years (1982–2004). The original study was a 4-year intervention project, utilizing a field experiment. The two follow-up studies were carried out 6 years after the end of the original study and again 12 years later.
- The sample of the study was a low-income and low-education semiurban group of families in Istanbul. Two cohorts of children, 3 and 5 years old, and their mothers were included in the study, totaling 255 mothers and children.
- The research design was of three (context: custodial, educational, home care) by two (age: 3 or 5) by two (mother training or no mother training) factorial design.
- The study investigated the effect of mother training and educational day care, custodial day care, or no day care (home care) on the overall development of children.
- After establishing baseline assessments in the 1st year, mother training was given to a randomly selected sample of mothers in the 2nd and 3rd years of the study.
- Mother training was the main independent variable, the other being preschool context. Mothers who received the training constituted the experimental group whereas mothers not receiving the training program were the control group.
- In the 4th year of the study, reassessments and interviews were carried out to establish both pre- and post- and experimental–control group differences.
- The 4th-year assessments of the study showed positive effects of mother training and educational day care in children's cognitive development, school-related achievement, socioemotional development, mother's orientation toward the child, and on mothers' outlooks.
- A follow-up study was conducted 6 years after the completion of the original study, assessing the overall condition of the children (who were now adolescents), their mothers, and their families.
- Gains from mother-training program regarding cognitive development, school performance, academic orientation, socioemotional development, social integration, and family relations (compared to control group) were observed in the first follow-up. More of the gains from mother training were sustained compared with those from educational day care for school attainment, school achievement, academic orientation, socioemotional development, and social adjustment/integration of children.

- Twenty-two years after the beginning of the original study, and 10 years after the first follow-up study, a second follow-up study was conducted. Early intervention (mother training, educational day care, or both together) showed sustained gains in academic and socioeconomic success. Specific effects of mother training were also seen in cognitive/school and socioeconomic outcome variables.
- The main finding of the second follow-up is that early childhood educational intervention has positive effects on the overall development of the child that carry over into adult life.
- This project has led to wide-scale applications all over Turkey and abroad.

## DISCUSSION QUESTIONS

1. What is the rationale behind the factorial design of the TEEP?
2. What are the reasons for conducting follow-up studies?
3. Discuss why more of the gains of mother-training program were sustained in adolescence compared with those from educational day care.
4. How do you explain the considerable difference between the experiment and control groups? How do you think the study achieved these? What were some important factors?
5. What are the scientific and policy implications of TEEP?

# 10

# Immigration and Acculturation

"Dutch children are on top of their mothers' heads!" This is a quote by a Chinese immigrant mother living in the Netherlands (Dekoviç et al., 2006). It is a rare case of a recorded view from the "other side," that is, a view of the host culture held by the immigrant. Commonly, we hear of how immigrants are viewed by the host society, but of course perceptions are reciprocal, though often quite different from one another. This quote reminds us of that fact. The present chapter deals with such issues and others that inhere in human relations in the context of immigration. Following on from the last chapter, this is the second chapter that deals with the implications of our knowledge in a field of study for social issues and applications.

Chapters 8 and 9 presented early intervention focusing on early childhood education as an applied area of developmental science that can promote competence and overall well-being. It was shown that, particularly in contexts of socioeconomic disadvantage, early intervention can make a difference and provide sustained gains. The focus there was on the development of competence, and it built on the theoretical perspectives in chapters 2 and 3, in particular. The present chapter focuses on the self in the context of immigration and **acculturation.** It builds on the theoretical perspectives covered mainly in chapters 4, 5, and 6.

Acculturation is studied both in its own right, and also as an applied field, in particular with respect to policy-relevant applications. Such applications can cover wide ground, from education to health, from social security to reducing prejudice and improving intergroup relations. Given the policy-relevant nature and applied significance of the topic, this chapter has been placed in the second part of the volume. As literally hundreds of studies have been carried out on immigration and acculturation, what we have here is a selective coverage of some topics and issues that are of relevance to the other topics covered in the volume.

## IMMIGRATION

Immigration is a global human phenomenon. Throughout history, individuals and groups have moved and resettled in other places, for a myriad of reasons from war to famine, from seeking refuge to seeking employment. As a social phenomenon, immigration has been studied extensively by the social sciences. Most work conducted on it has been at the macro level of analysis, focusing on its economic, social, and political aspects, often with policy implications (Kağitçibaşi, 2006a). Psychological work on immigration is of more recent origin, which is ironic, because this is a human phenomenon. We see here again the effects of the individual focus of the psychologist interfering with addressing a social phenomenon.

### Historical Background

Ethnic issues and intergroup relations rather than immigration as such were studied early on in sociology and social psychology. A pioneering study was *The Polish Peasant* by Thomas and Znaniecki (1918–1920), which looked into the attitudes and worldviews of the Polish immigrants in the United States. An important sociological study into culture conflict and personality was Stonequist's *The Marginal Man* (1937). The precursors of some of the acculturation strategies currently used in the field (Berry, 1990, 2001) are found in Stonequist's work. For example *assimilation* and *nationalism* (in the sense of separation from the dominant society and reasserting one's heritage culture) were first presented in this work as opposite acculturation strategies of the immigrant or the marginal man.

The 1950s marked early studies on attitudes as the hallmark of intergroup relations. From a psychoanalytic perspective, *The Authoritarian Personality* (Adorno et al., 1950) searched for the psychological basis of the rise of fascism in Europe and studied ethnic prejudice, mainly anti-Semitism, as a component of the "authoritarian personality syndrome." Extensive work on attitudes and stereotypes in the United States focused mainly on racial and ethnic prejudice against Jews and African Americans (Allport, 1980; Pettigrew, 1979). A series of studies on ethnic stereotypes conducted with American university students over a period of some 50 years pointed to the persistence of stereotypes in people's minds over time (Gilbert, 1951; Karlins, Coffman, & Walters, 1969; Katz & Braly, 1933; Singleton & Kerber, 1980). Recent work on stereotypes reflects a renewed interest in them. Studies find continuing consensus on national stereotypes (McAndrew et al., 2000; Peabody, 1985; Stephan et al., 1996).

From early on, a main issue was whether individual personality factors or situational factors explained prejudiced attitudes. The personality emphasis popularized by the authoritarian personality theory was challenged by studies in the 1950s and 1960s. Pettigrew (1958, 1959) showed regional differences and the effect of sociocultural factors in prejudice that override individual characteristics. Sherif's well-known studies of intergroup competition and cooperation in children's groups also pointed to the powerful role of situational factors (Sherif et al., 1961). The dispositional versus situational perspectives are still with us, and they reflect the relative emphases of the personality and social psychological explanations in general (see P. B. Smith et al., 2006). However, they are increasingly seen as complementary and as relatively more relevant to explaining individual differences and group differences, respectively.

Early studies of intergroup attitudes and prejudice in the United States thus were not studies conducted in an ungoing immigration context, as the ethnic and racial groups that were the targets of prejudice were not newcomers. Only more recently have psychological studies of ethnic migrants in the United States been carried out, in response to the immigration of large numbers of Latin and Asian Americans. To a large extent, studies now focus more on the acculturation of the immigrants (Berry, 1997; Berry & Sam, 1997; Ward, 2001; Ward & Kennedy, 1996).

Psychological studies of immigration have also been conducted in other countries, mostly those in Western Europe. However, immigration to Europe has been very different from that to the United States. Whereas the United States was a nation of immigrants from the very beginning, European societies were historically unicultural. They first experienced large-scale immigration as late as the 1950s, though there had been a continuous flow of immigration from former colonies, particularly to the United Kingdom.

Immigration into Europe was largely labor migration, recruited by the Northern European governments to rebuild their economies following the devastation of the Second World War. Both the "host" societies and also the migrants, themselves, saw this as a temporary stay, thus the German term *Gastarbeiten* (guest workers). It started out as a welcome and much-needed labor migration that contributed greatly to economic growth. It may be stated that Western Europe owes its great economic progress in the decades following the Second World War in no small measure to this imported labor. This is because it was a non-demanding, nonunionized, cheap, and hardworking labor force, which was available where and when needed and willing to undertake the least desirable tasks that the host society population was reluctant to do (Kağitçibaşi, 1987b, 1997d).

After the first few decades of labor migration, family reunions were allowed, bringing in the dependents of the workers and leading to sharp increases in ethnic-minority populations. It took a while for the European public to realize that what was assumed to be a temporary state was really a permanent one, that the "guest" workers were not guests but minorities, and that the European societies had in fact become heterogeneous, that is, plural, not homogenous.

The reactions of the core population have been mixed, ranging from tolerance to ambivalence to overt resentment and prejudice. The adaptation of the immigrants to the host societies and of the host populations to the transformation of their societies from unicultural to multicultural emerged as significant social and psychological issues. Economic difficulties, especially following the oil crisis of 1973, worsened the host-society sentiments toward the "outsiders," who were seen as competitors for employment and social services. Psychological studies took off rather late, mostly in response to these issues and others.

Immigration to other affluent "immigration" countries, such as Australia, Canada, and Israel, has also been extensive, and some research has also been carried out in these countries. However, this chapter examines mainly the recent American and European studies representing research conducted in two rather different immigration contexts but at the same time involving some common themes.

An important common theme is that these are *psychological* studies, utilizing individual, family, and interpersonal levels of analyses rather than macro perspectives. The latter are employed more by other social science research using mainly aggregate data. A second common theme is *psychological acculturation,* which is examined in most of the studies. This entails a focus on the immigrant's adaptation to the new environment, rather than the host society's adaptation to the immigrant, and is in keeping with a micropsychological approach.

Notwithstanding the psychological focus of the studies, these considerations remind us that the specific features of the larger immigration *context* should not be ignored. Different aspects of the environment may assume varying degrees of importance (Liebkind, 2003). For example, in culture contact situations, some values or conventions may clash but others may not, leading to demands for change in some behavior patterns and outlooks but not in others.

## ACCULTURATION

Originally, acculturation meant the adaptation of groups and/or individuals in culture contact situations. Thus, the classic definition of the term by anthropologists Redfield, Linton, and Herskovits (1936) entails a situation where "groups of individuals having different cultures come into continuous first-hand contact, with subsequent changes in the original culture patterns of either or both groups" (p. 149). However, the focus of the subsequent studies of acculturation has been mainly on the immigrant acculturating group, rather than the dominant society. Additionally, *psychological* acculturation has been studied extensively, rather than other forms of acculturation, such as political, economic, and so on. This is understandable given psychologists' interests.

Acculturation conceived in a general sense as culture contact involves a myriad of factors in dynamic interplay. From a social-psychological perspective, many have been examined in countless studies on prejudice and intergroup relations, ethnic stereotypes, adaptation processes, and so on. The circumstances involved in different types of culture contact can be extremely varied. For example, consider the experiences of foreign university students, seasonal migrant labor, expatriate business executives, diplomats, visiting professors, immigrants, and asylum seekers. Add to these the further variability of from which country to which country each incident occurs, the varied ages and personality characteristics of the participants, and so on. The emerging picture becomes so complex that it would appear to be difficult to point to any commonality among their experiences. Additionally, our understanding is necessarily constrained by what researchers have chosen to study. So what we have in our hands are just "clues," and this field may be seen to be "at its infancy stage" (Hong, Roisman, & Chen, 2006) despite the voluminous research that has already been carried out.

Notwithstanding the daunting complexity of this issue, each clue is valuable, and a great deal has been accomplished. In particular, theoretical schemes have been developed that help bring in order and make sense out of this complexity.

## Theoretical Perspectives

A heuristic grouping of theoretical approaches to the study of **acculturation** has been proposed by Ward (2001). These are the stress and coping, culture learning, and social identity approaches, corresponding to the affective, behavioral, and cognitive (A, B, C's) domains, respectively. These domains or spheres of psychological functioning have a long-standing position in psychology, especially in social psychology, and have been used extensively, particularly in the study of attitudes (Rosenberg & Hovland, 1960). In the context of culture contact, Ward points to work on acculturative stress and coping as emphasizing the emotional or affective aspects of acculturation. The behavioral sphere has been studied extensively in the "culture learning" approach, focusing on obtaining culture-specific knowledge, such as language, and a culture-appropriate behavior repertoire for successful adaptation. Finally, the cognitive outcomes referring to cultural identity and intergroup perceptions are studied within social identity approaches to acculturation, based on social cognition (Ward, 2001). This grouping does not mean that specific studies fit neatly into one or the other theoretical perspective. Often, several aspects of the acculturation process are studied together. Nevertheless, it is useful in detecting the main thrust of different theoretical approaches.

A fourth approach has been proposed to be added to Ward's A, B, and C—D for development (Sam, 2006; Sam, Kosic, & Oppedal, 2003). Often, the development of children and adolescents in immigration contexts is studied in acculturation studies. However, acculturation and development processes at times overlap, and it is not easy to untangle them. For example, the intergenerational conflict that is often observed in ethnic-minority families may be reflecting either the different acculturation levels of parents and children or just more common generational differences, or both. A developmental approach helps disentangle such overlapping processes (Phinney, 2003).

*Types of Intercultural Adaptation.* A further distinction has been made by Ward (Searle & Ward, 1990; Ward, 2001; Ward & Kennedy, 1996) between psychological and **sociocultural adaptation** in the context of intercultural acculturation. The former has to do more with an individual sense of well-being and self-satisfaction; the latter is more concerned with success in social integration in the dominant society as, for example, in school and work situations. Looking into the theoretical approaches mentioned previously, **psychological adaptation** outcomes are studied mainly from stress and coping theoretical perspectives. Sociocultural adaptation outcomes are examined mainly from culture-learning theoretical viewpoints. The theoretical emphasis has been more on acculturation stress (Berry, 1990, 1997); however, more recently sociocultural adaptation is also getting more attention.

Another aspect of adaptation, namely economic adaptation, has been proposed by Aycan and Berry (1996). Though related to the more general sociocultural adaptation, economic adaptation is more focused and was found to be predicted specifically by migration motivation, perception of relative deprivation, and status loss through immigration. Indeed, one common finding is status loss for the immigrants as a result of having to work at jobs with lower prestige and income level in the country of immigration compared with their experiences in their country of origin. There can be many reasons for this. The immigrant's educational qualifications, including diplomas, are often not considered on a par with the dominant society ones. Although this judgment can be due to a realistic assessment, more often it appears to be due to a lack of knowledge about the sending country, or to prejudice. Beyond this, for recruitment into equally paying jobs, locals are often preferred over immigrants.

Clearly, the course of adaptation to new environmental demands and lifestyles in the context of culture contact is highly varied. In a sense, there are as many different adaptation processes as there are migrants; that is, each individual's experience is unique. On the other hand, there also appear to be some common patterns that reflect systematic variations across individuals, groups, and psychological domains. The challenge is to unravel such patterns and discover their underpinnings to reach a better understanding of the apparent complexity. The theoretical perspectives are helpful in doing this.

*Acculturation Strategies.* A rather simple conceptualization of acculturation has been unidimensional. This view assumes that as a migrant adapts to the dominant culture, that is, acculturates; she or he gives up and is estranged from his or her original culture. In the bipolar view, the adoption of the new culture is assumed to take place at the expense of the culture of origin. In other words, it is assumed that there is a transformation of identity from that of the country of emigration to that of immigration. This is a common view and underlies the concept of assimilation, which, for example, was for a long time the general ideology of the American "melting pot," regardless of whether or how much it corresponded to the reality of immigration.

This view has been heavily challenged by scholarship into acculturation processes, even in the United States. A **bidimensional view** has been proposed by Berry (1990, 1997, 2001; Berry & Sam, 1997) to replace the unidimensional one. Acceptance (or not) of the dominant culture and maintenance (or not) of the heritage culture are seen as two independent dimensions here. So a fourfold categorization is possible, such that the resultant strategies are **integration** if both are high; **marginalization** if both are low; **assimilation** if the former is high and the latter low; and **separation** if the reverse is the case. These four categories have been used extensively in acculturation research (see Berry, 1997, Berry & Sam, 1997; Berry et al., 2002, for reviews).

A problem with this approach is that it tends to focus on the acculturating individual or group and assumes that these fourfold strategies are choices available to them, which may not always be the case (Kağitçibaşi, 1997d). In discriminating environments, assimilation or integration strategies may not be possible to pursue. Or where there is pressure for assimilation, integration may not be possible. Integration

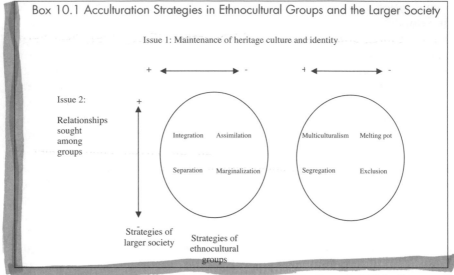

Box 10.1 Acculturation Strategies in Ethnocultural Groups and the Larger Society

Issue 1: Maintenance of heritage culture and identity

Issue 2:

Relationships sought among groups

Integration    Assimilation

Separation    Marginalization

Multiculturalism    Melting pot

Segregation    Exclusion

Strategies of larger society    Strategies of ethnocultural groups

*Note.* From Cross-cultural psychology. research and applications *(p.354)* by Berry, Poortinga, Segal, & Dasen, 2002, Cambridge UK: Cambridge University Press.

is possible only in host societies where cultural diversity is tolerated. Indeed, Berry recognized this constraint early on (1974; cited in Berry, 1990). He added to the model the dominant group orientations toward the immigrants as a third dimension. Here the dominant society orientations parallel those of the individual. Thus, for example, if the dominant group wants to keep the immigrant group separate from the main society, it segregates them. Box 9.1 gives the full scheme that also incorporates the strategies of the dominant society with regard to the acculturating groups.

Although the significance of the dominant society attitudes and policies is recognized, still the emphasis of much research in the field has been on the strategies of the acculturating groups. This is again due to the individual focus of psychology that tends to neglect the contextual/situational factors. It may also be the case that dominant-society strategies are not as easily studied by psychological tools. They may range from tolerance to overt or "blatant" prejudice (Pettigrew & Meertens, 1995) and may be reflected in different social, political, and economic policies on multiculturalism, citizenship rights, education, social security and unemployment benefits, and so on. Nevertheless, there is a great need to study aspects of the dominant culture in order to develop a better understanding of the acculturation phenomenon.

Whether due mainly to individual preference or the dominant-society policy, a considerable amount of research points to the greater adaptive value of *integration*, also labeled biculturalism (Berry, 1997, 2006; Berry & Sam, 1997; Berry et al., 2002). However, there are also exceptions and contradictory findings on acculturation and psychological adjustment (Lopez & Contreras, 2005). Particularly in situations where the immigrant group feels rejected by the society, *separation* reflected in greater family solidarity and enhancement of heritage culture appears to be associated with lower acculturative stress and better psychological adjustment (e.g., Arends-Tóth & Van de Vijver, 2006; Phalet & Swyngedouw, 2004 ), but sociocultural adaptation may suffer. In contexts where immigrants are well accepted, *assimilation* can work better concerning sociocultural adaptation. It is generally agreed that *integration* involves a more enriching acculturation strategy, as it involves sustaining both the culture of heritage and the host culture. Nevertheless, what aspects of this acculturative strategy account for this outcome need to be better understood. For example, Lopez and Contreras found that although both biculturality (integration) and linguistic balance (higher level of proficiency in the nonmother tongue) are associated with psychological adjustment, the latter showed a stronger association.

Though generally accepted, Berry's model has also been criticized for being categorical and for focusing on the end states rather than on the process of acculturation (Hong et al., 2006). Additionally, Birman (2006) has noted that the measures used in the fourfold two-dimensional model become unwieldy in the computation of acculturation gaps between parents and children. She proposes an orthogonal interaction model to better handle acculturation gaps in the immigrant family.

It is also possible that there may be alternative acculturation pathways other than the four strategies proposed in the model. For example, a **fusion model** has been proposed that brings in a third dimension to the acculturation process (Arends-Tóth, 2003; Arends-Tóth & Van de Vijver, 2006). This can be a synthesis or a mixture of the two cultures, the dominant culture and the heritage culture, resulting in a new entity. It needs to be seen, however, if this is different from integration or biculturalism. Finally, there can be other possible strategies, such as immigrant youth identifying with the global "hip hop" youth culture (Kaya, 2001), or highly individualistic groups not maintaining links with either the original culture or the host culture, but nevertheless being quite content with their life and not having adaptation problems, unlike the *marginalization* strategy (Van Oudenhoven, Van der Zee, & Bakker, 2002).

*Content of Acculturation.*    The emphasis on the process of acculturation, mainly in terms of acculturation strategies, has rendered the *content* of acculturation of secondary importance in theory and research. As mentioned earlier, what actually changes in acculturation provides insight into the everyday reality of the culture contact situation. Thus the content of acculturation needs to be studied above and beyond the process of acculturation. For example, Bornstein and Cote (2006) showed that publicly observable parental behaviors get changed and assimilated more than parental cognitions. Thus, cultural practices may be more open to change than attitudes. Also differences between groups tend to be greater than differences between individuals; group-level differences are more influenced by acculturation.

A great deal of diversity enters the picture here, based on individual differences, situation-and domain-specificity of behavior, and variations across attitudes, cognitions, and behaviors. Studies show that the public and the private domains need to be distinguished where significantly different behavioral patterns emerge ranging from language and identity to choice of friends and food habits. For example, Arends-Tóth (2003) found that Turkish immigrants in the Netherlands preferred integration in public domains but separation in private domains.

Within the different domains, a myriad of situations involving families, peers, schools, and communities create links and gaps in acculturation (Cooper, 2003). Generation is also important, later-generation immigrants being more acculturated in general than first-generation ones. For example, Harwood and Feng (2006) found that second-generation Puerto Rican mothers in the United States prefer to use English, are adopting American values, and are not likely to maintain Puerto Rican traditions. Still, they have active attachment to Puerto Rican culture, have relatives living with them and state that their ethnic heritage is important. Thus the picture emerging in the context of immigration is not uniform change.

A person acts differently in different contexts and with different people. Though this is a common human complexity that challenges the assumed generality of traits across situations, it becomes even more marked in culture contact contexts. This is because there is a greater range of variation in culture contact situations. Thus, it may be claimed that the more people are exposed to different salient situations (cultures) that make different demands on them, the more their behavior will show situational variation. For example, a young person acting in a cooperative manner in the family or the kin group may become competitive in the school context.

Furthermore, the same behavior may carry different meanings. For example, the academic achievement of immigrant adolescents may reflect their collectivistic tendencies to please parents, to show gratitude to them, and to "give back" to family and community (Liebkind, 2003; Phalet & Schonpflug, 2001). Or it may be a tool for individualistic

*can be see either way*

enhancement, and at times a route to abandonment of the ethnic group and assimilation to the dominant society.

Beyond situation- and domain-specificity, those behavioral patterns that are generally adaptive for sociocultural adaptation (Ward & Kennedy, 1992), that is, fitting in and functioning in the dominant society, are more likely to change than those that are closer to home and more private. This would result in integration, even assimilation in the public domain but separation in the private domain, as found by Arends-Tóth (2003) in the case of Turkish Dutch, mentioned before. On the other hand, some behaviors of immigrants may face more pressure to change than other behaviors that might be tolerated better by the host society. For example, though certain religious traditions of Moslem minorities in Europe are frowned on by the dominant society, their ethnic food is tolerated, even celebrated as multiculturalism. Thus, a great deal of variation occurs within integration (Arends-Tóth & Van de Vijver, 2006). The variations derive both from the dominant society, in terms of what it tolerates and demands, and also from the minorities in terms of their aspirations. The relative *adaptive* function of change and maintenance of behavior patterns, values, and interpersonal relations plays a role in the outcome of acculturation.

## FAMILY AND PARENTING IN ACCULTURATION

For psychologists, a key area of study is the acculturating family. There is a growing body of research on the family and parent–child relations in the **acculturation** context. As Western societies are becoming more aware of their multicultural social structures and as ethnic minorities are becoming more visible because of their increasing numbers, more cross-cultural (or cross-ethnic) studies appear to be conducted by Western psychologists within Western societies than among different national societies. Such research, in turn, promises to shed light on our understanding of family dynamics in general and provides precious empirical evidence for theories. In this section, I examine some of this research as it relates to the theoretical perspectives put forward in chapters 4, 5, and 6.

*again research gap*

In the acculturation context, the family shows a dynamic complexity. Spousal and intergenerational relations as well as gaps in their respective acculturation processes may create conflicts in some domains but not in others. This may result in changes in some aspects of family relations whereas others are maintained. For example, Kwak (2003), reviewing a great deal of research with immigrant adolescent–parent relations in the United States, showed that in general the generational conflicts between immigrants adolescents and parents revolved around autonomy but not around relatedness. In other words, as mentioned in chapter 6 also, immigrant adolescents wanted to have more autonomy than their parents were willing to grant them, but they were content with being closely related to their parents and didn't want to separate from them. This finding further points to the need to examine the specific content of acculturation and its resulting conflicts. It shows the complexity of parent–child interactions occasionally involving smooth relations in one aspect and problematic ones in another.

## Self and Family Change Model in Acculturation Context

We can better understand this situation in terms of the theoretical perspective presented in chapter 5. The basic issue is culture contact between the **culture of relatedness** of ethnic minorities originating from collectivistic societies and the **culture of separateness** of the individualistic dominant society. For example, the aspirations of adolescents in Kwak's review (2003) appear to be the **autonomous–related self** and the **family model of psychological/emotional interdependence** (Kağitçibaşi, 2003). Autonomy is adaptive in school and everyday situations that adolescents experience. **Social comparison process** also plays a role here. That is, when they compare themselves to the adolescents in the dominant society, the ethnic-minority adolescents see that the dominant-society adolescents enjoy more autonomy than they themselves do. On the other hand, relatedness with parents satisfies their need for relatedness and provides them with warmth and security. That is why it does not create conflict. Research points to the adaptive role of relatedness with parents and parent–child bonding in the context of immigration while autonomy is attained by the adolescents (Buriel, Love, & Ment, 2006; Chao, 2006).

Indeed, Leyendecker, Scholmerich, and Citlak (2006) found that second-generation Turkish immigrant parents in Germany expect their children to maintain close relationships with family, *and* they also endorse autonomy. No difference is found between second-generation Turkish mothers and German mothers in terms of autonomy goals, whereas first-generation Turkish mothers value conformity goals. So, both relatedness and autonomy are aspired for. A similar picture is drawn by Nijsten (2006) regarding Turkish immigrant parents in the Netherlands, the vast majority of which no longer think that authoritarian control is the proper type of discipline. Especially those with more education prefer to reason with their children and explain rather than use power assertion techniques. These findings provide evidence for the emergence of the **family model of psychological/emotional interdependence** in the context of immigration.

However, some parents, especially those with less education, tend to be reluctant to grant their children autonomy, because they see this as a sign of independence, disrespect, and **separation.** There is a "culture lag" here, with the traditional outlooks of the **family model of** (total) **interdependence** still persisting even though they are not adaptive in the immigration context, that is, urban technological society. There is a conflict between on the one hand the autonomous–related self and the family model of psychological/emotional interdependence that adolescents prefer and, on the other hand, the **heteronomous-related self** and the family model of (total) interdependence these parents prefer. Because the former is more adaptive in the immigration context, it is likely that it will prevail. In other words, adolescents may be expected to get what they want, but it may not be a smooth process of change.

This process can be facilitated and families can be supported if the nature of the problem is well understood by professionals such as psychologists, social workers, and the like. For example, parents may be helped to understand that autonomy of the child/adolescent is adaptive for success in school, that autonomy does not result in disrespect for parents, and that it does not necessitate separation from parents. This is often not done however, because these professionals tend not to think in these terms. Given the dominant psychological perspectives they know, they are more likely to uphold the **autonomous–separate self** and the **family model of independence** as the ideal or healthy models, and to impose these on the immigrants. The result is a lack of understanding and support.

Culture conflict and the different outlooks of parents and professionals (host society) manifest themselves in other ways, also. For example, Dekoviç et al. (2006) in their study of several ethnic minorities in the Netherlands find strict parental discipline to be prevalent. However, they also find these parents to be warm toward their children. They call this "an unlikely combination." This interpretation derives from the dominant assumption in Western psychology, based on psychoanalytic views, that **parental control** is not associated with **parental warmth** but rather with parental hostility.

As discussed earlier in chapters 2 and 6, recent research with African American families (Deater-Deckart & Dodge, 1997; Lansford et al., 2003) and with ethnic minorities in the United States and Europe (Chao, 1994; Dekoviç et al., 2006; Harwood et al., 2001) serves as a corrective here. These studies show that family control and connectedness (warmth) can and do coexist (Jose et al, 2000; Kwak, 2003).

Thus Gonzales et al. (1996) note that often ethnic minority parents are too readily labeled authoritarian because they appear too controlling. Yet, as I discussed in chapter 2, parental control and parental warmth are independent dimensions of parenting; therefore they can coexist (Deković et al., 2006; L. W. Hoffman, 2003; Kağitçibaşi, 1970; Rohner & Pettengill, 1985; Trommsdorff, 1985). We saw many examples of such coexistence in research covered in chapter 5 that provide support for the family model of psychological/emotional interdependence.

Some researchers, who label ethnic minority parenting as authoritarian, still note that it can coexist with parental warmth. For example, Rudy and Grusec (2001) comparing Egyptian Canadian with Anglo-Canadian parents found that whereas in both groups collectivism predicted **authoritarian parenting,** lack of warmth was also predicted by it in the Anglo group but not in the Egyptian group. They noted that, as was true of the Egyptian sample, higher authoritarianism may not be associated with lack of warmth or negative orientations to the child, such as using dispositional attributions for childrens' mistakes (blaming, derogating the child). Thus, as seen in the aforementioned examples, especially when strict parental discipline is normative, that is, common and accepted in a group, it does not have the negative meaning it carries in contexts where the norm is more permissive parenting.

What appears to be of key importance is not whether there is firm parental control but rather whether it is accompanied by parental warmth; what is normative in a community is also crucial. Given the social comparison process that underlies what is "normal" and what is not, in sociocultural contexts where firm parental discipline is the accepted norm, it may not reflect parental hostility. Consequently, it may not lead to maladaptive consequences.

Also, the way in which control is manifested in parenting is vital. If parents use firm control for the benefit of the child, especially communicating to the child their values and promoting the internalization by the child of those values, this is not associated with negative child outcomes (Deater-Deckart & Dodge, 1997; L. W. Hoffman, 2003, Lansford et al., 2003; Rudy & Grusec, 2001). However, if strict control occurs together with and therefore reflects parental hostility, domination, and lack of warmth, then it is maladaptive. Indeed, only this latter pattern should be labeled "authoritarian" because ever since the publication of the *Authoritarian Personality* (Adorno et al., 1950), this has been seen as the maladaptive authoritarian parenting style.

A related issue is the respect ethnic-minority parents expect of their children. This is interpreted by dominant-society professionals as domineering hierarchy. This may be the case especially if there is domineering control that does not grant any autonomy to the child. On the other hand, it may rather reflect a different understanding of decency (Kağitçibaşi, 2006a, 2006b). For example, "proper demeanor" (Harwood et al., 2002) as a childrearing goal may reflect not a simplistic obedience orientation but rather an upholding of family integrity as well as social awareness and sensitivity to others' needs (Fuligni, Tseng, & Lam, 1999; see also chap. 6, this volume). This may also be seen as a different understanding of morality. In this latter case, there may be coexistence of parental control and granting of some autonomy. This is what is construed for the family model of psychological/emotional interdependence. There is also a combination of parental control and warmth in this model. Many immigrant parents with a **culture of relatedness** show this pattern. It is more prevalent among the more educated and more acculturated parents because they understand the adaptive value of autonomy for succeeding in an urban technological society. It would be preferable to accept this disposition and to support these parents in their parenting orientation. On the other hand, as discussed earlier, other ethnic-minority parents may insist on following their traditional ways reflecting the family model of (total) interdependence with obedience-oriented parenting. This would more likely be the case among the less educated and less acculturated ethnic-minority parents. These parents would benefit from consciousness raising regarding the adaptive value of autonomy for their children in succeeding in the host society.

In turn, host-society professionals and others dealing with immigrant groups would do well to develop insights into the differences between these two parenting patterns. Although the pattern fitting into the **family model of interdependence** would need to be modified, that fitting into the family model of psychological/emotional interdependence would need to be supported. In the case of the latter, we have a healthy-functioning family that satisfies both basic needs for autonomy and relatedness. Indeed, it could serve as a model for the host society, also. Immigrants have a great deal to learn from the host society, but the host society could, in turn, also learn from them; in particular, they could learn the value of close family relations.

Close family ties nourish the need for relatedness and should be supported. Parental warmth and close parent–child/adolescent relations also promote the transmission of values between generations and the internalization of these values by the child, as mentioned previously. As proposed by self-determination theory, autonomy also emerges in the context of close parent–child relatedness (Chirkov et al., 2003; Ryan et al., 1995; Ryan & Lynch, 1989; see also chaps. 4 and 6, this volume).

*Cultural Transmission of Values.*    Considerable research has been conducted on the transmission of values in the acculturation context. Cultural transmission entails variations in cultural values, and such variation is more notable in immigration situations as it involves culture contact. Collectivistic orientations, familistic values, and attitudes toward family obligations are some spheres in which intergenerational cultural transmission takes place.

Continuing family loyalties are found in research with immigrants from cultures of relatedness. Thus, Fuligni et al. (1999) showed that Filipino, Chinese, Mexican, and Latin American immigrant adolescents in the United States possessed stronger values and greater expectations regarding their duty to support and respect their families compared with Euro-American adolescents. These differences were substantial and consistent across gender, family composition, socioeconomic status, and generation in the host country. It is notable that these family loyalties did not decrease in the second- and third-generation youth. Thus, transmission of values regarding family integrity and family obligations is sustained over time. Furthermore, the researchers also found that such collectivistic family values do not have a negative impact on young peoples' development in an individualistic society that emphasizes adolescent independence.

A series of studies conducted with Turkish immigrant families in Western Europe provide further insights into intergenerational transmission of values in the acculturation context. Phalet and Schonpflug (2001) showed that parental collectivism and achievement values were effectively transmitted to adolescents in the Netherlands and Germany. Collectivistic and aspiring Turkish parents who stressed conformity socialized their children toward a **collectivistic achievement motivation** (see chap. 4) involving achievement motivation with sustained commitment to the family. More collectivistic parents were found to stress conformity more and thereby enhanced transmission of achievement values. The researchers note that such achievement motivation is adaptive in an individualistic society for the survival of the immigrant family and community. Similarly, Phalet and Swyngedouw (2004) in their study with Turkish and Moroccan immigrants in Belgium found that conformity-tradition values and heritage-culture maintenance led to preferences for family, rather than individual mobility, whereas adoption of host-culture values led to weaker preference for family mobility.

There may be different implications of intergenerational cultural transmission for psychological and **sociocultural adaptation** (Searle & Ward, 1990; Ward, 2001; Ward & Kennedy, 1996) in the immigration context. Gungor (2007) with Turkish immigrant adolescents in Belgium found that collectivism and enhanced heritage-culture maintenance were associated with better psychological adjustment, whereas individualism reduced psychological adjustment (involving higher levels of somatization and depression-hostility). On the other hand, individualism increased the adoption of host culture and led to better sociocultural adaptation. Thus, psychological and sociocultural adaptation can proceed in opposite directions. Private and public domains present different affordances and challenges to the acculturating youth.

Finally, intergroup relations, and in particular whether the immigrants perceive discrimination by the dominant culture, play a role in how values mediate acculturation orientations. Studying gender orientations in immigrant adolescents, Idema and Phalet (2006) found that sons' perception of discrimination by the host society and religious **socialization** led to less egalitarian gender orientations and reinforced collectivism. On the other hand, more contact with the host society (for sons) and better dominant-language mastery (for daughters) led to more egalitarian gender values. These findings bring us to examine further the larger contextual factors, that is, the host society.

## Contextual Factors That Play a Role in Acculturation

As is obvious from the foregoing, a myriad of factors beyond the family play a role in **acculturation.** I have already touched on some of these as influencing acculturation. Here I elaborate on factors that provide us with some insights into the larger complex picture. These concern intergroup relations and perceptions of the dominant society or the minority group or both.

*Perceived Acceptance.* A great deal of research points to the crucial role played by the perceptions of the acculturating group regarding the degree of acceptance by the dominant society. This is found to be important in any type of acculturation, of sojourners, immigrants, refugees, and so on. In general, the more the perceived acceptance, the more positive is the experience of acculturation and **psychological adaptation.** For example, in an early study I conducted with Turkish exchange students who spent a year in the United States, I found that because these students stayed with families who had volunteered to host them and, by definition, were accepting of them, the students had a very positive growth experience (Kağitçibaşi, 1978). Contrast this with the experience of some Turkish immigrant families in Solingen, Germany, who lost some members in houses set on fire by violent fascist gangs. Between the extremes, there are different levels of perceived acceptance that set the stage for different acculturation experiences.

Obviously, this factor is significant in all intergroup relations, particularly between the more powerful and less powerful groups, and underlies many research findings on the behavior of the vulnerable group. It can also create situations that resemble self-fulfilling prophesies in the sense that those individuals or groups feeling belittled tend to behave in ways confirming these condescending attitudes of the more powerful others. For example, research in the United States on *stereotype threat* (Steele & Aronson, 1995) shows that when negative racial stereotypes against them are made salient, African American students do less well in academic tasks.

Perceived prejudice and discrimination is the main cause. As discussed earlier, U.S. research on stereotypes over a long period has produced much information on these "images in our minds," showing additionally that these are persistent images that resist change. They are based on history, myth, economic and political competition, and conflict. They have to do with the "us–them" distinctions that are at the basis of social identity and intergroup relations.

What gives people feelings of lack of acceptance in immigration contexts? Given the long-standing stereotypes, it is often quite clear that some minority groups are less well accepted than others. For example, Schalk-Soekar and Van de Vijver (2004) refer to the ethnic hierarchy among European immigrant groups. For the members of those minority groups low in this hierarchy, *status loss* is a salient experience in every aspect of their lives, not only in terms of economic or employment disadvantages mentioned before. This has a profound effect on their acculturation trajectories.

*Perceived Difference.* Underlying this hierarchy is often the perceived difference between the dominant society and the immigrant. The greater the perceived difference on some key attributes, the lower is the status of the immigrant group in the ethnic hierarchy, and the stronger is the rejection of the group by the dominant society. For example, an early study in France (Malewska-Peyre, 1980) showed a greater rejection of the North African immigrants than Portugese immigrants even though the former spoke French and the latter did not. Subsequent research corroborated the finding that perceived difference is a very important factor in discrimination (Arends-Tóth & Van de Vijver, 2006; Berry et al., 2002; Mirdal & Ryynnen-Karjalainen, 2004; Montreuil & Bourhis, 2001; Ward, 2001).

Indeed, in social psychology since the very beginning of the study of attitudes, stereotypes, and the Bogardus (1925) Scale of Social Distance, we know that the more "different" the other is seen as, the larger the preferred social distance between self and the other. Social identity theory (Tajfel & Turner, 1979) also points to the same phenomenon. Stereotypes serve to *reinforce* the difference of the *other* and thus to increase the social distance between the host/dominant society and the ethnic minorities. Stereotypes also tend to mask in-group diversity and individual differences and therefore may take the form of "pathologizing" immigrants, such as seen in assertions that the immigrants are "of

*[margin annotations: "huge issue in U.S. + Denmark!!"; "social distance + current events"]*

poor-quality stock." Such negative stereotypes are common despite evidence regarding many cases of the positive sociocultural adaptation of immigrants, for example, immigrant children doing well in Canadian and American schools despite various problems (Beiser, Hou, Hyman, & Tousignabt, 2002; Fuligni, 1997, 1998, 2003; Kwak, 2003) or Turkish immigrants being successful entrepreneurs, artists, filmmakers, and the like in Germany.

The type of acculturation strategy demanded of the migrant group by the main society is also influenced by stereotypic attitudes. For favored minorities, integration is endorsed, which maintains the cultural features of the group. However, for rejected groups' assimilation, segregation or exclusion are preferred. Thus their cultural features are not welcome in the host society; they should either vanish through full assimilation, or the groups should be excluded from the main society. Studies conducted in Canada regarding European French immigrants compared with Haitians (Montreuil & Bourhis, 2001) and in Israel regarding Russian and Ethiopian Jews compared with Israeli Arabs (Bourhis & Dayan, 2004) confirm these sentiments.

*also U.S. !!*

Beyond the perceived (and real) cultural differences, socioeconomic differences are also important. In most cases, there is an overlap between ethnic-minority status and low-SES status. This is especially the case in Europe where the original labor migration policies of European governments entailed the recruitment of unqualified work migrants with low levels of education, often from rural and less developed areas of the sending countries. Also, for many decades it was mostly the poor populations with few resources who were willing to leave their homes and search for employment elsewhere (Abadan-Unat, 1986; Kağitçibaşi, 1987b). This has been the case for both rural to urban migration within the same country and also for international migration.

At times the lower SES standing of the ethnic minorities is ignored and their various behaviors and characteristics are attributed to their "culture." Thus, if, for example, their children are not doing well in school, it is because of their culture. Yet, for quite a long time research has shown that what is assumed to be a cultural difference may be a social-class difference. For example, as discussed in chapter 2, Cashmore and Goodnow (1986) found that the differences among ethnic groups in Australia on parental orientations disappeared when social class was controlled. Similar results were reported by other research in 1980s (Lambert, 1987; Laosa, 1980; Podmore & St. George, 1986). More recent work corroborates earlier findings. For example, studies comparing Turkish minority children and Dutch children in the Netherlands found that socioeconomic status explained most of the ethnic differences in problem behaviors (Bengi-Arslan, Verhulst, & Crijnen, 2002; Crijnen, 2003).

*What kind of problem behaviors?*

## The Macro Context

Particularly when the macro context of **acculturation** is characterized by negative stereotypes, social distance, and discrimination, the less than optimal strategies of **separation** or even **marginalization** may emerge in the ethnic-minority groups (Berry, 2006), often as a reaction to status loss (Kağitçibaşi, 1997d). The issues may transcend psychological spheres and may assume political overtones. A better understanding of these issues would then require the multidisciplinary research of psychologists collaborating with other social scientists. In particular, when group mobilizations take place, more comprehensive macro perspectives may be needed.

Islamic mobilization in Europe is a case in point. This is a highly debated current political/social issue that carries the seeds of serious intergroup conflict, as reflected by recent events on an international scale. When people talk about multiculturalism in Europe, they refer mainly to Islam (Mirdal & Ryynanen-Karjalainen, 2004; Weller, 2004). Peach (2002) states, "Religion is the new key to unraveling ethnic identity in the West" (p. 255). Though religion is only one aspect of culture, in the eyes of the host society, Islam *is* the culture of the Moslem immigrants, and there are widespread negative sentiments regarding it, emerging out of historical roots.

Western European governments have been providing funds to Moslem minorities to establish their own religious schools and to carry out other religious activities in accordance with constitutional provisions in Western Europe upholding religious tolerance. However, there is a dilemma here because such tolerant policies do not in fact foster tolerance in the host society and do not benefit the minorities for a number of reasons. First of all, the increased Moslem identification renders these minorities even more *different* than the host society in appearance and behavior. Their "otherness" is accentuated, further fueling rejection by the dominant society (Kağitçibaşi, 1997d; Kaya, 2001). Thus, in the name of tolerance, in effect intolerance is nourished against Moslem minorities.

Second, in response to perceived rejection by the host society, Moslem immigrants cling to their religion as an affirmation of their own group identity and worth. Indeed, research shows that religiosity and group identity increase as a *consequence* of perceived prejudice (Baumgartl, 1994). This can even make some migrants vulnerable to radical fundamentalist mobilization, as in fact has been found to be the case in Western Europe. Thus, multicultural policies tend to result in increased separation rather than **integration** of the Moslem minorities.

Third, when minority children go to Moslem schools, rather than regular public schools, they do not interact with children of the host society and do not learn the host-society language adequately. This is a problem with serious consequences such as minority children's lower levels of schooling, lower social integration, and resultant lower life chances in the country of immigration. Thus, a chain of overlapping negative influences turning into a vicious cycle aggravates the problem. To prevent negative outcomes, the vicious cycle has to be broken by effective measures and informed socioeconomic policies (Guiraudon et al., 2005; see also chap. 7 for a more general discussion of schooling and the issue of religious education).

## POLICY IMPLICATIONS

The considerations just discussed have some policy implications regarding improving intergroup relations and the plight of migrants. A basic point deriving from what research shows us is that *both* the immigrant and the dominant populations need to be targeted. Although the immigrants can be helped and supported to develop the resources they need for psychological and **sociocultural adaptation,** sensitization and awareness-raising efforts directed at the host society can be helpful in easing intergroup tensions and reducing prejudice. For example, as mentioned before, Arends-Tóth (2003) found that the Turkish Dutch make a distinction between the private domain and the public domain, preferring different acculturation strategies in these. The Dutch majority, on the other hand, does not make such a distinction and demands assimilation in all domains. If such different views are recognized, then strategies toward solutions can be searched.

In both research and applications such as support programs, the main attention has typically focused on the migrant. Though such attention can be helpful, it has too often taken on a problem-oriented stance, at times even pathologizing the migrant (Sam et al., 2003). There needs to be a shift from emphasizing deficits to recognizing and optimizing strengths. For example, families can be helped to understand the ways in which they can support their children's school adjustment and performance. Often, migrants with low education levels have high educational aspirations for their children but are not sure how and through which routes this can be facilitated. For example, in chapter 2 we saw how immigrant parents' views that quietness and obedience in school leads to success do not match school expectations.

Migrant children and adolescents can also be helped directly through guidance. Success stories point to bridging the multiple worlds of immigrant adolescents and youth for better overall development, competence, and adjustment (Cooper, 2003). It is of utmost significance to

*Turkish early education program*

build on the existing strengths and to develop resources for the enhancement of competence. Interventions such as TEEP, described in the last chapter, can contribute toward this goal. Several of the points raised in chapters 2, 3, 8, and 9 regarding development in context, development of competence, and related applications are also relevant in the immigration context.

*this is partially the reason for the education achievement gap in CA !!*

As discussed before, the focus on the migrants may divert attention from the host society. General "sensitization" efforts reinforcing an appreciation of differences, rather than seeing what is different as deficient would go a long way in supporting multicultural policies. In particular, teachers can be helped to be sensitive toward tendencies to expect less from migrant children, which can serve as self-fulfilling prophesies, and to channel them to less academic tracks. Similarly, professionals like social workers and psychologists can be made more sensitive to different family cultures, especially the family model of psychological/emotional interdependence, so that they do not attribute pathology inappropriately when they observe close family ties and strict parental discipline.

Such sensitization can also help resolve even more serious problems with regard to possible conflicts between the traditional practices of immigrant parents and the legal stipulations in the country of immigration. For example, Azar and Cote (2002) point to the importance of sociocultural factors in custody decisions regarding immigrant children in the United States.

*is this true ??.*
*I'm not sure...*

As for the development of the self in the context of **acculturation,** we can say that nourishing the development of the **autonomous–related self** would enhance the well-being and **psychological adaptation** of the immigrant child. This is because this type of self is adaptive in the face of environmental demands for autonomous action as well as benefiting from the psychological support provided by close relationships. This could be realized only if parents with a *culture of relatedness* are supported to appreciate the value of autonomy and understand that it can and should coexist with relatedness. Professionals also need to have this understanding in order to help the acculturating minorities. It is to be noted that relatedness with the family is not a hindrance for adaptive development but can be a source of strength so long as it also nourishes autonomy.

*encouraging autonomy*

Thus self and family are at the core of the acculturation process. Immigration and culture contact create new environments, which cause changes in self–family dynamics above and beyond the common developmental changes. Studying these processes sheds light on the psychology of acculturation as well as provides a better understanding of the self in changing contexts.

## SUMMARY AND MAIN POINTS

- This chapter deals with some issues that inhere in human relations in the context of immigration.
- Early studies on attitudes were conducted in the United States to understand intergroup relations. A main issue was whether personality factors or situational factors were important to explain prejudiced attitudes. More recently, the attention has shifted from attitudes to the acculturation of immigrants.
- In recent American and European studies, *psychological* perspectives are used with individual, family, and interpersonal levels of analyses rather than macro perspectives. *Psychological* acculturation is studied more than other forms of acculturation, such as political, economic, and so on.
- A heuristic grouping of theoretical approaches to the study of acculturation has been proposed by Ward. It includes stress and coping, culture learning, and social identity approaches, corresponding to the affective, behavioral, and cognitive (A, B, C's) domains, respectively. A fourth approach has been added —D for development.
- A further distinction has been made between psychological and sociocultural adaptation. Economic adaptation has also been proposed.
- The unidimensional acculturation view, claiming that adaptation to the dominant culture means giving up the original culture, has been challenged. A bidimensional view, proposed by Berry, is widely accepted. Here, the resultant strategies are *integration, marginalization, assimilation,* and *separation.* These strategies may not always be choices available to the immigrant groups; therefore, the dominant group orientations toward the immigrants are also addressed in the revised model.
- What actually changes in acculturation provides insight into the everyday reality of the culture contact situation. A great deal of diversity enters the picture here, based on individual differences, situation- and domain-specificity of behavior, and variations across attitudes, cognitions, and behaviors.
- For psychologists, a key area of study is the acculturating family. The family context shows a dynamic complexity. Spousal and intergenerational relations as well as gaps in their respective acculturation processes create conflicts in some domains but not in others. This may result in some aspects of family relations to change and others to be maintained.

- Research points to the adaptive role of the *autonomous–related self* and the *family model of emotional/psychological interdependence*. However, at times there is conflict between on the one hand the autonomous–related self and the family model of psychological interdependence adolescents prefer, and on the other hand the heteronomous-related self and the family model of (total) interdependence traditional parents prefer. The process of change can be facilitated and families can be supported if the nature of the problem is well understood by professionals.
- Parental control and parental warmth are independent dimensions of parenting. Coexistence of parental control and autonomy is seen in some immigrant parents with culture of relatedness, especially among more educated ones.
- Transmission of values regarding family integrity and family obligations is sustained over time. There may be different implications of intergenerational transmission of cultural values for psychological and sociocultural adaptation.
- A myriad of factors beyond the family play a role in acculturation. The perception of the acculturating group regarding the degree of acceptance by the dominant society is crucially important. The more the perceived acceptance, the more positive is the experience of acculturation and psychological adaptation.
- The greater the perceived difference between the dominant society and the immigrant group, the lower is the status of the immigrant group on ethnic hierarchy and the greater is the rejection group by the dominant society.
- Particularly when the macro context of acculturation is characterized by negative stereotypes, social distance, and discrimination, the less than optimal strategies of separation or even marginalization may emerge in the ethnic-minority groups, often as a reaction to status loss.
- Although the immigrants can be helped and supported to develop the resources they need for psychological and sociocultural adaptation, sensitization and awareness-raising efforts directed at the host society can also be helpful to ease intergroup tensions and to reduce prejudice.

## DISCUSSION QUESTIONS

1. What are the main constructs used in acculturation studies?
2. How is the unidimensional view of acculturation challenged by Berry? What is the problem with Berry's original approach?

3. What is the main conflict between adolescents and their parents in the immigration context? How is the conflict conceptualized? How can it be solved?
4. Discuss the proposed and observed coexistence of parental control and warmth.
5. What different implications do intergenerational transmission of cultural values have for psychological and sociocultural adaptation?
6. What macro-environmental factors beyond the family are important in acculturation?

# 11

# Search for Integration and Policy Implications

Where do we stand now and what next? This book has covered a wide ground. On the one hand, I examined the theoretical issues involved in human development, family, and culture interfaces; on the other hand, I delved into applications designed to induce change. I attempted to bridge the gap between theory and application by presenting early intervention in general and the **Turkish Early Enrichment Project (TEEP)** as a case in point, as well as examining the implications of immigration and **acculturation** research. In this final chapter, I summarize what I have done and further attempt to verify my theoretical formulations of the development of the self and of human competence in the (changing) family. I also discuss emerging perspectives from TEEP and immigration/acculturation work and use these perspectives and research results as guidelines for drawing policy-relevant conclusions. In providing a synopsis and **integration** of the main points discussed in the previous chapters, I follow more or less the same order as in the presentation of the chapters.

## SUMMARY AND CRITICAL ISSUES

From the very start, I laid out some priorities in my orientation to psychology, namely, an involvement with interpersonal relations and social relevance. Then a **contextual-developmental-functional approach** was used in establishing the linkages between the self, family, and society on the one hand and between theory and application on the other. Furthermore, this approach was located within a cultural and **cross-cultural perspective.** This is a synoptic characterization of the general theoretical orientation used in this book.

Human development and the self were examined in context with this theoretical orientation. First, context was analyzed as a source of meaning, involving societal and parental beliefs, goals, and values regarding children. The functional underpinnings of these aspects of context emerged as important. Then **socialization** for competence and the self were examined within family and culture. The development of **cognitive competence** and of the self form the core topics in this book from both a theoretical and an applied perspective. They are subject to far-reaching cultural influences.

In particular, the distinction between the **related self** and the **separate self**, along the (inter)dependence–independence dimension, constitutes a key to an understanding of the functional links between culture, family, and the self and of family change through socioeconomic development. I distinguished between three different human/family patterns and proposed a general shift toward the model of emotional interdependence. This reflects a different type of convergence than what is commonly assumed by modernization views.

The next step was consideration of the role of psychology in promoting human development, at both the individual and societal levels. Issues such as setting comparative standards versus **relativism,** nature–nurture underpinnings, and the social-political implications of psychological research came to the fore. I then looked at early childhood care and education **(ECD)** as an area of induced change and examined the research and application issues involved. **TEEP** was then presented as a case study of induced change. Finally, immigration and **acculturation** was studied as a powerful example of environmental change and culture contact with direct implications for changes in family and self.

Thus, the first part of the book dealt mainly with theoretical issues regarding the family, human development, and the self in a cultural context. The second part examined induced change and the role of psychology, focusing on early enrichment and acculturation. Throughout the discussions, several important questions and issues emerged. I dwell on these further in an attempt to integrate the material presented in the different chapters. In particular, I try to relate theoretical considerations in the first part with the applied work in the second, especially the TEEP.

## Integrative Syntheses

Throughout the volume, several integrative syntheses have been posited. They have helped to weave some coherence among the numerous concepts used in the field and to link contextual perspectives with universal ones. They constitute some of the main theoretical contributions of this work.

An **integrative synthesis** is an attempt to qualify or change a construct or approach by combining it with another one arising from another context. Typically, a theory or construct that is claimed to be universal but is based on research in a particular sociocultural context, typically the United States, is combined with another one arising from a different context. The outcome promises to shed new light on global variations or commonalities in human phenomena.

Some such integrative syntheses emerging from cross-cultural research were described in earlier chapters. For example, the **socially oriented achievement motive** (Agarwal & Misra, 1986; Phalet & Claeys, 1993; Yu & Yang, 1994) is an integrative synthesis that combines the need for achievement and the need for extension, that is, the need to relate to others (J. B. P. Sinha, 1985; see also chap. 4). It is a different construct from the individualistically construed competitive achievement motivation traditionally found in mainstream psychology (McClelland & Winters, 1969). This construct integrates a universal need for achievement with the need for relatedness that shows cultural (contextual) variation. It helps explain why traditionally measures of (individualistically oriented) achievement motivation showed early on that people in cultures of relatedness lack achievement (Bradburn, 1963; Rosen, 1962). It also seems to underlie the aspirations for family mobility rather than individual mobility observed in current immigration contexts (Phalet & Swyngedouw, 2004).

In this book, I have put forward several such integrative syntheses. Most are theoretical constructs; one concerns my methodological approach. Starting with the latter, I reiterate and summarize them here.

*Combining Cultural Contextualism With Universal Standards.* The main methodological perspective I have utilized in this volume strives to combine **cultural contextualism** with universal standards of human development and well-being. This can be seen as an integrative synthesis in approach. It is the reason why, even though cultural diversity is stressed and context emerges as important in the theorizing used here, it does not result in cultural **relativism.** How can we combine and integrate cultural contextualism with universal standards so that we don't end up with relativism? As discussed at length throughout the volume, this is made possible through a number of measures. First of all, paying attention to context is not to claim that each context is unique. Rather, contexts can have common properties and can be compared (see chap. 1; Kağitçibaşi, 2000a). Such recognition helps us look for the underlying reasons for social change. It also allows us to recognize similarities in changing environmental conditions and thus the similar demands these changing environments put on people. In turn, this leads to a better understanding of the adaptations to social change.

Such an integrative synthesis in approaching behavior in culture can occur through innovative conceptualization and methodology. For example, the following measures can be helpful in integrating the contextual and the universal in the study of human development:

- Construing culturally valid and relevant human development and environmental indicators pointing to possibly universal shared attributes.
- Depicting what is adaptive and what is not, and the changes in these as a result of changing environmental demands (**functional approach**).
- Conducting culturally sensitive research involving local experts informed by indigenous knowledge and research participants sharing in the decision making.
- Utilizing culturally sensitive and valid assessment.
- Considering contextual factors in the interpretation of the research results.

*Family Model of Psychological-Emotional Interdependence.* The family model of psychological-emotional interdependence is one of the main *integrative syntheses* proposed in this volume (see chap. 5). It emerges as the synthesis of the prototypical family models of *independence* and *interdependence*. A number of syntheses are observed in this family model in family structure, socialization values, and the values attributed to children (voc). Most important, parenting orientation involves the combination of control, autonomy, and relatedness (warmth). As discussed at length, this type of parenting manifests a synthesis of presumably conflicting characteristics. Originally deriving from a psychoanalytic perspective, and accepted as "common wisdom" in psychological teaching, parental control (strict discipline) is assumed to reflect **authoritarian parenting** that does not include warmth. Thus, when **parental warmth** and **control** are observed to coexist, for example, in ethnic-minority families in Europe, this is labeled an "unlikely combination" (Dekoviç et al, 2006). In this family model, however, there is indeed a synthesis of these parenting orientations.

In chapters 5, 6, and 10 we saw that the **family model of psychological/emotional interdependence** develops in response to changing lifestyles involving urbanization, with increased education, specialization, and so on. These environmental changes require autonomy and individual decision making. At the same time, however, the **culture of relatedness** is sustained because it is not incompatible with the new lifestyles. This family model, as an integrative synthesis, is of particular relevance in the context of socioeconomic development in the **Majority**

**World** and in the immigration context in the Minority World. It helps us understand which family characteristics are adaptive in changing life circumstances and why. Furthermore, given the commonalities in changes in lifestyles, the family model of psychological/emotional interdependence is proposed as the model toward which there is a global convergence.

*The Autonomous–Related Self.* Emerging mostly in the family model of psychological/emotional interdependence, the **autonomous-related self** is another main integrative synthesis posited in this volume. Discussed at length in chapter 6, the autonomous–related **self-construal** combines two attributes, autonomy and relatedness, that a considerable body of theoretical work in psychology assume to be conflicting and mutually exclusive, albeit basic. Two pathways of thinking and research have led to this construct. One of these is my **family change theory,** based on the **Value of Children Study.** The autonomous–related self emerges in the family model of psychological/emotional interdependence, and this family model emerges in the context of global social change toward urban lifestyles, including international migration. Thus this type of self is adaptive to changing lifestyles. The other pathway derives from two basic human needs, those for **agency** (autonomy) and relatedness. Their combination, the autonomous–related self, thus emerges as an optimal human model. Both of these pathways imply a convergence toward the autonomous–related self as a healthy human model (see Box 6.4).

The autonomous–related self emerges as a healthy human model for at least two important reasons. First of all, it recognizes and fulfills both of the two basic needs for autonomy (agency) and relatedness. Second, fulfillment of these needs is adaptive to living in a modern technological society. In particular, autonomy is functional for success in school and specialized work in an urban technological society, toward which there is a global shift. Relatedness, in turn, provides the psychological support needed for healthy human development.

*Social/Cognitive Intelligence.* In discussing the development of competence, social and **cognitive competence** emerged as important. Considerable cultural variation was noted in chapter 3 regarding the relative significance of **social intelligence** in preindustrial societies, accompanied by practical skills. This is contrasted with cognitive school-like competence being valued and promoted in technological society. Research conducted particularly within an **everyday cognition paradigm** appears to pit one of these competencies against the other one. The claims that they are alternative ways of learning, each valuable in its own right and within its own context, recognize and praise diversity but do not deal with global urbanization and changing lifestyles. Success and social mobility in an urban technological society require cognitive/school-like skills; therefore, they have to be promoted. Practical skills alone are insufficient for success in changing lifestyles. Social intelligence, however, continues to be valuable, especially in cultures of relatedness.

Thus what appears to be needed is the *addition* of cognitive competence to social intelligence, not its replacement (see chap. 3). Therefore, an integrative synthesis of **social/cognitive competence** would be called for in the context of socioeconomic development with continuing closely knit human ties. This construct is in the realm of competence; however, it appears to be parallel to the autonomous–related self. Autonomous action would benefit from cognitive competence, and the **related self** would build on social sensitivity to others' needs and social responsibility, that is, social intelligence.

The preceding integrative syntheses have formed the backbones of the theoretical perspectives put forward in this volume. They represent thinking that benefits from both universal scholarship in the field, as well as indigenous knowledge arising out of different cultural experiences. Thus, they can be seen as examples of "endogenous" thinking as discussed in chapter 7. Originally proposed by UNESCO, **endogenous development** refers to encompassing both the culturally relevant and the globally shared knowledge (Huynh, 1979; Tripathi, 1988); thus, it is an integrative synthesis. It is this synthesis of the contextual with the universal that distinguishes this perspective from a purely indigenous one, involving only the contextual.

## Critical Issues in Early Intervention

A key question that emerged in the discussions in this book is whether there is an optimal fit between societal values/practices and children's "developmental trajectories." This is a legitimate question if we do not subscribe to a rampant **relativism.** It is answered necessarily affirmatively by an extreme functionalist-deterministic-relativistic stance in the sense that whatever a society needs, it values and practices, and therefore by definition, the outcome of this practice (e.g., childrearing) fits optimally with society's prerogatives.

There are some serious problems with this view, however. First of all, there is never full control or consensus in any society, and deviance exists everywhere. Therefore there is no such thing as a perfect fit between societal values/practices and behavioral outcomes. Second, even though functional analysis is enlightening, it has its limitations. If it is used in a deterministic fashion, it can deteriorate into circular reasoning and assume a static, nonchanging society. For example, obedience-oriented childrearing may be adaptive in agrarian lifestyles and thus becomes part of the family culture. However, being part of family culture does not render it adaptive or legitimizes its use in a changed context (urban living).

Assuming that because some behavior is a part of culture, then it must be adaptive is false in the face of constant ongoing change in all societies. Through societal change, what used to be a functional, optimal fit can turn into a dysfunctional relationship requiring correction.

This latter assertion is based on the assumption that decisions such as what is optimal, what is not; what is correct, what is not; what is good, what is not, *can* be made. It brings up the related issues of standards/relativism and the role of psychology in inducing change, which have been discussed at length in this book.

The general stand I take on this issue is that the original question, whether the fit between societal values/practices and children's developmental trajectories is optimal, is a legitimate question and that psychology has accumulated adequate knowledge and expertise to answer it. However, to do this, psychology must be prepared to establish some basic standards of human development while at the same time being sensitive to culture. This may appear as a contradiction in terms, but it is not, as I have argued in this book. A culturally sensitive stance does not mean the uniqueness of each culture or the impossibility of comparative standards. What it means is that assessment (evaluation) is done correctly, by utilizing culturally valid and relevant standards of shared attributes that can be applied in a comparative way. Thus, as I discussed earlier, a balance is needed between "emic" and "etic" orientations, in line with the "derived etic" concept, which benefits from both (Berry, 1989).

This stand underlies intervention research in general. It is quite clear in the area of the promotion of **cognitive competence** where certain standards such as "school preparedness" and school achievement can be used. These standards are applied in both specific realms of intervention, such as in enhancing preliteracy and prenumeracy skills, and also in the outcome measures used in evaluation. They are based on the psychological knowledge about the development of cognitive competence, school requirements, and school-related achievement criteria. Though less clear than cognitive/school-related indicators, indicators of healthy socioemotional development can also be established.

*Turkish Early Enrichment Project (TEEP) as a Case in Point.*   To give the example of **TEEP,** these indicators of healthy socioemotional development ment were based mainly on the theoretical views discussed in chapters 4,

5, and 6 regarding the two basic human needs of autonomy and related-ness and the human/**family model of psychological/emotional interdependence** that integrates them. Specifically, as we were dealing in the case of Turkey with a **culture of relatedness,** with a high value put on relatedness and closely knit human bonds, this basic human need for relatedness was considered well met, but the other basic need—the need for autonomy—was considered not adequately recognized and fulfilled. This was in fact found to be the case from the initial baseline assessments of mothers' child-rearing orientations, valuing relatedness and disapproving autonomy. It was also evidenced by other Turkish research (e.g., Fisek, 1991). Thus, a main goal of the intervention in the socioemotional realm was the acceptance of autonomy in childrearing and the resultant promotion of autonomy in children.

Another related issue emerging in this book is the role of psychology in the face of a less than optimal fit between cultural values/practices and children's developmental trajectories. I have made it clear that the psychologist has a role in *inducing* change where needed, in addition to analyzing, understanding, and explaining the situation. This is obviously implicated by any intervention research. The further issue of *how* to bring about change, or the most effective strategy to be used, is an empirical question.

The **contextual approach,** stressed throughout this book, informed our choices regarding this issue in TEEP. The main intervention introduced in the project had to do with changing the family context of the child, focusing on the mother. Thus, we applied a home-based early enrichment intervention together with and in comparison to a center-based intervention that was already under way.

The general approach utilized in the intervention introduced by the project was one of "empowerment" rather than ameliorating "deficiency." This is another issue of both theoretical and applied significance. Not subscribing to a "deficiency" model does not imply that the existing conditions are optimal for the development of children. If this were so, there would be no need for intervention. It rather means that the agent of change builds on the existing strengths in changing the conditions to promote optimal development. Empowerment refers, in effect, to strengthening what is adaptive in order to change what is mal-adaptive. Again, this kind of approach requires that the psychologist, first of all, accepts a role as an agent of change and, second, is willing to make decisions, based on scientific evidence, of what is to change. In other words, some standards (norms/criteria) of optimal development need to be accepted.

Obviously some risks are taken in making such decisions. However, as discussed before, these risks can be decreased if an effort is made to understand better the "realities" of the situation, aspirations of the people concerned, and so on. Furthermore, *not* making any decisions and *not* getting involved also carry risks in the sense that this may entail, in effect, a "decision by indecision" in perpetuating the status quo.

Also important is the guidance of sound theory, supported by research. The intervention of TEEP was informed by the theory of family change that I have developed, as well as by culturally relevant theory and research in developmental psychology discussed before. There was an attempt to combine **cultural contextualism** with universal standards, as I have already discussed in some detail (see chaps. 2, 3, 5, and 7). The socioeconomic context of the intervention was the changing lifestyles of formerly rural families whose children were to attend urban schools. Based on the aforementioned considerations, some decisions were made to induce change, focused on modifying maternal orientations/behavior and introducing new elements into it. They were designed to promote better mother–child interactions for greater cognitive competence (and school achievement) and more healthy socioemotional development of the child. They included such specific changes as increased verbalization, more effective communication, responsiveness, and perspective taking by the mother; more induction and authoritative (rather than authoritarian) discipline; better acceptance of the child and greater appreciation of his or her autonomy by the mother; more supportive parenting; higher educational aspirations; and carrying out a systematic program of school preparation with the child.

These induced changes were based on psychological knowledge regarding age-specific cognitive development and school preparedness, on the one hand, and the family model of psychological/emotional interdependence (see chap. 5), on the other. The research and theory I discussed in the first part of the book are relevant here. For example, the main goal of mother training was to induce the kind of stimulating parental orientation called "**parental modernity**" by Goodnow (1988) and found to contribute to children's cognitive development and school success (see chaps. 2 and 3). Another goal was to instill autonomy into the development of the **related self,** balancing the needs for **agency** and relatedness (see chaps. 4, 5, and 6).

As mentioned before, these goals were considered to fit with the psychological/ emotional interdependence family model, which is proposed to lead to the synthesis of the **autonomous–related self**. There may be the objection that rather than moving toward such a synthesis of the interdependent and independent developmental pathways, we have induced independence (individualism). However, as seen from the findings of TEEP, relational orientations were *not* weakened whereas a more positive orientation toward autonomy emerged among some of the mothers. This is a different change than one toward complete individualism/**separation.** It may be claimed that the beginnings of a move toward a synthesis of autonomy and related-ness are being seen here.

A contextual orientation was used in inducing change. Group discussion (group dynamics in general) was utilized as the instrument of change. Lewin's early work (1951, 1958), though not adequately appreciated today, clearly showed the facilitation of attitude and behavior change through group processes. The same facilitating effects were seen in our project. In small groups that meet regularly, individuals identify with the group and internalize its norms as their own, because they are its active participants. Thus, they feel the responsibility for carrying out group decisions; this seems to be a process that facilitates attitude and behavior change. Furthermore, because the group members feel the group support even when they are not in the group, they are empowered to resist others' possible opposition better than if they were carrying out their own individual decisions, alone. This appears to underlie group effects being sustained over time.

A culture-sensitive approach also favored a group process. In the traditional Turkish culture, women's kin and neighborhood groups serve an important support function (Kiray, 1981; Olson, 1982). Thus, utilizing such a familiar social structure meant building on an existing cultural strength. Indeed, women's support networks have been observed to be important in many cultural contexts, ranging from patriarchal Mediterranean societies with limited sharing of activities between males and females (Peristiany, 1976) to woman-headed African American families in the United States (Coll, 1990; Garbarino, 1990; Harrison et al., 1990; Stevens, 1988). Thus, Slaughter (1983) claimed that group discussion is a more culturally consonant intervention approach than individual home visits for low-income Black mothers. In any culture of relatedness with closely knit human bonds (as in Turkish society), it makes good sense to capitalize on groups as support mechanisms and as agents of change.

Finally, group training is more cost-effective than individual training. In terms of investment of time, personnel, and service per person, the group setting is clearly more economical than targeting persons individually. For all these reasons, a group orientation was utilized in TEEP. Thus, *contextuality* characterized our main theoretical and methodological approach in this project at two different levels, both in dealing with the development of the child in a family context (through the mother) and also in dealing with the mother in the group setting—micro- and meso-systems, respectively, in Bronfenbrenner's terms (1979).

Our contextual orientation, in working with the mother, also entailed an induced change in the conceptualization of the mother's role. Among lower-SES groups, rural people and ethnic minorities occupying marginal positions in urban society, the commonly held definition of parenting involves mainly loving and caring but *not* preparing the child for school, contrasted with the middle-class definitions including also the latter (see chaps. 2 and 3). A great deal of research, reviewed in this book, showed the latter, more comprehensive definition of parenthood to be more favorable for the child's school preparedness and school performance (Chao, 2000; Chao & Tseng, 2002; Coll, 1990; Goodnow, 1988; Jose et al., 2000; Laosa, 1984; LeVine & White, 1986; Slaughter, 1988). We therefore introduced cognitively oriented mother-focused intervention in our intervention. What has emerged here is the parent-as-teacher role.

TEEP applications and results demonstrate that cultural definitions of parenthood *can* change, and such change can even be brought about through intervention. Our long-term findings also showed that such change can be favorable for children's developmental trajectories.

Together with changes in the definitions of parental roles, there were changes also in conceptions of ("competent" and "good") children by parents. As discussed in chapters 3 and 4, in contexts where a relational conceptualization of the self and closely knit human bonds are prevalent, a social definition of intelligence prevails. Here a compliant and socially responsible child is highly valued. The 1st-year baseline assessments of TEEP also showed this. The project intervention stressing cognitive competence and autonomy, however, expanded this conceptualization to include also these latter elements. The change was apparent, for example, in more of the trained mothers accepting the autonomy of their children, expecting their children to do school-related activities on their own, and aspiring to higher levels of education and educational achievement for their children, compared with the nontrained mothers.

Such "new" values, however, seemed *not* to replace values of relatedness but to be *added* to them, as evidenced by the continued stress put on relatedness by the trained mothers. These results provide some evidence for the validity of the family model of psychological/emotional interdependence (see chap. 5). They also demonstrate that such a model of human relations can be induced through intervention.

This discussion of the critical issues and their reflections in TEEP shows that many of the theoretical considerations covered in the first part of the book were of relevance for the applications covered in the second part. Also the general **contextual-developmental-functional approach** that I adopted in linking human development/self, family, and society also underlay our Project.

## Critical Issues in Immigration

A key question that has emerged in this book is concerned with convergence in family/human models in conjunction with socioeconomic change. It asked whether there is a general shift toward the **family model of psychological/emotional interdependence** and the model of **autonomous–related self,** accompanying global trends toward urban technological lifestyles, because these models are more adaptive to these new lifestyles. Both the theoretical perspective proposed here as well as related empirical evidence provide an affirmative answer to this question.

This **family change theory** derived originally from the comparative Value of Children (VOC) Study conducted in nine countries with variations in socioeconomic development and demographic transition, including various fertility levels. The cross-country variations as well as social-class differences within Turkey pointed to systematic patterns of familial functioning that the family change theory helped explain. These were discussed at length in chapter 5.

Societal change is normally a slow process; the same is the case for culture change. Thus it is difficult to trace such changes empirically in research. However, the same changes occur at an accelerated pace in the context of immigration. Particularly in international migration, there are shifts in lifestyles from rural/agrarian/traditional ones to urban/technological ones. Culture contact accompanies these shifts and is manifested even in culture conflict between the **culture of relatedness** and the **culture of separateness.** Thus immigration constitutes a social change at the community, family, and individual levels. What normally takes many generations to come about in a society can occur within one or two generations in the context of culture contact. Thus, immigration provides us with a social laboratory to examine changes in family/human patterns through **acculturation.** Just as is true of societal change, immigration also brings about a shift toward the family model of psychological/emotional interdependence and the autonomous–related self.

It appears that autonomy and relatedness are both valuable for acculturation. Autonomy would appear to be particularly conducive to **sociocultural adaptation** and relatedness to **psychological adaptation.** Sociocultural adaptation requires the **agency** that the autonomous self can manifest in successfully coping with the demands of the urban/technological society involving educational and occupational achievement. A generally submissive and obedient orientation that comes with heteronomy would not get very far for social mobility in technological or posttechnological society. Relatedness, in turn, would appear to be conducive to psychological adaptation because relatedness with family, in particular, provides the acculturating person with the emotional support that is needed to cope with stressful environments. This view is in line with the empirical research conducted on adaptation in immigration (Arends-Tóth & Van de Vijver, 2006; Gungor, 2007; Phalet & Swyngedouw, 2004; Kwak, 2003; Ward, 2001; Ward & Kennedy, 1996).

Thus, the autonomous–related self that we considered to be the human model toward which there appears to be a universal convergence (see chap. 6) also emerges as the adaptive model in the immigration and acculturation context. In that context the adaptability of the autonomous–related self is even more noticeable. This is not surprising given the similar changes that occur in conjunction with societal socioeconomic development and international migration. In both cases, there is a shift from mostly rural/traditional to urban/modern lifestyles. Accordingly, the family model of psychological/emotional interdependence would also appear to be the most adaptive one in the context of immigration. This is because this model involves both parental (order-setting) control and autonomy granting in childrearing together with relatedness. It is therefore conducive to the development of the autonomous–related self.

Thus, the immigration context further affirms the autonomous–related self and the family model of psychological/emotional interdependence as healthy human models. Policies and interventions designed to promote better **integration** of immigrants and ethnic minorities need to aim toward these healthy models. For example, they should endeavor to promote awareness of the desirability of these models in both the dominant society and the minority groups.

We are now ready to complement Box 3.1, concerned with the change in **socialization** for competence, by adding the changes in family and self. Box 11.1 presents the fuller picture of changes in conjunction with both societal socioeconomic development and with migration from a traditional rural society to the technological society of the country of immigration.

The similarities in the lifestyles of the developed urban contexts in the **Majority World** and the Western immigration countries warrant dealing with them together as the context *toward which* there is a shift. In both of them, however, together with the changes in competence, there are also changes in the self. In the family and the self, we still see the reflections of the culture of relatedness that the former peasants/immigrants carry with them, but modified to adapt to changed lifestyles. The result is often an **integrative synthesis.** The changes presented in Box 11.1 reflect those manifested in the family model of psychological/emotional interdependence (see chap. 5, Box 5.4).

Box 11.1 Social Change and Changes in competence , family and self

| | Traditional/ Rural Subsistence | | Urban/Higher.SES Technological (Immigration) Society |
|---|---|---|---|
| **Context** | Less specialized work No/low schooling | → | More specialized work Increased schooling |
| **Teaching & Learning** | Demonstration and modeling Apprenticeship | → | Verbal explanation School-like learning |
| **Competence** | Social intelligence Practical/manual skills | → | Social + Cognitive Intelligence School-like skills |
| **Family** | Interdependence Model Material interdependencies Economic/utilitarian VOC | → | Psychological/ Emotional Inter-dependence Model Decreased material interdependencies Psychological VOC |
| **Child Rearing** | Obedience oriented childrearing | → | Control + Autonomy |
| **Self Development** | Heteronomous Related Self | → | Autonomous Related Self |

## PSYCHOLOGY AND SOCIAL POLICY

In what directions do these discussions lead? When we ask this question, we come to policy implications. There is much to be said about the policy relevance of the material covered in this book. However, I would first like to examine the relation between psychology and social policy.

Unlike other social scientists such as political scientists and economists, psychologists have not been typically much involved with social (public) policy (see chap. 7). This is not surprising given the individual focus in psychological analysis and a general lack of interest in issues of societal development, as discussed before. I have argued in this book that this has to change and psychology has to assume social accountability together with scientific rigor.

In the United States where psychology is well recognized and well established, it has some tradition of social involvement, mainly as a mental health profession. Yet even in the United States it is seen not to have realized its potential as an agent of change in the "public interest" (M. B. Smith, 1990). Nevertheless, there is a growing awareness of the need for psychological scientists to get involved with policy issues (Ceci & Papierno, 2005; Lerner, 2001; Shonkoff, 2000; Zimbardo, 2002), and there are signs that this may have started. The American Psychological Association (APA) endeavored to address policy issues ranging from national health care reform (*APA Monitor,* 1994) to efforts to strengthen **Head Start** to international human rights. It has declared 2000–2010 the "Decade of Behavior" as an initiative to meet "some of society's most significant challenges" (www.decadeofbehavior.org). In other countries and particularly in the **Majority World,** psychology has typically been less involved in policy matters.

Policy relevance of research and theory is the key here. Some time ago Bronfenbrenner (1979) stated it clearly: "Basic science needs public policy even more than public policy needs basic science. Moreover, what is required is not merely a complementary relation between these two domains but their functional integration" (p. 8). And M. B. Smith (1991) noted:

> The contribution of psychology is not limited to reporting conclusive research data (data are seldom if ever conclusive); it is also and maybe more importantly the redefining of policy questions by raising awareness of unconsidered possibilities or by reconceptualizing familiar dilemmas. (p. xviii)

Public policy has an impact on human conditions and human behavior, which psychology studies. In turn, policies often reflect the ideologies, cultural values, and social-structural characteristics of a society. Thus, they form an important aspect of the context in which human development and human behavior take place. Yet, policies can and should be based on scientific knowledge also and should be modifiable to serve changing human needs.

Many examples can be given of both cultural/ideological basis of policies and also their influence on human conditions. For example, in the social welfare states of the Nordic countries of Europe, it is considered the responsibility of the state to provide **ECD** to all children. In Sweden, every child is "entitled" to child-care service after the end of parental leave from about 1 year of age (Kağitçibaşi et al., 1994; Kamerman, 1991). This type of a social welfare ideology leads to a cogent child-care policy with universal coverage. The universal availability of high-quality child care, in turn, serves as a factor contributing to women's labor force participation, which in Sweden is 85% (the highest in the world). This is to be contrasted, for example, with the situation in the United States where child care is not seen as a societal responsibility but as "essentially an individual and private problem" (Huston, 1991, p. 306), with the resultant lack of comprehensive child-care policies in the United States (Bogenschneider, 2000; Dohrn, 1993; Duncan & Brooks-Gunn, 2000; Kamerman, 1991; McLoyd, 1997).

Another example is social policies in Western Europe that may serve as centrifugal factors encouraging **separation** from the family. The whole social security system in most Western European countries is individual based. Thus, a Council of Europe Study Group on "The Interaction Between the Providers of Family Services" (Kağitçibaşi et al., 1994) noted that even the so-called "family services" in Europe are basically services to individuals. This is so commonplace that in some cases it is more advantageous (financially) to live alone than to cohabit. The reflections of the **culture of separateness** are clear, reinforcing separateness.

These examples, particularly when viewed from a global **cross-cultural perspective,** point to the mutual influences and functional **integration** between cultural values and policies on the one hand, and objective human conditions on the other. The scientific study of these conditions, therefore, must take policy into consideration. Any applied research, inducing change, needs to attend to the policy implications. Thus, psychology should assume a place next to other social sciences in addressing policy issues. It needs to consider social policy–human behavior–human condition interfaces; it should work to inform social policies; and it should undertake to help establish or change policies in order to enhance human well-being.

## POLICY RELEVANCE

I now discuss briefly some of the main policy implications of the material I have covered in this book, and particularly of the **Turkish Early Enrichment Project (TEEP)**. I examine policy relevance both in general terms and also with regard to specific applications. Thus I reiterate and elaborate here what I have discussed before in specific chapters.

### Policies to Enhance Early Human Development

Probably the single most important policy implication of the deliberations in both the first and second parts of this book is the need to address early human development and investment in early childhood development (ECD) to build resources toward healthy human development. This does not imply a deterministic view of early years as a "critical period." There is indeed evidence pointing to the resilience of children who are able to function normally after early deprivation (Thompson & Nelson, 2001; Tizard, 1991). Nevertheless, there are limits to resilience from adverse conditions. For example, chronic and severe protein-calorie malnutrition particularly during the first years of life, when there is rapid growth of the brain and the body, can result in permanent mental and physical damage or even death; the same is found to be true for the deficiency of micronutrients (specifically, iodine, iron, and vitamin A) (J. L. Evans & Shah, 1994; R. Pollitt, Gorman, Engle, Martorell, & Rivera, 1993; World Bank Population, Health, and Nutrition Department, 1993). Though I have not dealt with malnutrition in this book, it is important to keep it in mind, so that we do not forget that there are limits to recovery from severe adversity. Recent neuropsychological research also points to the deleterious effects of early deprivation (Duncan et al, 2003; L. W. Hoffman, 2003; Mustard, 2002; see chaps. 2 and 7, this volume).

Furthermore, whether recovery or resilience occurs, is itself influenced by the immediate environment of the child. As discussed earlier (see chap. 7), there is an interaction between the environmental care/psychosocial stimulation and nutrition to produce so-called "**positive deviance.**" The children who survive, even thrive in adverse conditions do so with the support of a caring and stimulating environment with closely knit human bonds (Carvioto, 1981; Ceballo & McLoyd, 2002; Kotchabhakdi et al., 1987; Levinger, 1992; Weiss & Jacobs, 1988; Zeitlin, 1991; Zeitlin et al., 1990). Even the deleterious effects of undernutrition on mental development can be ameliorated by "appropriate stimulation in the home" (L. Eisenberg, 1982, p. 63). All this evidence calls for policies to focus on early human development and especially to enhance the environmental support provided to the child. The synergy between nutrition, health, and psychosocial aspects of development needs to be recognized. As parents become better informed about children's multiple needs and multifaceted development, they can contribute positively to this complex process.

Investing in ECD to promote more healthy human development is justified on many grounds. Myers (1992) listed a number of them. First and foremost among these is the basic human rights argument of children being "entitled to grow and develop to their full potential," as spelled out in the Declaration of the Rights of the Child, adopted unanimously in 1959 by the United Nations General Assembly. Thirty years later, in 1989, a Convention on the Rights of the Child was ratified, urging the signatories to ensure child survival *and development* and to provide services for the care of children. Indeed, this is adequate justification for any policy aiming to promote early human well-being. Nevertheless, because we are far from this ideal, often more specific justifications are needed to enact policies to invest in ECD. They cover a wide ground of scientific arguments (about the importance of early years for long-term effects) to economic ones (of long-term benefits to society from increased production and cost savings); from social-equity reasons (to provide a fair start to disadvantaged children) to programmatic ones (increasing the efficiency of women's programs, e.g., by combining them with ECD programs). More recent discussions focus on narrowing the gap for poor children and the political challenge that is presented by commitment to ECD (Doryan, Gautam, & Foege, 2002; Iglesias & Shalala, 2002).

Policies enhancing early development also have a direct educational impact, through increased "school preparedness." This is, in turn, another basic human right—the right to education (Article 26 of the Universal Declaration of Human Rights). Thus, allowing arrested development and lack of schooling to disable millions of young children, although this could be prevented, is a violation of basic human rights. Recent increased efforts to invest in alternative models of ECD in the **Majority World** (see chaps. 8 and 9) are steps taken in the right direction. The resurgence of interest and increased investment in the **Head Start Program** in the United States (Brooks-Gunn, 2003; Kassebaum, 1994; Zigler, 2003; Zigler & Styfco, 1994) also point to a growing recognition of the need to focus on early human development in the context of increasing poverty within some technological societies.

## Holistic, Multipurpose Policies

A great deal of discussion in this book about the importance of the environment has implications for a holistic, contextual policy orientation to early human development and **ECD**. The weight of the evidence from ECD and intervention research, covered in chapter 8, and from the

**Turkish Early Enrichment Project** (**TEEP**; see chap. 9) points to the greater effectiveness of a contextual-holistic, rather than an individual-focused, approach to intervention. Parental/caregiver involvement appears to be the key here.

This does not mean child-focused approaches are ineffective. An effective intervention with long-term benefits—the Perry Preschool Project (Berrueta-Clement et al., 1984; Schweinhart et al., 1994, 2005)—was a child-focused study, though it had some parent involvement, also. The point is that a **contextual approach** is bound to contribute to greater gains, because it supports the environment together with the child. This would especially be the case where the environment, for any reason, is not providing the child the amount and quality of support that it potentially could.

A contextual/holistic policy is particularly useful in targeting multiple goals. Thus, multipurpose programs addressing, for example, health, nutrition, development, and the school readiness of children, as well as the needs of mothers (e.g., health, family planning, income generation, etc.) tend to create greater motivation and participation, to be cost-effective, and to have expanding effects. For example, TEEP, combined ECD with adult education, was cost-effective and had enduring effects. It also had nutrition, health, and family-planning components. Mothers were provided information on all these topics designed to increase their awareness and knowledge as well as to help them get the services they needed.

The points just discussed are particularly relevant for the **Majority World** where unmet multiple, intersecting needs abound, and resources are limited. Multipurpose policies that are family and community based, while targeting ECD, have the potential to set into action mutually reinforcing and self-perpetuating virtuous cycles of development.

With regard to children in poverty in the United States, Schorr (1991) pointed to a number of characteristics: "Successful programs *see the child in the context of family and the family in the context of its surroundings*" (p. 267, emphasis in the original). Thus, successful programs, even if they start out focusing on the child or on the parent, evolve into *two-generational* programs; some evolve to even three generations (Hadeed, 2005; Zigler & Styfco, 1994). Furthermore, successful programs are also found to emphasize the importance of *relationships* (with the recipients) in a *flexible* structure with a *coherent, integrated broad spectrum of services, adapted to the needs of the people they serve* (Schorr, 1991, pp. 267–269, emphasis in the original).

In too many cases child-care programs, particularly in the Majority World, are based on the goal of providing custodial care for the children of working mothers (Huston, 1991; Myers, 1992; Phillips, 1991). This is often what is demanded. Yet, ECD program evaluations (see chap. 8) and particularly the follow-up results of the Turkish Early Enrichment Project (see chap. 9) show that custodial care is inadequate at best and can even be detrimental to the overall development of children. Thus, even policies focusing on supporting women's employment have to also adopt child development goals to be of benefit to all concerned. This calls for multipurpose policies again as well as for policies aiming at "quality care."

Center-based care, even starting in infancy, *can* be of high quality, with demonstrated long-term benefits, as evidenced by research in Sweden (Andersson, 1992). This shows that if child-care policies stress "quality" and "developmental goals" sufficiently, different types of programs (center or home/community based) can be beneficial. Nevertheless, the fact of the matter is that Sweden has the highest quality of care in the world (Kamerman, 1991), and particularly in the Majority World such a level of care appears a very remote possibility. Therefore, especially when the home conditions are not conducive to the optimal development of the child, not much sustained benefit can be expected from center-based approaches. Accordingly, a general policy implication might be that when the home provides the early stimulation and support the child needs (as in many middle-class contexts), center-based ECD would be appropriate; however, if not, then a contextual approach involving parents/family would be in order.

Another policy implication and challenge has to do with the potential for the wide-scale implementation of ECD programs. The more cost-effective approaches are more likely to evolve into large-scale policies and applications. Nonformal, group-oriented, home- and community-based programs are more promising particularly in the Majority World to "go to scale," though *low-cost* center-based programs have the potential to increase in coverage also.

*Policy and Program Impact of TEEP.* Just as policies engender programs, successful programs that find wide applications can also impact policy. For example, TEEP and the applications deriving from it have influenced educational policy and have helped formulate new policy in Turkey. ECD was conceptualized traditionally only as formal preschools, with the resultant grossly inadequate coverage, as described earlier (see chaps. 8 and 9). With the example of TEEP as an alternative nonformal model of ECD, this narrow definition of the field has been expanded to include a new policy of integrating ECD into the widespread adult education services, *in addition to* the preschool centers. The project has also helped to form cooperation among agencies and government bodies that normally do not work together but provide noncoordinated piecemeal services, noted to be a real problem for service provision in general (Huston, 1991; Kağitçibaşi et al., 2006; Myers, 1992; Schorr, 1991). Thus, in Turkey two different ministries and a private foundation, the **Mother-Child Education Foundation (MOCEF),** are involved in the large-scale implementation of the **Mother-Child Education Program (MOCEP),** deriving from TEEP.

As described in chapter 9, expanding applications of MOCEP over the last decade have reached hundreds of thousands of mothers and children. Programs have moved beyond the borders of Turkey into application with ethnic minorities in Western Europe and in some Middle Eastern countries. With new programs of MOCEF, thousands of fathers have also been reached by father support programs in Turkey. Preschool teachers, parents, and children have been supported through preschool-based programs deriving from MOCEP. Finally, MOCEP has been adapted to television and has been produced and aired on public television in Turkey, also reaching beyond its borders. Several evaluation programs of the different applications show significant benefits of the large-scale implementations (Bekman, 1998a) and the TV adaptation (Baydar, Kağitçibaşi, Goksen, & Kuntay, in press).

This is an example of how scientific research can inform and impact policy and applications. This work has also helped increase the recognition and prestige of psychology in public opinion and among policymakers in Turkey as an important scientific discipline that is relevant for development. As already discussed (chap. 7), in many parts of the Majority World social development lags behind economic development mainly because "development" is still conceived mainly in economic/technological terms. Culturally appropriate and relevant psychological research can go a long way in bridging this gap, especially with regard to initiating new human policies and programs.

## Policy Implications of the Model of Emotional Interdependence

There are policy implications of the **family model of psychological/emotional interdependence,** as well. I have noted that there is a shift toward this model in the **Majority World** with socioeconomic development. This is because in the urban, more developed contexts in the Majority World, with universal schooling and increased social welfare, the economic and old-age security value of children decrease, and their economic costs increase. This process of change decreases material dependence on children and grown-up offspring. This, in turn, allows for autonomy to enter into childrearing, because complete interdependence is no longer the goal. Also, autonomy proves to be adaptive in the lifestyles in an urban, developed context.

However, this process is sometimes too slow to take place and cultural lags can occur. Thus, even when material interdependence in the family decreases with changing socioeconomic conditions, expectations of complete obedience from children and rejection of autonomy can persist as cultural values. Such persistence of **authoritarian parenting** could be dysfunctional in more developed urban contexts of the Majority World where individual decision making and autonomy of the growing person are adaptive in changing lifestyles.

Educational policies are implicated here that could encourage and facilitate changes in child care and education. For example, in schools and particularly in adult education programs autonomy can be introduced as a goal, together with relatedness. Because autonomy of the growing child in the changing family should no longer be threatening to the family integrity, with decreased **material dependencies,** such an induced change need not encounter great resistance. Thus, the family model of emotional interdependence that produces the **autonomous–related self** has specific policy/program implications, as used in the **Mother Support Program** of the Turkish Early Enrichment Project (TEEP).

Other aspects of family change entailed in the model of psychological/emotional interdependence also have relevance for policy. A very important aspect is the change in the intrafamily status of the woman. With increased education and urbanization, decreased fertility, decreased importance of patrilineage, and decreased **son preference**, goes increased woman's status. Social and educational policies upholding women's status and well-being can further facilitate this process of change. This was done, for example, through an empowerment program (Mother Support Program) in **TEEP.**

Similarly, family-planning programs designed to decrease fertility would further help promote the higher **intrafamily status of the woman.** In many societies, woman's status is negatively associated with fertility (Kağitçibaşi, 1982a, 1998a). High fertility is further associated with poor health of both women and children. Thus, educational programs on family planning, nutrition, and health, as, for example, integrated in the Mother Support Program, promote women's well-being and higher intrafamily status.

Thus, different aspects of the model of psychological/emotional interdependence have implications for policies. Some of these were reflected in the general approach and the specific programs used in TEEP, going beyond the cognitive enrichment program of school preparation.

*Relevance for the Immigration Context.* The family model of psychological/emotional interdependence has considerable relevance for the immigration context, also. As discussed extensively in chapter 10, the psychological study of immigration has focused on **acculturation,** acculturative stress, and psychological and **sociocultural adaptation.** In these processes, the family plays a crucial role and needs to be studied extensively. With regard to policies addressing immigration issues, family can also be an optimal target for support.

The family model of psychological/emotional interdependence is adaptive in the immigration context. This is because it is conducive to the development of the autonomous–related self, which is again optimally adaptive in this context. As already discussed at some length, autonomy is particularly functional for sociocultural adaptation and relatedness for **psychological adaptation.** The family model of psychological/emotional interdependence allows for the development of autonomy within a context of relatedness. This is done through the type of childrearing that integrates **parental control** with relatedness and tolerance, even encouragement of autonomy.

If this is well understood and appreciated, then policies designed to promote human well-being in immigration contexts can support this family model with programs informing all concerned about its benefits. All concerned are the immigrants themselves as well as the dominant society. For example, discussions with immigrant parents can sensitize them to the value of autonomy for their children's success in school and in later work life. Sensitization efforts can also be directed toward the dominant society in pointing to the value of relatedness commonly observed in immigrant families. In particular, the professionals dealing with immigrants, such as teachers, social workers, and psychologists, would benefit from such sensitization. In turn, they can help with the solution of some of the human problems in immigration.

It is also possible that the family model of psychological/emotional interdependence would serve as a model for the dominant society. Such cultural diffusion from the immigrants to the dominant society would be a rare case of learning from the less powerful (immigrants). Even if this may be unlikely, there are signs that the family model of psychological/emotional interdependence, and the autonomous–related self are finding greater acceptance in Western individualistic societies also (e.g., Georgas et al, 2006; Inglehart, 2003; Kegan, 1994; Mascolo & Li, 2004; Silk et al., 2003; see chaps. 5, 6, and 10).

## CONCLUSIONS: A HEALTHY HUMAN MODEL

This book has examined and presented some basic theoretical and applied issues. From a theoretical perspective two parallel developmental trajectories—*the development of the self* (and of human relations) on the one hand, and *the development of human competence* on the other— have formed focal topics of study. Family has emerged as of key importance in engendering culturally varying characteristics of the self and of self–other relations. Family change, in turn, assumed significance in mediating between social change and the individual. Family and childrearing are also found to impact the development of human competence. The role of cultural/parental values, beliefs, and behaviors emerged as influential, particularly in the early years.

The powerful impact of the context, as mediated by the family, is evident in these two basic spheres of human development—that of the self and that of competence. Given the centrality of the early environment and particularly of the family for these developmental spheres, the implications for induced change also point toward the early environment and the family.

From an applied perspective, the field of **ECD** was taken up as an area of induced change. This field is quite fitting with a focus on the early environment and the family, especially when viewed from a contextual orientation, rather than an individualistic one. The weight of evidence points to a **contextual approach** in early intervention, particularly in adverse socioeconomic conditions where there is less than adequate family support for human development.

In line with the theoretical considerations regarding the two parallel developmental processes—of the self and of **cognitive competence**— specific interventions were pursued in **TEEP.** Basically, these entailed introducing *autonomy* into a family **culture of relatedness** and *cognitive emphasis* into a social-relational orientation to childrearing. One goal was to create a new synthesis in line with the theoretical **family model of psychological/emotional interdependence.** This is considered more optimal for human development than the models of independence and (total) interdependence. Another goal was to expand the conceptualization of parenting and of the good (and competent) child to also include cognitive aspects in addition to social-relational ones.

The long-term beneficial results call for efforts to support the proximal environment and the family and to build on existing strengths for promoting more optimal human development. It is important to understand and enhance the potential of the family for contributing to human well-being, ranging from nutrition and health to cognitive development, from individual accomplishment to emotional support. It should be noted that this is not at all a call for conservative family ideology. Indeed, in the family model of (total) interdependence, which typically carries a conservative worldview, suppressing individual autonomy is not deemed a healthy model. It is, in fact, undergoing change in conjunction with social change and development. This is, rather, a call for the emerging model of psychological/emotional interdependence, which promises to uphold individual autonomy *within* relatedness—engendering the development of the **autonomous–related self.**

Psychology has much to offer to an understanding of the mechanisms involved and to contribute to their better functioning. Psychology, especially in some of its professional applications, is a *prescriptive* science. In other words, it tells people what to do; it prescribes certain behaviors, measures, and so on. To do this, it needs to have a *healthy human model.*

Psychology has in fact traditionally held a healthy human model. This model has had a few interrelated characteristics. The first one is that this has been a model of the *individual,* designed for individual-level analysis and interventions. Second, it has been an *individualistic* model, influenced by the Western individualistic ethos. Third, it has often been *implicit,* tacitly accepted rather than made explicit. For a long time, the model held by clinical psychology, counseling, family therapy, and the like, that is, the more prescriptive professional psychology, has been the Western individualistic model, deriving mainly from psychoanalytic perspectives. As discussed in chapters 4, 5, and 6, this model upholds the **autonomous–separate self.** Yet this **self-construal** leaves something to be desired, because it does not fulfill the basic human need for relatedness. Also, in such an approach psychology does not emerge as a policy science that can address issues beyond the individual.

I have argued in this book that at the individual level the autonomous–related self is a healthy human model and needs to be upheld through psychological teaching. It may not be the *only* healthy human model. We can think of other assets and positive outlooks, such as democratic orientation, tolerance, aesthetic and humanitarian outlooks, and others. Still, on the basis of the considerable research reviewed in this book, we know that the autonomous–related self *is* one such healthy human model. It is certainly more optimal than the autonomous-separate self traditionally upheld in psychology. Other research concurs (see chaps. 5 and 6).

Furthermore, the autonomous–related self is a healthy model *in context.* This context is the urban, modern society, which requires autonomous action for adaptation to environmental demands. The proximal context for the development of this type of self is the psychologically/emotionally interdependent family. Thus, the healthy model in this psychological perspective does not refer to the individual alone, but has direct implications for family in sociocultural-socioeconomic context. This more expansive outlook makes this perspective more relevant at the familial and societal levels with implications for policies. For example, education and social-support policies in immigration contexts can be formulated to promote the healthy human model at the level both of the individual self and of the family. It may be promising for policies to also promote this convergence toward the healthy model of self/family in the individualistic societies (see Box 11.2).

Box 11.2 schematically presents the main thesis of this book regarding the theory of family change as well as the model of self. This is a thesis of convergence toward the more healthy family model of psychological/ emotional interdependence and the autonomous–related self. The policy implications of this convergence are immense.

Inducing change, as, for example, in intervention research, carries the weight of responsibility. This is particularly problematic when the knowledge base from which to act is not well established. This is one of the reasons underlying the hesitation of psychologists to get involved in policy-relevant issues. Indeed, there is "a tension between action and research in any area of applied scholarship" (Huston, 1991, p. 307; see also Schonkoff, 2000). On the one hand, we have accumulated knowledge on which to act, and problems cannot wait for solutions indefinitely. On the other hand, rushing into policy decisions without sound knowledge can be wasteful and even harmful. This is why research (science) and action (policy) have to be set in a mutually reinforcing complementary relationship.

We should also keep in mind, however, that policies are enacted because there are human problems requiring solutions, whether psychologists are involved or not. When psychologists or other social scientists do not get involved, policies are made by others, such as politicians; and when not informed by scientific knowledge, they turn out to be less than adequate. Therefore, notwithstanding the need to improve our insufficient database and our theories, we have to take on the heavy responsibility to get involved in action. This is a role that psychology may be getting ready to assume if it aspires to contribute to human well-being, not only at the level of the individual, but also globally. The myriad of issues considered and the knowledge accumulated in this volume should provide us with some basis on which to endeavor to face the challenge.

## SUMMARY AND MAIN POINTS

- An integrative synthesis combining cultural contextualism with universal standards of human development and well-being claims that contexts can have common properties and can be compared. It also helps the recognition of the underlying reasons for social change, the increasingly similar demands created by environmental changes, and a better understanding of the adaptations to social change.

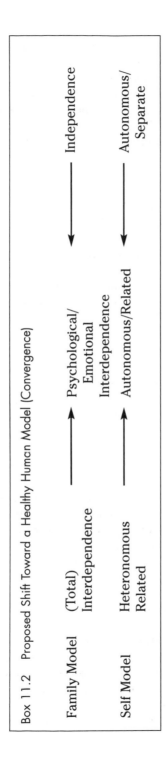

Box 11.2 Proposed Shift Toward a Healthy Human Model (Convergence)

Family Model    (Total)
                Interdependence    ⟶    Psychological/
                                         Emotional
                                         Interdependence    ⟶    Independence

Self Model      Heteronomous
                Related            ⟶    Autonomous/Related    ⟶    Autonomous/
                                                                    Separate

- The family model of psychological /emotional interdependence is one of the main integrative syntheses that is proposed as the model toward which there is a global convergence, given the commonalities in changing in lifestyles. The autonomous–related self is a healthy human model emerging mostly in this family model.
- There are conceptual parallels between the two integrative syntheses of social-cognitive competence and the autonomous–related self.
- Psychology can address the question whether there is an optimal fit between societal values/practices and children's developmental trajectories by establishing some basic standards of human development while at the same time being sensitive to culture. This would constitute a balance between "emic" and "etic" orientations.
- The Turkish Early Enrichment Project (TEEP) is significant in demonstrating that cultural conceptions of parenthood can be changed through intervention, and such change can be favorable for children's developmental trajectories.
- Convergence in family/human models in conjunction with socioeconomic development appears also with international migration, so the family model of psychological/emotional interdependence and the autonomous–related self appear to be the most adaptive models in the immigration and acculturation context. Specifically, autonomy is particularly functional for sociocultural adaptation, and relatedness for psychological adaptation.
- Policies to enhance early human development should address the synergy between nutrition, health, and psychosocial development.
- Evidence from early childhood development (ECD), intervention research, and TEEP shows that a contextual/holistic approach is more effective in the long run than a child-focused approach and that parental/caregiver involvement is the key here.
- The family model of psychological/emotional interdependence, engendering the autonomous–related self, has implications for policies designed to promote human well-being in immigration contexts as well as in the increasingly similar contexts of developed socioeconomic contexts.

## DISCUSSION QUESTIONS

1. Describe the integrative synthesis of social/cognitive competence and its relation to the autonomous–related self particularly in the context of immigration.

2. How do the results of the Turkish Early Enrichment Project (TEEP) imply the family model of psychological/emotional interdependence?
3. Compare the individual/child-focused approach and the contextual-holistic approach to early intervention. Discuss in what ways and why one is more effective in the long run, especially in the context of familial disadvantage. What are the policy implications?
4. In what sense psychology is a prescriptive science? What does psychology prescribe as a healthy human model? On the basis of the evidence provided in this volume, how should this prescription change?

# Glossary

**Acculturation:** Adaptation of groups and/or individuals in culture contact situations.

**Agency (autonomy–heteronomy):** One dimension of self–other dynamics referring to being an agent, extending from autonomy on the one pole to heteronomy on the other.

**Anticipatory socialization:** Parents socialize their children in such a way as to prepare them for their eventual adult roles in society.

**Assimilation:** One of the four acculturation strategies (Berry); implies that the acceptance of the dominant culture is high and maintenance of the heritage culture is low.

**Authoritarian parenting:** The type of parenting where there is an obedience orientation and no autonomy is provided to the child (from a psychoanalytic perspective, there is also a lack of warmth).

**Authoritative parenting:** The type of parenting where the child's autonomy is valued, and there is induction, that is, control with reasoning.

**Autonomous–related self:** The resultant self of the person developing in the family model of psychological/emotional interdependence and satisfying two basic needs, autonomy and relatedness.

**Autonomous–separate self:** The autonomous but not related self pattern, leaving the relatedness need unfulfilled; develops in the family model of independence.

**Bidimensional view of acculturation:** A conceptualization of acculturation in which acceptance (or not) of the dominant culture and maintenance (or not) of the heritage culture are seen as two independent dimensions.

**Central processor model:** considers cognitive competence (intelligence) as a basic psychological process, internal to the individual, and treats it as independent of sociocultural processes.

**Cognitive competence:** Competence in the cognitive realm.

**Cognitive Training Program:** A program designed to promote children's cognitive development (adaptation of HIPPY in TEEP).

**Collective self:** Cognitions concerning a view of the self that is a part of a collective, such as the family.

**Collectivistic achievement motivation:** See *socially oriented achievement motive*.

**Contextual approach:** An approach to the study of the person and human development that implicates the family and culture as the context and thus features the family explicitly in the conceptualization.

**Contextual-developmental-functional approach:** The approach (of this book) that involves the context, and considers developmental processes and functional (adaptive) relations.

**Contextual-interactionist perspective:** The approach that stresses contextual factors and their interactions with self.

**Convergence hypothesis:** The modernization theory claims that there is a general tendency in family/human patterns toward the family model of independence and the separate self.

**Correspondence bias/fundamental attribution error:** The tendency to explain others' behaviors in terms of individual characteristics (making dispositional attributions) without taking the situational factors into account.

**Cross-cultural perspective:** The comparative study of similarities and differences in individual psychological functioning in various cultural and ethnic groups; and of the relationships between psychological, sociocultural, and ecological variables.

**Cultural contextualism:** Paying attention to culture as context in the study of psychological phenomena.

**Culture and Personality School/psychological anthropology:** An out-growth of Boas's early introduction of psychological themes into anthropology starting in the late 1920s and 1930s and continuing for about three decades. Anthropologists looked into the interrelationships between culture and personality, mostly to reveal the basic personality structure of a society.

**Culture of relatedness:** Contexts (cultural-familial) and interpersonal patterns identified by relations between connected, expanding and therefore partially overlapping selves with diffuse boundaries. Used by Kagitçibasi to refer to (relational) collectivism.

**Culture of separateness:** Contexts (cultural-familial) and interpersonal patterns characterized by relations between separate selves, with clearly defined boundaries. Used by Kagitçibasi to refer to (relational) individualism.

**Developmental niche:** A construct proposed by Super and Harkness to study child development in the sociocultural context, including the physical and social setting, childrearing practices, and the psychology of the caretakers.

**"Dominating" parental control:** Restrictive discipline aiming to dominate the child rather than providing (moral) guidelines for action and regulation.

**Early child development (ECD):** Refers to early childhood development, education, and care (programs).

**Ecological theory:** Originally proposed by Bronfenbrenner; has become a generic term for a contextual approach to the study of human development and behavior.

**Economic/utilitarian value of children (voc):** Children's economic/material contribution to the family while they are young, and as adults (see *old-age security voc*).

**Egocentrism:** The inability to step into another's shoes and understand the other person's point of view.

**Emic approach:** The study of behavior in one culture, from within, often emphasizing culture-specific aspects.

**Endogenous development:** Societal development encompassing both the culturally relevant and the globally shared knowledge; approach with a focus on the characteristics and strengths of the societies involved.

**Environmental stimulation index:** An index that includes components such as father's and mother's education, mother's language skills, frequency of reading/telling stories to child, number of toys present, and whether there are any books in the home (used in TEEP).

**Etic approach:** The comparative study of behavior across cultures, often assuming some form of universality of the psychological underpinnings of behavior.

**Everyday cognition paradigm:** Seen particularly in anthropology and cultural psychology, a perspective that considers context as crucial and studies the constructive interface between informal learning experience and cognitive skills that are adaptive to the environment.

**False uniformity:** When a finding obtained in one sociocultural context is assumed to have universal validity, this may be false and needs empirical verification.

**False uniqueness:** When a finding obtained in one sociocultural context is assumed to be unique to that context, this may be false and needs empirical verification.

**Family change theory:** The theory of Kagitçibasi that predicts that the family model of psychological/emotional interdependence emerges in the context of global social change in cultures of relatedness toward urban lifestyles, including international migration; the autonomous–related self emerges in this family model. A shift to this model is also proposed in individualistic industrial society.

**Family model of independence:** A family model commonly seen in affluent, urban/industrial technological societies, with the culture of separateness (individualism). It is characterized by intergenerational and interpersonal independence, low son preference, emphasis on psychological voc, low fertility, higher intrafamily status of women, independence and self-reliance orientation in childrearing, and relatively permissive parenting.

**Family model of interdependence:** A family model commonly seen in rural/agrarian traditional societies with closely knit human/family relations, characterized by culture of relatedness (collectivism), in which material dependencies between generations promote economic and old-age security voc, as well as son preference, high fertility, low intrafamily status of women, obedience orientation in childrearing, and authoritarian parenting.

**Family model of psychological/emotional interdependence:** A synthesis of two family prototypical models (independent and interdependent); it is characterized by psychological/emotional interdependencies between generations, diminished economic voc, salient psychological voc, increased women's status, lower fertility, lower son preference, socialization values emphasizing family/group loyalties as well as individual loyalties, and childrearing entailing autonomy together with parental control (see *family change theory*).

**Familial self:** A self-construal observed among the Japanese and the Indians, "where the experiential sense of self is a 'we-self,'" including the family.

**Functional approach:** An approach is functional if adaptive social and psychological mechanisms are invoked to explain *why* a particular type of development occurs, rather than another one.

**Functionally extended family:** Even though the household may be nuclear, the family functions as if it was extended, carrying out different tasks jointly with kin.

**Genotype → environment theory:** A theoretical perspective that claims that the genotype shapes the environment and the environment has an influence on developmental variability only at the extremes (Scarr).

**Gesellschaft:** The original German term of Tonnies to refer to society.

**Gemeinschaft:** The original German term of Tonnies to refer to community.

**GNP:** Gross National Product; it is the value of all final goods and services produced within a nation in a given year.

**"Hands-on":** Involved stance, applied orientation, where the researcher gets involved in applications.

**HDI:** The UN Human Development Index is a comparative measure of social development including health, education, and income indicators.

**Head Start:** Large-scale ECD programs in the United States aimed to enhance the school readiness of young children in low-income families.

**Heritability (H):** Proportion of phenotypic variation in a population that is attributable to genetic variation among individuals.

**Heteronomous-related self:** The self-pattern leaving the autonomy need unfulfilled; related but not autonomous.

**Heteronomous–separate self:** The self-pattern characterized by low levels of autonomy and relatedness.

**Horizontal/vertical I–C:** The distinction addressing whether the individual is or should be subordinate to the group or not.

**Idiocentric (self-contained) self-construal:** Construal of self as self-sufficient and separate from others.

**Independent/separate self:** The self with clearly defined boundaries developing in the family/human model of independence.

**Indigenous psychology:** Purports that each culture should be studied in itself, as it forms the all-important context of psychological phenomena and provides meaning to them.

**Integrative synthesis:** A construct attempting to qualify or change a concept or approach by combining it with another one arising from another context.

**Integration:** One of the four acculturation strategies (Berry); implies both the acceptance of the dominant culture and maintenance of the heritage culture.

**Interdependent/relational self:** The self typically developing in the family/human model of interdependence that is closely related to significant others and may lack autonomy.

**Interpersonal distance (separateness–relatedness):** One dimension of self–other dynamics dealing with self–other distance, specifically with the degree of connectedness with others. It extends from separateness to relatedness.

**Intuitive parenting:** Parenting, especially mothering, of the young infant that is not taught/learned but comes "naturall"; considered to have an evolutionary base and survival value for the child.

**Marginalization:** One of the four acculturation strategies (Berry); implies that both the acceptance of the dominant culture and maintenance of the heritage culture are low.

**Material dependencies:** Intergenerational dependencies focused on material benefits, especially *old age security* needs of elderly parents; seen in Family Model of Interdependence.

**Majority World:** A descriptive term referring to the majority of the world's population outside of industrialized (Western) countries (Kagitçibasi); formerly called the Third World.

**Mechanistic model:** A behaviorist model (of learning) based on the machinelike characteristic of the human body responding to the (limited) environment as proximal stimulus.

**Minority World:** A descriptive term referring to the minority of the world's population living in industrialized (Western) countries (Kagitçibasi); formerly called the First World.

**MOCEF:** Mother-Child Education Foundation.

**MOCEP:** Mother-Child Education Program; a home/community-based parent-child education program that supports mothers, builds parenting skill, enhances children's overall development, and prepares them for school. It is the outgrowth of TEEP in Turkey and conducted by MOCEF.

**Modernization theory:** The prediction that there is a convergence of the diverse patterns in the world toward the Western prototypical pattern; whatever is different from this pattern is expected to be modified in time to resemble it.

**Mother Support Program:** The component of the Mother Child Education Program (MOCEP) that entails group discussions on several aspects of childrearing, communication skills, and so on.

**Naive theories:** Lay theories or beliefs parents have regarding various aspects of the development of children (see *parental enthnotheories*).

**Nomothetic approach:** An approach to the study of behavior that makes generalizations to groups or conditions; contrasted with an *idiographic* approach, which stresses the uniqueness of each individual case.

**Normative collectivism:** A values orientation to collectivism that emphasizes the priority of the group or collectivity that serves as the person's "in-group" (Kagitçibasi).

**Normative individualism:** A values orientation to individualism that upholds individual needs, rights and prerogatives (Kagitçibasi).

**"Order-keeping" parental control:** Parental control that is not domineering but, rather, provides order and regulation to the child.

**Organismic model:** A generic term for human development models that stress biological maturation (e.g., Piaget) often at the expense of environmental factors.

**Old-age security value of children (voc):** The value (grown) children have for their parents as their providers in old age (see *economic/utilitarian voc*). Elderly parents depend on their children's contribution to the family economy for their livelihood.

**Parental control:** Parental discipline.

**Parental ethnotheories:** Cultural beliefs that parents hold regarding the nature of children, their development, parenting, and the family (see *naive theories*).

**Parental modernity:** A parental outlook associated with "stimulating academic behavior""stimulating language" and"encouraging social maturit" (Goodnow).

**Parental warmth:** Parental affection to and acceptance of children (Rohner).

**Positive deviance:** Refers to children who survive, even thrive in adverse environments, whereas others don't make it.

**Private self:** Cognitions that involve traits or behaviors of the person.

**"Psychic unity" view:** The universalistic view of human psychological functioning, particularly cognitive capacity; first proposed by Boas (see universalism).

**Psychological acculturation:** The immigrant's adaptation to the dominant culture, rather than the host society's adaptation to the immigrant, and is in keeping with a micro psychological approach; refers to psychological well-being (see *psychological adaptation*).

**Psychological adaptation** (to culture contact): Adaptation to a new cultural context by someone from a different cultural context, as indicated by the reported subjective experiences of the newcomer, for instance, by measures of anxiety, strain, depression, and relationship difficulties.

**Psychological/emotional dependencies:** Not material but psychological dependencies and connectedness of selves in the family, especially between generations.

**Psychology of relatedness:** The psychological domain that has to do with general self–other relations and their integration with how the self is conceptualized.

**Psychological value of children (voc):** The nonmaterial psychological satisfactions children provide to their parents; parents attributing this type of value to children.

**Public self:** Cognitions concerning generalized others' view of the self.

**Reflection-enhancing communication:** The orientation that involves both inductive/authoritative reasoning with the child and also complex (elaborated) language.

**Relational I–C:** An orientation to I–C concerning self-construal and self–other relations; it refers to interpersonal distance dimension and the degree of separateness–connectedness of selves (Kagitçibasi).

**Relativism:** A theoretical orientation that assumes human behavior is strongly influenced (even determined) by culture and that it can be studied only by taking a person's culture into account.

**Scaffolding:** A Vygotskian concept referring to adults' *guided participation* of children's learning by extending children's actual level of development upward toward the limits of their potential but within their *zone of proximal development.*

**Self-construal:** How the self is understood or constructed by oneself and/or by others.

**Self-contained individualism:** The prototype of the Western and especially American construal of the self with firm boundaries between self and nonself; involving self-sufficiency and personal control.

**Separation:** One of the four acculturation strategies (Berry); implies that the acceptance of the dominant culture is low and maintenance of the heritage culture is high.

**Separation-individuation:** A psychoanalytic construct (Mahler) concerning a necessary process of early separation from mother; extended also to adolescence as a requisite of becoming an independent, autonomous individual.

**Sleeper effect:** Effect that is not found immediately but emerges later on.

**Sociocultural adaptation:** Adaptation to a new cultural context by learning how the local system operates and acquiring the necessary skills and procedures to get things done in that less familiar cultural context.

**Social/cognitive competence:** Social competence (intelligence) supplemented by cognitive (school-like) competence.

**Social comparison process:** The tendency to compare oneself with others. One tends to assume that the behavior or experience that is different from others' is "not norma"; can thus serve as a yardstick for normality or deviance from the norm.

**Socialization:** The human infant becoming social or the process through which the human infant becomes a member of the society.

**Social intelligence (social competence):** Social skills, social responsibility, and sensitivity to others seen as reflecting intelligence.

**Social selfhood:** Socially defined self; diffuse and expanding self boundaries to include close others.

**Social(ly oriented) achievement motive:** An integrative synthesis combining the need for achievement and the need for extension, which is the need to relate to others. It extends to and includes close others.

**Social value of children (voc):** The social benefits, particularly social recognition and acceptance, parents gain from having children (especially boys in traditional patriarchal societies).

**Sociocentric self-construal:** Relational self, connected and overlapping with close others.

**Son preference:** Preferring sons over daughters mainly because sons provide parents with economic support (in old age) as well as social acceptance in patriarchal family systems.

**Specific learning model:** A contextual approach that stresses informal everyday learning adaptive to and supported by specific context and therefore not easily transferable to other, dissimilar contexts (see *everyday cognition paradigm*).

**Stereotype threat:** When a stereotype alleges important negative qualities, this apprehension can have critically disruptive effects on behavior.

**TEEP:** Turkish Early Enrichment Project; a longitudinal project involving an ECD intervention program targeting the overall development of the child through training and supporting the mother.

**To go to scale:** To reach large proportions.

**UNDP:** United Nations Development Program; it is the UN's global development network.

**Unidimensional acculturation view:** The view that assumes that as a migrant adapts to the dominant culture, that is, acculturates, he or she gives up and is estranged from his or her original culture.

**Universalism:** A theoretical orientation that considers basic psychological process as shared characteristics of all people, and culture as influencing their development and manifestation.

**Value of children (VOC Study):** The value placed on having children; in other words, the types of satisfactions children provide to their parents and families. The cross-cultural study investigated these values.

**Wealth flows:** Material investments.

**Whole child approach:** A broader approach to child policies in ECD interventions that targets the child's overall development, not just cognitive development.

**Woman's intrafamily status:** The status of the woman in the home in terms of communication, role sharing, and decision making with the spouse.

**Zone of proximal development:** The learning potential of the child extended upward through the *guided participation* of an adult or someone more capable (see *scaffolding*).

# References

Abadan-Unat, N. (1986). Turkish migration to Europe and the Middle East: Its impact on social structure and social legislation. In L. O. Michalak & J. W. Salacuse (Eds.), *Social legislation in the contemporary Middle East* (pp. 325–369). Berkeley: University of California Press.

Adair, J. G. (1992). Empirical studies of indigenization and development of the discipline in developing countries. In S. Iwawaki, Y. Kashima, & K. Leung (Eds.), *Innovations in cross-cultural psychology* (pp. 62–74). Lisse, Netherlands: Swets & Zeitlinger.

Adair, J. G., & Diaz-Loving, R. (1999). Indigenous psychologies: The meaning of the concept and its assessment: Introduction. *Applied Psychology: An International Review, 48,* 397–402.

Adorno, T. W., Frenkel-Brunswik, E., Levinson, D. J., & Sanford, R. N. (1950). *The authoritarian personality.* New York: Harper.

Agarwal, R., & Misra, G. (1986). A factor analytical study of achievement goals and means: An Indian view. *International Journal of Psychology, 21,* 717–731.

Ainsworth, M. D. S. (1963). The development of infant–mother interaction among the Ganda. In B. M. Foss (Ed.), *The determinants of infant behaviour II* (pp. 67–112). London: Methuen.

Ainsworth, M. D. S. (1976). *System for rating maternal care behavior.* Princeton, NJ: ETS Test Collection.

Aksu-Koç, A. (2005). Role of the home-context in the relations between narrative abilities and literacy practices. In D. Ravid & H. Bat-Zeev Shyldkrot (Eds.), *Perspectives on language and language development* (pp. 257–274). Dordrecht, Netherlands: Kluwer.

Aksu-Koç, A., & Kuscul, H. (1994, April 4–8). *A comparison of Turkish middle- and working-class homes as a preliteracy environment.* Paper presented at the meeting of the American Educational Research Association International Symposium, New Orleans, LA.

Allen, J. P., McElhaney, K. B., Land, D. J., Kuperminc, G. P., Moore, C. W., O'Beirne-Kelly, H., et al. (2003). A secure base in child adolescence: Markers of attachment security in the mother–adolescent relationship. *Child Development, 74,* 292–307.

Allik, J., & Realo, A. (2004). Individualism-collectivism and social capital. *Journal of cross-Cultural Psychology, 35,* 29–49.

Allport, G. W. (1937). *Personality: A psychological interpretation*. New York: Holt.
Allport, G. W. (1959). The historical background of modern social psychology. In G. Lindzey (Ed), *Handbook of social psychology* (Vol. 1, pp. 3–56). Reading, MA: Addison-Wesley.
Allport, G. (1980). *The nature of prejudice*. Reading, MA: Addison-Wesley.
*American Psychologist* (1994). Special section on Head Start (pp. 120–139).
Anandalaksmy, S. (1994). *The girl child and the family: An action research study*. New Delhi, India: Department of Women and Child Development, Ministry of Human Resources Development.
Anandalaksmy, S., & Bajaj, M. (1981). Childhood in the weavers' community in Varanasi: Socialization for adult roles. In D. Sinha (Ed.), *Socialization of the Indian child* (pp. 31–38). New Delhi, India: Concept.
Anastasi, A. (1958). Heredity, environment, and the question "how?" *Psychological Review, 65,* 197–208.
Anastasi, A. (1992). A century of psychological science. *American Psychologist, 47,* 842–843.
Andersson, B. E. (1992). Effects of day-care on cognitive and socioemotional competence of thirteen-year-old Swedish schoolchildren. *Child Development, 63,* 20–36.
Angyal, A. (1951). A theoretical model for personality studies. *Journal of Personality, 20,* 131–142.
*The APA Monitor.* (1994, January). Vol. 25(1).
Applegate, J. L., Burleson, B. R., & Delia, J. G. (1992) Reflection enhancing parenting as an antecedent to children's social-cognitive and communicative development. In I. E. Sigel, A. V. McGillicuddy DeLisi, & J. J. Goodnow (Eds.), *Parental belief systems* (pp. 3–40). Hillsdale, NJ: Lawrence Erlbaum Associates.
Arends-Tóth, J. (2003). *Psychological acculturation of Turkish migrants in the Netherlands: Issues in theory and assessment*. Amsterdam: Dutch University Press.
Arends-Tóth, J., & van de Vijver, F. J. R. (2006). Issues in conceptualization and assessment of acculturation. In M. H. Bornstein & L. R. Cote (Eds.), *Acculturation and parent–child relationships: Measurement and development* (pp. 33–62). Mahwah, NJ: Lawrence Erlbaum Associates.
Aries, P. (1962). *Centuries of childhood: A social history of family life* (R. Baldick, Trans.). New York: Knopf.
Aries, P. (1980). Two successive motivations for the declining birth rate in the West. *Population and Development Review, 6,* 645–650.
Armecin, G., Behrman, J., Duazo, P., Ghuman, S., Gultiano, S., King, E. M., et al. (2005). *Early childhood development programs and children's health, nutrition, and psycho-social development: Evidence from the Philippines*. Cebu City, Philippines: Office of Population Studies, University of San Carlos.
Aronson, E. (1968). Dissonance theory: Progress and problems. In R. P. Abelson, E. Aronson, W. J. McGuire, T. M. Newcomb, M. J. Rosenberg, & P. H. Tannenbaum (Eds.), *Theories of cognitive consistency: A sourcebook* (pp. 5–27). Chicago: Rand McNally.
Aronson, E., Stephan, C., Sikes, J., Blaney, N., & Snapp, M. (1978). *The jigsaw classroom*. Beverly Hills, CA: Sage.

Assor, A., Kaplan, H., & Roth, G. (2002). Choice is good but relevance is excellent: Autonomy affecting teacher behaviors that predict students' engagement in learning, *British Journal of Educational Psychology, 72,* 261–278.

Aycan, Z. (2006). Paternalism: Towards conceptual refinement and operationalization. In U. Kim, K.-S. Yang, & K.-K. Hwang (Eds.), *Scientific advances in indigenous psychologies: Empirical, philosophical, and cultural contributions* (pp. 445–466). London: Cambridge University Press.

Aycicegi, A. (1993). *The effects of the mother training program.* Unpublished master's thesis, Bogazici University, Istanbul.

Aycan, Z., & Berry, J. W. (1996). Impact of employment-related experiences on immigrants' psychological well-being and adaptation to Canada. *Canadian Journal of Behavioral Science, 28,* 240–251.

Aydin, B., & Oztutuncu, F. (2001). Examination of adolescents' negative thoughts, depressive mood, and family environment. *Adolescence, 36,* 77–83.

Azar, S. T., & Cote, L. R. (2002). Sociocultural issues in the evaluation of the needs of children in custody decision-making: What do our current frameworks for evaluating parenting practices have to offer? *International Journal of Law and Psychiatry, 25,* 193–217.

Azmitia, M. (1988) Peer interaction and problem solving: When are two heads better than one? *Child Development, 59,* 87–96.

Azuma, H. (1984). Secondary control as a heterogeneous category. *American Psychologist, 39,* 970–971.

Azuma, H. (1986). Why study child development in Japan? In H. Stevenson, H. Azuma, & K. Hakuta (Eds.), *Child development and education in Japan* (pp. 3–12). New York: Freeman.

Bakan, D. (1966). *The duality of human existence.* Chicago: Rand McNally.

Bakan, D. (1968). *Disease, pain, and sacrifice.* Chicago: University of Chicago Press.

Baldwin, J. M. (1895). *Mental development in the child and the race.* New York: Macmillan.

Baldwin, J. M. (1909). *Darwin and the humanities.* Baltimore: Review.

Baltes, P. B. (1987). Theoretical propositions of life-span developmental psychology: On the dynamics between growth and decline. *Developmental Psychology, 23,* 611–626.

Baltes, P. B., Reese, H. W., & Lipsitt, L. P. (1980). Life-span developmental psychology. *Annual Review of Psychology, 31,* 65–110.

Bandura, A. (1962). Social learning through imitation. In M. R. Jones (Ed.), *Nebraska Symposium on Motivation* (Vol. 10, pp. 211–271). Lincoln: University of Nebraska Press.

Bandura, A. (1977). *Social learning theory.* Englewood Cliffs, NJ: Prentice-Hall

Bandura, A. (1986). *Social foundations of thought and action: A social cognitive theory.* Englewood Cliffs, NJ: Prentice-Hall.

Bandura, A. (1989). Human agency in social cognitive theory. *American psychologist, 44,* 1175–1184.

Barciauskas, R. C., & Hull, D. B. (1989). *Loving and working: Reweaving women's public and private lives.* Bloomington, IN: Meyer-Stone Books.

Barker, R. G. (1968). *Ecological psychology.* Stanford, CA: Stanford University Press.

Barros, R. P., & Mendonca, R. (1999). Costs and benefits of preschool education in Brazil. Background study commissioned to IPEA by the World Bank. Rio de Janeiro, Institute of Applied Economic Research.

Barnett, W. S. (1995). Long-term effects of early childhood programs on cognitive and school outcomes. *The Future of Children, 5,* 25–50.

Barry, H., Bacon, M., & Child, I. (1957). A cross-cultural survey of some sex differences in socialization. *Journal of Abnormal and Social Psychology, 55,* 327–332.

Barry, H., Child, I., & Bacon, M. (1959). Relation of child training to subsistence economy. *American Anthropologist, 61,* 31–63.

Bartle, S. E., & Anderson, S. (1991). Similarity between parents' and adolescents' levels of individuation. *Adolescence, 26,* 913–925.

Batson, C. D. (1990). How social an animal? *American Psychologist, 45,* 336–346.

Baumeister, R. F. (1986). *Identity: Culture change and the struggle for self.* New York: Oxford University Press.

Baumeister, R. F. (1991). *Meanings of life.* New York: Guilford.

Baumeister, R., & Leary, M. R. (1995). The need to belong: Desire for interpersonal attachments as a fundamental human motivation. *Psychological Bulletin, 117,* 497–529.

Baumrind, D. (1971). Current patterns of parental authority. *Developmental Psychology Monographs,* 4(1, Pt. 2).

Baumrind, D. (1980). New directions in socialization research. *American Psychologist, 35,* 639–652.

Baumrind, D. (1989). Rearing competent children. In W. Damon (Ed.), *Child development today and tomorrow* (pp. 349–378). San Francisco: Jossey-Bass.

Baydar, N., Kağitçibaşi, Ç., Kuntay, A., & Goksen, F. (in press). Effects of an educational television program on preschoolers: Variability in benefits. *Journal of Applied Developmental Psychology.* Manuscript submitted for publication.

Befu, H. (1986). The social and cultural background of child development in Japan and the United States. In H. Stevenson, H. Azuma, & K. Hakuta (Eds.), *Child development and education in Japan* (pp. 13–25). New York: Freeman.

Behrman, J. R., Cheng, Y., & Todd, P. E. (2004). Evaluating preschool programs when length of exposure to the program varies: A nonparametric approach. *The Review of Economics and Statistics, 86,* 108–132.

Behrman, J. R., & Hoddinott, J. (2005). Programme evaluation with unobserved heterogeneity and selective implementation: The Mexican PROGRESA impact on child nutrition. *Oxford Bulletin of Economics and Statistics, 67*(4), 547–569.

Beiser, M., Hou, F., Hyman, I., & Tousignant, M. (2002). Poverty, family process and the mental health of immigrant children in Canada. *American Journal of Public Health, 92,* 220–227.

Bekman, S. (1993) The preschool education system in Turkey revisited. *OMEP International Journal of Early Childhood, 25,* 13–19.

Bekman, S. (1998a). *A fair start: An evaluation of the Mother–Child Education Program. Istanbul, Turkey: MOCEF.*

Bekman, S. (1998b). Long-term effects of the Turkish Home-Based Early Intervention Program. In U. Gielen & A. L. Comunian (Eds.), *The family and family therapy in international perspective* (pp. 401–417). Trieste, Italy: Edizioni Lint.

Bellah, R. N., Madsen, R., Sullivan, W. M., Swidler, A., & Tipton, S. M. (1985). *Habits of the heart: Individualism and commitment in American life*. Berkeley: University of California Press.

Belsky, J., & Pensky, E. (1988). Developmental history, personality, and family relationships: Toward an emergent family system. In R. A. Hinde & J. S. Hinde (Eds.), *Relationships within families* (pp. 193–217). Oxford, England: Clarendon.

Bendix, R. (1967). Tradition and modernity reconsidered. *Comparative Studies in Society and History, 9,* 292–346.

Benedict, R. (1934). *Patterns of culture*. New York: Mentor.

Benedict, R. (1970). Patterns of the good culture. *Psychology Today, 4,* 53–55.

Bengi-Arslan, L., Verhulst, F. C., & Crijnen, A. A. M. (2002). Prevalence and determinants of minor pediatric disorder in Turkish immigrants living in the Netherlands. *Social Psychiatry Psychiatric Epidemology, 37,* 118–124.

Bennett, J. (1984). The tie that binds: Peasant marriage and families in late medieval England. *Journal of Interdisciplinary History, 15,* 111–129.

Bennett, J. M. (1993). Jomtien revisited: A plea for a differentiated approach. In L. Eldering & P. Leseman (Eds.), *Early intervention and culture* (pp. 11–19). Paris: UNESCO.

Berger, P. L., & Luckmann, T. (1967). *The social construction of reality*. New York: Doubleday.

Berman, J. J. (Ed.). (1990). *Cross-cultural perspectives: Nebraska Symposium on Motivation 1989*. Lincoln: University of Nebraska Press.

Bernstein, B. (1974). *Class, codes, and control: Theoretical studies toward a sociology of language* (Rev. ed.). New York: Shocken.

Berrueta-Clement, J. R., Schweinhart, L. L., Barnett, W., Epstein, A. & Weikart, D. (1984). *Changed lives: The effects of the Perry Preschool Programme on youths through age 19*. Ypsilanti, MI: High/Scope Press.

Berry, J. W. (1976). *Human ecology and cognitive style: Comparative studies in cultural and psychological adaptation*. New York: Sage/Halsted.

Berry, J. W. (1979). A cultural ecology of social behaviour. In L. Berkowitz (Ed.), *Advances in experimental social psychology* (pp. 177–206). New York: Academic Press.

Berry, J. W. (1980). Ecological analyses for cross-cultural psychology. In N. Warren (Ed.). *Studies in cross-cultural psychology* (Vol. 2, pp. 157–189). New York: Academic Press.

Berry, J. W. (1985). Cultural psychology and ethnic psychology: A comparative analysis. In I. Reyes-Lagunes & Y. Poortinga (Eds.), *From a different perspective* (pp. 3–15). Lisse, Netherlands: Swets & Zeitlinger.

Berry, J. W. (1989). Imposed etics-emics-derived etics: The operationalization of a compelling idea. *International Journal of Psychology, 24,* 721–735.

Berry, J. W. (1990). Psychology of acculturation. In J. Berman (Ed.), *Cross-cultural perspectives: Nebraska Symposium on Motivation* (Vol. 37, pp. 201–34). Lincoln: University of Nebraska Press.

Berry, J. W. (1997). Immigration, acculturation and adaptation. *Applied Psychology: An International Review, 46,* 5–68.

Berry, J. W. (2001). A psychology of immigration. *Journal of Social Issues, 57,* 615–31.

Berry, J. (2006). Acculturation: A conceptual overview. In M. H. Bornstein & L. R. Cote (Eds.), *Acculturation and parent–child relationships: Measurement and development* (pp. 13–30). Mahwah, NJ: Lawrence Erlbaum Associates.

Berry, J. W., & Bennett, J. A. (1992). Cree conceptions of cognitive competence. *International Journal of Psychology, 27,* 73–88.

Berry, J. W., & Dasen, P. R. (Eds.). (1974). *Culture and cognition: Readings in cross-cutural psychology.* London: Methuen.

Berry J. W., Dasen, P. R., Saraswathi, T. H., Poortinga, Y. H., Pandey, J., Segall, M. H., et al. (1997), *Handbook of cross-cultural psychology* (3 vols.). Boston: Allyn & Bacon.

Berry, J. W., Irvine, S. H., & Hunt, E. B. (Eds.). (1988). *Indigenous cognition: Functioning in cultural context.* Dordrecht, Netherlands: Nijhoff.

Berry, J. W., Poortinga, Y. H., Pandey, J., Dasen, P. R., Saraswathi, T. S., Segall, M. H., et al. (1997). *Handbook of cross-cultural psychology* (Vols. 1–3). London: Allyn & Bacon.

Berry, J. W., Poortinga, Y. H., Segall, M. H., & Dasen, P. R. (2002). C*ross-cultural psychology. research and applications* (2nd ed.). Cambridge, England: Cambridge University Press.

Berry, J. W., & Sam, D. L. (1997). Acculturation and adaptation. In J. W. Berry, M. H. Segall, & Ç. Kağitçibaşi (Eds.), *Handbook of cross-cultural psychology* (pp. 291–326). London: Allyn & Bacon.

Beyers, W., & Goossens, L. (1999). Emotional autonomy, psychological adjustment, and parenting: Interactions, moderating, and mediating effects. *Journal of Research on Adolescence, 22,* 753–769.

Beyers, W., Goossens, L., Vansant, I., & Moors, E. (2003). A structural model of autonomy in the middle and late adolescence: Connectedness, separation, detachment, and agency. *Journal of Youth and Adolescence, 32,* 351–365.

Birman, D. (2006). Measurement of the "acculturation gap" in immigrant and refugee families. In M. H. Bornstein & L. R. Cote (Eds.), *Acculturation and parent–child relationships: Measurement and development* (pp. 97–112). Mahwah, NJ: Lawrence Erlbaum Associates.

Bisht, S., & Sinha, D. (1981). Socialization, family and psychological differentiation. In D. Sinha (Ed.) *Socialization of the Indian child* (pp. 41–54). New Delhi, India: Concept.

Black, J. E., Jones, T. A., Nelson, C. A. & Greenough, W. T. (1998). Neuronal plasticity and the developing brain. In N. E. Alessi, J. T. Coyle, S. I. Harrison, & S. Eth (Eds.), *Handbook of child and adolescent psychiatry: Vol. 6. Basic psychiatric science and treatment.* New York: Wiley.

Blair, A. L., Blair, M. C. L., & Madamba, A. B. (1999). Racial/ethnic differences in high school students' academic performance: Understanding the interweave of social class and ethnicity in the family context. *Journal of Comparative Family Studies, 30,* 539–555.

Blatt, S., & Blass, R. B. (1996). Relatedness and self-definition: A dialectic model of personality development. In G. G. Noam & K. W. Fischer (Eds.), *Development and vulnerability in close relationship* (pp. 309–338). Mahwah, NJ: Lawrence Erlbaum Associates.

Blok, H., Fukkink, R. G., Gebhardt, E. D., & Leseman, P. P. M. (2005). The relevance of delivery mode and other program characteristics for the effectiveness of early childhood intervention. *International Journal of Behavioral Development, 29,* 35–47.

Blos, P. (1979). *The adolescent passage.* New York: International Universities Press.

Boas, F. (1911). *The mind of primitive man.* New York: Macmillan.

Bock, P. K. (1988). *Rethinking psychological anthropology: Continuity and change in the study of human actions.* New York: Freeman.

Bogardus, E. S. (1925). Measuring social distance. *Journal of Applied Sociology, 2,* 299–308.

Bogenschneider, K. (2000). Has family policy come of age? A decade review of the state of US family policy in the 1990s. *Journal of Marriage and the Family, 62,* 1136–1159.

Bolger, K. E., Patterson, C. J., Thompson, W. W., & Kupersmidt, J. B. (1995). Psychosocial adjustment among children experiencing persistent and intermittent family economic hardship. *Child Development, 66,* 1107–1129.

Bond, M. H. (Ed.). (1986). *The psychology of the Chinese people.* Hong Kong: Oxford University Press.

Bond, M. H. (1988). Finding universal dimensions of individual variation in multicultural surveys of values: The Rokeach and Chinese value surveys. *Journal of Personality and Social Psychology, 55,* 1009–15.

Bond, M. H. (1994). Into the heart of collectivism: A personal and scientific journey. In U. Kim, H. C. Triandis, Ç. Kağitçibaşi, S. C. Choi, & G. Yoon (Eds.), *Individualism and collectivism: Theory, method, and applications* (pp. 66–76). Thousand Oaks CA: Sage.

Bond, M. H. (2002). Reclaiming the individual from Hofstede's ecological analysis. A 20-year odyssey. *Psychological Bulletin, 128,* 73–77.

Bond, M. H., & Cheung, T. S. (1983). The spontaneous self-concept of college students in Hong Kong, Japan, and the United States. *Journal of Cross-Cultural Psychology, 14,* 153–171.

Bond, M. H., Leung, K., & 67 coauthors (2004). Culture-level dimensions of social axioms and their correlates across 41 cultures. *Journal of Cross-Cultural Psychology, 35,* 548–570.

Bond, M. H., Leung, K., & Wan, K. C. (1982). How does cultural collectivism operate? The impact of task and maintenance contributions on reward distribution. *Journal of Cross-Cultural Psychology, 13,* 186–200.

Bond, R., & Smith, P. B. (1996). Culture and conformity: A meta-analysis of studies using Asch's (1952b, 1956) line judgment task. *Psychological Bulletin, 119,* 111–137.

Bornstein, M. H. (1984). Cross-cultural developmental psychology. In M. H. Bornstein & M. E. Lamb (Eds.), *Developmental psychology: An advanced textbook* (pp. 231–281). London: Lawrence Erlbaum Associates.

Bornstein, M. H. (1989). Between caretakers and their young: Two modes of interaction and their consequences for cognitive growth. In M. H. Bornstein & J. S. Bruner (Eds.), *Interaction in human development* (pp. 197–214). Hillsdale, NJ: Lawrence Erlbaum Associates.

Bornstein, M. H., & Bradley, R. H. (2003). *Socioeconomic status, parenting, and child development*. Mahwah, NJ: Lawrence Erlbaum Associates.

Bornstein, M. H. & Cote, L. R. (2006). Parenting cognitions and practices in the acculturative process. In M. H. Bornstein & L. R. Cote (Eds.), *Acculturation and parent–child relationships: Measurement and development* (pp. 173–196). Mahwah, NJ: Lawrence Erlbaum Associates.

Bornstein, M. H., Tal, J., & Tamis-LeMonda, C. (1991). Parenting in cross-cultural perspective: The United States, France and Japan. In M. H. Bornstein (Ed.), *Cultural approaches to parenting* (pp. 69–89). London: Lawrence Erlbaum Associates.

Bornstein, M. H., & Tamis-LeMonda, C. (1990). Activities and interactions of mothers and their first born infants in the first six months of life. *Child Development, 61,* 1206–1217.

Bornstein, M. H., Tamis-LeMonda, C. S., Tal, J., Ludemann, P., Toda S., Rahn, C. W., et al. (1992). Maternal responsiveness to infants in three societies: The United States, France, and Japan. *Child Development, 63,* 808–821.

Bourhis, R. Y., & Dayan, J. (2004). Acculturation orientations towards Israeli arabs and Jewish immigrants. *International Journal of Psychology, 39,* 118–131.

Bowlby, J. (1973). *Attachment and loss: Vol. 2. Separation: Anxiety and anger.* New York: Basic Books.

Bowlby, J. (1969/1982). *Attachment and loss: Vol. 1. Attachment.* New York: Basic Books.

Boyden, J. (1990). Childhood and the policy makers: A comparative perspective on the globalization of childhood. In A. James & A. Prout (Eds.), *Constructing and reconstructing childhood* (pp. 184–215). New York: Palmer Press.

Bradburn, N. M. (1963). Need achievement and father dominance in Turkey. *Journal of Abnormal and Social Psychology, 67,* 464–468.

Bradley, R., & Caldwell, B., (1988, March-April). Using the HOME inventory to assess the family environment. *Pediatric Nursing, 14*(2).

Brazelton, B. T. (1982). Early intervention: What does it mean? In H. E. Fitzgerald (Ed.), *Theory and research in behavioral pediatrics* (pp. 1–34). New York: Plenum.

Bretherton, I. (1987). New perspectives on attachment relations: Security, communication and internal working models. In J. Osofsky (Ed.), *Handbook of infant development* (pp. 1016–1100). New York: Wiley.

Bridges, M., Fuller, B., Rumberger, R., & Tran, L. (2004). *Preschool for California's children: Promising benefits, unequal access* (Policy Brief No. 04-9). Berkeley: Policy Analysis for California Education.

Brislin, R. W. (1983). Cross-cultural research in psychology. *Annual Review of Psychology, 34,* 363–400.

Bronfenbrenner, U. (1974). *Is early intervention effective?* (Unpublished report). Washington, DC: U. S. Department of Health, Education, and Welfare.

Bronfenbrenner, U. (1979). *The ecology of human development: Experiments by nature and design.* Cambridge, MA: Harvard University Press.

Bronfenbrenner, U. (1986). Ecology of the family as a context for human development: Research perspectives. *Developmental Psychology, 22,* 723–742.

Bronfenbrenner, U. (1998). The ecology of developmental process. In R. M. Lerner (Ed.), *Handbook of child psychology: Vol. 1. Theoretical models of human development* (5th ed., pp. 993–1028). New York: Wiley.

Bronfenbrenner, U., & Weiss, H. B. (1983). Beyond policies without people: An ecological perspective on child and family policy. In E. F. Zigler, S. L. Kagan, & E. Klugman (Eds.), children, families and government: Perspectives on American social policy (pp. 393–414). New York: Cambridge University Press.

Bronfenbrenner, U. (1999). Environments in developmental perspective: Theoretical and operational models. In S. L. Friedman & T. D. Wachs (Eds.), *Measuring environment across the life span* (pp. 3–30). Washington, DC: American Psychological Association.

Bronfenbrenner, U., & Ceci, S. J. (1993). Heredity, environment, and the question "how?"—A first approximation. In R. Plomin & G. E. McClearn (Eds.), *Nature–nurture* (pp. 313–324). Washington, DC: American Psychological Association.

Bronfenbrenner, U., & Evans, G. W. (2000). Developmental science in the 21st century: Emerging questions, theoretical models, research designs and empirical findings. *Social Development, 9,* 115–125.

Bronfenbrenner, U., & Morris, P. (1998). The ecology of developmental processes. In R. M. Lerner (Ed.), *Handbook of child psychology: Vol. 1. Theoretical models of human development* (5th ed.). New York: Wiley.

Bronfenbrenner, U., & Weiss, H. B. (1983). Beyond policies without people: An ecological perspective on child and family policy. In E. F. Zigler, S. L. Kagan, & E. Klugman (Eds.), *Children, families* and *government: Perspectives on American social* policy (pp. 393–414). New York: Cambridge University Press.

Brooks-Gunn, J. (2003). Do you believe in magic?: What we can expect from early childhood intervention programs. *Social Policy Report, 17,* 3–14.

Brooks-Gunn, J., & Duncan, G. (1997). The effects of poverty on children and youth. *The Future of Children, 7,* 55–71.

Brooks-Gunn, J., Schley, S., & Hardy, J. (2000) Marriage and the baby carriage: historical change and intergenerational continuity in early parenthood. In L. J. Crockett & R. K. Silbereisen (Eds.), *Negotiating adolescence in times of social change* (pp. 36–57). Cambridge, England: Cambridge University Press.

Brunswik, R. (1955). Representative design and probabilistic theory. *Psychological Review, 62,* 236–242.

Bulatao, R. A. (1979). *On the nature of the transition in the value of children.* Honolulu, HI: East–West Population Institute.

Buriel, R., Love, J., & De Ment, T. (2006). The relation of language brokering to depression and parent–child bonding among Latino adolescents. In M. H. Bornstein & L. R. Cote (Eds.), *Acculturation and parent–child relationships: Measurement and development* (pp. 249–270). Mahwah, NJ: Lawrence Erlbaum Associates.

Caldwell, J. C. (1977). Towards a restatement of demographic transition theory. In J. C. Caldwell (Ed.), *The persistence of high fertility* (pp. 25–122). Canberra: Australian National University.

Caldwell, J. C. (1979). Education as a factor in mortality decline: An examination of Nigerian data. *Population Studies, 33,* 395–413.

Caldwell, J. C. (1980). Mass education as a determinant of the timing of fertility decline. *Population and Development Review, 6,* 225–256.

Campbell, D. T. (1975). On the conflicts between biological and social evolution and between psychology and moral tradition. *American Psychologist, 30,* 103–1126.

Campbell, F. A., Ramey, C. T., Pungello, E., Sparling, J., & Miller-Johnson, S. (2002). Early childhood education: Young adult outcomes from the Abecedarian Project. *Applied Developmental Science, 6,* 42–57.

Carlson, V. J., & Harwood, R. L. (2003). Attachment, culture, and the caregiving system: The cultural patterning of everyday experiences among Anglo and Puerto Rican mother–infant pairs. *Infant Mental Health Journal, 24,* 53–73.

Carraher, T. N., Schliemann, A. D., & Carraher, D. W. (1988). Mathematical concepts in everyday life. In G. B. Saxe & M. Gearhart (Eds.), *Children's mathematics: New directions in child development* (pp. 71–87). San Francisco: Jossey-Bass.

Carvioto, J. (1981). *Nutrition, stimulation, mental development and learning.* W. O. Atwater Memorial Lecture presented at the 12th International Congress of Nutrition, San Diego, CA.

Cashmore, J. A., & Goodnow, J. J. (1986). Influences on Australian parents' values: Ethnicity versus socioeconomic status. *Journal of Cross-Cultural Psychology, 17,* 441–454.

Caudill, W. A., & Frost, L. (1973). A comparison of maternal care and infant behavior in Japanese-American, American and Japanese families. In W. P. Lebra (Ed.), *Mental health research in Asia and the Pacific* (Vol. 3). Honolulu: University Press of Hawaii.

Caudill, W. A., & Schooler, C. (1973). Child behavior and child rearing in Japan and the United States: An interim report. *Journal of Nervous and Mental Disease, 157,* 323–338.

Ceballo, R., & McLoyd, V. C. (2002). Social support and parenting in poor, dangerous neighborhoods. *Child Development, 73,* 1310–1321.

Ceci, S. J. (1991). How much does schooling influence general intelligence and its cognitive components? A reassesment of the evidence. *Developmental Psychology, 27,* 703–722.

Ceci, S. J. (1999). Schooling and intelligence. In S. J. Ceci & W. M. Williams (Eds.), *The nature–nurture debate: The essential readings* (pp. 168–176). Malden, MA: Blackwell.

Ceci, S. J., & Papierno, P. B. (2005). The rhetoric and reality of gap closing: When the "have-nots" gain but the "haves" gain even more. *American Psychologist, 60,* 149–160.

Ceci, S. J., & Williams, W. M. (1997). Schooling, intelligence, and income. *American Psychologist, 52,* 1051–1058.

Ceci, S. J., & Williams, W. M. (1999). Born vs. made: Nature–Nurture in the new millennium. In S. J. Ceci & W. M. Williams (Eds.), *The nature–nurture debate: The essential readings* (pp. 1–11). Malden, MA: Blackwell.

Cha, J. H. (1994). Changes in value, belief, attitude and behavior of the Koreans over the past 100 years. *Korean Journal of Psychology: Social, 8,* 40–58.

Chamoux, M. N. (1986). Apprendre autrement: Aspects des pédagogies dites informelles chex les Indiens du Méxique [A different type of learning: Aspects of informal pedagogy among Mexican Indians]. In P. Rossel (Ed.), *Demain l'artisanat?* Paris: Cahiers: IUED.

Chao, R. K. (1994). *Chinese and European-American mothers' views about the role of parenting upon children's school success.* Unpublished manuscript.

Chao, R. K. (2000). Cultural explanations for the role of parenting in the school success of Asian-American children. In R. Taylor & M. Wang (Eds.), *Resilience across contexts: Family, work, culture, and community* (pp. 333–363). Mahwah, NJ: Lawrence Erlbaum Associates.

Chao, R. K. (2006). The prevalence and consequences of adolescents' language brokering for their immigrant parents. In M. H. Bornstein & L. R. Cote (Eds.), *Acculturation and parent–child relationships: Measurement and development* (pp. 271–296). Mahwah, NJ: Lawrence Erlbaum Associates.

Chao, R. K., & Tseng, V. (2002). Parenting of Asians. In M. H. Bornstein (Ed.), *Handbook of parenting: Vol. 4. Social conditions and applied parenting* (2nd ed., pp. 59–93). Mahwah, NJ: Lawrence Erlbaum Associates.

Chaturvedi, E., Srivastava, B. C., Singh, J. V., & Prasad, M. (1987). Impact of six years exposure to ICDS scheme on psycho-social development. *Indian Pediatrics, 24,* 153–160.

Chavajay, P., & Rogoff, B. (2002). Schooling and traditional collaborative social organization of problem solving by Mayan mothers and children. *Developmental Psychology, 38,* 55–66.

Chen, Z., & Dornbusch, S. M. (1998). Relating aspects of adolescent emotional autonomy to academic achievement and deviant behavior. *Journal of Research on Adolescence, 13,* 293–319.

Chinese Culture Connection. (1987). Chinese values and the search for culture-free dimensions of culture. *Journal of Cross-Cultural Psychology, 18,* 143–64.

Chirkov, V., Ryan, R., Kim, Y., & Kaplan, U. (2003). Differentiating autonomy from individualism and independence: A self-determination theory perspective on internalization of cultural orientations and well being, *Journal of Personality and Social Psychology, 84,* 97–110.

Chodorow, N. (1974). Family structure and feminine personality. In M. Z. Rosaldo & L. Lamphere (Eds.), *Women, culture and society* (pp. 43–66). Stanford, CA: Stanford University Press.

Chodorow, N. (1978). *The reproduction of mothering: Psychoanalysis and the sociology of gender.* Berkeley: University of California Press.

Chodorow, N. (1989). *Feminism and psychoanalytic theory.* New Haven, CT: Yale University Press.

Choi, I., & Choi, Y. (2002). Culture and self-concept flexibility. *Personality & Social Psychology Bulletin, 28,* 1508–1517.

Choi, S. H. (1992). Communicative socialization processes: Korea and Canada. In S. Iwawaki, Y. Kashima, & K. Leung (Eds.), *Innovations in cross-cultural psychology* (pp. 103–121). Lisse, Netherlands: Swets & Zeitlinger.

Chou, K.-L. (2000). Emotional autonomy and depression among Chinese adolescents. *Journal of Genetic Psychology, 161,* 161–169.

Christie, R., & Jahoda, M. (1954). *Studies in the scope and method of "the authoritarian personality."* Glencoe, IL: The Free Press.

Cicirelli, V. G., Evans, J. W., & Schiller, J. S. (1969). *The impact of Head Start: An evaluation of the effects of Head Start on children's cognitive and affective development.* Washington, DC: Westinghouse Learning Corporation, Ohio University.

Clarke, A., & Clarke, A. (1999). Early experience and the life path. In S. J. Ceci & W. M. Williams (Eds.), *The nature–nurture debate: The essential readings* (Vol. 9, pp. 136–147). Oxford, England: Blackwell.

Cochrane, S. H. (1979). *Fertility and education: What do we really know?* Baltimore: Johns Hopkins University Press.

Cochrane, S., & Mehra, K. (1983). Socioeconomic determinants of infant and child mortality in developing countries. In O. A. Wagner (Ed.), *Child development and international development: Research–policy interfaces* (pp. 27–44). San Francisco: Jossey-Bass.

Coe, C. L. (1999). Psychosocial factors and psychoneuroimmunology within a lifespan perspective. In D. Keating & C. Hertzman (Eds.), *Developmental health and the wealth of nations* (pp. 638–641). New York: Guilford.

Cohler, B., & Geyer, S. (1982). Psychological autonomy and interdependence within the family. In F. Walsh (Ed.). *Normal family processes* (pp. 196–227). New York: Guilford.

Cohler, B., & Grunebaum, H. (1981). *Mothers, grandmothers, and daughters: Personality and child-care in three-generation families.* New York: Wiley.

Cole, M. (1996). *Cultural psychology: A once and future discipline.* Cambridge, MA: Belknap.

Cole, M. (2005). Cultural-historical activity theory in the family of socio-cultural approaches. *International Society for the Study of Behavioural Development Newsletter, 1,* 47.

Cole, M., & Cole, S. R. (2001). *The development of children* (4th ed.). New York: Worth.

Cole, M., Sharp, D., & Lave, C. (1976). The cognitive consequences of education: Some empirical evidence and theoretical misgivings. *Urban Review, 9,* 218–233.

Cole, P. M., & Tamang, B. L. (2001). Nepali children's ideas about emotional displays in hypothetical challenges. *Developmental Psychology, 34,* 640–646.

Coleman, J. S. (1990). *Foundations of social theory.* Cambridge, MA: Harvard University Press.

Coll, C. T. G. (1990). Developmental outcome of minority infants: A process-oriented look into our beginnings. *Child Development, 61,* 270–289.

Collins, R. C. (1990). *Head Start salaries: 1989–90 staff salary survey.* Alexandria, VA: National Head Start Program.

Conger, K. J., Rueter, M. A., & Conger, R. D. (2000). The role of economic pressure in the lives of parents and their adolescents: The family stress model. In L. J. Crockett & R. K. Silbereisen (Eds.), *Negotiating adolescence in times of social change* (pp. 201–223). Cambridge, England: Cambridge University Press.

Conger, R. D., Conger, J. K., & Elder, G. H., Jr. (1997). Family economic hardships and adolescent adjustment: Mediating and moderating processes. In J. G. Duncan & J. Brooks-Gunn (Eds.), *Consequences of growing up poor* (pp. 288–310). New York: Russell Sage Foundation.

Connolly, K. (1985). Can there be a psychology for the Third World? *Bulletin of the British Psychological Society, 38,* 249–257.

Consultative Group. (1986). *Measuring early childhood development: A review of instruments and measures* (Report). New York.

Cooley, C. H. (1902). *Human nature and the social order*. New York: Scribner's.

Cooper, C. R. (2003). Bridging multiple worlds: Immigrant youth identity and pathways to college. *International Society for the Study of Behavioural Development Newsletter, 2,* 1–4.

Cooper, C. R., & Denner, J. (1998). Theories linking culture and psychology: Universal and community-specific processes. *Annual Review of Psychology, 49,* 559–84.

Copple, C., Cline, M., & Smith, A. (1987). *Paths to the future: Long-term effects of Head Start in Philadelphia school district*. Washington, DC: U.S. Department of Health and Human Services.

Correa-Chávez, M., & Rogoff, B. (2005). Cultural research has transformed our ideas of cognitive development. *International Society for the Study of Behavioural Development, 1,* 47.

Cousins, S. (1989). Culture and selfhood in Japan and the U.S. *Journal of Personality and Social Psychology, 56,* 124–131.

Crijnen, A. A. M. (2003). Emotional and behavioral problems of Turkish immigrant children, adolescents and their parents living in the Netherlands—an overview. *International Society for the Study of Behavioural Development Newsletter, 2*(44), 7–9.

Crijnen, A. A. M., Bengi-Arslan, L., Verhulst, F. C. (2000). Teacher-reported problem behavior in Turkish immigrant and Dutch children: A cross-cultural comparison. *Acta Psychiatry Scan, 102,* 439–444.

Crittenden, P. M. (2000). A dynamic-maturational exploration of the meaning of security and adaptation. In P. M. Crittenden & A. H. Claussen (Eds.), *The organization of attachment relationships: Maturation, culture and context* (pp. 358–383). Cambridge, England: Cambridge University Press.

Crocker, J., & Luhtanen, R. (1990). Collective self-esteem and ingroup bias. *Journal of Personality and Social Psychology, 58,* 60–67.

Crockett, L. J., & Silbereisen, R. K. (Eds.). (2000). *Negotiating adolescence in times of social change*. Cambridge, England: Cambridge University Press.

Cross, S. E., & Madson, L. (1997). Models of the self: Self-construals and gender. *Psychological Bulletin, 122,* 5–37.

Cross, S. E., Morris, M. L., & Gore, J. S. (2002) Thinking about oneself and others: The relational-interdependent self-construal and social cognition. In *Journal of Personality and Social Psychology, 82,* 399–418.

Curran, V. H. (Ed.). (1984). *Nigerian children: Developmental perspectives*. London: Routledge & Kegan Paul.

Cushman, P. (1990). Why the self is empty: Toward a historically situated psychology. *American Psychologist, 45,* 599–611.

Dalal, A. K. (1990). India: Psychology in Asia and the Pacific. In G. Shouksmith & E. A. Shouksmith (Eds.), *Status reports on teaching research in eleven countries*. Bangkok. Thailand: UNESCO.

D'Andrade, R. G., & Strauss, C. (Eds.). (1992). *Human motives and cultural models*. Cambridge, England: Cambridge University Press.

Daniels, J. A. (1990). Adolescent separation-individuation and family. *Adolescence, 25,* 105–117.

Darroch, R., Meyer, P. A., & Singarimbun, M. (1981). *Two are not enough: The value of children to Javanese and Sundanese parents.* Honolulu, HI: East–West Population Institute.

Dasen, P. R. (1984). The cross-cultural study of intelligence: Piaget and the Baoule. *International Journal of Psychology, 19,* 407–434.

Dasen, P. R. (1988a). Cultures et développement cognitif: La recherche et ses applications [Culture and cognitive development: Research and its applications]. In R. Bureau & D. de Saivre (Eds.), Apprentissages et cultures: les manières d'apprendre (Colloque de Cerisy)(pp. 123–141). Paris: Karthala.

Dasen, P. R. (1988b). Developpement psychologique et activités quotidiennes ches des enfants Africains [Psychological development and daily activities of African children). *Enfance, 41,* 3–24.

Dasen, P. R. (2003). Theoretical frameworks in cross-cultural developmental psychology: An Attempt at integration. In T. S. Saraswathi (Ed.), *Cross-cultural perspectives in human development: Theory, research and applications* (pp. 128–166). New Delhi, India: Sage.

Dasen, P. R., Berry, J. W., & Sartorius, N. (Eds.). (1988). *Health and cross-cultural psychology: Toward applications.* London: Sage.

Dasen, P. R., & Jahoda, G. (1986). Cross-cultural human development. *International Journal of Behavioral Development, 9,* 413–416.

Dawson, J. L. M. (1967). Traditional versus Western attitudes in West Africa: The construction, validation and application of a measuring device. *British Journal of Social and Clinical Psychology, 6,* 81–96.

Dawson, J. L. M. et al. (2000, November). Cited in D. Phillips (2004). *Early experience and the developing brain.* Paper presented at the International Step by Step Association Conference, Budapest, Hungary.

Dearing, E., McCartney, K., & Taylor, B. A. (2001). Change in family income-to-needs matters more for children with less. *Child Development, 72,* 1779–1794.

Deater-Deckard, K., & Dodge, K. A. (1997). Externalizing behaviour problems and discipline revisited: Nonlinear effects and variation by culture, context, and gender. *Psychological Inquiry, 8,* 161–175.

Decade of Behavior: 2000–2010. (2006). *Behavior matters: How research improves our lives.* Retrieved May 17, 2005, from http://www.decadeofbehavior.org

Deci, E. L., & Ryan, R. M. (1995). Human autonomy: The basis for true self-esteem. In M. H. Kernis (Ed.), *Efficacy, agency, and self-esteem.* New York: Plenum.

Dekovic, M., Pels, T., & Model, S. (Eds.). (2006). *Unity and diversity in child rearing: Family life in a multicultural society.* Lewiston, NY: Edwin Mellen Press.

Dennis, T. A., Cole, P. M., Zahn-Waxler, C., & Mizuta, I. (2002). Self in context: Autonomy and relatedness in Japanese and U.S. mother–preschooler dyads. *Child Development, 73,* 1803–1817.

De Silva, M., Nikapota, A., Vidyasagara, N. W. (1988). Advocacy and opportunity: Planning for child mental health in Sri Lanka. *Health, Policy and Planning, 3,* 302–307.

De Vos, G. (1968). Achievement and innovation in culture and personality. In E. Norbeck, D. Price-Williams, & E. W. McCord (Eds.), *The study of personality* (pp. 348–370). New York: Holt, Rinehart & Winston.

De Vos, G. (1985). Dimensions of the self in Japanese culture. In M. G. De Vos & F. L. K. Hsu (Eds.), *Culture and self*. New York: Tavistock.

De Wolff, M. S., & van Ijzendoorn, M. H. (1997). Sensitivity and attachment: A meta-analysis on parental antecedents of infant attachment. *Child Development, 68*, 571–592.

Dearing, E., McCartney, K., & Taylor, B. A. (2001). Change in family income-to-needs matters more for children with less. *Child Development, 72*, 1779–1794.

Deater-Deckard, K., & Dodge, K. A. (1997). Externalizing behaviour problems and discipline revisited: Nonlinear effects and variation by culture, context , and gender. *Psychological Inquiry, 8*, 161–175.

Decade of Behavior: 2000–2010. (2006). *Behavior matters: How research improves our lives*. Retrieved MONTH DAY, YEAR from http://www.decadeofbehavior.org

Deci, E. L., & Ryan, R. M. (1995). Human autonomy: The basis for true self-esteem. In M. H. Kernis (Ed.), *Efficacy, agency, and self-esteem*. New York: Plenum.

Dekovi, M., Pels, T., & Model, S. (Eds.). (2006). *Unity and diversity in child rearing: Family life in a multicultural society*. Lewiston, NY: Edwin Mellen Press.

Dennis, T. A., Cole, P. M., Zahn-Waxler, C., & Mizuta, I. (2002). Self in context: Autonomy and relatedness in Japanese and U.S. mother–preschooler dyads. *Child Development, 73*, 1803–1817.

Deutsch, M. (1962). Cooperation and trust: Some theoretical notes. In M. R. Jones (Ed.), *Nebraska Symposium on Motivation* (pp. 275–319). Lincoln: University of Nebraska Press.

Diaz-Guerrero, R. (Ed.). (1975). *Psychology of the Mexican: Culture and personality* (The Texas Pan American Series). Austin: University of Texas Press.

Diaz-Guerrero, R. (1991). Historic-sociocultural premises (HSCPs) and global change. *International Journal of Psychology, 26*, 665–673.

Diener, M. L., Nievar, M. A., & Wright, C. (2003). Attachment security among mothers and their young children living in poverty: Associations with maternal, child, and contextual characteristics. *Merrill–Palmer Quarterly, 49*, 154–182.

Dohrn, B. (1993). "Leastwise of the land": Children and the law. In K. Ekberg & P. E. Mjaavatn (Eds.), *Children at risk: Selected papers* (pp. 18–33). Trondheim: Norwegian Centre for Child Research.

Doi, L. A. (1974). Amae: A key concept for understanding Japanese personality structure. In R. A. LeVine (Ed.), *Culture and personality* (pp. 307–314). Chicago: Aldine.

Doi, T. (1973). *Anatomy of dependence*. Tokyo: Kodansha International.

Doob, L. W. (1967). Scales for assaying psychological modernization in Africa. *Public Opinion Quarterly, 31*, 414–421.

Dornbusch, S. M., Ritter, P. L., Leiderman, P. H., Roberts, O. F., & Fraleigh, M. J. (1987). The relation of parenting style to adolescent school performance. *Child Development, 58*, 1244–1257.

Douvan, E., & Adelson, J. (1996). *The adolescent experience*. New York: Wiley.

Drenth, P. J. D. (1991, July). *Scientific and social responsibility: A dilemma for the psychologist as a scientist*. Paper presented at the 2nd European Congress, Budapest, Hungary.

Duben, A. (1982). The significance of family and kinship in urban Turkey. In Ç. Kağitçibaşi (Ed.), *Sex, roles, family and community in Turkey* (pp. 73–99). Bloomington: Indiana University Press.

DuBois, C. (1944). *The people of Alor.* New York: Harper & Row.

Duncan, G. J., & Brooks-Gunn, J. (Eds.). (1997). *Consequences of growing up poor.* New York: Russell Sage Foundation.

Duncan, G. J., & Brooks-Gunn, J. (2000). Family poverty, welfare reform, and child development. *Child Development, 71,* 188–196.

Duncan, G., & Magnuson, K. A. (2003). Off with Hollingshead: Socioeconomic resources, parenting, and child development. In M. H. Bornstein & R. H. Bradley (Eds.), *Socioeconomic status, parenting, and child development* (pp. 83–107). Mahwah, NJ: Lawrence Erlbaum Associates.

Dym, B. (1988). Ecological perspectives on change in families. In H. B. Weiss & F. H. Jacobs (Eds.), *Evaluating family programs* (pp. 477–496). New York: Aldine.

Earley, C. P. (1989). Social loafing and collectivism: A comparison of the United States and the People's Republic of China. *Administrative Science Quarterly, 34,* 565–581.

Earley, C. P. (1993). East meets West meets Mideast: Further explorations of collectivistic and individualistic work groups. *Academy of Management Journal, 36,* 219–348.

Eccles, J. S., & Harold, R. D. (1993). Parent–school involvement during the early adolescent years. *Teachers College Report, 94,* 568–587.

Eckensberger, L. (1990). On the necessity of the culture concept in psychology: A view from cross-cultural psychology. In F. J. R. van de Vijver & G. J. M. Hutschemaekers (Eds.), *The investigation of culture* (pp. 153–177). Tilburg, Netherlands: Tilburg University Press.

Eckensberger, L. H. (1995). Activity or action: Two different roads towards an integration of culture into psychology? *Culture and Psychology, 1,* 67–80.

Eckensberger, L. H. (2003). Wanted: A contextualized psychology: Plea for a cultural psychology based on action theory. In T. S. Saraswathi (Ed.), *Cross-cultural perspectives in human development: Theory, research and applications* (pp. 70–102). New Delhi, India: Sage.

Eisenberg, L. (1982). Conceptual issues on biobehavioral interactions. In D. L. Parron & L. Eisenberg (Eds.), *Infants at risk for developmental dysfunction* (pp. 57–68). Washington, DC: National Academy of Sciences, Institute of Medicine.

Eisenberg, N., & Zhou, Q. (2001). Regulation from a developmental perspective. *Psychological Inquiry, 11,* 166–171.

Ekstrand, L. H., & Ekstrand, G. (1987). Children's perceptions of nonns and sanctions in two cultures. In Ç. Kağitçibaşi (Ed.). *Growth and progress in cross-cultural psychology* (pp. 171–180). Lisse, Netherlands: Swets & Zeitlinger.

Elder, G. H., Jr. (1985). The life course as developmental theory. *Child Development, 69,* 1–12.

Elder, G. H., Jr. (1995). Life trajectories in changing societies. In A. Bandura (Ed.), *Self-efficacy in changing societies* (pp. 46–57). New York: Cambridge University Press.

Elder, G. H., Jr. (1998) The life course and human development. In W. Damon (Series Ed.) & R. M. Lerner (Vol. Ed.), *Handbook of child psychology: Vol. 1. Theoretical models of human development* (pp. 939–991). New York: Wiley.

Eldering, L., & Leseman, P. (1993). *Early intervention and culture: Preparation for literacy. The Interface between theory and practice.* Netherlands National Commission for UNESCO.

Eldering, L., & Vedder, P. (1993) culture-sensitive home intervention: The Dutch hippy experiment. In L. Eldering & P. Leseman (Eds.), *Early intervention and culture* (pp. 231–252). Paris: UNESCO.

Eliram, T., & Schwarzwald, J. (1987). Social orientation among Israeli youth. *Journal of Cross-Cultural Psychology, 18,* 31–44.

Engle, P. L. (1986). *The intersecting needs of working mothers and their young children: 1980 to 1985.* Unpublished manuscript, California Polytechnic State University, San Luis Obispo.

Enriquez, V. G. (1988). The structure of Philippine social values: towards integrating indigenous values and appropriate technology. In D. Sinha & H. S. R. Kao (Eds.), *Social values and development: Asian perspectives* (pp. 124–148). Newbury Park, CA: Sage.

Enriquez, G. E. (1990). *Indigenous psychology.* Manila, Philippines: New Horizons Press.

Ercan, S. (1993). *The short-term effects of the Home Intervention Program on the cognitive development of children.* Unpublished master's thesis, Bogaziçi University, Istanbul.

Erelçin, F. G. (1988). *Collectivistic norms in Turkey: Tendency to give and receive support.* Unpublished master's thesis, Bogaziçi University, Istanbul.

Erikson, E. H. (1959). Identity and the life cycle. *Psychological Issues, 1*(1),

Erikson, E. H. (1968). *Identity: Youth and crisis.* New York: Norton.

Etzioni, A. (1993). *Spirit of community. Rights, responsibilities and the communitarian agenda.* New York: Crown.

Evans, G. W. (2004). The environment of childhood poverty. *American Psychologist, 59,* 77–92.

Evans, J. L., & Myers, R. G. (1985). *Improving program actions to meet the intersecting needs of women and children in developing countries: A policy and program review.* Ipsilanti, MI: The Consultative Group on Early Childhood Care and Development, High/Scope Educational Research Foundation.

Evans, J. L., & Shah, P. M. (1994). *Child care programmes as an entry point for maternal and child health components of primary health care.* Geneva, Switzerland: World Health Organization.

Farran, D. C. (1990). Effects of intervention with disadvantaged and disabled children: a decade review. In S. J. Meisels & J. P. Shonkoff (Eds.), *Handbook of early childhood intervention* (pp. 501–540). Cambridge, England: Cambridge University Press.

Fawcett, J. T. (1983). Perceptions of the value of children: Satisfactions and costs. In R. Bulatao, R. D. Lee, P. E. Hollerbach, & J. Bongaarts (Eds.), *Determinants of fertility in developing countries* (Vol. 1, pp. 347–369). Washington, DC: National Academy Press.

Featherman, D. L., & Lerner, R. M. (1985). Ontogenesis and sociogenesis: Problematics for theory and research about development and socialization across lifespan. *American Sociological Review, 50,* 659–676.

Festinger, L. (1954). A theory of social comparison processes. *Human Relations, 8,* 117–140.

Fiati, T. A. (1992) Cross-cultural variation in the structure of children's thought. In R. Case (Ed.), *The mind's staircase: Exploring the conceptual underpinnings of children's thought and knowledge* (pp. 319–42). Hillsdale, NJ: Lawrence Erlbaum Associates.

Fisek, G. O. (1991). A cross-cultural examination of proximity and hierarchy as dimensions of family structure. *Family Process, 30,* 121–133.

Forgas, J. P., & Bond, M. H. (1985). Cultural influences on the perception of interaction episodes. *Personality and Social Psychology Bulletin, 11,* 75–88.

Frank, S. J., Avery, C. B., & Laman, M. S. (1988). Young adults' perceptions of their relationships with their parents: Individual differences in connectedness, competence and emotional autonomy. *Developmental Psychology, 24,* 729–737.

Franz, C. E., & White, K. M. (1985). Individuation and attachment in personality development: Extending Erikson's theory. *Journal of Personality, 53,* 224–256.

Freud, A. (1958). *Adolescence. Psychoanalytic Study of the Child, 13, 255–278.*

Friedlmeier, W. (2005). Emotional development and culture: Reciprocal contributions of cross-cultural research and developmental psychology. In W. Friedlmeier, P. Chakkarath, & B. Schwarz (Eds.), *Culture and human development: The importance of cross-cultural research to the social sciences.* New York: Psychology Press.

Friedlmeier, W., Chakkarath, P., & Schwarz, B. (Eds.). (2005). *Culture and human development: The importance of cross-cultural research for the social sciences.* New York: Psychology Press.

Fromm, E. (1941). *Escape from freedom.* New York: Farrar & Rinehart.

Fu, V. R., Hinkle, D. E., & Hanna, M. A. (1986). A three-generational study of the development of individual dependence and family interdependence. *Genetic, Social and General Psychology Monographs, 112,* 153–171.

Fujinaga, T. (1991). *Development of personality among Japanese children.* Paper presented at the International Society for the Study of Behavioural Development, Workshop on Asian Perspectives of Psychology, Ann Arbor, MI.

Fuligni, A. J. (1997). The academic achievement of adolescents from immigrant families: The roles of family background, attitudes, and behavior. *Child Development, 68,* 261–273.

Fuligni, A. J. (1998). The adjustment of children from immigrant families. *Current Directions in Psychological Science, 7,* 99–103.

Fuligni, A. J. (2003). The adaptation of children from immigrant families. *International Society for the Study of Behavioural Development Newsletter, 2*(44), 9–11.

Fuligni, A. G., Tseng, V., & Lam, M. (1999). Attitudes toward family obligations among American Adolescents with Asian, Latin American and European backgrounds. *Child Development, 70*(4), 1030–1044.

Furstenberg, F. F., Jr. (1966). Industrialization and the American family: A look backward. *American Sociological Review, 31,* 326–337.

Gabrenya, W. K., Wang, Y., & Latane, B. (1985). Social loafing on an optimizing task: Cross-cultural differences among Chinese and Americans. *Journal of Cross-Cultural Psychology, 16,* 223–242.

Gaines, A. D. (1984). Cultural definitions, behavior and the person in American psychiatry. In A. J. Marsella & G. M. White (Eds.), *Cultural conceptions of mental health and therapy* (pp. 167–192). Dordrecht, Netherlands: D. Reidel.

Garbarino, J. (1990). The human ecology of early risk. In S. J. Meisels & J. P. Shonkoff (Eds.), *Handbook of early childhood intervention* (pp. 78–96). Cambridge, England: Cambridge University Press.

Garber, J., & Little, S. A. (2001). Emotional autonomy and adolescent adjustment. *Journal of Research on Adolescence, 16,* 355–371.

Gardiner, H. W., & Kosmitzki, C. (2005). *Lives across cultures: Cross-cultural human development* (3rd ed.). New York: Allyn & Bacon.

Gardner, W. L., Gabriel, S., & Lee, A. Y. (1999). "I" value freedom, but "we" value relationships: Self-construal priming mirrors cultural differences in judgment. *Psychological Science, 10*(4), 321–326.

Gay, J., & Cole, M. (1967). *The new mathematics and an old culture.* New York: Holt, Rinehart & Winston.

Geertz, C. (1975). On the nature of anthropological understanding. *American Scientist, 63,* 47–53.

Gellner, E. (1992). *Postmodernism, reason and religion.* London: Routledge.

Gennetian, L. A., & Miller, C. (2002). Children and welfare reform: A view from an experimental welfare program in Minnesota. *Child Development, 73,* 601–620.

Georgas, J. (1988). An ecological and social cross-cultural model: The case of Greece. In J. W. Berry, S. H. Irvine, & E. B. Hunt (Eds.), *Indigenous cognition: Functioning in cultural context* (pp. 105–123). Dordrecht, Netherlands: Nijhoff.

Georgas, J. (1989). Changing family values in Greece: From collectivistic to individualistic. *Journal of Cross-Cultural Psychology, 20,* 80–91.

Georgas, J. (1993). Ecological-social model of Greek psychology. In U. Kim & J. W. Berry (Eds.), *Indigenous psychology: Research and experience in cultural context* (pp. 56–78). Newbury Park, CA: Sage.

Georgas, J., Berry, J. W., van de Vijver, F., Kağitçibaşi, Ç., & Poortinga, Y. H. (Eds.). (2006). *Families across cultures: A 30-nation psychological study.* Cambridge, England: Cambridge University Press.

Gerard, H. B., & Rabbie, J. M. (1961). Fear and social comparison. *Journal of Abnormal and Social Psychology, 62,* 586–592.

Gergen, K. J. (1973). Social psychology as history. *Journal of Personality and Social Psychology, 26,* 309–320.

Gergen, K. J. (1985). Social constructionist inquiry: Context and implications. In K. J. Gergen & K. E. Davis (Eds.), *The social construction of the person* (pp. 3–18). New York: Springer-Verlag.

Gergen, K. J. (1991). *The saturated self: Dilemmas of identity in contemporary life.* New York: Basic Books.

Gheorghiu, M. A., & Vignoles, V. L. (2005). *Individual and nation level predictors of social trust in 21 nations.* Paper presented at University of Sussex, Sussex, England.

Gheorghiu, M. A., & Vignoles, V. L. (2005, MONTH). *Individual and nation level predictors of social trust in 21 nations.* Paper presented at the meeting of the NAME OF GROUP, Sussex, England.

Gilbert, G. M. (1951). Stereotype persistence and change among college students. *Journal of Abnormal and Social Psychology, 46,* 245–254.

Gillespie, J. M., & Allport, G. W. (1955). *Youth's outlook on the future: A cross national study.* Garden City, NY: Doubleday.

Gilligan, C. (1982). *In a different voice: Psychological theory and women's development.* Cambridge, MA: Harvard University Press.

Göncü, A. (1993). Guided participation in Kecioren. In B. Rogoff, J. Mistry, A. Göncü, & C. Moiser (Eds.), *Guided participation in cultural activity by toddlers and caregivers* (Vol. 236, pp. 126–147). Monographs of the Society for Research in Child Development.

Gonzales, N. A., Cauce, A. M., & Mason, C. A. (1996). Interobserver agreement in the assessment of parental behavior and parent–adolescent conflict: African American mothers, daughters, and independent observers. *Child Development, 67,* 1483–1498.

Goodnow, J. J. (1988). Parents' ideas, actions, and feeling: Models and methods from developmental and social psychology. *Child Development, 59,* 286–320.

Goodson, B. D., Layer, J. L., St. Pierre, R. G., Bernstein, L. S., & Lopez, M. (2000). Effectiveness of a comprehensive family support programme for low-income children and their families: Findings from the Comprehensive Child Development Programme. *Early Childhood Research Quarterly, 15,* 5–39.

Gorer, G., & Rickman, J. (1949). *The people of great Russia.* New York: Norton.

Gottfried, A. E., Fleming, J. S., & Gottfried, A. W. (1998). Role of cognitively stimulating home environment in children's academic intrinsic motivation: A longitudinal study. *Child Development, 69,* 1448–1460.

Gray, S., Ramey, B., & Klaus, R. (1983). The early training project 1962–1980. In Consortium for Longitudional Studies (Ed.), *As the twig is bent* (pp. 33–70). Hillsdale, NJ: Lawrence Erlbaum Associates.

Greenfield, P. M. (1994). Independence and interdependence as developmental scripts: implications for theory, research and practice. In P. M. Greenfield & R. R. Cocking (Eds.), *Cross-cultural roots of minority child development* (pp. 1–40). Hillsdale, NJ: Lawrence Erlbaum Associates.

Greenfield, P. M. (1996). Culture as process: Empirical methods for cultural psychology. In J. W. Berry, Y. H. Poortinga, & J. Pandey (Eds.), *Handbook of cross-cultural psychology: Vol. 1. Theory and method* (2nd ed., pp. 301–346). Boston: Allyn & Bacon.

Greenfield, P. M. (1999). Cultural change and human development. *New Directions for Child and Adolescent Development, 83,* 37–59.

Greenfield, P. M. (2000). Culture and universals: Integrating social and cognitive development. In L. Nucci, G. Saxe, & E. Turiel (Eds.), *Culture, thought, and development* (pp. 231–277). Mahwah, NJ: Lawrence Erlbaum Associates.

Greenfield, P. M., & Childs, C. P. (1977). Weaving, color terms, and pattern representation: Cultural influences and cognitive development among the Zinacantecos of Southern Mexico. *International Journal of Psychology, 11,* 23–48.

Greenfield, P. M., & Cocking, R. R. (Eds.). (1994). *Cross-cultural roots of minority child development.* Hillsdale, NJ: Lawrence Erlbaum Associates.

Greenfield, P. M., Keller, H., Fuligni, A., & Maynard, A. (2003). Cultural pathways through universal development. *Annual Review of Psychology, 54,* 461–490.

Greenfield, P. M., & Lave, J. (1982). Cognitive aspects of informal education. In D. Wagner & H. Stevenson (Eds.), *Cultural perspectives on child development* (pp. 181–207). San Francisco: Freeman.

Greenfield, P. M., Maynard, A. E., & Childs, C. P. (2003). Historical change, cultural learning, and cognitive representation in Zinacantec Maya children. *Cognitive Development, 18,* 455–487.

Greenfield, P. M., & Suzuki, L. (1998). Culture and human development: Implications for parenting, education, pediatrics, and mental health. In I. E. Sigel & K. A. Renninger (Eds.), *Handbook of child psychology: Vol. 4. Child psychology in practice* (5th ed., pp. 1059–1109). NewYork: Wiley.

Greenwald, A. G., & Pratkanis, A. R. (1984). The self. In R. S. Wyer & T. K. Srull (Eds.), *Handbook of social cognition* (Vol. 3, pp. 129–178). Hillsdale, NJ: Lawrence Erlbaum Associates.

Greulich, W. W. (1957). A comparison of the physical growth and development of American-born and Japanese children. *American Journal of Physical Anthropology, 15,* 489–515.

Grigorenko, E. L., Wenzel Geissler, P., Prince, R., Okatcha, F., Nokes, C., Kenny, D. A., et al. (2001). The organisation of Luo conceptions of intelligence: A study of implicit theories in a Kenyan village. *International Journal of Behavioral Development, 25,* 367–378.

Grossmann, K. E., Grossmann, K., & Keppler, A. (2005). Universal and culture-specific aspects of human behavior: The case of attachment. In W. Friedlmeier, P. Chakkarath, & B. Schwarz (Eds.), *Culture and human development: The importance of cross-cultural research for the social sciences* (pp. 75–97). Hove, England: Psychology Press.

Grotevant, H. D., & Cooper, C. R. (1986). Individuation in family relationships. *Human Development, 29,* 82–100.

Gudykunst, W. B., Bond, M. H. (1997). Intergroup relations across cultures. In J. W. Berry, M. H. Segall, & Ç. Kağitçibaşi (Eds.), *Handbook of cross-cultural psychology* (Vol. 3, pp. 119–162). Boston: Allyn & Bacon.

Gudykunst, W. B., Matsumoto, Y., Ting-Toomey, S., & Nishida, T. (1996). The influence of cultural individualism-collectivism, self-construals, and individual values on communication styles accross cultures. *Human Communication Research, 22,* 510–543.

Guerin, P. J. (1976). Family therapy: The first twenty-five years. In P. J. Guerin (Ed.), *Family therapy: Theory and practice* (pp. 2–22). New York: Gardner.

Guiraudon, V., Phalet, K., & ter Wal, J. (2005). Monitoring ethnic minorities in the Netherlands. *International Social Science Journal, 183,* 75–87.

Guisinger, S., & Blatt, S. J. (1994). Individuality and relatedness; Evolution of a fundamental dialectic. *American Psychologist, 49,* 104–111.

Gulgoz, S. (2004). *Psychometric properties of the Turkish Vocabulary Test.* Unpublished manuscript, Koç University, Istanbul, Turkey.

Güngör, D. (2007). *The meaning of parental control across migrant, sending, and host communities: Adaptation or persistence?* Manuscript submitted for publication.

Güngör, D., Kağitçibaşi, Ç., & Phalet, K. (2006). *Values, intercultural relations and acculturation among Turkish migrant youth in Belgium: A comparison across migrant, sending and host communities.* Unpublished research proposal.

Gunnar, M. R. (2000). Early adversity and the development of stress reactivity and regulation. In C. A. Nelson (Ed.), *The Minnesota Symposia on Child Psychology,* (Vol. 3., pp. 163–200). Mahwah, NJ: Lawrence Erlbaum Associates.

Gusfield, J. R. (1967). Tradition and modernity: Misplaced polarities in the study of social change. *American Journal of Sociology, 73,* 351–362.

Gutierrez, J., Sameroff, A. J., & Karrer, B. M. (1988). Acculturation and SES effects on Mexican-American parents' concepts of development. *Child Development, 59,* 250–255.

Haddad, L. (2002). *An integrated approach to early childhood education and care* (Early Childhood & Family Policy Series, Vol. 3). Paris: UNESCO.

Hadeed, J. (2005). *Poverty begins at home: The Mother-Child Education Programme (MOCEP) in the Kingdom of Bahrain.* New York: Peter Lang.

Hagiwara, S. (1992). The concept of responsibility and determinants of responsibility judgment in the Japanese context. *International Journal of Psychology, 27,* 143–156.

Haglund, E. (1982). The problem of the match: Cognitive transition between early childhood and primary school: Nigeria. *Journal of Developing Areas, 17,* 77–92.

Haight, W. L., Parke, R. D., & Black, J. E. (1997). Mothers' and fathers' beliefs about and spontaneous participation in their toddlers' pretend play. *Merrill–Palmer Quarterly, 43,* 271–290.

Halpern, R. (1990). Community based early intervention. In S. J. Meisels & J. P. Shonkoff (Eds.), *Handbook of early childhood intervention* (pp. 469–498). Cambridge, England: Cambridge University Press.

Hamaguchi, E. (1985). *Culture and experience.* Philadelphia: University of Pennsylvania Press.

Hamilton, C. E. (2000). Continuity and discontinuity of attachment from infancy through adolescence. *Child Development, 71,* 690–694.

Hanawalt, B. A. (1986). *The ties that bound: Peasant families in medieval England.* New York: Oxford University Press.

Hanawalt, B. A. (2002). Medievalists and the study of childhood. In *Ariès, centuries of childhood. Speculum, 77,* 440–461.

Hantal, B., Kağitçibaşi, C., & Ataca, B. (2006, June). *Does parental acceptance-rejection constitute a unidimensional construct? A Turkish-German comparison.* Paper presented at the First international Congress on Interpersonal Acceptance and Rejection, Istanbul, Turkey.

Harkness, S., Edwards, C. P., & Super, C. M. (1981). Social roles and moral reasoning: A case study in a rural African community. *Developmental Psychology, 17,* 595–603.

Harkness, S., & Super, C. (1993). The developmental niche: Implications for children's literacy development. In L. Eldering & P. Leseman (Eds.), *Early intervention and culture* (pp. 115–132). Paris: UNESCO.

Harkness, S., & Super, C. M. (1996). *Parents' cultural belief systems: Their origins, expressions, and consequences.* New York: Guilford.

Harkness, S., & Super, C., & van Tijen, N. (2000). Individualism and the "Western mind" reconsidered: American and Dutch parents' ethnotheories of the child. *New Directions for Child and Adolescent Development, 87,* 23–29.

Harris, R., Terrel, D., & Allen, G. (1999). The influence of education context and beliefs on the stimulating behavior of African American mothers. *Journal of Black Psychology, 25,* 490–503.

Harrison A. D., Wilson, M. N., Pine, C. J., Chan, S. R., & Buriel, R. (1990). Family ecologies of ethnic minority children. *Child Development, 61,* 347–362.

Hart, B., & Risley, T. R. (1995). *Meaningful differences in the everyday experiences of young American children.* Baltimore: Brookes.

Hart, B., & Risley, T. R. (2003, Spring). The early catastrophe: The 30 million word gap by age 3. *American Educator.* Retrieved March, 2, 2005, from http://www.aft.org

Hartman, H. (1958). *Ego psychology and the problem of adaptation* (D. Rapaport, Trans.). New York: International Universities Press. (Original work published 1939)

Harwood, R., & Feng, X. (2006). Studies of acculturation among Latinos in the United States. In M. H. Bornstein & L. R. Cote (Eds.), *Acculturation and parent–child relationships: Measurement and development* Mahwah, NJ: Lawrence Erlbaum Associates.

Harwood, R. L., Handwerker, W. P., Schoelmerich, A., & Leyendecker, B. (2001). Ethnic category labels, parental beliefs, and the contextualized individual: An exploration of the individualism-sociocentrism debate. *Parenting: Science and Practice, 1,* 217–236.

Harwood, R., Leyendecker, B., Carlson, V., Asencio, M., & Miller, A. (2002). Parenting among Latino families in the U.S. In M. H. Bornstein (Ed.), *Handbook of parenting: Vol. 4. Social conditions and applied parenting* (pp. 21–46). Mahwah, NJ: Lawrence Erlbaum Associates.

Harwood, R., Miller, J. G., & Lucca Irizarry, N. (1995). *Culture and attachment: Perceptions of the child in context.* New York: Guilford.

Hatano, G. (1982). Cognitive consequences of practice in culture specific procedural skills. *Quarterly Newsletter of the Laboratory of Comparative Human Cognition, 4,* 15–18.

Hatano, G., & Inagaki, K. (1998). Cultural context of schooling revisited: A review of the learning gap from a cultural psychology perspective. In S. G. Paris & H. M. Wellman (Eds.), *Global prospects for education: Development, culture and schooling* (pp. 79–104). Washington, DC: American Psychological Association.

Hatano, G., & Inagaki, K. (2000). Domain-specific constrains of conceptual development. *Journal of Behavioral Development, 24,* 267–275.

Hebbeler, K. (1985). An old and a new question on the effects of early education for children from low income families. *Educational Evaluation and Policy Analysis, 7,* 207–216.

Heelas, P., & Lock, A. (Eds.). (1981). *Indigenous psychologies: The anthropology of the self.* London: Academic Press.

Heine, S. J., Kitayama, S., Lehman, D. R., & Takata, T. (2001). Divergent consequences of success and failure in Japan and North America: An investigation of self-improving motivations and malleable selves. *Journal of Personality and Social Psychology, 81,* 599–615.

Heine, S. J., & Lehman, D. R. (1997). Culture, dissonance, and self-affirmation. *Personality and Social Psychology Bulletin, 23,* 389–400.

Heine, S. J., Lehman, D. R., Markus, H. R., & Kitayama, S. (1999). Is there a universal need for self-regard? *Psychological Review, 106,* 766–94.

Helling, G. A. (1966). *The Turkish village as a social system.* Los Angeles: Occidental College.

Hendrix, L. (1985). Economy and child training reexamined. *Ethos, 13,* 246–261.

Hernnstein, R. J., & Murray, C. (1994). *The bell curve: Intelligence and class structure in American life.* New York: Free Press.

Hess, R. D., & Shipman, V. C. (1965). Early experience and the socialization of cognitive modes in children. *Child Development, 36,* 869–888.

Ho, D. Y.-F., & Chiu, C.-Y. (1994). Component ideas of individualism, collectivism and social organisation: An application in the study of Chinese culture. In U. Kim, H. C. Triandis, Ç. Kağitçibaşi, S.-C. Choi, & G. Yoon (Eds.), *Individualism and collectivism: Theory, method and applications* (pp. 137–156). Thousand Oaks, CA: Sage.

Hockenberger, E., Goldstein, H., & Sirianni Haas, L. (1999). Effects of commenting during joint book reading by mothers with low SES. *Topics in Early Childhood Special Education, 19, 62,* 15–27.

Hodgins, H., Koeatner, R., & Duncan, N. (1996). On the compatibility of autonomy and relatedness. *Personality and Social Psychology Bulletin, 22,* 227–237.

Hoff, E. (2003) The specificity of environmental influence: Socioeconomic status affects early vocabulary development via maternal speech. *Child Development, 74,* 1368–1378.

Hoffman, J. A. (1984). Psychological separation of late adolescents from their parents. *Journal of Counseling Psychology, 31,* 170–178.

Hoffman, L. W. (1987). The value of children to parents and child rearing patterns. In Ç. Kağitçibaşi (Ed.), *Growth and progress in cross-cultural psychology* (pp. 159–170). Lisse, Netherlands: Swets & Zeitlinger.

Hoffman, L. W. (2003). Methodological issues in studies of SES, parenting, and child development. In M. H. Bornstein & R. H. Bradley (Eds.), *Socioeconomic status, parenting, and child development* (pp. 125–143). Mahwah, NJ: Lawrence Erlbaum Associates.

Hoffman, L. W., & Hoffman, M. L. (1973). The value of children to parents. In J. T. Fawcett (Ed.), *Psychological perspectives on education* (pp. 19–76). New York: Basic Books.

Hoffman, L. W., & Youngblade, L. M. (1998). Maternal employment, morale, and parenting style: Social class comparisons. *Journal of Applied Developmental Psychology, 19,* 389–413.

Hoffman, M. L. (1977). Moral internalization: Current theory and research. In L. Berkowitz (Ed.), *Advances in experimental social psychology* (pp. 85–133). New York: Academic Press.

Hoffman, M. L. (1989). Developmental issues, college students and the 1990s. *Journal of College Student Psychotherapy, 4,* 3–12.

Hofstede, G. (1980). *Culture's consequences.* Beverly Hills, CA: Sage.

Hofstede, G. (1991). *Cultures and organizations: Software of the mind.* London: McGraw-Hill.

Hofstede, G. (2001). *Culture's consequences: Comparing values, behaviours, institutions and organizations across nations* (2nd ed.). Thousand Oaks, CA: Sage.

Hogan, R. (1975). Theoretical egocentrism and the problem of compliance. *American Psychologist, 30,* 533–540.

Home visiting: Recent program evaluations. (1999). Whole Issue). *The Future of Children, 9*(1). Retrieved August 8, 2000, from http://www.futureof children.org/hv2/index.htm

Hong, Y., Roisman, G. I., & Chen, J. (2006). A model of cultural attachment: A new approach for studying bicultural experience. In M. H. Bornstein & L. R. Cote (Eds.), *Acculturation and parent–child relationships: Measurement and development* (pp. 135–172). Mahwah, NJ: Lawrence Erlbaum Associates.

Horowitz, F. D. (1993). The need for a comprehensive new environmentalism. In R. Plomin & G. E. C. McClearn (Eds.), *Nature–nurture* (pp. 341–354). Washington, DC: American Psychological Association.

Hoselitz, B. (1965). *Economics and the idea of mankind.* New York: Columbia University Press.

Hsu, F. L. K. (Ed). (1961). *Psychological anthropology* (1st ed.). Homewood, IL: Dorsey.

Hsu, F. L. K. (1985). The self in cross-cultural perspective. In A. J. Marsella, G. DeVos, & F. L. K. Hsu (Eds.), *Culture and self: Asian and Western perspectives* (pp. 24–55). New York: Tavistock.

Hui, C. H., & Yee, C. (1994). The shortened individualism–collectivism scale: Its relationship to demographic and work related variables. *Journal of Research in Personality, 28,* 409–424.

Huiberts, A., Oosterwegel, A., van der Valk, I., Vollebergh, W., & Meeus, W. (2006). Connectedness with parents and behavioural autonomy among Dutch and Moroccan adolescents. *Ethnic & Racial Studies, 29*(2), 315–330.

Hurrelman, K. (1988). *Social structure and personality development: The individual as a productive processor of reality.* New York: Cambridge University Press.

Huston, A. C. (1991). Antecedents, consequences, and possible solutions for poverty among children. In A. C. Huston (Ed.), *Children in poverty: Child development and public policy* (pp. 282–315). Cambridge, England: Cambridge University Press.

Huston, A. C., Duncan, G. J., Granger, R., Bos, J., McLoyd, V., Mistry, R., et al. (2001). Work-based antipoverty programs for parents to enhance the school performance and social behaviour of children. *Child Development, 72,* 318–336.

Huynh, C. T. (1979). *The concept of endogenous development centered on man.* Paris: UNESCO.

Hyman, S. (1999). Susceptibility and "second hits." In R. Conlan (Ed.), *States of mind: New discoveries about how our brains make us who we are.* New York: Wiley.

Idema, H., & Phalet, K. (2006). Transmission of gender-role values in Turkish-German migrant families: The role of gender, intergenerational and intercultural Relations. *Zeitschrift für Familienforschung.* (Special issue on migrant families).

Iglesias, E. V., & Shalala, D. E. (2002) Narrowing the gap for poor children. In M. E.Young (Ed.), *From early childhood development to human development* (pp. 363–374). Washington, DC: World Bank.

Imamoglu, E. O. (1987). An interdependence model of human development. In Ç. Kağitçibaşi (Ed.), *Growth and progress* (pp. 138–145). Lisse, Netherlands: Swets & Zeitlinger.

Imamoglu, E. O. (1998). Individualism and collectivism in a model and scale of balanced differentiation and integration. *Journal of Psychology, 132,* 95–105.

Imamoglu, E. O. (2003). Individuation and relatedness: Not opposing, but distinct and complementary. *Genetic, Social, and General Psychology Monographs, 129,* 367–402.

Inglehart, R. (2003). *Human values and social change: Findings from the values surveys* (International Studies in Sociology and Social Anthropology). Leiden, Netherlands: Brill.

Inkeles, A. (1969). Making men modern: On the causes and consequences of individual change in six developing countries. *American Journal of Sociology, 75,* 208–225.

Inkeles, A. (1977). Understanding and misunderstanding individual modernity. *Journal of Cross-Cultural Psychology, 8,* 135–176.

Inkeles, A., & Levinson, D. J. (1954). The study of modal personality and socio-cultural systems. In G. Lindzey (Ed.), *Handbook of social psychology* (Vol. 2, pp. 977–1020). Reading, MA: Addison-Wesley.

Inkeles, A., & Smith, D. H. (1974). *Becoming modern: Individual changes in six developing countries.* Cambridge, MA: Harvard University Press.

International Labor Organization. (2002). *The 2002 global report on child labour.* Geneva, Switzerland: Author.

Irvine, S. H. (1970). Affect and construct—a cross-cultural check on theories of intelligence. *Journal of Social Psychology, 80,* 23–30.

Iwawaki, S. (1986). Achievement motivation and socialization. In S. E. Newstead, S. M. Irvine, & P. L. Dann (Eds.), *Human assessment: Cognition and motivation.* Boston: Martinus Nijhoff.

Jackson, A. P., Brooks-Gunn, J., Huang, C.-C., & Glassman, M. (2000). Single mothers in low-wage jobs: Financial strain, parenting, and preschoolers' outcomes. *Child Development, 71,* 1409–1423.

Jahoda, G. (1975). Applying cross-cultural psychology to the Third World. In J. W. Berry & W. J. Lonner (Eds.), *Applied cross-cultural psychology* (pp. 3–7). Lisse, Netherlands: Swets & Zeitlinger.

Jahoda, G. (1986). A cross-cultural perspective on developmental psychology. *International Journal of Behavioral Development, 9,* 417–437.

Jahoda, G., & Dasen, P. R. (Eds.). (1986). *International Journal of Behavioral Development, 9*(4), 413–416.

Jolly, R. (1988). Deprivation in the child's environment: Seeking advantage in adversity. *Canadian Journal of Public Health Supplement, 20.*

Jones, E. E. (1990). *Interpersonal perception.* New York: Macmillan.

Jose, P. E., Huntsinger, C. S., Huntsinger, P. R., & Liaw, F.-R. (2000). Parental values and practices relevant to young children's social development in Taiwan and the United States. *Journal of Cross-Cultural Psychology, 31,* 677–702.

Kagan, J. (1984). *Nature of the child.* New York: Basic Books.

Kağitçibaşi, Ç. (1970). Social norms and authoritarianism: A Turkish–American comparison. *Journal of Personality & Social Psychology, 16,* 444–451.

Kağitçibaşi, Ç. (1973). Psychological aspects of modernization in Turkey. *Journal of Cross-Cultural Psychology, 4,* 157–174.

Kağitçibaşi, Ç. (1978). Cross-national encounters: Turkish Students in the US. *International Journal of Intercultural Relations, 2,* 141–160.

Kağitçibaşi, Ç. (1982a). *The changing value of children in Turkey* (Pub. No. 60-E). Honolulu, HI: East–West Center.

Kağitçibaşi, Ç. (1982b). Old-age security value of children: Cross-national socio-economic evidence. *Journal of Cross-Cultural Psychology, 13,* 29–42.

Kağitçibaşi, Ç. (1984). Socialization in traditional society: A challenge to psychology. *International Journal of Psychology, 19,* 145–157.

Kağitçibaşi, Ç. (1985a). Culture of separateness-culture of relatedness. *1984 Vision and Reality: Papers in Comparative Studies, 4,* 91–99.

Kağitçibaşi, Ç. (1985b). A model of family change through development: The Turkish family in comparative perspective. In R. Lagunes & Y. H. Poortinga (Eds.), *From a different perspective: Studies of behavior across cultures* (pp. 120–135). Lisse, Netherlands: Swets & Zeitlinger.

Kağitçibaşi, Ç. (1987a). Alienation of the outsider: The plight of migrants. *International Migration, 25,* 195–210.

Kağitçibaşi, Ç. (1987b). Individual and group loyalties: Are they compatible? In Ç. Kağitçibaşi (Ed.), *Growth and progress in cross-cultural psychology* (pp. 94–103). Lisse, Netherlands: Swets & Zeitlinger.

Kağitçibaşi, Ç. (1990). Family and socialization in cross-cultural perspective: A model of change. In J. Berman (Ed.), *Cross-cultural perspectives: Nebraska Symposium on Motivation, 1989* (pp. 135–200). Lindoln: University of Nebraska Press.

Kağitçibaşi, Ç. (1991). Decreasing infant mortality as a global demographic change: A challenge to psychology. *International Journal of Psychology, 26,* 649–664.

Kağitçibaşi, Ç. (1992a). Linking the indigenous and universalist orientations. In S. Iwawaki, Y. Kashima, & K. Leung (Eds.), *Innovations in cross-cultural psychology* (pp. 29–37). Lisse, Netherlands: Swets & Zeitlinger.

Kağitçibaşi, Ç. (1992b). Research on parenting and child development in cross-cultural perspective. In M. Rosenzweig (Ed.), *International psychological science* (pp. 137–160). Washington, DC: American Psychological Association.

Kağitçibaşi, Ç. (1994a). A critical appraisal of individualism and collectivism: Toward a new formulation. In U. Kim, H. Triandis, Ç. Kağitçibaşi, S. Choi, & G. Yoon (Eds.), *Individualism and collectivism: Theory, method and applications* (pp. 52–65). Newbury Park, CA: Sage.

Kağitçibaşi, Ç. (1994b). Human development and societal development. In A.-M. Bouvy, F. J. R. van der Vijver, & P. Boski (Eds.), *Journeys in cross-cultural psychology* (pp. 3–24). Lisse, Netherlands: Swets & Zeitlinger.

Kağitçibaşi, Ç. (1995). Is psychology relevant to global human development issues? *American Psychologist, 50,* 293–300.

Kağitçibaşi, Ç. (1996a). The autonomous-relational self: A new synthesis. *European Psychologist, 1,* 180–186.

Kağitçibaşi, Ç. (1996b). *Family and human development across cultures: A view from the other side.* Mahwah, NJ: Lawrence Erlbaum Associates.

Kağitçibaşi, Ç. (1997a). Individualism and collectivism. In J. W. Berry, M. H. Segall, & Ç. Kağitçibaşi (Eds.), *Handbook of cross-cultural psychology* (2nd ed., Vol. 3, pp. 1–50). Boston: Allyn & Bacon.

Kağitçibaşi, Ç. (1997b). Interactive mediated learning: the Turkish experience. *International Journal of Early Childhood, 29,* 22–32.

Kağitçibaşi, Ç. (1997c). Whither multiculturalism? *Applied Psychology: An International Review, 44,* 44–49.

Kağitçibaşi, Ç. (1998a). The value of children: A key to gender issues. *International Child Health, 9,* 15–24.

Kağitçibaşi, Ç. (1998b). Whatever happened to modernization? *Cross-Cultural Psychology Bulletin, 32,* 8–12.

Kağitçibaşi, Ç. (2000a). Indigenous psychology and indigenous approaches to developmental research. *International Society for the Study of Behavioural Development Newsletter, 37,* 6–9.

Kağitçibaşi, Ç. (2000b). Cultural contextualism without complete relativism in the study of human development. In A. L. Comunian & U. Gielen (Eds.), *International perspectives on human development* (pp. 97–115). Rome: Pabst Science.

Kağitçibaşi, Ç. (2002). Psychology and human competence development. *Applied Psychology: An International Review, 51,* 5–22.

Kağitçibaşi, Ç. (2003). Autonomy, embeddedness and adaptability in immigration contexts. *Human Development, 46,* 145–150.

Kağitçibaşi, Ç. (2004). Culture and child development. In C. Spielberger (Ed.), *Encyclopedia of applied psychology.* London: Academic Press.

Kağitçibaşi, Ç. (2005a). Autonomy and relatedness in cultural context: Implications for self and family. *Journal of Cross-Cultural Psychology, 36,* 403–422.

Kağitçibaşi, Ç. (2005b). Modernization does not mean Westernization: Emergence of a different pattern. In W. Friedmeier, P. Chakkarath, & B. Shwarz (Eds.), *Culture and human development* (pp. 255–272). Hove, England: Psychology Press.

Kağitçibaşi, Ç. (2006a). An overview of acculturation and parent–child relationships. In M. H. Bornstein & L. R. Cote (Eds.), *Acculturation and parent–child relationships: Measurement and development* (pp. 319–332). Mahwah, NJ: Lawrence Erlbaum Associates.

Kağitçibaşi, Ç. (2006b). Preface. In M. Dekovich, T. Pels, & S. Model (Eds.), *Child rearing in six ethnic families: The multi-cultural Dutch experience* (pp. 9–15). Lewiston, NY: Edwin Mellen Press.

Kağitçibaşi, Ç., & Ataca, B. (2005). Value of children and family change: A three-decade portrait from Turkey. *Applied Psychology: An International Review, 54,* 317–338.

Kağitçibaşi, Ç., Ataca, B., & Diri, A. (2005). The Turkish family and the value of children : Trends over time. In G. Trommsdorff & B. Nauck (Eds.), *The value of children in cross-cultural perspective* (pp. 91–120). Berlin: Pabst Science.

Kağitçibaşi, Ç., Baydar, N., Aycicegi, A., Cheung, F. M., Cheung, S. F., Johnson, M., et al. (2007). *Meanings attached to relatedness and autonomy: An exploratory study.* Manuscript submitted for publication.

Kağitçibaşi, Ç., Baydar, N., & Cemalcilar, Z. (2006). *Autonomy and relatedness scales* (Progress report). Istanbul, Koç University.

Kağitçibaşi, Ç., Benedek, L., Dubois, A., Carney, C., Jallinoja, A., & Vlaardingerbroek, P. (1994). *The interaction between the providers of family services.* Strasbourg, France: Council of Europe.

Kağitçibaşi, Ç., & Berry, J. W. (1989). Cross-cultural psychology: Current research and trends. *Annual Review of Psychology, 40,* 493–531.

Kağitçibaşi, Ç., & Savasir, I. (1988). Human abilities in the eastern mediterranean. In S. H. Irvine & I. W. Berry (Eds.), *Human abilities in cultural contat* (pp. 232–262). Cambridge, England: Cambridge University Press.

Kağitçibaşi, Ç., Sunar, D., & Bekman, S. (2001). Long-term effects of early intervention: Turkish low-income mothers and children. *Journal of Applied Development Psychology, 22,* 333–361.

Kağitçibaşi, Ç., Sunar, D., Bekman, S., & Baydar, N. (2007). *Journal of Applied Developmental Psychology.* Manuscript submitted for publication.

Kağitçibaşi, Ç., Sunar, D., Bekman, S., & Cemalcilar, Z. (2007). *Continuing effects of early intervention in adult life: The Turkish Early Enrichment Project 22 years later.* Manuscript submitted for publication.

Kakar, S. (1978). *The inner world: A psychoanalytic study of childhood and society in India.* Oxford, England: Oxford University Press.

Kamerman, S. B. (1991). Child care policies and programs: An international overview. *Journal of Social Issues, 47,* 179–196.

Kao, H. S. R., & Hong, N. S. (1988). Minimal 'self' and Chinese work behavior: Psychology of the grass-roots. In D. Sinha & H. S. R. Kao (Eds.), *Social values and development: Asian perspectives* (pp. 254–272). London: Sage.

Kapadia, S., & Miller, J. (2005). Parent–adolescent relationships in the context of interpersonal diasgreements: View from a collectivist culture. *Psychology and Developing Societies, 17,* 33–50.

Kardiner, A., & Linton, R. (1945). *The individual and his society.* New York: Columbia University Press.

Karlins, M., Coffman, T. L., & Walters, G. (1969). On the finding of social stereotypes: Studies in three generations of college students. *Journal of Personality and Social Psychology, 13,* 1–16.

Karpov, Y. V. (2005). Psychological tools, internalization and mediation: The neo-Vygotskian elaboration of Vygotsky's notions. *International Society for the Study of Behavioural Development, 1,* 47.

Kashima, E. S., & Hardie, E. A. (2000). The development and validation of the relational, individual and collective self-aspects (RIC) scale. *Asian Journal of Social Psychology, 3,* 19–48.

Kashima, Y., Siegel, M., Tanaka, K., & Isaka, H. (1988). Universalism in lay conceptions of distributive justice: A cross-cultural examination. *International Journal of Psychology, 23,* 51–64.

Kashima, Y., & Triandis, H. C. (1986). The self-serving bias in attributions as a coping strategy: A cross-cultural study. *Journal of Cross-Cultural Psychology, 17,* 83–97.

Kassebaum, N. L. (1994) Head Start: Only the best for America's children. *American Psychologist, 49,* 123–126.

Katz, D., & Braly, K. W. (1933). Racial stereotypes of one hundred college students. *Journal of Abnormal and Social Psychology, 28,* 280–290.

Kaya, A. (2001). *"Zicher in Kreuzberg." Constructing diasporas: Turkish hip-hop youth in Berlin.* London: Transaction.

Kaytaz, M. (2005). *A cost benefit analysis of preschool education in Turkey.* İstanbul, Turkey: AÇEV.

Keating, D. P., & Hertzman, C. (1999). *Developmental health and the wealth of nations: Social, biological and educational dynamics.* New York: Guilford.

Kegan, R. (1994). *In over our heads. The mental demands of modern life.* Cambridge, MA: Harvard University Press.

Keller, H. (1997). Evolutionary approaches. In J. W. Berry, Y. Poortinga, & J. Pandey (Eds.), *Handbook of cross-cultural psychology* (2nd ed., Vol. 1, pp. 215–56). Needham Heights, MA: Allyn & Bacon.

Keller, H. (2003). Socialization for competence: Cultural models of infancy. *Human Development, 46,* 288–311.

Keller, H., & Greenfield, P. M. (2000). History and future of development in cross-cultural psychology. *Journal of Cross-Cultural Psychology, 31,* 52–62.

Keller, H., & Lamm, B. (2005). Parenting as the expression of socio-historical time: The case of German individualisation. *International Journal of Behavioral Development, 29,* 238–46.

Keller, H., Lohaus, A., Völker, S., Cappenberg, M., & Chasiotis, A. (1999). Temporal contingency as an independent component of parenting behaviour. *Child Development, 70,* 474–85.

Keller, H., Papaligoura, Z., Kunsemuller, P., Voelker, S., Papaeliou, C., Lohaus, A., et al. (2003). Concepts of mother–infant interaction in Greece and Germany. *Journal of Cross-Cultural Psychology, 34*(6), 677–689.

Keller, H., Poortinga, Y. H., & Schölmerich, A. (2002). *Between culture and biology: Perspectives on ontogenetic development.* Cambridge, England: Cambridge University Press.

Keller, H., Schölmerich, A., & Eibl-Eibesfeldt, I. (1988) Communication patterns in adult–infant interactions in Western and non-Western cultures. *Journal of Cross-Cultural Psychology, 19,* 427–445.

Keniston, K. (1985). The myth of family independence. In J. M. Henslin (Ed.), *Marriage and family in a changing society* (2nd ed., pp. 27–33). New York: The Free Press.

Kessen, W. (1991). The American child and other cultural inventions. In M. Woodhead, P. Light, & R. Carr (Eds.), *Growing up in a changing society* (pp. 37–53). London: Routledge.

Killen, M. (1997). Culture, self, and development: Are cultural templates useful or stereotypic? *Developmental Review, 17,* 239–249.

Kim, U., & Berry, J. W. (1993). *Indigenous psychologies: Research and experience in cultural context.* Newbury Park, CA: Sage.

Kim, U., Butzel, J. S., & Ryan, R. M. (1998). *Interdependence and well-being: A function of culture and relatedness needs.* Paper presented at the International Society for the Study of Personal Relationships. Saratoga Spring, NY.

Kim, U., Park, Y.-S., Kwon, Y.-E., & Koo, J. (2005). Values of children, parent–child relationship, and social change in Korea: Indigenous, cultural, and psychological analysis. *Applied Psychology: An International Review, 54,* 338–355.

Kim, U., Triandis, H. C., Kağitçibaşi, Ç., Choi, S.-C., & Yoon, G. (Eds.). (1994). *Individualism and collectivism: Theory method applications.* Newbury Park, CA: Sage.

Kim, U., Yang, K.-S., & Hwang, K.-K. (2006). *Indigenous and cultural psychology: Understanding people in context.* New York: Springer.

Kiray, M. B. (1981). The women of small town. In N. Abadan-Unat (Ed.), *Women in Turkish society* (pp. 259–274). Leiden, Netherlands: Brill.

Kirkpatrick, J., & White, G. M. (1985). Exploring ethnopsychologies. In G. M. White & J. Kirkpatrick (Eds.). *Person, self and experience: Exploring Pacific ethnopsychologies.* Berkeley: University of California Press.

Kirpal, S. (2002). Communities can make a difference: Five cases across continents. In M. E.Young (Ed.), *From early childhood development to human development* (pp. 293–360). Washington, DC: World Bank.

Kitayama, S., Markus, H. R., & Kurokawa, M. (2000). Culture, emotion and well-being: Good feelings in Japan and the U.S. *Cognition and Emotion, 14,* 93–124.

Kitayama, S., Markus, H. R., Kurokawa, M., Tummala, P., & Kato, K. (1991). *Self–other similarity judgements depend on culture* (Tech. Rep. No. 91–17). Eugene: University of Oregon, Institute of Cognitive Decision Sciences,.

Kitayama, S., Markus, H. R., & Matsumoto, H. (1995). Culture, self, and emotion: A cultural perspective on "self-conscious" emotions. In J. P. Tangney & K. Fischer (Eds.), *Self-conscious emotions: The psychology of shame, guilt, embarrassment, and pride* (pp. 439–464). New York: Guilford.

Kitayama, S., Markus, H. R., Matsumoto, H., & Norasakkunkit, V. (1997). Individual and collective processes in the construction of the self: Self-enhancement in the United States and self-criticism in Japan. *Journal of Personality and Social Psychology, 72,* 1245–1267.

Kitayama, S., Snibbe, A. C., Markus, H. R., & Suzuki, T. (2004). Is there any "free" choice? *Psychological Science, 15,* 527–534.

Klaus, D., Nauck, B., & Klein, T. (2005). Families and the value of children in Germany. In G. Trommsdorff & B. Nauck (Eds.), *The value of children in cross-cultural perspective: Case studies from eight societies* (pp. 17–41). Berlin: Pabst Science.

Klaus, R. A., & Gray, S. W. (1968). The early training project for disadvantaged children. *Monographs of the Society for Research in Child Development, 33*(4, Serial No. 120).

Kluckhohn, C. (1957). *Mirror for man.* New York: Premier Books.

Kluckhohn, F. R., & Strodtbeck, F. L. (1961). *Variations in value orientations.* Evanston, IL: Row, Peterson.

Kohen, D. E., Brooks-Gunn, J., Leventhal, T., & Hertzman, C. (2002). Neighborhood income and physical and social disorder in Canada: Associations with young children's competencies. *Child Development, 73,* 1844–1860.

Kohlberg, L. (1969). Stage and sequence: The cognitive-developmental approach to socialization. In D. A. Goslin (Ed.), *Handbook of socialization theory* (pp. 347–380). Chicago: Rand McNally.

Kohlberg, L. (1984). *The psychology of moral development: The nature and validity of moral stages* (Essays on moral development, Vol. 2). San Francisco: Harper & Row.

Kohn, M. L. (1969). *Class and conformity: A study in values.* New York: Dorsey.

Kohut, H. (1977). *The restoration of the self.* New York: International Universities Press.

Kohut, H. (1984). *How does analysis cure?* Chicago: University of Chicago Press.

Koppitz, E. M. (1968). Psychological evaluation of children's human figure drawings. New York: Grune & Stratton.

Korenman, S., Miller, J., & Sjaastad, J. (1995). Long-term poverty and child development in the United States: Results from the NLSY. *Children and Youth Services Review, 17,* 127–155.

Kornadt, H. J. (1987). The aggression motive and personality development: Japan and Germany. In F. Halish & J. Kuhl (Eds.), *Motivation, intention and volition.* Berlin: Springer-Verlag.

Kotchabhakdi, N. J., Winichagoon, P., Smitasiri, S., Dhanamitta, S., & Valya-Sevi, A. (1987). The integration of psychosocial components in nutrition education in northeastern Thai villages. *Asia Pacific Journal of Publich Health, 2,* 16–25.

Koutrelakos, J. (2004). Acculturation of Greek Americans: Change and continuity in cognitive schemas guiding intimate relationships. *International Journal of Psychology, 39,* 95–105.

Kroeber, A. L., & Kluckhohn, C. (1952). *Culture* (Part III: Papers of the Peabody Museum of Harvard University). New York: Meridian Books.

Kroger, J. (1998). Adolescence as a second separation-individuation process: Critical review of an object relations approach. In E. E. A. Skoe & A. L. von der Lippe (Eds.), *Personality development in adolescence: A cross-national and life span perspective. Adolescence and society* (pp. 172–192). New York: Routledge.

Kuhn, M. H., & McPartland, T. S. (1954). An empirical investigation of self-attitudes. *American Sociological Review, 19,* 68–76.

Kurman, J. (2001). Self-enhancement: Is it restricted to individualistic cultures? *Personality and Social Psychology Bulletin, 27,* 1705–1716.

Kwak, K. (2003). Adolescents and their parents: A review of intergenerational family relations for immigrant and non-immigrant families. *Human Development, 46,* 15–36.

Lakoff, G., & Johnson, M. (1980). *Metaphors we live by.* Chicago: University of Chicago Press.

Lambert, W. E. (1987). The fate of old-country values in a new land: A cross-national study of childrearing. *Canadian Psychology, 28,* 9–20.

Lamborn, S. D., Mounts, N., Steinberg, L., & Dornbusch, S. M. (1991). Patterns of competence and adjustment among adolescents from authoritative, authoritarian, indulgent, and neglectful families. *Child Development, 62,* 1049–1065.

Landers, C., & Kağitçibaşi, Ç. (1990). *Measuring the psychosocial development of young children.* Florence, Italy: Innocenti (UNICEF).

Lansford, J. E., Deater-Deckard, K., Dodge, K. A., Bates, J. E., & Pettit, G. S. (2003). Ethnic differences in the link between physical discipline and later adolescent externalizing behaviors. *Journal of Child Psychology and Psychiatry, 44,* 1–13.

Laosa, L. M. (1978). Maternal teaching strategies in Chicano families of varied educational and socioeconomic levels. *Child Development, 49,* 1129–1135.

Laosa, L. M. (1980). Maternal teaching strategies in Chicano and Anglo-American families: The influence of culture and education on maternal behavior. *Child Development, 51,* 759–765.

Laosa, L. M. (1982). Families as facilitators of children's intellectual development at 3 years of age. In L. M. Laosa & I. E. Sigel (Eds.), *Families as learning environments for children* (pp. 1–45). New York: Plenum.

Laosa, L. M. (1984). Ethnic, socioeconomic, and home language influences upon early performance on measures of abilities. *Journal of Educational Psychology, 76,* 1178–1198.

Laosa, L. M., & Sigel, I. E. (1982). *Families as learning environments for children.* New York: Plenum.

Larson, R., Verma, S., & Dworkin, J. (2003). Adolescence without family disengagement: The daily family lives of Indian middle class teenagers. In T. S. Saraswathi (Ed.), *Cross-cultural perspectives in human development: Theory, research and applications* (pp. 258–287). New Delhi, India: Sage.

Lasch, C. (1978). *The culture of narcissism.* New York: Norton.

Lasch, C. (1984). *The minimal self: Psychic survival in troubled times.* New York: Norton.

Laslett, P. (1977). Characteristics of the Western family considered over time. In P. Laslett (Ed.), *Family and illicit love in earlier generations* (pp. 12–50). London: Cambridge University Press.

Lau, S., & Cheung, P. C. (1987). Relations between Chinese adolescents' perception of parental control and organization and their perception of parental warmth. *Developmental Psychology, 23,* 726–729.

Lau, S., Lew, W. J., Hau, K. T., Cheung, P. C., Berndt, T. J. (1990). Relations among perceived parental control, warmth, indulgence, and family harmony of Chinese in Mainland China. *Developmental Psychology, 26,* 674–677.

Layzer, J., Goodson, B., Bernstein, L. & Price, C. (2001). *National evaluation of family support programmes. Final report Volume A: The meta-analysis.* Cambridge, MA: ABT Associates, Inc. Retrieved December 3, 2004, from http://www.abtassoc.com

Lazar, I., Darlington, R. B., Murray, H. W., & Snipper, A.S. (1982) Lasting effects of early education: A report from the consortium for longitudinal studies. *Monographs of Society for Research in Child Development, 33*(120).

Leahy, R. L. (1990). The development of concepts of economic and social inequality. In V. C. McLoyd & C. A. Flanagan (Eds.), *Economic stress: Effects on family life and child development* (pp. 107–120). San Francisco: Jossey-Bass.

Lebra, T. S. (1976). *Japanese patterns of behavior.* Honolulu: University of Hawaii Press.

Lee, A. Y., Aaker, J. L., & Gardner, W. L. (2000). The pleasures and pains of distinct self-construals: The role of interdependence in regulatory focus. *Journal of Personality & Social Psychology, 78,* 1122–1134.

Lee, V., & Croninger, R. (1994). The relative importance of home and school in the development of literacy skills for middle-grade students. *American Journal of Education, 102,* 286–329.

Lerner, R. M. (1989). Developmental contextualism and the lifespan view of person–context interaction. In M. H. Bornstein & J. S. Bruner (Eds.), *Interaction in human development* (pp. 217–143). Hillsdale, NJ: Lawrence Erlbaum Associates.

Lerner, R. M. (1998). Towards a science for and of the people: Promoting civil society through the application of developmental science. *Child Development, 7*, 11–20.

Lerner, R. M. (2001). Toward a democratic ethnotheory of parenting for families and policy makers: A developmental systems perspective. *Parenting: Science and Practice, 1*, 339–351.

Lerner, R. M., Hultsch, D. F., & Dixon, R. A. (1983). Contextualism and the character of developmental psychology in the 1970s. *Annals of the New York Academy of Sciences, 412*, 101–128.

Leseman, P., (1993). How parents provide young children with access to literacy. In L. Eldering & P. Leseman (Eds.), *Early intervention and culture* (pp. 149–172). Paris: UNESCO.

Lerner, R. M., Rothbaum, F., Boulos, S., & Castellino, D. R. (2002). Developmental systems perspective on parenting. In M. H. Bornstein (Ed.), *Handbook of parenting: Vol. 2. Biology and ecology of parenting* (2nd ed., pp. 315–345). Mahwah, NJ: Lawrence Erlbaum Associates.

Leseman, P. (1993). How parents provide young children with access to literacy. In L. Eldering & P. Leseman (Eds.), *Early intervention and culture* (pp. 149–172). The Hague, Netherlands: UNESCO.

Lesthaeghe, R. (1980). On the social control of human reproduction. *Population and Development Review, 6*, 527–548.

Lesthaeghe, R. (1983). A century of demographic and cultural change in Western Europe: An exploration of underlying dimensions. *Population and Development Review, 9*, 411–437.

Lesthaeghe, R., & Surkyn, J. (1988). Cultural dynamics and economic theories of fertility change. *Population and Development Review, 14*, 1–47.

Leung, K. (1987). Some determinants of reactions to procedural models for conflict resolution. A cross national study. *Journal of Personality and Social Psychology, 53*, 898–908.

Leung, K. (1997). Negotiation and reward allocations across cultures. In P. C. Earley & M. Erez (Eds.), *New perspectives on international industrial/organizational psychology* (pp. 640–675). San Francisco: Jossey-Bass.

Leung, K., & Bond, M. H. (1984). The impact of cultural collectivism on reward allocation. *Journal of Personality and Social Psychology, 47*, 793–804.

Levenstein, P., O'Hara, J., & Madden, J. (1983). The mother–child home program of the verbal interaction project. In Consortium for Longitudinal Studies (Ed.), *As the twig is bent* (pp. 237–263). Hillsdale, NJ: Lawrence Erlbaum Associates.

LeVine, R. A. (1974). Parental goals: A cross-cultural view. *Teachers' College Record, 76*, 226–239.

LeVine, R. A. (1983). Fertility and child development: An anthropological approach. In D. A. Wagner (Ed.), *Child development and international development: Research–policy interfaces* (pp. 45–56). San Francisco: Jossey-Bass.

LeVine, R. A. (1988). Human parental care: Universal goals, cultural strategies, individual behavior. *New Directions in Child Development, 40*, 37–50.

LeVine, R. A. (1989). Cultural environments in child development. In N. Damon (Ed.), *Child development today and tomorrow* (pp. 349–378). San Francisco: Jossey-Bass.

LeVine, R. A. (2004). Challenging expert knowledge: Findings from an African study of infant care and development. In U. P. Gielen & J. L. Roopnarine (Eds.), *Childhood and adolescence: Cross-cultural perspectives and applications.* Westport, CT: Praeger/Greenwood.

LeVine, R. A., & LeVine, B. (1966). *Nyansongo: A Gusii community in Kenya.* New York: Wiley.

LeVine, R. A., & Norman, K. (2001). The infant's acquisition of culture: Early attachment re-examined in anthropological perspective. In C. C. Mors & H. F. Matthews (Eds.), *The psychology of cultural experience* (pp. 83–104). Cambridge, England: Cambridge University Press.

LeVine, R. A., & White, M. I. (1986). *Human conditions: The cultural basis of educational development.* London: Routledge & Kegan.

LeVine, R. A., & White, M. I. (1991). Revolution in parenthood. In M. Woodhead, P. Light, & R. Carr (Eds.), *Growing up in a changing society* (pp. 5–25). London: Routledge.

Levinger, B. (1992). *Promoting child quality: Issues, trends and strategies.* Washington, DC: Academy for Educational Development.

Lévy-Bruhl, L. (1910). *Les fonctions mentales dans les sociétés inférieures* [How natives think]. Paris: Alcan.

Lévy-Bruhl, L. (1922). *Mentalité primitive* [Primitive mentality]. Paris: Alcan.

Lewin, K. (1951). *Field theory in social science.* New York: Harper.

Lewin, L. (1958). Group decision and social change. In E. E. Maccoby, T. M. Newcomb, & E. L. Hartley (Eds.), *Readings in social psychology* (pp. 197–211). New York: Holt, Rinehart.

Lewis, M., Feiring, C., & Rosenthal, S. (2000). Attachment over time. *Child Development, 71,* 707–720.

Leyendecker, B., Schoelmerich, A., & Citlak, B. (2006). Similarities and differences between first- and second-generation Turkish migrant mothers in Germany: The acculturation gap. In M. H. Bornstein & L. R. Cote (Eds.), *Acculturation and parent–child relationships: Measurement and development* (pp. 297–315). Mahwah, NJ: Lawrence Erlbaum Associates.

Li, J. (1995). China's one child policy: How and how well has it worked? A case study of Hebei Province, 1979–88. *Population and Development Review, 21,* 563–584.

Liebkind, K. (2003). Gaps in the research on ethnic minority youth. *International Society for the Study of Behavioural Development Newsletter, 2*(44), 15–16.

Lightfoot, C., & Valsiner, J. (1992). Parental belief systems under the influence: Social guidance of the construction of personal cultures. In I. E. Sigel, A. McGillicuddy, & J. Goodnow (Eds.), *Parental belief systems* (pp. 393–414). Hillsdale, NJ: Lawrence Erlbaum Associates.

Liljestrom, R., & Ozdalga, E. (2002a). *Autonomy and dependency in the family: Turkey and Sweden in critical perspective.* Istanbul & Stockholm: Swedish Research Institute.

Liljestrom, R., & Ozdalga, E. (2002b). Epilogue: Seeing oneself through the eyes of the other. In R. Liljestrom & E.Ozdalga (Eds.), *Autonomy and dependency in the family: Turkey and Sweden in critical perspective* (pp. 263–271). Istanbul & Stockholm: Swedish Research Institute.

Lin, C.-Y. C., & Fu, V. R. (1990). A comparison of child-rearing practices among Chinese, immigrant Chinese, and Caucasian-American parents. *Child Development, 61,* 429–433.

Lin, J., & Wang, Q. (2002, August). *I want to be like Carol: US and Chinese preschoolers talk about learning and achievement.* Paper presented at the 17th Biennial meeting of the ISSBD, Ottawa, Canada.

Linver, M. R., Brooks-Gunn, J., & Kohen, D. E. (2002). Family processes as pathways from income to young children's development. *Developmental Psychology, 38,* 719–734.

Lombard, A. (1981). *Success begins at home.* Lexington, MA: Lexington.

Lonner, W. J., & Malpass, R. S. (Eds.). (1994). *Psychology and culture.* Boston: Allyn & Bacon.

Lopez, I. R., & Contreras, J. M. (2005). The best of both worlds: Biculturality, acculturation, and adjustment among young mainland Puerto Rican mothers. *Journal of Cross-Cultural Psychology, 36,* 192–208.

Love, J. M., Schochet, P. Z., & Meckstroth, A. L. (2002). Investing in effective childcare and education: Lessons from research. In M. E. Young (Ed.), *From early child development to human development: Investing in our children's future* (pp. 145–194). Washington, DC: World Bank.

Luria, A. R. (1976). *Cognitive development: Its cultural and social foundations.* Cambridge, MA: Harvard University Press.

Lykes, M. B. (1985). Gender and individualistic vs. collectivistic bases for notions about the self. *Journal of Personality, 53,* 356–383.

Ma, H. K. (1997). The affective and cognitive aspects of moral development: A Chinese perspective. In D. Sinha (Ed.), *Asian perspectives on psychology* (pp. 93–109). Thousand Oaks, CA: Sage.

Maccoby, E. E., & Martin, J. A. (1983). Socialization in the context of the family: Parent–child interaction. In E. M. Hetherington (Ed.), *Handbook of child psychology: Socialization, personality, and social development* (Vol. 4, pp. 1–102). New York: Wiley.

MacFarlane, A. (1978). *The origins of English individualism.* Oxford, England: Blackwell.

MacFarlane, A. (1987). The culture of capitalism. Oxford, England: Basil Blackwell.

Macro. (1993). *Ailede cocuk egitimi arastirmasi* [Child training in the family]. Ankara, Turkey: Aile Arastirma Kurumu.

Madden, N., Slavin, R., Karweit, N. L., Dolan, L., & Wasik, B. A. (1993). Success for all. *Phi Delta Kappan, 72,* 593–600.

Mahler, M. (1972). On the first three phases of the separation-individuation process. *International Journal of Psychoanalysis, 53,* 333–338.

Mahler, M., Pine, F., & Bergman, A. (1975). *The psychological birth of the human infant.* New York: Basic Books.

Malewska-Peyre, H. (1980). *Conflictual cultural identity of second generation immigrants.* Paper presented at the Workshop on Cultural Identity and Structural Marginalization of Migrant Workers, European Science Foundation.

Marin, G. (1985). The preference for equity when judging the attractiveness and fairness of an allocator: The role of familiarity and culture. *Journal of Social Psychology, 125,* 543–549.

Markus, H. R., & Kitayama, S. (1991). Culture and the self: Implications for cognition, emotion, and motivation. *Psychological Review, 98,* 224–253.

Markus, H. R., & Kitayama, S. (1992). The what, why and how of cultural psychology: A review of Shweder's "Thinking Through Cultures." *Psychological Inquiry, 3,* 357–364.

Markus, H. R., & Kitayama, S. (1994). The cultural construction of self and emotion: implications for social behaviour. In S. Kitayama & M. R. Markus (Eds.), *Emotion and culture: Empirical studies of mutual influence* (pp. 89–130). Washington, DC: American Psychological Asssociation.

Markus, H. R., & Kitayama, S. (2003). Models of agency: Sociocultural diversity in the construction of action. In V. M. Berman & J. J. Berman (Eds.), *The Nebraska Symposium on Motivation: Cross-cultural differences in perspectives on the self* (Vol. 49, pp. 1–58). Lincoln: University of Nebraska Press.

Marsella, A. J., DeVos, G., & Hsu, F. L. K. (Eds.). (1985). *Culture and self: Asian and Western perspectives.* New York: Tavistock.

Marsella, A. J., & White, G. M. (1984). *Cultural conceptions of mental health and therapy.* Dordrecht, Netherlands: D. Reidel.

Martini, M. (1995). Features of home environments associated with children's school success. *Early Child Development and Care, 111,* 49–68.

Martini, M. (1996). "What's new?" at the dinner table: Family dynamics during meal times in two cultural groups in Hawaii. *Early Development and Parenting, 5,* 23–34.

Martini, M., & Mistry, J. (1993). The relationship between talking at home and test taking at school: A study of Hawaiian preschool children. In R. N. Roberts (Ed.), *Coming home to preschool: The sociocultural context of early education: Vol. 7. Advances in applied developmental psychology.* Norwood, NJ: Ablex.

Mascolo, M. F., & Li, J. (2004). *Culture and developing selves: Beyond dichotomization* (New Directions for Child and Adolescent Development, 104). London: Jossey-Bass.

Masse, L. N., & Barnett, W. S. (2002). A benefit–cost analysis of the Abecedarian early childhood intervention. *American Journal of Orthopsychiatry, 63,* 500–508.

Masten, A. S., & Coatsworth, J. D. (1998). The development of competence in favorable environments: Lessons from research on successful children. *American Psychologist, 53,* 205–220.

Matsumoto, D. (1999). Culture and self: An empirical assessment of Markus and Kitayama's theory of independent and interdependent self-construal. *Asian Journal of Social Psychology, 2,* 289–310.

Matsumoto, D. (2001a). Culture and emotion. In D. Matsumoto (Ed.), *The handbook of culture and psychology* (pp. 171–194). New York: Oxford University Press.

Matsumoto, D. (2001b). *The handbook of culture and psychology.* Oxford, England: Oxford University Press.

Matsumoto, D., & Juang, L. (2004). *Culture and psychology* (3rd ed.). Melbourne, Australia: Thomson Wadsworth.

Matsumoto, D., Weissman, M. D., Preston, K., Brown, B. R., & Kupperbusch, C. (1997). Context-specific measurement of individualism-collectivism on the individual level: The individualism–collectivism interpersonal assessment inventory. *Journal of Cross-Cultural Psychology, 28,* 743–767.

Mayer, B., Albert, I., Trommsdorff, G., & Schwartz, B. (2005). Value of children in Germany: Dimensions, comparison of generations, and relevance for parenting. In G. Trommsdorff & B. Nauck (Eds.), *The value of children in cross-cultural perspective: Case studies from eight societies* (pp. 43–65). Lengerich: Pabst Science Publishers.

Mayer, S. (1997). *What money can't buy: The effect of parental income on children's outcomes.* Cambridge, MA: Harvard University Press.

Mazrui, A. (1968). From social Darwinism to current theories of modernization. *World Politics, 21,* 69–83.

McAndrew, F. T., Akande, A., Bridgstock, R., Mealey, L., Gordon, S. C., Scheib, J. E., et al. (2000). A multicultural study of stereotyping in English-speaking countries. *Journal of Social Psychology, 140,* 487–502.

McClelland, D. C., Atkinson, J. W., Clark, R. A., & Lowell, E. L. (1953). *The achievement motive.* New York: Appleton–Century–Crofts.

McClelland, D. C., & Winters, D. G. (1969). *Monitoring economic achievement.* New York: Free Press.

McGoldrick, M., & Carter, E. A. (1982). The family life cycle. In F. Walsh (Ed.), *Normal family processes* (pp. 167–195). New York: Guilford.

McKey, R. H., Condelli, L., Ganson, H., Barret, B. J., McConkey, C., & Plantz, M. C. (1985). *The impact of Head Start on children, families and communities* (Final report). Washington, DC: Head Start Evaluation, Synthesis and Utilization Project.

McLoyd, V. C. (1990). The impact of economic hardship on Black families and children: Psychological distress, parenting, and socioemotional development. *Child Development, 61,* 311–346.

McLoyd, V. C. (1997). Socioeconomic disadvantage and child development. *American Psychologist, 53,* 185–204.

McLoyd, V. (1998). Socioeconomic disadvantage and child development. *American Psychologist, 53,* 185–204.

Mcloyd, V. C., & Wilson, L. (1990). Maternal behavior, social support, and economic conditions as predictors of distress in children. In V. C. McLoyd & C. Flanagan (Eds.), *Economic stress: Effects on family life and child development* (pp. 49–70). San Francisco: Jossey-Bass.

Mead, G. H. (1934). *Mind, self, and society.* Chicago: University of Chicago Press.

Mead, M. (1928). *Coming of age in Samoa.* New York: Morrow.

Meeus, W., Oosterweegel, A., & Vollebergh, W. (2002). Parental and peer attachment and identity development in adolescence. *Journal of Adolescence, 25,* 93–106.

Meisels, S. J., & Shonkoff, J. P. (Eds.). (1990). *Handbook of early childhood intervention.* Cambridge, England: Cambridge University Press.

Menon, U., & Shweder, R. A. (1998). The return of the "White man's burden": The moral discourse of anthropology and the domestic life of Hindu women. In R. A. Shweder (Ed.), *Welcome to middle age! (And other cultural fictions)* (pp. 139–188). Chicago: University of Chicago Press.

Miller, A. M., & Harwood, R. L. (2002). The cultural organization of parenting: Change and stability of behavior patterns during feeding and social play across the first year of life. *Parenting: Science and Practice, 2,* 241–273.

Miller, J. G. (1984). Culture and the development of everyday social explanation. *Journal of Personality and Social Psychology, 46,* 961–978.

Miller, J. G. (1994). Cultural diversity in the morality of caring: Individually oriented versus duty-based interpersonal moral codes. *Cross-Cultural Research: The Journal of Comparative Social Science, 28,* 3–39.

Miller, J. G. (2001). Culture and moral development. In D. Matsumoto (Ed.), *The handbook of culture and psychology* (pp. 151–171). Oxford, England: Oxford University Press.

Miller, J. G. (2002). Bringing culture to basic psychological theory—beyond individualism and collectivism: Comment on Oyserman et al. *Psychological Bulletin, 128,* 97–109.

Miller, J. G. (2003).Culture and agency: Implications for psychological theories of motivation and social development. In V. M. Berman & J. J. Berman (Eds.), *Nebraska Symposium on Motivation: Cross-cultural differences in perspectives on the self* (Vol. 49, pp. 59–101). Lincoln: University of Nebraska Press.

Miller, J. G., Bersoff, D. M., & Harwood, R. L. (1990). Perceptions of social responsibilities in India and the United States: moral imperatives or personal decisions? *Journal of Personality and Social Psychology, 58,* 33–47.

Miller, J. G., & Chen, X. (2005). Introduction to sociocultural perspectives on cognitive development. *International Society for the Study of Behavioural Development Newsletter, 1,* 47.

Miller, J. G., Schaberg, L., Bachman, M., & Conner, A. (2006).*Culture, agency, and interpersonal motivation.* Manuscript submitted for publication.

Miller, S. A. (1988). Parents' beliefs about children's cognitive development. *Child Development, 59,* 259–285.

Min, K. F. (1994). *Empowering women through formal education.* The Hague, Netherlands: CESO.

Minturn, L., & Lambert, W. W. (1964). *Mothers of six cultures.* New York: Wiley.

Minuchin, S. (1974). *Families and family therapy.* Cambridge, MA: Harvard University Press.

Mirdal, G. M., & Rynanen-Karjalainen,, L. (2004, October). *Migration and transcultural identities* (ESF Forward Look Report No. 2). Strasbourg, France: European Science Foundation.

Mishra, R., Mayer, B., Trommsdorff, G., Albert, I., & Schwartz, B. (2005) Background and empirical results. In G. Trommsdorff & B. Nauck (Eds.), *The value of children in cross-cultural perspective: Case studies from eight societies* (pp. 143–170). Berlin: Pabst Science.

Mistry, J., & Saraswathi, T. S. (2003). The cultural context of child development. In R. M. Lerner, M. A. Easterbrooks, & J. Mistry (Eds.), *Handbook of psychology: Developmental psychology* (pp. 267–291). New York: Wiley.

Mistry, R. S., Vandewater, E. A., Huston A. C., & McLoyd, V. C. (2002). Economic well-being and children's social adjustment: The role of family process in an ethnically diverse low-income sample. *Child Development, 73,* 935–951.

Miyake, K. (1993). Temperament, mother–infant interaction, and early emotional development. *Japanese Journal of Research and Emotions, 1,* 48–55.

Miyake, K., Chen, S., & Campos, J. J. (1985). Infant temperament, mother's mode of interaction, and attachment in Japan: An interim report. In I. Bretherton &

E. Waters (Eds.), *Growing points of attachment theory. Monographs of the Society for Research in Child Development, 50*(1–2, Serial No. 209).

Moghaddam, F. M. (1990). Modulative and generative orientations in psychology: Implications for psychology in the three worlds. *Journal of Social Issues, 1,* 21–41.

Moghaddam, F., & Taylor, D. M. (1986). What constitutes an "appropriate psychology" for the developing world? *International Journal of Psychology, 21,* 253–267.

Moghaddam, F. M., Taylor, D. M., & Wright, S. C. (1993). *Social psychology in cross-cultural perspective.* New York: Freeman.

Molfese, V. J., Molfese, D. L., & Modgline, A. A. (2001). Newborn and preschool predictors of second-grade reading scores: An evaluation of categorical and continuous scores. *Journal of Learning Disabilities, 34,* 545–555.

Montreuil, A., & Bourhis, R. Y. (2001). Majority acculturation orientations toward 'valued' and 'devalued' immigrants. *Journal of Cross-Cultural Psychology, 32,* 698–719.

Moos, R. H., & Moos, B. S. (1981). *Family environment scale manual.* Palo Alto, CA: Consulting Psychologists Press.

Morelli, G., Rogoff, B., & Angellilo, C. (2003). Cultural variation in young children's access to work or involvement in specialized child-focused activities. *International Journal of Behavioral Development, 27,* 264–275.

Morsbach, H. (1980). Major psychological factors influencing Japanese interpersonal relations. In N. Warren (Ed.), *Studies in cross-cultural psychology* (Vol. 2, pp. 317–344). London: Academic Press.

Mulhall, S., & Swift, A. (1982). *Liberals & Communitarians.* London: Blackwell.

Mundy-Castle, A. (1974). Social and technological intelligence in Western and non-Western cultures. In S. Pilowsky (Ed.), *Cultures in collision.* Adelaide: Australian National Association of Mental Health.

Munroe, R. L., Munroe, R. H., & Shimmin, H. (1984) Children's work in four cultures: Determinants and consequences. *American Anthropologist, 86,* 342–348.

Munroe, R. L., Munroe, R. H., & Whiting, B. B. (Eds.). (1981). *Handbook of cross-cultural human development.* New York: Garland.

Murphy, G. (1947). *Personality: A biosocial approach to origins and structure.* New York: Harper.

Murphy-Berman, V. A., & Berman, J. J. (Eds.). (2003). *Cross-cultural differences in perspectives on the self. The Nebraska Symposium on Motivation* (Vol. 49). Lincoln: University of Nebraska Press.

Mustard, J. F. (2002). Early child development and the brain—the base for health, learning, and behavior throughout life. In M. E. Young (Ed.), *From early child development to human development: Investing in our children's future* (pp. 23–61). Washington, DC: World Bank.

Myers, R. G. (1992). *The twelve who survive.* London: Routledge.

Naidu, R. K. (1983, December). *A developing program of stress research.* Paper presented at the seminar on stress, anxiety and mental health, Allahabad, India.

Nauck, B., & Kohlmann, A. (1999). Kinship as social capital: Network relationships in Turkish migrant families. In R. Richter & S. Supper (Eds.), *New qualities of the life course: Intercultural aspects* (pp. 199–218). Würzburg, Germany: Ergon.

Neff, K. (2003). Understanding how universal goals of independence and interdependence are manifested within particular cultural contexts. *Human Development, 46,* 312–318.

Neisser, U., Boodoo, G., Bouchard, T. J., Jr., Boykin, A. W., Brody, N., Ceci, S. J., et al. (1996). Intelligence: Knowns and unknowns. *American Psychologist, 51,* 77–101.

Neki, J. S. (1976). An examination of the cultural relativism of dependence as a dynamic of social and therapeutic relationships. *British Journal of Medical Psychology, 49,* 1–10.

Neubauer, G., & Hurrelmann, K. (1995). Introduction: Comments on the individualization theorem. In G. Neubauer & K. Hurrelmann (Eds.), *Individualization in childhood and adolescence* (pp. 1–12). Berlin: deGruyter.

Nijsten, C. C. (2006). Coming from the East: Child rearing in Turkish families. In M. Dekovi , T. Pels, & S. Model (Eds.), *Unity and diversity in child rearing: Family life in a multicultural society* (pp. 25–57). Ceredigion, England: Edwin Mellen Press.

Nikapota, A. D. (1990). *Case study for Sri Lanka—child development in primary care.* Paper prepared for UNICEF and Ministry of Health, Sri Lanka, and presented to the Innocenti Technical Workshop on Psychosocial Development, Florence, Italy.

Noom, M. (1999). *Adolescent autonomy: Characteristics and correlates.* Delft, Netherlands: Eburon.

Novikoff, A. B. (1945) The concept of integrative levels of biology. *Science, 62,* 209–215.

Nsamenang, A. B. (1992). *Human development in cultural context: A Third World perspective.* Newbury Park, CA: Sage.

Nsamenang, A. B. (1993). Psychology in Sub-Saharan Africa. *Psychology and Developing Societies, 5,* 171–184.

Nsamenang, A. B., & Lamb, M. E. (1994). Socialization of Nso children in the Bamenda grassfields of Northwest Cameroon. In P. M. Greenfield & R. R. Cocking (Eds.), *Cross-cultural roots of minority child development* (pp. 133–146). Hillsdale, NJ: Lawrence Erlbaum Associates.

Nucci, L., Saxe, G., & Turiel, E. (Eds.). (2000). *Culture, thought, and development.* Mahwah, NJ: Lawrence Erlbaum Associates.

Nunes, T. (1993). Psychology in Latin America: The case of Brazil. *Psychology and Developing Societies, 5,* 123–134.

Nunes, T. (2005). What we learn in school: The socialization of cognition. *International Society for the Study of Behavioural Development Bulletin, 1,* 47.

Nunes, T., Schliemann, A. D., & Carraher, D. W. (1993). *Street mathematics and school mathematics.* New York: Cambridge University Press.

Obermeyer, I. (1973). *The relationship between moral development and role-taking during the years 10 to 20.* Unpublished master's thesis, American University, Beirut, Lebanon.

Ochs, E., & Schieffelin, B. B. (1984). Language acquisition and socialization: Three developmental stories and their implications. In R. Schweder & R. LeVine (Eds.), *Culture and its acquisition.* Chicago: University of Chicago Press.

Ogbu, J. U. (1990). Cultural model, identity, and literacy. In J. W. Stigler, R. A. Shweder, & G. Herdt (Eds.), *Cultural psychology: Essays on comparative human development* (pp. 520–541). Cambridge, England: Cambridge University Press.

Ohbuchi, K., Fukushima, O., & Tedeschi, J. T. (1999). Cultural values in conflict management: Goal orientation, goal attainment, and tactical decision, *Journal of Cross-Cultural Psychology, 30,* 51–71.

Okagaki, L., & Sternberg, R. J. (1993). Parental beliefs and children's school performance. *Child Development, 64,* 36–56.

Okman, F. (1982). *The determinants of cognitive style: An investigation on adolescents* [in Turkish]. Unpublished thesis, Bo aziçi University, Istanbul, Turkey.

Oloko, B. A. (1994). Children's street work in urban Nigeria: Dilemma of modernizing tradition. In P. M. Greenfield & R. R. Cocking (Eds.), *Cross-cultural roots of minority child development* (pp. 97–224). Hillsdale, NJ: Lawrence Erlbaum Associates.

Olson, E. (1982). Duofocal family structure and an alternative model of husband–wife relationship. In Ç. Kağitçibaşi (Ed.), *Sex roles, family and community in Turkey* (pp. 33–72). Bloomington: Indiana University Press.

Oosterwegel, M. W., & Vollebergh, A. (2002). Parental and peer attachment and identity in adolescence. *Journal of Adolescence, 25,* 93–106.

Orme, N. (2001). *Medieval children.* New Haven, CT: Yale University Press.

Osterweil, Z., & Nagano, K. N. (1991). Maternal views on autonomy: Japan and Israel. *Journal of Cross-Cultural Psychology, 22,* 363–375.

Oyserman, D., Kemmelmeier, M., & Coon, H. (2002a). Cultural psychology, a new look: Reply to Bond (2002), Fiske (2002), Kitayama (2002), and Miller (2002). *Psychological Bulletin, 128,* 110–117.

Oyserman, D., Kemmelmeier, M., & Coon, H. (2002b). Rethinking individualism and collectivism: Evaluation of theoretical assumptions and meta-analyses. *Psychological Bulletin, 128,* 3–72.

Padilla, A. M. (Ed.). (1995). *Hispanic psychology: Critical issues in theory and research.* Thousand Oaks, CA: Sage.

Padilla, E. (2000). In retrospect: The "we feeling" among Puerto Ricans. *Cento Journal, 12,* 96–115.

Pandey, J. (Ed.). (1988). *Psychology in India: The state-of-the-art* (Vols. 1–3). New Delhi, India: Sage.

Panel (1973a). The experience of separation-individuation in infancy and its reverbarations through the course of life: 1. Infancy and childhood. *Journal of the American Psychoanalytic Association, 21,* 135–154.

Panel. (1973b). The experience of separation-individuation in infancy and its reverbarations through the course of life: 2. Adolescence and maturity. *Journal of the American Psychoanalytic Association, 21,* 155–167.

Papoušek, H., & Papoušek, M. (1991). Innate and cultural guidance of infants' integrative competencies: China, the United States, and Germany. In M. H. Bornstein (Ed.), *Cultural approaches to parenting* (pp. 23–44). Hillsdale, NJ: Lawrence Erlbaum Associates.

Papoušek, H., & Papoušek, M. (2002). Intuitive parenting. In M. H. Bornstein (Ed.), *Handbook of parenting: Vol. 2. Biology and ecology of parenting* (pp. 23–44). Mahwah NJ: Lawrence Erlbaum Associates.

Patterson, G. R., & Dishion, T. J. (1988) Multilevel family process models: Traits, interactions, and relationships. In R. A. Hinde & J. Hinde (Eds.), *Relationships within families* (pp. 283–310). Oxford, England: Clarendon.

Pawlik, K., & Rosenzweig, M. R. (Eds.). (2000). *International handbook of psychology.* London: Sage.

Peabody, D. (1985). *National characteristics.* Cambridge, England: Cambridge University Press.

Peach, C. (2002). Social geography: New religions and ethnoburbs—contrasts with cultural geography. *Progress in Human Geography, 26,* 252–260.

Pepitone, A. (1987). The role of culture in theories of social psychology. In Ç. Kağitçibaşi (Ed.), *Growth and progress in cross-cultural psychology* (pp. 12–22). Lisse, Netherlands: Swets & Zeitlinger.

Peralta de Mendoza, O. A., & Irice, R. A. (1995). Developmental changes and socioeconomic differences in mother–infant picture book reading. *European Journal of Psychology of Education, 10,* 261–272.

Perez, W., & Padilla, A. M. (2000). Cultural orientation across three generations of Hispanic students. *Hispanic Journal of Behavioral Psychology, 22,* 390–398.

Peristiany, J. C. (1976). *Mediterranean family structures.* London: Cambridge University Press.

Pettigrew, T. F. (1958). Personality and sociocultural factors and intergroup attitudes: A cross-national comparison. *Journal of Conflict Resolution, 2,* 29–42.

Pettigrew, T. F. (1959). Regional differences in anti-Negro prejudice. *Journal of Abnormal and Social Psychology, 59,* 28–36.

Pettigrew, T. F. (1979). The ultimate attribution error: Extending Allport's cognitive analysis of prejudice. *Personality and Social Psychology Bulletin, 5,* 461–476.

Pettigrew, T. F., & Meertens, R. W. (1995). Subtle and blatant prejudice in Western Europe. *European Journal of Social Psychology, 25,* 57–75.

Phalet, K., & Claeys, W. (1993). A comparative study of Turkish and Belgian youth. *Journal of Cross-Cultural Psychology, 24,* 319–343.

Phalet, K., & Schonpflug, U. (2001). Intergenerational transmission of collectivism and achievement values in two acculturation contexts: The case of Turkish families in Germany and Turkish and Moroccan families in the Netherlands. *Journal of Cross-Cultural Psychology, 32,* 186–201.

Phalet, K., & Swyngedouw, M. (2004). A cross-cultural analysis of immigrant and host acculturation and value orientations. In H. Vinken, G. Soeters, & P. Ester (Eds.), *Comparing cultures* (pp. 183–212). Leiden, Netherlands: Brill.

Phillips, D. A. (1991). With a little help: Children in poverty and child care. In A. C. Huston (Ed.), *Children in poverty: Child development and public policy* (pp. 158–189). Cambridge, England: Cambridge University Press.

Phillips, D. A. (2004, November). *Early experience and the developing brain.* Paper presented at the International Step by Step Association Conference, Budapest, Hungary.

Phinney, J. S. (2003). What is developmental about immigration? *International Society for the Study of Behavioural Development Newsletter, 2*(4), 14–15.

Piaget, J. (1948). *The moral judgment of the child.* Glencloe, IL: The Free Press.

Plomin, R. (1989). Environment and genes: determinants of behavior. *American Psychologist, 44,* 105–111.

Podmore, V. N., & St. George, R. (1986). New Zealand Maori and European mothers and their 3-year-old children: Interactive behaviors in pre-school settings. *Journal of Applied Developmental Psychology, 7,* 373–382.

Pollitt, E., & Metallinos-Katsaras, E. (1990). Iron deficiency and behavior: Constructs, methods and validity of the findings. In R. Wurtman & J. Wurtman (Eds.), *Nutrition and the brain: Vol. 8. Behavioral effects of metals, and their biochemical mechanisms* (pp. 101–146). New York: Raven.

Pollitt, R., Gorman, K. S., Engle, P. L., Martorell, R., & Rivera, J. (1993). Early supplementary feeding and cognition. *Monographs of the Society for Research in Child Development, 58.*

Pomerlau, A., Malcuit, G., & Sabatier, C. (1991). Child-rearing practices and parental beliefs in three cultural groups of Montreal: Quebeçois, Vietnamese, Haitian. In M. Bornstein (Ed.), *Cultural approaches to parenting* (pp. 56–68). London: Lawrence Erlbaum Associates.

Poortinga, Y. H. (1992). Towards a conceptualization of culture for psychology. In S. Iwawaki, Y. Kashima, & K. Leung (Eds.), *Innovations in cross-cultural psychology* (pp. 3–17). Lisse, Netherlands: Swets & Zeitlinger.

Poortinga, Y. H., van de Vijver, F. J. R., Joe, R. C., & van de Koppel, J. M. H. (1987). Peeling the onion called culture: A sypnosis. In Ç. Kağitçibaşi (Ed.), *Growth and progress in cross-cultural psychology* (pp. 22–34). Lisse, Netherlands: Swets & Zeitlinger.

Posada, G., Jacobs, A., Richmond, M. K., Carbonell, O. A., Alzate, G., Bustamante, M. R., et al. (2002). Maternal caregiving and infant security in two cultures. *Developmental Psychology, 38,* 67–78.

Price-Williams, D. (1980). Toward the idea of a cultural psychology: A superordinate theme for study. *Journal of Cross-Cultural Psychology, 11,* 75–88.

Quintana, S. M., & Kerr, J. (1993). Relational needs in late adolescent separation-individuation. *Journal of Counseling & Development, 71,* 349–354.

Raeff, C. (1997). Individuals in relationships: Cultural values, children's social interactions, and the development of an American individualistic self. *Developmental Review, 17,* 205–238.

Raeff, C. (2004). Within-culture complexities: Multifaceted and interrelated autonomy and connectedness characteristics in late adolescent selves. In M. F. Mascolo & J. Li (Eds.), *Culture and developing selves: Beyond dichotomization* (pp. 61–79). San Francisco: Jossey-Bass.

Ramey, C. T., Campbell, F. A., Burchinal, M., Skinner, M. L., Gardner, D. M., & Ramey, S. L. (2000). Persistent effects of early childhood education on high-risk children and their mothers. *Applied Developmental Science, 4,* 2–14.

Ramey, C. T., & Ramey, S. L.(1998). Early intervention and early experience. *American Psychologist, 53,* 109–120.

Rank, O. (1929). *The trauma of birth.* New York: Knopf.

Rank, O. (1945). *Will therapy and truth and reality.* New York: Knopf.

Razí, Z. (1993). The myth of the immutable English family. *Past & Present: A Journal of Historical Studies, 140,* 3–44.

Realo, A., Koido, K., Ceulemans, E., & Allik, J. (2002). Three components of individualism. *European Journal of Personality, 16,* 163–184.

Redfield, R., Linton, R., & Herskovits, M. J. (1936). Memorandum on the study of acculturation. *American Anthropologist, 38,* 149–52.

Reynolds, A. J. (2004). Research on early childhood interventions in the confirmatory mode. *Children and Youth Services Review, 26,* 15–38.

Reynolds, A. J., Chang, H., & Temple, J. A. (1998). Early childhood intervention and juvenile delinquency. *Evaluation Review, 22,* 341–373.

Reynolds, A. J., & Ou, S.-R. (2004). Alterable predictors of child well-being in the Chicago Longitudinal Study. *Children and Youth Services Review, 26,* 1–14.

Reynolds, A. J., Wang, M. C., & Walberg, H. J. (2003). *Early childhood programs for a new century.* Washington, DC: Child Welfare League of America.

Rhee, E., Uleman, J. S., & Lee, H. K. (1996). Variations in collectivism and individualism by ingroup and culture: Confirmatory factor analyses. *Journal of Personality and Social Psychology, 71,* 1037–1054.

Rogoff, B. (1990). *Apprenticeship in thinking: Cognitive development in social context.* New York: Oxford University Press.

Rogoff, B. (2003). *The cultural nature of human development.* New York: Oxford University Press.

Rogoff, B., Ellis, S., & Gardner, W. (1984). Adjustment of adult–child instruction according to child's age and task. *Developmental Psychology, 20,* 193–199.

Rogoff, B., Gauvain, M., & Ellis, S. (1984). Development viewed in its cultural context. In M. H. Bornstein & M. E. Lamb (Eds.), *Developmental psychology: An advanced textbook* (pp. 533–571). London: Lawrence Erlbaum Associates.

Rogoff, B., & Lave, L. (1984). *Everyday cognition: Its development in social context.* Cambridge, MA: Harvard University Press.

Rogoff, B., Mistry, J., Göncü, A., & Mosier, C. (1991). Cultural variation in the role relations of toddlers and their families. In M. H. Bornstein (Ed.), *Cultural approaches to parenting* (pp. 173–183). London: Lawrence Erlbaum Associates.

Rogoff, B., & Morelli, G. (1989). Perspectives on children's development from cultural psychology. *American Psychologist, 44*(2), 343–348.

Rohner, R. (1980). *Handbook for the study of parental acceptance and rejection* (3rd ed.) Storrs: University of Connecticut.

Rohner, R. (1984). Toward a conception of culture for cross-cultural psychology. *Journal of Cross-Cultural Psychology, 15, 111–138.*

Rohner, R. P., & Pettengill, S. M. (1985). Perceived parental acceptance-rejection and parental control among Korean adolescents. *Child Development, 56,* 524–528.

Rohner, R. P., & Rohner, E. C. (1978). Unpublished research data. Storrs: Center for the Study of Parental Acceptance and Rejection, University of Connecticut.

Roland, A. (1988). *In search of self in India and Japan.* Princeton, NJ: Princeton University Press.

Roopnarine, J. L., & Talukder, E. (1990). Characteristics of holding, patterns of play, and social behaviors between parents and infants in New Delhi, India. *Developmental Psychology, 26,* 667–673.

Rosen, B. C. (1962). Socialization and achievement motivation in Brazil. *American Sociological Review, 27,* 612–624.

Rosenberg, B. G., & Jing, Q. (1996). A revolution in family life: The political and social structural impact of China's one child policy. *Journal of Social Issues, 53,* 51–69.

Rosenberg, M. J., & Hovland, C. I. (1960). Cognitive, affective and behavioral components of attitudes. In M. J. Rosenberg et al. (Eds.), *Attitude organization and change* (pp. 1–14). New Haven, CT: Yale University Press.

Rosenthal, R., & Jacobson, L. (1968). *Pygmalion in the classroom: Teacher expectation and pupils' intellectual development.* New York: Holt, Rinehart & Winston.

Rotenberg, M. (1977). Alienating-individualism and reciprocal-individualism: A cross-cultural conceptualisation. *Journal of Humanistic Psychology, 3,* 3–17.

Rothbaum, F., & Morelli, G. (2005). Attachment and culture: Bridging relativism and universalism. In W. Friedlmeier, P. Chakkarath, & B. Schwarz (Eds.), *Culture and human development: The importance of cross-cultural research for the social sciences* (pp. 99–124). New York: Psychology Press.

Rothbaum, F., Pott, M., Azuma, H., Miyake, K., & Weisz, J. (2000). The development of close relationships in Japan and the United States: Paths of symbiotic harmony and generative tension. *Child Development, 71,* 1121–1142.

Rothbaum, F., & Trommsdorff, G. (2007). Do roots and wings complement or oppose one another? The socialization of relatedness and autonomy in cultural context. In J. Grusec & P. Hastings (Eds.), *Handbook of socialization: Theory and Research* (pp. 461–489). New York: Guilford Press.

Rothbaum, F., Weisz, J., Pott, M., Miyake, K., & Morelli, G. (2000b). Attachment and culture: Security in the United States and Japan. *American Psychologist, 55,* 1093–1104.

Rotter, J. B. (1966). Generalized expectancies for internal versus external control of reinforcement. *Psychological Monographs, 80*(Whole No. 609), 1–28.

Rotter, J. B. (1990). Internal versus external control of reinforcement: A case history of a variable. *American Psychologist, 45,* 489–493.

Rudy, D., & Grusec, J. E. (2001). Correlates of authoritarian parenting in individualist and collectivist cultures and implications for understanding the transmission of values. *Journal of Cross-Cultural Psychology, 32,* 202–212.

Rutter, M., & the English and Romanian Adoptees (ERA) study team. (1999). Developmental catch-up, and deficit, following adoption after severe global early privation. In S. J. Ceci & W. M. Williams (Eds.), *The nature–nurture debate: The essential readings* (Vol. 8, pp. 108–135). London: Blackwell.

Ryan, R. M., & Deci, E. L. (2000). Self-determination theory and the facilitation of intrinsic motivation, social development, and well-being. *American Psychologist, 55,* 68–78.

Ryan, R. M., Deci, E. L., & Grolnick, W. S. (1995). Autonomy, relatedness, and the self: Their relation to development and psychopathology. In D. Cicchetti & D. J. Cohen. (Eds.), *Developmental psychopathology* (pp. 618–655). New York: Wiley.

Ryan, R. M., & Lynch, J. H. (1989). Emotional autonomy versus detachment: Revisiting the vicissitudes of adolescence and young adulthood. *Child Development, 60,* 340–356.

Saal, C. D. (1987). Alternative forms of living and housing. In L. Shamgar-Handelman & R. Palomba (Eds.), *Alternative patterns of family life in modern societies.* Rome: Collana Monografie.

Sabatier, C. (1986). Le mere et son bebe. Variations culturelles: Analyse critique de la litterature [Mother and her baby: Cultural variations: Critical analysis of literature]. *Journal of International Psychology, 21,* 513–533.

Sabatier, C., & Lannegrand-Willems, L. (2005). Transmission of family values and attachment: A French three-generation study. *Applied Psychology: An International Review, 54,* 356–378.

Sabogal, F., Marín, G., Otero-Sabogal, R., Marín, B. V., & Perez-Stable, E. J. (1987). Hispanic familism and acculturation: What changes and what doesn't? *Hispanic Journal of Behavioral Sciences, 9,* 397–412.

Sagi, A., Lamb, M. E., Lewkowicz, K. S., Shoham, R., Dvir, R., & Estes, D. (1985). Security of infant–mother, –father, and metapelet attachments among kibbutz reared Israeli children. In I. Bretherton & E. Waters (Eds.), *Growing point in attachment theory. Monographs of the Society for Research in Child Development, 50*(1–2), (Serial No. 209).

Sam, D. L. (2006). Adaptation of children and adolescents with immigrant background: Acculturation or development? In M. H. Bornstein & L. R. Cote (Eds.), *Acculturation and parent–child relationships: Measurement and development* (pp. 97–111). Mahwah, NJ: Lawrence Erlbaum Associates.

Sam, D. L., Kosic, A. & Oppedal, B. (2003). Where is "development" in acculturation theories? *International Society for the Study of Behavioural Development Newsletter, 2*(44), 4–7.

Sam, D., Peltzer, K., & Mayer, B. (2005). The changing values of children and preferences regarding family size in South Africa. *Applied Psychology: An International Review, 54,* 355–377.

Sameroff, A. J., & Fiese, B. H. (1992). Family representations of development. In I. E. Sigel, A. V. McGillicuddy-DeLisi, & J. J. Goodnow (Eds.), *Parental belief systems* (pp. 347–369). Hillsdale, NJ: Lawrence Erlbaum Associates.

Sameroff, A. J., Seifer, R., Barocas, B., Zax, M., & Greenspan, S. (1987). IQ scores of 4-year-old children: Social environmental risk factors. *Pediatrics, 79,* 343–350.

Sampson, E. E. (1977). Psychology and the American ideal. *Journal of Personality and Social Psychology, 35,* 767–782.

Sampson, E. E. (1987). Individuation and domination: Undermining the social bond. In Ç. Kağitçibaşi (Ed.), *Growth and progress in cross-cultural psychology* (pp. 84–93). Lisse, Netherlands: Swets & Zeitlinger.

Sampson, E. E. (1988). The debate on individualism: Indigenious psychologies of the individual and their role in personal and societal functioning. *American Psychologist, 43,* 15–22.

Sampson, E. E. (1989). The challenge of social change for psychology: Globalization and psychology's theory of the person. *American Psychologist, 44,* 914–921.

Sarason, S. B. (1981). *Psychology misdirected.* New York: The Free Press.

Sarason, S. B. (1988). *The making of an American psychologist: An autobiography.* San Francisco: Jossey-Bass.

Saraswathi, T. S. (2003). *Cross-cultural perspectives in human development: Theory, research and applications.* New Delhi, India: Sage.

Saraswathi, T. S., & Dutta, R. (1987). *Developmental psychology in India, 1975–1986: An annotated bibliography.* New Delhi, India: Sage.

Saraswathi, T. S., & Ganapathy, H. (2002). Indian parents: Ethnotheories as reflections of the Hindu scheme of child and human development. In H. Keller, Y. H.

Poortinga, & A. Schölmerich (Eds.), *Between biology and culture: Perspectives on onthogenetic development* (pp. 79–88). Cambridge, England: Cambridge University Press.

Saraswathi, T. S., & Kaur, B. (1993). *Human development and family studies in India*. New Delhi, India: Sage.

Savasir, I., & Sahin, N. (1988). *Weschler çocuk zekâ ölçegi (WISC–R)* [Weschler Intelligence Scale for Children]. Ankara, Turkey: Milli Egitim Basimevi.

Savasir, I., Sezgin, N. & Erol, N. (1992). 0–6 Yas Cocuklari icin gelisim tarama envanteri gelistirilmesi [Devising a developmental screening inventory for 0–6 year children]. *Türk Psikiyatri Dergisi, 3,* 33–38.

Saxe, G. B., & Esmonde, I. (2005). Studying cognition in flux: The case of "fu" in the social history of Oksapmin mathematics. *Mind, Culture, and Activity, 12,* 225–275.

Scarr, S. (1992). Developmental theories for the 1990s. *Child Development, 63,* 1–19.

Scarr, S., & McCartney, K. (1988). Far from home: An experimental evaluation of the mother–child home program in Bermuda. *Child Development, 59,* 531–544.

Schalk-Soekar, R. G. S., & van de Vivjer, F. J. R. (2004). Attitudes toward multiculturalism of immigrants and majority members in the Netherlands. *International Journal of Intercultural Relations,* 28, 533–550.

Schieffelin, B. B., & Eisenberg, A. R. (1984). Cultural variation in children's conversations. In R. Schiefelbusch & J. Pickar (Eds.), *The acquisition of communicative competence.* Baltimore: University Park Press.

Schimmack, U., Oishi, S., & Diener, E. (2005). Individualism: A valid and important dimension of cultural differences between nations. *Personality and Social Psychology Review, 9,* 17–31.

Schlegel, A. (2003). Modernization and changes in adolescent social life. In T. S. Saraswathi (Ed.), *Cross-cultural perspectives in human development: Theory, research and application* (pp. 236–258). New Delhi, India: Sage.

Schliemann, A., Carraher, D., & Ceci, S. (1997). Everyday cognition. In J. W. Berry, P. R. Dasen, & T. S. Saraswathi (Eds.), *Handbook of cross-cultural psychology: Vol. 2. Basic process and human development* (pp. 177–216). Boston: Allyn & Bacon.

Schmitz, M. F., & Baer, J. C. (2001). The vicissitudes of measurement: A confirmatory factor analysis of the emotional autonomy scale. *Child Development, 72,* 207–220.

Schonkoff, J. P. (2000). Science, policy and practice: Three cultures in search of a shared mission. *Child Development, 71,* 181–187.

Schorr, L. B. (1991). Effective programs for children growing up in concentrated poverty. In A. C. Huston (Ed.), *Children in poverty: Child development and public policy* (pp. 260–281). Cambridge, England: Cambridge University Press.

Schwartz, B. (2000). Self-determination: The tyranny of freedom. *American Psychologist, 55,* 79–88.

Schwartz, S. H. (1992). Universals in the content and structure of values: Theoretical advances and empirical tests in 20 countries. In M. Zanna (Ed.), *Advances in experimental social psychology* (Vol. *25,* pp. 1–65). Orlando, FL: Academic Press.

Schwartz, S. H. (1994). Beyond individualism and collectivism: New cultural dimensions of values. In U. Kim, H. C. Triandis, Ç. Kağitçibaşi, S. C. Choi, & G. Yoon (Eds.), *Individualism and collectivism: Theory, method and applications* (pp. 85–119). Thousand Oaks, CA: Sage.

Schwartz, S. H. (2004). Mapping and interpreting cultural differences around the world. In H. Vinken, J. Soeters, & P. Ester (Eds.), *Comparing cultures: Dimensions of culture in a comparative perspective* (pp. 43–73). Leiden, Netherlands: Brill.

Schwartz, S. H., & Bardi, A. (2001). Value hierarchies across cultures: Taking a similarities perspective. *Journal of Cross-Cultural Psychology, 32,* 268–290.

Schwartz, S. H., & Bilsky, W. (1990). Toward a theory of the universal content and structure of values: Extensions and cross-cultural replications. *Journal of Personality and Social Psychology, 58,* 878–891.

Schwartz, T. (1981). The acquisition of culture. *Ethos, 9,* 4–17.

Schweinhart, L. J., Barnes, H. V., Weikart, D. P., Barnett, W. S., & Epstein, A. S. (1994). *Significant benefits: The High/Scope Perry Preschool Study through age 27.* Ypsilanti, MI: High/Scope Press.

Schweinhart, L. J., Montie, J., Xiang, Z., Barnett, W. S., Belfield, C. R., & Nores, M. (2005). *Lifetime effects: The High/Scope Perry Preschool study through age 40* (Monographs of the High/Scope Educational Research Foundation, 14). Ypsilanti, MI: High/Scope Press.

Scott-McDonald, K. (2002). Elements of quality in home visiting programs: Three Jamaican models. In M. E. Young (Ed.), *From early childhood development to human development* (pp. 233–253). Washington, DC: World Bank.

Scribner, S., & Cole, M. (1981). *The psychology of literacy.* Cambridge, MA: Harvard University Press.

Searle, W., & Ward, C. (1990). The prediction of psychological and sociocultural adjustment during cross-cultural transitions. *International Journal of Intercultural Relations, 14,* 449–64.

Sedikides, C., Gaertner, J. & Toguchi, Y. (2003). Pan-cultural self-enhancement. *Journal of Personality and Social Psychology, 84,* 60–79.

Segall, M. H. (1983). On the search for the independent variable in cross-cultural psychology. In S. H. Irvine & J. W. Berry (Eds.), *Human assessment and cultural factors* (pp. 127–138). New York: Plenum.

Segall, M. H. (1984). More than we need to know about culture, but are afraid not to ask. *Journal of Cross-Cultural Psychology, 15,* 153–162.

Segall, M. H., Dasen, P. R., Berry, J. W., & Poortinga, Y. H. (1999). *Human behavior in global perspective. An introduction to cross-cultural psychology* (2nd ed.). Boston: Allyn & Bacon.

Seitz, V., & Provence, S. (1990). Caregiver-focused models of early intervention. In S. J. Meisels & J. P. Shonkoff (Eds.), *Handbook of early childhood intervention* (pp. 400–427). New York: Cambridge University Press.

Seitz, V., Rosenbaum, L. K., & Apfel, N. H. (1985). Effects of family support intervention: A ten-year follow-up. *Child Development, 56,* 376–391.

Selman, R. L. (1989). Fostering intimacy and autonomy. In W. Damon (Ed.), *Child development today and tomorrow* (pp. 409–436). San Francisco: Jossey-Bass.

Sen, A. K. (1999, March 14). *Investing in early childhood: Its role in development.* Keynote address presented at the annual meeting of the Board of Governors of the Inter-American Development Bank and the Inter-American Investment Corporation, Paris. Retrieved January 9, 2003, from http://www.iadb.org/sds/soc

Sénécal, M., & LeFevre, J. A. (2002). Parental involvement in the development of children's reading skill: A five-year longitudinal study. *Child Development, 73,* 445–460.

Serpell, R. (1976). *Culture's influence on behavior.* London: Methuen.

Serpell, R. (1977). Strategies for investigating intelligence in its cultural context. *Quarterly Newsletter, Institute for Comparative Human Development, 3,* 11–15.

Serpell, R. (1993). *Significance of schooling.* Cambridge, England: Cambridge University Press.

Seshadri, S., & Gopaldas, T. (1989). Impact of iron supplementation on cognitive functions in pre-school and school-aged children: The Indian experience. *American Journal of Clinical Nutrition, 50,* 675–686.

Sherif, M., Harvey, O. J., White, B. J., Hood, W., & Sherif, C. (1961). *Intergroup conflict and cooperation: The Robbers Cave experiment.* Norman: University of Oklahoma, Institute of Intergroup Relations.

Shand, N. (1985) Culture's influence in Japanese and American maternal role perception and confidence. *Psychiatry, 48,* 52–67.

Shonkoff, J. P. (2000). Science, policy, and practice: Three cultures in search of a shared mission. *Child Development, 71,* 181–187.

Shweder, R. A. (1984). Anthropology's romantic rebellion against the enlightenment, or there's more to the thinking than reason and evidence. In R. A. Shweder & R. A. LeVine (Eds.), *Culture theory: Essays on mind, self; and emotion* (pp. 1–27). Cambridge, England: Cambridge University Press.

Shweder, R. A. (1990). Cultural psychology—what is it? In J. W. Stigler, R. A. Shweder, & G. Herdt (Eds.), *Cultural psychology: Essays on comparative human development* (pp. 1–43). Cambridge, England: Cambridge University Press.

Shweder, R. A. (1991). *Thinking through cultures: Expeditions in cultural psychology.* Cambridge, MA: Harvard University Press.

Shweder, R. A., & Bourne, E. J. (1984). Does the concept of the person vary cross-culturally? In R. A. Shweder & R.A. LeVine (Eds.), *Culture theory: Essays on mind, self and emotion* (pp. 158–199). Cambridge, England: Cambridge University Press.

Shweder, R. A., Goodnow, J., Hatano, G., Le Vine, R. A., Markus, H., & Miller, P. (1998). The cultural psychology of development: One mind, many mentalities. In W. Damon (Chief Ed.) & R. M. Lerner (Vol. Ed.), *Handbook of child psychology: Vol. 1. Theoretical models of human development* (5th ed., pp. 865–923). New York: Wiley.

Shweder, R. A., & LeVine, R. (1984). *Culture theory.* Cambridge, England: Cambridge University Press.

Shweder, R. A., & Sullivan, M. A. (1993). Cultural psychology: Who needs it? *Annual Review of Psychology, 44,* 497–523.

Sigel, I. E. (1985). A conceptual analysis of beliefs. In I. E. Sigel (Ed.), *Parental belief systems* (pp. 345–371). Hillsdale, NJ: Lawrence Erlbaum Associates.

Sigel, I. E. (1992). The belief–behavior connection: A resolvable dilemma? In I. E. Sigel, A. McGillicuddy-Delisi, & J. J. Goodnow (Eds.), *Parental belief systems* (pp. 433–456). Hillsdale, NJ: Lawrence Erlbaum Associates.

Sigel, I. E., McGillicuddy-DeLisi, A., & Goodnow, J. (1992). *Parental belief systems.* Hillsdale, NJ: Lawrence Erlbaum Associates.

Sigman, M., & Wachs, T. D. (1991). Structure, continuity, and nutritional correlates of caregiver behavior patterns in Kenya and Egypt. In M. H. Bornstein (Ed.), *Cultural approaches to parenting* (pp. 123–136). Hillsdale, NJ: Lawrence Erlbaum Associates.

Silk, J. S., Morris, A.S., Kanaya, T., & Steinberg, L. (2003). Psychological control and autonomy granting: Opposite ends of a continuum or distinct constructs? *Journal of Research on Adolescence, 13,* 113–128.

Simons, R. L., Whitbeck, L. B., Conger, R. D., & Chyi, I. W. (1991). Intergenerational transmission of harsh parenting. *Developmental Psychology, 27,* 159–171.

Singelis, T. M. (1994). The measurement of independent and interdependent self-construals. *Personality and Social Psychology Bulletin, 20,* 580–591.

Singelis, T. M., Triandis, H. C., Bhawuk, D. S., & Gelfand, M. (1995). Horizontal and vertical dimensions of individualism and collectivism: A theoretical and measurement refinement. *Cross-Cultural Research, 29,* 240–275.

Singleton, R., Jr., & Kerber, K. W. (1980). Topics in social psychology: Further classroom demonstrations. *Teaching Sociology, 7,* 439–452.

Sinha, D. (1983). Cross-cultural psychology: A view from the Third World. In J. B. Deregowski, S. Dziuraviec, & R. C. Annis (Eds.), *Expiscations in cross-cultural psychology* (pp. 3–17). Lisse, Netherlands: Swets & Zeitlinger

Sinha, D. (1986). *Psychology in a Third World country: The Indian experience.* New Delhi, India: Sage.

Sinha, D. (1988). The family scenario in a developing country and its implications for mental health: The case of India. In P. R. Dasen, J. W. Berry, & N. Sartorious (Eds.), *Health and cross-cultural psychology: Toward applications* (pp. 48–70). Newbury Park, CA: Sage.

Sinha, D. (1989). Cross-cultural psychology and the process of indigenisation: A second view from the Third World. In D. M. Keats, D. M. Munro, & L. Mann (Eds.), *Heterogeneity in cross-cultural psychology* (pp. 24–40). Lisse, Netherlands: Swets & Zeitlinger.

Sinha, D. (1992). Appropriate indigenous psychology in India: A search for new identity. In S. Iwawaki, Y. Kashima, & K. Leung (Eds.), *Innovations in cross-cultural psychology* (pp. 38–48). Lisse, Netherlands: Swets & Zeitlinger.

Sinha, D. (1997). Indigenizing psychology. In J. W. Berry, Y. P. Poortinga, J. Pandey, & H. Needham (Eds.). *Handbook of cross-cultural psychology: Vol. 1. Theory and method* (2nd ed., pp. 129–169). Needham Heights, MA: Allyn & Bacon.

Sinha, D., & Kao, H. S. R. (1988). *Social values and development: Asian perspectives.* Newbury Park, CA: Sage.

Sinha, D., & Tripathi, R. C. (1994). Individualism in a collectivist culture: A case of coexistence of opposites. In U. Kim, H. C. Triandis, Ç. Kağitçibaşi, S.-C. Choi, & G. Yoon (Eds.), *Individualism and collectivism: Theory, method and applications* (pp. 123–138). Newbury Park, CA: Sage.

Sinha, J. B. P. (1980). *The nurturant task leader.* New Delhi, India: Concept.

Sinha, J. B. P. (1985). Collectivism, social energy, and development in India. In I. R. Lagunes & Y. H. Poortinga (Eds.), *From a different perspective: Studies of behavior across cultures* (pp. 120–135). Lisse, Netherlands: Swets & Zeitlinger.

Sinha, J. B. P. (1993). The bulk and the front of psychology in India. *Psychology and Developing Societies, 5,* 135–150.

Slaughter, D. T. (1983). Early intervention and its effects upon maternal and child development. *Monographs of the Society for Research in Child Development, 48.*

Slaughter, D. T. (1988). Black children, schooling, and educational interventions. In D. T. Slaughter (Ed.). *Black children and poverty: A developmental perspective* (pp. 109–116). San Francisco: Jossey-Bass.

Slobin, D. I. (1972). Children and language: They learn the same way all around the world. *Psychology Today, 6,* 71–74, 82.

Smetana, J., & Gaines, C. (1999). Adolescent–parent conflict in middle class African American families. *Child Development, 70,* 1447–1463.

Smilansky, M. (1979). *Priorities in education: Preschool evidence and conclusions* (World Bank Staff Working Paper No. 323). Washington, DC: World Bank.

Smith, M. B. (1968). Competence and socialization. In J. A. Clausen (Ed.), *Socialization and society* (pp. 270–320). Boston: Little, Brown.

Smith, M. B. (1978). Perspectives on selfhood. *American Psychologist, 33,* 1053–1063.

Smith, M. B. (1990). Psychology in the public interest: What have we done? What can we do? *American Psychologist, 45,* 530–536.

Smith, M. B. (1991). *Values, self, and society.* New Brunswick, NJ: Transaction.

Smith, M. B. (1993). *Selfhood at risk: Post-modern perils and the perils of post-modernism.* Murray Award Address at the meeting of the American Psychological Association, Toronto, Ontario.

Smith, M. B. (1994). Selfhood at risk: Post-modern perils and the perils of post-modernism. *American Psychologist, 49,* 405–411.

Smith, M. B. (2003). *For a significant social psychology: The collected writings of M. Brewster Smith.* New York: New York University Press.

Smith, P. B., Bond, M. H., & Kağitçibaşi, Ç. (2006). *Understanding social psychology across cultures.* London: Sage.

Smith, P. B., Dugan, S., & Trompenaars, F. (1996). National culture and the values of organizational employees. *Journal of Cross-Cultural Psychology, 27,* 231–64.

Smith, P. B., & Schwartz, S. H. (1997). Values. In J. W. Berry, M. H. Segall, & Ç. Kağitçibaşi (Eds.), *Handbook of cross-cultural psychology* (2nd ed., Vol. 3, pp. 77–108). Needham Heights, MA: Allyn & Bacon.

Snow, C. E. (1991). The theoretical basis for relationships between language and literacy in development. *Journal of Research in Childhood Education, 6,* 5–10.

Snow, C. E. (1993). Linguistic development as related to literacy. In L. Eldering & P. Leseman (Eds.), *Early intervention and culture* (pp. 133–148). Delft, Netherlands: UNESCO.

Sockalingam, S., Zeitlin, M., & Satoto, C. N. (1990). *Study to encourage positive indigenous caretaking behaviour in improving child nutrition and health.* A paper available from the Consultative Group on Early Child Care and Development, New York.

Solomon, M. (1993). Transmission of cultural goals: Social network influences on infant socialization. In J. Demick, K. Bursik, & R. DiBiase (Eds.), *Parental development* (pp. 135–156). Hillsdale, NJ: Lawrence Erlbaum Associates.

Spence, J. T. (1985). Achievement American style. *American Psychologist, 12,* 1285–1295.

Spielberger, C. (2004). *Encyclopedia of applied psychology.* San Diego, CA: Academic Press.

Staub, S., & Green, P. (Eds.). (1992). *Psychology and social responsibility: Facing global challenges.* New York: New York University Press.

Steele, C. M., & Aronson, J. (1995). Stereotype threat and the intellectual test performance of African Americans. *Journal of Personality and Social Psychology, 69,* 797–811.

Steinberg, L., Elmen, J. D., & Mounts, N. S. (1989). Authoritative parenting, psychosocial maturity, and academic success among adolescents. *Child Development, 60,* 1424–1436.

Steinberg, L., & Silverberg, S. B. (1986). The vicissitudes of autonomy in early adolescence. *Child Development, 57,* 841–851.

Stephan, W. G., Stephan, C. W., Abalakina, M., Ageyev, V., Blanco, A., Bond, M., et al. (1996). Distinctiveness effects in intergroup perceptions: An international study. In H. Grad, A. Blanco, & J. Georgas (Eds.), *Key issues in cross-cultural psychology* (pp. 298–308). Lisse, Netherlands: Swets & Zeitlinger.

Stevens, J. H. (1988). Social support, locus of control and parenting in three low-income groups of mothers: Black teenagers, Black adults, and White adults. *Child Development, 59,* 635–642.

Stevenson, H., Azuma, H., & Hakuta, K. (Eds.) (1986). *Child development and education in Japan.* New York: Freeman.

Stewart, S. M., Bond, M. H., Deeds, O., & Chung, S. F. (1999). Intergenerational patterns of values and autonomy expectations in cultures of relatedness and separateness. *Journal of Cross-Cultural Psychology, 30,* 575–593.

Stigler, J. W., Shweder, R. A., & Herdt, G. (1990). *Cultural psychology.* Cambridge, England: Cambridge University Press.

Stone, J., & Cooper, J. (2001). A self-standards model of cognitive dissonance. *Journal of Experimental Social Psychology, 37,* 228–243.

Stonequist, E.V. (1937). *The marginal man: A study in personality and culture conflict.* New York: Scribner's.

Suckow, J. (2005). The value of children among Jews and Muslims in Israel: Methods and results from the VOC field study. In G. Trommsdorff & B. Nauck (Eds.), *The value of children in cross-cultural perspective: Case studies from eight societies* (pp. 121–142). Berlin: Pabst Science.

Suedfeld, P., & Tetlock, P. E. (Eds.). (1992). Psychologists as policy advocates: The roots of controversy. In P. Suedfeld & P. E. Tetlock (Eds.), *Psychology and social policy* (pp. 1–30). New York: Hemisphere.

Suina, J. H., & Smolkin, L. B. (1994). From natal culture to school culture to dominant society culture: Supporting transitions for Pueblo Indian students. In P. M. Greenfield & R. R. Cocking (Eds.), *Cross-cultural roots of minority child development* (pp. 115–130). Hillsdale, NJ: Lawrence Erlbaum Associates.

Suizzo, M.-A. (2002). French parents' cultural models and childrearing beliefs. *International Journal of Behavioral Development, 26,* 297–307.

Sun, L. K. (1991). Contemporary Chinese culture: Structure and emotionality. *The Australian Journal of Chinese Affairs, 26,* 1–41.

Suomi, S. J. (2000). A biobehavioral perspective on developmental psychopathology. In A. J. Sameroff, M. Lewis, & S. M. Miller (Eds.), *Handbook of developmental psychopathology* (pp. 237–256). New York: Kluwer Academic.

Super, C. M., & Harkness, S. (1986). The developmental niche: A conceptualization at the interface of child and culture. *International Journal of Behavioral Development, 9,* 545–570.

Super, C. M., & Harkness, S. (1994). The developmental niche. In W. J. Lonner & R. Malpass (Eds.), *Psychology and culture* (pp. 95–99). Boston: Allyn & Bacon.

Super, C. M., & Harkness, S. (1997). The cultural structuring of child development. In J. W. Berry, P. R. Dasen, & T. S. Saraswathi (Eds.), *Handbook of cross-cultural psychology* (2nd ed.,Vol. 2, pp. 1–39). Boston: Allyn & Bacon.

Super, C. M,. & Harkness, S. (1999). The environment as culture in developmental research. In S. L. Friedman & T. D. Wachs (Eds.), *Measuring environment across the life span.* Washington, DC: American Psychological Association.

Super, C. M., & Harkness, S. (2002). Culture structures the environment for development. *Human Development, 45,* 270–274.

Suvannathat, C., Bhanthumnavin, D., Bhuapirom, L., & Keats, D. M. (1985). *Handbook of Asian child develapment and child rearing practices.* Bangkok, Thailand: Behavioral Science Research Institute.

Suzuki, T. (1984). Ways of life and social milieus in Japan and the United States: A comparative study. *Behaviormetrika, 15,* 77–108.

Sweet, M. A., & Appelbaum, M. (2004). Is home visiting an effective strategy? *Child Development, 75,* 1435–1456.

Szapocznik, J., & Kurtines, W. M. (1993). Family psychology and cultural diversity. *American Psychologist, 48,* 400–407.

Tajfel, H., & Turner, J. C. (1979). An integrative theory of intergroup conflict. In W. G. Austin & S. Worchel (Eds.), *The social psychology of intergroup relations.* Monterey, CA: Brooks-Cole.

Takano, Y., & Osaka, E. (1999). An unsupported common view: Comparing Japan and the U.S. on individualism/collectivism. *Asian Journal of Social Psychology, 2,* 311–341.

Tamis-LeMonda, C. S., Bornstein, M. H., & Baumwell, L. (1996). Responsive parenting in the second year: Specific influences on children's language and play. *Early Development & Parenting, 5,* 173–183.

Tanon, F. (1994). *A cultural view on planning: The case of weaving in Ivory Coast.* Tilburg, Netherlands: Tilburg University Press.

Taylor, C. (1989). *Sources of the self: The making of the modern identity.* Cambridge, MA: Harvard University Press.

Taylor, R. D., & Roberts, D. (1995). Kinship support and maternal and adolescent well-being in economically disadvantaged African-American families. *Child Development, 66,* 1585–1597.

Teasdale, G. R., Teasdale, J.I. (1992). Culture and curriculum: Dilemmas in the schooling of Australian Aboriginal children. In S. Iwawaki, Y. Kashima, &

K. Leung (Eds.), *Innovations in cross-cultural psychology* (pp. 442–457). Lisse, Netherlands: Swets & Zeitlinger.

Thadani, V. (1978). The logic of sentiment: The family and social change. *Population and Development Review, 4,* 457–499.

Thomas, W., & Znaniecki, F. (1918–1919). *The Polish peasant in Europe and America* (5 vols.). Boston: Badger.

Thomas, W., & Znaniecki, F. (1927). *The Polish peasant in Europe and America.* New York: Knopf.

Thompson, R. A., & Nelson, C. A. (2001). Developmental science and the media: Early brain development. *American Psychologist, 56,* 5–15.

Thorton, A. (1984). Modernization and family change. In *Social change and family policies* Proceedings of the 20th International CFR Seminar, Melbourne: Australian Institute of Family Studies.

Thorton, A., & Fricke, T. E. (1987). Social change and the family: Comparative perspectives from the West, China, and South Asia. *Sociological Forum, 2,* 746–779.

Tizard, B. (1991). Working mothers and the care of young children. In M. Woodhead, P. Light, & R. Caar (Eds.), *Growing up in a changing society* (pp. 61–77). London: Routledge.

Tönnies, F. (1957). *Community and society.* (C. P. Loomis, Trans.). East Lansing: Michigan State University Press.

Triandis, H. C. (1980) Reflections on trends in cross-cultural research. *Journal of Cross-Cultural Psychology, 11,* 35–58.

Triandis, H. C. (1988). Collectivism and individualism: A reconceptualization of a basic concept in cross-cultural psychology. In G. K. Verma & C. Bagley (Eds.), *Personality, attitudes, and cognitions* (pp. 60–95). London: Macmillan.

Triandis, H. C. (1989). The self and social behavior in differing cultural contexts. *Psychological Review, 96,* 506–520.

Triandis, H. C. (1990). Cross-cultural studies of individualism and collectivism. In J. J. Berman (Ed.), *Cross-cultural perspectives: Nebraska Symposium on Motivation* (pp. 41–134). Lincoln: University of Nebraska Press.

Triandis, H. C. (1994). *Culture and social behavior.* New York: McGraw-Hill.

Triandis, H. C. (1995). *Individualism and collectivism.* Boulder, CO: Westview Press.

Triandis, H. C., Bontempo, R., Villareal, M. J., Asai, M., & Lucca, N. (1988). Individualism and collectivism: Cross-cultural perspectives on self-ingroup relationships. *Journal of Personality and Social Psychology, 54,* 323–338.

Triandis, H. C., Leung, K., Villareal, M. V., & Clack, F. L. (1985). Allocentric versus idiocentric tendencies: Convergent and discriminant validation. *Journal of Research in Personality, 19,* 395–415.

Triandis, H. C., McCusker, C., & Hui, C. H. (1990). Multimethod probes of individualism and collectivism. *Journal of Personality and Social Psychology, 59,* 1006–1020.

Triandis, H. C., & Suh, E. M. (2002). Cultural influences on personality. *Annual Review of Personality, 53,* 133–160.

Tripathi, R. C. (1988). Aligning development to values in India. In D. Sinha & H. S. R. Kao (Eds.), *Social values and development* (pp. 315–333). Newbury Park, CA: Sage.

Trommsdorf, G. (1985). Some comparative aspects of socialization in Japan and Germany. In I. R. Lagunes & Y. H. Poortinga (Eds.), *From a different perspective: Studies of behavior across cultures* (pp. 231–240). Lisse, Netherlands: Swets & Zeitlinger.

Trommsdorff, G., & B. Nauck (Eds.). (2005). *The value of children in cross-cultural perspective: case studies from eight societies.* Berlin: Pabst Science.

Trommsdorff, G., Kim, U., & Nauck, B. (2005). Factors influencing value of children and intergenerational relations in times of social change: Analyses from psychological and socio-cultural perspectives [Special issue]. *Applied Psychology: An International Review, 54*(3).

Tuncer, G. (2006). *The effect of the self in family context and traditional family values on attitudes toward paternalistic leadership style.* Unpublished master's thesis, Koç University, Istanbul, Turkey.

Uleman, J. S., Rhee, E., Bardoliwalla, N., Semin, G., & Toyama, M. (2000). The relational self: Closeness to ingroups depends on who they are, culture, and the type of closeness. *Asian Journal of Social Psychology, 3,* 1–17.

UNESCO. (1982). *Different theories and practices of development.* Paris: Author.

UNESCO. (1991). *World education report.* Paris. Author.

UNESCO. (2002). *Illiteracy: The obstacle to an Arab Renaissance.* UNESCO: Education. Retrieved January 10, 2003, from http://portal.unesco.org/education/

UNESCO. (2004). Repetition at high cost in Latin America and the Caribbean. *Education Today, 8,* 15.

UNESCO. (2005). *Institute of Statistics.* Retrieved April 5, 2006, from http://portal.unesco.org/education/

UNICEF. (1991). *The state of the world's children.* New York: Author.

UNICEF. (2000). *The state of the world's children.* New York: Author.

UNICEF. (2005). *Child development questions* (Integrated Early Childhood Development). New York: Author.

Uskul, A. K., Hynie, M., & Lalonde, R. N. (2004). Interdependence as a mediator between culture and interpersonal closeness for Euro-Canadians and Turks. *Journal of Cross-Cultural Psychology, 35,* 174–191.

Valsiner, J. (1989). *Child development in cultural context.* Toronto, Canada: Hogrefe.

Valsiner, J. (1994). Comparative-cultural and constructivist perspectives. Norwood, NJ: Ablex.

Valsiner, J. (2000). Cultural psychology. In A. Kazdin (Ed.), *Encyclopedia of psychology* (Vol. 2, pp. 389–392). Washington, DC: American Psychological Association.

van der Gaag, J., & Tan, J. P. (1998). *The benefits of early child development programs: An economic analysis.* Washington, DC: World Bank.

van der Gaag, J. (2002). From child development to human development. In M. E. Young (Ed.), *From early childhood development to human development* (pp. 63–78). Washington, DC: World Bank.

van de Vijver, F. J. R., & Hutschemaekers, G. J. M. (Eds.). (1990). *The investigation of culture.* Tilburg, Netherlands: Tilburg University Press.

van de Vijver, F. J. R., & Poortinga, Y. H. (1990). A taxonomy of cultural differences. In J. R. van de Vijver & G. J. M. Hutschemaekers (Eds.), *The investigation of culture: Current issues in cultural psychology* (pp. 91–114). Tilburg, Netherlands: Tilburg University Press.

van Ijzendoorn, M. H., & Sagi, A. (1999). Cross-cultural patterns of attachment: Universal and contextual dimensions. In J. Cassidy & P. R. Shaver (Eds.), *Handbook of attachment: Theory, research, and clinical applications* (pp. 713–734). New York: Guilford.

van Oudenhoven, J. P. L., van der Zee, K., & Bakker, W. (2002). Culture, identity, adaptation strategy and well being. In D. Gorter & K. van der Zee (Eds.), *Frisian abroad* (pp. 46–56). Ljouwert, Netherlands: Fryske Akademy.

van Oudenhoven, N. (1989). Children at risk and community response (UNESCO). *Notes, Comments, 187.*

van Tuijl, C., & Leseman, P. P. M. (2004). Improving mother–child interaction in low-income Turkish-Dutch families: A study of mechanisms mediating improvements resulting from participating in a home-based preschool intervention program. *Infant and Child Development, 13,* 323–340.

van Tuijl, C., Leseman, P. P. M., & Rispens, J. (2001). Efficacy of an intensive home-based educational intervention programme for 4- to 6-year-old ethnic minority children in the Netherlands. *International Journal of Behavioral Development, 25,* 148–159.

Vannoy, D. (1991). Social differentiation, contemporary marriage, and human development. *Journal of Family Issues, 12,* 251–267.

Verhoeven, L., Rood, V. R., & van der Laan, C. (Eds.). (1991). *Attaining functional literacy: A cross-cultural perspective.* The Hague, Netherlands: UNESCO.

von Bertalanffy, L. (1933). *Modern theories of development.* London: Oxford University Press.

Völker, S., Yovsi, R., & Keller, H. (1998). *Maternal interactional quality as assessed by non-trained raters from different cultural backgrounds.* Paper presented at the XVth Biennial ISSBD Meetings, Bern, Switzerland.

Vygotsky, L. S. (1978). *Mind in society: The development of higher psychological processes.* Cambridge, MA: Harvard University Press.

Vygotsky, L. S. (1986). *Thought and language* (Trans./rev. by A. Kozulin). Cambridge, MA: MIT Press. (Original work published 1934)

Wachs, T. D. (1987). Specificity of environmental action as manifested in environmental correlates of infant's mastery motivation. *Development Psychology, 23,* 782–790.

Wachs, T. D. (1993). Determinants of intellectual development: Single determinant research in a multideterminant universe. *Intelligence, 17,* 1–10.

Wachs, T. D., & Gruen, G. (1982). *Early experience and human development.* New York: Wiley.

Wagar, B., & Cohen, D. (2003). Culture, memory, and the self: An analysis of the personal and collective self in long-term memory. *Journal of Experimental Social Psychology, 39,* 468–475.

Wagner, D. A. (Ed.). (1983). *Child development and international development: Research–policy interfaces.* San Francisco: Jossey-Bass.

Wagner, D. A. (Ed.). (1986). Child development research and the Third World. *American Psychologist, 41,* 298–301.

Wagner, D. A. (1988). Appropriate education and literacy in the Third World. In P. R. Dasen, J. W. Berry, & N. Sartorious (Eds.), *Health and cross-cultural psychology* (pp. 93–111). Newbury Park, CA: Sage.

Wagner, D. A., & Spratt, J. E. (1987). Cognitive consequences of contrasting pedagogies: The effects of Quranic preschooling in Morocco. *Child Development, 58,* 1207–1219.

Wagner, D. A., & Stevenson, H. W. (Eds.). (1982). *Cultural perspectives on child development.* San Francisco: Freeman.

Wallach, M. A., & Wallach, L. (1983). *Psychology's sanction for selfishness: The error of egoism in theory and therapy.* New York: Freeman.

Wallach, M. A., & Wallach, L. (1990). *Rethinking goodness.* Albany: State University of New York Press.

Wang, Q. (2004). The emergence of cultural self-constructs: Autobiographical memory and self-description in European American and Chinese children. *Developmental Psychology, 40*(1), 3–15.

Wang, Q. (2006). Earliest recollections of self and others in European American and Taiwanese young adults. *Psychological Science.*

Wang, Q., & Conway, M. A. (2004). The stories we keep: Autobiographical memory in American and Chinese middle-aged adults. *Journal of Personality, 72,* 911–938.

Wang, Q., & Tamis-LeMonda, C. S. (2003). Do child-rearing values in Taiwan and the United States reflect cultural values of collectivism and individualism? *Journal of Cross-Cultural Psychology, 34,* 629–642.

Wang, Z. M. (1993). New Chinese approach in psychological research. *Psychology and Developing Societies, 5,* 151–170.

Ward, C. (2001). The A, B, Cs of acculturation. In D. Matsumoto (Ed.), *The handbook of culture and psychology* (pp. 411–446). Oxford, England: Oxford University Press.

Ward, C., & Kennedy, A. (1992). Locus of control, mood disturbance and social difficulty during cross-cultural transitions. *International Journal of Intercultural Relations, 16,* 175–194.

Ward, C., & Kennedy, A. (1996). Crossing cultures: The relationship between psychological and sociocultural dimensions of cross-cultural adjustment. In J. Pandey, D. Sinha, & D. P. S. Bhawuk (Eds.), *Asian contributions to cross-cultural psychology* (pp. 289–306). New Delhi, India: Sage.

Washington, V. (1988). Historical and contemporary linkages between Black child development and social policy. In D. T. Slaughter (Ed.), *Black children and poverty: A developmental perspective* (pp. 934–1108). San Francisco: Jossey-Bass.

Wasik, B. H., Ramey, C. T., Bryant, D. M., & Sparling, J. J. (1990). A longitudinal study of two early intervention strategies: Project care. *Child Development, 61,* 1682–1696.

Waters, E., Merrick, S., Treboux, D., Crowell, J., & Albersheim, L. (2000) Attachment security in infancy and early adulthood: A twenty-year longitudinal study. *Child Development, 71,* 684–689.

Weil, S. (1987). Proximal households as alternatives to joint families in Israel. In L. Shamgar-Handelman & R. Palomba (Eds.), *Alternative patterns of family life in modern societies*. Rome: Collana Monografie.

Weinfield, N., Sroufe, L.A., & Egeland, B. (2000). Attachment from infancy to early adulthood in a high-risk sample: Continuity, discontinuity, and their correlates. *Child Development, 71,* 695–702.

Weisner, T. S. (2002). Ecocultural pathways, family values, and parenting. *Parenting: Science and Practice, 2,* 325–334.

Weiss, H. B., & Jacobs, F. H. (1988). Family support and education programs: Challenges and opportunities. In H. B. Weiss & F. H. Jacobs (Eds.), *Evaluating family programs* (pp. xix–xxix). New York: Aldine.

Weisz, J. R., Rothbaum, F. M., & Blackburn, T. C. (1984). Standing out and standing in. *American Psychologist, 39,* 955–969.

Weller, P. (2004). Identity, politics, and the future(s) of religion in the UK: The case of the religion questions in the 2001 decennial census. *Journal of Contemporary Religion, 19,* 3–21.

Westen, D. (1985). *Self and society.* Cambridge, England: Cambridge University Press.

White, G., & Kirkpatrick, J. (Eds.). (1985). *Person, self, and experience: Exploring Pacific ethnopsychologies.* Berkeley: University of California Press.

Whitehurst, G. J., Arnold, D. S., Epstein, J. N., Angell, A. L., Smith, M., & Fischel, J. E. (1994). A picture book reading intervention in day care and home for children from low-income families. *Developmental Psychology, 30,* 679–689.

Whitehurst, G. J., & Fischel, J. E. (1999). A developmental model of reading and language impairments arising in conditions of economic poverty. In D. Bishop & L. L. Lenard (Eds.), *Speech and language impairments in children: Causes, characteristics, intervention, and outcomes* (pp. 53–71). East Sussex, England: Psychology Press.

Whitehurst, G. J, Zevenbergen, A. A., Crone, D. A., Schultz, M. D., & Velting, O. N. (1999). Outcomes of an emergent literacy intervention from head start through second grade. *Journal of Educational Psychology, 91,* 261–272.

Whiting, B. B. (Ed.). (1963). *Six cultures: Studies in child rearing.* New York: Wiley.

Whiting, B. B., & Whiting J. W. (1975). *Children of six cultures: A psychocultural analysis.* Cambridge, MA: Harvard University Press.

Whiting J. W., & Child, I. (1953). *Child training and personality.* New Haven, CT: Yale University Press.

Wiggins, J. S., & Trapnell, P. D. (1996). A dyadic-interactional perspective on the five-factor model. In J. S. Wiggins (Ed.), *The five-factor model of personality: Theoretical perspectives* (pp. 88–162). New York: Guilford.

Willms, J. D. (2002). Standards of care: Investments to improve children's educational outcomes in Latin America. In M. E. Young (Ed.), *From early child development to human development* (pp. 81–122). Washington, DC: The World Bank.

Winkvist, A., & Akhtar, H. Z. (2000) God should give daughters to rich families only: attitudes towards childbearing among low-income women in Punjab, Pakistan. *Social Science & Medicine, 51,* 73–81.

Witkin, H., & Berry, J. W. (1975). Psychological differentiation in cross-cultural perspective. *Journal of Cross-Cultural Psychology, 6,* 4–87.

Woodhead, M. (1985). Pre-school education has long term effects: But can they be generalized? *Oxford Review of Education, 11,* 133–155.

Woodhead, M. (1988). When psychology informs public policy. *American Psychologist, 43,* 443–454.

Woodhead, M. (1991). Psychology and the cultural construction of children's needs. In M. Woodhead, P., Light, & R. Carr (Eds.), *Growing up in a changing society* (pp. 37–57). London: Routledge.

World Bank. (1988). *Education in sub-Saharan Africa: Policies for adjustment, revitalization, and expansion.* Washington, DC: Author.

World Bank Population, Health and Nutrition Department. (1993). *Best practices in addressing micronutrient malnutrition.* Washington, DC: World Bank.

World Bank. (2001). Arab Republic of Egypt: An economic analysis of early childhood education/development.Washington, DC: Author.

World Energy Council. (1999, May). London

World Health Organization. (1986). *Protocols for the development and field testing of techniques for monitoring physical growth and psychosocial development* (WHO/MCH/MNH/86.1). Geneva, Switzerland: Author.

World Health Organization. (1990). *Progress report on the activities of physical growth and psycho-social development (September 1988–April 1990)* (Programme of Maternal and Child Health). Geneva, Switzerland: Author.

Yamagishi, T. (2002). The structure of trust: An evolutionary game of mind and society. *Hokkaido Behavioral Science Report, SP–13,* 1–157.

Yamagishi, T., Cook, K. S., & Watabe, M. (1998). Uncertainty, trust, and commitment formation in the United States and Japan. *American Journal of Sociology, 104,* 165–194.

Yamaguchi, S. (1994). Collectivism among the Japanese: A perspective from the self. In U. Kim, H. C. Triandis, Ç. Kağitçibaşi, S.-C. Choi, & G. Yoon (Eds.), *Individualism and collectivism: Theory, method and applications* (pp. 175–188). Thousand Oaks, CA: Sage.

Yamaguchi, S. (2001). Culture and control orientations. In D. Matsumoto (Ed.), *The handbook of culture and psychology* (pp. 223–243). New York: Oxford University Press.

Yang, C. F. (1988). Familism and development: An examination of the role of family in contemporary China Mainland, Hong Kong, and Taiwan. In D. Sinha & H. S. R. Kao (Eds.), *Social values and development: Asian perspectives* (pp. 93–123). London: Sage.

Yang, K.-S. (1986). Chinese personality and its change. In M. H. Bond (Ed.), *The psychology of the Chinese people* (pp. 106–170). New York: Oxford University Press.

Yang, K.-S. (1988). Will societal modernization eventually eliminate cross-cultural psychological differences? In M. H. Bond (Ed.). *The cross-cultural challenge to social psychology* (pp. 67–85). London: Sage.

Yang, S., & Sternberg, R. J. (1997). Taiwanese Chinese people's conception of intelligence. *Intelligence, 25,* 21–36.

Yau, J., & Smetana, J. G. (1996). Adolescent–parent conflict among Chinese adolescents in Hong Kong. *Child Development, 67,* 1262–1275.

Yeung, W. J., Linver, M. R., & Brooks-Gunn, J. (2002). How money matters for young children's development: Parental investment and family processes. *Child Development, 73,* 1861–1879.

Yoshida, T., Kojo, K., & Kaku, H. (1982). A study on the development of self-presentation in children. *Japanese Journal of Educational Psychology, 30,* 30–37.

Yoshikawa, H. (1994). Prevention as cumulative protection: Effects of early family support and education on chronic delinquency and its risks. *Psychological Bulletin, 115,* 27–54.

Young, M. E. (1997). *Early child development: Investing in our children's future* (International Congress Series 1137). Amsterdam: Elsevier Science.

Young, M. E. (Ed.). (2002). *From early child development to human development: Investing in our children's future.* Washington, DC: World Bank.

Young, M. E., & van der Gaag, J. (2002). *Ready to learn? An assessment of needs and programs for children ages 4–6 in Jordan.* Washington, DC: World Bank.

Young, N. (1992). Postmodern self-psychology mirrored in science and the arts. In S. Kvale (Ed.), *Psychology and postmodernism* (pp. 135–145). London: Sage.

Yovsi, R. D. (2001). *Ethnotheories about breastfeeding and mother–infant interaction: The case of sedentary Nso farmers and nomadic Fulani pastrals with their infants 3–6 months of age in Mbvem subdivision of the Northwest providence of Cameroon, Africa.* Unpublished doctoral dissertation, University of Osnabrück, Germany.

Yu, A.-B., & Yang, K.-S. (1994). The nature of achievement motivation in collectivistic societies. In U. Kim, H. C. Triandis, Ç. Kağitçibaşi, S.-C. Choi, & G. Yoon (Eds.), *Individualism and collectivism: Theory, method, and applications* (pp. 239–250). Newbury Park, CA: Sage.

Zeitlin, M. (1991). Nutritional resilience in a hostile environment: Positive deviance in child nutrition. *Nutrition Review, 49,* 259–268.

Zeitlin, M. (1996). My child is my crown: Yoruba parental theories and practices in early childhood. In S. Harkness & C. M. Super (Eds.), *Parents' cultural belief systems: Their origins, expressions, and consequences* (pp. 407–427). New York: Guilford.

Zeitlin, M., Ghassemi, H., & Mansour, M. (1990). *Positive deviance in child nutrition, with emphasis on psychosocial and behavioral aspects and implications for development.* Tokyo: United Nations University.

Zheng, G., Shi, S., & Tang, H. (2005). Population development and the value of children in the People's Republic of China. In G. Trommsdorff & B. Nauck (Eds.), *The value of children in cross-cultural perspective: Case studies from eight societies* (pp. 239–281). Berlin: Pabst Science.

Zigler, E. (2003). Forty years of believing in magic is enough. *Social Policy Report, 17,* 10.

Zigler, E., & Berman, W. (1983). Discerning the future of early childhood intervention. *American Psychologist, 38,* 894–906.

Zigler, E., & Styfco, S. J. ( 1994). Head Start: Criticism in a constructive context. *American Psychologist, 49,* 127–132.

Zigler, E., Taussig, C., & Black, K. (1992). Early childhood intervention: a promising preventative for juvenile delinquency. *American Psychologist, 47,* 997–1006.

Zigler, E., & Weiss, H. (1985). Family support systems: An ecological approach to child development. In R. Rapaport (Ed.), *Children, youth, and families: The action–research relationship* (pp. 166–205). Cambridge, England: Cambridge University Press.

Zimbardo, P. G. (2002). Psychology in the public service. *American Psychologist, 57*(6), 431–433.

Zimmerman, B. J., & Rosenthal, T. L. (1974). Observational learning of rule-governed behavior by children. *Psychological Bulletin, 81,* 29–42.

# Author Index

## C

# Subject Index